NAMES IN THE HISTORY OF PSYCHOLOGY
A Biographical Sourcebook

NAMES IN THE HISTORY OF PSYCHOLOGY
A Biographical Sourcebook

LEONARD ZUSNE
Department of Psychology
University of Tulsa

HEMISPHERE PUBLISHING
CORPORATION
Washington, D. C.

A HALSTED PRESS BOOK

JOHN WILEY & SONS

New York   London   Sydney   Toronto

Hemisphere Publishing Corporation
1025 Vermont Ave., N.W., Washington, D.C. 20005

Distributed solely by Halsted Press, a Division of John Wiley & Sons, Inc.,
New York.

Library of Congress Cataloging in Publication Data
Zusne, Leonard, 1924-
    Names in the history of psychology.
    A biographical sourcebook.

    1. Psychologists—Biography. 2. Psychology—
History. I. Title. [DNLM: 1. Psychology—Biography.
2. Psychology—History. BF109.A1 Z96n]
BF109.A1Z85   150′.92′2   74-26643
ISBN 0-470-98676-X

Printed in the United States of America

PREFACE

Just before his death in 1968, Edwin Garrigues Boring, the historian of psychology *par excellence*, was preparing to write a biographic dictionary of deceased psychologists and individuals from other fields who had made a contribution to the development of psychology. Each biography was to follow a standard format. The idea for the present volume was conceived independently of Boring, but bears considerable resemblance to his.

Boring was planning to write a short statement on each of 538 individuals whose contributions to psychology had been rated by a panel of nine judges.* The list of 538 names came into existence in the following fashion. Desiring to create a roster of psychologists of rated eminence for the use of individuals both in psychology and outside of it, Boring and another historian of psychology, Robert I. Watson, had compiled an initial list of 1,040 names from various sources. The names were those of deceased individuals who had made some contribution to the development of psychology in the course of history. To obtain a more manageable list, Boring and Watson had a panel of nine judges rate the contributions of these 1,040 individuals. The panel consisted of Boring, Watson, and seven other prominent American and foreign psychologists. The rating procedure followed by a judge was to give an individual zero points if he did not recognize his name as belonging in the history of psychology, one point if he did so recognize his name, two points if, in addition, he could identify the contribution that the individual had made to psychology, and three points if he thought that the individual should be included in a list of the 500 most prominent psychologists of all times. Thus, if none of the nine judges recognized an individual's name, he received the lowest possible score of zero, or, if all had rated him highly, the highest possible score of 27. The 538 individuals in Boring's list were those whose ratings were 11 or more. The cutoff score of 11 was decided upon quite arbitrarily, and was dictated by the need to have a final list of approximately 500 individuals.

*E. L. Annin, E. G. Boring, & R. I. Watson. Important psychologists, 1600–1967. *Journal of the History of the Behavioral Sciences*, 1968, 4, 303–315.

Our list totals 526. The statements describing these individuals are not standard biographies or even short, dictionary versions of standard biographies. They have one main function, namely, to explain the specific contribution or contributions the subject made to psychology. The biographic data include only dates and places of birth and death, a chronology of highest degree or education, professional positions and relevant offices held, and recognitions received. The entries present the main points of philosophy, theory, discoveries made, methodologies initiated, books written, research conducted, influence exercised, and other contributions made to the development of psychology as a natural or social science. At the end of each statement, references are given to the best, most extensive, or most readily available biographies and autobiographies that may be consulted for supplementary material.

By bringing together in one place all the names in the history of psychology within a wide range of historic significance and by gathering from scattered sources information for each name, this volume becomes the first sourcebook of its kind for the history of psychology.

It is a kind of Who's Who in psychology, to be consulted by anyone interested in the historical antecedents of the subject. The book, however, is primarily for the use of students of the history or systems of psychology. They will readily recognize that the information presented is of the sort that they themselves, perhaps, have been putting together in preparing for examinations. The instructor, on the other hand, will recognize that uniform sets of information on a large number of individuals measured on a certain attribute (eminence) lend themselves to numerous tabulations, comparisons, and other instructional exercises.

Readers in general, and the teacher and student of the history of psychology in particular, should find the index of subjects and names that appears on pages 477–489 a particularly useful feature, not often encountered in biographical collections or dictionaries. Its main purpose is to relate those biographees who have contributed to the same specialty or field of research in psychology, have used or worked on the same fundamental concepts, have belonged to the same school of psychology or subscribed to the same philosophical doctrine or have shared a teacher-student relationship.

I want to express my thanks to Dr. Robert I. Watson of the University of New Hampshire Psychology Department for his interest, encouragement, and help in the preparation of this book. The Reference Department staff of the University of Tulsa McFarlin Library, particularly Margaret Patty, have been especially helpful to me, both in this and my other writing ventures—my gratitude to them also.

Leonard Zusne

EXPLANATORY NOTES

Entries are arranged chronologically, according to birth dates.* The number in brackets with the subject's name is the order number (1 through 526), and all references to entries within the text and in the Index are to these numbers rather than to page numbers.

Rating. The procedure by which the ratings were made is explained in the Preface. With two exceptions, the ratings range from 11 to 27. "Unrated" means that the individual was not included among those rated and reported on by Annin, Boring, and Watson because he was born before 1600, died after 1967, or is one of the six other names added to the list by the author.

Born, Died. In a few instances the day and month of either birth or death or both were either unknown or unavailable at the time this book was written. Such individuals' names are entered by year of birth alone and are placed ahead of others born in the same year. Places of birth and death of persons other than Americans are further identified by county, *department*, or province, unless the location is a well-known city; they are identified by country only where it differs from the person's nationality. Large, well-known regions in Central and Eastern Europe that were partitioned after World War I and now belong to different countries are not further identified.

Highest degree. Both the Ph.D. and M.D. degrees are given, if applicable. The name of the major professor is given only for individuals who received their doctorate in psychology.

Positions. This is not a complete list of all positions held. Only those are mentioned that are relevant to the individual's contribution to psychology. "Editorial work" encompasses any kind of editorial position, regardless of rank.

Biographic data. The biographic sources are English-language sources, if such are available. If sources in other languages are listed, it is because they are ample and more detailed than the English-language sources, or because they are the only ones available. Extensive and factual biographic sources are listed in preference to brief or discursive ones. Standard reference works in

---

*An exception is the biography of G. Stanley Hall, which was inadvertently placed out of chronological order. Now numbered [418], it falls chronologically between [195] and [196].

which more or less extensive biographies may be found for a considerable number of the subjects are also cited. The abbreviations used are:

DNB *Dictionary of National Biography* (1885–1912 edition)

DSB *Dictionary of Scientific Biography* (only eight volumes had been published by the time this manuscript was finished)

EP *Encyclopedia of Philosophy*

HPA *History of Psychology in Autobiography*

IESS *International Encyclopedia of Social Sciences*

NCAB *National Cyclopedia of American Biography*

The list of sources is by no means exhaustive. Other reference works contain additional biographies, which may also be extensive but not as numerous as in the works mentioned above. Standard encylopedias are such a source. Among additional useful references are the *Enciclopedia universal ilustrada* (in Spanish), *Enciclopedia italiana* (in Italian), *Enciclopedia Judaica*, and the *Catholic Encyclopedia*, as well as various specialized biographic dictionaries.

ALPHABETIC LIST OF NAMES

(Numbers in brackets are biography numbers, not page numbers.)

Bowditch, Henry Pickering [180]
Braid, James [114]
Brentano, Franz [176]
Brett, George Sidney [388]
Breuer, Josef [185]
Bridgman, Percy William [409]
Brill, Abraham Arden [354]
Broca, Paul [149]
Brown, Thomas [103]
Brown, Warner [407]
Brown, William [406]
Brown-Séquard, Charles-Edouard [133]
Brücke, Ernst Wilhelm von [141]
Brunswik, Egon [508]
Bryan, William Lowe [258]
Buffon, George Louis Leclerc de [48]
Bühler, Karl [385]
Burt, Sir Cyril Lodowic [414]
Bykov, Konstantin Mikhaĭlovich [437]

Cabanis, Pierre Jean Georges [80]
Calkins, Mary Whiton [271]
Cannon, Walter Bradford [332]
Carlson, Anton Julius [356]
Carmichael, Leonard [494]
Carpenter, William Benjamin [132]
Carr, Harvey A. [344]
Cattell, James McKeen [256]
Charcot, Jean-Martin [152]
Claparède, Edouard [342]
Coghill, George Ellett [335]
Comenius, Joann Amos [27]
Comte, (Isadore) Auguste (Marie
    François) [117]
Condillac, Etienne Bonnot de [57]
Condorcet, Marie Jean Antoine [67]
Cooley, Charles Horton [281]
Coué, Emile [228]
Cousin, Victor [112]
Crozier, William John [477]
Cuvier, Georges Léopold Chrétien Fréderic
    Dagobert, Baron [88]

Dallenbach, Karl M. [451]
Dalton, John [85]
Darwin, Charles [127]

Darwin, Erasmus [61]
Dearborn, Walter Fenno [379]
Decroly, Ovide Jean [330]
Delabarre, Edmund Burke [275]
Delboeuf, Joseph Rémi Leopold [159]
Democritus [5]
De Sanctis, Sante [263]
Descartes, René [28]
Dessoir, Max [295]
Destutt de Tracy, Antoine Louis
    Claude [79]
Dewey, John [253]
Diderot, Denis [54]
Dilthey, Wilhelm [164]
Dix, Dorothea Lynde [124]
Dodge, Raymond [327]
Donaldson, Henry Herbert [234]
Donders, Franciscus Cornelius [137]
Downey, June Etta [359]
Drever, James, Sr., [343]
Driesch, Hans Adolf Eduard [301]
Du Bois-Reymond, Emil [140]
Dumas, Georges [288]
Duncker, Karl [507]
Dunlap, Knight [360]
Durkheim, Emile [241]
Dusser de Barenne, Joannes Gregorius [433]

Ebbinghaus, Hermann [207]
Edwards, Jonathan [44]
Ehrenfels, Christian von [250]
Elliotson, John [111]
Ellis, (Henry) Havelock [246]
Emmert, Emil [195]
Empedocles [3]
English, Horace Bidwell [479]
Erasistratus [11]
Erdmann, Benno [210]
Esdaile, James [126]
Esquirol, Jean Etienne Dominique [91]
Ewald, Ernst Julius Richard [222]
Exner, Sigmund [198]

Fabre, Jean Henri [148]
Farrand, Livingston [298]
Fearing, Franklin [480]

Fechner, Gustav Theodor [120]
Fenichel, Otto [489]
Féré, Charles S. [213]
Ferenczi, Sándor [339]
Fernberger, Samuel Weiller [449]
Ferree, Clarence Errol [371]
Feuerbach, Paul Johann Anselm von [100]
Fichte, Johann Gottlieb [83]
Fisher, Sir Ronald Aylmer [464]
Fitts, Paul Morris [525]
Flechsig, Paul Emil [200]
Flourens, Pierre Jean Marie [113]
Flournoy, Théodore [220]
Flugel, John Carl [426]
Forel, August Henri [204]
Fourier, François Charles Marie [92]
Franklin, Benjamin [46]
Franz, Shepherd Ivory [350]
Freeman, Frank Nugent [392]
Frenkel-Brunswik, Else [522]
Freud, Sigmund [224]
Frey, Maximilian Ruppert Franz von [217]
Fritsch, Gustav Theodor [175]
Fröbel, Friedrich Wilhelm August [104]
Fröbes, Joseph [291]
Fromm-Reichmann, Frieda [461]
Fullerton, George Stuart [251]
Fulton, John Farquhar [497]

Galen [12]
Galilei, Galileo [21]
Gall, Franz Joseph [81]
Galton, Sir Francis [144]
Galvani, Luigi [65]
Gassendi, Pierre [26]
Gauss, Karl Friedrich [99]
Gelb, Adhémar Maximilian Maurice [452]
Gemelli, Agostino (Edoardo) [376]
Gesell, Arnold Lucius [394]
Geulincx, Arnold [31]
Goddard, Henry Herbert [290]
Goethe, Johann Wolfgang von [77]
Goldscheider, Alfred [244]
Goldstein, Kurt [380]
Golgi, Camillo [193]
Goltz, Friedrich Leopold [168]

Goodenough, Florence Laura [441]
Gosset, William Sealy [365]
Graham, Clarence Henry [515]
Groos, Karl Theodor [262]
Gruhle, Hans Walther [397]
Guillaume, Paul [377]
Guthrie, Edwin Ray [436]

Haeckel, Ernst Heinrich [165]
Hall, Granville Stanley [418]
Hall, Marshall [110]
Haller, Albrecht von [49]
Hamilton, Sir William [109]
Hartley, David [45]
Hartmann, Eduard von [187]
Harvey, William [23]
Head, Sir Henry [261]
Healy, William [307]
Hecht, Selig [473]
Hegel, Georg Wilhelm Friedrich [89]
Hellpach, Willy [370]
Helmholtz, Hermann Ludwig Ferdinand
    von [143]
Helvétius, Claude Adrien [56]
Henning, Hans [431]
Henri, Victor [334]
Heraclitus [1]
Herbart, Johann Friedrich [101]
Herder, Johann Gottfried [69]
Hering, Ewald [167]
Herophilus [10]
Herrick, Charles Judson [306]
Herskovits, Melville Jean [486]
Heymans, Gerardus [231]
Hippocrates [6]
Hitzig, Eduard [173]
Hobbes, Thomas [24]
Hobhouse, Leonard Trelawney [282]
Höffding, Harald [191]
Hollingworth, Harry Levi [393]
Hollingworth, Leta Stetter [440]
Holt, Edwin Bissell [348]
Holzinger, Karl John [478]
Hornbostel, Erich M. von [369]
Horney, Karen [434]
Hovland, Carl Iver [526]

Huarte (y Navarro), Juan [19]
Hull, Clark Leonard [423]
Humboldt, Wilhelm von [87]
Hume, David [52]
Humphrey, George [460]
Hunter, Walter Samuel [457]
Husserl, Edmund [248]
Huxley, Thomas Henry [151]
Huygens, Christian [32]

Itard, Jean (Marie-Gaspard) [98]

Jackson, John Hughlings [171]
Jaensch, Erich Rudolf [413]
James, William [184]
Janet, Pierre [249]
Jastrow, Joseph [269]
Jennings, Herbert Spencer [303]
Jodl, Friedrich [205]
Johnson, Samuel [43]
Jones, (Alfred) Ernest [382]
Jost, Adolph [352]
Judd, Charles Hubbard [340]
Jung, Carl Gustav [358]

Kafka, Gustav [415]
Kant, Immanuel [60]
Katz, David [428]
Kelley, Truman Lee [424]
Kelly, George Alexander [514]
Kent, Grace (Helen) [357]
Kepler, Johannes [22]
Kiesow, Federico [240]
Kinsey, Alfred Charles [484]
Klages, Ludwig [338]
Klein, Melanie [408]
Klemm, Gustav Otto [419]
Kluckhohn, Clyde Kay Maben [512]
Koffka, Kurt [438]
Köhler, Wolfgang [447]
König, Arthur [225]
Kornilov, Konstantin Nikolaevich [383]
Kraepelin, Emil [223]
Kretschmer, Ernst [456]
Kries, Johannes von [219]
Kris, Ernst [498]

Kroh, Oswald [454]
Krüger, Felix (E.) [351]
Kuhlmann, Frederick [361]
Külpe, Oswald [265]

Ladd, George Trumbull [186]
Ladd-Franklin, Christine [201]
Lamarck, Jean Baptiste Pierre Antoine de
    Monet [68]
La Mettrie, Julien Offray de [50]
Landis, Carney [490]
Lange, Carl Georg [169]
Lange, Ludwig [268]
Langfeld, Herbert Sidney [387]
Lapicque, Louis [289]
Laplace, Pierre Simon de [75]
Lashley, Karl Spencer [466]
Lavater, Johann Caspar [66]
Lazarus, Moritz [150]
Le Bon, Gustave [182]
Lehmann, Alfred Georg Ludwig [239]
Leibniz, Gottfried Wilhelm von [37]
Lenin, Vladimir Ilyich [318]
Leuba, James Henry [304]
Lévy-Bruhl, Lucien [230]
Lewes, George Henry [134]
Lewin, Kurt [468]
Liébeault, Ambroise August [145]
Lindworsky, Johannes [355]
Linnaeus, Carolus [47]
Linton, Ralph [481]
Lipps, Theodor [211]
Locke, John [33]
Loeb, Jacques [247]
Lombroso, Cesare [172]
Lorge, Irving [513]
Lotze, Rudolf Hermann [135]
Louttit, Chauncey McKinley [504]
Lubbock, Sir John (Baron Avebury) [166]

McCosh, James [128]
McDougall, William [329]
McGeoch, John Alexander [492]
Mach, Ernst [174]
Magendie, François [105]
Maine de Biran, Marie François Pierre
    Gouthier [86]

Malebranche, Nicolas de [35]
Malinowski, Bronislaw Kasper [420]
Malthus, Thomas Robert [84]
Marbe, Karl [311]
Mariotte, Edmé [29]
Marquis, Donald G. [521]
Marx, Karl Henrich [136]
Maslow, Abraham Harold [520]
Matsumoto, Matataro [284]
Maudsley, Henry [170]
Maxwell, James Clerk [160]
Mayo, (George) Elton [398]
Mead, George Herbert [270]
Meinong, Alexius von [218]
Meissner, Georg [157]
Mercier, Désiré Felicien François
    Joseph [212]
Merleau-Ponty, Maurice [519]
Mersenne, Marin [25]
Mesmer, Franz Anton [63]
Messer, August [296]
Meumann, Ernst [266]
Meyer, Adolf [292]
Meyer, Max Frederick [346]
Meynert, Theodor Hermann [163]
Michotte (van den Berck), Baron Albert
    Edward [405]
Mill, James [93]
Mill, John Stuart [125]
Moede, Walter [455]
Moll, Albert [264]
Molyneux, William [38]
Montessori, Maria [324]
Morgan, Conwy Lloyd [214]
Muenzinger, Karl Friedrich [432]
Müller, Georg Elias [208]
Müller, Johannes Peter [121]
Müller-Freienfels, Richard [412]
Müller-Lyer, Franz (Carl) [227]
Münsterberg, Hugo [272]
Murchison, Carl [453]
Myers, Charles Samuel [341]

Nagel, Wilibald (A.) [322]
Newton, Sir Isaac [36]

Nietzsche, Friedrich Wilhelm [196]
Nissen, Henry Wieghorst [502]

Obonai, Torao [495]
Ogden, Robert Morris [373]
Orth, Johannes [199]

Paracelsus [17]
Parsons, Sir John Herbert [305]
Pascal, Blaise [30]
Paterson, Donald Gildersleeve [472]
Pavlov, Ivan Petrovich [206]
Pearson, Karl [229]
Peckham, George William [197]
Peirce, Charles Santiago Sanders [177]
Pestalozzi, Johann Heinrich [72]
Peter of Spain [15]
Pflüger, Eduard Friedrich Wilhelm [155]
Piéron, Henri [404]
Pillsbury, Walter Bowers [337]
Pinel, Philippe [71]
Pintner, Rudolf [430]
Plateau, Joseph Antoine Ferdinand [122]
Plato [7]
Plotinus [13]
Polyak, Stephen [462]
Ponzo, Mario [410]
Poppelreuter, Walther [435]
Porter, Noah [129]
Preyer, Wilhelm Thierry [183]
Priestley, Joseph [62]
Prince, Morton [221]
Prochaska, Georg [76]
Purkinje, Jan Evangelista [107]

Quételet, (Lambert) Adolphe (Jacques) [116]

Ramón y Cajal, Santiago [215]
Rank, Otto [421]
Ranschburg, Paul [315]
Rapaport, David [524]
Rayleigh, John William Strutt,
    3rd baron [189]
Razran, Gregory [503]
Reid, Thomas [51]
Révész, Géza [381]

Reymert, Martin Luther [416]
Ribot, Théodule Armand [179]
Richet, Charles Robert [209]
Rignano, Eugenio [320]
Rivers, Baron William Halse Rivers [278]
Roback, Abraham Aaron [467]
Robinson, Edward Stevens [482]
Róheim, Géza [471]
Rolando, Luigi [95]
Romanes, George John [203]
Rorschach, Hermann [429]
Rosanoff, Aaron Joshua [378]
Ross, Edward Alsworth [293]
Rousseau, Jean Jacques [53]
Rubin, Edgar John [443]
Rubinshteĭn, Sergeĭ Leonidovich [459]
Ruckmick, Christian Alban [442]
Rush, Benjamin [70]

Sachs, Hanns [399]
Sanford, Edmund Clark [254]
Sapir, Edward [417]
Saudek, Robert [403]
Scheerer, Martin [500]
Schelling, Friedrich Wilhelm Joseph
    von [97]
Schiller, Johann Christopher Friedrich [82]
Schlosberg, Harold [510]
Schneierla, Theodore C. [506]
Schopenhauer, Arthur [108]
Schumann, Friedrich [273]
Scott, Walter Dill [308]
Scripture, Edward Wheeler [280]
Seashore, Carl Emil [286]
Seashore, Harold Gustav [516]
Sechenov, Ivan Mikhaĭlovich [156]
Seguin, Edouard [130]
Selz, Otto [400]
Sherrington, Sir Charles Scott [238]
Sidis, Boris [300]
Simon, Théodore [347]
Small, Willard Stanton [323]
Smith, Adam [59]
Smuts, Jan Christian [319]
Socrates [4]
Spearman, Charles Edward [274]

Spence, Kenneth Wartenbe [518]
Spencer, Herbert [142]
Spinoza, Benedictus de [34]
Spranger, Eduard [411]
Spurzheim, Johann Kaspar [102]
Starbuck, Edwin Diller [287]
Steinthal, Heymann [147]
Stekel, Wilhelm [302]
Stern, (Louis) William [328]
Stevens, S. Smith [517]
Stewart, Dugald [78]
Stoelting, Christian (H.) [276]
Stone, Calvin Perry [475]
Störring, Gustav [257]
Stouffer, Samuel Andrew [499]
Stout, George Frederick [255]
Stratton, George Malcolm [285]
Strong, Jr., Edward Kellog [427]
Stumpf, Carl [202]
Sullivan, Harry Stack [474]
Sully, James [188]
Swedenborg, Emanuel [41]
Symonds, Percival Mallon [483]

Taine, Hippolyte Adolphe [154]
Tarde, Gabriel [192]
Teplov, Boris Mikhaĭlovich [488]
Terman, Lewis Madison [368]
Tetens, Johann Nikolas [64]
Theophrastus [9]
Thomson, Sir Godfrey Hilton [401]
Thorndike, Edward Lee [353]
Thurstone, Louis Leon [448]
Tiedemann, Dietrich [74]
Titchener, Edward Bradford [294]
Tolman, Edward Chace [439]
Troland, Leonard Thompson [458]
Twitmyer, Edwin Burket [349]
Tylor, Sir Edward Burnett [162]

Uexküll, Baron Jakob Johann von [277]
Urban, Francis M. [313]
Uznadze, Dimitriĭ Nikolaevich [446]

Vaihinger, Hans [216]
Valentine, Charles Wilfrid [389]

Valentine, Willard Lee [511]
Vierordt, Karl von [139]
Vives, Juan Luis [18]
Volkmann, Alfred Wilhelm [119]
Voltaire [42]
Vygotskiĭ, Leon Semenovich [487]

Wallace, Alfred Russel [146]
Wallas, Graham [242]
Wallon, Henri Paul Hyacinthe [384]
Ward, James [190]
Warden, Carl John [465]
Warner, Lucien Hynes [501]
Warren, Howard Crosby [297]
Washburn, Margaret Floy [331]
Watson, John Broadus [374]
Watt, Henry Jackson [386]
Weber, Ernst Heinrich [115]
Weber, Max [279]
Weiss, Albert Paul [390]
Wells, Frederick Lyman [422]
Werner, Heinz [463]
Wertheimer, Max [391]
Wheatstone, Sir Charles [123]

Wheeler, Raymond Holder [476]
Wheeler, William Morton [283]
Whipple, Guy Montrose [364]
White, William Alanson [316]
Whithead, Alfred North [260]
Whytt, Robert [55]
Wiener, Norbert [485]
Wiersma, Enno Dirk [245]
Wirth, Wilhelm [366]
Wissler, Clark [325]
Witasek, Stephan [314]
Witmer, Lightner [299]
Wolff, Baron Christian von [39]
Woodworth, Robert Sessions [312]
Wundt, Wilhelm (Maximilian) [161]

Yerkes, Robert Mearns [363]
Young, Thomas [94]
Yule, George Udny [326]

Zener, Karl Edward [509]
Ziehen, Theodor [267]
Zilboorg, Gregory [469]
Zwaardemaker, Hendrick [233]

ACKNOWLEDGMENTS

Photographs accompanying biographies 1, 2, 3, 5, 6, 17, 20, 21, 22, 23, 36, 37, 45, 46, 47, 48, 50, 56, 58, 61, 62, 63, 65, 73, 77, 80, 81, 84, 87, 90, 91, 98, 103, 105, 110, 111, 113, 118, 121, 124, 131, 132, 133, 137, 138, 140, 141, 148, 149, 151, 152, 153, 178, 180, 181, 185, 190, 207, 208, 223, 228, 232, 237, 243, 269, 294, 297, 317, 331, 332, 336, 341, 345, 354, 356, 358, 372, 395, 408, 429, 437, 438, 445, 447, 461, 469, 474, 492, and 496 are used by permission of the National Library of Medicine, Bethesda, Maryland.

Photographs accompanying biographies 7, 12, 24, 28, 34, 40, 52, 53, 60, 68, 71, 94, 96, 115, 125, 127, 135, 142, 143, 144, 167, 176, 184, 224, 236, 238, and 247 are used by permission of the Library of Congress.

Photographs accompanying biographies 191, 202, 214, 231, 233, 240, 249, 262, 263, 267, 271, 274, 280, 291, 311, 312, 328, 329, 343, 344, 350, 363, 366, 368, 374, 401, 404, 418, 419, 423, 428, 439, 444, and 448 are from the first four volumes of *A History of Psychology in Autobiography* and are used by permission of the publisher, Clark University Press, Worcester, Massachusetts.

Photographs accompanying the following biographies are from *Scientific Monthly*: 256 (1929, 28, 25), 272 (1930, 30, 120), and 466 (1930, 30, 571). They are used by permission from the American Association for the Advancement of Science.

Photographs accompanying the following biographies are from the *Psychological Review*: 161 (1921, 28), 259 (1935, 42), 353 (1949, 56), 391 (1944, 51), 443 (1951, 58), and 468 (1948, 55). The photograph accompanying biography 517 is from the *American Psychologist,* 1960, 15, 794. The pictures are used by permission from the American Psychological Association.

Pictures accompanying biographies 33, 156, 206, and 226 are from Soviet sources.

The picture accompanying biography 187 is from *Founders of Modern Psychology,* by G. S. Hall, D. Appleton & Company, 1912.

The photograph accompanying biography 8 was taken by Leonard Zusne.

The photographs accompanying biographies 253 and 309 are used by permission of Underwood & Underwood.

NAMES IN THE HISTORY
OF PSYCHOLOGY
A Biographical Sourcebook

Greek philosopher
Rating: (unrated)
Born: Ephesus, ca. 540 B.C.
Died: Ephesus (?), ca. 475 B.C.

A philosopher of the Ionian school, Heraclitus postulated change as the only reality (the proposition that one cannot step into the same river twice is Heraclitus'), and fire (energy ?) as the basic principle or primary substance. He equated the soul with fire, did not give it any bodily localization, but did relate it to movement. Like most Greek philosophers, he thought of existence as constant motion or even strife: "Strife is the father of all things." He can thus be considered a primitive evolutionist. Knowledge Heraclitus thought to be derived from the senses, but believed only mind was able to understand the law of change.

Biographic data: *DSB* 6:289; *EP* 3:477; Diogenes Laertius. *Lives and Opinions of Eminent Philosophers*. Translated by R. D. Dicks, 1925

Greek physician
Rating: (unrated)
Born: Croton, southern Italy, ca. 500 B.C.
Died: Place and date unknown

Almost nothing is known of Alcmaeon's life, and only some fragments of his writings remain. Alcmaeon was a Pythagorean and somewhat of a mystic, but a good observer nevertheless. He is reported to have been the first to dissect a human body. Surgical operations were the basis for his observations on sensory functioning, although the inferences he made from anatomical observations to function are mostly incorrect. Alcmaeon was first to extirpate the human eye, as a result of which he discovered the connection between the eye and the brain. He developed theories of vision, hearing, smell, and taste, and concluded that the brain receives sensory impressions, is the seat of thought, as well as the central or vital point of the organism. While former philosophers had located the perishable aspect of the soul (*thymos*) in the lungs and the immortal aspect (*psyche*) in the head, Alcmaeon unified both and located them in the brain. To Alcmaeon, mind could exist only as long as the brain remained undamaged. Alcmaeon made a distinction between man and animals, attributing to man both perception and understanding, but perception only, to animals. Although he considered perception and understanding to be separate processes, he made them inhere in the one soul.

Biographic data: *DSB* 1:103–104; *EP* 1:67; Diogenes Laertius, *Lives and Opinions of Eminent Philosophers*. Translated by R. D. Dicks, 1925

[3]

EMPEDOCLES OF AKRAGAS

Greek philosopher
Rating: (unrated)
Born: Akragas, Sicily, ca, 490 B.C.
Died: Peloponnesus, ca. 430 B.C.

Empedocles, a pre-Socratic philosopher, argued for the existence of four elements of which everything is composed: earth, fire, air, and water. Upon decomposition of objects, the elements return to their original state, unchanged. Empedocles endowed all things with life and the power of thought, man differing from other things by his greater power of thought. He believed thinking occurred in the blood, and equated the soul with thinking. He considered the body to be mortal, the soul immortal. According to Empedocles the soul lives on to inhabit other bodies (metampsychosis). Perception was explained by Empedocles in terms of objects giving off emanations which affect the sense organs of perceivers. In various forms, this view came to be held by other Greek philosophers as well as philosophers of later centuries. One positive discovery that is attributed to Empedocles is that of the inner ear.

Biographic data: *DSB* 4:367; *EP* 2:496; Diogenes Laertius, *Lives and Opinions of Eminent Philosophers*. Translated by R. D. Dicks, 1925

Greek philosopher
Rating: (unrated)
Born: Ca. 470 B.C.
Died: Athens, Greece, ca. 399 B.C.

Socrates devised a method of sharpening truth and exposing
ignorance and falsehood in a dialogue. The Socratic method was
designed to bring out the knowledge that resides in each person.
Recognition of one's own ignorance results in self-knowledge.
This method and its results stood in contrast to the method of
the Sophists who insisted that truth was relative and that true
knowledge could not be had, and also resulted in the addition of
self-knowledge to the total of all knowledge. The Socratic
injunction to "know thyself" was to be achieved by the use of
introspection. Socrates was thus one of the first systematic users
of introspection, a method used later by Plotinus [13], St.
Augustine [14] and, much later, by the first scientific psychologists, such as Wundt [161] and Külpe [265]. One truth that
Socrates discovered was that the soul of man is more important
than his body because it enables him to tell good from evil.
Socrates was a dualist and was the first philosopher to identify
the consciousness of one's existence with the soul. The psychological views of Socrates were recorded by Plato [7] in his
dialogues. His contributions that go beyond the above cannot,
however, be distinguished from those of Plato since Socrates
himself never wrote anything down.

Biographic data: *EP* 7:480

Greek philosopher
Rating: (unrated)
Born: Abdera, Thrace, ca. 470 B.C.
Died: Ca. 370 B.C.

Democritus, one of the most eminent of the ancient Greek
philosophers, was a materialist, determinist, and atomist. He is
particularly celebrated for his atomic view of the world. Although
his atoms were not those of modern physics, they were tiny, in

ceaseless motion, and constituted all matter, including the mind. The atoms of the mind were round, fiery, slippery, moved very fast, and showed "subtlety of action." Following Empedocles [3], Democritus held that sensation and perception occur as atoms outside the body come in contact with atoms of the body, including those of the mind. The notion of sensory thresholds was adumbrated by Democritus when he stated that the nonbodily atoms had to possess certain strength before they could make an impression on the body. Democritus held that the shape of the atoms impinging upon the sense organs determined the quality of the sensations produced by them, but that all senses were basically touch because the essence of sensation was the contact between external and bodily atoms. This included vision: visual objects, said Democritus, continuously emit images of themselves which mold the atoms of the air accordingly. The aerial copy of the object creates visual impression upon contact with the eye. This original statment of the representative theory of perception persisted in scientific circles through the 19th century, and still lingers in the conception of vision of the "man in the street." Since the atoms that emanate from the sensible objects may mix with others before reaching the perceiver, the senses may distort reality. In addition, since sensation is only the movement of atoms, sensations are only subjective experiences to which nothing real corresponds outside the perceiver. They are what was from the 17th century onward called the "secondary qualities" of real objects, important to Locke [33], Descartes [28], and others.

Biographic data: *DSB* 4:30; Diogenes Laertius, *Lives and Opinions of Eminent Philosophers*. Translated by R. D. Dicks, 1925

[6]

HIPPOCRATES

Greek physician
Rating: (unrated)
Born: Island of Cos, ca. 460 B.C.
Died: Larissa, Thessaly, ca. 370 B.C.

Hippocrates, the "father of medicine," exercised a tremendous influence on the development of medicine. He was first to separate medicine from religion, magic, and superstition, espousing the more naturalistic notion that imbalance in the four bodily humors, blood, phlegm, yellow bile, and black bile, was the cause of disease.

Hippocrates placed all of man's conscious life in the brain. He included here the emotions. Too much bile, he thought, caused overheating of the brain, which led to terror and fear (because the face is flushed); too much phlegm caused overcooling, leading to anxiety and grief. Hippocrates' doctrine of the humors was later applied by Galen [12] to explain differences in human temperament.

Hippocrates left behind a considerable number of writings, although not all of the Hippocratic writings may be attributed directly to him. A treatise that is of importance to psychology deals with epilepsy, titled *On the Sacred Disease*. Hippocrates denied this disease was any more sacred than other diseases, asserted that its origin was in the brain, but related it to humoral congestion. He strongly believed in the virtue of observation and in Nature's way of curing diseases. As a founder of medicine, Hippocrates may be said also to have propounded one of the basic assumptions on which modern psychology rests, namely, that the functioning of man's physical body can be understood.

Biographic data: DSB 6:418; EP 4:6

PLATO

Greek philosopher
Rating: (unrated)
Born: Athens, 428 or 427 B.C.
Died: Athens, 348 or 347 B.C.
Education: Studied philosophy in Athens under Socrates [4], between 408 and 400 B.C.
Positions: Ca. 387 established the Academy in Athens; taught philosophy there for 40 years

Plato's views on psychology are entwined with his views on metaphysics, social theory, and related matters, and are subordinate to those matters. Plato was a dualist both in the sense that he recognized the body and the soul as two independent entities as well as in the sense of recognizing a phenomenal but "unreal" world of the senses and physical processes and a "real" world of ideal Forms, of which the former are only a shadow cast by the latter. Plato's philosophy has been influential throughout the centuries, and the habit of talking of a body and a soul and of positing a separate and distinct kind of existence for the soul may be attributed to Plato.

To Plato, only the soul can know the ideal Forms. When soul and body unite, body interferes with the soul and with its recall of the Forms. When the soul does recall the Forms, it is through an effort. Plato called this process reminiscence. Reason, feeling, and appetite are three aspects of the soul. Reason is related to the immortal (rational) soul and resides in the brain; feeling and appetite belong to the mortal (irrational) soul, reside in the chest and the abdomen. All three are connected by the spinal cord. The immortal soul is also connected to the heart. In case of wrongdoing, the heart is agitated and its agitation is carried to the rest of the body by the blood vessels, which Plato thought served the general purpose of transmitting sensations.

The essence of the soul is motion. The diverse psychological processes arise as a result of the motions of the soul, which in turn are caused by diverse external motions. Mind is an inner activity and acts on externally produced motions of the soul, as when the "fire of the eyes" meets the light of an object. Will, confidence, fear, pleasure, and other emotions, motives, and cognitions are also motions of the soul. Strong motion that conforms to nature is positive emotion; one that does not is unpleasant or painful emotion. Reason is the highest aspect of the soul. Knowledge is not given by the senses but acquired through them as reason organizes and makes sense out of that which is perceived. It reveals the ideal Forms behind appearances. The second aspect of the soul has the properties of drive or will, the third that of emotion, desire, and bodily needs. The two are likened by Plato to two horses which the charioteer (reason) must guide to a goal, which he alone knows. The role of reason is to achieve harmony among the aspects of the soul, but reason must prevail nevertheless. Reason, spirit, and appetite are each like a drive themselves, drives for wisdom, for success, or for satisfaction. Reaching a goal brings about a state of pleasure. Thus on the level of reason or of the immortal soul the drive is to achieve union with the ideal Form. Reaching that goal is pure love.

The irrational aspect of man was placed by Plato in the soul itself. Plato viewed much of man's actions as the result of a conflict between the rational and the irrational aspect. While nothing was made of this side of Plato's philosophy for 2500 years, this view of man is clearly present in Freud's [224] conflict theory of neuroses and his personality theory. Through Neoplatonism and St. Augustine [14], Plato's thinking colored Christian thought until the 13th century when Aristotle [8] began to dominate, but without displacing Plato. In today's psychology, thinking that is characterized as "clinical" or "tender-minded" reflects Plato's view of man, while the Aristotelean model of man lives in the "scientific" and "tough-minded" psychology. As to science and psychological science in general, Plato rendered both a service and a disservice. He was against experimentation and empirically derived or inductive knowledge. His stand on this issue was responsible for the absence of psychological enquiry until the emergence of Aristotelean thinking in the 13th century. Plato was not against rational science, one derived deductively from a consideration of ideal Forms. What psychology there was between his time and that of Thomas Aquinas [16] was deductive and introspective.

Biographic data: *EP* 6:314; *IESS* 12:159

ARISTOTLE [8]

Greek philosopher
Rating: (unrated)
Born: Stagira, 384 B.C.
Died: Chalcis, Euboea, 323 B.C.
Education: Probably studied in Plato's [7] Academy and was Plato's student.
Positions: The years 367 to 347, Aristotle spent in Athens, but little is known about his activities there; 347–344, teacher, writer, scientific collector at Assus (Asia Minor); 344–342, same at Mitylene (Lesbos); 342–336, tutor of Alexander the Great at Pella (Macedonia); 335–323, in Athens, established his school, the Lyceum, completed most of his psychological writings.

Regarded by many as the greatest mind that ever lived, Aristotle contributed to prescientific psychology in both quantity and quality more than any other individual. Up to the time of Descartes [28] 1400 years later, psychology was essentially Aristotelean psychology. Aristotle is therefore regarded by many as the first psychologist. In his writings, biology and psychology are given the amplest treatment, about one-third of the pages. Aristotle's main psychological work is *Peri Psyches*, better known under its Latin title, *De Anima*. Shorter works (On the Senses and the Sensible, On Memory and Reminiscence, On Sleep and Sleeplessness, and On Dreams) are included under the common title of Short Physical Treatises (*Parva Naturalia*). *De Anima* was the first systematic treatise on psychology.

While at first Aristotle was a Platonist, he gradually became convinced of the necessity of empirical observation, and began to modify existing views, including those of Plato, to conform to the results of his empirical observations. In this and many other respects (such as Aristotle's rejection of the Platonic doctrine of ideal Forms) the philosophies of Plato and Aristotle are antithetical. They represent a basic divergence in the way man and the world may be viewed, a modern parallel being the difference between the clinical and the experimental psychologist.

Aristotle defined the psyche as a substance capable of receiving knowledge. Knowledge of the psyche he held to be the most valuable knowledge. Although the senses are necessary to acquire knowledge, knowledge is received only through the psyche's faculty of intelligence. Since only man has intelligence, animals are incapable of acquiring knowledge. To Aristotle, the psyche was the form aspect of existence. He held it to be the vital principle that distinguishes inorganic from organic matter. In contrast to Democritus [5], who was a mechanist, Aristotle was a vitalist. Psyche to Aristotle meant life, and mental activities he held to be basically biological. Aristotle maintained, however, that body and psyche form a unity, a view that was later termed the hylomorphic view. The main center of action of the psyche is the heart, Aristotle having rejected the brain as its seat because of his observation that the brain did not seem to respond to stimulation. The functions of the psyche are the nutritive, sensitive, and the rational functions, a division that Aristotle used for convenience's sake as he believed in the unity of the psyche.

The listing of the five senses begins with Aristotle. In addition to vision, audition, smell, taste, and touch, Aristotle envisioned also a common sense or a central, coordinating sense faculty as well as one that perceives the common sensibles, such as size or number. Sensitivity is aroused by events in the environment, and memory is the persistence of sense impressions. Recall, present in man only, is active search for memory traces and requires deliberation or thinking. Recall occurs as one idea leads to another. Similarity, contrast, and contiguity are relationships which facilitate the association of ideas. Repetition, emotion, and organization also facilitate recall. The pleasure-pain aspect of sensation causes desire, which leads to movement. An activity that is pleasurable will be repeated. This beginning of a learning theory was not to be developed until the end of the 19th century.

Aristotle believed that thinking requires the use of images. While some animals can imagine, only man thinks. Knowing (*nous*) differs from thinking in that it is an active, creative process leading to the recognition of universals; it is akin to intuition, it does not cause movement, and it is independent of the other functions of the psyche. Since Aristotle's thinking underwent considerable changes in time, it is possible to interpret some of his statements in different ways, especially those concerning the nature of the psyche and of the *nous*. A metaphysical interpretation made Aristotle acceptable to the medieval Christian world. Today's Thomistic psychology of Catholicism is based, by way of St. Thomas Aquinas [16], on Aristotle. Many of Aristotle's ideas, in and out of psychology, have withstood time so well that today the thinking of both the layman and the psychologist alike shows them quite clearly.

Biographic data: *DSB* 1:250; *EP* 1:151; *IESS* 1:407; Diogenes Laertius, *Lives and Opinions of Eminent Philosophers*. Translated by R. D. Dicks, 1925

THEOPHRASTUS [9]

Greek philosopher
Rating: (unrated)
Born: Eresus, Lesbos, 371 to 370 B.C.
Died: Athens, 288 to 287 B.C.
Education: Studied in Athens under Aristotle

Theophrastus, a faithful disciple of Aristotle [8], headed the Lyceum for 35 years after Aristotle's departure from Athens. He was even more naturalistically and empirically oriented than Aristotle. He wrote numerous treatises on a wide variety of subjects. For his work in botany he is considered to be the founder of that science. In his discussion of Aristotle's teachings, Theophrastus tried to minimize the Platonic elements. One important modification was his rejection of the search for final causes, stressed by Aristotle, and the emphasis on efficient causes in science. Also, unlike Aristotle, in his treatise *On the Senses*, Theophrastus placed intelligence in the brain. In that treatise of physiological psychology may be found detailed descriptions of sensations, perceptions, and affects. Theophrastus believed that under normal circumstances the senses inform us correctly about the nature of the material universe and that the material universe exists independently of our senses. He followed Aristotle in stating that external objects affect our senses, not directly or through emanations but through intervening media. Sensory qualities are not experienced until the activity of the sense organs affects the brain, a view that Aristotle held with regard to some of the sense modalities only.

Theophrastus is better known for a collection of thirty personality sketches, called *Characters*, in which he describes the behavior of the typical flatterer, miser, and other types. Another volume of sketches of positive characters written by Theophrastus has been lost.

Biographic data: *EP* 8:99

[10]

HEROPHILUS

Greek anatomist
Rating: (unrated)
Born: Chalcedon, Bithynia, ca. 320 B.C.
Died: Place and date unknown
Education: Studied medicine with Chrysippus and Praxagoras of
  Cos

Herophilus was one of the founders of anatomy. Together with Erasistratus [11], his pupil, he founded the Alexandrian school of anatomy. His many discoveries and excellent knowledge of anatomy was in no small measure owing to the freedom he had to perform human dissections. Concerning the nervous system he knew that the nerves were different from the tendons and that they were sensitive to environmental stimulation. He also divided the nerves into sensory and motor kinds. Herophilus described and named the retina. He assigned a central role to the brain in the functioning of the nervous system and believed that the brain and not the heart (according to Aristotle [8]) was the seat of intelligence. A notion of Herophilus' that was accepted by Erasistratus and enjoyed widespread acceptance through antiquity was that the ventricles of the brain were containers of the vital forces.

Biographic data: *DSB* 6:316

[11]

ERASISTRATUS

Greek physician and anatomist
Rating: (unrated)
Born: Iulus, Island of Chios, ca. 304 B.C.

Died: Samos, ca. 250 B.C.

Education: Studied in Athens under Metrodorus and Theophrastus [9]

Positions: Court physician for Seleucus Nicator, king of Syria, at Antioch; physician and anatomist at Alexandria, where he and Herophilus [10] established a school of anatomy

Erasistratus is considered the father of physiology. Among Erasistratus' many discoveries and speculations concerning anatomy and physiology those important to psychology are the following. Air from the lungs passes to the heart, where it becomes vital spirits. Through the blood stream, vital spirits are distributed as the "breath of life." In the brain, vital spirits are transformed into animal spirits and stored in the ventricles of the brain. The nerves, which Erasistratus distinguished from the blood vessels, carry the animal spirits (*pneuma*) involved in sensation and motion. Muscular contraction is caused by the expansion of the *pneuma*. Descartes [28], among others, accepted this teaching. Erasistratus distinguished between motor and sensory nerves, a distinction that had to be rediscovered by Bell and Magendie in the 19th century. He also traced both kinds of nerves to the brain. He thought the brain to be the seat of the intellect and that functions were localized in the brain. Erasistratus compared the convolutions of the brain in man and animals and concluded that the convolutions were related to intelligence. After Herophilus died, Erasistratus continued his work, but his own death brought about a decline of the Alexandrian school.

Biographic data: DSB 4:382

GALEN
[12]

Greek-Roman physician

Rating: (unrated)

Born: Pergamum, Asia Minor, 130 A.D.

Died: Possibly in Sicily, ca. 200 A.D.

Education: Studied philosophy and medicine at Pergamum between 145 and 150

Positions: 150–158, travel and study; 158–161, surgeon to gladiators at Pergamum; 161, physician to emperors at Rome

Galen was the first experimental physiologist. He had wide and good knowledge of anatomy, and his medical work was so

impressive that it was being held as valid for thirteen centuries. Concerning the soul, Galen adhered to Plato, holding that the brain and the nervous system are the seat of intelligence. Galen also accepted the pneumatistic doctrine of Erasistratus [11]. To the four ventricles of the brain Galen assigned the function of producing and directing, through the nerves, animal spirits of the soul. The flow of animal spirits caused movement of the muscles, he thought.

Galen knew the effects of cutting the spinal cord, such as loss of sensation and motor disturbances, and that some nerves mediated motion while others were involved in sensation. He described the cerebral aqueduct, and attributed the correct function to the optic chiasma, the production of singleness of binocular vision. Galen took from Hippocrates [6] the association established by the latter between the four elements of Empedocles and the four bodily humors—blood, black bile, yellow bile, phlegm—and developed it into a systematic theory, the fourfold typology of the sanguine, melancholic, choleric, and phlegmatic temperaments. The fourfold division was used by Galen primarily to explain pathology, and only secondarily behavior, but in the hands of his epigones it became the first personality theory, surviving until the 19th century. Pavlov's [206] identification of four types of nervous system, albeit on a totally different basis, and his reference to sanguine and phlegmatic dogs gave the Galenic temperaments a new lease on life.

Biographic data: *DSB* 5:227; *EP* 3:261; G. Sarton, *Galen of Pergamon*, 1954

[13]

PLOTINUS

Roman philosopher
Rating: (unrated)
Born: 205 A.D., birth place unknown
Died: Rome, 270
Education: Studied philosophy at Alexandria, 234–245, under Ammonius Saccas
Positions: 245–270, teacher of philosophy at Rome

Sworn to secrecy by his master, Plotinus did not write anything down until about 263. During the last six years of his life he produced the six *Enneads*. As the foremost Neoplatonist, Plotinus proclaimed the doctrine of overcoming the senses and the mortal self for the immortal soul to unite with the source of all, the ultimate good. This goal, he asserted, could be achieved while in the physical body. The dualism of Plato [7] was further accentuated by Plotinus, who placed the soul in the middle between the physical body as the prison of the soul and the spirit toward which the soul was to escape. His thinking concerning body-soul relationship predominated for the next 1000 years. While Plato's soul resided in the body and was connected to it through internal organs, Plotinus' soul was only correlated with the body since it was immaterial. Plotinus held that while the soul knows about the experiences of the body, only the body actually has the experiences. The soul performs the functions of sensing, reflecting, and contemplating. In the latter activity, the soul transcends the body to dwell on things eternal. Reflection involves awareness of both the object of reflection and of the subject, hence self-awareness. In contemplation, the object-subject separation is absent; in its highest state contemplation is reunion with the ultimate. Plotinus attempted to contact Eastern philosophers, but he got only as far as Mesopotamia before being forced to return. The similarity between Plotinus and Indian religious philosophies is thus even more remarkable.

To demonstrate that a greater, ineffable reality lay beyond the sensory world, Plotinus resorted to phenomenological analysis of mental activity, which was open to introspection and could be understood. It is said by some that Plotinus was the first one to use the concept of the subconscious. By being a very skillful introspectionist, Plotinus helped to establish introspection as a method in psychology, next to be used as proficiently by St. Augustine [14]. Plotinus' introspection led him to raise many psychological questions that received an adequate answer only centuries later. His own answers were less provocative than the questions he raised. Plotinus' questions concerned the seat of emotions, suspension of consciousness by drugs, differences between actual and remembered sensations, the nature of love, the nature of beauty, and distance vision. Concerning the nature of matter, Plotinus suggested an answer that anticipated that of Berkeley [40], as well as J. S. Mill's [125] reaction to Berkeley.

Biographic data: *EP* 6:351; Porphyry's introduction to the *Enneads* contains a biography of Plotinus

AUGUSTINE, SAINT, OF HIPPO (AURELIUS AUGUSTINUS)

Roman Church father
Rating: (unrated)
Born: Tagaste, Numidia, November 13, 354
Died: Hippo Regius, Numidia, August 28, 430
Education: Studied rhetoric at Carthage, 370–373
Positions: 373–388, teacher of rhetoric in Carthage, Milan, and Rome; 399–430, priest, later bishop of Hippo

St. Augustine's contribution to psychology stems from his intense self-analysis, triggered by his sudden conversion to Christianity in 386, following a life of pleasure and dissipation, and after excursions into philosophy, Manicheism, and Neoplatonism. His psychological views are passionately but unsystematically presented in his famous autobiography, *Confessions* (ca. 406).

Augustine's attitude toward science was ambivalent. He was convinced, however, of the certainty of inner experience—contemplation, ecstasy, prayer, adoration, and the like. His insightful descriptions of subjective events (e.g., the will, experienced freedom of the will, the self) begin the tradition of introspection and phenomenology in psychology. Augustine discussed the perception of time and concluded that time is an inner experience, i.e., it is psychological. He anticipated Descartes [28] concerning the proof of self-existence: to doubt is to think, and to think is to exist ("For if I am deceived, I am"). Man arrives at knowledge not from sense impressions but from his awareness of himself. The mind is a unity, but it does have several functions or faculties: reason, memory, will, and imagination. Since Augustine talked of these faculties as relatively independent entities, faculty psychology may be said to have started with Augustine. Concerning the body-soul relationship, Augustine sided with Plato [7] and the Neoplatonists in that he considered the soul to be immaterial and immortal and the body material and mortal. Since Aristotle [8] was for the time being "lost," and Augustine became a Church father and a saint, his psychology was the only accepted psychology through the Dark Ages and the medieval period until the rise of scholastic Aristoteleanism.

Biographic data: *DSB* 1:333–338; *EP* 1:198; *IESS* 1:468

PETER OF SPAIN (PETRUS HISPANUS)

Spanish-Italian philosopher, physician, and psychologist
Rating: (unrated)
Born: Lisbon, Portugal, between 1210 and 1220
Died: Rome, March 16, 1277
Education: Studied medicine, theology, and Aristotelean physics
 and metaphysics until 1245
Positions: 1246–1250, University of Sienna; elected cardinal
 1273; crowned Pope John XXI in 1276

A contemporary of Thomas Aquinas [16], Peter of Spain also
wrote a commentary on Aristotle's [8] *De Anima*, as well as a
treatise called *De Anima* which, unlike Aquinas's work, was not a
commentary, but an original treatise on psychology, the first one
to appear since antiquity. It was written some time between 1245
and 1250 and contained, among other topics of psychological
interest, a history of psychology. Peter of Spain also wrote a very
popular logic and a very popular medical textbook. In another
health manual, *Commentaries on Isaac*, Peter of Spain, in
speaking of medicines, compares the rational and experimental
methods of gaining knowledge and gives six steps that are
necessary to conduct an experiment on the efficacy of medicines.
These steps implicitly show an understanding of the nature of the
scientific experiment. Peter of Spain's contributions, however,
stand in isolation, since the climate for the development of
science was yet some 300 years in the future.

Biographic data: EP 6:125

AQUINAS, SAINT THOMAS

Italian theologian
Rating: (unrated)
Born: Roccasecca, near Aquino, ca. 1225
Died: Fossanova Abbey, March 7, 1274
Education: University of Naples, liberal arts; University of Paris,
 Dominican House of Studies; Cologne, theology, under Albert
 the Great
Positions: 1252–1259, teacher at University of Paris; 1259–1268,
 teacher at various places in Italy; 1268–1272, University of
 Paris; 1272–1273, University of Naples

In psychological matters, Aquinas followed Aristotle [8], although he disagreed with him on a number of points. Aquinas also interpreted Aristotle so as to fit his ideas to the Christian theological framework. Aristotle's *nous*, the active, creative reason, was said by Aquinas to be immortal, as was the rational soul. Like Aristotle, Aquinas held the hylomorphic view of the unity of body and soul. The faculties of the soul are, from the highest to the lowest, the rational, sensitive, and the vegetative faculty. The rational faculty consists of the active and the passive intellect and the will. To the five Aristotelean senses Aquinas added the interior senses. Animals are endowed with an estimative power that allows them to appreciate nonsensory relationships without the use of reason. In man, reason is involved in this function, and the corresponding interior sense is called the cogitative power. Imagination and memory are two additional interior senses. Appetites are the sensitive appetites (the concupiscible and the irrascible) and the will. Since man has free will, desire comes from the will and not from without. The possible intellect, through the power of the senses, understands, judges, and reasons about objects. It is the agent intellect, however, that makes experience intelligible by abstracting from it general, nonsensory qualities.

The Thomistic philosophy gained acceptance slowly, becoming the official philosophy of the Roman Catholic church in 1897. Thomistic psychology is also the "official" psychology of Roman Catholicism, and is being taught in Catholic schools. Aquinas's psychological views are contained in the *Summa de Homine*, which is part of his *Summa Theologica* (1266–1273).

Biographic data: Many editions of the *Summa Theologica* include a biography of St. Thomas Aquinas. There are also several separate biographies available, such as *The Life of St. Thomas Aquinas* by K. Foster (1959); *DSB* 1:196; *EP* 8:105; *IESS* 1:375

[17]

PARACELSUS (THEOPHRASTUS PHILIPPUS AUREOLUS BOMBAST VON HOHENHEIM)

German physician and theosophist
Rating: (unrated)
Born: Near Einsiedeln, Schwytz, Switzerland, ca. 1490
Died: Salzburg, Austria, September 24, 1541
Education: Studied medicine at the University of Basel
Positions: 1526–1529, professor of medicine at the University of Basel

Paracelsus, like Hippocrates[6], did not believe that mental illness is caused by demoniacal possession, and had other correct insights concerning mental disorders, such as the relationship between head injury and paralysis, cretinism and goiter (*The Diseases That Deprive Man of His Reason*, ca. 1567). Paracelsus is also credited with the explicit recognition of the influence of unconscious motivation upon behavior. While Paracelsus was a Neoplatonist, mystic, cabbalist, and believed in astrology and alchemy, he also believed that truth could be arrived at only through observation rather than reliance on authority. In this respect Paracelsus represents a stage of development of scientific thought intermediate between that of, for instance, Albert the Great and Francis Bacon [20]. By rejecting medical dogma (in stressing the use of minerals and metals rather than medicines derived from plants, he introduced chemistry in medicine), teaching medicine in German, and teaching the practice of medicine rather than theory and definitions, Paracelsus earned his expulsion from the University of Basel.

Biographic data: EP 6:38

VIVES, JUAN LUIS

[18]

Spanish philosopher
Rating: (unrated)
Born: Valencia, March 6, 1492
Died: Bruges, Belgium, May 6, 1540
Education: Graduated from University of Paris in 1512
Positions: 1519, University of Louvain; 1523–1527, Oxford University

Vives, a Renaissance humanist, was separated from Thomas Aquinas [16] by a span of some 200 years, while Descartes [28] was another 100 years in coming. Although Vives anticipated several later developments in psychology, his work did not connect directly to the psychological work of others, and he stands alone as a forerunner of modern psychology that began with Descartes.

Vives wrote several works on education that went through many editions, and in which he advocated education for women. His psychological volume is *De anima et vita libri tres* (1538). Among the points that Vives makes are: psychology should be used in education; philosophical and psychological truths are to be discovered inductively rather than deductively, avoiding speculation; a knowledge of the essence of the soul is unimportant, but to know what the manifestations of the soul are is of great importance; knowledge is of value only when it is used. Vives therefore does not concern himself with the essence of mind but with how it works. A functionalist frame of mind is clearly evident in Vives's *De anima*, 350 years before Spencer [142], James [184], and the functionalist school. Among the specific topics discussed in Vives's book are the association of ideas, memory and forgetting, emotions and passions, and intelligence. The emotions and passions are treated extensively by Vives. He stresses their manifold character, temporal variations, interaction with temperament and habit patterns, the coloring of perceptions by emotions, and their influence in creating for a person a special world, all his own.

Biographic data: F. Watson, The father of modern psychology. *Psychological Review*, 1915, 22, 333–353

[19]

HUARTE (Y NAVARRO), JUAN

Spanish physician and author
Rating: (unrated)
Born: Saint-Jean-Pied-Port, Navarre, Between 1530 and 1535
Died: Probably at Baeza, Spain, 1592
Education: Studied medicine at the University of Huesca
Positions: Practiced medicine in various places in Spain, in Baeza between 1566 and 1592

Huarte may be considered to have written the first text of differential psychology. The text, *Examen de los ingenios para las scienzias* (1575) saw forty printings in Spanish and was translated into several other languages (English title: *The Tryal of Wits, Discovering the Great Differences of Wits Among Men and What Sort of Learning Suits Best With Each Genius*). Huarte believed that most people are engaged in activities for which they lack the necessary ability. He recommended that tests of ability be administered and vocational counseling be conducted to ensure the best match between a person and his occupation. In considering the origin of individual differences in intelligence, Huarte listed humors, climate, the brain, and many other conditions as factors. In anticipation of the view that became generally accepted through Herder's [69] endorsement, Huarte asserted that intelligence and therefore the higher cultures could flourish only in the moderate climatic zones. Because he attributed individual differences to bodily build, among other things, Gall [81] and Lavater [66] considered him to be a precursor of phrenology and physiognomy, respectively.

Biographic data: *Enciclopedia universal ilustrada*, vol. 28

BACON, FRANCIS

[20]

English philosopher
Rating: 23
Born: London, January 22, 1561
Died: London, April 9, 1626
Education: Admitted an outer barrister at Gray's Inn, Cambridge, 1582
Positions: In various capacities in the royal service, including that of Lord Chancellor

In science, Bacon stood on the threshold between the Middle Ages and the birth of modern science in the 17th century. The grand purpose of Bacon's writings was to restore to man the knowledge of and power over nature that he originally had possessed. Science was to be founded again, but it was to be a new science, and the means whereby its body of knowledge would be acquired was to be new as well. Bacon analyzed the obstacles (the four idols or preconceptions) that prevented man from bringing forth a science that would yield tangible benefits and power over nature. He described the features of a natural philosophy that was based on the mind's capacity to remember, imagine, and reason, and whose aim was to discover the forms of nature, or the permanent causes beyond observable phenomena. The Baconian method for uncovering the forms of nature was to prepare exhaustive, comparative listings or tables of apparently unrelated concrete instances and, by stripping away all inessential characteristics, to arrive eventually at the one common underlying form or cause of the phenomenon studied. Basically inductive, Bacon's method differed fundamentally from the deductive method of the schoolmen, who disdained empiricism. Bacon endorsed the experimental method without qualification. Bacon's empiricism provided the basis for John Locke's [33] psychological theorizing. The spirit of Bacon's *Novum organum* (1620), his major work, pervades Locke's *Essay Concerning Human Understanding*, and the postulate that the contents of the mind are sensations and reflections and nothing else is present in the first aphorism of Bacon's book. Bacon was thus a forerunner of the psychological speculations of the philosophers in the British school of empiricism and the formulator of some of the fundamental tenets of modern science, including psychology.

Biographic data: *DNB* 2:328; *EP* 1:325; *IESS* 1:494; numerous biographic monographs in different languages

[21]

GALILEI, GALILEO

Italian mathematician, astronomer, and physicist
Rating: 22
Born: Pisa, February 15, 1564
Died: Arcetri, January 8, 1642
Education: Studied medicine, mathematics, and science at the University of Pisa, 1581–1585
Positions: 1589, University of Pisa; 1592, University of Padua; 1610–1616, first philosopher and mathematician of the Grand Duke of Tuscany

Of Galileo's three major contributions to the development of modern science—the demonstration of heliocentrism, the introduction of experimental mechanics and physics, and the founding of the modern experimental method in science—the latter is of significance to psychology. By asserting that the "book of nature is written in mathematical characters" and that only those versed in mathematics could read it, Galileo pitted mathematical rationalism against Aristotle's [8] logical and verbal rationalism. The mathematical approach to nature was the foundation of the scientific method, which Galileo himself consistently used. By way of the natural sciences the scientific method found its way into psychology, since the early practitioners of scientific psychology were natural scientists themselves.

Galileo's first full discussion of the scientific method is found in a polemic reply titled *Saggiatore* . . . , published in 1623. In this book may also be found Galileo's discussion of primary and secondary qualities, although the terms themselves were coined by John Locke [33]. Galileo took Democritus' [5] view that sensations are nothing but subjective experiences to which nothing real corresponds in the outside world and developed it further, separating the psychological from the physical and asserting that, since sensations are a subjective phenomenon, they are not a proper object of study for the natural scientist. Galileo overlooked the fact that, for instance, his own telescopic observations were based entirely on his own visual sensations, but the attitude that subjective experience is somehow not as real as the reality "out there" persists even today. A specific contribution of Galileo's to the psychology of acoustics was his discovery and demonstration that pitch depends on the frequency of vibrations of the sound-producing body.

Biographic data: *DSB* 5:237; *EP* 3:262

KEPLER, JOHANNES

German astronomer and mathematician
Rating: **19**
Born: Weil der Stadt, Württemberg, December 27, 1571
Died: Regensburg, Bavaria, November 15, 1630
Highest degree: M.S., University of Tübingen, 1591
Positions: 1594, University of Graz, professor of astronomy; 1597, University of Prague

Kepler, the discoverer of the elliptic course of planetary motion, also founded modern optics through his experiments with telescopes, the refraction of light, and the properties of lenses. Of significance to psychology was his work on vision. In *Ad vitellionem paralipomena*...(1604) (and later in *Dioptrice*, 1611), he proposed a theory of vision that replaced the prevailing one according to which the lens of the eye was an organ of visual sensation. Kepler asserted correctly that the lens acts only as a lens, that it casts an inverted image on the retina, and that "sight is a sensation of the stimulation of the retina." He noted the existence of afterimages, theorized that light effects a chemical reaction in the retina, assumed that the retinal image had to be transmitted beyond the retina to the brain to be perceived, and correctly interpreted the function of the accomodation of the lens. Kepler also raised for the first time the question of why the world appears to be right side up when the retinal image is upside down.

Biographic data: *DSB* 7:289; *EP* 4:329

HARVEY, WILLIAM

English physician
Rating: **20**
Born: Folkeston, Kent, April 1, 1578
Died: London, June 3, 1657
Highest degree: Doctor of medicine, University of Padua, 1602
Positions: 1602–1609, practicing medicine in London; 1609–1629, St. Bartholomew's Hospital, London, physician extraordinary to James I, physician in ordinary to Charles I; 1636–1646, practice of medicine in London and Oxford

Harvey's discovery of the circulation of the blood (*Exercitatio anatomica de motu cordis et sanguinis in animalibus*, 1628) was a turning point in the development of physiology and medicine since much in these disciplines had been based on assumptions, mostly inherited from Galen [12], about the blood. Harvey was more of an Aristotelean than Galenic physician, especially in subscribing to the view that the soul was not something separate or added to the body but was its form. To Harvey, blood was practically identical with the soul or life, the body being merely an appendage to it. Harvey did not, however, accept Aristotle unquestioningly but used him as a starting point for a radical departure from the traditional ways of thinking about human bodily functions. Very important also was his method of scientific observation of animal bodies, which later anatomists and physiologists sought to emulate.

More specifically psychological was Harvey's study of sensation and locomotion (*De motu locali animalium*, begun in 1627 but left unfinished). Instead of viewing the brain as a distribution center of vital spirits that moved the muscles, Harvey held the correct view that the brain serves to process sensory information and to coordinate muscular movements, the muscles themselves having the power of sensation and contraction. The nerves are to convey messages to the brain, the brain is to make judgments. The brain is the Aristotelean *sensorium commune* that compares the different senses and unifies them. In anticipation of the concept of reflex action, Harvey recognized the difference between conscious sensations, mediated by the brain, and unconscious ones, shown by the direct response of individual bodily parts to stimulation, where the organism is not aware of the processes involved.

Biographic data: DNB 25:94; DSB 6:150; EP 3:426

English philosopher
Rating: 24
Born: Westport near Bristol, April 5, 1588
Died: Devonshire, December 4, 1679
Education: B.A., Oxford University, 1608

Although Hobbes's fame rests on his social philosophy, he made significant contributions to psychological thought also. Hobbes is considered to be the first in the line of British empiricists. His psychological ideas are to be found mainly in his *Humaine Nature* (1650) and *Leviathan* (1651). The latter work deals with state and government, but it is based on what Hobbes considered to be a prerequisite to the understanding of state and government, the psychology of the individual. Hobbes's treatment of the relationship between the individual and society makes him the first social psychologist of the modern era.

The seemingly pessimistic Hobbesian view of mankind that sees man governed by selfishness, lust, greed, and aggression whenever reason or the restraints placed upon him by government do not control him is counterbalanced by the implication that, in spite of the sordid passions that govern man, he is constantly striving to control them through the exercise of reason or governmental restraints. But even the agreement among men to institute a government is guided by selfishness, however enlightened. Man's motives are based on the expectations of pleasure or pain, the most important motive being fear. The Hobbesian doctrine that man's behavior is guided by self-interest came to be known as psychological hedonism. On it Hobbes bases man's social behavior and social organization.

Hobbes rejected supernaturalism and conceived of mental functions in a mechanistic fashion. Mental processes to him were motions of brain atoms, aroused by motions in the external world. Hobbes used the concept of motion even where no motion was apparent: thinking, emotions, sensations, and consciousness itself. He had found a single, materialistic explanatory principle underlying all phenomena. Materialistic and monistic, Hobbes was also an empiricist in that he held that sensations lead to all simple ideas, and simple ideas combine to form complex ideas. Basically, all cognitions are transformed sensations. Memory and imagination are slowly decaying sensations. On this matter Hobbes opposed Descartes [28] and Descartes's philosophy of innate ideas. Sensations he held to inhere in the perceiver, not in the object, although they are caused by the objects. Sensations are motions of the brain.

Hobbes clearly stated the principle of association of ideas in terms of temporal sequences or "trains" of thought, but he did not develop it any further. Hobbes does mention "coherence" (i.e., contiguity) as a factor in association, habit and desire as guides of attention, repetition as a factor in association, and distinguishes between free and controlled association of ideas. As to emotions, Hobbes stressed the motivational aspect of passions and desires, especially the desire for power. He mentions the fact that passions may distort reason, distinguishes between innate and acquired emotions, and even outlines a theory of humor and laughter. Hobbes did not have disciples or epigones, but many of the lines of thinking that he started were soon developed more fully by the British associationists and empiricists as well as by all those who believed that man was part of the natural order, both physically and psychologically.

Biographic data: *DNB* 27:37; *DSB* 6:444; *EP* 4:30; *IESS* 6:481

[25]

MERSENNE, MARIN

French mathematician and theologian
Rating: **11**
Born: Oizé, Maine, September 8, 1588
Died: Paris, September 1, 1648
Education: Studied theology at the Jesuit college at La Flèche, 1604–1609, at the Sorbonne, 1609–1611

Mersenne is noted for his having acted as an intermediary between scientists and philosophers, especially between Descartes [28] and other philosophers, encouraging them to exchange ideas. He defended Descartes and Galileo [21], from within the ranks of the Catholic church (he was a Minim friar). Mersenne maintained contact with Descartes for many years, being the only person who ever knew where Descartes was. He collected other philosophers' criticisms of Descartes's philosophy, to which Descartes replied in subsequent editions of his works. Like Galileo, Mersenne studied sound. He investigated the nature of vibrating strings, noting the existence of overtones. His was one of the first measurements of the velocity of sound. Using the echo, he obtained the figure of 1038 feet per second and the velocity of sound in the air (*Traitez de la nature des sons et des mouvements de toutes sortes de corps,* 1636).

Biographic data: DSB 9:316; EP 5:282

GASSENDI, PIERRE [26]

French philosopher and scientist
Rating: 11
Born: Champtercier, Provence, January 22, 1592
Died: Paris, October 24, 1655
Highest degree: Doctorate in philosophy, University of Avignon, 1616
Positions: 1617–1644, University of Aix; 1645–1648, Royal College of France, teaching mathematics

While Descartes [28] tried to ignore the ancient philosophers, including Aristotle [8], Gassendi, a contemporary of Descartes, wrote a book opposing Aristotle. He also opposed Descartes, though, on the most fundamental issue, that of the origin of knowledge. Gassendi believed that sensory perception was more fundamental than intuition. In this he anticipated Locke [33] and Berkeley [40], though not the latter's radical mentalism. Gassendi also made a contribution to sensory psychology by being first to measure the velocity of sound (in 1624), and by showing that, contrary to Aristotle's opinion, sound travels at the same rate regardless of pitch.

Biographic data: EP 3:269; DSB 5:284

COMENIUS, JOANN AMOS [27]
(JAN AMOS KOMENSKY)

Moravian educator
Rating: 15
Born: Nivnice, March 28, 1592
Died: Amsterdam, the Netherlands, November 15, 1670
Education: Graduated from University of Heidelberg, in 1614

His intense interest in practical education and the religious persecution of the times combined to send Comenius on educational missions to various European countries where he spent some 40 years of his life. He wrote widely on his theories of practical education. Their philosophical basis was materialistic sensationalism. Comenius stressed learning through experience and teaching by means of demonstrations and illustrations. He made up the first picture book for children in 1658. In his most famous work, *The Great Didactic*, Comenius lays down such educational principles as learning with understanding, the use of concrete examples to demonstrate abstract principles, gradualness and sequentiality in the presentation of materials, "from the concrete to the abstract, " "from the specific to the general," "from the easy to the difficult," "from the better known to the less known," "from that which is close to that which is away," and others. Comenius also stressed the presentation of materials in accordance with the child's developmental level, the avoidance of physical punishment in school, and teaching in the child's native language. Many of the main features of the contemporary system of teaching children, such as group instruction in classrooms, classes, exercises and tests in the classroom, and the planned school year, were introduced by Comenius.

Biographic data: *DSB* 3:359; *EP* 2:146; M. Spinka, *Joann Amos Comenius, That Incomparable Moravian*, 1943

[28]

DESCARTES, RENE

French philosopher
Rating: 27
Born: La Haye, Touraine, March 31, 1596
Died: Stockholm, Sweden, February 11, 1650
Highest degree: Law degree from University of Poitiers, 1616

Descartes was the first great thinker of the modern age. He represents a break away from the scholasticism that had dominated philosophy in the Middle Ages. Since much of Descartes's thinking is psychological in nature, he may also be called the first great psychologist of the modern age. Descartes arrived at epistemological certainty by, first, doubting everything, then realizing that one certainty did remain, namely that of his own existence, because he could not doubt that he was thinking, and that meant that he existed. From the fact of his own existence Descartes arrived at the conclusion that God exists and, since God was perfect and therefore would not deceive man, that the world was real and could be studied confidently. Descartes believed that mind and body were two separate things. Mind is unextended substance whose nature is thought; it can exist independently of the extended substance of the body. Descartes was thus a dualist; he believed, however, that mind and body interact and that this interaction takes place in a particular site in the body, the pineal gland.

The mind has faculties or powers, volition and understanding. Thinking leads to ideas, which are either derived or innate. One innate idea is that of the freedom of will. Volition is thus unlimited, while understanding is limited. Other innate ideas include those of God, infinity, unity, the geometric axioms, and the like. Understanding is the fundamental aspect of thought. It alone can perceive truth. Memory, imagination, and the senses are aids to understanding, but they are subject to error. Even though sense impressions are not as reliable as understanding, they are convenient guides to reality and not mere copies or pictures of objects. Descartes thus dismissed the representative theory of perception as false.

Descartes failed to endow animals with a mind. Animals were to be considered mere machines, with no thought and no freedom of will. Man's body is likewise to be explained in mechanistic terms. Much of our motor behavior is reflexive and not dependent on mind. In Descartes may be found one of the first statements of the reflex theory of action. Descartes also did some actual physiological work, such as demonstrating the inversion, by the lens, of the visual image in the retina of a bull's eye. A portion of Descartes's *Treatise on the World* called *L'Homme* (1662) may be considered the first systematic attempt at presenting a physiological psychology. Additional statements concerning physiological psychology were made by Descartes in his *Dioptric* (1637), a treatise on optics and the eye (including the theory that distance is estimated by feeling the angle between converging eyes, accomodation, from aerial perspective and size constancy, as well as the correct hypothesis that retinal images are focused as the curvature of the lens changes) and *Passions of the Soul* (1649). The latter volume deals with emotions and motives. Motion of vital spirits of the body affect the mind, but the mind also directs the flow of vital spirits to the various parts of the body to produce action. The function of the passions is to excite the will to action, although the will must control the passions. The conflict between the will and the activity of vital spirits in the body gives rise to passions.

Descartes's influence on later psychological thinking lies in his interactional dualism (developed into a parallelism by Wundt [161] and Titchener [294]) and his emphasis on the cognitive and intellectual (and therefore existential and phenomenological) aspect of mental life in contrast to its conative aspects. This influence, including the notion of innate ideas, persisted to the end of the 19th century. His physiological work and views of the functioning of the brain, the nervous system, and the body established him as a precursor of physiological psychology and, in spite of himself, as the father of the mechanistic and materialistic view of man that developed in 18th-century France.

Biographic data: *DSB* 4:51; *EP* 2:344; *IESS* 4:127

[29]   **MARIOTTE, EDME**

French physicist
Rating: **22**
Born: Probably Chazeuil, Burgundy, ca. 1620
Died: Paris, May 12, 1684
Education: Self-taught

Mariotte was an ordained Roman Catholic priest and also one of the founders of experimental physics in France. In 1668 (*Nouvelle découverte touchant la veüe*), Mariotte discovered the blind spot in the retina where the optic nerve enters it, and showed how it can be located by directing the gaze in a certain way. He described the macula lutea and other parts of the eye. Mariotte also performed experiments to study the nature of light, color, and vision (*De la nature de la couleur*, 1681).

Biographic data: *DSB* 9:114

[30]   **PASCAL, BLAISE**

French philosopher
Rating: **19**
Born: Clermont-Ferrand, Puy de Dôme, June 19, 1623
Died: Paris, August 19, 1662
Education: Educated by father

In response to the queries of a gentleman gambler, Pascal and Fermat worked out the answers as to why he was losing money in games of dice. From these beginnings, which included the famous

Pascal triangle, probability calculus arose, of immense importance to science since it allowed predictions in the face of uncertainty. Because behavioral events are eminently uncertain, Pascal's work was of utmost importance to the development of psychology as a science, especially after subsequent elaborations of Pascal's work by such men as Quételet [116], Gauss [99], and Galton [144].

Biographic data: EP 6:51

GEULINCX, ARNOLD [31]

Flemish philosopher
Rating: 11
Born: Antwerp, Flanders, 1624 (baptized January 31)
Died: Leiden, the Netherlands, November, 1669
Highest degree: Doctor of medicine, University of Leiden, 1658
Positions: 1646–1658, University of Louvain; 1662–1669, University of Leiden

The problem of how body, an extended substance, and mind, an unextended substance, interact was never solved by Descartes [28]. A Cartesian philosopher, Geulincx, solved this problem by asserting that there was no contact between body and mind: God, who was neither body nor mind but comprised both, was the cause of all action. Body and mind are like two clocks that keep perfect time. Although they do not affect each other, they give the appearance of interaction. Two events, A and B, which seem to be causally connected, are only an occasion for God, when event A occurs, to cause event B. Hence Geulincx's view came to be called occasionalism, a form of dualistic parallelism.

Biographic data: EP 3:323

HUYGENS, CHRISTIAN [32]

Dutch astronomer and mathematician
Rating: 14
Born: The Hague, April 14, 1629
Died: The Hague, June 8, 1695
Education: Studied at the University of Leiden

Huygens's main achievement was the formulation of the wave theory of light, but he contributed many other important new inventions and discoveries in the areas of astronomy, mathematics, mechanics, and optics. To psychology, Huygens is important for two things: the invention of the pendulum clock in 1656, and the writing, in 1657, of a first book on probability (*Tractatus de ratiociniis in aleae ludo*). His treatise on probability remained the only such work until the 18th century. The pendulum clock allowed precise time measurements for the first time. This was important to astronomy, but problems concerning time measurement in astronomy led directly to the reaction time experiment in psychology in the 19th century. French and German mathematicians developed the theory of probability in the 18th and 19th centuries, preparing for modern psychology its most important tool.

Biographic data: *DSB* 6:597

[33]

LOCKE, JOHN

English philosopher
Rating: 27
Born: Wrington, near Bristol, August 29, 1632
Died: Oates, Essex, October 28, 1704
Education: M.A., Christ Church, Oxford University, 1658, B.M. 1675

Empiricism was launched in England by Locke, who thus laid the foundations of comtemporary psychology. Locke's psychological views are to be found in *An Essay Concerning Human Understanding*, first published in 1690. The essay is based on the proposition that understanding the way in which the human mind works is a prerequisite to understanding anything else. Psychology in Locke thus became propaedeutic to all other knowledge. Locke asserted with Aristotle and Thomas Aquinas that there are no innate ideas in the human mind; that the notion that there are such ideas comes from habit; that the mind is at first like blank paper or an empty cabinet that is gradually filled with ideas; and that these ideas are entirely the result of experience. Ideas are units of mind and arise from the working of the senses. The senses supply the simple, indivisible sensory ideas. Primary sensible qualities are solidity, form, substance, and motion. Colors, tastes, smells, and the like are secondary qualities since they do not inhere in the sensible objects themselves but produce sensations as modes of appearance of the primary qualities. To illustrate the nature of the secondary qualities, Locke used the famous example of the reversed sensations produced in a cold and a warm hand when both are placed in a basin of water at room temperature. In addition to sensory ideas there are also ideas that arise from reflection (such as perception and thinking), although the raw material that reflection works upon is supplied by the sense organs. Sensory ideas and those that come from reflection constitute the totality of mental activities. Simple ideas resulting from sensation and simple ideas resulting from reflection may combine to form complex ideas. Pain and pleasure are simple ideas. They occur simultaneously with the experience of sensations or reflection, and emotions are derived from the experience of pleasure and pain.

Locke coined the expression "association of ideas," but used it only to to explain how wrong ideas become associated with each other, whereas the associationists that followed him used it to explain how any two ideas combine and therefore to explain the structure of mind itself. In the various aspects of Locke's treatment of mind—its analysis into the elements of ideas, the distinction between primary and secondary qualities, the careful and systematic use of introspection, denial of innateness of ideas, reflection as an inner sense, the association of ideas, and the referral of all mental life to experience—may be found the beginning of several trends and lines of thought that were to flourish in psychology in later centuries: associationism, structuralism, act psychology, and behaviorism, and through which Locke continues to exercise his influence even today.

Biographic data: *DNB* 34:27; *DSB* 8:436; *EP* 4:487; *IESS* 9:464; H. R. Fox Bourne, *The Life of John Locke*, 2 vol., 1876; M. Cranston. *John Locke: a Biography*, 1957

SPINOZA, BENEDICTUS (OR, BARUCH) DE   [34]

Dutch philosopher
Rating: 24
Born: Amsterdam, November 24,1632
Died: The Hague, February 20, 1677
Education: No university education

To Spinoza, lens grinder and philosopher, psychology was a stepping-stone in the development of a system of ethics, which, in

turn, was part of a great metaphysical system. Spinoza developed further the Cartesian system of philosophy and introduced changes and solutions to Cartesian difficulties. Like Descartes [28], Spinoza bases his metaphysics in the idea of God. Unlike Descartes's, Spinoza's philosophy is based on monistic parallelism, rather than a dualism and interactionism. The only substance is God. Human body and mind are only two aspects of the same reality, God. The modern version of Spinoza's double-aspect theory is the double-language theory, where the same event is described in one language by the subject in terms of his subjective experience and in another by an outside observer of the same event. Spinoza was also completely deterministic. Willing takes place when one thinks of the course of action that is to be followed. The illusion of free willing occurs when there is ignorance of antecedent causes. A corollary of this view is that both body and mind are subject to natural law. Man can follow ethical dictates even in the face of complete determinism because man can improve his understanding of nature and act in accordance with it. Freedom is acting in the light of necessity.

Everything obeys the fundamental law of nature, which is self-preservation. This endeavor (*conatus*) to persist manifests itself as appetite on the bodily side and as desire on the mental side. Desire plus joy and grief are the primary emotions. When man strives to achieve a greater understanding, active joy is the accompanying result. Freedom exists only when the emotions are active rather than passive. Freedom is relative: man is free if he can think clearly, control his environment, and remain in an active state as long as possible. This is difficult because of the dominance of the passive emotions. Freedom is achieved as the causes of the passive emotions are understood.

While Freud [224] was not directly influenced by him, Spinoza, in his emphasis on striving and the acquisition of emotional freedom through the understanding of emotions, anticipated two cardinal points of psychoanalysis and, in general, qualifies as a forerunner of the dynamic view in psychology. The direct influence of Spinoza on psychology, however, has been slight.

Biographic data: *EP* 7:530; A. Wolf, *Spinoza: His Life and Treatise on God and Man*, 1916; A. Wolf, *The Oldest Biography of Spinoza*, 1927

French philosopher and physicist
Rating: 21
Born: Paris, August 8, 1638
Died: Paris, October 13, 1715
Education: Studied philosophy at Collège de la Marche and theology at Sorbonne

Malebranche was a Cartesian philosopher who sought to complete Descartes's [28] philosophy with regard to body-mind interaction so that it would be compatible with Catholic theology and St. Augustine's [14] teachings. In Descartes's system, body and mind were completely separate, yet they interacted in the pineal gland. The problem created by Descartes of how the soul, an unextended substance, could influence the body, an extended substance, was solved by Malebranche by referring causation to God: if one event seems to cause another it is because the first event gives the occasion for God to cause the second (*De recherches de la vérité où l'on traite de la nature de l'esprit de l'homme et de l'usage qu'il en doit faire pour éviter l'erreur dans les sciences*, 1674–1675). The soul mediates between God and the body, but its light comes mainly from the light of God. The bond to the body results in sense impressions, the bond to God in an insight into God's ideas. True cognition arises only from the latter bond, thus all sense impressions are deceitful and of practical use only. About the nature of the soul one cannot have either ideas or knowledge in a strict sense, thus there cannot be a strong science of the soul. Still, Malebranche valued inner knowledge above that of sense impressions. Knowledge about other souls may be obtained on the assumption that all souls are the same. While incomplete, inner knowledge of the workings of the soul offers the possibility of having a science of mental life since introspection carries with it the seal of indubitable truth.

The soul has two kinds of faculties: understanding and will. Understanding is passive and includes sense impressions, imagination, and memory. The will manifests itself in attitudes, inclinations, and the "passions of the soul." Concerning psychophysical relationships Malebranche held that to mental phenomena there correspond traces in the brain and that the brain is the nodal point in the mind-body relationship. The brain contains both mental and physical processes, hence it is possible to correlate the qualities of inner experience and physical quantities.

In addition to writing on philosophical phychology, Malebranche did research on light and vision, including the phenomena of color, and the psychological determinants of visual perception, such as the moon illusion (*Réflexions sur la lumière et les couleurs et sur la génération du feu*, 1688).

Biographic data: *DSB* 9:47; *EP* 5:140

[36]

NEWTON, SIR ISAAC

English scientist and mathematician
Rating: **26**
Born: Woolsthorpe, Lincolnshire, December 25, 1642
Died: London, March 20, 1727
Highest degree : B.A., Cambridge University, 1665
Positions, honors: 1667, Cambridge University; 1703–1727, President, Royal Society; knighted 1705

Newton, one of the greatest scientists of all times, contributed to psychology directly through his research and discoveries in the area of light and indirectly by postulating the principle of determinism. Some time between 1665 and 1667, by breaking white light into chromatic components with a prism, recombing them into white light, and breaking it down again, Newton demonstrated the nature of white light and produced the first and entirely original theory of color. It explained why objects have different colors when illuminated by white light. Newton explained all colors as some combination of the spectral seven, described the nature of the complementarity of colors, described the color circle, formulated two laws of color mixture, and identified the whiteness of light with its intensity. Newton also knew that single objects are seen in binocular vision because of fusion of sensations from nerve fibers arising in corresponding points in the two eyes. Newton first described the nature of light in a paper presented to the Royal Society. All of his work on light and color was published in *Opticks*, which appeared in 1704.

In his principal work, *Philosophiae naturalis principia mathematica* (1687), Newton outlines the laws of the material universe that were the ones accepted by the scientific world for the next 200 years. He expressed the hope of deriving all phenomena of nature from the laws that he had formulated concerning the motion of bodies. Although the term "determinism" was not used until the 19th century, Newton was the first to state clearly the propositions on which scientific determinism came to be based. Newton's "phenomena of nature" were eventually interpreted by some to include mental phenomena as well. In scientific psychology today the hypothesis that all mental events and behaviors have a cause is accepted, and must be accepted in order to proceed with psychology as a scientific enterprise.

Biographic data: DNB 40:370; EP 5:489; many biographic monographs

LEIBNIZ, GOTTFRIED WILHELM VON [37]

German philosopher
Rating: **26**
Born: Leipzig, June 21, 1646
Died: Hannover, November 14, 1716
Education: Law degree from the University of Altdorf, 1666

To the scientific world Leibniz is important as mathematician, while his psychological view of reality left a mark in the history of psychology. Leibniz viewed reality as activity. Substance, according to Leibniz, is being. Substance may be simple or compound. Simple substance is called the monads. The monads are indestructible, uncreated, and immutable elements of all being, hence their essence is also activity. Although monads develop, they do not affect each other. The world is thus an infinite set of independent monads, which precludes causation. Causation is mere coincidences in time and space. The activity of the monads is akin to perception. Thus monadal development implies the clarification of perception, and substance shows degrees of consciousness. Even the unconscious is only relatively so, for it is potentially capable of being perceived, just as the totality of countless drops of water is heard as the splash of a wave (apperception), although no single drop of water makes a perceptible sound (*petites perceptions*).

Leibniz's emphasis on activity places him as the forerunner of all the activity psychologies that came later, such as act psychology. The notion that mind is a unitary, albeit developing entity is also found in later psychologies, such as the Gestalt theory. Leibniz also stands at the beginning of the development of the idea of the unconcious that, through Herbart [101], Fechner [120], and Wundt [161], reached its culmination in Freud [224]. In the question of mind-body relationship, Leibniz's acausality helped strengthen the doctrine of psychophysical parallelism, to which a number of prominent psychologists later subscribed. In this view body and mind are in agreement not because of some external intervention or causal act but because they obey parallel laws.

Biographic data: DSB 8:149; *EP* 4:422

[38]

MOLYNEUX, WILLIAM

Irish astronomer and mathematician
Rating: **13**
Born: Dublin, April 17, 1656
Died: Dublin, October 11, 1698
Highest degree: B.A., Trinity College, Dublin, 1675
Positions, honors: 1695, University of Dublin; honorary LL.D., Trinity College

In *Dioptrica nova: Treatise on Dioptricks* (1692), the first English work on optics, Molyneux provided the definitive answer to the question of how we see the world right side up when the retinal image is upside down, namely that up and down are terms that refer to the gravitational pull and that vision takes no account of this since the mind does not look at the retinal image and its relation to the outside world. It was in this context that Molyneux directed his famous query in a letter to his friend John Locke [33] concerning the visual experiences of a hypothetical individual who, having been born blind, sees for the first time as an adult. Molyneux himself supplied the answer and Locke confirmed it by saying that such a person indeed would not be able to identify objects by sight alone. Molyneux was thus one of the first thinkers to suggest that meaning accrues to perception through experience.

Biographic data: DNB 38:138

[39]

WOLFF, BARON CHRISTIAN VON

German philosopher
Rating: **25**
Born: Breslau, Silesia, January 24, 1679
Died: Halle, Saxony-Anhalt, April 9, 1754
Education: Studied at Jena (mathematics, physics, philosophy) and Leipzig (teaching), graduated from Leipzig University in 1703

Wolff was a prominent systematizer of philosophy and the foremost exponent of faculty psychology in the 18th century. He had considerable influence on other philosophers, such as Kant [60], in the way they conceptualized philosophical problems. In psychology, Wolff wrote two volumes, *Psychologia empirica* (1732) and *Psychologia rationalis* (1734). This particular subdivision of psychology begins with Wolff. Rational psychology comes from metaphysics and from the experience of the soul's activities, and it depends more on reason than experience; empirical psychology is about man (soul-body) and depends more on experience than reason. Wolff held that rational psychology is superior to empirical psychology in that it gives clear and distinct ideas, in contrast to empirical psychology whose product is vague, obscure ideas and sensations.

The soul is one, but it has different powers or faculties: feeling, desire, and knowing, the latter consisting of perception, memory, understanding, and reason. The most important function of the soul is to represent the world. Since the soul it tied to the body, the location of the body and nature of the sense organs determine the way in which the world is perceived. In his *Psychologia empirica*, Wolff relies more on Descartes [28] and relates the existence of the I to the fact of self-awareness. Consciousness is the first datum that we come across in our attempts to find a basis for psychology. Without consciousness it is impossible to know anything about the activity of the soul. Still, not all activity is conscious. Ideas can exist with or without consciousness. There is consciousness when the soul is aware of its own activities, but there is no consciousness in sleep. Sensations can likewise be obscure or clear and thus be conscious or unconscious. While Wolff's psychology was oversimplified, his terminology and conceptualization of mental processes is still present in the thinking of the man in the street.

Biographic data: *EP* 8:340

BERKELEY, GEORGE   [40]

English philosopher
Rating: 25
Born: Near Kilkenny, Ireland, March 12, 1685
Died: Oxford, England, January 14, 1753

Highest degree: M.A. in philosophy, Trinity College, Dublin, 1707

Positions: No academic positions; various ecclesiastic (Bishop of Cloyne)

Berkeley was a philosopher in the British empiricist school. His main arguments for his views were psychological in nature. Berkeley also contributed to psychology substantive thinking concerning problems of vision. His first major publication, *An Essay Toward a New Theory of Vision* (1709), dealt with that subject. A year later, *A Treatise Concerning the Principles of Human Knowledge* was published, second of Berkeley's works of importance to psychology. Both show the influence of Locke [33]. Sense experience is the source of knowledge, but the only thing we can know is our experiences and ideas. Being, in fact, is perception. This view, later called mentalism, insists that while objects are real, their reality lies in the mind of God. The appearances of objects is all we can know, but the appearances are also real since God guarantees their reality through the reality of the physical world. In our minds, the object and its appearance fuse.

In the mind, there are the sensory ideas aroused by the passions and imagination, but nothing that could be called abstract ideas. Such ideas are derived from the senses. Ideas are only perceptions and images, both of them particular, not abstract. Ideas from different sources, such as ideas arising in the different sense departments, are combined by experience into wholes. Idea are simultaneously associated when sensations occur contiguously. Berkeley also distinguished successive association and differentiated between association by similarity, causality, and coexistence. With Locke, he agreed that a person lacking previous experience would be unable to identify objects, but disagreed with him concerning the nature of the primary and secondary qualities of objects. To Berkeley, primary qualities were actually secondary qualities since experience can know only itself and not something that was not derived from experience.

Berkeley's essay on vision was the first monograph in psychology. In it he argues for immateriality, using the avenue of perception. Distance, depth, and size are not seen directly, "out there." Rather, we learn about spatial qualities by associating visual, tactual, and kinesthetic sensations. Depth is not a sensation but an additional property of the visual world, "suggested to the mind by the mediation of some other idea which is itself perceived in the act of seeing." Some of these ideas are what later came to be called the psychological or secondary depth cues, with the exception of motion parallax, which

Berkeley does not mention. The primary cues of convergence, accomodation, and blurring receive a discussion from Berkeley, but the role he assigns them is a mentalistic, not a materialistic one: one feels the position of the eyes, not the angle between them. Berkeley's account of how sight and touch combine to produce perception of space was a landmark in the development of an empiricist theory of perception.

Biographic data: DNB 4:348; *DSB* 2:16; *EP* 1:295; *IESS* 2:62; J. O. Wisdom, An outline of Berkeley's life. *British Journal of the Philosophy of Science* , 1953, 4, 78–87; A. A. Luce, *The Life of George Berkeley, Bishop of Cloyne*, 1949

SWEDENBORG, EMANUEL [41]

Swedish scientist, inventor, philosopher, and theologian
Rating: **11**
Born: Stockholm, January 29, 1688
Died: London, England, March 29, 1772
Highest degree: Master's degree from the University of Uppsala, 1709

Swedenborg's psychological views are found in his three-volume treatise, *Oeconomia regni animalis in transactiones divisa* (1740-1741), and subsequent shorter works, first collected and published in 1846 and translated into English as *Psychological Transactions by Emanuel Swedenborg* (1920). They constitute only a fraction of the 20,000 handwritten pages he left behind. To Swedenborg, consciousness has four functions: *anima* , which is the highest and of which we can have no direct knowledge; *mens rationalis* or reason; *animus*, similar to Aristotle's [8] vegatative soul; and the sense organs. This functional division shows the influence of St. Augustine [14]. Influenced to some extent also by Locke [33] and Leibniz [37], Swedenborg achieved a compromise between the *tabula rasa* and the innate ideas positions. At first only covert mystic, Swedenborg made significant contributions to science and technology during the first half of his adult life. He spent several years studying the brain, and is credited with being the first to place psychological functions in the cortex of the brain. In his later attempts to account for body-soul interaction, Swedenborg drew on his knowledge of physiology, which was good. To him, the soul was a separate intity, inherited from Adam through the semen of each individual's father. It is the life principle of the individual and possesses a store of wisdom from conception. There is no reason in the newborn child, though. This he acquires through experience. The *mens* thus becomes increasingly like the *anima,* and the *anima* reciprocates. The communication between reason and soul occurs through fibers and fluids, which Swedenborg attempted to explain in quasi-physiological terms in a manner reminiscent of Descartes [28]. Also, like Descartes, Swedenborg asserted that the body obeyed natural laws, which were mechanical. Unlike Descartes, to his physiology Swedenborg added mysticism instead of philosophy. In 1745 he experienced illumination that told him to abandom science and take up the interpretation of the Bible. Swedenborg acquired fame throughout Europe through his accounts of visits to the spirit world. The father of William James [184] was a Swedenborg enthusiast. James's own interest in psychic research was partly because of his father's influence.

Biographic data: *EP* 8:48 E. Swift, *Swedenborg, the Man and His Works,* 1932; G. Trobridge, *Emanuel Swedenborg, Life and Teaching,* 1944; S. Toksvig, *Emanuel Swedenborg,* 1948; J. Jonsson, *Emanuel Swedenborg,* 1971

[42] ## VOLTAIRE (PSEUDONYM OF FRANCOIS MARIE AROUET)

French author and philospher
Rating: **19**
Born: Paris, November 21, 1694
Died: Paris, May 30, 1778
Education: Attended the Jesuit school of Collège Louis-le-Grand between 1704 and 1711

Voltaire, one of the greatest figures in French letters and thought, never wrote anything specifically psychological. In the classic *Lettres philosophiques* (1734), however, Voltaire, by espousing and presenting the Lockean point of view, performed the service of acquainting Europe, and especially France, with the Lockean doctrine. Voltaire admired Newton [36], opposed Descartes [28] and professed ignorance concerning the nature of the soul, advocated empiricism, sensationism, and the scientific method, but did not go to the extreme of atheism, as did such French materialists as de la Mettrie [50], whom he influenced.

Biographic data: *EP* 8:262

American philosopher and educator
Rating: **12**
Born: Guilford, Connecticut, October 14, 1696
Died: Stratford, Connecticut, June 6, 1772
Education: Graduated from College of New Haven (Yale University) in 1714
Positions, honors: 1754–1763, President, King's College (Columbia University); three honorary degrees

In the first textbook of philosophy published in America, *Elementa philosophica* (1752), Johnson considered such psychological topics as sensation, perception, emotions, and the will, as well as some anatomy and physiology of the nervous system. He made comments on the possibility of a genetic and comparative psychology. The treatise basically followed the British empiricists, Johnson having become a disciple of Berkeley [40] after the latter's visit to America, but contained an admixture of Christian theology and the notion of innate ideas: Johnson proved the existence of God by the existence of eternal truths in the mind that did not depend on experience. The will Johnson held to be free, unlike his pupil Jonathan Edwards [44] who believed that all decisions were made by God.

Biographic data: *EP* 4:290; *NCAB* 6:341

American philosopher and theologian
Rating: **11**
Born: East Windsor, Connecticut, October 5, 1703
Died: Princeton, New Jersey, March 22, 1758
Highest degree: M. A., Yale College, 1722
Positions: 1722–1723, minister, New York State; 1724–1725, instructor, Yale College; 1726–1750, pastor, Northampton, Massachusetts; 1751–1756, missionary, Stockbridge, Massachusetts; 1757–1758 (6 months), President, College of New Jersey

Edwards was the most important pre-Revolutionary American thinker. He wrote on psychological questions in relation to religion, the emotions (*A Treatise Concerning Religious Affections*, 1746), the freedom of the will (*Inquiry Into the*

Freedom of the Will, 1757), and occasionally treated his parishoners' emotional problems with psychological techniques. His *Treatise* and *Inquiry* may be considered to be the first psychological works written by an American. Edwards was influenced by Locke [33], but also showed some originality of ideas. In his *Inquiry* Edwards, like Hume [52] and Spinoza [34], argues not only that there is no free will but that all choices made by man are actually those of God. In a sermon, "Men Naturally God's Enemies," he adumbrates Freud's [224] idea of the hate of the father as a symbol of authority and the unconscious desire of those led to kill the leader.

Biographic data: *EP* 2:460; *NCAB* 5:464, 7:169; C. H. Faust and T. H. Johnson, *Jonathan Edwards*, 1935; O. E. Winslow, *Jonathan Edwards*, 1940; P. Miller, *Jonathan Edwards*, 1949

[45]

HARTLEY, DAVID

English philosopher
Rating: 24
Born: Armley, Yorkshire, August 30, 1705
Died: Bath, Somersetshire, August 28, 1757
Highest degree: M.A. Cambridge University, 1729
Positions: Private practice of medicine at Newark, Bury, St. Edmunds, 1730–1735, London, 1735–1742, Bath, 1742–1757

Although Hartley was less original than Locke [33], Hobbes [24], Hume [52], or Berkeley [40], Hartley's systematic presentation of the views of the British empiricists and associationists earned him the title of the founder of the British school of association psychology. His main work is *Observations on Man* (1749), in which, for the first time, the mind of the associationist doctrine is related to the body. Although Hartley's physiology was mostly theoretical, he consistently and consecutively stated his propositions in mental and physical terminology. One important statement that Hartley made was that often repeated sensory vibrations left their impress as simple ideas, or, conversely, that often repeated sensory vibrations predisposed the brain to repeat similar but minute vibrations (vibratiuncles). Hartley subscribed to psychophysical parallelism in that he held that cerebral vibrations and the rise of ideas, while occurring simultaneously, were not the cause of each other. In line with Locke, Hartley said that at birth the mind is blank and that sensations arise from external impressions. Sensations, in turn, give rise to ideas. Simultaneous and successive contiguity is the main principle of association of sensations and ideas. Hartley consistently used the law of contiguity to explain all other mental phenomena. The fainter vibrations left in the wake of sensory vibrations are the basis of memory and imagination. One vibration, either sensory or its fainter trace in the brain, evokes another if they are associated. In this notion Hartley included motor acts, voluntary and involuntary, that could be evoked by ideas and vice versa.

Biographic data: *DNB* 25:66; *DSB* 6:138; *EP* 3:418; *IESS* 6:324

FRANKLIN, BENJAMIN

[46]

American philosopher, printer, diplomat
Rating: 13
Born: Boston, Massachusetts, January 6, 1706
Died: Philadelphia, Pennsylvania, April 17, 1790

Franklin's name enters the history of psychology in two contexts. In 1765, he showed that an afterimage may be positive when seen with closed eyes but negative when seen with open eyes on a light field. The demonstration came to be known as the "Franklin experiment" and was much discussed by scientists.

During his stay in France as the American ambassador Franklin was appointed by the French government to the first of several commissions to investigate August Mesmer [63], who was active in Paris at that time. The commission's findings was that "imagination" was responsible for Mesmer's alleged cures. When a follower of Mesmer, Puységur, claimed to have achieved cures by having afflicted persons stand under trees that he had "magnetized," Franklin performed the experiment of telling some peasants that certain trees had been "magnetized." Those who stood under these trees were cured as effectively as Puységur's patients, which confirmed to Franklin the commission's previous conclusion that "imagination" or suggestion was at work.

Biographic data: *DSB* 5:129; *NCAB* 1:328; *Autobiography*

LINNAEUS, CAROLUS

Swedish botanist
Rating: **19**
Born: Råshult, May 23, 1707
Died: Uppsala, January 10, 1778
Education: Studied medicine at University of Uppsala and University of Lund; M.D., University of Harderwijk, Holland, 1736
Positions: 1732–1778, University of Uppsala, teaching botany

The name of Linnaeus, the founder of taxonomy in botany and zoology, is one of the famous names in biology. One direct contribution of Linnaeus to psychology was the classification of odors that he proposed in a 1752 paper. Linnaeus suggested the classification of odors into the aromatic, fragrant, ambrosiac alliaceous, hircine, foul, and nauseous. With minor variations, this classification has been retained to this day through the work of such investigators of smell as Zwaardemaker [233] and Henning [431].

In a more general way, the classificatory work of Linnaeus made classification and description in science, including psychology, important. The classificatory and phenomenological tradition in psychology continued through such men as Goethe [77] in the 18th century, Purkinje [107] and Hering [167] in the 19th, and the Gestalt psychologists in the 20th century. Linnaeus himself opposed any idea of organic evolution. His taxonomic trees of plants and animals, however, stimulated thought along evolution lines. Systematic evolutionary thought began after Linnaeus, leading to Darwin [127] and the evolutionary theory.

Biographic data: *DSB* 8:374

BUFFON, GEORGE LOUIS LECLERC DE

French naturalist
Rating: **13**
Born: Montbard, Côte d'Or, September 7, 1707
Died: Paris, April 16, 1788
Education: Studied law at University of Dijon, 1723–1726, possibly medicine and botany at Collège de l'Oratoire, Angers, 1728–1730

Buffon created original ideas in many areas of natural science. He anticipated, for instance, Lamarck's [68] idea of the inheritance of acquired characteristics. In his *Histoire naturelle de l'homme* (1749), Buffon approached man in the same way he approached animals, including man's social and intelligent behavior. While recognizing that man is superior to animals by virtue of reason, he showed that it was the evolution of the biological organism that made reason possible. Reason developed from language, and language developed because man lived in a society. Society, in turn, was necessary because of man's slow physical development and long period of dependency in early life. Buffon applied the same reasoning to animals, demonstrating how the nature of their social life determined their level of intelligence. More generally, Buffon presented a speculative but bold theory of organic evolution which, while postulating the original creation of species, assumed, nevertheless, that they undergo chance variation, improvement, and deterioration from generation to generation. Buffon thus contributed to the several streams of evolutionary thinking that came together in Darwin's [127] evolutionary theory.

In a 1743 paper, Buffon used the phrase "accidental colors" to denote afterimages, flight of colors, color contrast, and other events in which color is seen without an adequate color stimulus. He was first to describe in detail the formation of successive color contrast.

Biographic data: DSB 2:576–582

HALLER, ALBRECHT VON [49]

Swiss antomist, physiologist, and botanist
Rating: 17
Born: Berne, October 16, 1708
Died: Berne, December 17, 1777
Highest degree: Medical degree, University of Leiden, 1727
Positions: 1736–1753, University of Göttingen

Haller, the father of experimental physiology of the modern era, established physiology as an independent science. His greatest work, *Elementa physiologiae corporis humani* (1757–1766), remained *the* treatise on physiology for a century. Of importance to psychology are several of his discoveries and demonstrations concerning the action of nerves and muscles. He showed that muscles shortened when stimulated, then returned to their original length. He labelled this property irritability (*vis insita*) and recognized it as essential in heart action and the action of the intestines. He thought of the nerves as tubes, however, and of vital spirits as a sort of watery juice flowing through them. Haller showed that body tissues are not of themselves capable of sensation, but that sensation depends on the presence of nerves. He introduced the notion of the adequate stimulus, or the normal and appropriate stimulus which a sense organ is designed to respond to. He showed that all nerves converge upon the brain, and demonstrated the central role of the brain through experiments with lesions to the brain and the nerves. Haller also calculated, but did not measure, the velocity of the nerve impulse to be about 150 feet per second, which is very close to modern measurements.

Biographic data: *DSB* 6:61; *EP* 3:405

[50]

LA METTRIE, JULIEN OFFRAY DE

French philosopher
Rating: 26
Born: St. Malo, Ille et Vilaine, December 25, 1709
Died: Berlin, Germany, November 11, 1751
Highest degree: M.D., University of Reims, 1724

La Mettrie lived but 41 years. He nevertheless left his mark in the history of philosophy as well as psychology by pioneering in the materialistic conception of man. Although La Mettrie started out as a theologian, a severe fever during a military campaign convinced him that mental life is nothing but the result of the mechanical action of the nervous system, that soul and thinking could not be distinguished from each other, and that the former was just as perishable as the latter—without a body neither one had an existence. The volume, *L'homme machine*, published in 1748 (English translation 1750), places La Mettrie at the beginning of the line of descent of behaviorism. La Mettrie extended Descartes's [28] view of animals as reflexive automata and applied it to man. His physiology, however, was still speculative. He considered organisms to be mechanisms, made of matter that not only moved but had consciousness. To man, La Mettrie asserted, the only reality is his body. His apparent uniqueness is only due to the complexity of his actions.

La Mettrie's extreme views attracted attention, but also led to persecution, making him a landmark that signified the increasing materialism of 18th-century science.

Biographic data: *DSB* 7:605; *EP* 4:379; J. P. Damiron, *Mémoirs pour servir à l'histoire de la philosophie au XVIIIe siècle,* 1858, I, 1–14

REID, THOMAS   [51]

Scottish philosopher
Rating: 25
Born: Strachan, Kincardine, April 26, 1710
Died: Glasgow, October 7, 1796
Education: Studied theology at Marischal College, Aberdeen; licensed for ministry 1731
Positions: 1733–1736, librarian at Marischal College; 1737, minister at New Machar; 1751, Aberdeen University, philosophy instructor; 1764–1781, University of Glasgow, professor of moral philosophy

Reid came first in time among the philosophers who made up the so-called Scottish School. Reid and the Scottish School stood against associationism, especially Hume's [52] associationism, rejected references to physiology in any explanation of human behavior, and substituted for empiricist explanations of the perception of reality explanations that were in accord with Christian orthodoxy. The question of how the mind creates objects if the raw material available is only sensations, Reid answered by reference to "common sense" or the agreement of all people through the ages, as evidenced in their actual conduct in real situations and the "structure and grammar of all languages." Common sense informs us that it is self-evident physical objects exist. Reid added that, while the senses provide sensations, a divinely implanted belief in the existence of objects to which the sensations correspond, brings about the perception of the world as it is commonly experienced. The sensations "suggest" the physical objects.

Reid is also called a faculty psychologist, mainly because of the contents of two books that he wrote, *Essays on the Active Powers of the Human Mind* (1788) and *Essays on the Intellectual Powers of Man* (1785). Reid listed twenty-four active powers of the mind and six intellectual powers, similar to those proposed by

Wolff [39]. The phrenologist Gall [81] borrowed twenty-seven of these powers from Reid and Reid's disciple, Steward [78], and assigned them to twenty-seven brain areas. In addition to phrenology, Reid's influence was felt later (19th century) in France and in America, where pre-Jamesian psychology was largely of the Scottish variety. Reid's philosophy of common sense may be found expounded in his *Inquiry Into the Human Mind on the Principles of Common Sense* (1764).

Biographic data: DNB 47:436; EP 7:118

[52]

HUME, DAVID

Scottish philosopher
Rating: 27
Born: Edinburgh, April 26, 1711
Died: Edinburgh, August 25, 1776
Education: Entered University of Edinburgh in 1723, no degree

Hume was one of the great English philosophers-empiricists and a representative of the school of associationism. Hume never occupied an academic post but gained fame as a philosophic writer. He may be considered Berkeley's [40] philosophical successor in that he carried Berkeley's idealistic position a step further toward its ultimate extreme. Of importance to psychology are Hume's *Treatise of Human Nature* (1739–1740) and *An Enquiry Concerning Human Understanding* (1748), a revision of the first essay.

Hume tackled the question of cause and effect, which theretofore had been assumed to be a universal principle presenting no particular problem. Hume realized that while things may follow each other in a predictable sequence, the necessary connection between them cannot ever be observed. Yet, while we never have a percept of a cause, we all believe that there is such a thing. Hume then set out to establish what there was in human nature that made man think in terms of cause and effect. In the *Treatise* Hume shows that some things which were previously thought of as belonging to the universe are in fact a function of man's psychological makeup. All information is derived from experience. Sensing, feeling, and willing leave impressions as the first mental contents. When the sensory object is gone, impressions become ideas. The clear distinction between sense impressions and ideas was a major contribution of Hume to psychology. The main distinction between them lies, according to Hume, in their degree of vividness, ideas being relatively faint.

When two objects occur together repeatedly, the appearance of one object later will evoke the idea of the missing object through association. This is the basis for the belief that the world continues even though there are no direct sense impressions at the moment. It is also the basis for the belief in a continuing self. Memory and imagination are only two ways in which ideas work. The principles that the association of ideas obeys are similarity, contiguity, and causality. Later Hume reduced causality to a special case of similarity and contiguity. The idea of causality arises because we may experience events together repeatedly. Thus causality is a mental habit that arises from experience and not an innate idea or law of thought. In fact, Hume explained all human experiences as habits. The soul was reduced by Hume to impressions and ideas. The mind became nothing but a congeries of sensations.

Hume was a most important link in the development of psychological thought from empiricism to modern learning theory by way of associationism. His other contribution to psychology was his "very curious discovery" that the idea of causality was an acquired habit of thought. Philosophers and psychologists of later generations, especially those concerned with the philosophy of science and the logic of scientific enquiry, have had to contend with it in one way or another.

Biographic data: DNB 28:215; DSB 6:555; EP 4:74; IESS 6:546; D. Hume, *My Own Life*; J. H. Burton, *Life and Correspondence of David Hume*, 1846; T. H. Huxley, *Hume*, 1879; J. Orr, *Hume*, 1903

ROUSSEAU, JEAN JACQUES   [53]

Swiss-French moralist
Rating: 24
Born: Geneva, Switzerland, June 28, 1712
Died: Ermenonville, Oise, France, July 2, 1778

As a philosopher and moralist Rousseau exercised great influence on Western thought, even though he never had any formal education. On psychological thought Rousseau's influence was largely in the developmental and educational area. Rousseau's ideas here were so well accepted that the first radical deviation

from the benevolent conception of the child that Rousseau had presented did not occur until the advent of psychoanalysis, and Rousseau's ideas may be discerned even in some of Freud's [224] theorizing. In the 20th century, Hall's [418] recapitulation theory, the "rosebud" theory in education, the "progressive" schools, Freud's instinct theory, and the early work of Jean Piaget all reflected Rousseau's influence.

Rousseau's psychological ideas are contained mostly in his *Emile* (1762). For many psychologists child study as a body of knowledge starts with *Emile*. In it, the following propositions may be found: Childhood is a natural event, important in and of itself. The child is born with an innate sense of what is right and wrong. Attempts by adults to "finish God's work," as exemplified by prohibitions and restrictions, corrupt the child. The child is not a miniature adult. He is well adapted to his environment and his mental life is appropriate to his needs. The child will develop satisfactorily without much adult intervention since nature herself has provided him with a built-in mechanism for healthy growth. Therefore education must follow the spontaneous inclinations of the child and be guided by his natural development. Knowledge is not poured into children by adults; rather, children find it by actively interacting with the environment. The child develops through a number of stages that follow each other in an invariant order. In his own development, the child recapitulates the cultural evolution of mankind: the animal stage (to the age of five), the savage stage (ages five to twelve), the rational stage (ages twelve to fifteen), and social stage (ages fifteen to adulthood). The first few years of life are the most influential ones in the child's development.

Biographic data: *EP* 7:218; *IESS* 13:563

[54]

DIDEROT, DENIS

French philosopher
Rating: 19
Born: Langres, Haute-Marne, October 5, 1713
Died: Paris, July 30, 1784
Highest degree: Master of Arts, University of Paris, 1732

Diderot, the Encylopaedist of the Enlightenment, was philosophically a sensationalist, empiricist, materialist, and a believer in the scientific method. In his *Lettre sur les aveugles* (1749) and

Lettre sur les sourdes et muets (1751) he discusses communication on the basis of actual case histories of blind and deaf people. The former work may be considered the first scientific study of blindness. In concert with Condillac [57], Diderot considered thought to be the property of the brain, as well as memory. He believed memory was a material phenomenon and sought to provide a physiological basis to both memory and the Lockean association of ideas. In general, Diderot endeavored to provide psychology with a scientific and physiological basis. His thoughts on these matters may be found in his *Rêve de d'Alambert* (1769) and *Eléments de physiologie*. Of particular importance was the article *Psychology* that Diderot wrote for the great French *Encyclopédie*, of which he was the editor-in-chief, since as one of the great works of the Enlightenment the volumes of the Encyclopedia spread knowledge among both specialists and laymen.

Biographic data: *DSB* 4:84; *EP* 2:397

WHYTT, ROBERT   [55]

Scottish physiologist
Rating: **15**
Born: Edinburgh, September 6, 1714
Died: Edinburgh, April 15, 1766
Highest degree: M.D., University of Rheims, 1736; M.D., St. Andrews University, 1737
Positions: 1738, private practice of medicine; 1747, University of Edinburgh; 1761, first physician to King of Scotland

Whytt repeated and extended an experiment performed in 1730 by Stephen Hales in which the existence of reflexes was demonstrated. In doing so, Whytt coined the terms "stimulus" and "response" (*On the Vital and Other Involuntary Motions of Animals*, 1751). Whytt performed the first important experiments on the reflex. He was first to demonstrate that the pupillary response is a reflex to light. He showed that the spinal cord is not only nesessary but also sufficient to produce reflexes. Whytt also distinguished between voluntary and involuntary movements. He considered the reflex as involuntary but not quite unconscious, since it was a response by the "sentient principle" in the nervous system, which was part of the mind.

Biographic data: *DNB* 61:174

HELVETIUS, CLAUDE ADRIEN

French philosopher
Rating: **15**
Born: Paris, January 26, 1715
Died: Voré, December 26, 1771
Education: Collège Louis-le-Grand, graduated in 1738
Positions: No academic or scientific appointments

Helvétius was a French materialsit who followed La Mettrie [50] and Condillac [57]. He considered man's motivations hedonistically, and may be considered an early dynamic psychologist. In his works, *De l'esprit* (1758) and *De l'homme* (1773), Helvétius argues that all mental processes and capabilities may be reduced to sensations and that self-interest is the origin of all action and all affect since man is guided by the desire to avoid pain and seek pleasure.

Biographic data: *EP* 3:471

CONDILLAC, ETIENNE BONNOT DE

French philosopher
Rating: **25**
Born: Grenoble, September 30, 1715
Died: Beaugency, Loiret, August 3, 1780
Education: Studied theology at Saint Sulpice, Sorbonne, ordained 1740

As a philosophical empiricist and sensationalist, Condillac established Locke's [33] philosophy in France. His *Essai sur l'origine des connaissances humaines* (1746) presented Locke's ideas, but with the qualification that while Locke was right in saying that ideas arise from sensations, he probably was not when he said that ideas also arise from reflection. In his *Traité des systèmes* (1749) Condillac spoke out against the innate ideas, faculties, and monads of his philosophical predecessors. The *Traité des sensations* (1754) is Condillac's best known work. It includes the famous analogy of the statue, organized like man but with no previous experience, that, by starting out with a single sense, develops attention, memory, judgment, desire, aversion, imagination, and other mental processes. Condillac's style of writing, coupled with the susceptibility of the French to cold, analytic examination of human affairs at that time, were responsible for his success as a philosopher.

Biographic data: *DSB* 3:380; *EP* 2:180; *IESS* 3:211; Baguenalt de Puchesse, *Condillac, sa vie, sa philosophie, son influence*, 1910

BONNET, CHARLES

[58]

Swiss biologist and philosopher
Rating: 20
Born: Geneva, March 3, 1720
Died: Genthod near Geneva, May 20 1793
Highest degree: Doctorate in law, 1743

From law, Bonnet turned to biology where he made well known contributions to the study of insects. Failing eyesight made him turn to philosophy. In his philosophy, Bonnet repeated Condillac [57], including Condillac's parable of the sentient statue that develops memory, thinking, discrimination, judgment, desire, and aversion by being endowed originally with a single sense. Bonnet considered Condillac incomplete in that he believed that mere sequences of sensory impressions were insufficient to render a sentient being. He thus gave an organizing and creative role to an active soul. Bonnet also differed from Condillac by giving the statue nerves. Bonnet's neurophysiology was largely speculative, although in his speculations he anticipated such discoveries as the specificity of nerve energies. His neurophsiologically based empiricism makes him a precursor of the physiological psychology that was to develop in the 19th century. His works of psychological importance are *Essai de psychologie* (1754) and *Essai analytique sur les facultés de l'âme* (1760). Through his other philosophical writings that centered on biological themes, such as epigenesis, the principle of continuity in nature (he was first to use the term evolution), and the indestructability of organisms, Bonnet considerably influenced philosophical thought of his day.

Biographic data: *DSB* 2:286; *EP* 1:345

SMITH, ADAM

Scottish philosopher and political economist
Rating: **17**
Born: Kirkcaldy, Fife, baptized June 5, 1723
Died: Edinburgh, July 17, 1790
Highest degree: M.A., Oxford University, 1740
Positions: 1751–1763, Glasgow University

In his work, *The Theory of Moral Sentiments* (1759), Smith presents a psychology of moral feeling and moral behavior. The basic explanatory concept used by Smith is sympathy: "Whatever is the passion which arises from any object in the person principally concerned, an analogous emotion springs up at the thought of his situation, in the breast of every attentive spectator." It is our conception of the cause of the situation and not the actual situation that we witness that arouses emotion. Sympathy is the major factor that accounts for the existence of social groups.

In his major work, *The Wealth of Nations* (1776), Smith builds his explanation of economic behavior on a psychological basis also: trade, commerce, exchange of goods, and the resulting institutions are explained in terms of human motives. The utilitarian principle ("the greatest happiness of the greatest number") was first formulated by Smith. It was taken over by Bentham [73], who in turn influenced James Mill [93] and, through the latter, John Stuart Mill [125].

Biographic data: *DNB* 53:3; *EP* 7:461; *IESS* 14:322

KANT, IMMANUEL

German philosopher
Rating: **25**
Born: Königsberg, East Prussia, April 22, 1724
Died: Königsberg, February 12, 1804
Highest degree: Ph.D. in philosophy, University of Königsberg, 1775
Positions: 1755–1796, University of Königsberg

Kant, one of the greatest philosophers of all times, was rather orthodox in his approach to philosophy until he was aroused from his "dogmatic slumber" by the reading of Hume [52] and Hume's psychological analysis of causality. While Kant's main works are related to psychology, his approach to the problems of philosophy was not psychological. Kant thought of psychology as an empirical study of the laws of mental functioning. His psychological views are contained in his *Anthropology* (first published in German in 1798). His significant contributions to psychology are contained, however, in his critical volumes, especially the *Critique of Pure Reason* (1781), which deals with the process of knowing, but also to a lesser extent in his *Critique of Judgment* (1790) and *Critique of Practical Reason* (1788), which treat of feeling and willing.

Kant, avoiding the extremes of both the rationalists, such as Descartes [28], and of the empiricists, such as Locke [33], combined the views of both schools in a new and more complex system. While agreeing with the empiricists that objects are known through the senses and that the ultimate reality is unknowable, he argued that the mind brings to experience certain qualities of its own that order it. These are the twelve *a priori* categories of causality, unity, totality, and the like, and the *a priori* intuitions of time and space. While the mind has no substance, it is an active process that serves to convert raw sensory data into meaningful, ordered experiences. Kant named this process apperception. Things in themselves cannot be known, we perceive the world only the way our mind makes us do it, i.e., through the instrumentality of the innate mental categories. Kant thus accepted the notion of mental faculties—cognition, feeling, desire, understanding, judgment, and reason—and his treatment of them in his critique volumes sanctioned their acceptance and use by others.

Kant stated that since mental processes have no substance and have only the time dimension, it is impossible to measure them. For this reason Kant specifically denied the possibility of psychology as an experimental science. Because Kant was an extremely influential philosopher, this view of his delayed the emergence of psychology as an experimental science. On the other hand, his statement that mathematics is a source of scientific knowledge (because it is based on *a priori* axioms), and is basic to all science, led those who were seeking an experimental psychological science to introduce mathematics in psychology at an early date.

Another direct and important influence of Kant's on psychology was through his insistence that experience, particularly in the form of perception, is a unitary act. While the sensory elements of the associationists are there, the mind performs an integrative act that makes a coherent, meaningful experience out of them. This view undermined the associationists' position and contributed to the demise of associationism as a systematic school of thought.

Kant's stress on innate mental categories labels him as a nativist. By presenting time and space as innate intuitions, Kant gave support to nativist theories of space perception and was therefore the philosophical godfather of the forthcoming phenomenological and nativist schools of psychology, such as the Gestalt school.

Biographic data: *DSB* 7:224; *EP* 4:305; *IESS* 8:349; H. W. Stuckenberg, *The Life of Immanuel Kant*, 1882

[61]

DARWIN, ERASMUS

English physician and biologist
Rating: 16
Born: Elston Hall, Nottinghamshire, December 12, 1731
Died: Breadsall Priory near Derby, Derbyshire, April 18, 1802
Highest degree: M.D., University of Edinburgh, 1754

Darwin intimated the evolutionary theory, although he attributed the main role in evolution to purposeful adaptation, in anticipation of Lamarck's [68] theory. Fearing for his reputation, Darwin did not present his views until late in life. Since at least the initial works in which the idea was presented were written in verse, it was that much less effective. Darwin is also counted as one of the lesser British associationists. The doctrine of association of ideas is presented in his *Zoonomia* (1794). This work also presents one of the earliest accounts of vertigo and the apparent negative after-rotation. The 1801 edition of the work also introduces the (incorrect) theory that hunger is the quiescent state of the stomach when it has nothing to do.

Biographic data: *DNB* 14:84; *DSB* 3:577; *EP* 2:295

[62]

PRIESTLEY, JOSEPH

English theologian and chemist
Rating: 13
Born: Fieldhead, Yorkshire, March 13, 1733
Died: Northumberland, Pennsylvania, February 6, 1804

Education: Studied for Presbyterian ministry
Positions 1755–1794, various positions as minister and tutor in languages and literature; honorary LL.D., University of Edinburgh, 1764

Priestley was a versatile man who published scientific studies on the chemistry of gases (he discovered oxygen but, favoring the phlogiston theory, failed to recognize oxygen for what it was) and on electricity, as well as papers and books on education, philosophy, history of science, religion, and political theory. "An Essay on Government," published in 1768, contains a sentence seminal to Bentham's [73] famous principle of "the greatest happiness of the greatest number." His *Examination of Scottish Philosophy* (1774) was his first psychological essay. Priestley embraced associationism wholeheartedly, and placed Hartley [45], whom he had studied thoroughly, next to the Bible only. He published an abridged edition of Hartley's *Observations of Man*, to which he added three original essays of his own. An important pioneering work in the history of science as it relates to psychology was his *History and Present State of the Discoveries Relating to Vision, Light, and Colours* (1772). Priestley also wrote on education, opposing innate ideas and embracing education based on the formation of associative bonds (*Miscellaneous Observations Relating to Education,* 1778). His religious unorthodoxy forced him to leave England. Priestley came to the United States in 1794.

Biographic data: *DNB* 46:357; *EP* 6:451; R. E. Schofield, *Scientific Autobiography of Joseph Priestley,* 1966

MESMER, FRANZ ANTON [63]

Austrian physician
Rating: 25
Born: Iznang, Baden-Württemberg, Germany, May 23, 1734
Died: Meersburg, Baden-Württemberg, March 5, 1815
Highest degree: M.D., University of Vienna, 1766

Mesmer, at first a physician at Vienna, came under the influence of the occcult teachings of Paracelsus [17], believing that magnetism emanating from the stars affects human lives. His experiments on the effects of magnets on the human body led

him to the discovery that his passes made some people go into a trance. They also led him to assume that the magnetism of iron and of celestial bodies was similar to that possessed by living organisms. Mesmer therefore began to use the term animal magnetism, a term used by others before. In 1766, he published a work on the postulated relationships (*De planetarum influxu*), and, in 1779, an account of what later came to be called mesmerism (*Mémoire sur la découverte du magnétisme animal*). Although Mesmer never thought that he had any magical powers but, rather, that animal magnetism was a natural force, he was repeatedly accused of magic and charlatanism, and was forced to change residence several times. In 1778, Mesmer moved to Paris to continue the cures of neurotic individuals begun in Vienna. His séances around the baquet, a chest filled with chemicals that had iron protrusions his patients held on to, became famous in Paris society, and Mesmer achieved many hypnotic cures. Eventually, Mesmer fell into disrepute since he maintained his belief in animal magnetism but could not explain it satisfactorily to the scientists who investigated him and denied it had anything to do with the magnetism of ferric metals. Mesmerism continued to be practiced after Mesmer's death, and men like Elliotson [111] and Braid [114] began to explain it in scientific terms. Later, under the name of hypnosis, mesmerism became part of the psychiatrist's tools of trade.

Biographic data: DSB 9:325; IESS 10:260

[64]

TETENS, JOHANN NIKOLAS

German philosopher
Rating: **11**
Born: Tetenbüll, Schleswig-Holstein, September 16, 1736
Died: Copenhagen, Denmark, August 15, 1807
Highest degree: Master's degree, University of Rostock, 1759
Positions: 1763, Bützow Academy; 1776, University of Kiel; 1789, finance official, City of Copenhagen

Tetens was the most prominent German philosopher of the era of Enlightenment, and the only one to accept the empirical philosophy and psychology of Locke [33], Hume [52], and the associationists. He further emphasized the distinction made by von Wolff [39] between rational and empirical psychology, but stressing the importance of the latter. His most important philosophical work, *Philosophische Versuche über die menschliche Natur* (1777, English translation, *Essays on Human Nature*, 1913), is also the most important one to psychology. In it, Tetens asserts that a consideration of psychology must precede a consideration of metaphysics, and that the validity of the psychological considerations ultimately rests on the validity of empirical observations and experimentation. While accepting association, Tetens pointed out that sensations and other mental contents are not simple building blocks that are put together without loss of identity. Rather, complex interactions are the rule, and even the simplest-appearing thinking process can be actually extremely complex. Throughout his book Tetens produces empirical evidence for his statements concerning the nature of sensations, perception (especially aftersensations and illusions), memory, thinking, habit formation, and development. Kant [60] was considerably influenced by Tetens's philosophy, especially by Teten's attempts to state the principles governing the subjective *a priori* experiences and his threefold division of consciousness: feeling, will, and understanding.

Biographic data: EP 8:96

GALVANI, LUIGI   [65]

Italian physiologist
Rating: 20
Born: Bologna, September 9, 1737
Died: Bologna, December 4, 1798
Education: Degree in medicine and philosophy, University of Bologna, 1759
Positions: 1762–1791, University of Bologna, teaching anatomy

Galvani discovered that a frog's leg would twitch if a nerve at its cut end was connected to its outside by two pieces of different metals. While Galvani believed that it was animal tissue that generated electricity, he had actually built the first wet battery. Galvani described his experiment in 1791 ("De viribus electricitatis in motu musculari"). The belief in and investigation of animal electricity, started by Galvani, spread and eventually led to the correct view concerning the nature of the nerve impulse through the work of the great 19th-century physiologists. Volta, on the other hand, showed that animal tissue was not necessary to generate electricity. The inorganic voltaic battery, in turn, played an important role in the work of the neuranatomists and neurophysiologists as they studied the structure and functioning of the nervous system.

Biographic data: *DSB* 5:267

[66]

LAVATER, JOHANN CASPAR

Swiss pastor, writer, and patriot
Rating: **10**
Born: Zurich, November 11, 1741
Died: Zurich, January 2, 1801
Education: Degree in theology, University of Zurich, 1786
Positions: 1787, pastor, St. Peter's church in Zurich

Lavater was the founder of physiognomics. His interest in mesmerism and physiognomics was rooted in his religious convictions. It was an attempt to demonstrate visibly the divine in man and the interaction between mind and body. Lavater was part of an antirational movement that had strong religious and literary components, and the writing of *Von der Physiognomik* (1772) and the four volumes of *Physiognomische Fragmente zur Beförderung der Menschenkenntnis und Menschenliebe* (1775–1778; English translation, *Essays on Physiognomy*, 1789–1798) was prompted more by religious and metaphysical considerations than scientific curiosity. His *Essays* were translated into ten languages, won him a European reputation and the friendship of such people as Goethe [77]. Herder [69] collaborated with him on these volumes. Because Lavater's style was simple and readable and he related physiognomy and character in the description of well-known contemporary figures, his book was widely read and Lavater himself became the most publicized physiognomist in history. Lavater did not accept the assumption made by earlier physiognomists of a direct and simple correlation between animal and human physiognomy and character. His own physiognomy, in turn, may be seen appearing in a more sophisticated form in later German physiognomy, graphology, and characterology.

Biographic data: *EP* 4:401; G. Gesner, *Johann Caspar Lavaters Lebensbeschreibung*, 3 vol., 1802; F. Muncker, *Johann Caspar Lavater*, 1883; O. Guinaudeau, *Etudes sur Johann Caspar Lavater*, 1924; A. Vömel, *Johann Caspar Lavater, ein Lebensbild*, 2d ed., 1927, C. Janensky, *Johann Caspar Lavater*, 1928; M. Lavater-Slomann, *Genie des Herzens*, 1939

CONDORCET, MARIE JEAN ANTOINE (MARQUIS DE CONDORCET)

French philosopher and mathematician
Rating: **20**
Born: Ribemont, Aisne, September 17, 1743
Died: Bourg-la-Reine (Paris), April 8, 1794
Education: Degree in philosophy, Collège de Navarre, Paris, 1759

Condorcet was a precursor of the social sciences whose chief endeavor was to use the approach of natural sciences and especially of mathematics in the study of social problems. Since experience is probabilistic, the relationship between the physical sciences and those of man lie in probability calculus. In his *Essai sur l'application de l'analyse à la probabilité des décisions rendues à la pluralité des voix* (1785, 2d rev. ed. 1805 under the title *Eléments du calcul des probabilités et son application aux jeux de hasard, à la lotterie, et aux jugements des hommes*), Condorcet offered a probabilistic model of collective decision making. Condorcet believed that social mathematics and an exact analysis of ideas would work toward liberating man from passion and into reason in his dealings with fellow men. He demonstrated the power of reason in human affairs in his *Esquisse d'un tableau historique des progrès de l'esprit humain* (1795). A similar effort, "Tableau général de la science, qui a pour objet l'application du calcul aux sciences morales et politiques," published in a journal in 1793, remained unfinished.

Biographic data: *DSB* 3:383; *EP* 2:182; *IESS* 3:213; F. Arago, "Condorcet: A Biography," in Smithsonian Institution, *Annual Report of the Board of Regents*, 1878, pp. 180–235

LAMARCK, JEAN BAPTISTE PIERRE ANTOINE DE MONET

French biologist
Rating: **23**
Born: Bazentin, Somme, August 1, 1744
Died: Paris, December 18, 1829
Education: Studied medicine, metereology, botany at University of Paris
Positions: Various botanical appointments; from 1793 teaching invertebrate zoology at University of Paris

In addition to his very significant contributions to the development of animal taxonomy, Lamarck's name is most often associated with the doctrine of the genetic transmission of acquired characteristics. In his *Philosophie zoologique* (1809), Lamarck proposed a theory of evolution whose main tenet was that the use and disuse of organs leads to their modification, and that these changes are passed on to descendants (Lamarckian transmission). Lamarck was the first biologist of prominence to adopt the evolutionary point of view, even though his particular theory was soon proved to be wrong. The evolutionary viewpoint was at first opposed by such influential non-evolutionists as Cuvier [88], but it was to persist from then on. It asserted that animal species are not unchanging but may be modified by external influences, that, in spite of differences, unity underlies the differences among species, and that species develop continually. Lamarck was thus an important link in the development of evolutionary thought that reached its peak in Darwin's [127] theory.

Biographic data: DSB 7:584; EP 4:376

[69]

HERDER, JOHANN GOTTFRIED

German philosopher, critic, and writer
Rating: **11**
Born: Mohrungen, East Prussia, August 25, 1744
Died: Weimar, December 18, 1803
Education: Theological degree, University of Königsberg, 1764, ordained 1765
Positions: 1764–1769, Cathedral school, Riga; later worked as preacher, had ecclesiastic appointments in Germany

In his major treatise, *Ideen zur Philosophie der Geschichte der Menschheit* (1784–1791), Herder suggests ideas that were later developed by other philosophers and psychologists. He held that body and mind were inseparable (providing, incidently, a theoretical foundation for physiognomy) and that psychology was actually "physiology at every step." Nevertheless, all of his psychological writings are based on the metaphysical concept of *Kraft* (force), which he uses in a manner not unlike Heraclitus' [1] use of fire. The idea emerged later in the vitalistic philosophies of Schopenhauer [108] and Bergson [252]. Herder believed in the wholeness of man and the inseparability of his psychological functions, opposing the notion of psychological faculties. He also held that man's nature was active rather than passive (man has a soul only to the extent that he is active), for which he is held to be an early dynamic psychologist. Herder was one of the originators of that specifically German product, ethnopsychology (*Völkerpsychologie*) that was to reach its acme in Wilhelm Wundt's [161] multivolume opus. Herder believed that each people, even the smallest, develops its own spirit and laws. On this assumption, Herder attempted to write a history of the human psyche as it manifests itself in the different national groups and stages of historical development. His raw materials were the languages, literary monuments, and especially the folk songs of various ethnic groups, which Herder thought afforded an insight into and empathy with the spirit of these groups. Herder was also responsible for coining the terms *Naturvölker* and *Kulturvölker*, and contrasting them by ascribing innate goodness to the former, in a manner that Rousseau [53] had done. The most developed *Kulturvölker* flourished only in the temperate zone, a statement of Herder's that became very well known and was repeated by many in the years to come.

Biographic data: EP 3:486

RUSH, BENJAMIN

[70]

American physician and medical educator
Rating: 15
Born: Near Philadelphia, Pennsylvania, 1745
Died: Philadelphia, April 19, 1813
Highest degree: M.D., University of Edinburgh, 1768
Positions: 1769, professor of chemistry at the College of Philadelphia; 1791, professor of medicine, University of Pennsylvania; 1797, Treasurer of National Mint

Rush was one of the pioneers in American medicine, a medical reformer and educator, deeply involved in social causes, including the establishment of the United States of America: he was one of the signers of the Declaration of Independence. Psychiatry was also one of his concerns and, following the lead of Pinel [71] in France and Tuke in England, he advocated more humane treatment of the mentally ill, organized the first course in psychiatry in the United States, and wrote the first American medical treatise on psychiatry, *Medical Inquiries and Observations*

Upon the Diseases of the Mind (1812). For these achievements he is called the father of American psychiatry. He was, however, rather dogmatic in his treatment of mental patients, a believer in the meliorating powers of tranquilization, which in medical patients he achieved through debilitating treatments (purges, bloodletting) and an immobilizing device of his own invention (the "tranquilizer") in psychiatric patients. Although Rush represented an advance in comparison with the treatment accorded the mental patient before, he was also less progressive than Pinel.

Biographic data: *IESS* 13:588; *NCAB* 3:333; G. W. Corner (ed.), *The Autobiography of Benjamin Rush*, 1948; C. Binger, *Revolutionary Doctor: Benjamin Rush*, 1966

[71]

PINEL, PHILIPPE

French psychiatrist
Rating: **25**
Born: Saint-André, Tarne et Garonne, April 20, 1745
Died: Paris, October 25, 1826
Highest degree: M.D., University of Toulouse, 1773
Positions: 1792, chief physician, Bicêtre hospital, Paris; 1795, chief physician, La Salpêtrière hospital, Paris

Pinel turned his attention to psychiatry when a friend lost his mind, ran away, and was killed by wolves. On being appointed superintendent of the insane asylum at Bicêtre, he was appalled by the inhuman treatment of the insane, and at once appealed to the Revolutionary Committee and was allowed to remove the chains from some of the patients as an experiment. Instead of the expected chaos, a much more orderly and peaceful asylum resulted.

Pinel instituted a humane, psychological management of the insane, removed them from dungeons into well-lit rooms, placed them under the care of physicians, abolished such methods as bleeding and purging, and allowed physical exercise. He repeated the reorganization of treatment at La Salpêtrière with the same excellent results.

Pinel believed that severe abnormalities of behavior were due to brain disorders rather than wickedness or demoniacal possession. These views and a plea for a more humane treatment of mental patients were published in his *Traité médico-philosophique sur l'aliénation mentale* (1801). As word of Pinel's success spread, other humanitarians followed his lead, such as Tuke in England. Their success eventually revolutionized the treatment of the mentally ill in the Western world.

Biographic data: *IESS* 12:97

PESTALOZZI, JOHANN HEINRICH

[72]

Swiss educator
Rating: 22
Born: Zurich, January 12, 1746
Died: Brugg, Aargau, February 17, 1827
Education: Studied law and theology

Pestalozzi is honored as a humanitarian who throughout his life was concerned with the fate of underprivileged and orphaned children. He was convinced that human society could be bettered through education and the perfection of human nature. He presented his views in fictional form, *Lingard und Gertrude* (1801, English translation, *How Gertrude Teaches Her Children*). His guiding principle was the development of human capabilities in accordance with nature. This was to be accomplished through activity since activity is what is natural to the child. Activity should take the form of exercise. The first educator is the mother, then the school. The child's capacities need to be exercised in a sequential order. Pestalozzi's educational theory included physical, moral, and mental education. At the famous Yverdon boarding school that Pestalozzi established in 1805, he emphasized motor acts, such as singing, drawing, writing, and physical exercise, and activities such as collecting and model making. In moral development Pestalozzi thought the principal factor was the child's love for mother arising from the satisfaction of the child's needs by the mother. This love the child must transfer to family members, then to other people, and finally to all humanity. Important factors in moral development are the behavior of model adults and the practice of moral behavior. In mental education Pestalozzi stressed the accumulation of knowledge on the basis of sensory experience and the development of mental capacities. The principle of "sense impression" was the accurate relation of words and ideas to concrete objects and events so that thinking likewise may be accurate. Pestalozzi adjusted instruction to the difficulty level of the material and according to individual differences in ability. In developmental psychology, Pestalozzi is credited with having published for the first time observations on a child (his own three-and-a-half-year-old son) in a scientific journal (1774).

Biographic data: R. de Guimps, *Pestalozzi: His Life and Work*, 1880; J. A. Green, *Life and Work of Pestalozzi*, 1913

[73]

BENTHAM, JEREMY

English philosopher
Rating: 22
Born: London, February 15, 1748
Died: London, June 6, 1832
Education: Oxford University, law degree, 1763
Positions: No official positions

While Bentham was influenced by Helvetius [56] and Hume [52], his writings often sound like those of Hartley [45] (*Analysis of the Phenomena of the Human Mind*, 1829). Bentham promulgated the doctrine of ethical hedonism, which in terms of his "greatest happiness principle" states that the ethical goal is the greatest happiness for the greatest numbers. This later became the underlying principle of philosophical Utilitarianism. Bentham also believed that every individual acts so as to increase his own happiness and minimize pain (psychological hedonism). Several "sanctions" or reasons were postulated by Bentham to reconcile ethical and psychological hedonism. The law acts by manipulating these sanctions—by rewarding and punishing the citizens. Bentham's and his disciples' endeavors were directed toward showing that the interests of the individual and of society could be made to coincide. They took the motive of self-interest as their starting point. Under the influence of Bentham reforms were instituted and legal codes drawn up and adapted by various countries. After his death his work was carried on, but on a more literary level. Among the psychologically oriented philosophical Utilitarians who were influenced by Bentham were James Mill [93], John Stuart Mill [125], Alexander Bain [138], and Herbert Spencer [142].

Biographic data: DNB 4:268; EP 1:280; IESS 2:55

German philosopher
Rating: 11
Born: Bremervörde, Lower Saxony, April 3, 1748
Died: Marburg, Hessen, May 24, 1803
Education: Studied at University of Göttingen
Positions: 1786, University of Marburg

Tiedemann's observations on the development of the mental abilities of his own son, published in 1787 (*Beobachtungen über die Entwicklung der Seelenfähigkeit bei Kindern*), was the second (after Pestalozzi's [72]) instance of the publication of developmentat observations of children in a scientific journal. Other instances did not occur until about a hundred years later. Tiedemann also published a *Handbuch der Psychologie* (1804), but his most important work was done in philosophy rather than psychology.

Biographic data: *Enciclopedia universal ilustrada,* vol. 61

LAPLACE, PIERRE SIMON DE   [75]

French astronomer and mathematician
Rating: 17
Born: Beaumont-en-Auge, Calvados, March 28, 1749
Died: Paris, March 5, 1827
Education: Military school at Beaumont, University of Caen
Positions: 1767, Ecole Militaire, Paris; 1787, Ecole Polytechnique

Laplace was one of the top men of science of 18th-century France. His major contributions to science were in astronomy. He was also a first-rate mathematician. Laplace is important in the history of psychology because he formulated the normal law of error (1786), although the bell-shaped distribution of errors was already known to de Moivre. Laplace must also be credited with the application of this law to errors in scientific observation in general, rather than just to specific instances, such as gambling events or life expectancies. The importance of the concept of normal distribution in psychological statistics cannot be over-estimated.

Biographic data: *EP* 4:391; *IESS* 9:23

PROCHASKA, GEORG

Czech physiologist
Rating: 11
Born: Blizkovice, Moravia, April 10, 1749
Died: Vienna, Austria, July 17, 1820
Highest degree: M.D., University of Vienna, 1776
Positions: 1778, University of Prague; 1791–1819 University of
Vienna

One of the earliest investigators of reflex action, Prochaska
sectioned the spinal cord of frogs and observed their reactions to
stimulation (*De functionibus systematis nervosi*, 1784). He
contended that, while nervous energy was necessary for reflex
action, it also needed activation through the common sensorium
which exists in the brain and the spinal cord. Thus activated,
reflex responses are automatic. The concept of common sensorium originated with Prochaska. It was an important concept in
that it provided for a connection between stimulation and action
without the intervention of the will. Prochaska, however, did not
assume that all action was automatic, allowing also for voluntary
movements that are the result of the will. Prochaska's view of the
reflex was an advance over Whytt's [55] and contributed to the
development of the modern view of it.

Biographic data: *Enciclopedia italiana,* vol. 28

GOETHE, JOHANN WOLFGANG VON

German poet, author, and philosopher
Rating: 25
Born: Frankfurt-am-Main, August 28, 1749
Died: Weimar, March 22, 1832
Education: Studied law at Leipzig and Strasbourg, graduated in
1771

Goethe's contributions to science date from the period 1775–
1786 when he first became a friend and adviser to the Duke Karl
August of Weimar. Among them may be counted his principle of
metamorphosis of homologous parts in animals and plants, which
was a contribution to the theory of evolution, and his theory of
color. Goethe attacked Newton's [36] theory that white light is

composed of different chromatic lights, but his attacks were not accepted by scientists. Frustrated, Goethe produced in 1810 his own 1411-page work on the phenomenology of color vision (*Zur Farbenlehre*). While the theory itself played no major role in the history of color vision study, Goethe's book did stimulate color research. Purkinje [107] dedicated one of his volumes on vision to Goethe; it stimulated even Schopenhauer [108] to produce his own color vision theory. Goethe's work on color contains many valid and original observations on the perception of color, such as irradiation, dark and light adaptation, positive and negative afterimages, color contrast, colored shadows, color blindness, and others. His color theory was based on the observation that all colors are darker than white. He took blue and yellow as the two primary colors and related the rest to them. Even though the theory was sterile, Goethe was a famous figure and his theory continued to be cited through the first half of the 19th century while that of Thomas Young [94] was ignored.

Though Goethe's color theory was bad, his phenomenological observations were good. Goethe strongly believed that the method of science was intuitive observation and not experimentation. He may be said to have started the phenomenological tradition in modern psychology. Goethe also exercised some degree of influence on Sigmund Freud [224]: Freud acknowledged that an essay on nature by Goethe had been one of the factors that influenced him to take up the medical profession. In Goethe's writings certain aspects of Freud's libido theory also may be found.

Biographic data: *DSB* 5:442; *EP* 3:362; Goethe's *Dichtung und Wahrheit* is autobiographic, as are several other of his works, such as *Italienische Reise* and *Kampagne in Frankreich*

STEWART, DUGALD [78]

Scottish philosopher
Rating: 23
Born: Edinburgh, November 22, 1753
Died: Edinburgh, June 11, 1828
Education: Graduated from University of Edinburgh, 1769
Positions: 1772–1820, University of Edinburgh

Stewart, one of the three most prominent members of the Scottish school, was a disciple and follower of one of them,

Thomas Reid [51]. He did not add anything new to Reid's common sense philosophy, but was more influential than Reid as he interpreted and popularized Reid's philosophy. In Stewart's hands, Reid's faculty psychology became an easily absorbable doctrine, and Stewart was thus instrumental in spreading it, not only among the philosophers but also among laymen. Stewart's lectures at Edinburgh supplied the raw material for the psychological side of Gall's [81] and Spurzheim's [102] phrenology, the 27 human faculties that Gall and Spurzheim related to prominences on the human head. Stewart's most important books were *Elements of Philosophy of the Human Mind* in three volumes (1792, 1814, 1827) and *The Philosophy of the Active Moral Powers of Man* (1828).

Biographic data: DNB 54:282; EP 8:16; J. Veitch, "Life of Dugald Stewart," in D. Stewart, *Collected Works*, ed. by Sir William Hamilton, vol. 10, 1858, pp. 243–324

[79]   **DESTUTT DE TRACY, ANTOINE LOUIS CLAUDE**

French philosopher
Rating: **11**
Born: Province of Bourbonnais, July 20, 1754
Died: Paris, March 9, 1836
Education: Strasbourg University

One of the principal *Idéologues*, Destutt de Tracy called his philosophy "idealogy." Under the influence of Cabanis [80], another ideologue, Destutt de Tracy stressed the physiological aspect of sensation and included ideology under zoology. Perception, memory, judgment, and will are nothing but aspects of sensation. The brain "secretes" thought, just as other organs of the body secrete liquids. Thinking is all conscious processes, whereas immediate impressions, be they sensory, emotional, or intellectual, are feelings. Feelings are imageless; they are only awareness of content. The content is ideas: sensations, memories, judgment, and desires. The idea of touch assures us of the existence of an external world. Destutt de Tracy's main work was *Eléments d'idéologie* in four volumes (1801–1815).

Biographic data: EP 2:356

French physician and philosopher
Rating: 22
Born: Department of Corrèze, June 5, 1757
Died: Rueil, Hauts de Seine, May 5, 1808
Education: Studied medicine at the University of Paris, 1777–1783
Positions: Professor at the Académie at Warsaw; 1789, administrator of Paris hospitals; 1795, professor of hygiene at Paris; 1799, professor of legal medicine and the history of medicine at Paris

With Destutt de Tracy [79], Condorcet [67], Lavoisier, and Laplace [75], Cabanis was one of the leaders of the Idéologues, who held that the mind, like chemical composition, could be analyzed, reducing ideas to the original sensations; that the study of man could be reduced to the study of physics and physiology; and that the pursuit of pleasure, happiness, and self-preservation were the only motives. Cabanis is also sometimes called the father of physiological psychology (as an alternate to Descartes [28]), although his physiological psychology was not a systematic affair like that of Wundt's but rather an attempt to explain mental events in terms of physiological and anatomical knowledge.

Cabanis began to formulate ideas of importance to psychology when in 1795 he was asked to find out if a person was still conscious after having been guillotined. Cabanis decided that it is the brain that secretes thought, hence a decapitated body is not conscious. Cabanis organized his ideas on this and related matters in his *Rapports du physique et du moral de l'homme* (1802), his most important work. Cabanis was more materialistic than Descartes, whose dualism he rejected, but not as materialistic as La Mettrie [50], whose materialism in religious matters he could not accept. To Condillac's analysis of the origin of mental states Cabanis added the idea that mental states show developmental levels as a function of the individual's age. At any point in time the mind also shows levels of awareness: unconscious instincts, semiconscious states, and the conscious state which exists by virtue of the brain's activity. Cabanis thought that bodily sensations were essential to the development of awareness and that such senses as the smell alone would not be enough from which to develop a fully sentient being.

Biographic data: *DSB* 3:1; *EP* 2:3; In *Rapports*, 8th ed., 1844

GALL, FRANZ JOSEPH

German physician and anatomist
Rating: 24
Born: Tiefenbrunn, Baden, March 9, 1758
Died: Paris, France, August 22, 1828
Highest degree: M.D., University of Vienna, 1785
Positions: 1785, practicing medicine in Vienna; 1796, began lecturing on phrenology; 1807, practicing medicine in Paris

Attracted to the relationship between head shape and personality since boyhood, Gall established phrenology soon after he received his medical training, although the name was given it later by his collaborator Spurzheim [102]. Forbidden to lecture on phrenology in Vienna, Gall and Spurzheim went on a lecture tour in Germany, then settled in Paris, where Gall achieved fame.

Between 1810 and 1819 Gall published *Sur les fonctions du cerveau et sur celles de chacune de ses parties* in four volumes (the first two written with Spurzheim), of which the last three presented the phrenological doctrine. The first volume dealt with the nervous system in general and made several important contributions to science. Gall believed that mind could be divided into separate faculties. These Gall obtained from the Scottish psychologists Thomas Reid [51], and Dugald Stewart [78]. After Spurzheim's subsequent elaboration, a list of 37 such faculties was used in phrenology. Gall also believed that the faculties were discretely localized in the brain, and that the exercise or prominence of a faculty would enlarge the appropriate brain area which, in turn, would show up as a cranial prominence. The correlations between "bumps" on the skull and personality characteristics were obtained from persons with well-known and pronounced mental traits. Aided by Spurzheim's propaganda efforts, phrenology flourished for a century, with numerous phrenological societies and journals to further its work, although it was never accepted by orthodox science. The followers of Gall made phrenology into a folly, and the stigma of the quack became attached to him. The notions of faculties and exact cortical localizations of such faculties became immediately, and correctly, suspect among scientists.

The significance of phrenology and of Gall lies not so much in the doctrine as in the impetus they gave to scientific thought. Gall was correct in assigning the brain the role of the seat of mental activities, and he established the brain as such in the mind of even the common man. Gall was wrong in details because of faulty methodology, but the possiblity of the localization of brain functions could not be denied. Flourens's [113] work on the correct localization of brain functions stands out largely by contrast with phrenology. In opposing it, Flourens's own views seemed less radical than they actually were.

Biographic data: *DSB* 5:250; *IESS* 6:47; F. J. Gall, *Sur les fonctions* ... , vol. 1, 1–52; F. J. Möbius, *Franz Joseph Gall*, vol. 7 of Möbius's *Ausgewḧlte Werke*, 1905, 3–17

SCHILLER, JOHANN CHRISTOPHER FRIEDRICH [82]

German dramatist and poet
Rating: **13**
Born: Marbach, Baden-Württemberg, November 10, 1759
Died: Weimar, Thuringia, May 9, 1805
Education: Studied medicine at Karlsakademie, Stuttgart, graduating in 1780

Schiller, one of the greatest German poets, developed a typology of characters in his *Uber naive und sentimentalische Dichtung* (1795–1796). He recognized at least two major and opposed ways of viewing the world, not only on the part of the poet but in man in general. C. G. Jung [358] worked out Schiller's typology in his *Psychological Types*. More generally and philosophically, Schiller's influence may be seen in James [184], Dilthey [164], Nietzsche [196], Marx [136], and Dewey [253].

Biographic data: *EP* 7:312

FICHTE, JOHANN GOTTLIEB [83]

German philosopher
Rating: **16**
Born: Rammenau, Upper Lusatia, May 19, 1762
Died: Berlin, January 27, 1814
Education: Studied theology and philosophy at Jena and Leipzig
Positions: 1794–1799, University of Jena, professor of philosophy; 1805–1808, University of Erlangen; 1809–1812, University of Berlin

Fichte was a philosophical successor of Kant [60]. His philosophy centered on the a priori characteristics of the notions of time and space, which Helmholtz [143] felt called upon to combat. He was strongly interested in the practical or moral aspects of Kant's teachings, which led him to state that knowledge depends on moral convictions and acts. The world of non-self is a scene where man acts out his duties and which acquires its significance from the self. Individual differences determine the philosophy a person chooses, as well as the kinds of other interests he develops: "The kind of philosophy a man chooses depends upon the kind of person he is" (*Die Bestimmung des Menschen*, 1800).

Biographic data: *Encyclopaedia Britannica,* vol. 9.

[84]

MALTHUS, THOMAS ROBERT

English economist and demographer
Rating: **17**
Born: Dorking, Surrey, February 14, 1766
Died: St. Catherine's, near Bath, Somersetshire, December 23, 1834
Education: M.A., Cambridge University, 1791; took holy orders 1797
Positions: 1805, professor of history and political economy, College of Haileybury

Malthus's proposed the famous theory that while population increases on a geometric scale, food production increases on an arithmetic scale, and that for this reason humanity is destined to live in poverty (*An Essay on the Principle of Population*, 1798). While "vice and misery," including contraception, war, famine, and disease, may keep check on population growth, the fact that there is an excess of population in relation to the amount of food available implied a struggle for survival. In general, Malthus viewed human society in biological terms. Both Charles Darwin [127] and Wallace [146] read Malthus's *Essay* and were stimulated by it to begin thinking along evolutionary lines.

Biographic data: *DNB* 36:1; *DSB* 9:66; *EP* 5:145; *IESS* 9:549; J. Bonar, *Malthus and His Work,* 1885; J. M. Keynes, "Robert Malthus, the First of the Cambridge Economists," in *Essays in Biography,* 1933

English chemist
Rating: **23**
Born: Eaglesfield, Cumberland, September 6, 1766
Died: Manchester, Lancashire, July 27, 1844
Education: Largely self-taught; two honorary degrees
Positions: 1793, New College, Manchester, professor of mathematics and philosophy; 1799, private tutor

Dalton's scientific fame rests principally on his advocacy of the atomic theory in chemistry and his investigations of gases, vapor, and steam. In psychology, he is known for his study and description of color blindness. In a 1794 presentation to the Manchester Literary and Philosophical Society, Dalton described his own inability to see reds and greens. He theorized that it might be due to the absorption of these colors by the ocular media. A post-mortem examination of his eyes, for which he himself had provided, disproved his theory. The study and understanding of the nature of color blindness dates from 1794. For a time (since 1827) color blindness was called Daltonism. It is still called that in some languages.

Biographic data: *DNB* 13:428; *DSB* 3:537

MAINE DE BIRAN, MARIE FRANCOIS PIERRE GOUTHIER

French philosopher
Rating: **24**
Born: Bergerac, Dordogne, November 29, 1766
Died: Paris, July 16, 1824
Education: Studied at the Collège at Périgueux

As one of the Idéologues, Maine de Biran was part of the idealistic reaction to the French 18th-century materialism and mechanism. Maine de Biran was at first instrumental in spreading Lockian empiricism in France. He gradually discovered inadequacies in the Lockian view and added a metaphysical turn to his psychological thinking. In *Influences de l'habitude sur la faculté de penser* (1802), Maine de Biran argues that if the mind were only sensations, habituation would make one lose consciousness. It is the will, something besides mere sensations, that maintains a state of consciousness. In *Mémoire sur la décomposition de la pensée* (1804), Maine de Biran takes issue with Descartes [28]. The subject of experience, so ran his argument, is not only the external but also the internal world. Statements about the latter can be made with a far greater degree of certainty since the inner experiences are the first experiences. It is certain from these experiences that the self is active. The first and fundamental certainty is the activity of the self, the efforts of the will, the *ego*, not the *cogito* of Descartes. Since the self as substance is not the same as self as subject, the methods of the physical sciences are inadequate to study the self as subject. All cognitive acts are basically activity and will. While the self is at first not aware of its own existence, repeated experiences lead to a separation between the non-self and a self. The experience of resistance offered by the external world yields self-awareness as the will to respond to the environment is exercised. In his *Essai sur les fondements de la psychologie* (1812), Maine de Biran established the existence of a "hyperorganic" element in the psyche, an idea developed later in *Nouveaux essais d'anthropologie* (1823–1824) where he describes the development of the self through the stages of animal or sensory life, human life of will and freedom, and the spiritual life of transcended humanity. In spite of additional writing on psychological subjects, such as *L'apperception immédiate* (1807) and *Rapports du physique et du moral* (1814), Maine de Biran's influence on psychology in terms of the specifics of his philosophy was minimal, and his genetic approach to psychological questions were not emulated. His emphasis on activity and the will, however, left a legacy of a dynamic approach to psychology that has persisted in French psychology.

Biographic data: *EP* 5:134; P. Hallie, *Maine de Biran*: *Reformer of Empiricism*, 1959

[87]

HUMBOLDT, WILHELM VON

German philosopher
Rating: **17**
Born: Potsdam, Brandenburg, June 22, 1767
Died: Tegel, near Berlin, April 8, 1835
Education: Studied law, other areas at University of Frankfurt, University of Göttingen
Positions: No university positions; active in political life

Humboldt was one of the forerunners of social psychology. To designate the approach to social psychology that he was using, and that was typical of most later German social psychologists, Humboldt coined the term *Völkerpsychologie* or ethno-psychology. His work was in the area of comparative linguistics where his emphasis was on how to understand different peoples. He was first to make the explicit statement that language expresses the psychic reality of the speaker and that differences in languages parallel differences in their speakers. Humboldt asserted that the point where language originated historically was the point in time where nature and idea became connected. To him language was the uniquely human characteristic. The central concept in Humboldt's theory was the "inner form" of language, or the profoundly rooted subjective view of the world. The speaker of a language views the world through his language; it serves not only to reflect truth but to discover truth. Steinthal [147] in the 19th century and Whorf and Sapir [417] in the 20th developed very similar lines of thought. As a philosopher of history Humboldt also influenced Wilhelm Dilthey [164] through his idea of historical experience, or the development of empathy and understanding through the study of history.

Biographic data: *EP* 4:72; P. Binswanger, *Wilhelm von Humboldt* 1937; E. Howald, *Wilhelm von Humboldt,* 1944; F. Schaffstein, *Wilhelm von Humboldt: Ein Lebensbild,* 1952

CUVIER, GEORGES LEOPOLD CHRETIEN FREDERIC DAGOBERT, BARON

[88]

French biologist
Rating: 12
Born: Montbéliard, Doubs, August 23, 1769
Died: Paris, May 13, 1832
Education: Studied natural science for four years at the Stuttgart Academy
Positions: 1795, Assistant at the Museum of Natural History, Paris; 1799, Collège de France, professor of natural history

Cuvier played a leading role in the development of paleontology and comparative anatomy. His doctrine of the correlation of parts claimed that since the parts of an animal are functionally and structurally appropriately related (at creation, not through adaptation), the entire animal could be reconstructed from a single bone. He believed, however, in spontateous generation, the fixity of species, and the preformation of the embryo. His opposition to the idea of evolution was such that, when faced with the evidence of paleontology, he opted for the theory of catastrophism promulgated by Bonnet. Cuvet's influence in France was so great it was an obstacle to the acceptance of the point of view of the evolutionists, such as Lamarck [68]. Cuvier also appears to have been persuaded by Napoleon to reject (in 1808) the application of the phrenologist Gall [81] for membership in the Institut de France (later Académie de Science).

Biographic data: *DSB* 3:521

[89]

HEGEL, GEORG WILHELM FRIEDRICH

German philosopher
Rating: 18
Born: Stuttgart, August 27, 1770
Died: Berlin, November 14, 1831
Highest degree: Ph.D. in philosophy, University of Tübingen, 1790; certificate in theology, 1793
Positions 1797–1800, University of Frankfurt; 1801–1806, University of Jena; 1816, University of Heidelberg; 1818, University of Berlin

Hegel's *Die Phänomenologie des Geistes* (1807), one of his most important works, covers psychology—the development of the human mind from consciousness to self-consciousness, then to reason, spirit, religion, and, finally, absolute knowledge. While working in the Kantian tradition, Hegel differed from Kant [60] in that he admitted the possibility of absolute knowledge.

Of all his ideas, his dialectic (thesis, opposed by antithesis, both of which are resolved in synthesis, which, in turn, serves as thesis for the next cycle, and so on indefinitely) has had the greatest influence on the social sciences, including psychology, as the concept of dialectic was extended to the interaction between man and the environment that he creates for himself. By way of Marx [136] and Lenin [318], Hegelian dialectic became a cardinal principle of Soviet psychology.

Biographic data: *EP* 3:435; *IESS* 6:341

BICHAT, MARIE FRANCOIS XAVIER

French physician
Rating: **17**
Born: Thiorette, Jura, November 11, 1771
Died: Paris, July 22, 1802
Education: Studied anatomy at University of Lyon, surgery at the University of Paris
Positions: 1800, physician at the Hôtel Dieu

Bichat is considered the founder of histology. He was first to demonstrate that different organs have tissues (the term was of his coinage) and membranes in common and that disease affects tissue and not the individual organ. The then current view of anatomy as a complex of organs was changed by Bichat who stressed tissue as the fundamental building block. Bichat also emphasized the difference between conscious and unconscious life and identified two separate mechanisms in the body, the organic (vegetative) and relational (animal). In sensory physiology, Bichat proposed the existence of muscular sensibility before Bell [96] (*Anatomie générale appliquée à la physiologie et à la medicine*, 2d ed,. 1812).

Biographic data: *DSB* 2:122–123

ESQUIROL, JEAN ETIENNE DOMINIQUE

French psychiatrist
Rating: **18**
Born: Toulouse, February 3, 1772
Died: Paris, December 13, 1840
Highest degree: Docteur en médecine, La Salpêtrière, Paris
Positions: 1811, physician at La Salpêtrière; 1823, chief inspector, University of Paris; 1826, chief physician, asylum at Charenton

Esquirol continued Pinel's [71] efforts at bettering the life of the inmates of insane asylums. In 1817, Esquirol began lecturing on the treatment of the insane, which resulted in the appointment of a commission to investigate such treatment. Esquirol was responsible for planning the asylums at Rouen, Nantes, and Montpellier. He also wrote a cardinal work on mental disorders,

Des maladies mentales (1838). It constituted an advance away from speculation and superstition toward a more rational and objective view of mental disorders. It was a first work of this kind. In his book, Esquirol differentiated between hallucinations and illusions, emphasized environmental and age factors as precipitants of mental disorders and the role of emotions in such disorders. He continued to develop Pinel's statistical classification of inmates by age, disorder, and other characteristics. It later became the established practice to keep ample records on patients as one approach to the understanding of the origin of mental disorders.

Biographic data: M. K. Amdur & E. Messinger, Jean Etienne Dominique Esquirol. *American Journal of Psychiatry,* 1939, 96, 129–135

[92]

FOURIER, FRANCOIS CHARLES MARIE

French social reformer
Rating: **14**
Born: Besançon, Doubs, April 7, 1772
Died: Paris, October 10, 1837

Fourier first published his social-philosophical views in 1808 in a book titled *Théorie des quatre mouvements et des destinées générales*. All social ills Fourier attributed to individualistic competition, hence proposed that society be reorganized on the basis of cooperation. Fourier held that the repression of passions is responsible for human discontent, crime, and immorality and that, by allowing them free rein, behavior would naturally find the happy medium between extremes. Fourier's plan for reorganizing society involved groups of 1,600 persons, called *phalanges*, that would reside in the same building. Actual attempts at cooperative communal living were made in France and America, but they failed. What ties Fourier into the fabric of the development of psychology was a theory of human destiny that played its part in eventually producing the mainstream of evolutionary thinking in the 19th century. Fourier saw man as progressively improving himself and his lot throughout his evolutionary history, where each stage of development covers thousands of years.

Biographic data: EP 3:215; *IESS* 5:547

English historian, economist, and philosopher
Rating: **27**
Born: Northwater Bridge, Angus, Scotland, April 6, 1773
Died: London, June 23, 1836
Education: Studied theology, philosophy, the classics at University of Edinburgh from 1790; licensed as preacher in 1798
Positions: Editorial work, writing, with the East India Company from 1819 on

Mill's greatest achievement was the writing of *The History of British India* (1818); in philosophy he subscribed to the ideas of the utilitarian Jeremy Bentham [73]. His historical, political, and economic works reflect the principles of Utilitarianism or Philosophical Radicalism. Mill's psychology, which is contained in his 1829 volume, *Analysis of the Phenomena of the Human Mind*, also served the cause of Utilitarianism. The importance of this work to psychology lies in that in it Mill develops further the doctrine of associationism that began with Hartley [45]. According to Mill, there are only two kinds of mental contents, sensations and ideas. The latter remain when the former are removed. While sensation is primary, association occurs only among ideas. The association of two ideas, one of which is a word, gives the word its meaning (the associative theory of meaning). The association of ideas obeys one principle only, namely contiguity, successive or simultaneous. The strength of an association is determined by its frequency and vividness. Association cements previous experiences together, so that complex ideas contain all of the component simpler ideas, the most complex idea being that of "everything." Even though complex ideas may appear to be simple because the component ideas fuse together, analysis may still reveal their original structure. Mill's conception of association as a mechanical, noncreative, nonsynthesizing process marked the end of the logical development of a line of thinking—its culminating point and dead end at the same time.

Biographic data: *DNB* 37:382; *EP* 5:312: G. S. Bower, *Hartley and James Mill*, 1881, pp. 8–23; A. Bain, *James Mill*, 1882

YOUNG, THOMAS

English physicist
Rating: **23**
Born: Melverton, Somersetshire, June 13, 1773
Died: London, May 10, 1829
Highest degree: Doctor of Physics, University of Göttingen, 1796; M.D., Cambridge University, 1808
Positions: 1799–1801, physician in London; 1801–1803, Royal Institution, professor of physics; 1802–1829, Foreign Secretary, the Royal Society

In addition to his many contributions in physics, Young was also the founder of physiological optics. In 1793, he explained the phenomenon of accomodation, demonstrating experimentally that it was due to the changing curvature of the lens of the eye. In 1801, he described astigmatism and explained it in terms of irregularities of the cornea. In the same year Young also determined the extent of the visual field and described how acuity decreases toward the periphery of the field.

Young's most notable contribution to psychology was the formulation of a color vision theory in 1802. He developed Newton's [36] laws of color mixture, presented some 130 years earlier, and hypothesized that all colors could be produced if only the three principal ones—red, yellow, and blue—were mixed in the right proportion. Young assumed further that the retina was so constituted that, instead of an infinte number of different structures, each responding to its own color, only three kinds of structures were necessary. It was not until 1852 that Helmholtz [143] presented a full-fledged theory of color vision referring to Young's original formulation. It was named the Young-Helmholtz color-vision theory. Young's explanation of color vision also implied specificity of nerve-fiber action even before Bell [96] in 1811 and Johannes Müller [121] in 1826 had stated the general principle of specific nerve energies and before Helmholtz's definition of the specificity of nerve fibers in 1852.

Biographic data: *DNB* 63:393; A. Wood, *Thomas Young*, 1954

ROLANDO, LUIGI

Italian anatomist
Rating: **15**
Born: Turin, June 20, 1773

Died: Turin, April 20, 1831
Highest degree: M.D., University of Turin, 1793
Positions: 1804, University of Sassari; 1814, University of Turin

Rolando studied the anatomy and pathology of the brain. He published his findings on the localization of brain functions in 1809 (*Saggio sopra la vera struttura del cervello e sopra le funzione del sistema nervoso*), prior to Flourens. Some of the functions he assigned the various portions of the brain were incorrect, however, and his experiments were inadequately described. Nevertheless, since he steered away from phrenology, did actual experiments on the brain, and used post-mortem examinations, his work represents a definite advance in neurophysiology and neuranatomy. Rolando localized the higher mental functions in the cerebral hemispheres. He attributed brain activity, however, to the movement of the fibers, thought that the white matter of the brain was more important than the gray matter, and localized sensation in the medulla rather than the cortex. Long before Fritsch [175] and Hitzig [173], Rolando used the brand-new discovery of his countryman Volta, the electric pile, to stimulate brain tissue. Since he noticed that muscular contractions became more vigorous as he moved the electrodes closer to the cerebellum, he concluded, incorrectly, that the cerebellum was the source of nerve energy. The central fissure in each hemisphere of the brain as well as several other brain structures have been named after Rolando.

Biographic data: *Enciclopedia italiana,* vol. 29

BELL, CHARLES [96]

Scottish anatomist
Rating: 24
Born: Edinburgh, November, 1774
Died: Hallow Park near Worcester, Worcestershire, England, April 28, 1842
Highest degree: Medical degree, University of Edinburgh, 1799
Positions: 1804, private practitioner, lecturer; 1812, surgeon, Middlesex Hospital; 1836, chair of surgery, University of Edinburgh

Bell was one of the great physiologists of the early 19th century. He studied the nature of hearing and the comparative anatomy of the ear, identified the role of the small bones in the middle ear as well as that of the round window (1809). He also identified the papillae of the tongue as the taste organs and mapped the tongue for taste sensitivity. Bell was also the discoverer of the polarization of neurons, which was basic in connection with the concept of reflex. The third volume of Bell's *The Anatomy of the Human Body* (1803) deals with the nervous system and the sense organs.

Bell's greatest discovery, one of fundamental importance to neurophysiology, was that of the existence of two kinds of nerves, sensory and motor. Bell described his discovery in a privately published monograph (*Idea of a New Anatomy of the Brain*) in 1811 and it was not very well known nor its significance appreciated. François Magendie [105] described the distinction independently later and supported it with clearly described experiments. The principle that motor and sensory impulses are carried by separate nerves, the former leaving the spinal cord in its ventral roots and the latter entering it through its dorsal roots became known as the Bell-Magendie law. In the same monograph Bell suggested the existence of further specialization among the nerves, namely that the five senses are mediated by five kinds of nerves, but he failed to name this principle, and it remained for Johannes Müller [121] to elaborate it and state it as the law of specific nerve energies. In 1826, Bell added to the five a sixth sense, the muscle sense.

Biographic data: *DNB* 4:154; *IESS* 2:47–48; *DSB* 1:583; L. Carmichael, Sir Charles Bell: A Contribution to the History of Physiological Psychology. *Psychological Review,* 1926, 33, 188–217

[97]

SCHELLING, FRIEDRICH WILHELM JOSEPH VON

German philosopher
Rating: 15
Born: Leonberg, Baden-Württemberg, January 27, 1775
Died: Bad Ragaz, St. Gallen, Switzerland, August 20, 1854
Education: Studied theology and philosophy at Tübingen and Leipzig, graduated in 1792
Positions: 1798, University of Jena; 1803–1806, University of Würzburg; 1827, University of Munich; 1841–1845, University of Berlin

In his *Ideen zu einer Philosophie der Natur* (1797) and other writings, Schelling expressed ideas that influenced some of the fundamental conceptualizations of the analytical psychology of C. G. Jung [358]. Schelling's thesis was that the spiritual and the physical are only seemingly a pair of opposites. In reality they are two different manifestations of the absolute, and specifically the manifestations of force: attraction is objective, repulsion is subjective. The spiritual is the invisible form of the absolute and also the principle of life in all nature, both of the macrocosm and the microcosm in individual beings. Duality and opposition (male-female, dark-light, irritability-sensitivity) is the general law of nature. The unconscious is the source of all ideas. It exists everywhere, and only the upper layers of the mental world exist on the conscious level. The myth is the concrete manifestation of the unconscious and semiconscious forces of the spiritual world.

Biographic data: *EP* 7:305

ITARD, JEAN (MARIE-GASPARD)

[98]

French physician
Rating: 21
Born: Oraison, Basses Alpes, April 24, 1775
Died: Paris, July 5, 1838
Education: Acquired medical knowledge through practice
Positions: 1800–1838, Institute for Deaf-Mutes, Paris

Itard pioneered in the systematic study of mental deficiency when he undertook to train the "wild boy of Aveyron" (Kaspaar Hauser) in 1798. The boy had been found in the woods by hunters. He was brought to Itard to see if he could be civilized. The interest shown in the boy was owing to the then-current theory of the "noble savage." Itard worked with the boy between 1800 and 1806 using such testing techniques as having him obtain food that was out of reach (a technique to be used with apes more than a century later by Köhler [447]) and delayed reaction (to be used systematically by Hunter [457], also more than a century later). When, after much effort, the boy showed only slight progress, Itard decided that he must be a congenital idiot (as Pinel [71] had diagnosed him to be at the very outset) and abondoned his efforts, believing that idiots and imbeciles were incapable of training. Itard described his work in two reports to the Minister of the Interior, dated 1801 and 1806. Itard, however, had unknowingly established the methodology and principles of the reeducation of mental retardates that are in use today and are directed toward the development of the senses, the intellect, and affect.

As he worked with the wild boy of Aveyron, Itard also worked with deaf-mutes. In his *Traité des maladies de l'ouïe et de l'audition* (1821), he made, for the first time, the differentiation between the diseases of the ear and hearing disorders. Upon this work rests today's education of the deaf-mutes.

Biographic data: H. H. Hunsicker, Dr. Jean Marie-Gaspard Itard. *Medical Record*, 1934, 140, 682-684

[99]

GAUSS, KARL FRIEDRICH

German mathematician
Rating: 22
Born: Braunschweig, April 30, 1775
Died: Göttingen, February 23, 1855
Highest degree: Ph.D. in mathematics, University of Göttingen, 1799
Positions: 1807-1855, director of the Göttingen observatory

Although it was Laplace [75] and de Moivre who pioneered in the mathematical theory of errors, Gauss's developments were so important that the law and the curve (the normal curve) that goes with it are often called Gaussian. Gauss expanded the theory of errors in *Theoria motus corporum coelestium* (1809), an astronomical treatise. The role that the normal curve has played in inferential statistics and hence in psychological research cannot be overestimated. Gauss also discovered the method of least squares to fit a curve to a group of data, another mathematical device not infrequently resorted to by psychologists.

Biographic data: DSB 5:298; IESS 6:74-81

[100]

FEUERBACH, PAUL JOHAN ANSELM VON

German jurist
Rating: 14
Born: Hainichen near Jena, November 14, 1775
Died: Frankfurt-am-Main, May 29, 1833

Highest degree: Ph.D. in philosophy, University of Jena, 1795;
J.D., 1799
Positions: 1795, University of Jena; 1802, University of Kiel;
1804–1805, University of Landshut

Feuerbach advocated the Kantian doctrine that punishment
should be given for its own sake to enforce the law and to act as a
deterrent rather than to prevent wrongdoing individually. This
became known as the "psychological-coercive" or intimidation
theory of punishment.

Biographic data: *Enciclopedia universal ilustrada*, vol. 23

HERBART, JOHANN FRIEDRICH

[101]

German philosopher and educator
Rating: 27
Born: Oldenburg, Lower Saxony, May 4, 1776
Died: Göttingen, August 4, 1841
Highest degree: Ph.D. in philosophy, University of Göttingen,
1804
Positions: 1802, University of Göttingen; 1809–1832, University
of Königsburg; 1833, University of Göttingen

Herbart's philosophy, pedagogy, and psychology form a related
whole. Having evolved a system of ideas, Herbart also evolved a
system for teaching these ideas. It was based on psychological
considerations. Herbart's psychological views are found in his
Lehrbuch zur Psychologie (1816) and particularly his *Psychologie
als Wissenschaft neu gegründet auf Erfahrung, Metaphysik und
Mathematik* (1824–1825). Herbart's psychology was based upon
observation, metaphysics, and mathematics. He specifically denied
that it could be experimental. Neither was it analytic (he denied
the existence of mental faculties) nor physiological. It was,
however, scientific in that mental processes could be described in
mathematical terms. For his mathematical formulations Herbart
never supplied any empirical verification, though. His contribution
was to view psychology as separate from both philosophy and
physics, and thus to present it as an independent scientific
discipline.

Herbart's basic metaphysical tenet was that the universe consists of independent, unconscious elements, *the reals*. Despite his metaphysical bent, Herbart conceptualized the mind and psychology in general in mechanistic terms. Mental states are the result of interaction of ideas. Ideas are forces, however, and combine not in the rather passive fashion envisioned by the British associationists but dynamically and in a much more complicated manner. Ideas differ in quality and intensity. When ideas do not resist each other, they coalesce in the way postulated by the associationists. When ideas clash or contrast, they may not only fail to associate but one idea may expel another from consciousness. Inhibited ideas do not vanish, however, but remain as tendencies. The force of existing ideas Herbart called *apperceptive mass,* a term that was quite in vogue for some time after its introduction and for which Herbart is best known. When this force changes, a previously inhibited idea may return to consciousness. Herbart thus postulated the notion of threshold of consciousness and the existence of conscious and unconscious mental processes. Herbart was therefore in one of the several lines of development of thought that led to the modern notion of inhibition in learning and the dynamics of unconscious processes. The idea of the threshold and of mathematical measurement led to Fechner and psychophysics. In spite of himself, Herbart thus contributed also to the development of experimental psychology.

Herbart's theory of the apperceptive mass had the greatest influence in educational psychology, which he may be considered to have founded. Since new ideas that enter the mind have to contend with the existing apperceptive mass, or the individual's accumulated previous experience, for learning to take place in the easiest and most efficient way new ideas must be introduced so that they are related to what is already known. Herbart's reasoning eventually led educators to adopt teaching practices by which students were led from familiar to closely related but unfamiliar materials.

Biographic data: *DSB* 6:294; *EP* 3:481

[102]

SPURZHEIM, JOHANN KASPAR

Austrian physiologist
Rating: 21
Born: Near Trier, Rhineland-Palatinate, Germany, December 31, 1776
Died: Boston, Massachusetts, November 10, 1832

Highest degree: M.D., University of Vienna, 1804, validated at
  University of Paris, 1821

Franz Joseph Gall [81] was the originator of the doctrine of
phrenology. Spurzheim studied medicine under him, became his
chief disciple in 1800 and later the chief propagandist for the
doctrine. Spurzheim extended Gall's list of personality characteristics that could be localized on the cranium to thirty-seven.
These were grouped into the affective and intellectual faculties,
the former being in turn divided into propensities and sentiments,
the latter into perceptive and reflective faculties. Spurzheim
christened the new doctrine "phrenology."

Spurzheim traveled with Gall in Germany and France, settling
with him in France. In 1813 he separated from Gall and traveled
in France, England, and the United States (1813–1832) to spread
the doctrine. For this purpose he published a book in English,
The Physiognomical System of Gall and Spurzheim (1815). He
collaborated with Gall in preparing the first two volumes of the
magnum opus of phrenology, the *Anatomie et physiologie du
système nerveux en général, et du cerveau en particulier, avec
observations sur la possibilité de reconnaître plusiers dispositions
intellectuelles et morales de l'homme et des animaux par la
configuration de leurs têtes* (1810–1819). Spurzheim wrote
additional volumes on phrenology, elaborating the details and
revising the terminology: *Phrenology or the Doctrine of the
Human Mind* (1825), *The Anatomy of the Human Brain* (1826),
Manuel de phrenologie (1832), and others.

Biographic data: *Enciclopedia universal ilustrada*, vol. 57

BROWN, THOMAS   [103]

Scottish philosopher
Rating: 22
Born: Kirkmabreck, Kirkcudbright, January 9, 1778
Died: London, England, April 2, 1820
Highest degree: M.D., University of Edinburgh, 1803
Positions: 1810–1820, University of Edinburgh, professor of
  moral philosophy

Although Brown was trained in medicine, he soon turned to
philosophy and became Dugald Stewart's [78] disciple. He

prepared Stewart's lectures, which after Brown's death were published as *Lectures on the Philosophy of the Human Mind* (1820). While Brown may be counted with the Scottish school that opposed associationism, he resortd to associationistic principles anyway, but following Berkeley [40], used the term "suggestion." Also, while Reid [51], in denying the association of ideas, had to resort to God to make human sensations into perceptions, Brown solved the problem of objective reference by saying that it is the felt resistance in muscular exertion that supplies us with the idea of an external world. Brown's theory of space perception links Berkeley with Lotze [135] and Wundt [161] through its appeal to muscular sensations. Brown furthered associationism by postulating for the first time the secondary laws of association (or, as he called them, laws of suggestion): relative duration of the sensations, their relative liveliness, frequency, and recency, the reinforcement of one idea by many others, and individual differences in experience, makeup, health, bodily efficiency, and the attending circumstances. His primary laws were similarity, contrast, and spatial and temporal contiguity. From these simpler instances of "suggestion" Brown distinguished relative "suggestions," such as resemblance, difference, and proportion, which anticipated the recognition by future psychologists that mere association does not account for all cognitions. Relative suggestions supplemented the modulating effect of the secondary laws on the primary ones. Modern learning experiments study the effects on learning of the very factors postulated by Brown. Of Brown's secondary laws of association, a major contribution to the associationistic doctrine, only frequency had been suggested earlier (for instance by Aristotle [8]). It became the number-of-trials variable in Ebbinghaus's [207] studies of memory and, later, in learning experiments. The recognition of the complexity of the associative process was given further recognition by Brown when, in anticipation of John Sturart Mill's [125] contribution to the doctrine of association, he spoke of "mental chemistry" as the process of blending of ideas that results in a new and different idea.

Biographic data: *DNB* 7:31; *EP* 1:401; D. Welsh, *Accounts of the Life and Writings of Thomas Brown*, 1825 (reprinted since 1834 in all editions of Brown's *Lectures*)

FROBEL, FRIEDRICH WILHELM AUGUST

[104]

German educator
Rating: 13
Born: Oberweissbach, Thuringia, April 21, 1782

Died: Marienthal, Brunswick, June 21, 1852

Education: A few university courses at University of Jena and University of Göttingen

It was not until Fröbel was thirty-four years old that, having pursued a variety of occupations, he entered the field of education, establishing schools and training others in his method of education. Influenced by Rousseau [53] and Comenius [27], he was basically a follower of Pestalozzi [72]. Fröbel developed the idea of the *kindergarten* in 1836. In kindergartens, young children were to be educated to develop all of their potentialities, mainly through activities. Fröbel established the first kindergarten in Blankenburg in 1837, and spent the rest of his life as an educator of both children and of teachers who were to educate them in Fröbel's kindergartens.

Fröbel's educational philosophy was determined by his belief that life, nature, and spirit each have an inner unity. The development of nature shows itself in the development of the individual mind, and the educational process should reflect the natural inner development of the pupil. Education should unfold the whole person: religion unfolds his emotions, natural science reveals God, and mathematics shows the order that reigns in the universe. Self-activity and instructive play were to be the basic features of the kindergarten. Fröbel introduced toys and devices (called by him "gifts") to stimulate learning through play. *The Education of Man* (1826; English translation, 1885) is Fröbel's most important book.

Biographic data: EP 3:225; *Autobiography* (1903, English ed.)

MAGENDIE, FRANCOIS [105]

French physiologist

Rating: 25

Born: Bordeaux, October 15, 1783

Died: Sannois, near Paris, October 17, 1855

Highest degree: M.D., University of Paris, 1808

Positions: 1813–1831, private teacher of physiology; 1831–1855, professor of medicine at the Collège de France and physician at the Hôtel-Dieu hospital in Paris

In 1809, Magendie acquired a name by attacking in a paper Bichat's [90] doctrine of "vital properties." In the same year he conducted and reported on an experiment on the effects of certain vegetable poisons (later known to have contained strychnine) on animals, for which Magendie has been called the "father of experimental pharmacology." He is known, however, mostly for his discovery of the difference between sensory and motor nerves. Although Bell [96] had described the distinction first (1811), Magendie did his work independently of Bell and stated the experimentally established distinction between the two kinds of nerves with greater clarity than Bell had done (*Expériences sur les fonctions des racines des nerfs qui naissent de la moelle épinière*, 1822). The principle that the posterior spinal roots are afferent or sensory and that the ventral roots are efferent or motor was eventually named the *Bell-Magendie law*, but not until after a prolonged controversy over the question of priority between the two physiologists. Magendie made several other important contributions to physiology that were unrelated to behavior and founded, in 1821, the *Journal de physiologie expérimentale et pathologie*.

Biographic data: DSB 9:6; J. M. D. Olmsted, *François Magendie*, 1944

[106]

BESSEL, FRIEDRICH WILHELM

German astronomer
Rating: 23
Born: Minden, Westphalia, July 22, 1784
Died: Königsberg, East Prussia, March 17, 1846
Education: Self-educated
Positions: 1810, professor of astronomy and director (since 1813) of the observatory at Königsberg

When the astronomer royal at Greenwich, Maskelyne, dismissed his assistant, Kinnebrook, for alleged gross time errors made in the observation of stellar transits, the event was written up in a history of the observatory and published in 1816; Bessel read it but hypothesized that the error was in fact a matter of individual differences in reaction time between the two men. He systematically compared his own performance with those of several other astronomers over a period of years, confirming the hypothesis. He also showed that considerable variability in reaction time existed among individuals. Differences in reaction time between two astronomers were presented by Bessel in the form of an equation, $A - B = x$ sec., the "personal equation," which could be used to make the observations of the two astronomers comparable. The determination of personal equations became an important aspect of astronomical observations. In the 1860s and 1870s this work was extended to include the dependence of reaction time on such variables as the brightness of the celestial object and its rate of motion. Bessel's contribution was to recognize the psychological nature of the reaction time problem and to give impetus to the study of two important phenomena in the incipient experimental psychology: "reaction time" and the so-called "complications," or mental processes involving more than one sense modality.

Biographic data: *DSB* 2:97; C. T. Anger, *Erinnerungen an Bessels Leben und Wirken,* 1845; H. Durège, *Bessels Leben und Wirken,* 1861

PURKINJE (PURKYNE), JAN EVANGELISTA

Czech physiologist
Rating: 24
Born: Libochovice, Bohemia, December 17, 1787
Died: Prague, July 28, 1869
Highest degree: M.D., University of Prague, 1819
Positions: 1823, University of Breslau; 1850, Charles University, Prague

Purkinje did pioneer work in several different areas: experimental physiology, microtechnique, neuranatomy, histology, embryology, pharmacology, and vision. After him are named the large cells of the cerebellar cortex (*Purkinje's cells*), *Purkinje's fibers,* and other structures. In psychology, his name is associated mainly with the *Purkinje shift*, the change in the visibility of blue and red in twilight: as illumination decreases, blue appears lighter, while red begins to look black. Purkinje described this phenomenon in 1825, but is was not until the very end of the 19th century that a neurophysiological explanation of the phenomenon was provided.

Purkinje was first to observe the change in distance between the reflections of a flame in the anterior and posterior surfaces of the lens of the eye and the cornea as accommodation took place. The entoptically seen shadows of the retinal capillaries, which Purkinje first described, are called *Purkinje's figure*. Purkinje also observed that visual acuity decreases toward the periphery and that colors look gray in extreme peripheral vision. He coined the term "indirect vision." In addition, Purkinje described the phenomenology of a variety of other organismic states: vertigo, nystagmus, disturbances in sense organs, hearing (he discovered bone conduction in deaf-mutes), touch, sleep, and the effect of drugs (atropin, digitalis, camphor, and opium). Purkinje is thus one of the great figures in the phenomenological approach to sensation and perception, among whom are counted Goethe [77] and Hering [167]. Purkinje published his contributions to the phenomenology of vision in *Beobachtungen und Versuche zur Physiologie der Sinne* (vol. 1, 1819; vol. 2, 1825).

Biographic data: V. Robinson, Jan Evangelista Purkinje. *Scientific Monthly*, 1929, 29, 217–229; O. V. Hykes, The life of Jan Evangelista Purkinje. *Osiris*, 1936, 2, 464–471; W. J. Bishop, Jan Evangelista Purkinje. *British Medical Bulletin,* 1950, 7, 99–100

[108]

SCHOPENHAUER, ARTHUR

German philosopher
Rating: **22**
Born: Danzig, East Prussia, February 22, 1788
Died: Frankfurt-am-Main, September 20, 1860
Highest degree: Ph.D. in philosophy, University of Berlin, 1813
Positions: 1820–1822, University of Berlin

Schopenhauer contributed to psychology a color vision theory and a philosophical viewpoint that influenced a considerable number of psychologists in the 19th and 20th century, such as William James [184]. An admirer of Goethe [77], Schopenhauer emulated him in preparing a manuscript on vision and colors (*Uber das Sehen und die Farben,* 1816) and sent it to Goethe for approval. Before Helmholtz [143] and Hering [167], his theory and those of Goethe and Young [94] were the only color vision theories extant.

Philosophically, Schopenhauer was influenced mainly by Kant [60], but he disdained Hegel [89]. In his principal philosophical work, *Die Welt als Wille und Vorstellung* (1819; English translation, *The World as Will and Idea*, 1883), Schopenhauer argues that man is more than what is revealed to the senses, more than just a phenomenal object. Man is also aware that his actions are the result of his will. A person's activity can be explained ultimately as the manifestation of a force; so can everything else in nature. The best analogy of this force is the will. Will thus becomes the most fundamental metaphysical truth. It also makes for determinism since all of man's behavior is the expression of his will, and that is fixed. Self-realization is the result of observing one's own actions, but since these are determined, so is one's self-concept. There is no freedom to be this or that: one is what one is because of one's own unalterable will. In man, will reaches or can reach a conscious form. Conscious motives, however, do not explain all of man's behavior. There are unconscious motives which also affect behavior. Secondary motives are sometimes invented so as to explain one's unacceptable behavior which has been actually caused by other motives. This view relates Schopenhauer to Freud [224], in whom unconscious motivation became a major tenet of psychoanalysis.

Biographic data: *EP* 7:325

HAMILTON, SIR WILLIAM   [109]

Scottish philosopher
Rating: 21
Born: Glasgow, March 8, 1788
Died: Edinburgh, May 6, 1856
Education: M.A., Oxford University, 1814
Positions: 1821–1856, University of Edinburgh, teaching civil
  history until 1836, philosophy from 1836 on

Hamilton not only edited the works of both Thomas Reid [51] and Dugald Stewart [78] of the Scottish school but in many respects derived his own philosophy from them. At the same time his thinking was also considerably influenced by German transcendentalism. Hamilton acquired recognition by his 1829 essay on *The Philosophy of the Unconditioned*, in which a mixture of Kant [60] and British empiricism predominates. What the mind knows is not objective reality but objective reality conditioned by the number and nature of the senses. Judgment is not entirely objective either since it processes sensory data according to the rules of the mind. "To think is to condition." The ultimate reality (the unconditioned) is beyond the reach of philosophy. This latter Kantian notion Hamilton accepted, along with a faculty psychology of the Kantian variety.

Hamilton's most important contribution to psychology was his theory of memory and association. Its central concept is that of "redintegration," or the bringing back to consciousness, by a sense impression, of the entire situation of which it has been a part. The evocation of a whole rather than ideas in their associative sequence contrasted markedly with the notion of association of the British associationists, and anticipated 20th-century thinking.

Hamilton was primarily a philosopher, but because he was influenced by the more psychologically oriented Reid and Stewart and because he did discuss psychological topics, such as redintegration and the nature of consciousness (*Lectures on Metaphysics and Logic*, 1859), and was able to argue very competently the case of the Scottish school against British associationism, Hamilton had a measure of influence on the development of thought within the Scottish school of psychology. The Scottish school came to an end with Hamilton, but its philosophical ideas continued to live in the idealist movement.

Biographic data: *DNB* 24:227; *DSB* 6:80; *EP* 3:409

[110]

HALL, MARSHALL

English physiologist
Rating: 21
Born: Basford, Nottinghamshire, February 18, 1790
Died: Brighton, Sussex, August 11, 1857
Highest degree: M.D., University of Edinburgh, 1812
Positions: 1812–1816, various medical appointments; 1817–1826, private practice in Nottingham; 1826–1850, private practice in London, some lecturing

Hall pioneered in the study of reflex action. He studied it over a period of twenty-five years, beginning in 1832. In an 1833 report, Hall laid down the fundamentals of a theory of reflex action. While others (Whytt [55], von Haller [49], Prochaska [76]) had investigated the reflex, Hall showed it to be an essential function of the body, not just an isolated phenomenon. He made a distinction between voluntary and involuntary action, holding that reflexes are both involuntary and unconscious since the brain is not required to produce them. This stirred up considerable controversy, but for several decades Hall's convenient dichotomization of the conscious and the unconscious, voluntary and involuntary was adhered to. Hall's work on reflex action found no recognition in England during his time, although foreign scientists thought him to be the most outstanding name in the field.

Biographic data: *DNB* 24:80; *DSB* 6:58

ELLIOTSON, JOHN

[111]

English physician
Rating: 22
Born: London, October 29, 1791
Died: London, July 29, 1868
Highest degree: M.D., Cambridge University, 1821
Positions: 1817–1837, University College and University College Hospital, London, professor of practice of medicine and senior physician

Before 1837, when Elliotson saw a demonstration of mesmerism and became immediately enthused about its medical uses, he had introduced several innovations in medical practice in spite of the initial skepticism and even ridicule of other physicians. Elliotson's troubles with the medical profession continued to increase from here on. He began to apply mesmerism in treating his patients at the University College Hospital. Elliotson would "magnetize" an object, apply it to the affected spot, and a cure would be achieved. Demonstrations that belief on the part of the patient, i.e., suggestion was necessary, did not change Elliotson's attitude toward mesmerism. Mesmerism was in disrepute at the time, and the Council of the University College forbade its use at the College. Elliotson resigned and proceeded to study and use mesmerism on his own, in opposition to the medical establishment. In 1843, he began publishing a journal, the *Zoist*, to print papers on "cerebral physiology and mesmerism" that other journals would not accept. Elliotson not only had become quite interested in phrenology but believed that "magnetic" hands, as they touched parts of a person's head, would stimulate the underlying (according to the phrenologists) functionally specific area and faculty. *Zoist*, however, ceased publication in 1856. Some time during this period Elliotson also became interested in the anesthetic use of mesmerism as reports on James Esdaile's [126] operations performed on patients in mesmeric trance began to reach England. He founded a mesmeric hospital in 1849. The discovery of the anesthetic uses of ether, nitrous oxide, and chloroform in the mid-1840s, however, prevented the development of this application of mesmerism.

Biographic data: *DNB* 17:264; J. M. Bramwell, *Hypnotism, Its History, Practice, and Theory*, 1903, pp. 4–14; G. Newbold, Famous Names in Hypnotism: (2) John Elliotson, *British Journal of Medical Hypnotism*, 1950, 1(3), 2–7

[112]

COUSIN, VICTOR

French philosopher
Rating: 15
Born: Paris, November 28, 1792
Died: Cannes, January 13, 1867
Education: Graduated from Ecole Normale, Paris 1812
Positions: 1815–1821, Sorbonne; 1828–1830, Sorbonne, remained as professor until 1852; 1835–1840, director, Ecole Normale, Paris; from 1840 in political life

Cousin adopted the psychological approach to philosophy in the manner of Maine de Biran [86] and Thomas Reid [51], but in his later life was influenced by Schelling [97]. Cousin opposed the extreme sensationalism of Condillac [57] and the materialism and atheism that he thought resulted from it, but accepted the view that sensations inform us about the external world, as did the Scottish school of common-sense philosophy. From this psychological premise Cousin arrived at an ontology and the recognition of God as the ultimate causal substance.

Biographic data: *EP* 2:246

[113]

FLOURENS, PIERRE JEAN MARIE

French physiologist
Rating: 24
Born: Maureilhan, Hérault, April 1, 1794
Died: Montgeron near Paris, December 6, 1867
Highest degree: M.D., University of Montpellier, 1813

Positions: Collège de France; University of Paris; 1832, Museum of Jardin du Roi, professor of comparative anatomy; 1855, Collège de France, professor of natural history; elected permanent Secretary of the Academy of Sciences in 1833; elected to the French Academy in 1840

Flourens's main contribution was to physiological psychology, which he made through his work on the localization of brain functions. Using the method of extirpation, which he introduced, he concentrated on the cerebral hemispheres, the cerebellum, the corpora quadrigemina, the medulla oblongata, the spinal cord, and the nerves to isolate each from the other, to remove it cleanly, and so determine its function. Flourens correctly established the function of the six main divisions of the nervous system of animals: while each has a specific and unitary role (*action propre*), the brain also acts as a whole (*action commune*). In this Flourens anticipated the much later work of Lashley [466] and Franz [350]. In moving away from the speculations of the philosophers concerning brain function and at the same time rejecting the extreme specificity of the phrenologists (whom he severely criticized), Flourens, through the precision of his technique and his clear and forceful presentations materially advanced knowledge concerning the anatomical substrate of behavior. His main work is *Recherches expérimentales sur les propriétés et les fonctions du système nerveux dans les animaux vertébrés* (1824).

Biographic data: *DSB* 5:44; *IESS* 5:495

BRAID, JAMES [114]

Scottish physician
Rating: 21
Born: Rylaw House, Fife, ca. 1795
Died: Manchester, England, March 25, 1860
Highest degree: Degree in medicine, University of Edinburgh
Positions: Private practice of medicine in Manchester

Within five weeks after a mesmerist had given a stage demonstration at Manchester, Braid had his own theory of the nature of mesmerism. He presented his theory, along with a demonstration, on that same stage. Then and in his subsequent work, Braid was a moderate, seeking the middle ground between the mesmerists and the medical profession. Braid continued experimenting and writing, providing a scientific foundation for the phenomenon that he named hypnotism (developed from the term *neurypnology*, which was a contraction of neurohypnology). He published several books and many articles on hypnotism: *Neurypnology: or, the Rationale of Nervous Sleep, Considered in Relation with Animal Magnetism*, 1843; *The Power of the Mind over the Body*, 1846; *Observations on Trance*, 1850; *Magic, Witchcraft, Animal Magnetism, and Electro-Biology*, 1852; *Hypnotic Therapeutics, with an Appendix on Table-Moving and Spirit-Rapping*, 1853; *Observations on the Nature and Treatment of Certain Forms of Paralysis*, 1855. These eventually resulted in the acceptance of hypnotism as a valid phenomenon by the scientific world, as well as of Braid's explanation of the phenomenon. Braid's first theory stressed sensory fixation, later eyelid fatigue, then attentional fixation (monoideism), and finally, suggestion as the crucial factor in hypnotism. The scientific understanding of hypnotism that began with Braid was psychological in nature from the outset. The study and use of hypnotism in clinical settings spread first to France, where for some time (1860–1875) it was known as "Braidism."

Biographic data: *DNB* 6:198; a biography of Braid by A. E. Waite in Braid's *Neuropnology*, 1899 reprint

[115]

WEBER, ERNST HEINRICH

German physiologist
Rating: 27
Born: Wittenberg, June 24, 1795
Died: Leipzig, January 26, 1878
Highest degree: M.D., University of Wittenberg, 1815
Positions: 1817–1878, University of Leipzig

Weber worked on the physiology of the internal organs, but he is best known for his work on touch, on which subject he wrote a book (*De pulsu, resorptione, auditu et tactu: annotationes anatomicae et physiologicae*, 1834) and a chapter in R. Wagner's *Handwörterbuch der Physiologie* (1846, vol. 3). He made a major contribution here in determining two-point thresholds on the skin. Weber found that the size of the threshold varied according to the skin area stimulated, which he explained by the hypothesis of "sensory circles": for two points to be percieved as separate, the corresponding nerve fibers must be separated by at least one fiber that is not being stimulated. The idea of skin areas sending messages to the brain where discrimination took place anticipated Lotze's [135] theory of local signs.

Weber's other work was not as well known at the time, and his discovery of the just noticeable difference in sensation might also have passed unnoticed if Fechner [120], who at the time was also at Leipzig, had not made it into a cornerstone of psychophysics. Weber performed experiments in another, little studied area, the physiology of the muscle sense, and asked the question what would be the smallest difference between two weights that would be just noticeably different. He found that the absolute size of this difference varied depending on the size of the weights compared, but that the difference bore a constant relationship to the weight ($\delta S/S = k$). Weber determined that the relationship held also for the discrimination of the length of lines and the pitch of tones: for an increment in a stimulus to be just noticeably different, it had to be a certain proportion of the stimulus. To each sense modality there corresponded a different proportion. Fechner took Weber's formulation, assumed the just noticeable difference to be infinitely divisible and directly related to differences in sensation, integrated Weber's fraction, and introduced the logarithmic law of psychophysics, which he called *Weber's law*. That term is now reserved for the original Weber's fraction, and the logarithmic law bears Fechner's name.

Biographic data: IESS 16:493

QUETELET, (LAMBERT) ADOLPHE (JACQUES) [116]

Belgian mathematician, astronomer, and statistician
Rating: 24
Born: Ghent, February 22, 1796
Died: Brussels, February 17, 1874
Education: Graduated from University of Ghent in 1814
Positions: 1814, University of Ghent; 1828, Director, Royal Observatory in Brussels

In addition to important contributions to astronomy, Quételet was one of the fathers of modern statistics. The term "statistics" was coined by him. His main achievement was the application of probability theory and statistical computations to social and psychological data. Quételet obtained a large number of chest measurements of Scottish and French soldiers. He observed that they followed the same distribution as gaming events and other physical phenomena, subject to the laws of probability. Extending the work of Laplace [75] and Gauss [99] on human errors, Quételet applied the concept of normal distribution to human physical characteristics and other biological and social data, and statistical organization to such enterprises as census taking.

The deviation of shots from the bullseye and of errors from the correct value Quételet generalized to biological phenomena, considering the distributions of values about their mean as deviations by nature from a central ideal or the mean. He developed in his *Sur l'homme et le développement de ses facultés, ou Essai de physique sociale* (1835) the notion of the average man (*l'homme moyen*), whose measurements are the measures of central tendency about which the measurements of all other men vary according to the normal probability distribution. Quételet worked for international uniformity in statistics, and organized the first international conference on statistics.

Biographic data: IESS 13:247

[117]

COMTE, (ISADORE) AUGUSTE (MARIE FRANCOIS)

French philosopher
Rating: 25
Born: Montpellier, January 19, 1798
Died: Paris, September 5, 1857
Education: Studied science at Ecole Polytechnique in Paris, 1814–1816

In 1838, Comte coined the term "sociology" and attempted to systematize a new science under that name. He believed that individual behavior is largely the product of the society and not of the individual's experience or his personality. Likewise, data in science, he believed, are social and the study of one's own inner self through introspection is impossible. Man can be understood only in relation to other men, hence data in science are those that are arrived at by observation and concerning whose existence agreement exists. Data are therefore not inferred. Positive data are basic, observational, and preinferential. Comtian positivism thus doubted the validity of a science based on introspection. Even so, in his *Système de politique positive* (one of the six volumes of his main work, *Cours de philosophie positive*, published over the period 1830 to 1842) Comte presents a *Tableau cerebral* which relates cerebral areas and functions or faculties. Comte accepted Gall's [81] anatomy and, in a sense, may be seen as holding the views of a physiological psychologist. He denied that there could be function without organs and stated that the brain and the nervous system were the site of intellectual and emotional functions.

Comte represented the evolutionary viewpoint in the social sciences. He postulated three stages in human evolution: the theological, the methaphysical, and the positive (or scientific). John Stuart Mill [125] was instrumental in making Comte's views known. As the evolutionary viewpoint was gathering momentum in Comte's time, Comte exercised a tremendous influence on the development of thinking in the social sciences.

Biographic data: DSB 3:375; EP 2:173; IESS 3:201

BENEKE, FRIEDRICH EDUARD [118]

German philosopher
Rating: **17**
Born: Berlin, February 17, 1798
Died: Berlin, between March (when he disappeared) and June (when he was found dead), 1854
Education: Theology, University of Berlin, University of Halle
Positions: 1824–1827, University of Göttingen; 1832–1854, University of Berlin

Beneke, at a time when philosophical transcendentalism predominated, sought to offer an alternative view in the interpretation of psychological phenomena. He rejected the concept of innate ideas as well as that of mental faculties; neither did he accept the view that mental life is the result of associated mental experiences. In his book, *Lehrbuch der Psychologie als Naturwissenschaft* (1832), Beneke offers the view that the infant possesses the capacity for many different activities, or part functions, which are as yet undeveloped, but which develop into the adult's complex activities with age. His doctrine of traces states, although not in physiological terms, that an idea, upon disappearance from the mind, leaves behind a trace. The later retrieval or revival of this trace constitutes memory. Beneke used the same analytic approach to dismantle other "faculties" in addition to that of memory. This may be considered his most significant general contribution to psychology.

Beneke theorized that philosophy is based on empirical knowledge, and suggested that psychology should be restructured from the ground up and placed on a scientific basis. As an empirical science psychology would be propadeutic to all other sciences. Beneke insisted, however, that psychology does not have to use the data of other sciences. While it is true that the senses give us only a mediated knowledge of reality, we can apprehend our own mental processes directly through introspection. The inner life of others is understood by analogy with one's own. Other psychological texts of Beneke's are *Pragmatische Psychologie* (1832), *Psychologische Umrisse* (1825), and *Neue Psychologie* (1845).

Biographic data: *EP* 1:278

[119]   **VOLKMANN, ALFRED WILHELM**

German physiologist
Rating: 12
Born: Leipzig, Saxony, July 1, 1800
Died: Halle, Saxony-Anhalt, April 21, 1877
Highest degree: Ph.D. in physiology, University of Leipzig, 1826
Positions: 1837, University of Tartu; 1843–1873, University of Halle

Although Volkmann's first psychological publication was on animal magnetism (*Observatio biologico de magnetismo animali*, 1826), his major contributions were in the area of the physiology of vision where he wrote *Neue Beiträge zur Physiologie des Gesichtssinnes* (1836) and the section on vision in Rudolph Wagner's *Handwörterbuch der Physiologie* (1844–1846). Volkmann collaborated also with Fechner [120] in developing the psychophysical method of average error.

Biographic data: *Enciclopedia universal ilustrada*, vol. 69

[120]   **FECHNER, GUSTAV THEODOR**

German philosopher, physicist, and psychologist
Rating: 27
Born: Gross-Särchen, Lower Lusatia, April 19, 1801

Died: Leipzig, November 18, 1887

Highest degree: M.D., University of Leipzig, 1822

Positions: 1824–1887, University of Leipzig, teaching physics until 1840, pensioned in 1844 because of poor eyesight, engaged in philosophy

Scientific psychology begins with Fechner. He first made a name for himself as a physicist (an interest acquired after obtaining the medical degree), then became even more prominent by relating his interest in physics to his basic interest in philosophy and metaphysics. The field of psychophysics that developed therefrom was entirely a byproduct of his philosophical interests. He is celebrated, nevertheless, as a psychophysicist and not as a philosopher.

Stimulated by his desire to prove that mind and body are aspects of the same unity (the identity hypothesis), Fechner, on October 22, 1850, conceived of the idea of how to measure sensation. He reasoned that if the exact relationship between stimulus energy and the sensation it produced were known, then by measuring physical energy, which is easy, one could measure sensation. The physiologist Ernst Heinrich Weber [115] had just formulated the law that now bears his name, namely that the ratio of a just noticeable difference in a stimulus and the original stimulus is a constant. Fechner integrated Weber's fraction and arrived at the equation that shows that sensation is directly proportional to the logarithm of the stimulus: $R = k \log S$ (Fechner's law).

The program for the development of psychophysics Fechner described in 1851 in a philosophical treatise titled *Zend-Avesta*. Fechner then proceeded to work out the three basic psychophysical methods for establishing the lower (absolute) and upper (terminal) thresholds of sensation as well as the difference thresholds for deep pressure, visual brightness, and tactual and visual distance. The methods of limits, average error, and the constant method are still basic in psychophysics today. They were the first methods of mental measurement and therefore initiated the era of quantitative experimental psychology.

In 1860, Fechner published his theory and experimental findings in *Elemente der Psychophysik*, which treated of the "exact science of the functional relations of dependency between body and mind." Fechner then turned to experimental aesthetics, and spent the next ten years developing still another field of inquiry. He contributed a dozen papers on the subject, including one on the golden section and several on the authenticity of paintings. This work culminated in a book, *Vorschule der Aesthetik*

(1876), which laid the foundation for experimental aesthetics. By this time psychophysics was beginning to be incorporated in the "new" psychology, and Fechner published two more books and several articles on the subject. The *Elements*, however, remained his main psychological work and a cornerstone of the new scientific psychology that experimented and measured, not merely speculated.

In addition to Fechner's law, Fechner's name is associated with the following phenomena: *Fechner's colors* (subjective colors seen in relatively slowly rotating discs with black-and-white patterns) and *Fechner's paradox* (that a visual target viewed with two eyes will appear brighter if one eye is suddenly covered up).

Biographic data: *DSB* 4:556; *EP* 3:184; *IESS* 5:350; J. E. Kuntze, *Gustav Theodor Fechner*, 1892; K. Lasswitz, *Gustav Theodor Fechner*, 1896; G. S. Hall, *Founders of Modern Psychology*, 1912, pp. 123–177; O. Külpe, Gustav Theodor Fechner. *Vierteljahrsschrift für wissenschaftliche Philosophie*, 1901, 25, 191–217; C. Burt, Gustav Theodor Fechner: Elemente der Psychophysik, 1860–1960. *British Journal of Statistical Psychology*, 1960, 13, 1–10

[121]

MULLER, JOHANNES PETER

German physiologist
Rating: 25
Born: Koblenz, Rhineland-Palatinate, July 14, 1801
Died: Berlin, April 28, 1858
Highest degree: Ph.D. in physiology, University of Bonn, 1822
Positions: 1824, University of Bonn; 1833, University of Berlin

Müller was the foremost physiologist of his day. He wrote a compendium of physiological knowledge, the *Handbuch der Physiologie des Menschen* (1833–1840), which served as the primary reference text in physiology for some time. In it may be found not only a presentation of the state of knowledge of physiology of the time but also many of Müller's speculations, theories, research results, and conclusions. Müller shares with von Haller [49] the appellation "father of experimental physiology."

The fifth book of the *Handbuch* deals with the senses and contains the statement on the specificity of nerve energies (or qualities). While not entirely original with Müller, it was Müller who gave the principle a clear and precise formulation and made it known through his *Handbuch*. It states that we are not directly aware of objects themselves but of the quality of nerve activity that is triggered by the objects. There are five kinds of nerves, each conveying to the mind its own characteristic quality and not that of any others. The locus of specificity lies in the brain, however. Müller's doctrine led to such later formulations as the color vision theories of Young [94], Helmholtz [143], and Hering [167], all based on the notion of nerve fiber specificity, and the discovery of sensory spots in the skin. It was the most important law of physiology during the early 19th century.

The sixth book of Müller's *Handbuch* deals with a variety of psychological subjects, such as memory, thought, temperament, sleep, and others. Müller discussed hearing at length, made some sound conjectures concerning the function of the middle and inner ear, as well as some erroneous ones. He described Aguilonius's concept of the horopter so well that it came to be called *Müller's circle*. Earlier, Müller had written a text on the physiology of vision (*Zur vergleichenden Physiologie des Gesichtssinnes*, 1826) and one on perception (*Uber die phantastischen Gesichtserscheinungen*, 1826). In all of his writings Müller's approach to physiology was that of a physiological psychologist, as he repeatedly referred to the mind to explain physiological functions. In some respects Müller was old-fashioned and believed in vital forces and the instantaneous transmission of nerve impulses, but he was also an inspiring teacher, and many physiologists and psychologists, who later acquired fame themselves, had studied with him.

Biographic data: *DSB* 9:567; *IESS* 10:525; B. Chance, Johannes Müller; a Sketch of His Life and Ophthalmological Works. *Archives of Ophthalmology*, 1944, **32**, 395–402; U. Ebbecke, *Johannes Müller, der grosse rheinische Physiologe*, 1944

PLATEAU, JOSEPH ANTOINE FERDINAND   [122]

Belgian physicist
Rating: **18**
Born: Brussels, October 14, 1801
Died: Ghent, September 15, 1883
Highest degree: Doctorate in physics and mathematical sciences, University of Liège, 1829

Positions: 1835–1843, University of Ghent; after becoming
blind, continued research privately with the help of his son and
son-in-law

Plateau introduced the psychophysical method of bisection in the
1850s by having painters paint a gray that would be midway
between a given white and a given black. He published the results
in an 1872 article and proposed that instead of equal stimulus
distances yielding equal sense distances (*Fechner's* [120] *law*),
equal stimulus ratios yielded equal sense ratios (*power law*).
Later, Plateau agreed with Fechner since an equisection experiment with length (performed by Delboeuf [159]) did not yield a
power function. Fechner was the greater authority in psychophysics then, but Plateau was right since reflectance (from paint)
is an intensive continuum and subject to the power law, as shown
a century later by S. S. Stevens [517], while length is a
continuum whose perception relates to it one to one and hence
yields a rectilinear function in both a semilogarithm and a
logarithm–logarithm coordinate system.

In an 1829 paper, Plateau proposed the initial version of what
came to be called later the *Talbot-Plateau law* after Talbot used it
in photometric matches; Plateau wrote again, discussing it and
giving the principle specific formulation. The law deals with the
time–intensity relationship of intermittent stimuli perceived as
continuous.

Plateau also wrote a 266-page history of visual sensation in 1876.
In 1830 he invented a stroboscope, but did not publish its
description until 1833, by which time another version of the
stroboscope had been described by Faraday. In 1850, Plateau
described both the color sensations and the movement aftereffect
obtained by looking at a rotating spiral (*Plateau's spiral*). Both
the stroboscope and apparent movement played an important
role later in the history of the Gestalt school of psychology.

Biographic data: *Enciclopedia universal ilustrada*, vol. 45

WHEATSTONE, SIR CHARLES

English physicist
Rating: 14
Born: Gloucester, Gloucestershire, February, 1802
Died: Paris, France, October 19, 1875
Education: No university education

Positions, honors: 1834–1840, King's College, London, professor of experimental philosophy; honorary D.C.L., 1862, LL.D., 1864; knighted 1868

Among Wheatstone's numerous discoveries and other achievements in physics, two were of importance to psychology. In 1833, Wheatstone discovered that retinal disparity is converted by the nervous system into a single percept of three-dimensionality and that all that was needed for three-dimensional perception was a difference between the two retinal images. He demonstrated this by constructing what he called a stereoscope and publishing a description of it in 1838. Of the various types of stereoscopes, Wheatstone's prism stereoscope has proved to be the best. It has been used in psychological experiments on perception since Wheatstone's time.

In 1840, Wheatstone contructed a chronoscope to measure the velocity of cannon balls. It was used subsequently to measure reaction time in psychological laboratories.

Biographic data: DNB 60:435

DIX, DOROTHEA LYNDE

[124]

American humanitarian
Rating: **11**
Born: Hampden, Maine, April 4, 1802
Died: Trenton, New Jersey, July 17, 1887

In 1841, Dix became interested in the conditions prevailing at insane asylums as well as prisons and alms houses. The rest of her life was devoted to the betterment of the life of the inmates of these institutions. Dix started in the state of Massachusetts, and through her efforts legislation was passed to alleviate the conditions of the mentally ill, including the separate institutionalization of the mentally ill and of criminals. Her work eventually extended to other states and countries. For forty years Dix campaigned ceaselessly and energetically but in a subdued and dignified manner to achieve more humane conditions in asylums and other institutions. Through presentations to the Congress, journalism, and carefully chosen spokesmen, she was able to raise many millions of dollars for new and modern mental hospitals and to remove chains, ropes, and other indignities from mental patients. Because of her singular effort twenty states had established separate institutions for the insane within thirty years of the beginning of her work. She then performed the same service in Scotland and in thirteen other European countries.

Biographic data: NCAB 3:438, 6:388, 8:232, 10:431; H. E. Marshall, *Dorothea Dix: A Forgotten Samaritan*, 1937; S. Rypins, Dorothea Lynde Dix. *Psychiatric Quarterly Supplement*, 1948, **22**, 277–289; F. R. Taylor, Dorothea Lynde Dix: America's Greatest Woman. *North Carolina Medical Journal* 1949, **10**, 317–320

[125]

MILL, JOHN STUART

English philosopher and economist
Rating: **27**
Born: Pentonville (London), May 20, 1806
Died: Avignon, France, May 8, 1873
Education: Taught by father and self
Positions: East India Company

Mill, the eldest son of James Mill [93], was a lesser figure of a psychologist than his father. He exercised a far greater influence as a philosopher, logician, and economist. Mill's psychological views may be found in *A System of Logic, Ratiocinative and Inductive* (1843), *Examination of Sir William Hamilton's Philosophy* (1865), and the notes written for the 1869 edition of his father's *Analysis of the Phenomena of the Human Mind*. Mill did not accept his father's notion of infinite compounding of associations. Instead, he suggested that the mind's activity produces, in combining simple elements, something new that is not present in the original components. The whole is different from the sum of its parts, which is what Wundt [161] said later and the Gestalt psychologists made into a cardinal proposition in their system. Mill himself called this notion "mental chemistry . . . in which . . . the simple ideas generate, rather than they compose, the complex ones." Mill's contribution, as against his father's, was to demonstrate the need for empirical observation of the complex idea rather than assuming its identity with the sum of its parts. Mill thus called for the scientific study of associations. Like his father, Mill subscribed to the laws of similarity and contiguity in association; he added, however, intensity in his *Logic*, but later replaced it with frequency and inseparability (in his *Examination*).

Mill also offered a theory of perception, which was not unlike that of Berkeley [40]. The mind is able to have expectations. Having had actual sensations sets up the expectation in the mind that these sensations would reoccur, that is, the idea of possible sensations. Thus there are "permanent possibilities of sensations." The perception of matter is but a belief in the permanent possibilities of sensations, which makes it a matter of association and therefore a "psychological theory of the belief in an external world." In his *Logic* Mill also proposed some basic postulates for ascertaining truth. These have become fundamental in scientific research, including psychological research, such as the logic underlying the use of control groups in experimentation.

Biographic data: *DNB* 37:390; *DSB* 9:383; *EP* 5:314; *IESS* 10:340; J. S. Mill, *Autobiography*, 1873; A. Bain, *John Stuart Mill*, 1882; W. L. Courtney, *Life of John Stuart Mill*, 1889

ESDAILE, JAMES [126]

English surgeon
Rating: **20**
Born: Montrose, Angus, Scotland, February 6, 1808
Died: Sydenham (London), January 10, 1859
Highest degree: M.D., University of Edinburgh, 1830
Positions: 1831–1851, various appointments as surgeon in India

In 1845, after reading of Elliotson's [111] work with mesmerism, Esdaile tried it on a patient suffering from great pain. Finding that he was successful in eliminating pain by this method, Esdaile began to use mesmerism for anesthetic purposes in performing his operations. While the medical profession remained in opposition, he received some support from the government. Working in several hospitals, Esdaile performed 291 operations on patients in a mesmeric trance before he left India. His reports lay buried in government files, since the medical journals in both India and England refused to publish them. Esdaile published a book in 1846 (*Mesmerism in India, and Its Practical Application in Surgery and Medicine*) and still another in 1851 (*The Introduction of Mesmerism, as an Anesthetic and Curative Agent, Into the Hospitals of India*), both dealing with his work with mesmerism.

It remained for Braid [114], however, to attach a different label to mesmerism, hypnotism, and to give it scientific respectability.

Biographic data: *DNB* 18:1; J. M. Bramwell, *Hypnotism, Its History, Practice, and Theory*, 1903, pp. 14–21

[127]

DARWIN, CHARLES

English biologist
Rating: 27
Born: Shrewbury, Shropshire, February 12, 1809
Died: Down, Kent, April 19, 1882
Education: Studied medicine at University of Edinburgh and ministry at Cambridge University

Darwin's world fame is based on his theory of evolution. To psychology, his books *The Origin of Species* (1859), *The Descent of Man* (1871), and *The Expression of the Emotions in Man and Animals* (1872) are of particular importance. They spell out the basic assumption underlying psychology, namely that man is on a continuum with the rest of the animal world, and that, since animals can be studied by the scientific method, so can man. Evolutionary biology, founded by Darwin, gave impetus to phylogenetic or comparative psychology. The evolutionary viewpoint concerning the development of both structure and function, including the mental processes, is now the accepted and pervasive point of view in psychology. Ontogenetic psychology, which had its beginnings around 1880, was greatly influenced by Darwin's theory. G. Stanley Hall [418], who pioneered child study in the United States, did so along the lines of the evolutionary thoery, as did Baldwin [259]. The child's developmental history was seen by many as a key to the developmental history of mankind. Darwin himself contributed to the developmental psychology literature by writing a biography of his first-born son.

Biographic data: *DNB* 14:72; *DSB* 3:565; *EP* 2:294; *IESS* 4:7; F. Darwin, *Life and Letters of Charles Darwin*, 1887

MCCOSH, JAMES

Scottish-American philosopher
Rating: 13
Born: Southern Ayrshire, Scotland, April 1, 1811
Died: Princeton, New Jersey, November 16, 1894
Education: Studied theology at University of Edinburgh, licensed for ministry in 1834
Positions, honors: 1852–1868, Queen's College, Belfast, professor of logic and metaphysics; 1868–1888, College of New Jersey (Princeton College), professor of psychology, history, and philosophy; 1870–1892, president of the college; honorary M.A., University of Edinburgh, 1833

McCosh was a representative of the nonexperimental Scottish school of psychology. He represented it in the United States in his capacity as president of Princeton University. He wrote an exposition of the views of fifty philosophers of the Scottish school, *The Scottish Philosophy* (1875), a text on *The Emotions* (1880), in which he adumbrated Jame's [184] theory of emotions, and the last mental philosophy text to be published in America, *Psychology, the Cognitive Powers* (1833).

Biographic data: *EP* 5:225; *NCAB* 5:468

PORTER, NOAH   ⌈129⌉

American philosopher
Rating: 11
Born: Farmington, Connecticut, December 14, 1811
Died: New Haven, Connecticut, March 4, 1892
Highest degree: Graduated from Yale University in 1831
Positions, honors: 1847–1892, Yale University, professor of moral philosophy and metaphysics; 1871–1886, president; four honorary degrees

Porter and James McCosh [128] were the two best known representatives of the Scottish school of psychology in the United States. They were also the last. Porter wrote on *The Human Intellect* (1868) and a psychology text, *Elements of Intellectual Science* (1871).

Biographic data: *EP* 6:412; *NCAB* 1:171

SEGUIN, EDOUARD

French-American psychiatrist
Rating: **18**
Born: Clamecy, Nièvre, France, January 20, 1812
Died: Mt. Vernon, New York, October 28, 1880
Education: No university education; honorary M.D., University of the City of New York, 1861
Positions: 1846, head, Institution for the Training of the Feeble-Minded, Paris; 1850, School for Defectives, Randall's Island, New York

Séguin was a pioneer in the mental retardation area. At the time when Itard [98] was trying to improve the behavior of the wild boy of Aveyron, Séguin was his assistant. When Itard gave up, Séguin continued his efforts realizing that they were not a waste of time since they contributed to a better adjustment of the boy. Later, Séguin extended his work to retarded children in general, and was placed in charge of the first training school for the feeble-minded in the world. Séguin based his training and educational method on physiological considerations, especially stressing the development of the sense organs. In his main work, *Traitement moral, hygiène et éducation des idiots* (1846), Séquin states the main points of the training of the feeble-minded. Although such individuals cannot be brought to a level of normal intelligence, their existing capacities may be developed through the use of the "physiological method," or the stimulation of their senses and neuromuscular systems by the use of bright colors, repeated sounds, and muscular exercises requiring balance. Séguin came to the United States about 1850, was one of the organizers of the School for Defectives at Randall's Island, New York, and for two decades worked on the improvement of training methods for mentally retarded children and for the establishment of special schools for them.

Biographic data: *Enciclopedia universal ilustrada,* vol. 54; *New York Times*, 1880, Oct. 29, 2:3

BERNARD, CLAUDE

French physiologist
Rating: **25**
Born: Saint-Julien, Rhône, July 12, 1813

Died: Paris, February 10, 1878
Highest degree: M.D., Collège de France, 1843, D.Sc., 1853
Positions: 1841, Collège de France; 1854, Sorbonne, experimental physiology; 1855, Collège de France, experimental medicine; 1868, Museum of Natural History, Paris, general physiology; numerous honors

[128]

Bernard was the most famous of the four most prominent physiologists of the first half of the 19th century—Bell [96], Bernard, Johannes Müller [121], and Magendie [105]—but his contributions to psychology were the least significant. Bernard was a great experimental physiologist, founder of experimental medicine, and helped to introduce experimentation in French psychology (*Introduction à la étude de la médecine expérimentelle*, 1865). He is known for his work on the vascular system (he demonstrated the mechanisms of vasodilation and vasoconstriction) and digestion (he demonstrated that thirst is satisfied only if water is directed into the stomach, not when it bypasses it). He also studied the effects of curare, carbon monoxide, and other poisons on the nervous system. His discovery of and work on internal secretions paved the way to the discovery of hormones. Bernard formulated a fundamental concept in physiology, that of a *milieu intérieur* or internal environment (consisting of the humors, the blood, and the lymph), which remains stable despite changes within and without the organisms. When this environment or balance is disturbed the organism immediately sets to work to restore it. This concept anticipated Cannon's concept of homeostasis. The latter, in the form of the principle of drive reduction played an important role in psychological learning theories.

Biographic data: DSB 2:24; EP 1:304; Michel Foster, *Life of Bernard*, 1899; J. M. D. Olmsted, *Claude Bernard*, 1938

CARPENTER, WILLIAM BENJAMIN

[132]

English physiologist
Rating: 14
Born: Exeter, Devon, October 29, 1813
Died: London, November 19, 1885
Highest degree: M.D., University of Edinburgh, 1839

Positions, honors: 1844, Royal Institute, London, professor of physiology; University College, London, professor of forensic medicine; 1856–1879, registrar, University of London; LL.D., University of Edinburgh, 1871

Of Carpenter's numerous publications, his *Principles of Mental Physiology* (1874) is the most important to psychology. In this work, Carpenter coined the phrase "unconscious cerebration," which he defined in the terms "thought and feeling could be regarded as an expression of brain-change," the latter being sensations created by the brain itself and no less real than the external sensations that it interprets. The concept led to a fruitful controversy with Thomas Laycock who, while holding a view of the reflex function of the brain similar to that of Carpenter, asserted that the stimulus for the reflexes arose in the brain itself; Carpenter maintained that a physiological stimulus external to the brain was responsible.

Biographic data: DNB 9:166; DSB 3:87

[133]

BROWN–SEQUARD, CHARLES–EDOUARD

French physiologist
Rating: 14
Born: Port-Louis, Mauritius, April 8, 1817
Died: Sceaux, near Paris, April 2, 1894
Highest degree: M.D., University of Paris, 1846
Positions: 1859–1863, head of a hospital in London; 1864–1867, Harvard University, lecturer in physiology; for some years did research, lectured, and practiced medicine in France, United States, England, and other countries; 1878, Collège de France professor of physiology

Brown-Séquard's reputation as neurophysiologist started with his M.D. thesis on the spinal cord. His major contribution to physiology was the demonstration of the crossing over of sensory fibers in the spinal cord and the study of the consequences of experimental lesions in the nervous system, especially the spinal cord. The *Brown-Séquard syndrome* is a set of symptoms resulting from lateral hemisection of the spinal cord, such as the paralysis of one side of the body and contralateral anesthesia.

Brown-Séquard also did research on the sympathetic nervous system, epilepsy, paralysis, and the brain in general. He founded and edited the *Journal de physiologie de l'homme et des animaux.*

Biographic data: DSB 2:524; J. M. D. Olmsted, *Charles-Edouard Brown-Séquard, a 19th Century Neurologist and Endocrinologist,* 1946

LEWES, GEORGE HENRY

[134]

English philosopher
Rating: **11**
Born: London, April 18, 1817
Died: London, November 28, 1878

Lewes's education was spotty, but he was gifted and engaged in a number of different activities. He is known mainly for his efforts as a writer and critic. He stated more fully (in *Problems of Life and Mind: The Study of Psychology*, 5 volumes, 1873-1879) than Darwin [127] or Spencer [142] had done, the significance of the evolutionary theory for psychology, namely that man, being part of nature, can be studied, like any other animal by the scientific method. He added that, since man was also a social being, he must be studied also in his interaction with his social environment, as all mental activity is the result of the interaction of an organism with its physical and social environment. While describing human nature in associationistic and empiricist terms, Lewes avoided materialism, subscribing to the double aspect theory of body-mind relationship. He was a determinist who included free will in his world picture by stating that, while unpredictable events do occur, they occur so subject to the existing laws of nature. Only choices that are compatible with physical laws can be made. To illustrate his position he used the analogy of the sailor who is free to move about the ship, but cannot change the course of the ship.

Lewes also dabbled in physiology where he achieved minor standing by investigating the sensations of innervation (1878) and argued against the Bell-Magendie law, substituting for it the notion of the recurrent impulse to account for sensory and motor acts. In this area he wrote *Physiology of Common Life*, 2 volumes (1859–1860), and *Studies in Animal Life* (1862).

Biographic data: DNB 33:164; EP 4:451

LOTZE, RUDOLF HERMANN

German philosopher
Rating: 25
Born: Bautzen, Saxony, May 21, 1817
Died: Berlin, July 1, 1881
Highest degree: M.D., University of Leipzig, 1838
Positions: 1839, University of Leipzig, appointments in medicine and in philosophy; 1844, University of Göttingen

Lotze's contributions to psychology were his book, *Medizinische Psychologie oder Physiologie der Seele* (1852) and his theory of the local signs. His book was the first text of physiological psychology. While it was heavily metaphysical, it was his empiricism that became part of the "new" psychology that arrived with Wundt [161]. Of the topics included in the book, Lotze's theory of space perception was his most important and influential contribution. Although Lotze endowed the mind with the capacity to perceive space, the main point of the theory was that the mind produces spatial experience from nonspatial information, namely intensity. A pattern of pressure intensities creates a local sign for touch. Eye movements create patterns of experienced intensity of these movements, which are the visual local signs. Local signs identify locations in two-dimensional space. These are joined into a perception of solid space through experience, as movements of the body piece together these local signs. When no actual movement occurs, there may be a tendency set up for movement, which takes the place of actual movement. The spatial relating of local signs obtained through experience is accomplished by the mind's ability to interpret movement in terms of space, and thus to reestablish space from what was originally only a pattern of intensities. Lotze also held that, with repetition, local signs become unconscious, and visual space perception at least may be entirely nonexperiential, a notion akin to that of unconscious inference advanced by Helmholtz [143]. In addition to *Medizinische Psychologie*, Lotze also wrote *Grundzüge der Psychologie* (1881) and, in general, was an enthusiastic supporter of psychology. Carl Stumpf [202] and George Elias Müller [208] were his students.

Biographic data: DSB 8:513; *EP* 5:87; *IESS* 9:476; E. Rhenisch, *Revue philosophique*, 1881, 12, 321–336; R. Falckenberg, *Hermann Lotze,* 1901; M. Wentscher, *Hermann Lotze,* 1913

MARX, KARL HEINRICH

German philosopher
Rating: **16**
Born: Trier, Rhineland-Palatinate, May 5, 1818
Died: London, England, March 14, 1883
Highest degree: Ph.D. in philosophy and history, University of
  Jena, 1841

Marx, the philosopher of history, greatest socialist thinker, and
the ideological father of communism, influenced thinking in all of
the behavioral sciences, including psychology. The fundamental
assumptions of Marx's economic interpretation of history (*Misère
de la philosophie,* 1847, [English translation, *Poverty of Philosophy,* 1935] ; *Manifest der Kommunistischen Partei,* 1848 [English
translation, *The Communist Manifesto,* 1888]) earn him a place
in the history of psychology. One of his basic assumptions was
that economic development is the primary determining factor of
social development, and that it is social development that
produces the development of ideas, political, philosophical,
artistic, legal, and religious. Basically, consciousness is the
product of the economic conditions of life: as they change, so
does man's thinking. While ideas may also influence social and
economic development, economic changes are primary. Although
materialistic or selfish interests are important motivators, idealistic motives, such as altruism or patriotism, also play their part.
Nevertheless, they themselves are a product of the material
conditions of existence. The materialism of Marx and his
coworker Friedrich Engels was later elaborated by Lenin [318].
Lenin's doctrine of reflection became the fundamental principle
of Soviet psychology.

Biographic data: *EP* 5:171; *IESS* 10:34; F. Mehring, *Karl Marx*,
  1918 (English translation, 1935); O. Rühle, *Karl Marx, His Life
  and Work*, 1928 (English translation, 1929)

DONDERS, FRANCISCUS CORNELIUS

Dutch ophthalmologist
Rating: **19**
Born: Tilburg, May 27, 1818
Died: Utrecht, March 24, 1889
Highest degree: M.D., University of Utrecht, 1842

Positions: 1842, military school, Utrecht; 1852, University of Utrecht

Donders's initial work of interest to psychology was in the areas of eye movements, accomodation, and vowel sounds. In 1846, he stated the principle that for any direction of regard the eye always assumes the same position. This was later (1866) named *Donders's law* by Helmholtz [143]. In 1854, Donders was the cofounder, with A. von Gräfe, of *Archiv Für Ophthalmologie*, and in 1864 he published a book dealing with anomalies of refraction and accommodation. In an 1857 paper, Donders listed the resonance values of the mouth cavity for the vowels that he had determined. Not long before his death (1881), Donders proposed a color vision theory.

In the 1860s, Donders became interested in the measurement of reaction time. He published his first report on it in 1865. While he had been working on it before that date, Donders's reaction time work is usually dated from 1868 when his original Dutch article was published in German. After some work on simple reaction time it occured to Donders that if the simple task of giving a prescribed response to a single stimulus were complicated by adding, for instance, discrimination, and the reaction time were prolonged, this prolongation would be the measure of additional mental process required to perform the more complicated task. The subtraction of simple reaction time from the total reaction time in a compound reaction task gave Donders the duration of the mental process required to perform the task. The last three decades of the 19th century are sometimes called the age of *mental chronometry*. Initiated by Donders, mental chronometry was expanded by Wundt [161]. Although complicating the reaction time task does increase the time needed for its execution, the increase is not constant, and the subtraction method was later abandoned. Psychologists kept studying and using reaction time to an ever-increasing extent, however, and today reaction time is a standard response measure in the study of a great variety of psychological phenomena.

Biographic data: DSB 4:162; E. Clarke, *A Brief Review of the Work of Donders*, 1914

[138]

BAIN, ALEXANDER

Scottish psychologist
Rating: 26
Born: Aberdeen, June 11, 1818

Died: Aberdeen, September 18, 1903
Highest degree: B.A. in philosophy, Marischal College, 1840
Positions: 1840–1860, freelance in London and Scotland; 1860, University of Aberdeen; 1880–1887, Lord Rector, University of Aberdeen

Since Bain's life covered most of the 19th century, he belonged to both the outgoing school of British associationism and the new German scientific psychology. While much of the two of his most important texts written in the 1850s were in the Scottish tradition of moral philosophy, they, for the first time, established a solid connection between psychology and actual physiological fact. Bain considered Darwin [127] important and followed him in his own work on emotional expression in man and animals, but he did not accept the evolutionary theory entirely. Concerning association, Bain embraced a modified form of John Stuart Mill's [125] "mental chemistry" and took the principle of contiguity to be the primary, and similarity, a second principle. To the Aristotelean five senses he added the organic sense; there is an emphasis on the importance of movement, including reflexive movement. In regard to the body–mind problem, Bain was a psychophysical parallelist.

Bain wrote two texts that remained standard for the next fifty years because of their thoroughness of coverage. *The Senses and the Intellect* (1855) and *The Emotions and the Will* (1959) were his major work, two large, systematic psychological texts that saw repeated editions. Bain also wrote *On the Study of Character* (1861), *Manual of Mental and Moral Science* (1869), *Mind and Body* (1872), and, in 1876, founded the first philosophical psychology journal, *Mind*, which is still being published.

Biographic data: *DNB*, 2nd Suppl., vol. 1; *DSB* I:403; *EP* 1:243; *IESS* 1:503

VIERORDT, KARL VON [139]

German physiologist
Rating: 17
Born: Lahr, Württemberg, July 1, 1818
Died: Tübingen, Württemberg, November 22, 1884
Highest degree: M.D., University of Heidelberg, 1841
Positions: 1849–1884, University of Tübingen

In the area of psychophysics, Vierordt was first (1852) to use the method of right and wrong cases (the method of constant stimuli) to establish sensory thresholds. Fechner [120] was to develop this method later. In 1868, Vierordt published a volume on the psychology of time (*Der Zeitsinn*). In it, Vierordt introduced, among other things, the notion of the indifference point in time estimation (.75 seconds), where there is no constant error. Vierordt conducted many additional researches on vision, hearing, and somesthesis. In 1869, he measured the brightness of the solar spectrum. In the same and in the following year, he measured the two-point threshold, formulating this law, namely that the two-point threshold varies inversely with the mobility of the bodily part where it is measured (*Veirordt's law*).

Biographic data: *Enciclopedia universal ilustrada*, vol. 68

⌈140⌉

DU BOIS-REYMOND, EMIL

German physiologist
Rating: 23
Born: Berlin, November 7, 1818
Died: Berlin, December 26, 1896
Highest degree:, Ph.D. in physiology, University of Berlin, 1843
Positions: University of Berlin

Du Bois-Reymond played a prominent role in the development of neurophysiology in the 19th century. He became interested in the question of animal electricity and studied it using the newly invented galvanometer. His first paper on animal electricity appeared in 1843, followed by *Untersuchungen über thierische Elektricität* in two volumes (1848, 1849). This book marks the beginning of modern electrophysiology. Du Bois-Reymond's theory of the polarization of animal tissue eventually turned out to be wrong, but his work stimulated further research on the conduction of nerve impulses. He showed that explanations of nerve conduction in terms of animal spirits of activity of the soul were unnecessary since it was demonstrably a material phenomenon. He thus fulfilled the pledge that he and three other students of Johannes Müller [121] had made, namely to fight vitalism and to establish and compel acceptance of the truth that no forces other than the physical and chemical ones are active within the organism. To Helmholtz [143], Du Bois-Reymond's work suggested that the velocity of the nerve impulse was finite and measurable. When he succeeded in measuring it, he sent his paper to Du Bois-Reymond to read before the Physikalische Gesellschaft in Berlin. Several psychologists who later became famous were Du Bois-Reymond's students: Wundt [161], Sully [188], Hall [418], Bekhterev [226], and Sechenov [156], among others.

Biographic data: *DSB* 4:200; *EP* 2:421; H. Boruttan, *Emil Du Bois-Reymond,* 1922

BRUCKE, ERNST WILHELM VON [141]

German-Austrian physiologist
Rating: 20
Born: Berlin, Germany, June 6, 1819
Died: Vienna, Austria, January 7, 1892
Highest degree: M.D., University of Berlin, 1842
Positions: 1848, University of Königsberg; 1849–1891, University of Vienna

Brücke was one of Sigmund Freud's [224] teachers. In Brücke's Physiological Institute Freud acquired the view that man is an interacting energy system. Brücke, in turn, had adopted the idea as a student in his twenties when he, Ludwig, Du Bois-Reymond [140], and Helmholtz [143] had formed a pact to fight vitalism. Du Bois-Reymond and Brücke pledged between them the additional oath that they would prove and make it an accepted truth that "no other forces than common physical-chemical ones are active within the organism." This strict physicalist physiology Brücke passed on to his students, including Freud. Brücke also did work in psychophysics. Of enduring value was his thorough study (1878) of change in hue as a function of change in light intensity. Since Bezold had briefly described the phenomenon earlier (1873), it was named the *Bezold-Brücke phenomenon.* It refers to the shift toward either yellow or blue of spectral colors when their intensity is increased.

Biographic data: *DSB* 2:530

SPENCER, HERBERT

English philosopher
Rating: 27
Born: Derby, Derbyshire, April 27, 1820
Died: Brighton, Sussex, December 8, 1903
Education: Self-educated

Spencer at first accepted the Lamarckian view of evolution, then developed his own, just prior to the appearance of Darwin's [127] *Origin of Species*. He espoused Darwin's theory but, unlike Darwin, made the broadest possible generalization of it. Spencer's *Synthetic Philosophy* was an attempt to apply the idea of evolution to all human knowledge. The work appeared in ten volumes, between 1862 and 1893. The two volumes of *The Principles of Psychology* were revised several times.

According to Spencer, the course of evolution follows a movement from homogeneity to heterogeneity. As organic life increases in complexity, existence becomes increasedly marked by better adjustment of organisms to external conditions. With increasing complexity and specialization there arises consciousness and, later, increasing differentiation and complexity of consciousness. The constituents of consciousness are "feelings," or the most elementary units of consciousness, and relations between feelings. Emotions and sensations are primary feelings, memories and ideas of emotions and sensations are "ideal" feelings. They are fainter than the primary feelings; besides, while consciousness of sensory impressions is a continuous stream, consciousness of memories is easily disrupted. The feelings of relation are those of coexistence, sequence, and difference. While the associationists thought of these as the result of association, Spencer made them exist prior to the formation of associations. They played a role similar to that assigned them by the Würzburg school, and simplified the working out of associations that created a problem to the Mills [93, 125] and Bain [138]. Similarity, vividness, and repetition were the conditions stated by Spencer that furthered the formation of associations.

In Spencer's scheme, psychology as a whole is part of biology because psychology and physiological processes are correlated and behavior is a constant series of adjustments of the organism to the environment. The adjustment theme runs throughout Spencer's discussion. "The survival of the fittest" is a corollary of it and a phrase coined by Spencer. The function of intelligence is the adaptation of the organism to its environment. Intelligence increases in the course of evolution, representing increased flexibility in the use of the feelings of relation. This view of intelligence makes Spencer the forefather of the functionalist school of psychology that was to flourish later in America. Ontogenetically, the growth of intelligence shows itself in increasingly accurate adjustments to the environment and an increasing breadth and complexity of these adjustments. Association in Spencer's thinking becomes part of the evolutionary picture. Often repeated associations become part of the genetic material of the organism and are transmitted to offspring. The process is cumulative, more complex associations evolving from simple ones. Although the postulated transmission was Lamarckian in nature and failed of its validation, Spencer, along with Darwin, by emphasizing the continuity from animal to man, not only in structure but also in psychic functions, was laying the foundation for comparative psychology. As part of his evolutionary psychology, Spencer also anticipated a most important concept in psychology by stating that pleasant associations tend to be repeated and transmitted, while unpleasant ones are abandoned. In a different form, this principle later became known in learning theory as the *law of effect*.

Biographic data: *DNB,* 2nd Suppl., vol. III; *EP* 7:523; *IESS* 15:121; H. Spencer, *An Autobiography*, 1904

HELMHOLTZ, HERMANN LUDWIG FERDINAND VON

[143]

German physicist and physiologist
Rating: 27
Born: Potsdam, Brandenburg, August 31, 1821
Died: Charlottenburg, Brandenburg, September 8, 1894
Highest degree: M. D., Medico-Surgical Friedrich-Wilhelm Institute, Berlin, 1842
Positions: 1847–1854, University of Königsberg; 1855, University of Bonn; 1858–1870, University of Heidelberg; 1871, University of Berlin

Helmholtz was one of the great names in science. His genius encompassed theoretical physics, physiology, optics, and vision, acoustics, and the psychology of the senses. While he considered psychology to be related to philosophy, he made an exception of sensory psychology. Helmholtz's contributions to psychology lie in this area and that of neurophysiology. He was the first to measure the speed of nerve conduction. Although Helmholtz was interested only in the speed of the neural impulse, his measurements meant that mental processes did not occur instantaneously but took finite time. Since Helmholtz had used muscular contractions to measure the rate of nerve conductivity (he invented the *myograph* for this purpose), it also meant that motor acts could be used to measure the duration of mental events. The excellence of presentation and the amount of original work on visual physiology, sensation, and perception in Helmholtz's classic *Handbuch der physiologischen Optik* (1856–1866, reissued together in 1867; English translation, *Treatise on Phyiological Optics*, 1925) was such that much of it is still valid today. In it may be found such contributions as Helmhotz's theory of color vision (later named the *Young-Helmholtz theory*), and a theory of space perception. The basic features of the Young-Helmholtz theory remain undisputed today, the three-component theory having been basic to the development of color photography. With regard to space perception, Helmholtz's empiricist theory asserted that while each of the nerves pertaining to the various sense organs was characterized by a nerve energy specific to that sense, the sensations caused by them were meaningless until meaning was acquired through repeated associations. Perception of space was to Helmholtz the unconscious inference of relations from components whose meaning had been previously acquired. The doctrine of unconscious inference is still of more than just historic interest today.

Helmholtz also presented the first explanation of the additive and the subtractive color mixtures. There is a first recorded recognition of the role of motion parallax in depth perception in Helmholtz, and many other original contributions to the physiology and psychology of vision. In the area of auditory perception Helmholtz clarified the meaning of timbre as the third major dimension of the acoustic stimulus by conducting experiments with tuning forks and resonators (the *Helmholtz resonators*) that he had invented. He used the idea of resonance in his theory of hearing to explain how the basilar membrane, by having hair cells of graduated length through its extent, responds selectively in accordance with the sound wave frequency that stimulates it. Helmholtz's *Die Lehre von den Tonempfindungen als physiologische Grundlage für die Theorie der Musik* (1863), like his *Handbuch*, is another classic in the literature of the experimental psychology of sensation. In general. Helmholtz's research and his strong and successful arguments against the nativist and for the empiricist position (for instance, his demonstration that the geometric axioms are not innate ideas) gave a strong impetus to the emergence of experimental psychology.

Biographic data: *DSB* 6:241; *EP* 3:469; *IESS* 6:345; J. G. McKendrick, *Hermann Ludwig Friedrich von Helmholtz,* 1899; L. Koenigsberger, *Hermann von Helmholtz,* 3 vol., 1902–1903; J. Reiner, *Hermann von Helmholtz,* 1905; G. S. Hall, *Founders of Modern Psychology,* 1912, pp. 247–308

GALTON, SIR FRANCIS

[144]

English scientist
Rating: 27
Born: Birmingham, February 16, 1822
Died: Haslemere, Surrey, January 17, 1911
Highest degree:, B.A., Cambridge University, 1844
Positions, honors: No academic or official positions; knighted 1909

Although primarily a scientist-at-large, Galton's contributions to scientific psychology were such that he may be called one of its founding fathers. Specifically, he founded the study and measurement of individual differences, a field that saw its next major expansion in the hands of J. McK. Cattell [256]. The reading of Darwin's [127] *Origin of Species* led Galton to study anthropology and heredity. In 1869, he published *Hereditary Genius*, a study of the variability of human intellect through the biographies of eminent men. Galton's thesis was that eminence runs in families, that there are specific forms of eminence in the various fields of human endeavor, and that mental traits are inherited in the same way as physical traits are. The problems of heredity and the improvement of the human race were always Galton's first concern. In 1876, he also conducted the first behavioral study of twins in an effort to separate environmental from genetic influences. The juxtaposition of the terms "nature" and "nurture" first occurs in Galton's paper, and the problem of the inheritance of intelligence that still occupies psychology, was set up by Galton's work.

Quétlet [116] had applied the normal law of error of Laplace [75] and Gauss [99] to biological measures. Galton extended Quétlet's work to behavioral measurements and found it applicable. Galton concluded that statistical treatment of psychological measures in general was appropriate. His most important contribution here was the development of the statistical measure of correlation (in 1877) that was later elaborated by his student and biographer Karl Pearson [229]. The principle of the regression toward the mean is a formulation of Galton's. Galton then proceeded to collect a variety of psychological measurements on many individuals and to treat the data statistically. In 1882, he established a laboratory in London where physical measurements, sensory acuity measurements, and reaction time measurements were taken on those who applied, for a fee. It was the first mental test center in the world, and his activities there made Galton the first psychological practitioner. Several pieces of apparatus of Galton's invention were used there, among them the *Galton whistle* that produced tones between 6,500 and 84,000 cycles and the *Galton bar* for distance estimation. In 1901, Galton, Pearson, and W. F. R. Weldon founded the journal, *Biometrika*.

Galton's psychological contributions were published in 1883 in a volume titled *Inquiries into Human Faculty and Its Development*. Prominent among them, in addition to those already mentioned, are his study of imagery, the description of specific imagery types, and the discovery of synesthesia; work on reaction time in word association, which also demonstrated, for the first time, the importance of the effect of childhood experiences upon adult thinking; and the development of specifically mental tests. The methodology used by Galton included introspection, his own and that of others, and experimentation and measurement, but not of the elaborate type employed by Continental psychologists. Instead, he used tests, including mental tests. He was the first to use extensively the questionnaire method for gathering data in psychology. In sum, Galton's work in psychology spelled out the emergence of a fundamental assumption in psychological science, namely that all individuals differ among themselves, that they differ consistently, and that therefore these differences can be measured.

Biographic data: *DNB* 1901–1911; *DSB* 5:265; *IESS* 6:48; F. Galton, *Memories of My Life*, 1908; K. Pearson, *The Life, Letters, and Labors of Francis Galton*, vol. 1 (1914), vol. 2 (1924), vol. 3 (1930)

[145]   **LIEBEAULT, AMBROISE AUGUST**

French hypnotist
Rating: 21

Born: Farrières, Meurthe-Moselle, 1832
Died: Nancy, 1904
Highest degree: M.D.

At first a country doctor, Liébeault began to use hypnotism (in 1860) on those of his patients who agreed to it. In 1864, Liébeault moved to Nancy. He was successful in using hypnotic treatment, especially with a patient whom Hyppolite Bernhiem [181], a much better known physician, had failed to cure with orthodox treatment. This converted Berheim to hypnosis, and he and Liébeault together founded a clinic at Nancy where both practiced hypnotic treatment. In 1866, Liébeault published his first book on hypnosis, *Du sommeil et des états analogues, considérés surtout au point de vue de l'action de la morale sur le physique*. Liébeault's and Bernheim's explanation of the hypnotic state disagreed with that of the famous Charcot [152] at the La Salpêtrière hospital in Paris, and a rivalry between the two schools ensued, with the view of the Nancy school prevailing in the light of accumulating evidence.

Biographic data: No readily available biographies

WALLACE, ALFRED RUSSEL [146]

English biologist
Rating: 15
Born: Usk, Monmouthshire, January 8, 1823
Died: Broadstone, Dorsetshire, November 7, 1913
Education: Hertford Grammar School and self-education; honorary LL.D., University of Dublin, D.C.L., Oxford University

Wallace acquired fame for developing the evolutionary theory simultaneously with, but independently of, Darwin [127]. Wallace was stimulated by his reading of the *Essay on the Principle of Population* by Malthus [84]. He sent a manuscript of a paper on the topic to Darwin, who found that it contained ideas almost identical to his own. Darwin had Wallace's and his own ideas presented in a joint paper, read in 1858. A year later Darwin's *Origin of Species* appeared. Wallace later criticized Darwin's theory of sexual selection, and became, with Weissman, a leader in the neo-Darwinian movement.

Biographic data: *DNB* 1912–1921; *EP* 8:276; A. R. Wallace, *My Life*, 1905

STEINTHAL, HEYMANN

German philosopher and linguist
Rating: 12
Born: Gröbzig, Anhalt, May 16, 1823
Died: Berlin, March 14, 1899
Highest degree: Ph.D. in philosophy, University of Berlin, 1850
Positions: 1850, University of Berlin; 1859–1890, editor, *Zeitschrift für Völkerpsychologie und Sprachwissenschaft*

With his brother-in-law, Moritz Lazarus [150], Steinthal laid the foundation of *ethnopsychology*. The event that is often considered to have launched ethnopsychology was the founding, in 1859, of the journal *Zeitschrift für Völkerpsychologie und Sprachwissenschaft* by Steinthal and Lazarus. Materials on folklore, religion, myths, customs, and languages of different ethnic and national groups were presented there, the basic assumption being that such groups differ among themselves psychologically and hence perceive and react to reality in distinctive ways. Both Steinthal and Lazarus were linguists and disciples of Herbart [101]. Steinthal produced many publications on the philosophy of language, mythology, ethics, logic, comparative religion, and psychology. Quite often his ideas met opposition, especially the idea of a "group mind," by which he meant the integration of individual minds that, under given conditions, might function in a unitary fashion. Relevant to psychology is his work, *Grammatik, Logik und Psychologie* (1855).

Biographic data: *Encyclopedia of the Social Sciences* 14:384

FABRE, JEAN HENRI

French biologist
Rating: 20
Born: Saint-Léons, Aveyron, December 21, 1823
Died: Sérignac, Provence, October 11, 1915

While Fabre taught school most of his life (he did not have a university education), his one real interest had always been insects. He began to devote all of his time to insects in 1879, the year of his retirement, and continued collecting insects and describing their behavior for the next twenty-five years. He

published his observations in the ten-volume *Souvenirs entomolo-
giques* (1878–1907). Parts of it were translated into English under
the titles of *The Life and Love of the Insect* (1911), *Social Life in
the Insect World* (1912), *The Life of the Fly* (1913) and others.
Fabre thus contributed to the development of animal psychology
during its preexperimental period.

Biographic data: *DSB* 4:503

BROCA, PAUL

French surgeon and anthropologist
Rating: 24
Born: Sainte-Foy-la-Grande, Gironde, June 28, 1824
Died: Paris, July 9, 1880
Highest degree: M.D., University of Paris, 1849

On the basis of his theory of the cerebral localization of
functions, Broca predicted that a certain patient with a disorder
in speech articulation that had come to his attention would have
a lesion in the third left frontal convolution of the brain. When
the patient died, a postmortem confirmed Broca's prediction, and
Broca took the brain to the *Société de Anthropologie* for a
demonstration. (He published a paper on the case in 1861.) The
demonstration impressed scientists greatly, made a case for the
exact localization of brain functions, and made Broca himself
famous. The area of the brain involved was later named in his
honor. Broca continued to argue that the convolutions of the
cerebral cortex were the guides for localizing brain functions.

Broca made it a general practice to trephine the skull for brain
tumor operations on the basis of predictions made from
symptoms and his theory of brain functions. He is considered to
be the founder of modern brain surgery in France. Broca is even
better known for his work in physical anthrolopology, which
occupied him during the latter part of his life.

Biographic data: *DSB* 2:477; *IESS* 2:154

German philosopher
Rating: 13
Born: Filehne, Posen, September 15, 1824
Died: Merano, Italy, April 13, 1903
Education: Studied philosophy at the Braunschweiger Institut, 1844–1846; later philology, law, and history
Positions: 1860–1866, University of Bern; 1867–1873, Kriegs-akademie, Berlin; 1873–1897, University of Berlin

Lazarus was a Herbartian, but with the distinction of being also a social psychologist. He was a pioneer in ethnopsychology in the mid-19th century. He and Steinthal [147] used data from comparative linguistics and mythological research and applied to them ideas developed by Wilhelm von Humboldt [187], Herder [69], Hegel [89], and Herbart [101], especially the latter. Both Lazarus and Steinthal expected ethnopsychology to use exact scientific methods to study social psychological phenomena on the assumption that the mental phenomena to be studied existed only in their objective manifestations, such as religious practices and language. Lazarus accepted Kant's [60] idea that the categorical imperative exists universally but that no universal concrete ethical rules exist. The feelings of a person or a group of persons become behavior; these behaviors are imitated by others, institutionalized, and, in turn, determine the feelings of other individuals. The realized similarity in attitudes leads to a feeling of similarity and solidarity in general, hence to the formation of political entities, such as nations. Lazarus's ideas concerning the reality, autonomy, and influence of social groups influenced such thinkers as Durkheim [241]. In 1859, Lazarus and Steinthal founded the first journal of social psychology, the *Zeitschift für Völkerpsychologie, und Sprachwissenschaft*. In 1890 it was continued as the *Zeitschift des Vereins fur Volkskunde*. In 1862, the University of Bern created the first chair in ethnopsychology, and Lazarus was its first occupant. He wrote about a dozen books on ethnopsychological topics.

Biographic data: M. Lazarus, *Aus Meiner Jugend*, 1913; A. Leicht, *Lazarus, der Begrunder der Völkerpsychologie*, 1904; N. R. Lazarus and A. Leicht, *Lebenserinnerungen von Moritz Lazarus*, 1906; N. R. Lazarus, *Ein deutscher Professor in der Schweitz*, 1910

English biologist, lecturer, educator, and essayist
Rating: 18
Born: Ealing, Middlesex, May 4, 1825
Died: Eastbourne, Sussex, June 29, 1895
Highest degree: M.D., Charing Cross Hospital, 1845
Positions, honors: 1846–1854, various medical appointments with the Royal Navy; 1854–1892, teaching natural sciences, Royal School of Mines, London; from 1870 onward, numerous appointments on government commissions, boards; 1872–1874, Rector, University of Aberdeen; seven honorary degrees

To psychology, Huxley's significance lies in his advocacy and defense of Darwin's evolutionary theory. Immediately recognizing its value when it was published in 1859, he very ably defended it against the attack by Bishop Wilberforce at a famous meeting of the British Association for the Advancement of Science in Oxford a year later. The energetic defense of Darwin [127] earned him the nickname "Darwin's bulldog." Through his writings and lectures Huxley continued to defend science, the evolutionary theory, and to fight obscuritanism. While he was an agnostic, he asserted the certainty of determinism, albeit as an unprovable assumption necessary for science. The term *agnosticism* was coined by Huxley. To him it meant that the ultimate reality is unknowable and that speculation about it is useless. It also meant that one should not make statements and assert them to be true without being able to produce empirical evidence for them. His agnosticism hence rejected both materialistic and idealistic monism as unprovable, although Huxley accepted the use of materialistic language for scientific purposes. Huxley regarded animal and human bodies as mechanical systems. States of consciousness were real enough to him, but only as effects of bodily processes. Although Huxley admitted that this was a definite epiphenomenalistic view of the body-mind relationship, he asserted that he actually knew nothing and could not hope to know anything.

Biographic data: *DNB*, 1st Suppl., vol. III; *DSB* 6:589; *EP* 4:101; L. Huxley (ed.), *Life and Letters of T. H. Huxley*, 1900

CHARCOT, JEAN-MARTIN

French neurologist
Rating: 27
Born: Paris, November 29, 1825
Died: Paris, August 16, 1893
Highest degree: M.D., University of Paris, 1853
Positions: 1856, physician at Central Hospital bureau; 1860, University of Paris, professor of pathological anatomy; 1862, Salpêtrière, Paris, senior physician; president (honorary), First International Congress of Psychology, 1889

Charcot is often called the father of neurology because of his skill in relating patients' symtoms to the anatomy of the nervous system (*Leçons sur les maladies du système nerveux,* 5 volumes, 1872–1893). He was famous both as a physician and as a teacher. The neurological clinic that he established at La Salpêtrière hospital in Paris was the best in the 19th century. Janet [249] was his pupil. Freud [224] worked under Charcot for a year and would later refer to him as "my master." Freud learned hypnosis from Charcot and later used it in his own practice. It was Charcot who had planted in him the idea that sexual problems could underlie behavioral disorders.

When the phenomenon of hypnotism was declared to be genuine, Charcot began an intensive study of it. His demonstrations of hypnosis began in 1878. On observing that both in hysteria and in hypnosis a great variety of bodily symptoms were simulated, that the symptoms of hysteric patients could be modified by hypnosis, and that it was mostly hysteric patients who could be deeply hypnotized, Charcot concluded that hypnotic phenomena were caused by hysteria and that therefore only hysterics could be hypnotized. Charcot presented his view to the French Academy of Sciences in 1882, and it was completely accepted. A rivalry developed between Charcot and the Nancy school of hypnotism, represented by Liébeault [145] and Bernheim [181], who thought that there was no essential difference between hypnotism and sleep and considered the former a type of suggestibility and therefore a normal rather than a pathological phenomenon. Although later research supported the Nancy school, it was the contribution of Charcot that the neuroses were identified as a separate clinical entity that could be dealt with outside the walls of a mental hospital.

Biographic data: *DSB* 3:205; *IESS* 2:384; J.-L. Langlois, Charcot: clinician and teacher. *Bulletin of the Isaac Ray*

Medical Library, 1954, **2**, 1–14; J. C. Tomlinson and W. Haymaker, Jean-Martin Charcot. *AMA Archives of Neurology and Psychiatry*, 1957, **77**, 44–48

AUBERT, HERMANN [153]

German physiologist
Rating: 20
Born: Frankfurt-am-Main, November, 1826
Died: Rostock, Mecklenburg, February 12, 1892
Highest degree: M.D., University of Berlin, 1850
Positions: 1852, University of Breslau; 1862, University of Rostock; one of first editors of *Zeitschrift für Psychologie*

Aubert was a pioneer, along with Helmholtz, [143], in the area of physiological optics *(Physiologie der Netzhaut,* 1865; *Grundzüge der physiologischen Optik,* 1876). In the 1850s, he studied visual space perception. *Aubert's phenomenon* (a lighted vertical line appears to move in a dark room when the observer inclines his head, a starting point for the Werner-Wapner sensory-tonic field theory) and the *Aubert-Förster phenomenon* (with the visual angle constant, small and near objects occupy more retinal area than do large and distant objects) were named after him. In the same decade he published research on cutaneous space perception, and in the 1860s, one on psychophysics. First complete understanding of dark and light adaptation is found in Aubert (1865). He introduced both the term and the concept of adaptation and plotted the first curves of dark-adaptation. The first thorough experimental measurement of the retinal color zones was done by Aubert in 1865. His last contribution was to the understanding of bodily orientation (1888).

Biographic data: Enciclopedia universal ilustrada, vol. 6

TAINE, HIPPOLYTE ADOLPHE [154]

French philosopher, critic, and historian
Rating: 21
Born: Vouziers, Ardennes, April 21, 1828
Died: Paris, March 5, 1893

Highest degree: Doctor of letters, University of Paris, 1853
Positions: 1864–1884, professor of aesthetics, Ecole des Beaux-Arts, Paris

Taine was a convinced positivist. He believed that the scientific method should be applied not only in the sciences but also in sociology, psychology, the study of literature and art, philosophy, history, and even religion. He showed an interest in psychology very early, and his literary work is based on the theory of psychological determinism, stated in a two-volume work on psychology, *De l'intelligence* (1870). In it he rejects the concept of innate ideas and embraces empiricism. In his literary criticism Taine stressed the examination of literary documents so as to achieve an understanding of the psychology of the author, as well as the use of the author's biographic data and personality characteristics. This information, coupled with the author's ethnic, social, and political background should produce an insight into the author's or artist's work. Taine's *De l'intelligence* helped prepare a favorable climate for the development of scientific psychology in the second half of the 19th century. An additional, more limited and specific contribution of Taine's was a paper on the acquisition of language in a child, published in 1876. After the papers of Pestalozzi [72] and Tiedemann [74], published a century earlier, Taine's was the third paper in developmental psychology published in a scientific journal.

Biographic data: EP 8:76; *Life and Letters of Hippolyte Taine*, 3 vols., 1902–1908

[155]

PFLUGER, EDUARD FRIEDRICH WILHELM

German physiologist
Rating: 18
Born: Hanau, Hesse, June 7, 1829
Died: Bonn, March 16, 1910
Highest degree: M.D., University of Berlin, 1853
Positions: 1858, University of Berlin; 1859–1909 University of Bonn

Pflüger studied the effects of electrical stimulation on motor nerves, and was the first to formulate the laws governing such effects. He also studied the functions of the spinal cord and, in this connection, became involved in a controversy with Lotze [135] and Marshall Hall [110] concerning the question of whether spinal reflexes were conscious or not. Pflüger held that they were conscious because they were purposeful and, being purposeful, they must be conscious (*Die sensorischen Funktionen des Rückenmarks der Wirbelthiere nebst einer neuen Lehre über die Leitungsgesetze der Reflexionen,* 1853). In 1868, Pflüger established *Pflügers Archiv für die gesamte Physiologie des Menschen und der Thiere,* known simply as *Pflügers Archiv* and for many years an important forum for the works of both physiologists and psychologists who contributed significantly to the development of physiological psychology.

Biographic data: Enciclopedia universal ilustrada, vol. 44

SECHENOV, IVAN MIKHAILOVICH [156]

Russian physiologist
Rating: 26
Born: Teplyĭ Stan, Simbirsk, Russia, August 1, 1829
Died: Moscow, November 2, 1905
Highest degree: M.D., Military-Medical Academy, St. Petersburg, 1860
Positions: 1860, Military-Medical Academy, St. Petersburg; 1870, University of Odessa; 1876, University of St. Petersburg; 1888–1901, University of Moscow

After graduating as a physician in 1856 and 1860, Sechenov studied at Berlin and Heidelberg, worked on the inhibition of reflexes by the cortex, and, as a result of this work, was soon attempting to show that all mental processes have a physiological basis, namely that they are reflex activity, either innate or learned. Three years after receiving his doctorate he wrote his most important work, *Refleksy golovnogo mozga* (1863, English translation, *Reflexes of the Brain*). He implied that learned reflexes arise through association, contiguity playing the most important role. Sechenov considered thinking to be an inhibited reflex, or a reflex in which the motor response portion was missing. In general, he argued that mental life, being a function of the nervous system, is a physiological problem, that any mental activity expresses itself in some form of bodily activity, and that psychological problems ought to be studied by physiologists by studying the reflexes (*Who Must Investigate the Problems of*

Psychology and How, 1873). Sechenov developed an objective psychology that was materialistic, reflexological, associationistic, and stressed to the extreme the role of the environment in behavioral development.

Sechenov's views were thus very similar to those of Pavlov [206], except that Pavlov demonstrated experimentally the truth of Sechenov's theoretical contentions. In the 1860s, though, Sechenov was ahead of everybody in physiological thinking in his assignment to the reflexes of a major role in cognitive processes. To the czarist autocratic regime he was too much of a materialist and it was attempted to suppress his book. His views were, however, accepted by the educated class. Sechenov was the major figure in the rise of Russian physiology. He introduced, for instance, bioelectric research in Russian physiology and founded a physiological laboratory at St. Petersburg. His views played an important role in the development of Pavlov's thinking, although Pavlov did not study under Sechenov and did not observe conditioning in dogs until the 1890s. Sechenov's influence outside of Russia during his lifetime was small. In the United States this was mainly because his works were not translated until mid-20th century.

Biographic data: *IESS* 14:129; M. N. Shaternikov, "Ivan Mikhaĭlovich Sechenov," in *Selected Works of Ivan Mikhaĭlovich Sechenov*, 1935; N. Ishlondskiĭ, The Life and Work of I. M. Sechenov, *Journal of Nervous and Mental Diseases*, 1958, 126, 367–391

[157]

MEISSNER, GEORG

German physiologist
Rating: 11
Born: Hannover, November 19, 1829
Died: Göttigen, March 30, 1905
Highest degree: M.D., University of Göttingen, 1852
Positions: 1855, University of Basle; 1858, University of Freiburg; 1860, University of Göttigen

Meissner became known for his histological studies of the skin and the pressure receptors. He showed that the adequate stimulus for pressure receptors is not pressure itself but the deformation of the skin or changes in pressure pattern. Also, that if pressure is uniform it is not perceived except around the edges of the uniform pressure area, that is, at a pressure gradient contour. Meissner discovered touch receptors in hairless skin (palms and soles). These were named in his honor *Meissner corpuscles.* Meissner described his work on the skin in *Beiträge zur Anatomie und Physiologie der Haut* (1853). *Beiträge zur Physiologie des Sehorgans* (1854) reports on his work in physiological optics.

Biographic data: *DSB* 9:258; H. Boruttan, *Zum Andenken an Georg Meissner*, 1905

BEAUNIS, HENRI–ETIENNE [158]

French physiologist
Rating: 18
Born: Amboise, Indre et Loire, 1830
Died: Le Cannet, Alpes Maritimes, July 11, 1921
Positions: University of Strasbourg, University of Nancy; 1861– 1880, army surgeon; Collège de France; retired 1894

Beaunis was the co-founder, with Alfred Binet [236], of the first French psychological laboratory at the University of Paris in 1889; he was its first director. In 1895, he participated in founding, with Binet and Henri [334], the French psychological journal *L'Année psychologique*, and was a co-founder of the *Société de psychologie physiologique.* Beaunis wrote several medical books. His psychological research was mostly on hypnotism and the psychology of dreams. In hypnotism, he supported the views of the Nancy school and opposed those of the Salpêtriére (*Le somnambulisme provoqué*, 1886). He also wrote *De l'habitude en général* (1856), *Les sensations internes* (1889), and *Travaux de laboratoire de psychologie physiologique de la Sorbonne* (1892– 93). The drawing of a stack of cubes that can be seen in reversed perspective is called *Beaunis's cubes.*

Biographic data: *Enciclopedia universal ilustrada*, vol. 7

DELBOEUF, JOSEPH REMI LEOPOLD [159]

Belgian psychologist
Rating: 24
Born: Liège, September 30, 1831

Died: Bonn, Germany, August 14, 1896
Highest degree: Ph.D.
Positions: 1863, University of Ghent; 1866, University of Liège

Delboeuf began psychophysical experimentation on brightness in 1865, under the influence of Fechner [120]. In psychophysics, Delboeuf's contributions rank right after those of Fechner and G. E. Müller [208]. The most important idea that Delboeuf introduced was that of the sense distance (*contraste sensible*). Fechner had thought that sensations, like distances, were magnitudes, and that, like distances, they could have zero values. Objections were made to this notion, especially since introspectively sensations do not appear to have magnitude. Delboeuf modified Fechner's notion by asserting that, while sensations are not magnitudes, they can be ranked on a continuum, so that differences or distances between them may be established. This idea came to underlie the measurement of sensation in the 20th century.

Delboeuf published four critical monographs on psychophysics over a period of ten years: *Etude psychophysique* (1873), *Théorie générale de la sensibilité* (1876), (the last two were reprinted together as *Elements de psychophysique* in 1883), *Psychophysique* (1882), and *Examen critique de la loi psychophysique* (1883). Delboeuf's name is also attached to the illusion of contrasting circles, which Delboeuf first described in 1893. Many experiments have been performed on this illusion since that time. Finally, as a pioneer of psychology in Belgium, Delboeuf established a psychological laboratory at Liège. During the last years of his life, Delboeuf turned his attention to hypnotism, siding with the Nancy school of hypnotism. He wrote a volume in this area, *De l'origin des effets curatifs de l'hypnotisme* (1887).

Biographic data: *Enciclopedia universal ilustrada*, vol. 17

[160]

MAXWELL, JAMES CLERK

English physicist
Rating: **19**
Born: Edinburgh, Scotland, November 13, 1831
Died: Cambridge, England, November 5, 1879
Highest degree: Ph.D. in natural philosophy, Trinity College, Cambridge, 1854

Positions: 1856, Marischal College, Aberdeen; 1860–1865, King's College, London; 1871–1879, Cambridge University

Maxwell, famous for his work in physics and electricity, contributed to psychology during his two postgraduate years at Trinity College. During this time he worked out, for the first time (1855), the quantitative laws of color mixture, recognizing that in such mixtures the intensity of light had to be taken into account and that therefore a color mixture diagram had to be a solid rather than a plane figure. He also developed a method, used ever since, for mixing color using circles of colored paper that were cut along a radius and could be superimposed on each other on a rotating disc showing sectors of varying width. Maxwell accepted Helmholtz's [143] three-color theory, and computed from his color triangle the three excitation curves for the retina as well as those for a color-blind person. He wrote a number of significant papers on color and color vision, receiving for his work the Rumford Medal of the Royal Society.

Biographic data: *DNB* 37:118; *DSB* 9:198; *EP* 5:224; L. C. Campbell & W. Garnett, *Life of James Clerk Maxwell*, 1882; R. T. Glazebrook, *James Clerk Maxwell and Modern Physics*, 1901

WUNDT, WILHELM (MAXIMILIAN) [161]

German psychologist
Rating: 27
Born: Neckarau, Baden, August 16, 1832
Died: Grossbathen near Leipzig, Saxony, August 31, 1920
Highest degree: M.D., University of Heidelberg, 1856
Positions: 1857, University of Heidelberg; 1874, University of Zurich; 1875–1917, University of Leipzig

Wundt's interests began to shift to physiology even before he received his medical degree. His first teaching appointment at Heidelberg was in physiology. He began to publish in physiology in 1858. The *Beiträge zur Theorie der Sinneswahrnehmungen*, which was an outline of much that Wundt taught and published later, came out in installments between 1858 and 1862, and in one piece in 1862. In this work, Wundt makes the point that psychology, before tackling metaphysical problems, should start by trying to understand the simplest experiences, and that this should be done using the methods of physiology. In 1867, Wundt began teaching the first formal academic course in psychology, called "Physiological Psychology." The lecture notes were published in 1873 and 1874 in Wundt's most important book, *Grundzüge der physiologischen Psychologie,* which appeared in several enlarged editions. Upon his arrival at the University of Leipzig, Wundt established there, in 1875, the first psychological laboratory in the world. The laboratory became a famous training center for psychologists and the hub of what was soon to be known as the "new" psychology.

Using highly trained observers who introspected and reported on their experiences when presented visual, auditory, and other kinds of stimuli, Wundt collected data on the functioning of the senses, published them in the first purely psychological journal, *Philosophische Studien* (founded by him in 1881), and summarized the results in the changing editions of his *Grundzüge.* Most of the experimental studies were on sensation and perception, reaction time, attention, feeling, and association. About 100 experimental studies were published in *Philosophische Studien* during its publication, by Wundt and his students, among whom were to be found some of the most famous names in the history of modern psychology. Wundt's written production is close to the 500-item mark, with a total of some 54,000 printed pages. Some of the outstanding volumes were *Vorlesungen über die Menschen- und Thierseele* (1863), *Grundriss der Psychologie* (1896), and *Einführung in die Psychologie* (1911). Not all of Wundt's written output was experimental psychology. He wrote several volumes on philosophy and a ten-volume ethnopsychology (*Völkerpsychologie,* 1900–1920). While Wundt was opposed to any form of applied psychology, he accepted social psychology and used it to account for those psychic processes that were more complex than sensation or memory, and that could not, in his view, be studied experimentally.

Wundt's fame is based principally on his having founded an experimental psychological science. His systematic views are of lesser importance and constitute largely a descriptive system. Wundt saw the investigation of the contents of the mind as psychology's main task. The notion of consciousness consisting of elements and the method of introspection directed toward eliciting the elements put the mark of elementism on Wundt's psychology. Experience is always complex, and introspection must be used to break it down into elementary components, which are the sensations and feelings. Pure sensations differ in quality and intensity, feelings differ in pleasantness-unpleasantness, tension-relaxation, and excitement-depression (the three-dimensional theory of feeling). Sensations and feelings in combination become ideas and percepts. The latter acquire meaning only as apperceived, that is, combined with past experience and giving rise to feeling. This is active association. Basically, Wundt accepted the ideas of the associationists as to how successive ideas become passively associated. He added the notion of fusion to account for the tighter association between simultaneously occurring ideas as well as the notion of creative synthesis to explain how parts, in combining, may produce something different from a mere sum of the parts. Thus Wundt was somewhat inconsistent in that, in asserting the changing, dynamic nature of consciousness, he affirmed that it was not only content but also process. Wundt, however, did not further elaborate on this aspect of his psychology.

Wundt's elementism and the method of introspection did not survive the death of his truest disciple, E. B. Titchener [294]. His own students went on to establish branches of applied psychology. His theory of feeling reappeared in a modified form in later theories of emotion, and the idea of creative synthesis was made into a cardinal tenet of the Gestalt school of psychology, although it arose partly in opposition to Wundt's elementism. Wundt's greatest contribution, however, was to show that psychology could be an experimental science. The experimental study of thinking, which Wundt thought could not be done, was begun by others in his lifetime. Today, there is no area of human behavior that has not been studied experimentally, and experimentation is one of the cornerstones of the psychological edifice.

Biographic data: *EP* 8:349; *IESS* 16:581; W. Wundt, *Erlebtes und Erkanntes*, 1920; E. B. Titchener, Wilhelm Wundt. *American Journal of Psychology*, 1921, 32; 161–178, 577–580; [Various] in memory of Wilhelm Wundt. *Psychological Review*, 1921, 28, 153–188

TYLOR, (SIR) EDWARD BURNETT [162]

English anthropologist
Rating: **13**
Born: London, October 2, 1832
Died: Wellington, Somersetshire, January 2, 1917
Education: No university education; self-educated
Positions, honors: 1883, Oxford University; 1888, University of Aberdeen; 1896–1909, Oxford University, occupying first chair

of anthropology at Oxford; president, Anthropological Society, 1891; knighted 1912; honorary D.C.L., Oxford University, 1875

Tylor was a Darwinian anthropologist, known for his studies of mythology, magic, primitive mentality, and his pioneering work in developing anthropology as a science. In his work, Tylor used psychological methods. His best known work is *Primitive Culture* (1871). Tylor emphasized that the psychological makeup of humans is basic to their behavior and that a psychological approach to anthropology is therefore the best approach. His main contribution to psychology was the doctrine that religion evolves from primitive mentality. Since the primitive man is animistic, endowing all things with life and motives, he worships those things that seem to be powerful and affect his life. The primitive man considers the soul a separate entity that enters and leaves the body in sleep and dreams.

Biographic data: *DNB* 1912–1921

[163]

MEYNERT, THEODOR HERMANN

German-Austrian neurologist
Rating: **12**
Born: Dresden, Germany, June 15, 1833
Died: Vienna, Austria, May 31, 1892
Highest degree: M.D., University of Vienna, 1865
Positions: 1866, University of Vienna

As a researcher, Meynert contributed to the study of brain anatomy and brain functions. He wrote *Der Bau der Grosshirnrinde und seine örtlichen Verschiedenheiten* (1867–1868) and several other books in this area. Meynert described the association neuron and other brain structures, some of which have been named after him (*Meynert's fasciculus, Meynert's commisure*). As a practitioner, Meynert advocated mental hospitals with minimal restraints. He is known as one of Freud's [224] teachers. His concept of *das primäre ich*, or bodily consciousness, bears some resemblance to Freud's *id*.

Biographic data: *Enciclopedia universal ilustrada*, vol. 34

German philosopher
Rating: **22**
Born: Biebrich-am-Rhein, near Wiesbaden, November 19, 1833
Died: Seis, Austria, October 3, 1911
Highest degree: Ph.D. in philosophy, University of Berlin, 1864
Positions: 1866, University of Basel; University of Kiel; 1882, University of Berlin

Dilthey's domain was the philosophical understanding of history. He analyzed the process by which the historian himself apprehends history. The apprehension (*Verstehen*) enables the historian to grasp all cultural manifestations as expression of an underlying philosophy of life of the particular culture. His comprehension is thus determined by the "mind" of the cultural group to which he belongs. In addition to the emphasis on the importance of the whole cultural fabric in thinking, the total structure of mind rather than its elements, and on *Verstehen* rather than reasoning, Dilthey made the additional distinction between the natural sciences and the cultural sciences (*Geisteswissenschaften*) and classified psychology with the latter. In an 1894 paper (*Ideen über eine beschreibende und zergliedernde Psychologie*) Dilthey made the programmatic statement that human nature is qualitatively the same for all men, individual differences being merely quantitative, and that therefore a descriptive and classificatory psychology of personality is both possible and desirable. In this paper, Dilthey mentions five great areas of human activity, religion, art, economy, politics, and science, to which Eduard Spranger [411], a student of Dilthey's, added a sixth, the social sphere, and presented a sixfold classification of human types that was later the basis of the Allport-Vernon-Lindzey personality profile, *Study of Values*. Otherwise, Dilthey was opposed to the "new" Wundtian psychology and held that laboratory psychology was inadequate to understand man since such understanding could come only from the study of the total mental life. While natural science analyzes and refers to elements to explain, cultural science begins with wholes and, by describing them, understands. Dilthey and Spranger were the godfathers of that current in psychology which prefers synthesis to analysis, wholes to parts, insight to rational analysis, and emphasizes existence rather than essence.

Biographic data: *EP* 2:403; *IESS* 4:185

HAECKEL, ERNST HEINRICH

German biologist
Rating: 15
Born: Potsdam, Brandenburg, February 16, 1834
Died: Jena, August 9, 1919
Highest degree: M.D., University of Berlin, 1857
Positions: 1861, University of Jena

In 1866, Haeckel published a classic treatise of Darwinian biology, *Allgemeine Morphologie*, in which, among other things, he had formulated the principle that "ontogeny recapitulates phylogeny," or that during its developmental stages an organism repeats the evolutionary history of the species. G. Stanley Hall [418], who pioneered in developmental psychology under the aegis of Darwin [127], based his cultural recapitulation theory on Haeckel's principle, substituting the evolution of human civilization for biological evolution. The cultural recapitulation theory was never proven, while Haeckel's principle has been found to be applicable only to certain aspects of morphology.

Biographic data: DSB 6:6; EP 3:400

LUBBOCK, SIR JOHN (BARON AVEBURY)

English man of science and banker
Rating: 16
Born: London, April 30, 1834
Died: Kingsgate Castle, Kent, May 28, 1913

In addition to being a banker, Lubbock was a member of the British Parliament, worked in anthropology, geology, botany, popularized science (through his writings and be delivering numerous lectures on all subjects), and was a prolific writer (he wrote some twenty-five books and more than 100 articles). Lubbock pioneered in comparative psychology with his studies of insect behavior (*On the Senses, Instincts, and Intelligence in Animals* 1888; *Ants, Wasps, and Bees*, 1882). He investigated the social behavior as well as the sensory capacities and learning in insects. To observe ants in a controllable environment he devised the "Lubbock nest." Lubbock produced the first data on the longevity of ants, introduced the use of paint to identify individual animals, discovered the hearing organ in ants, used mazes and obstacles, tested color vision of ants, bees, and *Daphnia*, and otherwise broke ground in the area of comparative psychology some time before Morgan [214] and Thorndike [353].

Biographic data: DNB 1912–1921; *DSB* 8:527; *IESS* 9:487; H. G. Hutchinson, *Life of Sir John Lubbock, Lord Avebury,* 2 vol., 1914

HERING, EWALD [167]

German physiologist
Rating: 27
Born: Altgersdorf, Saxony, August 5, 1834
Died: Leipzig, January 26, 1918
Highest degree: M.D., University of Leipzig, 1858
Positions: 1862, University of Leipzig; 1865, Josephs-Akademie, Vienna; 1870, University of Prague; 1895, University of Leipzig

Hering began to practice medicine in 1860, but soon was devoting more time to science. The first ten years of his scientific career Hering spent studying space perception (*Bieträge zur Physiologie*: *Zur Lehre vom Ortsinn der Netzhaut*, 1861–1864; *Die Lehre vom binokularen Sehen*, 1868). He defended nativism in space perception, arguing that each retinal point has a local sign for height, one for right-left, and one for depth. In this he found himself opposing Helmholtz [143], who held to the empiricist position.

In the next decade, while working on vision, Hering opposed Helmholtz in his formulation of a color-vision theory (*Zur Lehre vom Lichtsinne*, 1872–1874). Instead of Helmholtz's three kinds of fibers, pigments, and basic colors, Helmholtz proposed that there are three visual pigments which, depending on whether they are metabolically broken down or reconstituted, produce the six opponent pairs of colors of black-white, blue-yellow, and red-green.

Hering's theory is still alive in the opponent-process color vision theory of Hurvich and Jameson, constituting a viable alternative to the Young-Helmholtz theory. Hering made several additional contributions to the phenomenology of visual perception. Among them are the *Hering illusion* (1861) and the concept of *memory color* or *color constancy* (1905). For temperature sensations Hering proposed, in 1880, a theory similar to his color vision theory. He suggested that warm and cold are a pair of opponent qualities, fluctuating about a physiological zero point and showing other phenomena similar to those of colors.

Hering's third contribution was his invention or modification of a large number of pieces of apparatus and materials for the study of color vision, such as the *Hering colored papers, Hering grays, Hering window, Hering binocular color mixer* and many others. The apparatus, used in many laboratories, did much to earn the "new psychology" the nickname of "brass-instrument psychology." In spite of the brass instruments, Hering was not an experimentalist as Wundt [161] was. His experiments were mostly phenomenologicial in nature, and he may be assigned to that psychological tradition to which belong Goethe [77], Purkinje [107], Dilthey [164], and the Gestalt psychologists.

Biographic data: *DSB* 6:299; *IESS* 6:351

[168]

GOLTZ, FRIEDRICH LEOPOLD

German physiologist
Rating: **12**
Born: Poznan, Poland, August 14, 1834
Died: Strasbourg, May 4, 1902
Education: Mainly self-taught
Positions: 1870, University of Halle; 1872, University of Strasbourg

An adherent of Flourens [113], Goltz worked on the localization of cerebral functions in dogs (*Uber die Verrichtungen des Grosshirns*, 1881) and on labyrinthine sensitivity. In 1870, Goltz showed that cold and hot water, applied externally to the ear, caused vertigo, nausea, and ocular nystagmus. He theorized that the semicircular canals were not involved in hearing but in equilibrium.

Biographic data: *DSB* 5:462

LANGE, CARL GEORG

Danish physiologist
Born: Vordingborg, December 4, 1834
Died: Copenhagen, May 29, 1900
Highest degree: M.D., University of Copenhagen, 1859
Positions: 1859–1875, various medical appointments in Denmark; 1869–1872, lecturer at the University of Copenhagen; 1875, University Hospital, Copenhagen, lecturer, later professor of pathological anatomy

At about the same time as James [184] offered his theory of emotion (1884) and independently of him, Lange conceived of a very similar theory. In studying the circulatory system, Lange came to the conclusion that emotion was the result of felt changes in the blood vessels and published his views in an 1885 paper. It appeared later in his *Om Sindsbevaegelser*, 1885, German translation, *Uber Gemüthsbewegungen*, 1887). Lange's theory was not quite as broad as James's and stressed vascular rather than all visceral changes. James republished his own theory in his *Principles of Psychology* in 1890, taking Lange's contribution into account. The theory became known as the James-Lange theory of emotion. Lange also wrote *Bidrag til mydelsernes fysiologi* (1889; English translation, *Contributions to the Physiology of Sensual Pleasure*, 1899), a study of pleasurable emotions that, in accordance with his theory of emotion, were the effect of vasomotor activity occurring during an aesthetic experience.

Biographic data: DSB 8:7; K. Faber, *Eridringer om C. Lange*, 1927; In V. Meisen, *Prominent Danish Scientists through the Ages*, 1932

MAUDSLEY, HENRY

English psychiatrist
Rating: 16
Born: Rome, near Settle, Yorkshire, 1835
Died: Bushey Heath, Hertsfordshire, January 23, 1918
Highest degree: M.D., University College, London, 1857
Positions, honors: 1856, Cheadle Royal, medical superintendent; 1859–1862, Manchester Royal Lunatic Hospital, medical

superintendent; 1864–1874, West London Hospital, physician; 1869–1879, University College, London, professor of medical jurisprudence; editor, *Journal of Mental Science*, 1862–1878; honorary LL.D

In addition to his medical contributions to psychiatry, Maudsley conceived the idea and advanced some money for the London University Psychiatric Hospital, completed in 1915, that now bears his name. His *Physiology and Pathology of the Mind* (1867, 3d edition in 2 volumes, *The Physiology of Mind*, 1867, *and The Pathology of Mind*, 1879) was an influential book that formed the foundation of British medical psychology. A Comtian positivist, Maudsley stressed the importance of considering those aspects of mind which are not accessible to introspection, that is, are unconscious, and believed that most behaviors are unconsciously motivated. Some of the psychological works that reflect Maudsley's viewpoint are *Body and Mind* (1870), *Responsibility in Mental Disease* (1874), *Body and Will* (1883), *Life in Mind and Conduct* (1902), *and Organic to Human, Psychological, and Sociological* (1917).

Biographic data: A. Lewis, The 25th Maudsley lecture–Henry Maudsley: His work and influence. *Journal of Mental Science*, 1951, **97**, 259–277

[171]

JACKSON, JOHN HUGHLINGS

English neurologist
Rating: **21**
Born: Green Hammerton, Yorkshire, April 4, 1835
Died: London, October 7, 1911
Highest degree: M.D., St. Andrews, 1860
Positions: From 1856 on, various hospital and medical appointments

Jackson was trained by Brown-Séquard [133] and took his scientific philosophy from Herbert Spencer [142]. He is known for his studies of epilepsy, aphasia, and paralysis. Jackson gave the classic descriptions of focal or hemiplegic epilepsy (*Jacksonian epilepsy*), relating cortical sites to movements in epilepsy. He identified sites of motor action, sensation, and language in the cortex, and was first to demonstrate the use of the ophthalmoscope, invented by Helmholtz [143], in the study of disorders of the nervous system.

Jackson conceived of a hierarchical relationship between nerve centers. Those that evolved later (higher centers) subserve more complex functions than those that evolved earlier (lower centers). Neurological disorders affect the higher nervous centers first and only then the lower centers (*Jackson's law*). Dissolution (Spencer's term), in contrast to evolution, characterizes nervous disease.

Because much of Jackson's work was advanced for his time, he laid the groundwork for future brain investigations. His doctrine of evolutionary levels in the brain and psychological functioning had a definite effect on physiological psychology, one of which was a de-emphasis on exact localization of brain functions and a stress on evolutionary levels in the brain and the complexity of the functions involved.

Biographic data: *DNB* 1901–1911; *DSB* 7:46

LOMBROSO, CESARE [172]

Italian psychiatrist and anthropologist
Rating: 20
Born: Verona, November 18, 1835
Died: Turin, October 19, 1909
Highest degree: M.D., University of Pavia, 1858
Positions: 1862, University of Pavia, professor of psychiatry; 1871, director, lunatic asylum at Pesaro; 1876, University of Turin, professor of forensic medicine and psychiatry

Lombroso developed the positive school of criminology which, in contrast to the classical school that concentrated on the crime, concentrated on the criminal. Lombroso saw criminal as an instance of physical degeneration and atavism. A criminal commits his criminal acts because he is a throwback to a more primitive state of development. Lombroso's was a theory of hereditary determinism. He believed that degeneration showed itself in certain physical characteristics, or stigmata, such as a narrow forehead, protruding ears, exaggerated facial bones, and the like, which permitted the identification of criminals (*L'Uomo delinquente*, 2 volumes, 1876; *La Donna delinquente*, 1893). Although Lombroso's theory was discredited and Lombroso himself later gave up his biological theory and attempted to explain crime by reference to psychological and social factors, the notion of the criminal as a physically identifiable "type" persisted for a long time. Lombroso's emphasis on the criminal rather than the crime was emulated by many sociologists and criminologists.

Biographic data: *IESS* 9:471; M. E. Wolfgang, "Cesare Lombroso," in H. Mannheim (ed.), *Pioneers in Criminology,* 1960

[173]

HITZIG, EDUARD

German psychiatrist
Rating: 18
Born: Berlin, February 6, 1838
Died: St. Blasien, Baden, August 21, 1907
Highest degree: M.D.
Positions: 1875, University of Zürich; 1879–1903, University of Halle

Hitzig is known for the famous experiment, performed with Gustav Fritsch [175], that established the electrical excitability of the brain tissue ("über die elektrische Erregbarkeit des Grosshirns," 1870). The prevailing doctrine had been that the brain tissue was insensitive and unexcitable. Hitzig first observed that the electrical stimulation of a patient's cortex produced eye movements. He confirmed his observations in a rabbit, then proceeded to study the phenomenon systematically, using dogs. Applying electric current to the dog's brain, Fritsch and Hitzig also established that muscular contractions were controlled by certain areas of the brain only, as well as the location of some of the more specific motor centers.

Biographic data: *Enciclopedia italiana*, vol. 18

[174]

MACH, ERNST

Austrian physicist
Rating: 25
Born: Chirlitz-Turas, Moravia, February 18, 1838
Died: Vaterstetten, near Haar, Bavaria, February 19, 1916
Highest degree: Ph.D. in physics, University of Vienna, 1860

Positions: 1864, University of Graz; 1867, University of Prague; 1895–1901, University of Vienna

Mach's contributions to psychology stem from his work as a philosopher of science as well as his purely psychological work. The latter included research on visual space perception, time perception, and his experimental work on the perception of rotation (*Lehre von den Bewegungsempfindungen*, 1875), which was his most significant empirical contribution to psychology. His theory of the functioning of the semicircular canals is yet to be replaced by another.

At Prague, Mach published his most important book, *Analyse der Empfindungen* (1886; English translation, *The Analysis of Sensations* 1897). In this book, Mach set forth the principles of a positivist philosophy of science. With Hume [52], Mach asserted that causality exists only as observed concomitant relationships, that all science is observational, and that the data of any science, including the "hard" sciences, are sensations. In echoing Berkeley [40], Mach insisted that the physical world exists only in the form of sensations and that these are to be taken as they occur, meaning, for instance, that there were no such things as illusions. Among the immediate data of consciousness, i.e., sensations, Mach included those of time and space, in contrast to Kant [60], who thought of time and space as innate reference systems with respect to which sensations were ordered, and Wundt [161], who thought in Kantian terms. Külpe [265], however, was influenced by Mach, and so, through him, was Gestalt psychology. Although Mach was a phenomenalist, the resemblance of his views to those of Berkeley made him appear an idealist, for which he was severely criticized by such materialists as Lenin [318].

The scientific study of form perception begins with *The Analysis of Sensations*, for, by making space a sensation that was correlated with the physical world, Mach made it amenable to scientific study. A form is recognized independently of other attributes, Mach said, hence there are form sensations. Mach also analyzed the physical form dimensions that determine the recognition of shape, such as rotation and reflection, made a contribution to the aesthetics of visual form, discovered the phenomenon known as Mach bands and, in relation to the latter, made a mathematical analysis to demonstrate the origin of contour perception. Mach's seminal ideas concerning the nature of form were developed by the school of form qualities, a transitional stage between Mach and the Gestalt psychologists.

Biographic data: *DSB* 8:595; *EP* 5:515; H. Henning, *Ernst Mach als Philosoph, Physiker und Psycholog*, 1915

FRITSCH, GUSTAV THEODOR

German anatomist and anthropologist
Rating: 18
Born: Cottbus, Saxony, March 5, 1838
Died: Berlin, June 12, 1927
Highest degree: M.D., University of Berlin, 1862
Positions: 1867, University of Berlin, 1899, honorary professor

Fritsch's contribution to psychology was the famous experiments, performed with E. Hitzig [173] ("Uber die elektrische Erregbarkeit des Grosshirns," 1870), that established the electrical excitability of the brain tissue. The dogma held by most authorities of the day was that the brain was insensitive and inexcitable. Applying electric current, rather than mechanical or chemical stimulation, to various portions of the brain of the dog, Fritsch and Hitzig established, in addition, that muscular contractions were controlled by certain areas of the brain only, as well as the exact location of some of the more specific motor centers.

Biographic data: DSB 5:195

BRENTANO, FRANZ

German philosopher and psychologist
Rating: 27
Born: Marienburg-am-Rhein, near Cologne, June 16, 1838
Died: Zurich, Switzerland, March 17, 1917
Highest degree: Ph.D. in philosophy, University of Tübingen, 1864
Positions: 1886, University of Würzburg; 1874–1894, University of Vienna

The history of Brentano as a psychologist begins with the publication, in 1874, of a book by which he is best known, *Psychologie vom empirischen Standpunkt*. It was a psychology intended to replace all existing psychologies. It was philosophical psychology (since Brentano saw no essential difference between philosophy and psychology), but with an empirical emphasis. To Brentano, "empirical" meant pure psychic activity or experience, and only indirectly referred to the Lockean notion of sense-derived knowledge. Brentano's reaction to Wundt's [161] *Physiologische*

Psychologie, published a year earlier, was to say that scientific psychology was not physiological psychology, although it may use the physiological approach as a method. Brentano argued but did not experiment. He argued that psychological phenomena possess immanent objectivity. Psychological phenomena are acts. The act of seeing is mental. What is seen, "inexists" in the act of seeing by intention. The quality of what is seen, the structure of experience (the content), belongs to the physical world. Brentano's philosophy was basically that of Aristotle [8], which he brought to bear upon contemporary psychological thinking.

Brentano wrote only seven other papers and books of importance to psychology: *Sinnespsychologie* (1907), *Von der Klassifikation der psychischen Phänomene* (1911), two articles on sensation, and three on optical illusions. In the latter, Brentano advanced the theory that the Müller-Lyer illusion is owing to the overestimation of acute angles and the underestimation of obtuse ones. Brentano exercised great influence on psychological thinking in Germany and abroad because of the effectiveness of his writings and his personality. "Act" psychology (also known as the Austrian school of psychology) became an alternative to Wundt's "content" psychology to those who favored phenomenological argument over experimentation. Brentano's thought, that the basis of experience is subjective perception, was basic to the imageless thought school of Würzburg and the development of the phenomenological branch of psychology.

Biographic data: EP 1:365; M. Puglisi, Brentano: a biographical sketch. *American Journal of Psychology,* 1924, 35, 414–419, A. C. Rancurello, *A Study of Franz Brentano,* 1968

PEIRCE, CHARLES SANTIAGO SANDERS [177]

American philosopher
Rating: 19
Born: Cambridge, Massachusetts, September 10, 1839
Died: Milford, Pennsylvania, April 14, 1914
Highest degree: A.M., Harvard University, 1860; Sc.B. in chemistry, Harvard University, 1863
Positions: 1879–1884, lectured at Harvard, Johns Hopkins, and other universities

Peirce created pragmatism (1878) in American philosophy, although it remained for James [184] to develop and popularize it. Peirce used the term pragmatism for the first time in the English language in an article on "How to Make Our Ideas Clear." The way to make an idea clear was to "consider what effects, that conceivably might have practical bearings we conceive the object of our conception to have. Then our conception of these effects is the whole of our conception of the object." Since the practical consequences of a concept can be experienced only through the senses, Peirce's pragmatism was a further development of empiricism; and since only that which is empirically observable can be measured, Peirce's definition of pragmatism anticipated the operational definition of Bridgman [409]. James's and Peirce's conceptualizations of pragmatism did not coincide completely, Peirce emphasizing the public nature of the criterion of "what works" while James's pragmatism was more subjective. Peirce considered that James's concept of pragmatism was that "the end of man is action," whereas Peirce's own doctrine was intended as a "theory of logical analysis." To distinguish his own definition of pragmatism from that of James's, Peirce called it "pragmaticism." It was, however, James's version that prevailed, and Peirce is now remembered more as an important developer of modern logic.

Biographic data: EP 6:70; *IESS* 11:511; *NCAB* 8:409

[178]

BERNSTEIN, JULIUS

German physiologist
Rating: 12
Born: Berlin, December 18, 1839
Died: Halle, February 6, 1917
Highest degree: M.D., University of Berlin, 1862
Positions: 1864, University of Heidelberg; 1871, University of Berlin; 1872–1917, University of Halle

In 1866, by measuring the polarization of nerves, Bernstein showed that the nerve impulse is a "wave of negativity." In 1902, he helped to establish the membrane theory of nerve conduction, when the "wave of negativity" became the wave of depolarization. In 1871, he stated the projection theory of nerve conduction, which postulated a point-to-point correspondence between the receptors stimulated and ganglion cells in brain centers upon which stimulation from the receptors is projected and from which stimulation irradiates along a gradient to adjacent brain cells. The theory went a long way toward explaining binocular vision, blind areas in cases of brain injury, phenomena of the cutaneous two-point threshold, the error of localization, and other nervous phenomena. There has been little improvement upon Bernstein's idea. Bernstein authored several books on neurophysiology and electrobiology.

Biographic data: Enciclopedia italiana, vol. 6; *Enciclopedia universal ilustrada,* vol. 8

RIBOT, THEODULE ARMAND   [179]

French psychologist
Rating: 26
Born: Guingamp, Côtes du Nord, December 18, 1839
Died: Paris, December 8, 1916
Highest degree: *Agrégé* in philosophy, École Normale Supérieure, 1865
Positions: 1865, teaching at various *lycées*; 1872, clinical studies of mental abnormalities, city of Paris; 1885, Sorbonne, teaching experimental psychology; 1889–1896, Collège de France; founder (1876) and editor of *Revue philosophique*

Ribot had interest in a wide variety of fields of psychology. He wrote a number of books that were well read by other French psychologists. These books introduced to them the ideas of evolution, the work of the German experimental psychologists, and the thinking of the English associationists (*La psychologie anglaise contemporaine*, 1870, English translation, *English Psychology of To-Day*, 1879; *La psychologie allemande contemporaine*, 1879, English translation, *German Psychology of To-Day*, 1886).

Although Ribot held the title of professor of experimental psychology at Collège de France, he was not an experimentalist. His pattern of interests resembled more that of the traditional French medical psychologist. His books on behavior disorders reflected that orientation (*Les maladies de la mémoire*, 1881; *Les maladies de la volonté*, 1883; *Les maladies de la personalité*, 1885). Ribot was one of the first psychologists to relate pathology to problem areas in general psychology. He strived to separate psychology from philosophy, especially metaphysics, yet he considered physiology to be a clearly separate discipline also. He used psychopathology to arrive at insights concerning general behavioral principles. Abnormal behavior was to him a form of disintegration of the normal, integrated personality. Ribot considered affects and emotions to be the basis of mental life. He was a pioneer in introducing dynamic psychology in France. Between 1896 and 1914 he wrote several volumes on affective states, such as *Essais sur les passions* (1907), *Problèmes de psychologie affective* (1910), and *La vie inconsciente et les mouvements* (1914). In pathological states, in his view, experiences, habits, learned reactions, and the will retreated into the background while the emotional life emerged unveiled. The most recently learned behaviors are the first to disappear in mental disorders. Ribot stressed the analysis of abnormal behavior so much that he recommended to his students that they combine their psychological studies with the study of medicine. In general, Ribot was very influential in France during his day, but he did not leave quite as deep an impression on psychology as did, for instance, Binet [236] and Janet [249].

Biographic data: *EP* 7:191; E. Claparède, Théodule Ribot. *Archives de Psychologie*, 1916, **16**, 194–196; J. W. Baird, Théodule Armand Ribot. *American Journal of Psychology*, 1917, **28**, 312–313

[180]

BOWDITCH, HENRY PICKERING

American physiologist
Rating: 12
Born: Boston, Massachusetts, April 4, 1840
Died: Boston, Massachusetts, March 13, 1911
Highest degree: M.D., Harvard University, 1866
Positions, honors: 1871–1893, Harvard University: editorial work, *Journal of Physiology*, 1877–1898; four honorary degrees

Bowditch opened the first American physiological laboratory at Harvard in 1871. He was an eclectic physiologist who collaborated with such psychologists as James [184] and Hall [418]. Hall, who received his degree from James, did his dissertation on the muscular sense in Bowditch's laboratory. Later (1882), Bowditch and Hall published a paper on apparent motion in which the waterfall illusion machine was described and used in psychology for the first time. Bowditch was first to demonstrate the all-or-none *law of nerve impulse transmission* in heart muscle fibers (1871). The principle that nerves cannot be fatigued is referred to as *Bowditch's law*.

Biographic data: *DSB* 2:365–368; *NCAB* 12:252

BERNHEIM, HIPPOLYTE

[181]

French neurologist and hypnotist
Rating: **23**
Born: Mulhouse, Haut Rhin, April 17, 1840
Died: Nancy, Meurthe et Moselle, 1919
Highest degree: M.D., University of Strasbourg
Positions: 1868, University of Strasbourg; 1872, University of Nancy; 1882, private practice, Nancy

Bernheim was a well-known physician at Nancy when Ambroise-Auguste Liébeault [145] happened to cure one of his patients of sciatica using hypnosis. Bernheim, who had failed with orthodox treatment, became a pupil of Liébeault's in 1882. Together, they founded a clinic at Nancy. In this clinic, treatment by hypnosis was prominent. The clinic soon became a rival of Charcot's [152] in Paris, both in terms of cases treated (Bernheim hypnotized some ten thousand persons during his clinical practice) and the ideas entertained concerning the nature of hypnosis (The "Nancy school" of hypnotism). While Charcot believed that hypnosis was the result of the hysteric makeup of a person, Bernheim thought that ordinary sleep and hypnotic sleep were similar and that most people could be hypnotized. Bernheim induced hypnotic sleep using suggestion of sleepiness and treated his patients on the assumption that medical cures could be achieved in a state of suggestibility. This was essentially a development of Braid's [114] view of hypnosis as suggestion.

Bernheim, along with Charcot, showed that hypnosis was a proper subject for scientific study; they also contributed to the development of clinical psychology by concentrating on neurotic cases and separating them from the more severe cases of abnormality that required hospitalization. Bernheim was first to treat neuroses hypnotically. Among his books on the subject are *De la suggestion dans l'état hypnotique et dans l'état de veille* (1884), *De la suggestion et ses applications à la thérapeutique* (1886), *Hypnotisme, suggestion, psychothérapie, études nouvelles*

(1891), and *L'hypnotisme et la suggestion dans leurs rapports avec la médicine légale et les maladies mentales* (1897).

Biographic data: DSB 2:35–36

[182]

LE BON, GUSTAVE

French sociologist
Rating: 24
Born: Nogent le Rotrou, Eure et Loire, May 7, 1841
Died: Marne-la-Coquette, near Paris, December 13, 1931
Highest degree: M.D., 1876

Le Bon felt no calling for the practice of medicine, and turned to archeology, sociology, and writing. In sociology, Le Bon influenced not only that field but also the thinking of the general public through his writings on the psychology of crowds and nations. *La psychologie des foules* (1895) saw many editions and was soon translated into English (*The crowd: A study of the popular mind*, 1897). His thesis was that mental phenomena that are easily controlled in individuals—strong emotions, affects, excitement—propagate and contaminate other individuals in unorganized groups, such as crowds, people in traffic jams, and groups of juveniles and children. These mental phenomena are contagious since a lowering of resistance takes place in groups. People in unorganized groups become uncritical and lose their ability to judge. At the same time a crowd possesses psychological unity (a collective mind).

Le Bon also believed in racial hierarchy. He placed the white race above the colored ones and the Teutons and Anglo-Saxons with their individuality and rationality above the Latins, who to him were overemotional and reflected mob psychology. After World War I Le Bon revised his opinion of the Teutons, however. Presented in such books as *Les lois psychologiques de l'évolution des peuples* (1894; English translation, *The psychology of peoples*, 1898). *La psychologie du socialisme* (1898; *The psychology of socialism*, 1899). *La revolution française et la psychologie des revolution* (1912; *The psychology of revolution*, 1913), and *La psychologie des temps nouveaux* (1920; *The world in revolt: A psychological study of our times*, 1921), these views, although unsupported by research, found wide readership because of Le Bon's facile style. Le Bon may be said to have continued and developed the sociological ideas of Tarde [192] and

Durkheim [241] concerning the nature of unorganized groups, as well as the views of the German ethnopsychologists, such as Herder [69].

Biographic data: *IESS* 9:82

PREYER, WILHELM THIERRY [183]

German physiologist
Rating: 22
Born: Moss Side, near Manchester, England, July 4, 1841
Died: Wiesbaden, Hessen, Germany, July 15, 1897
Highest degree: Ph.D. in physiology, University of Paris, 1865; M.D., 1867
Positions: 1865, University of Bonn, Privatdozent in zoochemistry and zoophysics; 1869, University of Jena, 1885–1893, University of Berlin; one of the original editors of *Zeitschrift für Psychologie*

As a physiologist, Preyer first did research on color vision and hearing. He invented the sound helmet for studying the localization of sound, wrote a number of papers on sensation, and a text, *Elemente der reinen Empfindungslehre* (1877). In the late 1870s, Preyer studied sleep (*Über die Ursache des Schlafes,* 1877), which led him to hypnosis. He translated Braid's [114] works into German (1882) and wrote a book on the subject, *Hypnotismus* (1890). Hypnosis, in turn, led to an enquiry into the origins of psychological functions and thus to the question of child development. *Die Seele des Kindes* (1882, English translation, *The Mind of the Child,* published in 1888–1889, saw its ninth edition by 1923) turned out to be his most important work. The book may be considered the first textbook of developmental psychology. It presented observations on the development of a child arranged by topic (sensory, motor, intellectual development, and the like). The observations made by Preyer were not as rigorously controlled as those that were made later by others. Also, being a Darwinian, he considered development to be merely a biological process. Nevertheless, Preyer's book provided the greatest single impetus to the development of modern ontogenetic psychology. It served as a textbook for a long time. Preyer also pioneered in the investigation of prenatal life in animals (*Specielle Physiologie des Embryo: Untersuchungen über die Lebenserscheinungen vor der Geburt,* 1885) and wrote an additional developmental text, *Die geistige Entwicklung der ersten Kindheit* (1893).

Biographic data: *Encyclopedia of Social Sciences,* 12:349

[184]

JAMES, WILLIAM

American philosopher and psychologist
Rating: 27
Born: New York, New York, January 11, 1842
Died: Chocorua, New Hamsphire, August 26, 1910
Highest degree: M.D., Harvard University, 1868
Positions: 1872–1907, Harvard University, taught physiology, then psychology, followed by philosophy; president, American Psychological Association, 1894 and 1904

James is still considered by many to be America's foremost psychologist. James achieved this distinction without founding a school, without formulating a comprehensive psychological theory, without performing any notable experiments, or without having his students, of which he had very few, perform them. James's contributions were several; they were all significant, and to a considerable extent continue to be significant.

Early in his career at Harvard, James established a psychological laboratory to give demonstrations. It was in the same year, 1875, that Wundt [161] established his at Leipzig. Although James recognized the importance of experimentation, he was not an experimentalist by nature and did little experimental work of his own. The historic significance of the founding of the laboratory was great, however, in that it signalled the introduction of the "new" psychology in the United States.

In 1890 James published his *Principles of Psychology*. James's influence on psychology and psychologists occurred mainly through his *Principles* as well as through his personal contacts and lectures. In one case the important factor was James's literary style, in the other his personality. The main distinction of James's book was not its originality (although many of James's ideas were original) or exhaustive treatment, but a style of writing that even today brings James as an individual close to the reader. In 1892, an abridged textbook version of *Principles* appeared that was used as a university text for many years.

James's psychological views lack systematicity, which may be explained by his conviction that psychology in its incipient stage did not need as much definitive conclusions as it needed suggestions and inspiration for the future. The term, "stream of consciousness," is of James's coinage. James contrasted this view of the nature of consciousness with that of Wundt and the structuralists who thought of it as consisting of discrete elements. James was thus supporting the new psychology in his book by presenting its findings, but he also criticized it by reinterpreting these findings in the light of his own view of the human psyche. James saw consciousness as continuous, personal, selective, constantly changing, and different from the objects of consciousness. Concerning association and memory, James held that these are physiological processes in the nervous system. What is associated is not ideas but physiological processes. While granting that Hartley [45] had adequately described the process of association, James nevertheless did not think that it explained everything about the human mind, and felt the need to assume the existence of inborn capacities of the mind to order reality. Habit was likewise treated by James as a phenomenon of the nervous system. Concerning emotion, James reversed the customary notion that emotion causes behavior. "We are afraid because we run" is a summary statement of what became known as the *James-Lange theory of emotion* since Carl Lange [169] came to similar conclusions at about the same time as did James. It is the only specific psychological theory of James that ever became famous. It produced much controversy and research. Although incomplete, the Jamesian theory in various modified forms is still current.

In the 1890s, James thought and wrote in a more philosophical vein. Thanks to his writings that appeared in the next decade (*Pragmatism*, 1907; *The Meaning of Truth*, 1909), pragmatism as a philosophical theory became important and James himself gained the distinction of being considered America's most oustanding philosopher. The doctrine of pragmatism that beliefs are true because they work, instead of the other way around, was germane to what later became known as the functionalist school of psychology in America, which stressed the adaptive functions of behavior. James himself stressed that the primary function of mind is the acquisition of knowledge. James's psychology of knowledge and its use made him a precursor of the functionalist school that flourished in America in the 1920s and 1930s. James sought to advance pragmatism as a solution to the recurring struggle between the rationalists and the empiricists. In the process of doing so, James labelled the monistic rationalists "tender-minded" and the pluralistic empiricists "tough-minded," terms which are a current coin of the psychological realm today. James himself advanced a monism that held the distinction between subject and object, between knowing and that which is known to be false. He proposed a radical empiricism to eliminate the subject–object dualism.

James wrote two additional books around the turn of the century, *Talks to Teachers* (1899) and *Varieties of Religious Experience* (1902). Both arose from his university lectures. The first reflects his pragmatic bent in that it is intended to bring psychology into the classroom by showing how psychology can be applied to everyday problems. The second book is a classic in the field of the psychology of religion. While showing that many religious experiences are correlated with psychopathology, James also asserted that mental stability was not a criterion of the value of religious experience.

Biographic data: *DSB* 7:67; *EP* 4:240; *IESS* 8:227; *NCAB* 18:31; E. Boutroux, *William James*, 1911 (English translation, 1912); R. B. Perry, *The Thought and Character of William James*, 1935; G. W. Allen, *William James*, 1967

[185]

BREUER, JOSEF

Austrian psychoanalyst
Rating: 23
Born: Vienna, January 15, 1842
Died: Vienna, June 20, 1925
Highest degree: M.D., University of Vienna, 1867
Positions: 1867, University of Vienna, 1871; private practice in Vienna

Breuer is known both as the discoverer (independently of Ernest Mach [174]) of the function of the semicircular canals (described in three papers, dated 1873, 1874, and 1875) and as Sigmund Freud's [224] intimate friend and father figure—more as the latter. Breuer reinforced Freud's biological orientation in interpreting psychic events in terms of related nervous and psychic excitation and organismic energy balance and surplus. Together they wrote papers on aphasia and hysteria. It was Breuer's famous patient, Anna O., who set Freud's thinking along lines that later became the foundation of psychoanalysis. Breuer had treated Anna O., a hysteric patient, using hypnosis and allowing her to talk freely of her problems under hypnosis. As a result, the symptoms decreased or disappeared. Breuer and Freud called the phenomenon *catharsis*. The treatment had begun in 1880. When

Anna O. developed transference to Breuer and Breuer discovered countertransference in himself, he terminated the treatment and Freud took it over. Eventually Freud abandoned hypnosis and began to rely on free association alone. The book by Breuer and Freud, *Studien über Hysterie* (1895), is held to mark the beginning of psychoanalysis. Within the next two years the relationship between Breuer and Freud cooled, however, and they went their separate ways.

Biographic data: *DSB* 2:445–450; C. P. Oberndorf, Autobiography of Josef Breuer. *International Journal of Psychoanalysis*, 1953, 34, 64–67

LADD, GEORGE TRUMBULL

[186]

American psychologist
Rating: 24
Born: Painesville, Ohio, January 19, 1842
Died: New Haven, Connecticut, August 8, 1921
Highest degree: Degree in divinity, Andover Theological Seminary, 1869
Positions: 1869–1879, minister; 1879, Bowdoin College, professor of mental philosophy; 1881–1905, Yale University, professor of mental philosophy; president, American Psychological Association, 1893

While influenced strongly by Lotze [135], Ladd was a pioneer of the "new" psychology who emphasized the functional aspects of mind and its biological and adaptive significance. Ladd's influence was felt, not through his theories or research, (though he and E. Scripture [280] founded the Yale psychological laboratory in 1892), but in the texbooks he wrote. *Elements of Physiological Psychology* (1887) was a compendium of the "new", or Wundtian, psychology, and represented the first survey of it in the English language. It remained one of the most important texts of the new psychology for some time, and appeared in updated from in 1911 when R. S. Woodworth [312] revised it. A short edition of the *Elements* appeared in 1891, then a larger *Psychology, Descriptive and Explanatory* (1894). Ladd's *Psychology* was another compendium of the "new" psychology, but it did not receive the acclaim of the 1887 text. It was, however, an important event in that Ladd's emphasis on the adaptive functions of mind was clearly evident, and the volume may thus be considered a cornerstone of the edifice of American function-alism that was to appear full-fledged later.

In his conception of psychology Ladd had a place for an active self. Consciousness he viewed as the activity of the self. Inasmuch as he felt that he had to describe consciousness also in terms of Wundt's contents, his view was similar to that of Külpe's [265], The function of the active self Ladd considered to be the solving of problems of adaptation. Consciousness to Ladd thus had a purpose. In 1894 Ladd published a *Primer of Psychology,* then *Philosophy of Mind* (1895). Afterward Ladd reverted to philosophy, so that his influence in psychology lasted only the eight or so years of his writing of the textbooks. That activity was important enough for him to have merited the appellation "the Sully [188] of America."

Biographic data: NCAB 33:561; A. C. Armstrong, George Trumbull Ladd. *Philosophical Review,* 1921, 30, 639 ff.; E. B. Titchener, George Trumbull Ladd. *American Journal of Psychology,* 1921, 32, 600–601; E. S. Mills, *George Trumbull Ladd: Pioneer American Psychologist,* 1969

[187]

HARTMANN, EDUARD VON

German philosopher
Rating: 15
Born: Berlin, February 23, 1842
Died: Berlin, June 5, 1906
Highest degree: Ph.D. in philosophy, University of Rostock, 1867
Positions: No official or academic positions

Hartmann evolved a metaphysics based on the notion of the unconscious (*Die Philosophie des Unbewussten,* 3 volumes, 1869; English translation, *The Philosophy of the Unconscious,* 1884), which he considered to be the ground of all existence. Even the lowest organisms possess the unconscious, as indicated by the presence of reflexes and instincts showing purpose. Of the purely psychological processes, emotions have the deepest roots in the unconscious. The will, a part of the unconscious, is in constant strife with reason. The genius arises also from the unconscious. In fact, the conscious only reflects the powers of the unconscious. While Ebbinghaus [207] wrote his doctoral dissertation on Hartmann's philosophy of the unconscious, Hartmann was not as influential in determining the course of development of the concept of the unconscious in psychology as were Herbart, [101], James [184], Janet [249], or Charcot [152].

Biographic data: *EP* 3:419

SULLY, JAMES [188]

English psychologist
Rating: 22
Born: Bridgwater, Somersetshire, March 3, 1842
Died: London, November 1, 1923
Highest degree: M.A., University of London
Positions: 1892, Grote professor of mind and logic, University of London

Sully acquired a name in the history of psychology not as a scientist or philosopher but as a writer of textbooks. After publishing books of more restricted scope, *Sensation and Intuition* (1874), *Pessimism* (1877), and *Illusions* (1881), he wrote *Outlines of Psychology* (1884), *Teacher's Handbook of Psychology* (1886), *The Human Mind* (1892), *Studies of Childhood* (1896), *Children's Ways* (1897), and *An Essay on Laughter* (1902). The *Outlines* and *Teacher's Handbook* were his most successful writing ventures, distinguished by lucidity and facility of style. They saw several editions and were used widely. Sully spread knowledge of psychological advances also among psychologists by writing on the achievements of German psychologists. He did this in the pages of *Mind,* beginning soon after the founding of that journal and continuing in this enterprise for some twenty years.

Biographic data: J. Sully, *My Life and Friends,* 1918

RAYLEIGH, JOHN WILLIAM STRUTT, 3D BARON [189]

English physicist
Rating: 18
Born: Maldon, Essex, November 12, 1842
Died: Witham, Essex, June 30, 1919
Education: Graduated from Trinity College, Cambridge University, in 1865

Positions, honors:　1879–1884, head Cavendish Laboratory at Cambridge; 1887, Royal Institution of Great Britain, professor of natural philosophy; president, Royal Society, 1905–1908; 1904 Nobel prize (for the discovery of argon); Royal Society Rumford medal, other honors

Rayleigh worked in almost every area of physics, producing, incidentally, some work of importance to psychology. He worked out (in 1881) an equation (Rayleigh equation) for color mixture to screen individuals for color blindness. It involved the matching of a yellow with a mixture of red and green. Rayleigh also studied auditory detection. He established that auditory localization is due to the binaural ratio of intensities, as well as other conditions of auditory localization. Later (1907), he added the theory ("phase theory") that with low tones phase relation, detectable through beats, allows auditory localization because intensity ratios are no longer (in comparison with higher tones) perceivable.

Biographic data:　DNB 1912–1921

[190]

WARD, JAMES

English psychologist
Rating: 24
Born: Kingston upon Hull, Yorkshire, January 27, 1843
Died: Cambridge, March 4, 1925
Highest degree: M.A. in philosophy, University of London, 1874
Positions: 1875–1925, University of Cambridge, fellow, lecturer, professor of mental philosophy

Ward continued the philosophical psychology tradition of Bain [138], but he was also influenced by Lotze [135], Brentano [176], and the evolutionary doctrine. While Ward was in favor of experimentation and even attempted to establish a laboratory at Cambridge, he was temperamentally not an experimentalist. His emphasis on the subject–object relationship and the activity of the subject is act–psychological in nature. Ward's mature views of psychology are found in his *Psychological Principles* (1918), but even at the appearance of the book Ward's views were anachronistic since, by being entirely philosophical, Ward failed to give account of the many advances that empirical psychology had been making. Ward's fame rested chiefly on the article on psychology that he had prepared for the ninth edition (1886) of the *Encyclopedia Britannica* (and revised for the eleventh edition of 1911), of which his *Psychological Principles* was an expanded version. The article was very influential, and to generations of Britannica users represented *the* view of what psychology was.

Biographic data: *DNB* 1922–1930; *EP* 8:277; *IESS* 16:472; W. R. Sorley, James Ward. *Mind*, 1925, 34, 273–279; F. C. Bartlett, James Ward. *American Journal of Psychology*, 1925, 36, 449–453

HOFFDING, HARALD

[191]

Danish philosopher
Rating: 24
Born: Copenhagen, March 11, 1843
Died: Copenhagen, July 2, 1931
Highest degree: Degree in theology, University of Copenhagen, 1865; Ph.D. in philosophy, University of Copenhagen, 1870

Although Höffding was a philosopher, his psychology was one "without soul," concerned with mental phenomena and their introspective investigation. Höffding was a determinist, and maintained the identity of the mental and the material. Mental elements (feeling, cognition, will) he regarded as abstractions rather than as elements in the Wundtian sense. Mental life, according to Höffding, has a passive and an active side. The active aspect is the synthesizing aspect. One form of its manifestation is the law of relativity which states that the existence and qualities of a sensation depend on its relation to other sensations from its very beginning. Höffding wrote the first psychological text in the Danish language in 1882 (English translation, *Outlines of Psychology*, 1892). It saw many editions and was translated into many other languages.

Biographic data: *EP* 4:48; *HPA* 2:196

TARDE, GABRIEL

[192]

French sociologist
Rating: 24
Born: Sarlat, Dordogne, March 12, 1843

Died: Paris, May 13, 1904
Highest degree: Law degree from University of Paris, 1869
Positions: 1900, professor of modern philosophy, Collège de France

Tarde, distinguished as a philosopher, psychologist, sociologist, and criminologist, pioneered in social psychology. His most important book, *The Laws of Imitation,* was published in 1890, and its English translation appeared in 1903, five years before McDougall's [329] *An Introduction to Social Psychology.* Tarde's theory of imitation and his study of crowd psychology (*Opinion and the Crowd,* 1901) and of the psychology of economic behavior (*Economic Psychology,* 1902) make him one of the founders of social psychology. Tarde saw imitation as the fashioner of all social interaction, although he estimated that only one person in a hundred would be inventive enough to serve as model for imitation. Society, nevertheless, is a group of people who imitate each other. The psychological processes underlying social and historic progress are repetition, opposition, and adaptation. Since inventions differ in the degree to which they are imitated (repeated) and the manner of imitation, opposition arises between different imitations as well as between tradition and innovation in culture. This leads to a resolution or adaptation, which is an invention in its own right and subject to imitation. These Hegelian dialectic cycles keep repeating themselves endlessly.

Biographic data: *IESS* 15:509; S. M. Wilson, Pioneers in criminology: I. Gabriel Tarde. *Journal of Criminal Law and Criminology*, 1954, 45, 3–11

[193]

GOLGI, CAMILLO

Italian histologist, neurologist, and pathologist
Rating: 14
Born: Cortona, Tuscany, July 7, 1843
Died: Pavia, January 21, 1926
Highest degree: M.D., University of Pavia, 1865
Positions, honors: 1875-1926, University of Pavia; Nobel prize in physiology and medicine, 1906

In 1873, Golgi used silver nitrate to stain nerve cells, which was a cornerstone in the study of the nervous system. He eventually developed a theory of the nervous system as a network formed by the axons and the dendrites. His studies of the nervous system were important enough to have several of its structures named after him, such as the *Golgi apparatus*. Golgi gave the first complete description (in 1880) and his name to the nerve endings in tendons, near the points of attachment for muscles (*Golgi tendon organ or Golgi spindle*), whose stimulation informs the organism concerning the position of its limbs. The *Golgi–Mazzoni corpuscle* is assumed to mediate pressure sensations. Golgi's work of importance to sensory psychology is described in his *Untersuchungen über den feineren Bau des centralen und peripherischen Nervensystems* (1894; published in Italian, 1885).

Biographic data: *DSB* 5:459

AVENARIUS, RICHARD HEINRICH LUDWIG [194]

German philosopher
Rating: **23**
Born: Paris, France, November 19, 1843
Died: Zürich, Switzerland, August 18, 1896
Highest degree: Ph.D. in philosophy, University of Leipzig, 1876
Positions: 1876, University of Leipzig; 1877, University of Zürich

Avenarius developed an epistemology (empiriocriticism) that influenced systematic thinking in psychology. It was essentially the same as Mach's [174], but Avenarius developed it independently. It is contained in his only important work, the two-volume *Kritik der reinen Erfahrung* (1888–1890). Avenarius's "System C" is a bodily system that is essential for the mind. Statements of experience (E-values) depend on System C, which in turn is affected by external stimuli or R-values. A constant process of equilibration between catabolism and anabolism occurs in System C, tending toward a state of vital balance along a course of "vital series." Two kinds of vital series are distinguished by Avenarius: independent series, or physical changes, and dependent series which parallel the former and depend on them. The latter are psychological in nature. The terms "independent" and "dependent" to signify physical and psychological facts are found later in Külpe [265] and Titchener [294]. Avenarius denied there was any difference between inner and outer experience, and substituted for them pure experience as the single fact of experience. Lenin [318], who opted for naive realism, criticized empiriocriticism, holding that the objective world exists independently of any experiencing entities and is the basis of all knowledge.

Biographic data: *EP* 1:218

[195]

EMMERT, EMIL

Swiss ophthalmologist
Rating: 17
Born: 1844
Died: 1911

In an 1881 article, Emmert formulated the following law: if l is the linear size of an object, d its distance from the observer, L the linear size of the object's afterimage, and D the distance between the observer and the surface on which the afterimage is seen, then $l/L = d/D$. This formulation was later named Emmert's law. Although Emmert wrote several books on vision (*Die Organe des Sehens der verschiedenen Thierkreisen,* 1872; *Uber funktionelle Störungen des menschlichen Auges,* 1876; *Uber Refraktionsund Accomodationsverhältnisse des menschlichen Auges,* 1876; *Auge und Schädel,* 1880), the *law of afterimage size* is his one lasting contribution to psychology.

Biographic data: None readily available

[196]

NIETZSCHE, FRIEDRICH WILHELM

German philosopher
Rating: 20
Born: Röcken, Saxony, October 15, 1844
Died: Weimar, Thuringia, August 25, 1900
Highest degree: Ph.D in classical philology, University of Leipzig, 1869
Positions: 1869–1879, University of Basel, teaching classical philology

Nietzche inspired many famous writers, poets, philosophers, and psychologists in Germany and France, although not in the

English-speaking countries. Freud [224] admired Nietzche for his psychological insights, and in the instinct theory of Freud's may be found ideas very similar to those of Nietzsche. Nietzsche saw the principal human motives not in thought and reason but in instincts and drives. Man tries to hide his nonrational nature by inventing a system of rational motives and considering such motives as primary. The "real" man is man with untamed drives, and consciousness and its acts are in the service of the drives. To see the real man, the mask of rationality must be removed. The European man deceives himself in that he considers "facts of consciousness" as the first givens. The drives are unconscious, and the emphasis on consciousness leads man astray. In another way, Nietzsche anticipated the recent emergence of a "third force" in psychology by voicing extreme criticism of the atomistic approach to the psyche shown by the experimental psychologists and by calling for a psychology "in the grand style" that would consider the entirety of man's psyche. He was convinced that psychology should consider the will to power as the primary motive and all other motives as derivations from it.

Biographic data: *EP* 5:504; G. Bianquis, "Nietzsche, sa vie et sa pensée." *Journal de psychologie*, 1932, 29,146–153

PECKHAM, GEORGE WILLIAMS

[197]

American biologist
Rating: 12
Born: Albany, New York, March 23, 1845
Died: Milwaukee, Wisconsin, January 10, 1914
Highest degree: M.D., University of Michigan, 1881

Peckham never held any university positions. He was a high school teacher and principal who contributed to psychology by way of his pioneer observations of animal behavior. He was interested mainly in spiders and wasps, and wrote a number of papers on them, such as an 1887 paper on the intelligence of spiders. A book, *On the Instincts and Habits of Solitary Wasps* (1898), that Peckham wrote with his wife, E. A. Peckham, was his main work and his main contribution to comparative psychology.

Biographic data: *NCAB* 12:346

EXNER, SIGMUND

Austrian physiologist
Rating: 18
Born: Vienna, April 5, 1846
Died: Vienna, February 5, 1926
Highest degree: M.D., University of Vienna, 1870
Positions, honors: 1870–1926, University of Vienna; editorial work for *Zeitschrift für Psychologie;* three honorary doctorates

Besides physiological work that has no direct implications for psychology, Exner did notable work on adaptation to hue (which supported the Young-Helmholtz theory of color vision), rate–threshold for pitch (or the continuum of noises and tones), and apparent movement. Exner named (in 1873) the *reaction time experiment*, and knew that it was affected by the subject's motivation. He also worked on the physiology of the senses, brain localization, illusions, color contrast, and the orientation of birds in flight. Exner wrote numerous papers. Of his books the following are relevant to psychology: *Die Localisation der Funktionen in der Grosshirnrinde des Menschen* (1881), *Die Physiologie der facettierten Augen von Krebsen und Insecten* (1891), *and Entwurf zu einer physiologischen Erklärung der psychischen Erscheinungen* (1894).

Biographic data: *World Who's Who in Science*, 1968, p. 538

ORTH, JOHANNES

German pathological anatomist
Rating: 13
Born: Wallmerod, Hessen-Nassau, January 14, 1847
Died: Berlin, January 13, 1923
Highest degree: M.D. University of Berlin, 1871
Positions: 1873, Wirchow Institute, Berlin; 1878, University of Göttingen; 1902, Pathological Institute, Berlin, director and professor of pathology

In 1901, Orth wrote a paper (with A. Mayer) on the qualitative nature of association that launched the writings from the Würzburg school of psychology. Orth stressed the importance of *Bewusstseinslagen* or conscious attitudes which, in addition to images and sensations, determine thinking. These, according to Orth, are imageless feelings. *Gefühl und Bewusstseinslage* (1903) was another contribution of Orth's to the body of writings form the Würzburg school.

Biographic data: Enciclopedia universal ilustrada, vol. 40

FLECHSIG, PAUL EMIL [200]

German neuranatomist and neurologist
Rating: 13
Born: Zwickau, Saxony, June 29, 1847
Died: Leipzig, July 22, 1929
Highest degree: M.D., University of Leipzig, 1870
Positions, honors: 1872–1921, University of Leipzig; two honorary doctorates

Flechsig originated the ontogenetic method of studying the structure of the central nervous system. By following the myelinization process in axons, he was able to isolate and identify functions of nerve tracts and of cortical projection areas. Based on this technique, Flechsig prepared a map of cortical localization. He distinguished between sensory projection areas and association areas of the cortex on the basis of their rates of maturation (myelinization). While the sensory projection system matures prenatally, the association system matures after birth and underlies the higher intellectual functions. Flechsig published about fifty titles. Those of importance to psychology are *Plan des menschlichen Gehirns* (1883), *Die Lokalisation der geistigen Vorgänge* (1896), and *Gehirn und Seele* (1896).

Biographic data: DSB 5:26; P. E. Flechsig. *Meine myelogenetische Hirnlehre,* 1927; R. A. Pfeifer, Paul Emil Flechsig. *Schweizerisches Archiv für Neurologie und Psychiatrie,* 1930, 26

LADD-FRANKLIN CHRISTINE [201]

American psychologist
Rating: 22
Born: Windsor, Connecticut, December 1, 1847
Died: New York, New York, March 5, 1930

Highest degree: Ph.D. in mathematics, Johns Hopkins University, 1926 (studied there between 1878 and 1882)

Positions, honors: 1904–1909, Johns Hopkins University, teaching logic and psychology; 1910–1930, Columbia University; honorary LL.D., Vassar College, 1887

Ladd-Franklin's interest in mathematics extended to the investigation of the *horopter* in 1886, which led to the study of color vision. Her work between 1891 and 1892 in Georg Müller's [208] laboratory at Göttingen and in Helmholtz's [143] laboratory at Berlin led her to develop a new theory of color vision, for which she is best known. In a paper published in 1892, Ladd-Franklin developed Hering's [167] hypothesis that the red-green visual substance was a later evolutionary development than the blue-yellow substance. Ladd-Franklin's theory was that black-white vision was the most primitive form of color vision, that white became differentiated into blue-yellow vision, and that later still in the evolutionary history, yellow differentiated into red-green vision. This differentiation she thought was represented in the decomposition products of a retinal color molecule. Red, green, and blue are fundamental colors. The simple colors are those that can be obtained by backtracking the evolutionary steps, for instance, yellow, which results from red and green. Other colors, such as purple, are complex colors. Much later Ladd-Franklin published a book on color vision, *Colour and Colour Theories* (1929).

Biographic data: NCAB 26:422, B:287; *Notable American Women 1607–1950*, 1971, vol. 2

[202]   **STUMPF, CARL**

German psychologist

Rating: 27

Born: Wiesentheid, Bavaria, April 21, 1848

Died: Berlin, December 25, 1936

Highest degree: Ph.D. in philosophy, University of Göttingen, 1868

Positions: 1870, University of Göttingen, 1873, University of Würzburg; 1879, University of Prague; 1884, University of Halle; 1889, University of Munich; 1894–1921, University of Berlin; joint president, International Congress of Psychology, 1896

Stumpf's most important work was on the psychology of music, but his first psychological book was on the origin of spatial perception, *Uber den psychologischen Ursprung der Raumvorstellung* (1873). It set forth a nativistic, nonexperimental theory that was related to that of his teacher, Lotze [135]. In 1875, Stumpf's early interest in music took a scientific form: he began to do experiments in the psychology of music and to write *Tonpsychologie*, his major contribution to psychology. Its first volume appeared in 1883, the second in 1890. In the second volume may be found the results of his important experimental investigations of tonal fusion. At Berlin University, Stumpf's laboratory eventually expanded into an institute. He published extensively on audition and music and was active in many other psychological projects, including the founding of a Verein für Kinderpsychologie. He investigated a child musical prodigy and a mind-reading horse, and established an archive of primitive music, Das phonographische Archiv, in 1900. The journal, *Beiträge zur Akustik und Musikwissenschaft,* was founded by Stumpf in 1898.

While Stumpf is remembered for his contributions in the narrower area of the psychology of tone and music, he also influenced the development of psychology systematically. As the incumbent of the most prestigious chair in psychology in Germany, Stumpf wrote two theoretical papers that placed the stamp of approval on the psychology of Brentano [176], whom Stumpf had accepted during his stay at the University of Würzburg. There was an impress of phenomenology on the Berlin laboratory, and Schumann [273], Köhler [447], and Koffka [438] of Gestalt psychological fame were Stumpf's students.

Biographic data: EP 8:28; *HPA* 1:389; *IESS* 15:350; II. S. Langfeld, Carl Stumpf. *American Journal of Psychology,* 1937, 49, 316–320; C. A. Ruckmick, Carl Stumpf. *Psychological Bulletin*, 1937, 34, 187–190; K. Lewin, Carl Stumpf. *Psychological Review*, 1937, 44, 189–194; M. Nadoleczny, Death of Carl Stumpf. *Journal of Speech Disorders*, 1938, 3, 76–80

ROMANES, GEORGE JOHN

[203]

English biologist
Rating: 25
Born: Kingston, Ontario, Canada, May 20, 1848
Died: Oxford, England. May 23, 1894

Highest degree: M.A., Oxford University, 1873
Positions, honors: 1886–1890, University of Edinburgh; 1888–1891, Royal Institution, Fullerian professor of physiology; LL.D., University of Aberdeen, 1882

In 1882, twenty-four years after the appearance of Darwin's [127] *Origin of Species,* Romanes wrote what is often considered to be the first text of comparative psychology, *Animal Intelligence.* (Hermann Reimarus had written a book on animal instincts in the 18th century.) In writing this book, Romanes's aim was to supply evidence for Darwin's theory by showing continuity between the mental processes of man and animals, especially regarding the presence, to different degrees, of reason in animals. To Romanes, comparative psychology meant the comparison of mental structures of organisms.

Romanes collected all available evidence on animals, from molluscs, through insects, to fishes and mammals, much of it supplied by pet owners, zoo keepers, and other individuals who dealt with animals. Romanes's contribution was to collect the material and to systematize it. The evidence was largely anecdotal, and Romanes did not avoid anthropomorphization by attributing, for instance, reason to animals where a simpler explanation in terms of instinct or habit would have been more appropriate. It was a direct result of Romanes's premise that psychology is the study of the mind, one's own mind, and that with animals (as well as with other people) inferences concerning mental processes based on analogy had to be made. Romanes's book was one of the stimuli for Morgan [214] to state his canon concerning the interpretation of animal behavior. Romanes kept pursuing his original aim of proving Darwin's theory by writing *Scientific Evidence of Organic Evolution* (1882), *Evolution in Animals* (1883), and *Mental Evolution in Man* (1888), but his first book has been the most important one to comparative psychology.

Biographic data: *DNB* 49:177; *EP* 7:205; E. Romanes, *Life and Letters of George John Romanes,* 1896

[204]

FOREL, AUGUST HENRI

Swiss psychiatrist and entomologist
Rating: 12
Born: La Gracieuse, Vaud, September 1, 1848

Died: Yvorne, Vaud, July 27, 1931
Highest degree: M.D., University of Lausanne, 1872
Positions: 1873, University of Munich; 1877, Monaco, *Privat-dozen* in psychiatry; 1879–1906, director, Burghölzli Hospital, professor of psychiatry, University of Zurich

While Forel worked as a psychiatrist and wrote books and papers on psychological subjects (alcoholism, memory, hypnotism and suggestion, sex) as well as on legal psychiatry and brain anatomy (he discovered the origin of the auditory nerve), he is known principally as an entomologist who very thoroughly studied ants and their behavior for almost fifty years. His opus magnum, *Le monde sociale des fourmis du globe, comparé a celui de l'homme,* came out in five volumes between 1921 and 1923. He wrote his first book on the ants of Switzerland in 1874, however. It was followed by a number of others, some of which made a contribution to comparative psychology: *Expériences et re-marques critiques sur les sensations des insects* (1887), *Die psychischen Fähigkeiten der Ameisen* (1901), and *Das Sinnes-leben der Insekten* (1910).

Biographic data: *DSB* 5:73; A. H. Forel, *Rückblick auf mein Leben,* 1935

JODL, FRIEDRICH

German-Austrian philosopher
Rating: 11
Born: Munich, Germany, August 23, 1849
Died: Vienna, Austria, January 26, 1914
Highest degree: Ph.D. in philosophy, University of Munich, 1871
Positions: 1880, University of Munich; 1885, University of Prague; 1896, University of Vienna

Jodl was a positivist, influenced by J. S. Mill [125] and Auguste Comte [117]. He rejected metaphysical speculation and asserted that the basis of both science and philosophy is experience. The factual existence of things beyond phenomenal appearance is guaranteed by the existence of fellowmen. In psychology *(Lehrbuch der Psychologie,* two volumes, 1896–1897), Jodl presented empirical facts without any metaphysical assumptions. He held consciousness to be an act, not a substance. The soul is integrated experience. The mental and the physical are not two different things but a linguistic convention to designate the same reality. The psyche is the internal experiencing of neural processes. These views of Jodl's gave direction and support to scientific psychology during its first stage of development.

Biographic data: *EP* 4:278; W. Börner, *Friedrich Jodl*, 1911; M. Jodl, *Friedrich Jodl, sein Leben und Wirken*, 1920

[206]

PAVLOV, IVAN PETROVICH

Russian physiologist
Rating: 27
Born: Ryazan', September 14, 1849
Died: Leningrad, February 27, 1936
Highest degree: M.D., University of St. Petersburg, 1883
Positions: 1890, Military Medical Academy; 1924, director, Physiological Institute, Russian Academy of Science

Pavlov was fifty-five when he received the Nobel prize for his work on the physiology of digestion. Before 1900, he had made the observation that dogs salivated not only when food was given them but also to other stimuli that accompanied feeding. By 1901, he had given the name of *conditioned reflex* to the reflexive response to a stimulus that had previously not been able to elicit it but had acquired that power through association. Pavlov spent the next three decades studying conditioning.

From the basic form of conditioning in which an unconditioned (innately effective) stimulus was paired with a conditioned stimulus (bell, metronome, light flash) until the latter alone came to elicit the reflex (conditioned reflex) and its temporal variants (backward conditioning, trace conditioning), Pavlov progressed to the study of the extinction of the conditioned response with repeated presentation of the conditioned stimulus alone, stimulus generalization (response to other, similar stimuli), discrimination learning (response to only a determined value of the stimulus, but not to others), spontaneous recovery of the conditioned response after a period of extinction, higher-order conditioning, and other phenomena. Pavlov sought their explanation in terms of postulated excitatory and inhibitory processes in the nervous system, and not in terms of any mental processes.

While Pavlov did not perform any human conditioning experiments, he did make some theoretical statements concerning the organization of the more complex human behaviors that made it possible later to base the entire system of Soviet psychology on his teachings. Pavlov visualized both the unconditioned and the conditioned reflexes as effecting a connection between the organism and its enviroment. The nervous activity involved in forming the temporal (conditioned) connections he called higher nervous activity, to distinguish it from lower nervous system activity, which served to integrate the organism in Sherrington's [238] sense. Environmental stimuli significant to the organism's survival constituted the first signal system. A second signal system had developed in man, Pavlov held, as a result of his practical experience. This system does not represent reality directly but rather through its data in the nervous system, which are then called thought or, in their physical manifestation, language. Rubinshteĭn [459] was instrumental in translating these Pavlovian premises into a new basis for Soviet psychology.

In studying discrimination learning, Pavlov observed that when forced to make very difficult or impossible discriminations, animals would begin to act in unusual or "neurotic" ways. This coincided with Freud's [224] clinical observations that conflicts underlay all neuroses, and thus opened a way for the experimental study of behavioral abnormalities. Between 1916 and 1936 Pavlov also studied types of the nervous system in terms of the innate relative predominance of the excitatory and inhibitory processes. He was prompted in this by the observed individual differences in his laboratory animals' behavior. While Pavlov at first referred to different temperaments in his dogs and thought there were four such temperaments, he stopped referring to behavior after 1927 and from then on considered only the physiological properties of the nervous system. The fourfold classification of behaviors was continued, however, by Soviet psychologists, especially since Pavlov had at one time described them using the names of the Galenic temperaments. Present-day Soviet personality theory is based on Pavlov's classification of nervous systems, as elaborated by his own students who survived him. Pavlov wrote numerous papers, but only a few books, such as *Conditioned Reflexes* (English translation, 1927) and *Lectures on Conditioned Reflexes* (English translation of 3d edition, 1928).

Pavlov had a rather pessimistic view of psychology, and tried to avoid making any mentalistic, subjective, or "psychological" references with regard to conditioning. Because of his own insistence that his work was physiology and not psychology, his influence on Russian psychology became significant only after 1950 as the result of an official move to "pavlovianize" science. Nevertheless, conditioning as the simplest kind of learning was one of the cornerstones on which the school of behaviorism was built, and its study and application (as in the conditioning therapies) by Pavlov's own numerous coworkers and students, as well as psychologists throughout the world, has become a substantial portion of the psychological edifice.

Biographic data: *EP* 6:61; *IESS* 11:480; I. Pavlov, Autobiography, in *Selected Works,* 1955, pp. 41–44; A. V. Hill, A tribute to Pavlov. *Science*, 1936, 83, 351–353; M. J. Sereisky, Ivan Petrovich Pavlov. *Character and Personality*, 1936, 4, 344–348; H. K. Wells, *Ivan Petrovich Pavlov*, 1956; B. P. Babkin, *Pavlov, a Biography*, 1951

[207]

EBBINGHAUS, HERMANN

German psychologist
Rating: 27
Born: Barmen (now part of Wuppertal), North Rhine-Westphalia, January 24, 1850
Died: Halle, February 26, 1909
Highest degree: Ph.D. in philosophy, University of Bonn, 1873
Positions: 1880–1893, University of Berlin; 1894, University of Breslau; 1905, University of Halle

After obtaining his Ph.D., Ebbinghaus studied independently for seven years. It was during this time that he came across a copy of Fechner's [120] *Elements of Psychophysics* and decided to apply the scientific method to the study of processes "higher" than sensation. The idea that the higher process should be memory Ebbinghaus got from the British associationists, as well as the idea that repetition, or frequency of association, should be the measure of memory. The method that Ebbinghaus used to study memory was his own invention. To avoid preestablished associations of ordinary verbal materials, Ebbinghaus devised some 2,300 consonant-vowel-consonant combinations or nonsense syllables. Using himself as the sole subject, Ebbinghaus learned lists of nonsense syllables (as well as poetry) to mastery, and recorded the amounts retained, or the trials necessary for relearning, after a passage of time. The nonsense syllables, the mastery method, and the savings method are still standard methodology in human learning laboratories today.

In 1885, Ebbinghaus published the classic monograph *Über das Gedächtnis* (English translation, *Memory*, 1913) which included, among other things, the famous *forgetting curve.*

Ebbinghaus had launched the scientific study of learning and memory entirely on his own and with a high degree of originality. He had done it even before opening the psychological laboratory at the University of Berlin in 1886. Ebbinghaus's ability to control sources of error and to quantify his results precisely was such that his work is still quoted today as valid research, rather than just because of its historical interest. To publish work emanating from places other than Wundt's [161] Leipzig laboratory, Ebbinghaus and A. König [225] founded the *Zeitschrift für Psychologie und Physiologie der Sinnersorgane* in 1890. After this, Ebbinghaus began to study vision (he published a color vision theory in 1893), content to let others, notably Georg Müller, [208] develop the breakthrough of experimental psychology into the area of the higher mental processes.

At Breslau, Ebbinghaus established another laboratory (in 1894), and published (in 1897) a new method for testing the mental ability of school children, the "Ebbinghaus completion test," which is still used. He thus made an original contribution to the study of another higher mental process at the same time Binet [236] was developing his mental test. In 1897, Ebbinghaus published the first volume of a highly successful textbook of psychology, *Grundzüge der Psychologie,* which saw three editions by 1911. In it (the 1902 edition) appear Ebbinghaus's further contributions to psychology, such as the first modern version of the double color pyramid, a standard graphic representation of the phenomenology of color perception. Ebbinghaus influenced his contemporaries by his personality and style, however, not by his systematic views or publications. Of lasting importance to psychology, therefore, is solely his work on human memory.

Biographic data: E. R. Jaensch, Hermann Ebbinghaus. *Zeitschrift für Psychologie*, 1909, **51**, i-vii; R. S. Woodworth, Hermann Ebbinghaus. *Journal of Philosophy, Psychology, and Scientific Methods*, 1909, **6**, 253–256; D. Shakov, Hermann Ebbinghaus. *American Journal of Psychology*, 1930, **42**, 505–518

MULLER, GEORG ELIAS [208]

German psychologist
Rating: 26
Born: Grimma, Saxony, July 20, 1850
Died: Göttingen, December 23, 1934
Highest degree: Ph.D. in philosophy, University of Göttingen, 1873

Positions:, 1876, University of Göttingen; 1880, University of Czernowitz; 1881–1921, University of Göttingen.

Müller's doctoral dissertation was the first empirical study of attention, and it was extensively cited by others, decades later. Müller next turned to psychophysics, and presented some new ideas on psychophysical measurement in his 1876 *Habilitationsschrift*. In an article published the following year he proposed the new psychophysical method of constant stimuli. The Müller-*Urban weights,* as they came to be known later, were to be used to find the ogive that best fits the data obtained by the method of constant stimuli and from which the difference threshold is determined. At Fechner's [120] death, Müller became the leading psychophysicist. Müller's laboratory at Göttingen, which he founded in 1881, was second only to Wundt's [161] laboratory at Leipzig.

The psychophysics of vision and memory were the two areas that Müller continued to work in for the rest of his life. *Zur Analyse der Unterschiedsempfindlichkeit* (1899) is a classic in psychophysics. Müller's theory of color vision is also well known. It incorporated Hering's [167] theory but with the difference that Müller postulated a cortical gray from which all color sensations differ, rather than absence of vision when the black-white, red-green, and blue-yellow processes are in an equilibrium. Müller published four important papers on vision in the 1890s. The last summary of his views on psychophysics was his 1903 book, *Gesichtspunkte und Tatsachen der psychophysischen Methodik*. His interest in color and vision continued, and only four years before his death he completed the two volumes of *Uber die Farbenempfindung: psychophysische Untersuchungen* (1930).

After Ebbinghaus [207] published his work on memory, Müller began studying learning. He worked out the "method of right associates," and his student Jost [352] developed a law concerning the strength of associations. While using Ebbinghaus's method of study, Müller added the introspective reports of the subjects and found that simple association by contiguity did not account for all that went on in learning, and that the learner's organizational activity, preparatory set (*Anlage*), and other internal processes affected learning. Müller's studies thus anticipated the findings of the Würzburg psychologists of the imageless thought school. On the technical side, Müller and Schumann [273] introduced the use of the memory drum in learning experiments, a device still in use today. Müller's experimental work on memory is brought together in the three volumes of *Zur Analyse der*

Gedächtnistätigkeit und des Vorstellungsverlaufes (1911, 1913, 1917).

Müller was more clearly a pure psychologist than Wundt or Stumpf [202], but he did not produce any systematic theoretical statement in book form. His Göttigen laboratory, like Wundt's laboratory at Leipzig, did become an institution producing many doctorates and individuals who were later to become well known. At a time when psychology as an experimental science was getting started, Müller and his students exercised almost as great an influence as did Wundt.

Biographic data: IESS 10:523; D. Katz, Georg Elias Müller. *Acta Psychologica*, 1935, 1, 234–240; D. Katz, Georg Elias Müller. *Psychological Bulletin*, 1935, 32, 377–380; E. G. Boring, Georg Elias Müller. *American Journal of Psychology*, 1935, 47, 344–348; O. Kroh, Georg Elias Müller, ein Nachruf. *Zeitschrift für Psychologie*, 1935, 134, 150–190

RICHET, CHARLES ROBERT [209]

French physiologist
Rating: 17
Born: Paris, August 26, 1850
Died: Paris, December 4, 1935
Highest degree: M.D., University of Paris, 1877
Positions, honors: 1877, Collège de France; 1877–1927, University of Paris; founder and first president, Institut Métaphysique International; 1913 Nobel prize (for work on hypersensitivity to foreign proteins)

Richet had manifold interests, within and outside of science. To French psychology he is important because of an 1875 article in which he made a positive evaluation of hypnotism and certified it to be a genuine phenomenon. A revival of interest in hypnotism started, and in 1878 Charcot [152] was already demonstrating it. Throughout his career Richet was engaged in various psychological and parapsychological studies, publishing a number of volumes along the way: *Recherches expérimentales et cliniques sur la sensibilité* (1877), *Les poisons de l'intelligence* (1877), *L'homme stupide* (1919), *Traité de metapsychique* (1923), *Le savant* (1923), *L'homme impuissant* (1927)

Biographic data: *Enciclopedia italiana*, vol. 29

ERDMANN, BENNO

German philosopher and psychologist
Rating: 12
Born: Guhren near Glogau, Silesia, May 30, 1851
Died: Berlin, June 7, 1921
Highest degree: Ph.D. in philosophy, University of Berlin, 1873
Positions: 1876, University of Berlin; 1878, University of Kiel; 1884, University of Breslau; 1890, University of Halle; 1898, University of Bonn; 1909, University of Berlin

As a psychologist, Erdmann was interested in thinking. He distinguished between thinking ("hypological thinking"), imagination ("discursive thinking"), and fantasy ("intuitive thinking"). Logic he held to be the norms of thinking, and that, for this reason, its problems cannot be resolved through experimental psychology. Experimental psychology cannot be ignored, however, and logic must maintain close contact with it. On the subject of thinking Erdmann wrote three books: *Umriss zur Psychologie des Denkens* (1900, 2d edition, 1908), *Die Funktionen der Phantasie im wissenschaftlinchen Denken* (1913), and *Grundzüge der Reproduktionspsychologie* (1920).

Biographic data: R. Dodge, Benno Erdmann. *American Journal of Psychology*, 1922, 33, 155–156

LIPPS, THEODOR

German psychologist
Rating: 23
Born: Wallhalben, Rhineland-Palatinate, July 28, 1851
Died: Munich, October 17, 1914
Highest degree: Ph.D. in psychology, University of Leipzig
Positions: 1877, University of Bonn; 1890, University of Breslau; 1894, University of Munich

Although Lipps was a student of Wundt's [161] and stated that the subject matter of psychology was content, he may also be counted as belonging to the Austrian act school, particularly because of his emphasis on empathy, which is an act. Lipps postulated that consciousness is a function of the interaction of previous experiences, which are unconscious, and present experiences (apperception). Mind is the totality of these past experiences, and as such determines the way in which present stimulation is experienced, organized, and retained.

Lipps is best known for his *empathy theory and aesthetics* (*Raumaesthetik und geometrisch-optische Täuschungen,* 1897). According to this theory, the perceiver perceives the nature of an object when he feels like that object, or projects himself into the object. Lipps applied this theory both to aesthetics and the geometric illusions. A form is beautiful if it fulfills the function assigned it, as when the empathy felt for a column in a building that is too thin makes one feel the stress it experiences, creating thus a negative aesthetic impression. The vertical line in the vertical-horizontal illusion, for instance, is experienced as being longer because the upward direction of the vertical makes the observer feel like stretching up, and that feeling is projected unto the vertical line.

In addition to *Raumaesthetik,* Lipps's *Grundtatsachen des Seelenlebens* (1883) was also well known. He produced several other books and many articles and monographs, although few of them are experimental in nature because Lipps was not an experimentalist.

Biographic data: EP 4:485; G. Anschütz, Theodor Lipps. *Archiv für die gesamte Psychologie,* 1915, 34, 1–13; E. V. Aster, Theodor Lipps. *Zeitschrift für Psychologie,* 1915, 70, 429–433; [Anon.] *American Journal of Psychology,* 1915, 26, 160

MERCIER, DESIRE FELICIEN FRANCOIS JOSEPH [212]

Belgian philosopher
Rating: 13
Born: Braine-l'Allend, November 21, 1851
Died: Brussels, January 23, 1926
Highest degree: Ph.D. in philosphy and theology; University of Louvain, 1882
Positions: 1877, Malines Seminary; 1882, University of Louvain

In response to the call of Pope Leo XIII to revive Christian philosophy, Mercier became a leader in the 19th-century revival of Thomistic philosophy (Neothomism), including neothomistic psychology. He wrote an account of psychology from the Thomistic point of view, *Psychologie* (1892), and another psychological text, *Les origins de la psychologie contemporaine* (1897; English translation 1918), both of which appeared in several editions and were translated into other languages. At Louvain, Mercier familiarized himself with the "new" psychology that was coming from Germany, and established a psychological laboratory at that university in 1891. To organize it and direct its work, Mercier put a student of Wundt's [161], Armand Thiéry, in charge of it. While Mercier considered experimental psychology to be a natural science, separate from philosophy, and believed that rational psychology needed experimental psychology, he also believed that experimental psychology without rational psychology would become materialistic, mechanistic, and cease to be a separate science.

Biographic data: *EP* 5:277; J. A. Gade, *The Life of Cardinal Mercier*, 1934; H. Misiak and V. S. Sexton, *Catholics in Psychology,* 1954, pp. 34–52

[213]

FERE, CHARLES SAMSON

French psychiatrist
Rating: 18
Born: Auffay, Seine Maritime, 1852
Died: Paris, 1907
Highest degree: Dr. en médecine, University of Paris, 1882
Positions: Bicêtre hospital

Féré was an early collaborator of Binet's [236]. With Binet, he wrote two books, one on *Le magnétisme animal* (1886), which stressed the increased sensitivity to touch in hypnotized animals, and one on reasoning, *La psychologie du raisonnement* (1886). In 1885, Féré discovered the changes that take place in the conductance of the skin during emotional arousal. It was named the psychogalvanic reflex, and renamed the *galvanic skin response (GSR)* later. It has been measured in innumerable psychological studies, and is the central measure taken in the polygraph technique.

In connection with his studies of fatigue, Féré built the first ergograph. These studies were conducted by Féré in relation to his *doctrine of dynamogenesis,* presented in his 1887 book, *Sensation et mouvement.* The theory originated from Féré's observation that the strength of muscular contractions is increased by external stimuli, even apparently irrelevant stimuli, so that they seem to release energy within the organism. Féré wrote many books on medicine, psychopathology, and hypnotism. His *Pathologie des emotions* (1892) was translated into English in 1899

Biographic data: *Enciclopedia universal ilustrada,* vol. 23

MORGAN, CONWY LLOYD

[214]

English psychologist and biologist
Rating: 27
Born: London, February 6, 1852
Died: Hastings, Sussex, March 6, 1936
Highest degree: D.Sc., University of Bristol, 1910
Positions, honors: 1878–1883, lectureship in South Africa; 1884–1909, University College, Bristol, professor of zoology and geology, appointed professor of psychology and education in 1901; 1910–1919, professor emeritus; 1919–1936, lecturer at Clark University and Harvard University; honorary LL.D

Morgan was one of the pioneers in comparative psychology. He performed the first psychological experiments on animals outside a laboratory and reported them in his early books, such as *Animal Life and Intelligence* (1890–1891), *Introduction to Comparative Psychology* (1894), *Habit and Instinct* (1896), and *Animal Behavior* (1900). His best known book is the *Introduction*. In it, to counteract the tendency that existed then of attributing reason, foresight, and other human mental functions to animals, Morgan stated a principle, to be applied in interpreting an animal's behavior: "In no case may we interpret an action as the outcome of the exercise of a higher psychical faculty, if it can be interpreted as the outcome of the exercise of one which stands lower in the psychological scale." As a form of the more general scientific law of parsimony, the principle came to be known as *Lloyd Morgan's canon,* and served as a guideline in avoiding the anthropomorphization of animal behavior when it could be explained in terms of instinct or simple learned habits. Although Morgan believed that psychology's business was the study of the mind, and that in comparative psychology one should proceed by observing the behavior of animals, then drawing inferences about mental processes by analogy from one's own introspections, the very important difference between Morgan and Romanes [203], who held identical views, and other Darwinians, was that Morgan adhered to the canon of parsimonious interpretation of behavior.

Morgan's *doctrine of emergent evolution* (*Emergent Evolution*, 1923) stated that higher evolutionary stages emerged from lower ones by chance, whenever the necessary elements happened to come together in the necessary constellation. Consciousness, he thought, must have emerged by chance rather than by design. This view created considerable discussion among scientists from different fields.

Among Morgan's other books in comparative psychology and related areas may be mentioned *The Interpretation of Nature* (1905), *Instinct and Experience* (1912), *Life, Mind, and Spirit* (1926), *Mind at the Crossways* (1929), *The Animal Mind* (1930), and *The Emergence of Novelty* (1933).

Biographic data: DNB 1931–1940; HPA 2:237; IESS 10:495; G. C. Grindley, Obituary notice: Professor Conwy Lloyd Morgan. *British Journal of Psychology*, 1936, 27, 1–3

[215]

RAMON Y CAJAL, SANTIAGO

Spanish histologist
Rating: 25
Born: Petilla de Aragón, Navarre, May 1, 1852
Died: Madrid, October 17, 1934
Highest degree: M.D., University of Zaragoza, 1873
Positions, honors: 1875, University of Zaragoza; 1883, University of Valencia; 1887, University of Barcelona; 1892–1922, University of Madrid; 1906 Nobel prize in physiology and medicine (shared with Camillo Golgi [193])

Ramón y Cajal, often considered the greatest of all neuranatomists, studied and described all parts of the nervous system using the cell staining method newly developed by Golgi. He studied the microscopic structure of the nervous system, the neuroglial cells, and the degeneration and regeneration of neurons in great detail. His 1904 book, *Textura del sistema nervioso del hombre y los vertebrados,* contained 1,800 pages and 887 original illustrations, many of which are still being reproduced in textbooks. Ramón y Cajal identified the function of the synapse and of the dendrites, but his greatest achievement was the establishment of the neuron as the building block of the nervous system (1889). The formulation was of fundamental importance not only to neuranatomy but to physiological psychology as well.

Biographical data: W. C. Gibson, Santiago Ramón y Cajal. *Annals of Medical History*, 1936, 8, 385–394; S. Ramón y Cajal, *Recollection of My Life*, 1937 (translation of *Recuerdo de mi vida*, 1901–1917); D. F. Cannon, *Explorer of the Human Brain: the Life of Santiago Ramón y Cajal*, 1949

VAIHINGER, HANS [216]

German philosopher
Rating: **11**
Born: Nehren, Württemberg, September 25, 1852
Died: Halle, Saxony-Anhalt, December 12, 1933
Highest degree: Ph.D. in philosophy, University of Tübingen, 1874
Positions: 1877, University of Strasbourg; 1884–1906, University of Halle

Vaihinger's name is mentioned in histories of psychology because a book that he wrote (*Die Philosophie des Als Ob,* 1911, English translation, *The Philosophy of "As If,"* 1925) influenced the development of Adler's [317] thinking. Vaihinger advanced the idea that while man may be striving to achieve goals or live by ideals that have no existence in reality, the mere striving for them and the pretense that they actually exist lends them some reality because they affect thereby his attitudes and behavior.

Biographic data: EP 8:221

FREY, MAXIMILIAN RUPPERT FRANZ VON [217]

German physiologist
Rating: **23**
Born: Salzburg, Austria, November 16, 1852
Died: Würzburg, Germany, January 25, 1932
Highest degree: M.D., University of Leipzig, 1877
Positions: 1882, University of Leipzig; 1898, University of Zurich; 1899, University of Würzburg

Frey is known for his authoritative work on haptic sensations. While practically nothing was known previously about the sensory physiology of the skin, Frey's papers, written between 1894 and 1897, provided textbook writers with the basic information. Frey confirmed the existence of sensory spots for warm, cold, and pressure; he established pain as an additional (fourth) haptic sense modality, and conducted quantitative studies relating stimulus characteristics and sensation. Frey discovered paradoxical cold, and that the nature of the stimulus for pressure is not simply force but tension of the area of the skin that is depressed. Frey found for each of the four haptic senses a specific end-organ in the skin, and invented two classical instruments for studying cutaneous sensitivity: the *limen-gauge* and the *stimulus-hair* or *hair aesthesiometer*. Frey wrote some fifty-two papers on the haptic system. Much of this information is collected in his *Vorlesungen über Physiologie* (1904), which was issued in three editions.

Biographic data: *DSB* 5:184; E. G. Boring, Max von Frey. *American Journal of Psychology*, 1932, 44, 584–586

[218]

MEINONG, ALEXIUS VON

Austrian philosopher
Rating: 24
Born: Lemberg (L'vov), Galicia, July 17, 1853
Died: Graz, Austria, November 27, 1920
Highest degree: Ph.D. in philosophy, University of Vienna, 1878
Positions: 1878, University of Vienna; 1882, University of Graz

Meinong was the leader of the Austrian school of psychology at the University of Graz. He was a philosopher, but contributed to theoretical psychology mainly in connection with the development of the school of form quality. Nevertheless, he established the first Austrian psychological laboratory at Graz in 1894 and was one of the editors of *Zeitschrift für Psychologie*. As a philosopher, Meinong attained celebrity with his *Gegenstandstheorie* or *object theory* which, stemming as it did from Brentano's philosophical psychology, had a psychological flavor. In this theory, as in Brentano's [176], mental states "intend" objects. They have two aspects, content and act, and may be classified into presentations, thought processes, emotions, and motives. The rest of the theory is concerned with different classes of mind-independent objects as a function of the type of mental act. In regard to the doctrine of form quality, Meinong's ideas did not differ substantially from those of Ehrenfels [250], who had formulated its basic propositions. Meinong introduced new terms for those used by Ehrenfels, however (*founding contents* for *Fundamente* and *founded contents* for form quality). The founding and founded contents together were complexions, of which there were two kinds: real complexions or perceptions and ideal complexions or concepts. Real complexions are determined primarily by stimulus characteristics whereas ideal complexions depend on the production process (*Produktionsvorgang*) that fuses sensory elements into unitary wholes, such as four straight lines of equal length into the unitary form of a square. Since Meinong was an important philosopher, his discussion of form quality helped to establish the school of form quality in psychology. Later, the Gestalt psychologists found much to criticize in Meinong's formulation.

Biographic data: *EP* 5:261; E. B. Titchener, Notes. *American Journal of Psychology*, 1921, 32,154; R. Schmidt, *Philosophie der Gegenwart in Selbstdarstellungen*, 1923, vol. 1, pp. 101–160

KRIES, JOHANNES VON [219]

German physiologist
Rating: 25
Born: Roggenhausen, West Prussia, October 6, 1853
Died: Freiburg-im-Breisgau, Baden-Württemberg, December 30, 1928
Highest degree: M.D., University of Leipzig
Positions: 1876, University of Berlin; 1877, University of Leipzig; 1880–1924, University of Freiburg

Kries's main contributions to psychology were in the area of the physiology of vision. Among these the most notable was his "duplicity" theory of vision (1894) that associated the rodlike cells of the retina to brightness discrimination and vision at reduced levels of illumination and the cone-shaped cells to daylight and color vision. Kries measured difference thresholds for hue, studied additive color mixture, color blindness and color weakness, identified and named *protanopia, deuteranopia, deuteranomalous trichromacy* and *protanomalous trichromacy*. He clarified the nature of color blindness and thereby reconciled the Hering and Young-Helmoltz theory concerning this phenomenon. Kries wrote a book on vision (*Die Gesichtsempfindungen und ihre*

Analyse, 1882), one on sensory physiology (*Allgemeine Sinnes-physiologie*, 1923), and sections on vision in books edited or compiled by others. He was also one of the first editors of the *Zeitschrift für Psychologie*.

Biographic data: E. von Skramlik, Johannes von Kries. *Zeitschrift für Sinnesphysiologie*, 1929, 60, 249–255

[220]

FLOURNOY, THEODORE

Swiss psychologist
Rating : 11
Born: Geneva, August 15, 1854
Died: Geneva, November 5, 1920
Highest degree: M.D., University of Strasbourg, 1878
Positions: 1908–1920, University of Geneva; president, Sixth International Congress of Psychology, 1909

Flournoy initiated scientific psychology in French-speaking Switzerland. With E. Claparède [342], he founded *Archives de psychologie* in 1901. In this journal he published many studies on different subjects. Flournoy also wrote several books on psychology, parapsychology, metaphysics, spiritualism, and religion: *Métaphysique et psychologie* (1890), *Des phénomènes de synopsie* (1893), *Les principes de la psychologie religieuse* (1903), *Esprits et mediums* (1911). The book that made him known was *Des Indes à la planète Mars: étude sur un cas de somnambulisme avec glossolalie* (1900), which was translated into English (*From India to the Planet Mars*) in the year it was published. It was a study of a bizarre case of dissociation, suggestion, and glossolaly, similar to that described by the Swiss psychiatrist C. G. Jung [358] in his doctoral dissertation in 1902.

Biographic data: E. B. Titchener, Notes. *American Journal of Psychology*, 1921, 32, 154

[221]

PRINCE, MORTON

American psychiatrist
Rating: 23
Born: Boston, Massachusetts, December 21, 1854

Died: Cambridge, Massachusetts, August 31, 1929

Highest degree: M.D., Harvard University, 1879

Positions: 1880–1902, various nonacademic medical appointments; 1902, Tufts University, professor of diseases of the nervous system; 1926, Harvard University, professor of abnormal and dynamic psychology; president and founder, American Psychopathological Association; president, American Neurological Association; editorial work for *American Journal of Psychology*, 1906–1929

One factor that turned Prince's interest from general practice to psychopathology was his wife's psychogenic symptoms. In the mid-1880s, Prince began to specialize in nervous and mental disorders, especially in unconscious phenomena and multiple personalities, along the lines of Janet [249] (*The Nature of Mind and Human Automatism,* 1885). He came across the famous case of Miss Beauchamp who showed five different personalities, and described it in one of his two best known books, *The Dissociation of a Personality* (1905). In it he also presented the concept of coconscious personalities. In a multiple personality one personality may function consciously and be the dominant one who sees, feels, and talks, while the other personality functions subconsciously and communicates indirectly, as through automatic writing. The coconscious personality is aware of the conscious personality, but the conscious personality knows nothing of the existence of the coconscious personality. The book was widely read. A year later Prince founded the *Journal of Abnormal Psychology*.

In 1910, Prince, along with Ribot [179], Janet, and Münsterberg [272], contributed to a famous symposium on subconscious phenomena. In 1913, Prince published another widely read book, *The Unconscious*. It described the scientific method in psychopathology, and distinguished clearly conscious and unconscious phenomena. It established Prince's reputation. While recognizing the importance of motivational factors in psychopathology, Prince did not join the psychoanalytic movement and was opposed to its speculative and symbolic aspects because they deviated from his ideal of scientific rigor and his goal of a marriage of clinical and academic psychology (*Clinical and Experimental Studies in Personality,* 1929). This goal Prince realized late in his life. Upon receiving his Harvard appointment and with money contributed by an anonymous donor, Prince proceeded to establish the Harvard Psychological Clinic in 1927. The donor had specified that the clinic should promote instruction and research in "abnormal and dynamic psychology." The term *dynamic psychology* appeared here for the first time in an official record and was incorporated in a psychology professor's (Prince's) title.

Biographic data: *NCAB* 25:313; M. Moore, Morton Prince, M.D. *Journal of Nervous and Mental Diseases,* 1938, 87, 701–710; H. A. Murray, Morton Prince: sketch of his life and work. *Journal of Abnormal and Social Psychology,* 1956, 52, 291–295

[222]   EWALD, ERNST JULIUS RICHARD

German physiologist
Rating: 17
Born: Berlin, February 14, 1855
Died: Konstanz, Baden-Württemberg, July 22, 1921
Education: Studied mathematics, physics, medicine, and physiology at University of Strasbourg, graduated in 1884
Positions: 1880–1921, University of Strasbourg; editorial work for *Zeitschrift für Psychologie und Physiologie der Sinnesorgane*

Ewald specialized in the physiology of the end organs and thus contributed to the understanding of sensation. He formulated (1899 and 1903) *the pressure-pattern theory of hearing.* He could make a demonstration of it because it was based on the observation that different tones produce different patterns in sand on plaques and membranes. Ewald postulated that for each combination of intensity and frequency there was a unique "acoustic image" which acted upon the basilar membrane, producing perception of the sound. Since the theory was less parsimonious than Helmholtz's [143], which assumed only that nerve fibers in the inner ear each resonate to a sound wave of the appropriate length, it did not prevail. Ewald also invented a "pneumatic hammer," a tiny cylinder and piston that could be used to stimulate directly the semicircular canals in experimental animals.

Biographic data: *World Who's Who in Science,* 1968

German psychiatrist
Rating: **27**
Born: Neustrelitz, Mecklenburg, February 15, 1856
Died: Munich, October 7, 1926
Highest degree: M.D., University of Leipzig, 1878
Positions: 1879, University of Munich; 1882, University of
    Leipzig; 1884, University of Tartu; 1890, University of Heidel-
    berg; 1903, University of Munich

Although Kraepelin's field was medicine, Wundt [161] was his
most revered teacher and influenced Kraepelin's work in psychiatry. Kraepelin applied psychology to psychiatry by extending
the use of the association experiment to psychiatric problems
(1895). He found that associations produced in states of fatigue
or alcoholic intoxication resemble those of psychotic patients in
that they are more superficial and determined by habit rather
than meaning. At Tartu, Kraepelin continued the work he had
begun in 1883 in Wundt's laboratory on psychopharmacology. It
allows the appellation of "father of psychopharmacology" to be
bestowed on him. Kraepelin tested the effects of ethyl alcohol,
morphine, and other substances on human behavior using
Wundt's experimental procedures.

Concerning the etiology of mental disorders, Kraepelin represented, and was instrumental in establishing, the organic view
point that stresses the importance of brain pathology. It was first
presented in his *Compendium der Psychiatrie* (1883). This work
was a major contribution to the development of psychiatry and
underlies the present-day classificatory system of mental disorders. Kraepelin presented a systematic classification of mental
disorders, introducing such terms as *manic-depressive psychosis,*
and *paranoia* in their present meaning. Kraepelin believed that,
since mental disorders were basically organic, a clear division of
disorders into categories was not only possible but that the course
of development of each disorder was predictable, even if it could
not be controlled. This led to the development of an interest in
the accurate description and classification in psychopathology.
Because of his contributions, Kraepelin is also known as the
"father of modern psychiatry."

Biographic data: *IESS* 8:449; W. Wirth, Emil Kraepelin zum
    Gedächtnis. *Archiv für die gesamte Psychologie,* 1927, 58,
    i–xxxii; E. Kahn, Emil Kraepelin. *American Journal of Psy-
    chiatry,* 1945, **113,** 289–294

FREUD, SIGMUND

Austrian psychoanalyst
Rating: 27
Born: Freiberg, Moravia, May 6, 1856
Died: London, England, September 23, 1939
Highest degree: M.D., University of Vienna, 1881
Positions: 1881–1938, University of Vienna, *Dozent* till 1901, then professor of neuropathology; in private practice in Vienna since 1882

As the founder of psychoanalysis, Freud contributed to psychological thought more than any other single individual in the 20th century. Freud began as a successful neurologist (he coined the term *agnosia*), associated himself with Joseph Breuer [185], who had been using hypnosis with hysteric patients, and began to use it himself. He found that hypnosis did not always work, however. A year spent studying with Charcot [152] gave him the idea that sexual problems may underlie hysteria. The study of one of Breuer's patients, Anna O., convinced him of this possibility, and in 1895 Freud and Breuer published *Studies in Hysteria*. The book contained many of the now classical concepts of psychoanalysis, such as defense, resistance, repression, and abreaction, and the psychoanalytical school of thought is often dated from it.

At about the same time Freud chanced upon the method of free association, and began to interpret his patients' dreams. Freud's greatest work was *Interpretation of Dreams*, published in 1900. The object of these techniques was to uncover the patient's unconscious motives as they manifested themselves in his speech, recovered memories, and dreams (*The Psychopathology of Everyday Life*, 1904). The role that Freud assigned the unconscious and unconscious motivation counts as his greatest contribution to psychology. His fame began to spread in the 1900's, when disciples also began to gather around him. In 1905, Freud published *Three Essays on the Theory of Sexuality*, which introduced the novel and startling idea that all children are born with a sexual drive. International recognition of Freud began when G. Stanley Hall [418] invited Freud and other psychoanalysts to the United States in 1909.

Although his most important disciples broke off their relationship with Freud a few years later, Freud's fame grew from here on as he elaborated his theory and kept publishing additional volumes on his theory of personality and psychosexual development. Like many of Freud's other notions, the idea that conscience is not implanted by God but develops through identification with a parent was an iconoclastic one, but it became accepted. Similarly, his view of infant sexuality destroyed the benevolent view of the child held since the time of Rousseau [53], but it did give parents finally a key to the understanding of the irrational behaviors of their offspring. The tripartite division of the psychological person (id, ego, superego), the oral, anal, and phallic stages of development and personality types, the Oedipus complex, libido, castration anxiety, and ego defense mechanisms are some of the ideas that are not only part of the vocabulary of the psychiatrist and the psychologist but the layman as well. In later years Freud's outlook widened, and psychoanalysis was applied to broad cultural phenomena, such as literature, religion, and civilization as such. *Beyond the Pleasure Principle* (1920), *The Future of an Illusion* (1928), *Civilization and Its Discontents* (1930), and *Moses and Monotheism* (1939) belong to this period of Freud's life. The standard edition of his collected works fills twenty-four volumes. What is in them has become part, not only of psychology's heritage, creating thousands of titles of research, observation, and theory, but of the heritage of Western culture.

Biographic data: *DSB* 5:171; *EP* 3:249; *IESS* 6:1; E. Jones, *The Life and Work of Sigmund Freud*, 1953–1957; S. Freud, An Autobiographical Study (in, e.g., *The Standard Edition of the Complete Psychological Works of Sigmund Freud*, 1959)

KONIG, ARTHUR · [225]

German physicist
Rating: 16
Born: Krefeld, North Rhine-Westphalia, September 13, 1856
Died: Berlin, October 26, 1901
Highest degree: Ph.D. in physics, University of Berlin, 1882
Positions: 1884, University of Berlin

In the 1800s and 1890s, König studied color vision. He measured changes in the Weber fraction for colors as a function of light intensity; established spectral mixtures (*König's color triangle*); showed brightness and sensitivity to be a joint function of wavelength and intensity (a generalization that brought brightness and the Purkinje phenomenon under the same heading); drew the first curves comparing color sensitivity of normal individuals and the color blind; defended the Young-Helmholtz theory of color vision; showed that total color blindness is blindness in the center of the retina; demonstrated that color confusion in red-blind and green-blind persons can be explained in terms of the Young-Helmholtz theory; and identified the role of the visual purple in the retinal rods. König published the second edition of Helmholtz's *Physiological Optics* after Helmholtz's [143] death, adding to it a 7,833-item bibliography on vision. He was a cofounder (1890) and editor, with Ebbinghaus [207], of *Zeitschrift für Psychologie und Physiologie der Sinnesorgane*.

Biographic data: *DSB* 7:457; H. Ebbinghaus and J. A. Barth, Arthur König. *Zeitschrift für Psychologie*, 1901, **27**, 145–147

[226]

BEKHTEREV, VLADIMIR MIKHAILOVICH

Russian psychiatrist and neuropathologist
Rating: 27
Born: Sorali, Vyatka province, January 20, 1857
Died: Moscow, December 24, 1927
Highest degree: M.D., Medical and Surgical Academy, St. Petersburg, 1881
Positions: 1884, postgraduate study with Charcot [152], Flechsig [200], and Wundt [161]; 1885, University of Kazan, psychiatry; 1894, Military Medical Academy, St. Petersburg, mental and nervous diseases; 1913, director, Psychoneurological Institute, St. Petersburg; 1918–1927, director, Brain Research Institute, Petrograd; 1927, scientist emeritus

Bekhterev contributed to the areas of neurophysiology, neuropathology, and the objective study of psychological phenomena. He studied the brain since 1883, demonstrating the control of vegetative functions by the thalamic regions and the existence of nerve centers that control the sympathetic nervous system. He also studied the reticular formation, the cerebellum, skin muscle centers, and demonstrated the existence of antagonistic nerve centers in the brain in 1895. Several brain structures are named in his honor.

Bekhterev published more than five hundred papers and books on neurology and psychiatry, some one hundred fifty of which are clinical publications. Significant among them are *Provodyashchie puti spinnogo i golovnogo mozga* (1893, 2d edition, 1896; translated into French and German as *The Nerve Currents in Brain and Spinal Cord*), *Osnovy ucheniya o funktsiyakh mozga*

(1903–1907, *Fundamentals of Brain Functioning*), *Funktsii nervnykh tsentrov* (1909, *The Functions of the Nervous Centers*), and *Obshchaya diagnostika bolezneĭ nervnoĭ sistemy* (1911–1915, *General Diagnosis of the Diseases of the Nervous System*). Bekhterev founded the first psychological laboratories in Russia, one at the University of Kazan in 1886 and another at St. Petersburg in 1895. He also founded a Psycho-neurological Institute in St. Petersburg in 1903 and two journals, the *Neurologicheskiĭ vestnik and Obzor psikhiatrii, nevropatologii i eksperimental'noĭ psikhologii*. The latter was the first journal ever to have the words "experimental psychology" in its title.

Bekhterev's psychology was strictly objective and based on the concept of reflex. In distinction from Pavlov [206], Bekhterev worked with both animals and humans. He used conditioned associative motor responses with humans in the belief that the salivary response was less objective than motor responses. Bekhterev first designated his view of psychology as objective psychology (*Ob"ektivnaya psikhologiya*, 1910, German and French translations in 1913), then coined the term reflexology (*Obshchie osnovy refleksologii cheloveka*, 1917: English translation, *General Principles of Human Reflexology*, 1932). Bekhterev argued against the use of introspection, mentalistic terms, and for an objective approach to psychological phenomena. He denied the reality of psychic processes as well as the need for psychology as an independent science, since all psychic processes were to be considered complexes of "associative reflexes," as he called the conditioned reflexes. Bekhterev also extended his conceptualization of psychology of the single individual to societal groups (*Kollektivnaya refleksologiya*, 1921).

Biographic data: *DSB* 1:579; *IESS* 2:45–47; V. P. Osipov, *Bekhterev. Zhizn' i deyatel'nost'*, 1947; N. I. Kasatkin, Vladimir Mikhaĭlovich Bekhterev. *Zhurnal vyssheĭ nervnoĭ deyatel'nosti*, 1957, 7, 148–156

MULLER-LYER, FRANZ (CARL) [227]

German psychiatrist, philosopher, psychologist, and sociologist
Rating: 19
Born: Baden-Baden, February 5, 1857
Died: Munich, October 29, 1916
Highest degree: M.D., University of Strasbourg, 1880
Positions: 1881–1883, University of Strasbourg, assistant director, psychiatric clinic; 1888, private practice in Munich

Between 1884 and 1888 Müller-Lyer studied psychology and sociology at the universities of Berlin, Vienna, Paris, and London. He is best known for his sociological writings. He established a sociological and cultural philosophical system based on an analysis of the social causes of suffering. It had many adherents. In psychology, Müller-Lyer wrote two monographs on psychophysics (*Physiologische Studien über Psychophysik*, 1886; *Psychophysische Untersuchungen*, 1889), but his name is firmly associated with a simple geometric illusion, first presented in 1889 ("Optische Urteiltäuschungen." *Archiv für Physiologie*, suppl. edition, 1889, pp. 263–270), rather than psychophysics or psychiatry. The *Müller-Lyer illusion* may be considered *the* geometric illusion since the largest number of studies by far have been done on it, and most theories of geometric illusions attempt to explain at least the Müller-Lyer illusion or take it to represent all other geometric illusions.

Biographic data: *Encyclopedia of the Social Sciences*, 1933, vol. 11, p. 83

[228]

COUE, EMILE

French hypnotist
Rating: 18
Born: Troyes, Aube, February 26, 1857
Died: Nancy, July 2, 1926
Education: Graduated in pharmacy and worked as a druggist from 1882 to 1901

Coué followed the apothecary trade for twenty-eight years, then became interested in suggestion and hypnotism (in 1901) and took up their study with Liébeault [145] and Bernheim [181] at Nancy. In 1910, he opened his own clinic at Nancy. Unlike other hypnotists, Coué taught his clients self-help. Self-help was accomplished through self-suggestion (he is thought to have coined the term *auto-suggestion*), as when a client was told to repeat to himself formulas expressing faith in self-improvement, such as "Every day in every way I am getting better and better." Coué presumed to cure even organic disorders by the power of imagination. He became famous, and went on lecture tours in England and the United States. He published a number of books, among them *Self-mastery through Conscious Autosuggestion* (1922) and *My System* (1923).

Biographic data: *Encyclopedia Britannica*, vol. 6

PEARSON, KARL

English mathematician
Rating: 27
Born: London, March 27, 1857
Died: London, April 27, 1936
Education: Studied mathematics, engineering, and law, among other subjects, at King's College, Cambridge, graduated in 1879
Positions, honors: 1884–1933, University College, London, since 1911 director of Department of Applied Statistics and Sir Francis Galton professor of eugenics; founder (1901) and editor of *Biometrika* (1902–1936); editor of *The Annals of Eugenics*, 1925–1936; honorary LL.D., University of St. Andrews, D.Sc., University of London; Darwin medal of Royal Society, 1898

Pearson was one of the fathers of modern statistics. Around 1890 he acquired an interest in heredity, eugenics, and biological problems in general and in the application of statistics to such problems. His aim was to verify Darwin's [127] evolutionary theory. He developed a number of statistical treatments of biological data that are among the most widely used ones today. Pearson was a student, companion, and biographer of Sir Francis Galton [144], and with the latter's encouragement developed the mathematical formulation of the idea of correlation that Galton had conceived. The result was the now widely used *Pearson product-moment correlation coefficient*. Another statistic developed by Pearson was the *chi square*. Pearson's work found such broad application in other fields besides eugenics that students from all over the world came to Cambridge to study under him. To psychology, the importance of the correlation coefficient and of the chi square statistic is such that much of psychological research work today would be unthinkable without them. They were first presented in a series of eighteen papers published between 1893 and 1912 under the title of *Mathematical Contributions to the Theory of Evolution*. Pearson shared with Hume [52] and Mach [174] their view of causality as concomitant variation (correlation). His views on the philosophy of science, presented in his early lectures, are to be found in the classic, *The Grammar of Science* (1892). Pearson published several other books and sets of statistical tables.

Biographic data: *DNB* 1931–1940; *EP* 6:68; *IESS* 11:496; E. S. Pearson, *Karl Pearson*, 1938

[230]

LÉVY-BRUHL, LUCIEN

French anthropologist
Rating: 23
Born: Paris, April 10, 1857
Died: Paris, March 13, 1939
Highest degree: Docteur des lettres, University of Paris, 1884
Positions: 1895–1939, Sorbonne, professor of philosophy

Lévy-Bruhl's main concern was to demonstrate the essential difference between the thinking of the civilized and the primitive man. He thought that the primitive man had no conception of physical causality, that his thinking was magic, confusing the natural with the supernatural, lacking in logic and the ability to form abstractions. All categories of logic, he thought, are produced by the collective consciousness. Lévy-Bruhl wrote several books on the mind of the primitive, among them *How Natives Think* (1919; English translation 1927), *La mentalité primitive* (1910; English translation, *Primitive Mentality*, 1922), *L'âme primitive* (1910; *The Soul of the Primitive*, 1927), and *The Supernatural and the Nature of the Primitive Mind* (English translation, 1931). Lévy-Bruhl's contention that the primitive mind is prelogical, unable to think logically, has been disproved, and he himself in his later life conceded that his theories were inadequate. In spite of that, his ideas influenced such minds as C. G. Jung's [358]. Jung repeatedly refers to Lévy-Bruhl, particularly his idea that the native, being unable to draw a clear line between himself and his environment, lives in a *participation mystique*; the notion of *abaissement du niveau mental*, a "lowering of the mental level" during which abnormal states of mind and abnormal mental phenomena ensue; the notion of *représentations collectives*, which became Jung's archetypes, and others.

Biographic data: *EP* 4:451; *IESS* 9:263; R. Lenoir, Lucien Lévy-Bruhl. *American Journal of Sociology*, 1939, 44, 980

HEYMANS, GERARDUS

Dutch psychologist
Rating: 17
Born: Ferrwerd, April 17, 1857
Died: Groningen, February 18, 1930
Highest degree: Ph.D. in philosophy, University of Freiburg, 1890
Positions: 1890–1926, University of Groningen; president, Eighth International Congress of Psychology, 1926

A philosophically inclined psychologist, Heymans subscribed to a philosophy of psychic monism, according to which the universe consists of one stuff, consciousness, of which each individual partakes. Heymans established the first psychological laboratory in Holland at the University of Groningen in 1893 and did some empirical research in a variety of areas: individual differences, personality, dreams, geometric illusions, inhibition. In the latter area, the law that the threshold for one stimulus is raised in direct proportion to the intensity of another, inhibitory stimulus acting upon the organism at the same time, bears his name.

Biographic data: HPA 2:153

BLEULER, (PAUL) EUGEN

Swiss psychiatrist
Rating: 25
Born: Zollikon, near Zurich, April 30, 1857
Died; Zollikon, July 15, 1939
Highest degree: M.D., University of Zurich
Positions: 1886, Psychiatric Hospital, Rheinau; 1898, University of Zurich, professor of psychiatry and director (until 1927) of its psychiatric clinic and University Hospital (Burghölzli)

Before Jung's [358] time, Bleuler was the best known psychiatrist in Switzerland. Bleuler was influenced by both Wundt [161] and Freud [224] and tried to reconcile the two in relation to psychopathology. In doing so, Bleuler pioneered in introducing Freudian thinking in psychiatry. Bleuler was particularly interested in *dementia precox*. In his monumental work, *Dementia precox, oder Gruppe der Schizophrenien* (1911), Bleuler coined the term schizophrenia and substituted it for *dementia precox*.

He also invented the term "autistic thinking" and others, and in general, described schizophrenia, arguing that it was a heterogeneous collection of disorders, not incurable, that mental deterioration in schizophrenia was not inevitable, and that individuals suffering from it did not lack emotionality. Bleuler emphasized the regressive behavior of schizophrenics, and thought that the etiology of delusions was to be sought in any discrepancy between aspiration and ability. He stressed conscious and unconscious motivational factors, adding the dynamic dimension to the etiology of schizophrenia. Bleuler published more than one hundred fifty psychiatric papers and books.

Biographic data: *IESS* 2:85; A. A. Brill, In memoriam: Eugen Bleuler. *American Journal of Psychiatry*, 1939, 96, 513–516; G. Zilboorg, Eugen Bleuler. *Psychoanalytic Quarterly,* 1939, 382–384; [Various] Zum Andenken an Eugen Bleuler. *Schweizerisches Archiv für Neurologie und Psychiatrie*, 1941, 46, 1–32

[233]

ZWAARDEMAKER, HENDRICK

Dutch otolaryngologist
Rating: 23
Born: Haarlem, May 10, 1857
Died: Utrecht, September 19, 1930
Highest degree: M.D., University of Amsterdam, 1883
Positions: 1897–1927, University of Utrecht

Zwaardemaker did his most important work on smell. His *Die Physiologie des Geruchs* (1895) was a classic and the first scientific treatise on smell. It remained the most significant treatise on smell during the first half of the 20th century and created much interest and research on smell. A revised version of it was published in French under the title of *L'odorat* (1925).

Zwaardemaker spent much of his professional life looking for the physical key that makes substances odorous, but he never succeeded in finding one. His successes include the invention of a device for the administration of measured amounts of odorous substances, the *olfactometer*, the design of the odor-proof room, measurement of olfactory thresholds, and the introduction of the unit of olfactory intensity, *the olfactie*. Zwaardemaker attempted to show that the same laws that hold for vision also hold for smell, namely those of mixture, adaptation, and compensation. He classified odors using the seven odors of Linnaeus [47] plus two additional ones, and introduced several subclasses of each. This classification prevailed until the time when Henning [431] introduced his smell prism.

Zwaardemaker also did important work on hearing. He studied speech sounds, measured pitch thresholds, formulated the law of presbyacusis and a theory of hearing.

Biographic data: *HPA* 1:491; A. K. M. Noyons, Hendrik Zwaardemaker. *American Journal of Psychology,* 1931, 43, 525–526; T. Baader, Hendrik Zwaardemaker, Nachruf und Verzeichnis sämtlicher Veröffentlichungen. *Archiv für die gesamte Phonetik,* 1938, Abt. 1, 2, 248–254

DONALDSON, HENRY HERBERT

[234]

American neurologist and psychologist
Rating: 15
Born: Yonkers, New York, May 12, 1857
Died: Philadelphia, Pennsylvania, January 23, 1938
Training and highest degree: Three years of neurological studies in the United States and Europe; Ph.D. in psychology, Johns Hopkins University, 1895, under G. S. Hall [418]
Positions, honors: 1883, Johns Hopkins University, biology; 1889, Clark University, neurology; 1892, University of Chicago, neurology; 1906–1930, Wistar Institute, neurology; honorary D.Sc., Yale University, 1906

Donaldson was internationally known as a neurologist. Between 1890 and 1891 he conducted one of the most thorough studies of a single human brain, that of the deaf-mute Laura Bridgman, and later published a volume on *The Growth of the Brain* (1895). He was one of the independent discoverers (in 1885) of differences in thermal sensitivity in the skin and of the punctiform nature of temperature sensitivity. He could not find any specialized nerve endings in the skin, however, which finding still stands. At the Wistar Institute, Donaldson was instrumental in introducing the albino rat as an experimental subject, developed the Wistar stock of rats, published a volume on *The Rat* (1924), and was one of Karl Lashley's [466] teachers.

Biographical data: *DSB* 4:160; *NCAB* 28:374; E. G. Conklin, Biographical memoir of Henry Herbert Donaldson. *Biographical Memoirs of the National Academy of Sciences*, 1938, 20, 229–243; K. M. Dallenbach, Henry Herbert Donaldson. *American*

Journal of Psychology, 1938, 51, 434–435; J. P. McMurrich and C. M. Jackson, Henry Herbert Donaldson. *Journal of Comparative Neurology*, 1938, 69, 172–179

[235]

ANGELL, FRANK

American psychologist
Rating: 16
Born: South Scituate, Rhode Island, July 8, 1857
Died: Palo Alto, California, November 2, 1939
Highest degree: Ph.D. in psychology, University of Leipzig, 1891, under Wundt [161]
Positions: 1891, Cornell University; 1892–1922, Stanford University; editor, *American Journal of Psychology*, 1895–1925

A Wundtian laboratory psychologist, Angell did most of his research in psychophysics. His major contributions to psychology were as a teacher, especially of the introductory undergraduate course, during the thirty years he spent at Stanford, and the establishment of two early experimental psychology laboratories in America: at Cornell in 1891, and at Stanford in 1893.

Biographic data: L. M. Terman, Frank Angell. *American Journal of Psychology*, 1940, 53, 138–141

[236]

BINET, ALFRED

French psychologist
Rating: 27
Born: Nice, July 8, 1857
Died: Paris, October 18, 1911
Highest degree: Law degree, Lycée St. Louis, Paris, 1878; Ph.D. in science, University of Paris, 1894
Positions: 1894, University of Paris, professor and director of psychological laboratory

Binet was the most prominent psychologist of his time. With Henri Beaunis [158], he was a cofounder of the first French psychological laboratory at the Sorbonne in 1889. With Victor

Henri [334], he founded *L'Année psychologique* in 1895. Binet became first interested in abnormal phenomena. He wrote a book on hypnotism (with C. S. Féré [213], *Le magnétisme animal*, 1886), abnormal personality (*Les altérations de la personalité*, 1892), and suggestibility (*La suggestibilité*, 1900), and was best known for his studies of suggestibility. In 1886, he wrote (with Féré) a book on thinking (*La psychologie du raisonnement*), but it was a largely theoretical work. In the 1890s he carried out a number of experiments on subjects in general psychology in the German tradition. In 1902, his book on intelligence (*L'étude expérimentale de l'intelligence*) already included empirical data on his two daughters and considerable discussion of the differences in intelligence between them. His interest in intelligence and individual differences in intelligence and thinking dates from around 1887. In the fall of 1904, the Minister of Public Instruction of France appointed a committee to study the problem of and make recommendations concerning the education of retarded children in Paris. In 1905, Binet and Théodore Simon [347] wrote a paper ("Sur la nécessité d'établir un diagnostic scientific des états inférieurs de l'intelligence") in which they urged the necessity to diagnose the intelligence of children in order to implement the committee's recommendation. The first intelligence test was constructed by Binet and Simon in 1905, although the preparatory work had already been done and published in a series of papers between 1894 and 1898. The 1905 test contained a single scale—a long series of tests of increasing difficulty. In 1908, Binet revised this instrument. The tests were arranged according to the different ages at which they were to be passed by normal children. With that revision there occurred a shift away from simple identification of retardation to the general problem of intelligence measurement. In 1911, Binet's last revision of the test appeared. It contained the important new idea of mental age.

Binet's work on intelligence led to the construction of the first *intelligence scale*, the precursor of the currently used *Stanford-Binet Intelligence Scale*, the best known and most researched individual intelligence test. The test introduced objective measurement of mental processes in child, developmental, and educational psychology, and advanced the understanding of the concept of intelligence. The amount of subsequent research and practical use of intelligence tests has been such that very few psychologists may be compared to Binet in the fruitfulness of their ideas.

Biographical data: *DSB* 2:131–132; *EP* 1:308; *IESS* 2:74–78; T. Simon, Alfred Binet. *L'Année psychologique*, 1912, 18, 1–14;

F. L. Bertrand, *Alfred Binet et son oeuvre*, 1930; J. Delay, La vie et l'oeuvre d'Alfred Binet. *Psychologie française*, 1958 (April), 3, 85–88; H. L. Silverman and K. Krenzel, Alfred Binet: Prolific Pioneer in Psychology. *Psychiatric Quarterly Supplement*, 1964, 38(2), 323–335

[237]

BABINSKI, JOSEPH FRANCOIS FELIX

French neurologist
Rating: 20
Born: Paris, November 17, 1857
Died: Paris, October 29, 1932
Highest degree: M.D., University of Paris, 1885
Positions: 1890–1927, director, Hôpital de la Pitié, Paris

Babinski described various pathological reflexes occurring in disorders of the central nervous system. By far the best known among them is the *Babinski reflex,* the fanning of the toes when the sole of the foot is stimulated, present in infants and individuals with a lesion in the pyramidal nerve tract. Babinski also distinguished between organic and hysteric hemiplegia. He limited hysteria to phenomena produced or abolished by suggestion. Babinski's other work is more directly related to neurology. It includes the foundings of the French neurological society, the *Societé de neurologie,* in 1907.

Biographic data: J. H. Talbot, *A Biographical History of Medicine,* 1970, p. 866; J. F. Fulton, Joseph François Félix Babinski. *Archives of Neurology and Psychiatry,* 1933, 29, 168–174

[238]

SHERRINGTON, SIR CHARLES SCOTT

English neurophysiologist
Rating: 27
Born: London, November 27, 1857
Died: Eastbourne, Sussex, March 4, 1952
Highest degree: M. B., University of Cambridge, 1885
Positions, honors: 1887–1893, fellow, lecturer at St. Thomas Hospital, London; 1891, University of London, professor of pathology; 1895, University of Liverpool, professor of physiology; 1913–1935, University of Oxford, professor of

physiology; president, Royal Society, 1920–1925; twenty-two honorary degrees; 1932 Nobel prize in medicine; knighted 1922; many other honors

Sherrington was a pioneer and leading researcher in most areas of neurophysiology. Much of what is known today about neurophysiology may be traced to the work of Sherrington. The areas in which Sherrington did his most significant work were inhibition, the physiology of synapses, reflexes, activity of the cerebral cortex, especially the mapping of the motor area, functions of the inner ear, and reciprocal innervation (reflex behavior of antagonistic muscles and how this results in, for instance, upright posture without conscious participation). He coined such terms as synapse, synaptic, perikaryion, proprioceptive, final common path, neurone pool, recruitment, occlusion, and subliminal fringe. The present-day concept of the integrative and coordinating role that the nervous system plays in the economy of the organism was stressed by Sherrington (*The Integrative Action of the Nervous System,* 1906). He considered the reflex not in isolation but as part of a functioning whole in which it may be controlled by higher levels of neural functioning. *The Integrative Action of the Nervous System* was the most influential and stimulating volume in the history of physiology.

Sherrington supported psychology by permitting psychologists to work in his Liverpool laboratory as researchers as well as lecturers, by lending his prestige to it, and by his work on sensory physiology (color vision, flicker fusion, tactual and muscular sensitivity—he demonstrated the presence of receptors in the muscles which, in turn, helped to explain the loss of coordination of motor acts in certain nervous disorders in terms of reduced feedback from the muscles).

Biographic data: DNB 1951–1960; *IESS* 14:233; D. Denny-Brown, Charles Scott Sherrington. *American Journal of Psychology,* 1952, 65, 474–477; J. F. Fulton, Sir Charles Scott Sherrington. *Journal of Neurophysiology,* 1952, 15, 167–190; R. S. Creed, Sir Charles Scott Sherrington. *British Journal of Psychology,* 1953, 44, 1–4

LEHMANN, ALFRED GEORG LUDWIG [239]

Danish psychologist
Rating: 16
Born: Copenhagen, 1858

Died: Copenhagen, 1921
Highest degree: Ph.D. in psychology
Positions: University of Copenhagen

Lehmann worked with Wundt [161] on brightness contrast (*Anwendung der Methode der mittleren Abstufungen auf den Lichtsinn*, 1886–1887), then worked out pulse and breathing curves and correlated them with psychological processes according to Wundt (the "method of expression"). This work was published in *Uber die Beziehung zwischen Athmung und Aufmerksamkeit* (1893), causing quite a stir because of its supposed accurate demonstration of the relationship between physiological and psychological processes.

Upon his return to Copenhagen, Lehmann founded the first Danish psychological laboratory at the University of Copenhagen in 1886. *Fundamental Laws of Human Affective Life* (German translation from the Danish in 1892) was his best known work, but he wrote also *Die Hypnose und die damit verwandten normalen Zustände* (1890), *Die köperlichen Ausserungen psychischer Zustände* (German translation from the Danish, 1898), *Die physischen Aequivalente der Bewusstseinserscheinungen* (1901), a manual of psychological methods in Danish (1906), as well as others.

Biographic data: A. Aall, Alfred Lehmann, in memoriam. *Scandinavian Scientific Review*, 1922

[240]

KIESOW, FEDERICO

German-Italian psychologist
Rating: 19
Born: Brüel near Schwerin, Mecklenburg, Germany, March 28, 1858
Died: December 9, 1940
Highest degree: Ph.D. in philosophy, University of Leipzig, 1894, under W. Wundt [161]
Positions, honors: 1895–1933, University of Turin; honorary LL.D., Wittenberg College

Before moving to Turin, Kiesow studied taste with Wundt. At Turin, Kiesow established a psychological laboratory (Institute of

Psychology) in 1895 and, in general, brought Wundtian experimental psychology to Turin. He worked there for 40 years, studying touch and other sensations, psychophysics, geometric illusions, eidetic imagery, and other phenomena. Kiesow produced numerous publications and for many years was Italy's most prominent experimental psychologist.

Biographic data: HPA 1:163; M. Ponzo, Obituary to Federico Kiesow. *Psychological Review*, 1941, 48, 268–269; M. Ponzo, Vite di psicologi, pagine di psicologia. Federico Kiesow, *Archivio di psicologia, neurologia e psichiatria*, 1942, 3, 3–25

DURKHEIM, EMILE [241]

French sociologist
Rating: 23
Born: Epinal, Vosges, April 15, 1858
Died: Paris, November 15, 1917
Highest degree: Ecole Normale Supérieure, Paris, *agrégé*, 1882
Positions: 1887, University of Bordeaux; 1902, University of Paris

A leader in French sociology at the turn of the century, Durkheim stressed the differences between sociology and psychology. Collective consciousness differs from individual consciousness. Collective representations, which constrain the individual, are outside him, and give members of a society the same view of the world. The society, however, plays no role in creating a person's individual representations. There are, as it were, two separate and almost opposite beings within each individual, the personal and the collective.

Durkheim presented an influential and enduring analysis of suicide. The causes of suicide are entirely social, be it egoistic, altruistic, or anomic or normless suicide. Likewise, the source of religion is society itself, and God is society personified. Religion, in turn, gives rise to categories of thought, such as class, force, space, or time. Psychologically relevant books written by Durkheim are *De la division du travail social* (1893), *Règles de la méthode sociologique* (1894), *Suicide* (1897), and *Les formes élémentaires de la vie religieuse* (1912).

Biographic data: EP 2:437; IESS 4:311; G. Davy, *Emile Durkheim*, 1927

WALLAS, GRAHAM

English sociologist
Rating: 11
Born: Sunderland, Durham, May 31, 1858
Died: Portloe, Cornwall, August 9, 1932
Education: Graduated from Oxford University in 1881
Positions, honors: Various civic and teaching positions; honorary degrees from Manchester University (1922) and Oxford University (1931)

Wallas was a speculative social psychologist. In *Human Nature in Politics* (1908), he expressed the view that students of politics should pay more attention to human nature and should not assume that all political decisions are made rationally. He pleaded for a closer relation between psychology and political studies. In *The Art of Thought* (1926), Wallas examined unconscious determinants of thought as viewed by nonpsychologists.

Biographic data: DNB 1931–1940; *IESS* 16:440

BOAS, FRANZ

German-American anthropologist
Rating: 19
Born: Minden, Westphalia, July 9, 1858
Died: New York, New York, December 21, 1942
Highest degree: Ph.D. in physics, University of Kiel, 1881
Positions: 1888–1892, Clark University; 1896–1937, Columbia University; many other nonteaching positions in anthropology; editorial work for anthropological journals; four honorary degrees; president, American Association for the Advancement of Science, 1931

In anthropology, Boas was an outstanding figure: he restructured anthropology by separating it into physical anthropology, linguistics, and ethnology, demonstrated the diffusion of cultural traits (rather than cultural evolution), wrote more than six hundred papers and several books, among them a monumental study of the Kwakiutl Indians, was one of the founders of the American Anthropological Society, and developed the Columbia

University Anthropology Department into one of the foremost in the country.

Boas was influenced by German psychology, especially by Wundt and his ethnopsychology. He performed some psychophysical experiments, finding that the previous experience of his subjects made a difference in the results. At Clark University, under the influence of G. Stanley Hall [418], Boas initiated the first American longitudinal growth study in 1891. His studies of the plasticity of the human organism (e.g., the demonstration of changes in skull shape in European emigrants brought about by environmental influence) also show Hall's influence. Toward the end of his life, Boas shifted his emphasis on psychological explanations of cultural phenomena and the psychological description of environmental conditions that modify a person's behavior. He investigated motor behavior, posture, walking, and gestures. Boas reversed Tylor's [162] rationalistic position by asserting that behavior is influenced by and occurs within a culture, that culture is not just the product of man's mind. Thinking and acting follow paths etched by the individual's culture from birth. Yet, while culture affects the individual, the individual also affects culture. To psychology, his most significant book is *The Mind of Primitive Man* (1911, 1938).

Biographic data: DSB 2:207; IESS 2:99 & 110; J. P. Foley, Jr., Franz Boas, psychologist. *Science,* 1943, 97, 330; F. C. Cole, In memoriam: Franz Boas. *American Journal of Sociology,* 1943, 48, 603; R. Benedict, Franz Boas. *Science,* 1943, 97, 60–62; M. J. Herskovitz, *Franz Boas,* 1953

GOLDSCHEIDER, ALFRED   [244]

German physiologist
Rating: 18
Born: Sommerfeld, Saxony, August 4, 1858
Died: Berlin, April 10, 1935
Highest degree: M.D., Friedrich-Wilhelm Institut, Berlin, 1881
Positions: 1894 directing physician, Moabit Hospital, Berlin; 1906, Virchow Hospital, Berlin; 1910–1933, director, Berlin Polyclinic

In 1884 and independently of Blix, Goldscheider discovered separate sensory spots in the skin that mediated the perception of warmth, cold, and pressure. Goldscheider believed pain was not a separate sensory modality but resulted from increased pressure (the intensive or summation theory of pain). In this view he was opposed by von Frey [217], who believed that pain was a separate sense modality. Frey's view eventually won out. Goldscheider also discovered, independently of Rubin [443], paradoxical warmth. In a series of papers on kinesthesis, published between 1887 and 1893, Goldscheider established, among other things, the present tripartite components of kinesthesis: muscles, tendons, and joints. He produced many papers on haptic sensations, aftersensations, and thresholds, as well as over a dozen books on physiology and medicine.

Biographic data: *Enciclopedia universal ilustrada,* vol. 26

[245]

WIERSMA, ENNO DIRK

Dutch psychiatrist
Rating: 12
Born: Pieterzyl, November 29, 1858
Died: The Netherlands, 1940
Highest degree: M.D., University of Groningen, 1886
Positions: 1897, University of Groningen

Wiersma was a close collaborator of G. Heymans [231], with whom he wrote, among other things, eight papers on "special psychology" between 1906 and 1918, but he was of a more experimental bent than Heymans (*The Psychological Experiment in Psychiatry*, 1903). Wiersma published a fair number of papers on physiological psychology, psychopathology, heredity, mental tests, statistical methods, sex differences, and other psychological topics.

Biographic data: *The Psychological Register,* vol. III, 1932

[246]

ELLIS, (HENRY) HAVELOCK

English psychologist
Rating: 23
Born: Croydon, Surrey, February 2, 1859
Died: Washbrook, Suffolk, July 8, 1939
Highest degree: Physician's license, St. Thomas Hospital, London, 1889

Ellis was principally a writer, his main topic, the psychology of sex. Ellis never held any academic or official positions and never delivered a lecture or address. His literary style won prominence for his books. They broke the silence that had long surrounded the topic of sex and promoted its scientific study. Ellis brought data to an area of speculation—numerous case histories from all over the world. Through his writings Ellis promoted a more natural, healthy, and liberal attitude toward sex and marriage. His most important work is the seven volumes of *Studies in the Psychology of Sex*, published between 1898 and 1928. Other books that Ellis wrote on the same subject are *Sexual Inversion* (1897), *Man and Woman* (1894), *Sex in Relation to Society* (1910), *The Erotic Rights of Women* (1918), *The Play-Function of Sex* (1921), *The Dance of Life* (1923), *Marriage Today and Tomorrow* (1929), and *More Essays on Love and Virtue* (1931). In *The World of Dreams* (1911) Ellis criticised the emphasis on sex in Freud's interpretation of dreams, and found time for a *Study of British Genius*, a study in the manner of Galton of 1,030 eminent British subjects.

Biographic data: *DNB* 1931–1940; *IESS* 5:29; H. Ellis, *My Life*, 1940; H. Peterson, *Havelock Ellis, Philosopher of Love*, 1928; I. Goldberg, *Havelock Ellis*, 1926; A. Calder-Marshall, *The Sage of Sex*: *A Life of Havelock Ellis*, 1960; J. C. Flugel, Henry Havelock Ellis. *British Journal of Educational Psychology*, 1941, **11**, 1–7

LOEB, JACQUES [247]

German-American physiologist
Rating: 26
Born: Mayen, Rhineland-Palatinate, Germany, April 7, 1859
Died: Hamilton, Bermuda, February 11, 1924
Highest degree: M.D., University of Strasbourg, 1884
Positions: 1881, University of Würzburg; 1888, University of Strasbourg; 1889, Naples Biological Station; 1891, Bryn Mawr College; 1892, University of Chicago; 1902, University of California at Berkeley; 1910, Rockefeller Institute for Medical Research, New York

Loeb headed the mechanistic school of animal psychology. In his theory of tropisms, presented in an 1890 paper ("Der Heliotropismus der Thiere und seine Uberstimmung mit dem

Heliotropismus der Pflanzen"), he proposed that tropisms existed not only in plants but also in animals, and that animal behavior was largely orienting movements determined by physical and chemical reactions in a field of force. Unlike Descartes [28], however, Loeb attributed consciousness to animals having "associative memory," thus denying it only to the lowest levels of animals on the phylogenetic scale. His tropistic psychology fit in well with and supported the objective psychology of Watson, under whose aegis behaviorism was beginning to emerge at the time Loeb was writing his books. In them he further expounded his mechanistic psychology: *The Mechanistic Conception of Life* (1912), *The Organism as a Whole* (1916), and *Forced Movements, Tropisms, and Animal Conduct* (1918). Earlier, Loeb had penned a text of comparative psychology stressing tropistic behavior on the basis of his observations of invertebrates (*Einleitung in die vergleichende Gehirnphysiologie und vergleichende Psychologie mit besonderer Berürcksichtigung der wirbellosen Thiere*, 1899; English translation, 1900). Toward the end of his career, Loeb founded, with W. J. V. Osterhout, the *Journal of General Physiology* (1918).

Biographic data: DSB 8:445; *EP* 4:503; W. J. V. Osterhout, Jacques Loeb: Biographical sketch. *Journal of General Physiology,* 1928, 8(1), pp. ix–xcii

[248]

HUSSERL, EDMUND

German philosopher
Rating: 26
Born: Prossnitz, Moravia, April 8, 1859
Died: Freiburg-im-Breisgau, April 26, 1938
Highest degree: Ph.D. in mathematics, University of Berlin, 1881
Positions: 1887, University of Halle; 1901, University of Göttingen; 1916–1928, University of Freiburg; editor, *Jahrbuch für Philosophie und phäneomenologische Forschung,* 1913–1930

After studying philosophy under Franz Brentano [176] at the University of Vienna (1884–1886), Husserl abandoned mathematics and turned to philosophy. Eventually, he brought about a radical change on the German philosophical scene by synthesizing, in his phenomenology, both the subjective and the objective viewpoints in philosophy. Since the philosophically oriented psychologist is constantly aware of the objective-subjective or inside-outside problem, Husserl's philosophy influenced psychologists, particularly since he began to write at a time when dissatisfaction with one form of phenomenological research, introspection, was beginning to find resolution in Wertheimer's [391] Gestaltist phenomenology and Watson's [374] behaviorism (*Logische Untersuchungen,* 1900–1901; *Ideen zu einer reinen Phänomenologie und phänomenologischen Philosophie,* 1913). In psychology, the term phenomenology was borrowed from Husserl. It means the description of immediate experience while keeping scientific biases at the lowest possible level. Husserl's phenomenology owes much to Brentano, such as his use of Brentano's intentionality concept, although with an altered content. According to Husserl, the mind can intuit what is not part of mind itself. From the data within it, consciousness synthesizes a meaningful universe. The objective universe is the ideal limit of the process of objectification. This transcendental productivity of consciousness works from inside out, instead of allowing objectivity to produce a view of the world from outside in, in a passive individual. Thus the phenomenological observation of subjective experiences is the key to the understanding of being. The phenomenological approach flourished in the Gestalt school of psychology. After the dominance period of the learning theories, Husserl experienced a revival in psychology, especially among the so-called third-force or humanistic psychologists.

Biographic data: *EP* 4:96; *IESS* 7:27

JANET, PIERRE

French psychologist
Rating: 27
Born: Paris, May 30, 1859
Died: Paris, February 24, 1947
Highest degree: Docteur dès lettres, University of Paris, 1889; M.D., University of Paris, 1893
Positions, honors: 1890–1894, director of psychological laboratory at the Salpêtrière Hospital, Paris; 1895, Sorbonne;1920–1936, Collège de France; general secretary, Fourth International Congress of Psychology; honorary president, Eleventh

International Congress of Psychology, 1937; three honorary doctorates

Janet was a systematic psychopathologist. He came to the attention of Charcot [152] through his interest in and report on the case of Léonie, a patient who could be hypnotized from a distance. Although Janet worked in Charcot's laboratory and Charcot was concerned with the neural bases of pathology, Janet thought of hysteria as a mental disease. He developed a system of psychology and of psychopathology which he called *psychologie de la conduite*. He attempted to systematize the existing knowledge about hysteria and to relate clinical and academic psychology to it. His major effort in this direction was *L'état mental des hystériques* (1892; English translation, *The Major Symptoms of Hysteria*, 1907). Janet saw hysteria as a disorder characterized by exaggerated suggestibility, faulty memory, and fixed ideas. Hysteric patients have a weakness. Fluctuations in psychic energy determine mental health and disease. "Lowered mental tension" means insufficient energy mobilized to cope with obstacles, leading to neurosis. Decrease in psychic energy was a central concept in Janet's explanation of mental disorders. To Janet, a healthy personality was one that had a stable, integrated system of ideas and emotions, the cardinal property of mind being its ability to integrate. Hysterical personalities lack integration. In extreme cases, a dissociation of the mind into conscious and unconscious portions occurs and multiple personalities may result. The hysteric experiences a narrowing of consciousness, as unacceptable mental contents are driven out of it. These contents are converted, however, into symbolic symptoms. This view bore considerable resemblance to that of Freud [224], and a controversy arose between Janet and Freud concerning priority in the use of the concept of the unconscious.

Janet wrote fifteen additional books, some of which have been also translated into English (*Principles of Psychotherapy*, 1924; *Psychological Healing*, 1925), and many articles, a total of about ninety titles. Many of the articles appeared in *Journal de psychologie*, founded by Janet in collaboration with Georges Dumas [288] in 1904, and of which he was the editor until 1937.

Biographic data: HPA 1:123; IESS 8:234; W. S. Taylor, Pierre Janet. *American Journal of Psychology*, 1947, 60, 637–645; E. R. Guthrie, Pierre Janet. *Psychological Review*, 1948, 55, 65–66

Austrian philosopher
Rating: 26
Born: Rodaun near Vienna, June 20, 1859
Died: Lichtenau, September 8, 1932
Highest degree: Ph.D. in philosophy, University of Vienna, 1885, under F. Brentano [176]
Positions: 1885–1888, University of Graz; 1889, University of Vienna; 1896, University of Prague

Ehrenfels was one of the important names in the Austrain school of act psychology, although only incidentally, because he was mainly a philosopher. Ehrenfels developed Mach's [174] idea that there are sensations of form. He decided that form is not a combination of other qualities but a new one, form quality (*Gestaltqualität*). The idea was presented in a paper, "Uber Gestaltqualitäten," in 1890. In the perception of the square, the four lines are the sensations or the foundation (*Fundamente*) of the perception of the square. This perception is not caused by any one of the lines alone but is experienced when all are brought together (*Grundlage*) and are perceived jointly. Form-quality may persist even when the elements change, hence all squares are perceived essentially the same, melodies are heard as the same when transposed to a different key, and the like. Form-qualities are temporal or spatial, and each may form the *Grundlage* for the experience of higher levels of form-quality.

Ehrenfels, by realizing that Wundt's [161] elementism failed to explain many aspects of perception, took a step toward what was later called Gestalt psychology. At the same time, unlike Max Wertheimer [391] who held that the original elements disappear in the perception of the whole, Ehrenfels still thought of form-quality as a derivative of the *Fundamente*, appearing as a new quality from them but not as a relationship among the primary elements and therefore not as independently given. With Alexius von Meinong [218] and Hans Cornelius, Ehrenfels originated the form-quality school, the immediate precursor of Gestalt psychology.

Biographic data: EP 2:467

FULLERTON, GEORGE STUART

American philosopher
Rating: 14
Born: Fatehgarh, India, August 18, 1859
Died: Poughkeepsie, New York, March 23, 1925
Highest degree: A.M., University of Pennsylvania, 1882
Positions, honors: 1883, University of Pennsylvania; 1904–1917, Columbia University; president, American Psychological Association, 1896; honorary Ph.D., LL.D., Muhlenberg College, 1900

With J. McK. Cattell [256] Fullerton published an important monograph, *On the Perception of Small Differences,* in 1892. Using the functionalist approach to a classical problem in psychophysics, Fullerton and Cattell concluded sensory variability is error in the perceiving organism as it strives to discriminate perfectly. They recommended the use of the probable error as a measure of discrimination rather than the usual measure of difference threshold, and that the critical point of discrimination be the 75 percent and not the 50 percent judgment level. The *Fullerton-Cattell law* reads that the errors of observation and just noticeable differences are proportional to the square root of the magnitude of the stimulus. It is also known as the *square root law*, and was proposed as a substitute for Weber's law.

Biographic data: NCAB 12:57

BERGSON, HENRI

French philosopher
Rating: 22
Born: Paris, October 18, 1859
Died: Paris, January 4, 1941
Education: Doctorate in philosophy from Ecole Normale Supérieure, Paris, 1881
Positions, honors: 1898, Ecole Normale Supérieure; 1900, Collège de France; Nobel prize in literature in 1928

Bergson opposed both associationism and Wundtian structuralism to the point of denying the possibility of a scientifically based psychology. In this he was voicing a position similar to that of Dilthey [164] and Nietzsche [196], but not necessarily therefore taking the position of phenomenology. Bergson opposed associationism because he believed that the associationists proceeded in a manner opposite to that dictated by the nature of mental processes. The components of inner experience cannot be treated like discrete things and the self as if it were a composite of such things. Inner experience and the outside world of facts are incommensurable, and inner experience cannot be described using the usual methods of acquisition of knowledge. Human intelligence, however, is directed toward external things. Its domain is the external world, which it seeks to manipulate and change. Intelligence can analyze it and synthesize it again, but it is inadequate to comprehend the inner world of experience. The mechanism whereby the stream of consciousness is apprehended Bergson calls intuition, which he contrasts with intelligence as a totally different phenomenon. What in animals is called instinct is intuition in man. It permits man to "live" his inner reality instead of just realizing, imagining, or otherwise representing it cognitively. The experience of time is made central in Bergson's philosophy. Using time as a vehicle for stating his case, Bergson presents his psychological views in, among other works, his *Essai sur les données immediates de la conscience* (1889; translated *Time and Free Will*, 1910).

Biographic data: DSB 2:8; EP 1:287; H. H. Price, Obituary: Henri Bergson. *Proceedings of the Society for Psychic Research, London*, 1941, 46, 271–276

DEWEY, JOHN [253]

American philosopher
Rating: 27
Born: Burlington, Vermont, October 20, 1859
Died: New York, New York, June 1, 1952
Highest degree: Ph.D. in philosophy, Johns Hopkins University, 1884
Positions: 1884, University of Michigan; 1894, University of Chicago; 1904–1929 Columbia University; president, American Psychological Association, 1899

Although Dewey's doctorate was in philosophy, he wrote his dissertation on Kant's [60] psychology. During his stay at Michigan, Dewey taught psychology as well as philosophy and wrote a text for the "new" psychology (*Psychology*, 1886). It was a philosophically sophisticated text, second in the English language (after Sully's [188] 1884 text), but was soon replaced by texts that stressed psychology more than philosophy.

The period of Dewey's impact on psychology coincided with his ten years' stay at Chicago. Dewey accepted the evolutionary point of view, and stood for social change, the use of philosophy to deal with problems of men, and the value of science and of experimentation. He held that ideas are plans for action, that they arise when an individual faces a problem, and accomplish their function by solving the problem. He laid the foundation of what was to become the functionalist school of psychology, influential during the 1920s and 1930s. Dewey's pragmatic philosophy and his personal brilliance influenced James Rowland Angell [309] who was at Chicago at that time. It was under the leadership of Angell that functionalism developed as a formal school.

Dewey's first important publication in the Chicago school was his 1896 paper on "The Reflex Arc Concept in Psychology." In it, Dewey argued against elementism's abstraction of the sensory and motor aspects of the reflex and against treating it as an open arc. Dewey insisted that the stimulus in a reflex is inseparable from the response, in that the response serves to modify the way the stimulus is perceived the next time, so that the reflex is actually a circular arrangement and serves to adapt the organism to the environment. Dewey pleaded for a psychology of acts and functions of the whole organism. After the Chicago period, Dewey's contributions to psychology declined, although he kept using psychology in his educational and philosophical writings.

Biographic data: *EP* 2:380; *IESS* 4:155; *NCAB* 40:1; *A*:547; E. G. Boring, John Dewey. *American Journal of Psychology*, 1953, 66, 145–147

[254]

SANFORD, EDMUND CLARK

American psychologist
Rating: 20
Born: Oakland, California, November 10, 1859
Died: Boston, Massachusetts, November 22, 1924
Highest degree: Ph.D. in psychology, Johns Hopkins University, 1888, under G. S. Hall [418]
Positions, honors: 1888, Johns Hopkins University; 1889, Clark University; 1909–1920, president, Clark College; 1920, Clark University, professor of psychology and education; editorial

work for *American Journal of Psychology*, 1888–1924; president, American Psychological Association, 1902; honorary degrees from Hobart College (1909), University of California (1912), and Clark University (1924)

After Sanford took his degree from Hall, he went with Hall from Johns Hopkins to Clark University, where he ran Hall's laboratory and published a series of twenty-two minor studies. He invented and built a vernier pendulum chronoscope that was used in reaction time work for some time. His most important contribution was the publication of a laboratory manual, which first came out in installments in the *American Journal of Psychology*, beginning in 1891, then in book form in 1898 (*Course in Experimental Psychology*). Although only Part 1 of the *Course* was ever published, Sanford's only book served as the standard laboratory manual for a long time. He published about thirty papers in psychology.

Biographic data: *NCAB* 12:272; W. H. Burnham, Edmund Clark Sanford. *Pedagogical Seminary*, 1925, *32*, 2–7; E. B. Titchener, Edmund Clark Sanford. *American Journal of Psychology*, 1925, *36*, 157–170

STOUT, GEORGE FREDERICK   [255]

English psychologist
Rating: 26
Born: South Shields, Durham, January 6, 1860
Died: Sydney, Australia, August 18, 1944
Highest degree: A.M. in philosophy, Cambridge Univeristy, 1885
Positions: 1883, Cambridge University, lecturer in moral science; 1896, University of Aberdeen, lecturer in comparative psychology; 1898, Oxford University, reader in mental philosophy; 1903, St. Andrews University, professor of metaphysic and logic; editor of *Mind*, 1891–1920

Stout's views on psychology were similar to those of Ward [190], his teacher, but Stout was more popular than Ward because he was easier to understand. He was influential because of his psychology texts; *Analytic Psychology* (1896, written for psychologists), *Manual of Psychology* (1898, written for students), *Groundwork of Psychology* (1903), and *Mind and Matter* (1931), but especially his *Manual*. Sanford's position in the history of psychology rests mainly on his reputation as textbook writer.

Stout rejected associationism in favor of a psychology that was a form of act psychology, like Ward's. In his doctrine of conation Stout emphasized the individual's activity. Stout held that the objects of mental processes are mental entities (sensations) also. The processes are cognition and interest. Interest means conation or striving, plus feelings and attitudes. The goal object of striving may be an immediate one, or else such goal object may be only instrumental in attaining a superordinate goal. In this connection Stout discussed unconscious attitudes as factors that determine activity in addition to conation.

Stout was very influential, mainly because he provided the empirical psychologist with an explicit statement of the kind of simple body-mind relationship that he subscribes to but does not consciously try to formulate, as well as for his ability to assimilate, synthesize, and present the divergent viewpoints of the different schools of psychology as *the* psychology.

Biographic data: *DNB* 1941–1950; *EP* 8:22; *IESS* 15:280; C. A. Mace, *George Frederick Stout*, 1948; C. A. Mace, George Frederick Stout. *British Journal of Psychology*, 1946, 36, 51–54

[256]

CATTELL, JAMES MC KEEN

American psychologist
Rating: 26
Born: Easton, Pennsylvania, May 25, 1860
Died: Lancaster, Pennsylvania, January 20, 1944
Highest degree: Ph.D. in psychology, University of Leipzig, 1886, under Wilhelm Wundt [161]
Positions: 1887, University of Pennsylvania; 1891, Columbia University; 1917, founder and president of Psychological Corporation; president, American Psychological Association, 1895; president, Ninth International Congress of Psychology, 1929; editor of *Science* (1904–1944), *Popular Science Monthly* (1900–1915), *Psychological Review* (1894–1903), *American Naturalist* (1907–1944), *Scientific Monthly* (1915–1943), and *School and Society* (1915–1939)

Cattell never wrote a text and was author of relatively few papers. His influence on psychology was very strong, nevertheless, mainly because of his personality and because he happened to represent the functionalist point of view in the form of mental tests when Americans were most ready to accept both. His ability and willingness to speak out fearlessly on issues, psychological and social, and to be involved in public affairs made him prominent.

Cattell was the first American to receive a doctorate from Wundt. While at Leipzig, Cattell, like Wundt, studied reaction time, but, unlike Wundt, related it to individual differences. Individual differences became the leitmotif of all of Cattell's subsequent work. He studied the tachistoscopic perception of objects, which introduced reaction time as a measure of sensory differences; reading time in different languages; and the latency of associations, which laid the foundation for future work on association. In this connection, Cattell invented the lip-key and the voice key. His work on reaction time was as important as Wundt's.

At the University of Pennsylvania Cattell came to occupy the world's first chair in psychology. He also established here a psychological laboratory in 1887, which was the first formally recognized psychological laboratory in the United States. At Pennsylvania, Cattell studied the difference threshold, with emphasis less on the size of the threshold and more on the size of the observer error. This work resulted in a well-known monograph that Cattell wrote with G. S. Fullerton [251] in 1892 (*On the Perception of Small Differences*). Cattell also proposed a substitute for Fechner's law in the form of $S = k\sqrt{R}$, where S was errors of judgment.

On his arrival at Columbia University, Cattell established a psychological laboratory there in 1891. He started promoting the idea of mental tests in the 1890s, and his time at Columbia is associated with the mental test movement. The term "mental test" was coined by Cattell in an 1890 article published in *Mind*. In the 1890s, Cattell published the results of tests given to a large number of Columbia University students in the manner of Galton [144]. Cattell measured such variables as reaction time and visual acuity, but these failed to correlate with the "higher mental processes" or even with grades. Cattell's "anthropometric test movement" died as other psychologists began to pay attention to Binet [236] who was developing direct measures of the "higher mental processes." The Psychological Corporation, founded by Cattell in 1921 for the promotion of applied psychology and still in existence, has played an important role in the development of psychometric instruments and of professional psychology in general.

Around 1903, Cattell started working on the scientific eminence of psychologists, and then on the eminence of scientists in general. The rankings he obtained were published in the form of stars after the names of scientists described in *American Men of Science,* a publication which Cattell edited between 1906 and 1938. In connection with this understaking, Cattell invented the method of order of merit.

Biographic data: DSB 3:130; *IESS* 2:344; R. S. Woodworth, James McKeen Cattell. *Psychological Review,* 1944, 51, 201–209; F. L. Wells, James McKeen Cattell. *American Journal of Psychology,* 1944, 57, 270–275

[257]

STORRING, GUSTAV

German psychologist and philosopher
Rating: 15
Born: Voerde, Westphalia, August 24, 1860
Died: Göttingen, December 1, 1946
Highest degree: Ph.D. in philosophy, University of Halle, 1890; M.D.
Positions: 1902, University of Zurich; 1911, University of Strasbourg; 1914, University of Bonn

Störring did some writing on emotions (*Zur Lehre vom Einfluss der Gefühle auf die Vorstellung,* 1896; *Psychologie des menschlichen Gefühlslebens,* 1916) and psychopathology (*Vorlesungen über Psychopathologie in ihrer Bedeutung für die normale Psychologie,* 1900), but he was mostly a philosopher. He emphasized the contribution of psychiatry and psychopathology to experimental psychology an, in turn, saw experimental psychology as the basis of both logic and epistemology. Störring wrote some forty papers and several books on philosophy and the development of morals.

Biographic data: W. Wirth, Gustav Störring zum 80. Geburtstag. *Archiv für die gesamte Psychologie,* 1940, 107, 384–391; K. Fischer, Über Gustav Störrings Lebenswerk. *Archiv für die gesamte Psychologie,* 1940, 107, 392–410

[258]

BRYAN, WILLIAM LOWE

American psychologist
Rating: 16
Born: Bloomington, Indiana, November 1, 1860

Died: Bloomington, Indiana, November 21, 1955

Highest degree: Ph.D. in psychology, Clark University, 1892, under G. S. Hall [418]

Positions: With the exception of two years abroad (University of Berlin, 1886–1887, University of Paris, University of Würzburg, 1900–1902), Bryan held positions at Indiana University, at first in fields other than psychology (1884–1892), then in psychology (1892–1902), and finally as president of Indiana University; president, American Psychological Association, 1903

In psychology, Bryan is known for having established a psychological laboratory at Indiana University in 1888 and for a study (published in two papers in 1897 and 1899), performed with N. Harter, of the acquisition of telegraphic skill. It showed an early example of a learning curve, including a learning plateau in the consolidation phase of two separate skills. Also, in the summer of 1902, Bryan performed experiments on abstraction with Oswald Külpe [265] at Würzburg. They cast in doubt the proposition that all attributes of a sense impression can exist simultaneously in the mind. Bryan produced only a moderate amount of research in psychology since he became an administrator quite early in his career. After After 1902, Bryan supported psychology financially and by personal encouragement.

Biographic data: NCAB 13:464; D. G. Ellson, William Lowe Bryan. *American Journal of Psychology,* 1956, 69, 325–327; J. R. Kantor, William Lowe Bryan, scientist, philosopher, educator. *Science,* 1956, **123,** 214

BALDWIN, JAMES MARK [259]

American psychologist

Rating: 25

Born: Columbia, South Carolina, January 12, 1861

Died: Paris, November 8, 1934

Highest degree: Ph.D. in philosophy, Princeton University, 1889

Positions: 1887, Lake Forest College; 1890, University of Toronto; 1893, Princeton University, psychology; 1903, Johns Hopkins University, psychology; 1909, National University,

[261]

Mexico City, advisor; 1913–1918, L'école des Hautes Etudes Sociales, Paris, psychology; president, American Psychological Association, 1897; honorary D.Sc., Oxford University, 1900; president, International Congress of Psychology, 1909–1913

Baldwin was a writer and speculative theorist. His contributions were in the areas of textbook writing, popularization of the evolutionary theory, developmental psychology, and psychological publications. His book, *The Story of the Mind* (1889), appeared in many editions. He also wrote *Senses and Intellect* (1889), *Handbook of Psychology* (1890), *Feeling and Will* (1891), and *History of Psychology* (1913). Because of their happy style, the books were well received. They emphasized the importance of the evolutionary theory to the human sciences. A theory put forth by Baldwin in this connection was that the individual is constantly learning to change his heredity through his own efforts. Baldwin applied the evolutionary concept in pioneering in the study of child development in the United States. While his developmental writings were largely theoretical, he, along with G. Stanley Hall [418] broke ground in this area. His developmental psychology texts include *Mental Development in the Child and the Race* (1895), *Social and Ethical Interpretations in Mental Development* (1897), and *Thought and Things or Genetic Logic* three volumes., 1906, 1911.

With Hall, Baldwin was a cofounder of the American Psychological Association. Although he did very little experimental work himself, he did found psychological laboratories at Toronto in 1889, at Princeton in 1893, and reestablished Hall's laboratory at Johns Hopkins. Baldwin founded the *Psychological Review* in 1894, *Psychological Bulletin* in 1904, as well as the *Psychological Index* and *Psychological Monographs*. Among his editorial efforts is also the publication of the four-volume *Dictionary of Philosophy and Psychology* in 1901-02, to which more than sixty philosophers and psychologists contributed. Baldwin's influence on American psychology lasted only about twenty years, however, approximately between 1889 and 1909 when Baldwin left the United States.

Biographic data: HPA 1:1; *IESS* 1:510; *NCAB,* 25:89; 34:338; J. M. Baldwin, *Between Two Wars, 1861–1921,* 1926; J. Jastrow, James Mark Baldwin. *Psychological Bulletin,* 1935, 32, 1–3; W. M. Urban, James Mark Baldwin, Coeditor of Psychological Review. *Psychological Review,* 1935, 42, 303–306; M. F. Washburn, James Mark Baldwin. *American Journal of Psychology,* 1935, 47, 168–169

English-American philosopher
Rating: 14
Born: Ramsgate, Kent, February 15, 1861
Died: Cambridge, Massachusetts, December 30, 1947
Highest degree: D.Sc. in mathematics, Cambridge University, 1905
Positions, honors: 1885, Cambridge University; 1911, University of London; 1924–1936, Harvard University; several honorary doctorates, medals, and prizes

While Whitehead did not present his psychological views in any specifically psychological paper or book, he discussed psychological problems to a considerable extent. Whitehead was in agreement on some points with the Gestalt, psychoanalytic, and dynamic schools, and in disagreement on others, so that no school label can be attached to him.

Although to Whitehead psychology is the basis of his metaphysics, he does not say much about psychology that others have not said before, albeit in different terms. Whitehead considers the experiencing subject mainly from the point of view of his affects and purposes. There is a close interrelation between the subject's body, himself, and the external world. Whitehead makes the distinction between perception in the mode of causal efficacy, which is perception as it relates to the past or the future, and perception in the mode of presentational immediacy, which is related to the here and now. Whitehead criticizes the stress placed on the latter mode and unrelated bits of sensory experience, and failure to consider the former. He thus rejects the Humean analysis of sense perception and his theory of the association of ideas. Whitehead's concept of thinking is very similar to that of Dewey's [253] in that he views thinking functionally and assigns it a pragmatic role of practical relevance. Whitehead believes, however, that much of our experience is unconscious and that the original source of knowledge is intuition.

Biographic data: *DNB* 1941–1950; *EP* 8:290; *IESS* 16:532

HEAD, SIR HENRY [261]

English neurologist
Rating: 25
Born: Stamford Hill, Lincolnshire, August 4, 1861

Died: Reading, Berkshire, October 8, 1940
Highest degree: M.D., Cambridge University, 1892
Positions, honors: Medical appointments in various hospitals, longest at London Hospital; LL.D. from University of Edinburgh, several medals and prizes; knighted 1927

Head's contributions lie in the area of sensory physiology. In his work Head collaborated with the psychologists W. R. R. Rivers [278] and F. C. Bartlett [444]. With the former, he performed experiments (in 1905 and 1908) on cutaneous sensitivity by cutting two nerves in his own arm and observing the return of sensitivity; On the basis of this experiment Head theorized that three different neural systems were involved in cutaneous sensitivity: deep sensitivity; protopathic sensitivity, a crude and strong system that is first to respond when a nerve regenerates; and epicritic sensitivity, a later and finer cutaneous discrimination. This and other experiments of Head's on the central nervous system in which he traced the passage of sensory nerves through the spinal cord, brain stem, and thalamus to the cortex, were thought to present evidence for Hughlings Jackson's [171] theory of the evolutionary levels of the nervous system. The results of Head's neurological work on the effects of lesions were published in 1920 in *Studies in Neurology*. After 1910, Head became interested in aphasia. Work on aphasic cases produced during World War I led to the publication of *Aphasia and Kindred Disorders of Speech,* two volumes, in 1926. His view of aphasia struck between the classic view of it as a loss of images and the view that it involves more than just language functions. Head classified aphasias into the verbal, the syntactical, the nominal, and the semantic. Jackson's theory of mental deterioration also led Head to formulate his theory of vigilance that is contained in this volume. It is concerned with the manner in which hierarchically organized neural levels activate each other.

Biographic data: DNB 1931–1940

[262]

GROOS, KARL THEODOR

German psychologist and philosopher
Rating: 16
Born: Heidelberg, December 10, 1861
Died: Tübingen, March 27, 1946

Highest degree: Ph.D. in philosophy, University of Heidelberg, 1884

Positions: 1892, University of Giessen; 1898, University of Basel; 1901, University of Giessen; 1911–1929, University of Tübingen

Groos concentrated on studying play and development in children, suggesting that play serves as training for serious activities in the future (*Die Spiele der Thiere*, 1896, English translation, 1898; *Die Spiele der Menschen,* 1899, English translation 1901; *Das Seelenleben des Kindes,* 1903, six editions by 1923). Groos's work was mainly a philosophical attempt to synthesize psychology, philosophy, and biology. Groos also produced work on aesthetics and the psychological analysis of documents.

Biographic data: HPA 2:115

DE SANCTIS, SANTE [263]

Italian psychiatrist
Rating: 13
Born: Parrano, Umbria, February 7, 1862
Died: Rome, February 20, 1935
Highest degree: M.D., 1886
Positions: 1892–1935, University of Rome, where for the first ten years he worked in the Psychiatric Clinic and taught psychiatry; he taught experimental psychology between 1907 and 1930, but he was also the director of the Psychiatric Clinic from 1910 to 1930 and director of the Neuropsychiatric Clinic for the last five years of his life

De Sanctis is credited with establishing experimental psychology and child psychiatry in Italy. In 1906, he established a psychological laboratory at the University of Rome, became the first graduate teacher of experimental psychology in Italy, and expanded considerably the teaching of experimental psychology at the University of Rome. Otherwise his main interest was the training and education of retarded children. De Sanctis organized the first school for retardates in Italy in 1899. He left behind numerous publications. Of importance to psychology are his books *I sogni* (1899), *La mimica del pensiero* (1904), *La conversione religiosa* (1924; English translation, *Religious Conversion*, 1927), and *Psicologia sperimentale* in two volumes (1929–1930).

Biographic data: *HPA* 3:83; M. Ponzo, La figura di Sante De Sanctis nella scienza e nella vita. *Archivio italiano di psicologia*, 1935, 13, 3-8

[264]

MOLL, ALBERT

German psychiatrist
Rating: 13
Born: Lissa, Prussia (now Leszno, Poland), May 4, 1862
Died: Berlin, September 23, 1939
Highest degree: M.D.
Positions: Private practice in Berlin; editor, *Zeitschrift für Psychotherapie und medizinische Psychologie*, 1902–1904

Moll introduced hypnotic psychotherapy in Germany (*Der Hypnotismus*, 1889, English translation, *Hypnotism*, 1902), studied sexual problems (*Die conträre Sexualempfindung*, 1891; *Das nervöse Weib*, 1898; *Das Sexualleben des Kindes*, 1909, English translation 1912; *Handbuch der Sexualwissenschaften*, two volumes, 1912, editor; *Behandlung der Homosexualität, biochemisch oder psychisch?* 1921; *Untersuchungen über die libido sexualis*, English translation, 1933), and wrote on psychic research, in which area he spoke out for scientific research (*Prophezeien und Hellsehen*, 1922; *Der Spiritismus*, 1924; *Psychologie und Charakterologie für Okkultisten*, 1929).

Biographic data: A. Moll, *Ein Leben als Arzt der Seele*, 1936

[265]

KULPE, OSWALD

German psychologist
Rating: 27
Born: Kandava, Latvia, August 3, 1862
Died: Munich, December 30, 1915
Highest degree: Ph.D. in psychology, University of Leipzig, 1887, under W. Wundt [161]

Positons, honors: 1887, University of Leipzig; 1894, University of Würzburg; 1909, University of Bonn; 1913, University of Munich; honorary medical degree, 1907, University of Giessen

Külpe began to take issue with Wundtian psychology publicly in 1893 when in his *Grundriss der Psychologie* (English translation, *Outlines of Psychology*, 1895) he criticized the subtractive procedure used by Wundt to measure the duration of thought processes. Külpe was at first strictly Wundtian. He elaborated on Wundt's notion of attributes in his doctrine of attributes (quality, intensity, duration, plus extension for vision and touch). It added an element of nativism (he thought space could not be constituted from nonspatial attributes) to his basically empiricist orientation. He made no mention of thinking but counted a very large number (12,000) of sensations. Külpe's reaction time work in Wundt's laboratory, however, started him on a line of thought that led eventually away from Wundtian psychology toward the experimental study of thought, which Wundt held to be an impossibility. Külpe applied the method of "systematic experimental introspection" to the investigation of thinking. Subjects performed some cognitive task and then analyzed their own thought processes used in the task.

Although Külpe established psychological laboratories at Würzburg (1896) and Bonn, he himself did little experimental work. He headed a group of psychologists, however, who did. The most important of these were Ach [333], Bühler [385], Marbe [311], and Watt [386]. They and their work came to be called the Würzburg school of imageless thought. The writings of the school began with a 1901 paper by Mayer and Orth. To Külpe, there were cognitive contents and cognitive acts. The cognitive acts were states of awareness of the existence of rules, relations, and intention, and could not be said to have a sensory content, representation, or image. It was imageless thought. Külpe's psychology included both content and function or act. In his own day Külpe and the Würzburg school made important new contributions to the study of thought. A broader additional effect that, through later psychologists, has continued to this day was the emphasis placed on the role of motivation, set, and the nature of the cognitive task on thinking, as well as the recognition that not only elements consciously present in mind could affect thinking but that unconscious determinants were at work also. The radical development of the latter proposition is to be found in Freud [224]. Külpe's criticism of Wundt's elementism and his inclusion of both content and act in psychology on the one hand, and his analysis of mental life that was still done in terms of elements, albeit nonsensory ones, on the other, placed Külpe midway between structuralism and Gestalt psychology. The originator of the Gestalt theory, Max Wertheimer [391], was a student of Külpe's.

Biographic data: *EP* 4:367; *IESS* 8:467; R. M. Ogden, Oswald Külpe and the Würzburg school. *American Journal of Psychology,* 1951, 64, 4–19

[266] MEUMANN, ERNST

German psychologist
Rating: 23
Born: Uerdingen bei Wesel, North Rhine-Westphalia, August 29, 1862
Died: Hamburg, April 15, 1915
Highest degree: Ph.D. in philosophy and theology, University of Tübingen, 1887
Positions: 1894, University of Leipzig; 1897, University of Zurich; 1905, University of Königsberg; 1908, University of Münster; 1909; University of Halle; 1910, University of Leipzig; 1911, University of Hamburg

Meumann became a leader in experimental education and educational psychology in Germany, after having done general-experimental work under Wundt [161], and later independently. Among his researches are those on organic sensations, done in 1907 and 1909 (he differentiated the sensations of stomach repletion and emptiness, cardiac oppression, and suffocation, which have been discarded since), on time perception (1892 to 1896), for the study of which he invented an important piece of apparatus, on rhythm (1894), memory, types of attention, and aesthetics. In the area of educational psychology, Meumann started the *Zeitschrift für experimentelle Pädagogik* (1905) later renamed *Zeitschrift für padagogische Psychologie und Jugendkunde,* founded and edited the *Archiv für die gesamte Psychologie,* and wrote *Uber Oekonomie und Technik des Lernens* (1903) and *Vorlesungen zur Einführung in die experimentelle Pädagogik und ihre psychologische Grundlagen* (1907–1914).

Biographic data: G. Störring, Nachruf für Ernst Meumann. *Archiv für die gesamte Psychologie,* 1915, 34, i–xiv; [Anon.]

Ernst Meumann. *American Journal of Psychology,* 1923, 34, 271–274

ZIEHEN, THEODOR

German psychiatrist
Rating: 18
Born: Frankfurt-am-Main, November 12, 1862
Died: Wiesbaden, Hesse, December 29, 1950
Highest degree: M.D., University of Berlin, 1885
Positions, honors: 1886, University of Jena; 1900, University of Utrecht; 1903, University of Halle; 1904–1912, University of Berlin; 1917–1930, University of Halle, honorary Ph.D., University of Berlin, 1910

Ziehen had an interest in both psychiatry and philosophy, as a result of which he wrote some successful books in psychology. While not contributing much that was original, Ziehen seldom used the ideas of others in their original form but modified them or disagreed with some aspect of them. This made him a successful textbook writer. His *Leitfaden der physiologischen Psychologie,* first published in 1891 had twelve (English translation, *Introduction to Physiological Psychology,* 1892), editions. Other successful books in psychology written by Ziehen were *Die Grundlagen der Psychologie,* two volumes (1915), *Die Beziehung der Lebenserscheinungen zum Bewusstsein* (1921), *Das Seelenleben der Jugendlichen* (1923), *Allgemeine Psychologie* (1923), and others. Ziehen's books, monographs, and articles in psychology, psychiatry, and philosophy were numerous.

Ziehen's view was that each science takes as its own a segment of the experientially given without the need to trace back its origin epistemologically. The knowledge of the epistemological origins of its raw material is, however, necessary for the psychologist because he must know what it is that is given for him. There is the difficulty of defining either that which is being experienced or to derive it from anything else. Ziehen called the mental givens "gignomena," in analogy to phenomena, and stressed the necessity of studying them so as to remain entirely within the realm of that which is immediately given (the principle of immanence), beyond mind-body dualism, but without becoming transcendental and thus losing the scientific ground of enquiry.

Biographic data: *EP* 8:379; *HPA* 1:471

[268]

LANGE, LUDWIG

German psychologist
Rating: 12
Born: 1863
Died: 1936
Highest degree: Ph.D. in psychology, University of Leipzig 1886, under W. Wundt [161]
Positions: University of Tübingen

Working in Wundt's laboratory, Lange established (in 1888) that some of the differences in reaction time between individuals was owing to their attending to either the stimulus (sensorial reaction) or the response (muscular reaction). In the latter case the reaction time was shorter. This clarified the nature of the personal equation devised by astronomers to account for individual differences between them in observing stellar transits. Külpe (265) used Lange's finding to support his contention that the subject's predisposition affects his sensory and motor responses. Lange's work created interest in the role of attention, as contrasted with simple reaction. Later, Lange was cited as a pioneer of experimental investigation of the dynamics of attitude.

Biographic data: *Enciclopedia universal ilustrada,* vol. 29

[269]

JASTROW, JOSEPH

American psychologist
Rating: 22
Born: Warsaw, Poland, January 30, 1863
Died: Stockbridge, Massachusetts, January 8, 1944
Highest degree: Ph.D. in psychology, Johns Hopkins University, 1886, under G. S. Hall [418]
Positions: 1888, University of Wisconsin; 1927–1933, New School of Social Research; president, American Psychological Association, 1900

Jastrow's was the first American doctorate taken specifically in psychology. His early work was in psychophysics. An important paper, written with C. S. Peirce [177] in 1884, anticipated the work of Fullerton [251] and Cattell [256] concerning the substitution of the probable error for the ordinary threshold measure and hence fixing the difference threshold at the point where the discrimination is made 75 percent rather than 50 percent of the time. After this, Jastrow published numerous papers on a variety of topics in general psychology, in line with his nonadherence to any school, and an eclectic borrowing of the best from all. At Wisconsin, Jastrow began publishing a series of "minor studies," a custom soon emulated by psychologists elsewhere. His own series numbered twenty-five studies. They resulted from his and his own students' work in the experimental psychology laboratory that Jastrow established there in 1888.

Jastrow is best known as a popularizer of the "new" psychology. In 1895, he arranged an exhibit of psychology at the Chicago World's Fair, which aroused popular interest in psychology. He wrote a column, "Keeping Mentally Fit," which was syndicated in many newspapers. He was skilled in presenting scientific psychology both orally and in writing in a way that appealed to the general public. Of his several books (*The Subconscious*, 1906; *Psychology of Conviction*, 1918; *Keeping Mentally Fit*, 1928; *The House That Freud Built*, 1932; *The Betrayal of Intelligence*, 1938), *Fact and Fable in Psychology* (1900) was most popular.

Biographic data: *HPA* 1:135; *NCAB* 11:373; C. L. Hull, Joseph Jastrow. *American Journal of Psychology*, 1944, 57, 581–585; W. B. Pillsbury, Joseph Jastrow. *Psychological Review*, 1944, 51, 261–265; V. A. C. Henmon, Joseph Jastrow. *Science*, 1944, 94, 193

MEAD, GEORGE HERBERT [270]

American philosopher
Rating: 19
Born: South Hadley, Massachusetts, February 27, 1863
Died: Chicago, Illinois, April 26, 1931
Education: Did graduate work at Harvard University, 1887–1888, studied psychology and philosophy in Europe, 1888–1891
Positions: 1891, University of Michigan; 1894, University of Chicago

Mead made a contribution to social psychology by way of his interpretation of the origin of the self. The self arises, according to Mead, from social interaction, and language plays a crucial part in its development. It is through language that a child, who at first has no innate self-consciousness, learns to play the role of other persons and experiences the social feedback from such role playing. As a result he learns to think of himself as an object, since others act toward him as an object, and he reacts in kind. Thus a notion of self can arise only in a social setting. In this way more than one self can develop.

Mead influenced considerably the thinking of a number of prominent psychologists, such as Sullivan [474], and psychological thinking in the area of the psychology of personality. Mead and Dewey [253] knew each other, were both pragmatists, went to Chicago from Michigan at the same time, and Dewey acknowledged his debt to Mead in the development of his own philosophy.

Biographic data: *EP* 5:231; *IESS* 10:83; D. L. Miller, *George Herbert Mead, Self, Language, and the World,* 1973, pp. xi-xxxviii

[271]

CALKINS, MARY WHITON

American psychologist
Rating: **20**
Born: Hartford, Connecticut, March 30, 1863
Died: Newton, Massachusetts, February 27, 1930
Highest degree: Ph.D. in psychology, Harvard University, 1895, under William James [184]
Positions, honors: 1891, Wellesley College; president, American Psychological Association, 1905

At Wellesley, Calkins set up the first psychological laboratory, and in 1896, published a paper in which the methodology for paired associates learning was first presented. The method was reinvented by Georg Müller [208] a few years later and has been used widely ever since. Her chief interest was psychology as a science of the self, which she opposed to the view of psychology as a succession of experiences. A paper expressing this view, "Psychology As a Science of Selves," published in 1900, raised criticism and objections by others. She answered the criticisms in her 1905 presidential address at the American Psychological Association meeting and in subsequent papers. Her views were gathered in a systematic treatise in 1910 when *A First Book in Psychology* (2d edition, 1914) appeared. Its main theme was the blending of conceptions of psychology of the self and psychology of succeeding mental events into a single conceptual framework. Calkins's concept of the psychic element and the doctrine of relational elements of experience also appear in her other books, *Introduction to Psychology* (1901, 2d edition, 1905) and *Der doppelte Standpunkt in Psychologie* (1905).

Biographic data: HPA 1:31; NCAB 13:75

MUNSTERBERG, HUGO

[272]

German-American psychologist
Rating: 24
Born: Danzig, East Prussia, June 1, 1863
Died: Cambridge, Massachusetts, December 16, 1916
Highest degree: Ph.D. in psychology, University of Leipzig, 1885, under W. Wundt [161]; M.D., University of Heidelberg, 1887
Positions: 1887, University of Freiburg; 1892–1895, 1897–1916, Harvard University; president, American Psychological Association, 1898

Although William James [184] started the first psychological laboratory in the United States at Harvard, he was tempermentally not an experimentalist and asked Münsterberg to take over the direction of the laboratory. Münsterberg at that time had attracted attention as an original experimenter (*Beiträge zur experimentellen Psychologie*, 1889–1892). Münsterberg directed the Harvard laboratory for a few years, but began to be involved in other things and neglected the laboratory. These other things, however, were his major contribution to psychology, namely the development of applied psychology in America. As his work as a researcher ended with the *Beiträge*, his work in applying psychological principles to industrial, educational, legal, medical, clinical, and business problems began. At a time when there was little application of psychological knowledge to practical affairs, Münsterberg wrote such volumes as *Psychology and the Teacher* (1909), *Psychotherapy* (1909), *On the Witness Stand* (1910), *Psychology and Industrial Efficiency* (1913), *Grundzüge der Psychotechnik* (1914), and *Psychology: General and Applied* (1914). Earlier, he had completed *Die Willenshandlung* (1888), an expanded version of his dissertation, *Psychology and Life* (1899), and *Grundzüge der Psychologie* (1900), in which he set forth his philosophical theory of psychology, "voluntaristic idealism." Neither his philosophical nor his psychological theories (action theory) attracted much attention at the time. Neither did they leave much of an imprint on psychology.

Much of Münsterberg's applied psychology was armchair psychology, but he himself and his students did some empirical work also, such as producing some of the first efforts to validate aptitude tests. Münsterberg contacted business people with suggestions on how they might use psychology. In the area of psychotherapy, Münsterberg was one of the early users of hypnotism. While in the area of education his influence was not so strong because others were working in that field already, his book on the psychology of witness testimony was a landmark publication, and no other such book was written in the next twenty years. It included the suggestion that veracity and blood pressure might be related, a relationship that is now incorporated in the polygraph.

Advocacy of applied psychology, combined with his involvement in psychic research, made Münsterberg a public figure. He not only showed people outside of psychology how psychology can work for them, but also convinced a small number of psychologists that applied psychology was a legitimate enterprise. This latter group has grown in size steadily ever since. Münsterberg's influence could have been greater had it not been for his vocal advocacy of things German and the beginning of the first World War soon after the publication of his applied psychology texts. Animosity toward Germans even precluded the publication of an appreciation upon his death.

Biographic data: *IESS* 10:561; *NCAB* 13:85; M. Münsterberg, *Hugo Münsterberg: His Life and Work,* 1922; W. Stern, Hugo Münsterberg. *Journal of Applied Psychology*, 1917,1, 186–188

[273]

SCHUMANN, FRIEDRICH

German psychologist
Rating: **19**
Born: Hildsheim, Lower Saxony, June 16, 1863
Died: Frankfurt-am-Main, January 10, 1940
Highest degree: Ph.D. in physics, University of Göttingen, 1885
Positions: 1885, University of Göttingen; 1894, University of Berlin; 1905, University of Zurich; 1910–1928, University of Frankfurt

In addition to physics, Schumann also studied psychology under G. E. Müller [208] at Göttingen. He conducted experiments and published with Müller studies on psychophysics, memory, sensory psychology, and perception. He constructed apparatus for studying time perception and a tachistoscope, and in general, influenced Müller to become a real experimenter. With Müller, Schumann was a cofounder of the Gesellschaft für experimentelle Psychologie, and when Ebbinghaus [207] died, took over the editorship of the *Zeitschrift für Psychologie*.

During the early 1900s, Schumann conducted a large number of experiments that make him a direct precursor of the founders of the Gestalt school of psychology ("Beiträge zur Analyse der Gesichtswahrnehmungen," published in *Zeitschrift für Psychologie* between 1900 and 1904). The experiments were phenomenological in nature, but represented a definite advance over the speculations of the form-quality school. Always relating his results to the physical properties of the stimuli and to the factor of attention, Schumann arrived at a number of conclusions that later became basic Gestalt laws: attention may either join the parts of a figure into a whole or else emphasize a part so that the perception of the whole becomes secondary; incomplete figures tend to be perceived as complete; nearness, as well as equal distances among the components makes for the grouping of visual components into larger wholes; vertical symmetry favors perceptual connectedness; ambiguous figures tend to be seen as "good" figures; properties of figures, such as grouping and organization, have their origin in both central and stimulus factors. In spite of his contributions to Gestalt psychology, Schumann is not counted among its founders since he made no attempt to go beyond his empirical findings and fit them into a theoretical framework.

Biographic data: W. Metzger, Friedrich Schumann, ein Nachruf. *Zeitschrift für Psychologie*, 1940, 148, 1–18

SPEARMAN, CHARLES EDWARD   [274]

English psychologist
Rating: 27
Born: London, September 10, 1863
Died: London, September 17, 1945

Highest degree: Ph.D. in psychology, University of Leipzig, 1904, under W. Wundt [161]

Positions: 1906–1931, University College, London; president, British Psychological Society, 1923–1926

Spearman had a late start in psychology, but he compensated for it by the thoroughness of his education (he spent several years in postdoctoral work with Külpe [265], G. E. Müller [208], and studying physiology) and the significance of his subsequent contributions. In 1904, he wrote two important papers, one on reliability measurements, the other on the structure of intelligence. By examining the intercorrelations of the scores on various intellectual tasks given school children he arrived at the conclusion that, since most such measures were correlated, a general intelligence factor underlay all intellectual tasks (the G factor), while several different specific factors (s factors) were involved, each pertaining to its particular task. Spearman theorized that intelligence is made up of these two kinds of factors (*the two-factor theory of intelligence*).

Spearman contributed not only to the theory of intelligence but also to the extension of the use of correlation measures to infer structures and processes, as well as to the development of the notion of statistical factors. Factor analysis, however, was not developed until the 1930s, and Spearman used a technique known as the *tetrad equation,* which he himself developed. Spearman summarized his work in a 1927 book, *The Abilities of Man,* in which he also related the G and s factors to attention, conation, and similar psychological processes. Spearman had always wanted to establish the fundamental laws of psychology. Seeing the scope of the concept of intelligence factors, Spearman wrote an article (in 1930) to show that the G concept represented a school to end all schools. The study of intelligence and the development of factor analysis have been closely related ever since, and the question of the structure of intelligence raised by Spearman has not been finally settled yet. Spearman's work in statistics yielded several well-known and widely used statistical measures, such as the *Spearman rank order correlation coefficient*, the *Spearman-Brown prophecy formula,* and *the correction for attenuation of the correlation coefficient.* In addition to *The Abilities of Man,* Spearman wrote *The Nature of Intelligence and the Principles of Cognition* (1923), *Creative Mind* (1931), and *Psychology Down the Ages* (1937).

Biographic data: *DNB* 1941–1950; *HPA* 1:299; *IESS* 15:108; E. L. Thorndike, Charles Edward Spearman. *American Journal of*

Psychology, 1945, 58, 558–560; J. C. Flugel, Charles Edward Spearman. *British Journal of Psychology*, 1946, 37, 1–6; C. Burt, Obituary: Professor Charles Edward Spearman. *Nature*, 1945, 156, 740–741

DELABARRE, EDMUND BURKE

[275]

American psychologist
Rating: 12
Born: Dover, Maine, September 25, 1863
Died: Providence, Rhode Island, March 16, 1945
Highest degree: Ph.D. in psychology, University of Freiburg, 1891, under H. Münsterberg [272]
Positions: 1892, Brown University; 1896, Harvard University; 1897–1932, Brown University

A year after obtaining his doctorate, Delabarre established a psychological laboratory at Brown University and became one of the twenty-six individuals who founded the American Psychological Association. From 1896 to 1897 he ran William James's [184] laboratory at Harvard. Delabarre published both experimental and theoretical papers on philosophical psychology, consciousness, visual perception, social psychology, and muscular sensations. He had formulated a motor theory of consciousness and planned to write a systematic treatise on it, but never did. He likewise failed to publish many of his experiments, involving hundreds of hours of work that he had spent observing muscular movements. For this purpose, Delabarre, invented the first long tape *kymograph* to record lengthy observations of muscular movements. In 1898 he also made the first eye movement recordings using a mechanical device—a cup on the eye traced paths on a kymograph tape. Because of his failure to publish much of his work Delabarre's influence of psychology was slight.

Biographic data: L. Carmichael, Edmund Burke Delabarre. *American Journal of Psychology*, 1945, 58, 406–409; H. Schlosberg, Edmund Burke Delabarre. *Psychological Review*, 1945, 53, 183–186; R. S. Woodworth, Edmund Burke Delabarre. *Science*, 1945, 102, 369

STOELTING, CHRISTIAN (H.)

American layman
Rating: 12
Born: 1864
Died: Chicago, March 18, 1943

For many years Stoelting was the president of the C. H. Stoelting Company of Chicago that manufactured instruments and materials for psychological laboratories. Stoelting was actively involved not only in the manufacture of apparatus and instruments but also in designing new ones on the basis of direct knowledge of the needs of researchers. He himself visited the various psychological laboratories and studied experimental methods and problems. He would sometimes spend days and weeks at a given laboratory, and would run into financial difficulties when a new piece of equipment took a long time to be developed. The manufacture of "brass instruments" for psychology had been a German enterprise since the beginning of laboratory psychology. Stoelting changed this by making America the prime source of apparatus and equipment for psychological laboratories.

Biographic data: [Anon.] Christian H. Stoelting. *American Journal of Psychology*, 1943, 56, 450

UEXKULL, (BARON) JAKOB JOHANN VON

German biologist
Rating: 19
Born: Estonia, 1864
Died: Capri, Italy, 1944
Education: Studied zoology at University of Tartu between 1884 and 1900, later at University of Heidelberg
Positions: 1925, director, Institut für Umweltforschung, Hamburg

Uexküll was one of the forerunners of ethology. Uexküll first attracted attention by publishing in 1899, with T. Beer and A. Bethe, a paper in which they recommended that, in discussing animal behavior, all psychological terms, such as sensation or memory, be discarded, and terms like reception and resonance be used instead. Independently of Jennings [303], Uexküll arrived at views rather similar to his. Uexküll insisted that the observation of all behaviors must precede any attempt to explain specific behavior items in an animal species. Uexküll's major contribution was the concept of *Umwelt* (*Umwelt und Innenwelt der Tiere*, 1909; *Streifzüge durch die Umwelten von Tieren und Menschen*, 1934). Uexküll realized that only certain aspects of the animal's physical environment (*Merkwelt* or the sum total of possible stimuli) have a significance for him. Only these stimuli (the releasers), either innately or through learning, release the animal's behaviors. The totality of such stimuli Uexküll named the animal's *Umwelt*. Each kind of animal lives in its special *Umwelt*. Internally, each animal has its *Innenwelt* or an internal orienting mechanism which conditions the animal's response to the *Umwelt* in such a way as to produce and maintain some optimum adjustment to it. The relationship between the animal and the stimuli of the *Umwelt* is reciprocal. As the animal reacts to them, the reaction changes the sensory qualities of the stimuli, which elicits a new reaction on the part of the animal. The symbolic representation of this circular interaction Uexküll called the *Funktionskreis* (functional circle), which represents the perfectly matched worlds of releasers and the world of the animal's responses to them.

Biographic data: EP 8:173

RIVERS, (BARON) WILLIAM HALSE RIVERS [278]

English psychologist and anthropologist
Rating: 19
Born: Luton, Kent, March 12, 1864
Died: Cambridge, June 4, 1922
Highest degree: M.D., St. Bartholomew's Hospital, London, 1886
Positions, honors: 1893–1922, Cambridge University, appointed to first lectureship in experimental and physiological psychology in 1897, first director of Cambridge psychological laboratory; 1914–1918, psychologist in Royal Air Force; honorary degrees from St. Andrews University and Manchester University

Upon receiving his appointment at Cambridge, Rivers did some work on vision. He then participated (1898) with McDougall [329] and Myers [341] in the Cambridge anthropological expedition to the Torres Straits, did some of the first measurements of individual differences in nontechnological societies, and reported on the color vision, perception of geometric illusions, and other visual phenomena in the Torres Straits aborigenes in 1901. Later, he visited southern India (1902) and reported on the color vision on the inhabitants of that area in 1905. In 1908 he visited Melanesia. Rivers's anthropological observations were published in two books, *The Todas* (1906) and *History of Melanesian Society* (1914). Between expeditions Rivers collaborated with Henry Head [261] on a famous experiment (published in 1905 and 1908) on sensitivity changes during the regeneration of a cut nerve in the arm (Rivers's arm). In 1904, Rivers, Myers [341], and Ward [190] founded the *British Journal of Psychology*. During World War I and in connection with his work with the Royal Air Force, Rivers became interested in neurological problems. He was concerned with problems in medical psychology until his death. During this period Rivers also published a book, *Instinct and the Unconscious* (1920), that was instrumental in providing a favorable reception of Freud's [224] psychoanalytic theory in England.

Biographic data: *IESS* 13:526; F. C. Bartlett, William Halse Rivers Rivers. *American Journal of Psychology*, 1923, 34 275–277; F. C. Bartlett, Cambridge, England, 1887–1937. *American Journal of Psychology*, 1937, **50**, 97–110, especially pp. 102–107

[279]

WEBER, MAX

German sociologist
Rating: 19
Born: Erfurt, Thuringia, April 21, 1864
Died: Munich, June 14, 1920
Highest degree: Ph.D., University of Berlin, 1889
Positions: 1893, University of Berlin; 1894, University of Freiburg; 1897, University of Heidelberg; 1919, University of Munich

Weber's sociology of understanding is based on psychological understanding, the understanding of human motivation. Social science differs from natural science, according to Weber, in that the latter is concerned with antecedent causes whereas the former is concerned with the future—the why and whither of human behavior. To formulate his hypotheses, the sociologist needs "ideal types." Ideal types are concepts formulated by abstracting and combining elements of reality into mental constructs that have no counterpart in reality but help to analyze reality. Of his many works, Weber's *Die protestantische Ethik und der Geist des Kapitalismus* (1904–1905, English translation, *The Protestant Ethic and the Spirit of Capitalism*, 1930) is the best known. In it, Weber, using such ideal types as "17th century Calvinism," "20th century capitalism," and "Protestant ethic," develops the thesis that when the relationship between the various world religions and economics is compared, a close relationship is found only between Calvinsim and the development of capitalism. The asceticism of the Middle Ages turned into an asceticism of the "inner world": work, activity, and entrepreneurship became behaviors willed by God. Human drives, instead of being suppressed are converted into work and the building of capital. Work thus becomes service to God and prosperity a visible manifestation of God's favor. Since Weber, it has become quite common to analyze Christian reform movements in terms of transformation or sublimation of human drives.

Biographic data: *EP* 8:282; *IESS* 16:493; Marianne Weber, *Max Weber*, 1950

SCRIPTURE, EDWARD WHEELER [280]

American psychologist
Rating: 23
Born: Mason, New Hampshire, May 21, 1864
Died: Henleaze, near Bristol, England, July 31, 1945
Highest degree: Ph.D. in psychology, University of Leipzig, 1891, under W. Wundt [161]; M.D., University of Munich, 1906
Positions: 1891, fellow at Clark University; 1892–1903, teaching psychology, director, Psychology Laboratory

A year after receiving his doctorate from Wundt, Scripture became one of the cofounders of the American Psychological Association. At Yale, Scripture took over the direction of the psychological laboratory from G. T. Ladd [186], and during his decade or so there, produced enough research to fill a yearly volume of articles (Scripture's complete bibliography contains 225 references). He did much of the work himself, especially in the area of reaction time measurement and hearing. In the latter area he invented a device (the *strobilion*) that made the human voice visible. At Yale, Scripture wrote *Thinking, Feeling, Doing*

(1895) and *The New Psychology* (1897). The "new psychology" was the scientific, experimental, physiological psychology of Helmholtz [143], Fechner [120], and Wundt [161], and Scripture's label came into general use. Scripture's interest gradually turned from psychology to phonetics, speech, and speech defects. He left not only psychology but America to work in Europe, where he held a number of nonpsychological appointments, including the professorship of experimental phonetics at the University of Vienna for ten years.

Biographic data: *HPA* 3:231; *NCAB* 10:310; E. G. Boring, Edward Wheeler Scripture. *American Journal of Psychology,* 1965, 78, 314–317

[281]

COOLEY, CHARLES HORTON

American sociologist
Rating: 13
Born: Ann Arbor, Michigan, August 17, 1864
Died: Ann Arbor, Michigan, May 8, 1929
Highest degree: Ph.D. in political economy, University of Michigan, 1894
Positions: 1894–1929, University of Michigan; president, American Sociological Society, 1918

Cooley's important psychological contributions were in the field of social psychology. He considered the self and the society as inseparable, each contributing to the identity of the other. Like James [184] and Baldwin [259], Cooley considered communication between individuals the essential characteristic of social relations. People respond to what they think the other person is, not what he actually is. The society exists therefore in an individual's mind. Likewise, the abstract individual, without reference to society, is inconceivable. Individuality is shaped by the primary groups: the family, peer group, neighborhood. Personality traits and attitudes arise in the course of interaction in such face-to-face relationships. The child sees himself as others see him (the "looking-glass self"). Society and the individual are "collective and distributive aspects of the same thing." Cooley's best known works are *Human Nature and the Social Order* (1902), *Social Organization* (1909), and *Social Process* (1918).

Biographic data: *IESS* 3:378

HOBHOUSE, LEONARD TRELAWNEY

English sociologist
Rating: **19**
Born: St. Ives. near Liskeard, Cornwall, September 8, 1864
Died: Alençon, Normandy, France, June 21, 1929
Education: Studied at Oxford University, 1883–1887
Positions, honors: 1890, Corpus Christi College, tutor; 1897–1907, editorial and newspaper work; 1907–1929, University, of London, teaching sociology; D. Litt., Durham University, 1913; LL.D., St. Andrews University, 1919

Most of Hobhouse's writings were in philosophy and sociology. Hobhouse's contribution to psychology stems from his having written, in 1901, the book *Mind in Evolution*. The reason for Hobhouse's venturing into psychology as well as other fields was that he considered sociology to be not just a discipline among others but a conceptual framework that helped to explain all social life, as well as biology and philosophy. Hobhouse's book summarized and systematized the work of Lubbock [166], Romanes [203], Morgan [214], and other early comparative psychologists, presented Hobhouse's own animal experiments, which were similar to those later performed by Köhler [447] with apes, and served *to found the science of phylogenetic psychology*. Hobhouse traced the psychological development of animals by examining the evolution of instincts, habits, and higher processes from the simplest organisms to man. He attempted to show that man's mind and body were the product of simultaneous evolution. *Mind in Evolution* was the first comprehensive treatment of such data and problems.

Biographic data: DNB 1922–1930; *EP* 4:46; *IESS* 6:481; M. Ginsberg and J. A. Hobson, *L.T. Hobhouse: His Life and Work*, 1931

WHEELER, WILLIAM MORTON

American biologist
Rating: **11**
Born: Milwaukee, Wisconsin, March 19, 1865
Died: Cambridge, Massachusetts, April 19, 1937
Highest degree: Ph.D. in biology, Clark University, 1892

Positions, honors: 1892, University of Chicago; 1899, University of Texas; 1903, American Museum of Natural History, curator of Invertebrate Zoology; 1908, Harvard University; four honorary degrees, two medals

Wheeler specialized in the biology of insects. He wrote several hundred papers in biology, most of them on ants and some on the behavior of ants. Books by Wheeler that were important to comparative psychology include *Ants, Their Structure, Development, and Behavior* (1910), *Social Life among the Insects* (1923), *Foibles of Insects and Men* (1928), and *The Social Insects, Their Origin and Evolution* (1928).

Biographic data: NCAB 27:395; G. H. Parker, Biographical memoir of William Morton Wheeler. *Biographical Memoirs of the National Academy of Science*, 1938, 19, 203–241

[284]

MATSUMOTO, MATATARO

Japanese psychologist
Rating: 11
Born: Takasaki, Gumma, September 15, 1865
Died: Tokyo, 1943
Highest degree: Ph.D. in psychology, Yale University, 1899, under E. W. Scripture [280]
Positions: 1900–1906, Tokyo Higher Normal School; 1900–1905, Tokyo Higher Female Normal School; 1901–1906, University of Tokyo; 1906–1916, University of Kyoto; 1910–1915, Kyoto Municipal Higher School for Fine and Technical Arts; 1913–1926, University of Tokyo, irregular member; 1920–1929, Aeronautical Research Institute; 1929–1943 Tokyo Bunrika University; 1929–1943, Japan Women's University, Institute of Child Study; editor, *Japanese Journal of Psychology;* editorial work for *Journal of General Psychology*

Matsumoto was an assistant at Yale for three years and did work with Scripture [280] in general experimental psychology. He was first to use the *sound cage* in the study of auditory perception. After obtaining his Ph.D. he worked for a year in the psychological laboratory at Leipzig. Upon his return to Japan, Matsumoto established a psychological laboratory at the University of Tokyo in 1903, and in 1908, another at the University of Kyoto. In spite of his training, Matsumoto gravitated toward experimental applied psychology. He may be credited with introducing experimental applied psychology in Japan, especially through his book *Psychocinematics* (1914), in which he described the objective study of purposive motor acts. His *Psychology of Intelligence* (1925) and *Psychology and Practical Life* (1926) were also works in applied psychology. In addition to applied psychology, Matsumoto was also interested in art and wrote *Psychological Interpretation of Modern Japanese Paintings* (1915) and *Psychology of Aesthetic Appreciation of Pictorial Arts* (1926). He also wrote *Lectures in Experimental Psychology* (1914), *Outlines of Psychology* (1923), *Psychical Dispositions* (1929), and *Psychology of Childhood* (1930). Matsumoto contributed to the development of psychology in Japan through his writings and research as well as in training almost all of the senior psychologists in Japan.

Biographic data: *The Psychological Register,* 1939, vol. 3

STRATTON, GEORGE MALCOLM [285]

American psychologist
Rating: 22
Born: Oakland, California, September 26, 1865
Died: Berkeley, California, October 8, 1957
Highest degree: Ph.D. in psychology, University of Leipzig, 1896, under W. Wundt [161]
Positions: 1896, University of California at Berkeley; 1904, Johns Hopkins University; 1908–1935, University of California; president, American Psychological Association, 1908

Stratton was part of the first crop of Wundtian experimentalists in America. With Wundt he performed experiments on pressure patterns on the skin, and on his arrival at the University of California, established there a psychological laboratory in 1899 and became its director. He is remembered mostly for having performed the first of the very few experiments on the effects of prolonged distortion of the visual field (Vision without inversion of the retinal image. *Psychological Review,* 1897, 4, 341–360, 463–481). By wearing lenses that inverted the visual world for eighty-seven hours, distributed over eight days, Stratton answered a question that theretofore had been given only a priori answers. While the world looked upside down at first and

Stratton was greatly hampered in his behavior, adjustment quickly took place, and while the world did not look quite right side up even after eight days, his behavior adapted as if it were. Vision and kinesthesis had found a new basis on which to act in harmony.

In 1902, Stratton performed a classic experiment that settled empirically another theoretical question. By recording eye movements of subjects who were examining symmetric and asymmetric art objects, Stratton was able to establish that aesthetic experience could not arise from the presumed smooth and symmetric eye movements as the eyes explored symmetric and regular contours, because eye movements in response to even perfectly symmetric objects were jerky, did not follow the contours exactly, and were far from symmetrically distributed between the two halves of the symmetric object.

Stratton's reputation is based mainly on his work on the inversion of the retinal image. He believed that there was a point beyond which science could not go and that a higher reality existed beyond the senses. Although Stratton himself considered his contributions as a social psychologist the most important, his writings on the subject have elicited little attention from psychologists. These include the books, *Psychology of Religious Life* (1911), *Theophrastus and the Greek Physiological Psychology* (1917), *Experimental Psychology and Its Bearing Upon Culture* (1903), *Anger: Its Religious and Moral Significance* (1923), *The Social Psychology of International Conduct* (1929), and quite a number of papers on social and political issues and their relation to human nature.

Biographic data: NCAB 13:551; O. Bridgman, George Malcolm Stratton. *American Journal of Psychology,* 1958, 71, 460–461; C. W. Brown, George Malcolm Stratton, social psychologist. *Science,* 1958, 127, 1432–1433

[286]

SEASHORE, CARL EMIL

American psychologist
Rating: 24
Born: Mörlunda, Sweden, January 28, 1866
Died: Lewiston, Idaho, October 16, 1949
Highest degree: Ph.D. in psychology Yale University, 1895, under E. W. Scripture [280]
Positions, honors: 1897–1938, from assistant professor of philosophy to dean of graduate college (from 1908); president,

American Psychological Association, 1911; three honorary degrees

At Iowa, Seashore established a psychological laboratory and the second psychological clinic in the United States. He was also instrumental in promoting the Iowa Child Welfare Research Station. He was its general supervisor until his death. During his time, the Station issued some 1,000 publications. Seashore wrote a number of general psychology texts, such as *Elementary Experiments in Psychology* (1908), *Psychology in Daily Life* (1918), *Introduction to Psychology* (1923), and *Pioneering in Psychology* (1923). He also contributed in the area of the psychology of speech and phonetics and in educational psychology. He was dean of the Graduate College at Iowa and helped to identify and measure special talent and scholastic aptitude. He produced the *Iowa Placement Examinations,* the *Meier-Seashore Art Judgment Test* (1930, with N. C. Meier), and the *Seashore Measures of Musical Talents* (rev. ed. 1939, preceded by his 1919 *Psychology of Musical Talent*). The latter is his best known and most widely used test. The recorded test consists of subtests measuring pitch, loudness, rhythm, time, and timbre discrimination, and tonal memory. Seashore also produced a complete, classic treatise on the psychology of music, *Psychology of Music* (1938), his lifelong interest. In this field Seashore's book finds few competitors even today.

Biographic data: *HPA* 1:225; *NCAB* A:227; G. D. Stoddard, Carl Emil Seashore. *American Journal of Psychology,* 1950, 63, 456–462; D. Starch, Carl Emil Seashore. *Journal of Educational Psychology,* 1950, 41, 217–218; J. Tiffin, Carl Emil Seashore. *Psychological Review,* 1950, 57, 1–2; M. Metfessel, Carl Emil Seashore. *Science,* 1950, 111, 713–717; W. R. Miles, Carl Emil Seashore. *National Academy of Sciences Biographical Memoirs,* 1956, 29, 265–316

STARBUCK, EDWIN DILLER [287]

American psychologist
Rating: 12
Born: Bridgeport, Indiana, February 20, 1866
Died: Los Angeles, California, November 18, 1947
Highest degree: Ph.D. in psychology, Clark University, 1897, under G. S. Hall [418]

Positions: 1897, Stanford University, education; 1904, Earlham College, Indiana, education; 1906, University of Iowa, philosophy; 1930–1943, University of Southern California; 1924–1947, director, Institute of Character Research

Starbuck's interests were in religion, philosophy, and education. He pioneered in the study of the psychology of religion both through research (such as the turn-of-the-century study of the phenomemon of religious conversion among young people) and writing (*The Psychology of Religion*, 1899). Starbuck was also first to offer university courses on character education, educational psychology, and tests and measurements. In these areas he wrote *Guide to Literature for Character Training*, (2 volumes, 1927, 1929), and *Moral Education in the Public Schools* (1904).

Biographic data: NCAB E:319

[288]   **DUMAS, GEORGES**

French psychologist
Rating: 21
Born: Lédignan, Provence, March 6, 1866
Died: Lédignan, February 13, 1946
Highest degree: *Agrégé* in philosophy, 1889 (under T. A. Ribot [179]), docteur en médecine, 1890, docteur des lettres, 1900, all from Ecole Normale Supérieure, Paris
Positions: 1894–1902, Collège Chapatal; 1897–1939, director of Psychological Laboratory, Clinic of Mental Disorders, Medical School, Sorbonne

Like those of his teacher, Ribot [179], Dumas's interests tended in the direction of abnormal psychology, in which area he wrote *Névroses et psychoses de guerre chez les Austro-Allemands* (1918), *Troubles mentaux et troubles nerveux de guerre* (1920), and *Les états intellectuels dans la mélancolie* (1894). His other books have dealt with emotion: *Tolstoi et la philosophie de l'amour* (1893), *La tristesse et la joie* (1900), *Psychologie de deux messies positivistes, Saint-Simon et Auguste Comte* (1905), and *La sourire, psychologie et physiologie* (1906). With Janet [249], Dumas founded the *Journal de psychologie normale et pathologique* in 1903, but he is best known as the author of a two-volume treatise on psychology, the *Traité de psychologie*

(1923–1924), which was later revised and expanded into a multivolume *Nouveau traité de psychologie.* Its publication began in 1930 and Dumas served as editor and coauthor.

Biographic data: L. Litwinski, Georges Dumas. *British Journal of Psychology,* 1946, 37, 6–7; [Anon.] Georges Dumas. *Revista de psicología general y aplicada,* 1948, 3, 417–423

LAPICQUE, LOUIS

[289]

French physiologist
Rating: 18
Born: Epinal, Vosges, August 1, 1866
Died: Paris, December 6, 1952
Highest degree: M.D., 1895, Sc.D., 1897, Sorbonne
Positions, honors: 1894–1936, Sorbonne; numerous medals, awards, other honors

Lapicque acquired distinction for his work in neurophysiology. Of importance to physiological psychology was his work on nervous excitability (*La machine nerveuse,* 1943), especially that on the chronaxie (the duration that an electric current, twice the intensity threshold value, required to produce stimulation), which he named (*La chronaxie chez l'homme,* 1923). *Chronaxie* allowed the direct measurement of the effects on the nervous system of drugs, anesthetics, and other agents, as well as the study of the progress of nerve degeneration or regeneration. In 1913 Lapicque predicted that the chronaxie of motor fibers would be in inverse ratio to the diameter. This was later confirmed through the use of electronic instruments.

Biographic data: DSB 8:28; A.-M. Monnier, Louis Lapicque. *Journal de psychologie normale et pathologique,* 1953, 46, 371–378; J. F. Fulton, Louis Lapicque. *Journal of Neurophysiology,* 1953, 16, 97–100

GODDARD, HENRY HERBERT

[290]

American psychologist
Rating: 19
Born: Vassalboro, Maine, August 14, 1866

Died: Santa Barbara, California, June 18, 1957

Highest degree:, Ph.D. in psychology, Clark University, 1899, under G. S. Hall [418]

Positions: 1899, Pennsylvania State Teachers College at Westchester; 1906–1917, director of research Vineland (New Jersey) Training School for the Feeble-Minded; 1918–1921, director, Ohio State Bureau of Juvenile Research; 1922–1938, Ohio State University

Goddard established the first laboratory for the psychological study of the feeble-minded (at Vineland, New Jersey), and is known principally for his study of feeblemindedness. At Vineland, the concept of feeblemindedness was extended to include borderline cases, since owing to their number they were seen as constituting a socioeconomic and educational problem. Goddard coined and applied the term "moron" to such cases.

Goddard wrote several books, most of them on feeblemindedness and intelligence (*Feeblemindedness, Its Cause and Consequences*, 1914; *School Training of Defective Children*, 1915; *Human Efficiency and Levels of Intelligence*, 1920; *School Training of Gifted Children*, 1928). The one for which he is best known is *The Kallikak Family* (1913), in which Goddard attempted to show that feeblemindedness is inherited and runs through successive generations. The book aroused considerable controversy. Through his books, activities (in 1910, he prepared his own revision of the Binet intelligence test to study feeblemindedness), and fervent presentations Goddard was, during his time, quite influential in psychological and sociological circles as well as with the general public. While he did believe that feeblemindedness was caused mainly by faulty heredity, his major contribution was also to show that mentally defective individuals can be trained to be usefully occupied.

Biographic data: NCAB 15:236; H. E. Burtt & S. L. Pressey, Henry Herbert Goddard, *American Journal of Psychology*, 1957, 70, 656–657

[291]   **FROBES, JOSEPH**

German-Dutch psychologist
Rating: 16
Born: Betzdorf, Rhineland-Palatinate, Germany, August 26, 1866

Died: Cologne, Germany, March 24, 1947
Education: 1886–1889, Jesuit training in philosophy; 1894–1899, theological training, ordained priest 1900; 1902–1904, University of Göttigen, psychology
Positions: 1904–1925, Ignatiuskolleg, Valkenburg (Limburg), · Holland

Fröbes was a neo-Thomist who, nevertheless, kept philosophical psychology separate from experimental psychology, holding that philosophical beliefs are irrelevant to the validity of experimental work. Even so, he made it his life's work to integrate philosophical and empirical psychology, believing that each would profit from a consideration of the other. Fröbes achieved this integration in his textbooks, especially those dealing with philosophical psychology. He was the first Catholic writer of psychological texts. His *Lehrbuch der experimentellen Psychologie* (vol. 1, 1915, rev. ed. 1923; vol. 2, 1920, rev. ed. 1929) was much used and may be considered his major accomplishment. His major texts of philosophical psychology were *Psychologia sensitiva* (1908), *Psychologia rationalis* (1911), and *Psychologia speculaitva* (1927). Fröbes also wrote many papers on diverse psychological subjects.

Biographic data: HPA 3:121

MEYER, ADOLF

Swiss-American psychiatrist
Rating: **21**
Born: Niederweningen, Zurich, Switzerland, September 13, 1866
Died: Baltimore, Maryland, March 17, 1950
Highest degree: M.D., University of Zurich, 1892
Positions: 1892, University of Chicago; 1893, Illinois Eastern Hospital for the Insane, Kankakee; 1895, Worcester Insane Hospital, Clark University; 1902–1910, director, Pathological Institute, New York State Hospital Service; 1904–1909, Cornell University; 1910–1941, Johns Hopkins University, professor of psychiatry and director of Henry Phipps Psychiatric Clinic

Meyer was an outstanding psychiatrist of his time ("dean of American psychiatry"). He revolutionized methods of treatment while at the New York State Hospital Service Pathological Institute, and developed that institute into a first-class training center for psychiatrists. Under his direction the Phipps Clinic at Johns Hopkins reached such levels of excellence that it became the foremost training center for English-speaking psychiatrists in the world.

Meyer made a substantial contribution to the promotion of the holistic view in psychopathology, in which both the organic and psychological factors are fused into a whole. Meyer's "psychobiology" is based on the assumptions that the behavior of a patient may be understood only if his total personality is understood, and that the patient's behavior is determined by a variety of factors—biological, psychological, and sociological—that acting and interacting produce the patient's maladjustment. Neurotic maladjustments result from levels of aspiration that are to high and the inability to accept oneself as one is. Failure to achieve unrealistic goals results in feelings of inferiority and the use of defense mechanisms. In neuroses only a part of the total personality is involved, in contrast to psychotic decompensation that involves the entire person. Meyer viewed schizophrenia as the result of faulty habits, accumulated over a long period of time and often complicated by organic and hereditary factors. Psychobiological therapy is an attempt at integrating and synthesizing the different aspects of the patient's personality by analyzing the psychological, sociological, and biological factors involved, keeping close to the patient's complaint, and achieving a combination of treatment methods that both the psychiatrist and the patient find satisfactory.

Meyer contributed a number of significant papers to the medical literature, suggested the term "mental hygiene," and was instrumental in furthering the mental hygiene movement originated by Clifford Beers [362]. His *Collected Papers* were published after his death (1950–1952), as was his *Psychobiology* (1957).

Biographic data: *IESS* 10:263; *NCAB* 38:45, E:26; E. G. Ebaugh, Memorial to past president: Adolf Meyer, M.D. *American Journal of Psychiatry*, 1950, **107**, 288–290; L. W. Crafts, Adolf Meyer. *American Journal of Psychology*, 1950, 63, 620–622; [Anon.] Professor Adolf Meyer. *British Medical Journal* 1950, **1**, 732–734; [Anon.] Adolf Meyer. *Journal of Nervous and Mental Diseases*, 1951, **113**, 89–91; J. C. Whitehorn, Adolf Meyer. *Bulletin of Johns Hopkins Hospital, Supplement*, 1951 (July), 89, 53–80

American sociologist
Rating: 11
Born: Virden, Illinois, December 12, 1866
Died: Madison, Wisconsin, July 22, 1951
Highest degree: Ph.D. in economics, Johns Hopkins University, 1891
Positions, honors: 1891–1895, taught economics briefly at Indiana University and Cornell University; 1895–1900, University of Stanford, turning to sociology; 1900–1906, University of Nebraska; 1906–1937, University of Wisconsin, chairman of the Departament of Sociology and Anthropology from 1929; LL.D., Coe College, 1911

In 1908, Ross wrote a *Social Psychology,* the first text in social psychology written in English. It appeared just a few months before McDougall's [329] text, but was quite different from the latter's: it was a psychological sociology. Ross wrote much for popular presentation and thereby stimulated interest in social psychology.

Biographic data: *IESS* 13:560; *NCAB* 18:98; E. A. Ross, *Seventy Years of It,* 1936; J. O. Hertzler, Edward Alsworth Ross: sociological pioneer and interpreter. *American Sociological Review*, 1951, 16, 597–613

American psychologist
Rating: 27
Born: Chichester, Sussex, England, January 11, 1867
Died: Ithaca, New York, August 3, 1927
Highest degree: Ph.D. in psychology, University of Leipzig, 1892, under W. Wundt [161]
Positions: 1892–1927, Cornell University; editor *American Journal of Psychology,* 1895–1927

Titchener considered Wundt to be of utmost importance to psychology, and he spent his life expounding and systematizing the Wundtian point of view and producing laboratory research

using Wundt's method of introspection. The school of structuralism was born at Cornell and had life in Titchener and the many doctoral students that he produced. In Titchener's view, psychology's first task was to study structure before embarking on the study of function. Functionalism in his view was premature. Structuralism, however, died with Titchener, for he refused to change his thinking as psychology changed. He refused to consider applied psychology a valid enterprise, and had no interest in studying animals, children, abnormalities of behavior, or individual differences in general. The organization of experimental psychologists that Titchener established in 1904, although intended to perpetuate Wundt's psychology, changed its name to Society of Experimental Psychologists after Titchener's death and used the introspective method only sparingly.

To Titchener, psychology was the study of experience from the point of view of the experiencing individual. Mental processes are not to be confused with the material causes of these processes. In an experiment, introspection consists of describing the conscious contents of experience. The tendency to describe the object instead is "stimulus error." Since psychology as a science depends on introspection as its method of observation, the avoidance of stimulus error is crucial. Mind is the totality of subjective experiences, past, present, conscious, and unconscious. It is correlated with the activity of the nervous system but is not caused by it (Wundt's psychophysical parallelism). Since nervous and mental processes parallel each other, the former may be used to explain the latter. Titchener, however, made no particular attempt to relate neurophysiology and experience. Neither did behavior play any particular role because Titchener relegated it to biology, considering it irrelevant to the psychology of consciousness.

The building blocks of consciousness were the sensations, images, and affections. These were the ultimate irreducibles that went on to make up the perceptions (from sensations), ideas (from images), and emotions (from affections). Titchener characterized mental processes as having quality, intensity, duration, clearness, and extensity, the last three being Titchener's addition to Wundt's list of the dimensions of mental processes. The addition of clearness assigned attention a systematic place, and eliminated some of the problems previously associated with its uncertain status.

Within the general framework of structuralism, Titchener provided one specific theory that became well known because it kept reappearing in different forms in the work of a number of psychologists and linguists. It is the core-context theory of meaning, according to which a new mental process (the core) acquires its meaning from the context of other mental processes

NAMES IN THE HISTORY OF PSYCHOLOGY

within which it occurs. In its simplest form, the context may be just one other mental element, and, besides, a person does not have to be aware of the context in order to assign meaning (unconscious context).

Titchener authored more than two hundred articles, eight books in psychology, and eleven translations of German psychological texts. His most important book is *Experimental Psychology,* four volumes, (1901–1905). The others are *Outline of Psychology* (1896), *Primer of Psychology* (1898), *Lectures on Elementary Psychology of Feeling and Attention* (1908), *Lectures on the Experimental Psychology of the Thought Processes* (1909), *A Textbook of Psychology* (1910), *Systematic Psychology: Prolegomena* (1929), and *A Beginner's Psychology* (1915).

Biographic data: *IESS* 16:88; *NCAB* 22:94; E. G. Boring, Edward Bradford Titchener. *American Journal of Psychology,* 1927, 38, 489–506

DESSOIR, MAX [295]

German psychologist
Rating: 18
Born: Berlin, February 8, 1867
Died: Königstein-im-Taunus, Hesse, July 19, 1947
Highest degree: Ph.D. in philosophy, University of Berlin, 1889, under W. Dilthey [164]; M.D., University of Würzburg, 1892
Positions: 1889–1933, University of Berlin

Dessoir's main interest was in aesthetics, in which area he published several books and articles, founded a journal in 1906 which he edited throughout his career, and exercised some influence, especially in the United States. In connection with his medical studies, Dessoir did research on cutaneous after-sensations, making a distinction (1892) between "continuous after-sensations" (primary after-sensations) and "intermittent after-sensations" (secondary after-sensations). Many of his writings are in the area between medicine and psychology, such as *Bibliographie des modernen Hypnotismus* (1888), *Das Doppel-Ich* (1890, 2d edition, 1896), and *Das Ich, der Traum, der Tod* (1947). One other area of interest to Dessoir was parapsychology, which he endeavored to clear of quackery, trickery, and superstition. In this area he wrote *Vom Jenseits der Seele* (1917) and a number of papers. In 1911, Dessoir published a history of psychology, *Abriss einer Geschichte der Psychologie,* which was immediately translated into English (*Outlines of the History of Psychology,* 1912) and became, to English-speaking psychologists, his best known book.

Biographic data: *EP* 2:354; C. Herrmann, *Max Dessoir: Mensch und Werk,* 1929; M. Dessoir, *Das Buch der Erinnerungen,* 1946; R. Schantz, In memoriam Max Dessoir. *Grenzgebiete der Medizin,* 1948, 1, 24–26

[296]

MESSER, AUGUST

German psychologist
Rating: 18
Born: Mainz, February 11, 1867
Died: Rostock, 1937
Highest degree: Ph.D. in philosophy, University of Giessen, 1892
Positions: 1899–1933, University of Giessen

Messer was a philosopher who, impressed by Külpe's [265] approach to both philosophy and psychology, spent a semester studying thinking under Külpe's direction at Würzburg. Messer immediately published a book-size monograph (*Experimentell-psychologische Untersuchungen über das Denken,* 1906), consistent with the position of the Würzburg school, still another book in 1908 (*Empfindung und Denken*), and, in 1914, a *Psychologie.* Messer developed a two-part psychology that Külpe himself was gravitating toward, namely one in which the content of Leipzig and the acts of Würzburg both found a place. According to Messer, each kind of intentional experience, knowing, feeling, and willing (the proper subject matter for psychology), involve activity that has a content. The contents of knowing are the sensations, images, time- and space-related contents, and the impressions or relational experiences. The acts of knowing are perception, memory, and imagination. The contents of feeling and willing are also sensations, while the acts of feeling are preferences and those of willing, desire and will.

Biographic data: In R. Schmidt, *Philosophie der Gegenwart in Selbstdarstellungen,* 1922, vol. 3, pp. 145–176

American psychologist
Rating: 23
Born: Montclair, New Jersey, June 12, 1867
Died: New York, New York, January 4, 1934
Highest degree: Ph.D. in psychology, Johns Hopkins University, 1917
Positions: 1890–1934, Princeton University; president, American Psychological Association, 1913

Warren was a first-generation American psychologist, Darwinian, materialistic, deterministic, but inclined toward introspection and an adherent of the double-aspect theory of mind-body relationship. At Princeton, he directed the psychology laboratory between 1904 and 1934, and in 1920 was able to establish a psychology department, separate from that of philosophy, becoming its first chairman.

Warren contributed few experimental papers. Most of his papers were of a theoretical nature because Warren's poor eyesight prevented him from engaging in experimental work. He had a particular interest in bibliography and lexicography, however, and made several imporant contributions in this area. He wrote a *Dictionary of Psychology* (1934), compiled the *Psychological Index* between 1894 and 1907 and again from 1910 to 1914, contributed to Baldwin's [259] *Dictionary of Philosophy and Psychology*, was on the American Psychological Association Committee on Psychological Bibliography since 1900 and chairman for many years of the APA Standing Committee on Psychological and Philosophical Terminology. Warren also contributed through editorial work and management of several psychological journals. He established the *Journal of Experimental Psychology* in 1916, was editor and business manager of *Psychological Review* from 1901 to 1934, and first editor of *Psychological Bulletin*, which he edited from 1904 to 1934. Eventually Warren's Psychological Review Company owned the *Psychological Review, Psychological Index, Psychological Monographs, Psychological Bulletin,* and *Journal of Experimental Psychology*. In 1922, Warren sold all of these to the American Psychological Association.

Warren's views on psychology may be found in his *Human Psychology* (1919), of which he published a simplified version in 1930 under the title of *Elements of Human Psychology*. He also penned a *History of the Association Psychology* in 1921.

Biographic data: *HPA* 1:443; *NCAB* 25:344; R. S. Woodworth, Howard Crosby Warren. *Psychological Review,* 1934, 41, 105–107; H.L. Langfeld, Howard Crosby Warren. *American Journal of Psychology,* 1934, 46, 340–342; S. W. Fernberger, Howard Crosby Warren. *Psychological Bulletin,* 1934, 31, 1–4

[298]

FARRAND, LIVINGSTON

American anthropologist
Rating: 11
Born: Newark, New Jersey, June 14, 1867
Died: New York, New York, November 8, 1939
Highest degree: M.D., Columbia University, 1891; two years of postdoctoral studies in physiological psychology at Cambridge University and University of Berlin
Positions, honors: 1893–1901, Columbia University, teaching psychology; 1901–1914, teaching anthropology; 1914–1919, president, University of Colorado; 1921–1937, president, Cornell University; thirteen honorary degrees, numerous medals and citations for public health and Red Cross–related work

In psychology, Farrand coauthored with Cattell [256] a classic study, begun in 1894, of the physical and mental measurements of Columbia University students, along the lines of Galton's [144] research. The purpose of the tests (known as the "freshman tests") was to study the development of abilities and personality and their correlation. The project continued for several years and represented one of the earliest correlational studies.

Biographic data: *NCAB* A:117, 40:494; R. S. Woodworth, Livingston Farrand. *American Journal of Psychology,* 1940, 53, 302

[299]

WITMER, LIGHTNER

American psychologist
Rating: 19
Born: Philadelphia, Pennsylvania, June 28, 1867
Died: Philadelphia, Pennsylvania, July 19, 1956
Highest degree: Ph.D. in psychology, University of Leipzig, 1892, under W. Wundt [161]

Positions, honors: 1893–1937, University of Pennsylvania; 1896–1898, Bryn Mawr College; 1903–1905, Lehigh University; honorary Sc.D., 1937

Although Witmer established a psychological laboratory at Bryn Mawr College in 1896 and another at Lehigh University in 1903, he did not remain experimentalist for very long. At the University of Pennsylvania, Witmer founded the first psychological clinic. It started without much planning, and its first patients were children. In 1896, which is taken as the year in which the clinic was established, Witmer reported on its operation to the American Psychological Association. He described its functioning, philosophy, and uses. He employed the terms "psychological clinic," "clinical psychology," and the "clinical method." In his clinic, the first service-oriented enterprise of this sort, Witmer used the talents of a multidisciplinary group: neurologists, physicians, social workers, and special education teachers. Through the clinic, Witmer opened up a new field of psychology, and its considered to be the "father" of clinical psychology.

Other activities of Witmer in this field include the founding of the journals *Analytical Psychology* in 1902 and *The Psychological Clinic* in 1907. He edited the second journal until it ceased publication in 1935. He also founded a hospital school at the University of Pennsylvania in 1907. It was later named the Orthogenic School, and was established to prepare personnel in education, medicine, and social work to train normal and retarded children. Witmer saw the school as training ground for a new profession, the psychological expert. The Witmer School, established in 1920, served as a educational institution for mentally retarded children. Among other test devices, the *Witmer Cylinder Test* and the *Witmer Form Board* were used in this school and elsewhere.

Biographic data: S. H. Tulchin, In memoriam, Lightner Witmer. *American Journal of Orthophychiatry*, 1957, 27, 200–201; L. Carmichael, Lightner Witmer. *Yearbook of the American Philosophical Society*, 1956, 132–133

SIDIS, BORIS [300]

American psychologist
Rating: 17
Born: Kiev, Ukraine, October 12, 1867

Died: Portsmouth, New Hampshire, October 24, 1923

Highest degree: Ph.D. in psychology, Harvard University, 1897, under H. Münsterberg [272]; M.D. Harvard University, 1908

Positions: 1896–1901, New York State hospitals; 1901, New York Infirmary for Women and Children; 1904, private practice in Boston; 1909, Sidis Psychotherapeutic Institute, Portsmouth, New Hampshire; editorial work for *Archives of Neurology and Psychopathology* and *Journal of Abnormal and Social Psychology*

Sidis pioneered, in the United States, in the scientific study of unconsciously motivated behavior. He disagreed with Freud [224], emphasizing environmental and social factors in mental disorders. He showed that abnormal behavior involves the same mechanisms as normal behavior, except that the social pattern within which the behavior occurs is different. Sidis thought that the study of the unconscious was important also to sociology because man is social insofar as he fears and is suggestible. Sidis published a number of books, most of them in the area of personality and abnormal behavior, such as *Multiple Personality* (1905, with S. P. Goodhart), *The Foundations of Normal and Abnormal Psychology* (1914), *Symptomatology, Psychognosis, and Diagnosis of Psychopathic Maladies* (1914), *The Causation and Treatment of Psychopathic Diseases* (1916), and *Nervous Ills, Their Cause and Cure* (1922). In his book, *The Psychology of Laughter* (1913), Sidis maintained that laughter was a social rather than a psychological phenomenon because it was caused by the unconventional.

Biographic data: NCAB 24:68; *Encyclopedia of the Social Sciences* 14:48; H. A. Bruce, Boris Sidis. *Journal of Abnormal Psychology*, 1923–1924, 18, 274–276

[301] **DRIESCH, HANS ADOLF EDUARD**

German biologist

Rating: 18

Born: Bad Kreuznach, Rhineland-Palatinate, October 28, 1867

Died: Leipzig, April 17, 1941

Highest degree: Ph.D. in natural sciences, University of Jena, 1889

Positions, honors: 1891–1900, Naples Zoological Station; 1906, Aberdeen University; 1909, University of Heidelberg; 1920,

University of Cologne; 1921, University of Leipzig; several honorary degrees

Driesch was a developmental physiologist and an exponent of vitalism. In a well publicized experiment, Driesch cut up the blastula of a sea urchin and observed any and all parts of the blastula develop into a complete organism. He therefore decided that life cannot be explained merely in physical, chemical, or mechanistic terms, and proposed a theory of organic development (*Analytische Theorie der organischen Entwicklung*, 1894) according to which an immaterial principle, *entelechy*, was responsible for the development of the egg. *In Die Lokalisation morphogenetischer Vorgänge: ein Beweis vitalistischen Geschehens* (1899) and *Die Seele als elementarer Naturfaktor* (1903), Driesch elaborated his theory further. In the 1920s, he turned to psychology and parapsychology, publishing a successful *Grundprobleme der Psychologie* (1925, 2d edition 1929), a *Parapsychologie* (1932, 2d edition 1952), and a number of philosophical works.

Biographic data: H. Driesch, *Lebenserinnerungen*, 1950

STEKEL, WILHELM [302]

Austrian psychoanalyst
Rating: 16
Born: Bojan, Bucovinia, March 18, 1868
Died: London, England, June 21, 1940
Highest degree: M.D., University of Vienna, 1897
Positions: 1898–1938, practicing medicine in Vienna; founder (1934) and editor of *Psychotherapeutische Praxis*

Stekel belonged to the original group of early Freudian psychoanalysts. Although he did not split off from this group to establish his own school, some of his interpretations of Freud [224] differed enough from Freud's own views to draw Freud's criticism. Stekel was basically an eclectic interpreter of Freud. Some of his views were very similar to Adler's [317]. He emphasized the importance of life style and life goals, and held that for diagnostic purposes it was important to identify such goals and to distinguish between genuine and false goals, but that an explanation of the patient's childhood problems was not always necessary. Stekel called his approach active analytic psychotherapy to emphasize the active partnership role of the therapist in the therapeutic situation. In his symbolic interpretation of behavior, however, Stekel outdid Freud in seeing sex in its pure or sublimated form in almost everything. Stekel was a prolific but unsystematic and redundant writer who authored many a psychoanalytic volume. Among them are *Die Sprache des Traumes* (1910), *Der Wille zum Schlaf* (1916), *The Homosexual Neurosis* (1922), *Sex and Dreams* (1922), *Frigidity in Women in Relation to Their Love Life* (1926), *Impotence in the Male* (1927), *Sexual Aberrations* (1930), *Fortschritte der Traumdeutung* (1935), *Störungen des Trieb- und Affektlebens,* ten volumes (1932), *The Interpretation of Dreams* (1943), and *Compulsion and Doubt* (1949).

Biographic data: [Anon.] Wilhelm Stekel: Obituary. *Psychoanalytic Review,* 1940, 27, 506; W. Schindler, Wilhelm Stekel. *Marriage Hygiene,* 1948, 1, 183–184; W. Stekel, Autobiography. *American Journal of Psychotherapy,* 1947, 1, 183–188, 338–346, 479–494; 1948, 2, 82–107, 256–282, 417–437, 624–649; 1949, 3, 46–73

[303]

JENNINGS, HERBERT SPENCER

American biologist
Rating: 25
Born: Tonica, Illinois, April 8, 1868
Died: Santa Monica, California, April 14, 1947
Highest degree: Ph.D. in zoology, Harvard University, 1896
Positions: 1897, Manhattan State College; 1898, Dartmouth College; 1900, University of Michigan; 1903, University of Pennsylvania; 1906–1936, Johns Hokpins University, professor of experimental zoology, director of zoological laboratory since 1910; president, American Zoological Society, 1908, American Society of Naturalists, 1910

Jennings is noted for his work on the physiology of microorganisms, genetics, and animal behavior. Jennings believed that the behavior of organisms on even the lowest level of the phylogenetic scale could not be explained entirely in mechanistic terms. He studied the behavior of protozoans and found it to be too adaptable to warrant the view that only simple chemical and physiological reactions were involved. In contrast to the view of Loeb [247] and others, Jennings proposed that modifiable behavior implies consciousness because the function of consciousness is adaptation. Jennings objected to Loeb's explanation of animal behavior in terms of tropisms. These he thought to be artifactual collections of certain selected behaviors only, while other significant behaviors had been omitted. Jennings insisted that "the organism responds as a whole, by a reaction involving all parts of the body." To study animal behavior, Jennings proposed as a guiding principle the study of an animal's action system, "the characteristic set of movements by which its behavior under all sorts of conditions is brought about." Jennings's important volume, *Behavior of the Lower Organisms* (1906), supported those who believed animal life meant consciousness. Jennings did not have an answer, though, to the question of whether continuity of psychological processes in the animal kingdom also meant continuity of subjective states. He left that answer to be worked out by the philosophers, being satisfied with providing experimental and other objective evidence for his statements concerning animal behavior. This attitude sets Jennings apart from such comparative psychologists as Romanes [203].

Biographic data: DSB 7:98; NCAB 47:92, A:278

LEUBA, JAMES HENRY [304]

American psychologist
Rating: 15
Born: Neuchatel, Switzerland, April 9, 1868
Died: Florida, December 8, 1946
Highest degree: Ph.D. in psychology, Clark University, 1895, under G. S. Hall [418]
Positions: 1898–1933, Bryn Mawr College, professor of psychology, head of Psychology Department, professor emeritus after 1933

The topic of Leuba's doctoral dissertation was the psychology of religion, a topic which he pursued throughout his career in spite of criticism from the press and from churchmen. His pioneer studies resulted in several books on the psychology of religion: *A Psychological Study of Religion, Its Origin, Nature, and Future* (1912, translated into French and Japanese), *The Belief in God and Immortality* (1916), *The Psychology of Religious Mysticism* (1925, translated into French and German), *God or Man? A Study of the Value of God to Man* (1933), and others. Leuba's other interests included perception, comparative psychology, and motivation. In the latter area he adhered to Janet [249] and McDougall [329], rather than Freud [224], whom he did not respect.

Biographic data: K. E. McBride, James Henry Leuba. *American Journal of Psychology,* 1947, 60, 645–646

[305]

PARSONS, (SIR) JOHN HERBERT

English ophthalmologist
Rating: 13
Born: Bristol, September 3, 1868
Died: London, October 7, 1957
Highest degree: M.B., St. Bartholomew's Hospital, London, 1892; D.Sc., University of London, 1904
Positions, honors: Various medical appointments, private practice; president, Illuminating Engineering Society, 1921; honorary D.Sc., University of Bristol, 1925; honorary LL.D., Edinburgh University, 1927; three medals from ophthalmological societies; knighted in 1922; other honors

After considerable clinical and research work on the eye and eye diseases, in which he became a world expert, in 1913 Parsons turned to the psychology of vision. In 1915, Parsons introduced the term *photopia* for daylight vision and *scotopia* for twilight vision. His *Introduction to the Study of Colour Vision* also appeared in that year. Later, in 1927, he wrote *An Introduction to the Theory of Perception.* Its main thesis was that perception can be studied only factually and materialistically, using the method of physiological experimentation, and that instrospection without biology is dangerous. Psychology outside of perception also attracted Parsons's interest, from the writing of *A Précis of Applied Psychology* in 1918 to *The Springs of Conduct* in 1950.

Biographic data: DNB 1951–1960:794

American physiologist
Rating: 16
Born: Minneapolis, Minnesota, October 6, 1868
Died: Grand Rapids, Michigan, January 29, 1960
Highest degree: Ph.D. in physiology, Columbia University, 1900
Positions: 1893, Denison University; 1907–1937, University of
    Chicago; editor *Journal of Comparative Neurology*, 1893–1948

Herrick contributed to the understanding of the histology of the
nervous system. He studied the vertebrate brain for forty years,
endeavoring to relate data from physiology, psychology, and
psychiatry. His principal conclusion was that the brain of the
lower animals is the basis of the brain structure of all higher
animals. His doctoral thesis on cranial nerves was a major
contribution to the establishment of the "American school" in
neurology, which considered the structure of the nervous system
in terms of its function. Herrick is therefore counted as one of
the University of Chicago functionalists, along with Angell [309]
and Carr [344]. Herrick wrote several volumes on neurology. Of
these, important to psychology are *Neurological Foundations of
Animal Behavior* (1924), *Brains of Rats and Men* (1926), *The
Thinking Machine* (1929), and *The Evolution of Human Nature*
(1956).

Biographic data: *NCAB* 47:90; G. W. Bartelmez, Charles Judson
    Herrick, neurologist. *Science,* 1960, 131, 1654–1655

American psychiatrist
Rating: 17
Born: Buckinghamshire, England, January 20, 1869
Died: Clearwater, Florida, March 15, 1963
Highest degree: M.D., University of Chicago, 1900
Positions: 1900–1906, Northwestern University, medical ap-
    pointments in various hospitals; 1906–1907, postgraduate study
    in Vienna, Berlin, and London; 1909–1917, director, Juvenile
    Psychopathic Institute, Chicago; 1917–1947, director, Judge
    Baker Foundation (Judge Baker Guidance Center)

In collaboration with his first wife, Grace Fernald, and later with his second wife, Augusta Bronner, both psychologists, Healy pioneered in the study of childhood delinquency. He organized and headed the first child guidance clinic in Chicago in 1909, the Chicago Juvenile Psychopathic Institute (Institute of Juvenile Research since 1920). It began as a treatment center for delinquent children, later began to accept nondelinquent but emotionally disturbed children to be treated by a full-time staff of psychiatric and social workers. After Chicago, Healy went to Boston's Judge Baker Clinic, where he conducted extensive research on delinquency. With Bronner, he wrote *New Light on Delinquency and Its Treatment* (1936) and *The Value of Treatment and What Happened Afterward* (1939). In his work with delinquent children Healy realized the need for performance tests to complement the more verbal types of intelligence test tasks of the Stanford-Binet Intelligence Scale. The result was the Healy-Fernald series of twenty-three tests, put in use in 1911. Some of these tests were incorporated into later intelligence scales and are still in use today, such as the *Healy Picture Completion Test* and the *Healy Puzzle*. Healy wrote many articles and fourteen books. Of these, the most significant was *The Individual Delinquent* (1915), in which Healy called for the application of psychology to broader things than just testing.

Biographic data: H. Meltzer, Contributions to the history of psychology: VI. Dr. William Healy, 1869 to 1963. The man in his time. *Psychological Reports,* 1967, 20, 1028–1030

[308]

SCOTT, WALTER DILL

American psychologist
Rating: 11
Born: Cooksville, Illinois, May 1, 1869
Died: Evanston, Illinois, September 23, 1955
Highest degree: Ph.D. in psychology, University of Leipzig, 1900, under W. Wundt [161]
Positions, honors: 1901–1939, Northwestern University, teaching psychology until 1920, president of Northwestern since 1920; 1912–1921, president of The Scott Co., a personnel consulting firm; 1916–1917, director of Salesmanship Research,

Carnegie Institute of Technology; president, American Psychological Association, 1919; chairman, American Council on Education, 1927; two honorary degrees, other honors

Although Scott received his degree from Wundt, he developed into an industrial and business psychologist with an emphasis on motivation; his first book was on *Die Psychologie der Triebe* (1900). He wrote a first text on the psychology of advertising (*Theory of Advertising,* 1903), followed by a series of other books on business and psychology: *Psychology of Public Speaking* (1907), *Psychology of Advertising* (1908), *Influencing Men in Business* (1911), *The Psychology of Agreement and Suggestion* (1911), *Increasing Human Efficiency* (1911), *Aids in Selecting Salesmen* (1916), *Psychology of Advertising in Theory and Practice* (1921), *Science and Common Sense in Working with Men* (1921), *Personnel Management* (1941). Scott authored or coauthored a number of other books. Between 1917 and 1919 he introduced the use of rating scales in the Army, contributed to the production of the ten volumes of *Personnel Specifications,* and coauthored the two volumes of *The Personnel System of the U.S. Army* and *The Personnel Manual.* Scott was the director of the Committee on Classification of Personnel in the Army, appointed by the Secretary of War and consisting of ten psychologists. The Committee prepared an Army personnel classification system, for which service Scott received the Distinguished Service Medal.

Biographic data: NCAB 42:328; J. Z. Jacobson, *Scott of Northwestern,* 1951: E. K. Strong, Jr., Walter Dill Scott. *American Journal of Psychology,* 1955, 68, 682–683; R. C. Clothier, Walter Dill Scott, pioneer in applied psychology. *Science,* 1956, 123, 408–409

ANGELL, JAMES ROWLAND

[309]

American psychologist
Rating: 27
Born: Burlington, Vermont, May 8, 1869
Died: Hamden, Connecticut, March 4, 1949
Highest degree: M.S., Harvard University, 1892; Ph.D. dissertation written, degree not completed, at University of Berlin
Positions, honors: 1893, University of Minnesota, philosophy; 1894–1919, University of Chicago, psychology, 1919–1921,

administration; during World War I among psychologists who worked on the classification of Army personnel; 1921–1937, president, Yale University; after retirement in 1937, educational counselor to NBC, others; president, American Psychological Association, 1906; chairman, National Research Council, 1919–1920; chairman, Board of Trustees, Carnegie Corporation, 1920–1921; twenty-three honorary doctorates

Titchener [294] gave functionalism its name by contrasting it with Wundt's [161] and his own structuralism, but Angell was the most prominent spokesman of functionalism. While functionalism was born gradually in the work of Darwin [127], Cattell [256], Dewey [253], and others, as a school of psychology functionalism was most closely associated with the name of Angell and the University of Chicago. Before coming to Chicago, Angell established a psychology laboratory at the University of Minnesota in 1893, and another one, with Dewey, at the University of Chicago in 1893–94.

In a book (*Psychology*, 1904, which saw four editions by 1908 and additional revised editions thereafter) and a paper (The province of functional psychology. *Psychological Review*, 1907, 14, 61–91) Angell outlined the point of view of functionalism. In his book, Angell was already accepting the observation of behavior as a valid method in psychology. His paper stated that functionalism is concerned with the how, why, and what of the psyche, that is, its function; that the mind was the mediator between the organism and its environment; and that it was psychophysical because it considered mental processes in relation to the body as these effected the body's adjustments to the environment. The useful or applied nature of mind was contrasted with questions concerning its nature or structure.

Angell was a very talented administrator. As president of Yale University he was known as the creator of the "new Yale"— through fund raising, building programs, and expanding of educational programs. He created the Yale Institute of Human Relations. As head of the Psychology Department at Chicago, Angell was also very effective, making the department the most influential one of its day.

Biographic data: HPA 3:1; *IESS* 1:287; *NCAB* E:5, 40:40; W. Miles, James Rowland Angell. *Science*, 1949, 110, 1–4; R. M. Yerkes, James Rowland Angell. *Yearbook of American Philosophical Society*, 1949, 294–301; W. S. Hunter, Biographical memoir of James Rowland Angell. *National Academy of Sciences, Biographical Memoirs*, 1950, 26(10), 191–208

BAIRD, JOHN WALLACE

Canadian-American psychologist
Rating: 17
Born: Motherwell, Ontario, May 21, 1869
Died: Baltimore, Maryland, February 2, 1919
Highest degree: Ph.D. in psychology, Cornell University, 1902, under E. B. Titchener [294]
Positions: 1903, Cornell University; 1904, Johns Hopkins University; 1906, University of Illinois; 1910, Clark University; president, American Psychological Association, 1918; on editorial boards of several psychological journals

Baird achieved recognition in psychology for a number of experimental investigations, the most notable of which was a thorough study, reported in 1903, of the role of accomodation and convergence in the perception of distance. Baird concluded that convergence was the more important clue in three-dimensional space perception.

Biographic data: NCAB, 22:213; [Anon.] John Wallace Baird. *American Journal of Psychology,* 1919, 30, 120

MARBE, KARL

German psychologist
Rating: 24
Born: Paris, France, August 31, 1869
Died: Würzburg, Germany, January 2, 1953
Highest degree: Ph.D. in psychology, University of Bonn, 1893
Positions: 1895, University of Würzburg; 1905, Academy of Social and Commercial Sciences at Frankfurt; 1909–1934, University of Würzburg

Marbe first worked on classical problems in psychophysics and perception, as well as speech and language problems. He made the first distinction between popular and unusual associations in word-association tests and devised a soot-writing method for recording speech intonations. At Würzburg, Marbe contributed to the development of the imageless thought school through his work on judgment (*Experimentell-philosophische Untersuchungen über*

das Urteil, eine Einleitung in die Logik, 1901). One of his important findings was that while the sensations and images produced by the stimulus being judged, such as a weight, were clearly present, the process whereby the judgment of "heavier" or "lighter" was arrived at could not be described by the subject. Marbe concluded that judgment is a logical and not a psychological concept. Later, he became disenchanted with Külpe's [265] "systematic experimental introspection", considered the then current discussions around the concept of Gestalten unproductive, and turned to applied psychology. He started using aptitude tests in the various occupations, studied business psychology, accident proneness, and other related problems (Fortschritte der Psychologie und ihre Anwendungen, an applied psychological journal, was founded by Marbe in 1913). During his career Marbe published eighteen books and more than one hundred articles. An additional 180 books and papers were authored by students and assistants who worked in his laboratory.

Biographic data: HPA 3:181; W. Peters, Karl Marbe. American Journal of Psychology, 1953, 66, 645–647

[312]

WOODWORTH, ROBERT SESSIONS

American psychologist
Rating 27
Born: Belchertown, Massachusetts, October 17, 1869
Died: New York, New York, July 4, 1962
Highest degree: Ph.D. in psychology, Columbia University, 1899, under J. McK. Cattell [256]
Positions, honors: 1899, New York University; 1902, University of Liverpool; 1903–1942, Columbia University, retired 1942; 1942–1958, lecturer on dynamics of behavior, Columbia University; president, American Psychological Association, 1914; editorial work for several psychological journals, such as Archives of Psychology (1906–1948); five honorary degrees; American Psychological Foundation Gold Medal, 1956

Woodworth did not formulate any special psychological theory or found any school of psychology. He taught and influenced by the example of his work as a general experimental psychologist. One of his first notable contributions was the publication of a piece of research on transfer of learning (1901, with E. L. Thorndike [353]) that effectively dismantled the doctrine of formal disciplines. This was followed by some 220 papers and 10 major books. Of the books, the most important ones were a revision of Ladd's [186] *Physiological Psychology* in 1911, which was the standard text in the area for many years; *Dynamic Psychology* (1918), a call for functional psychology and a treatise on the psychology of motivation; *Psychology* (1921), a very popular textbook that saw five editions and was far ahead of any other such text in sales; *Contemporary Schools of Psychology* (1931), a much used text; and *Experimental Psychology* (1938, revised in 1954, with H. Schlosberg [510]), one of the classic texts in psychology, on which generations on psychologists were brought up.

Woodworth called himself a dynamic psychologist. The term, "dynamic psychology," was actually coined by Woodworth. His *Dynamic Psychology* and subsequent articles show him emphasizing the study of cause-effect relationships and the use of motor behavior, physiology, or introspection in such study, depending on which method best fit the situation. Within this functionalist framework Woodworth wanted to study the motives that determine specific behaviors ("motivology"). Woodworth noted how behavioral mechanisms (cause-effect, S-R relations), once they get started, begin to act on their own accord ("the mechanism becomes the drive").

Biographic data: *HPA* 2:359; *IESS* 16:561; *NCAB* A:24, 48:546; A. J. Poffenberger, Robert Sessions Woodworth. *American Journal of Psychology*, 1962, 75, 677–689; G. Murphy, Robert Sessions Woodworth. *American Psychologist,* 1963, 18, 131–133

URBAN, FRANCIS M. [313]

American psychologist
Rating: 14
Born: Place and year unknown
Died: Brazil, in the 1950s
Highest degree: Ph.D.
Positions: University of Pennsylvania

Urban was a psychophysicist who contributed a book (*The Application of Statistical Methods to the Problem of Psychophysics,* 1908) and some fifty papers to the area. He is known for having introduced a correction in the table of weights furnished by G. E. Müller [208] in 1903 for fitting the psychometric function to data obtained using the method of right and wrong cases. The table was named the *Table of Müller-Urban weights.* Urban also contributed the concept of the psychometric function, the *phi-gamma function* (1910), which is a curve obtained by plotting percentages of responses in the categories "less," "more," or "equal" against stimulus values when the method of constant stimuli is used in establishing the difference or absolute threshold. It is stated in terms of h, an index of the dispersion of the responses about the mean. *The phi-gamma hypothesis* states that data obtained with the constant stimuli method will fit the phi-gamma function.

Biographic data: No biographic references available

[314]

WITASEK, STEPHAN

Austrian psychologist
Rating: 19
Born: Graz, 1870
Died: Graz, 1915
Highest degree: Ph.D. in philosophy, University of Graz, under A. Meinong [218]
Positions: 1900, University of Graz

A psychologist in the Austrian school of form quality, Witasek continued the work of Ehrenfels [250], Meinong [218], and Cornelius in the 1910s. Subscribing to a psychology that allowed room for both act and content, his systematic views centered on perception and the act of production (*Grundlinien der Psychologie*, 1908; *Psychologie der Raumwahrnehmung des Auges*, 1910). The psychological act of production results in simple or complex complexions. Complex complexions are determined both by the internal act of production and the physical properties of the stimulus object. Witasek's main interest, however, was aesthetics, in which area he published extensively. Here, too, he made contact with psychology by proposing a theory to explain the geometric illusions (1898).

Biographic data: *Enciclopedia universal ilustrada*, vol. 70

RANSCHBURG, PAUL

Hungarian psychiatrist and psychologist
Rating: 12
Born: Gyoer, January 3, 1870
Died: Budapest, January 18, 1945
Highest degree: M.D., University of Budapest, 1894
Positions: 1910, University of Budapest; editor, *Magyar psychologiai szemle*

Ranschburg contributed equally to the psychiatric and the psychological literature. Most of his approximately thirty papers in psychology are on memory and the pathology of memory. His single most important contribution was the experimental demonstration of retroactive inhibition in 1905. Ranschburg showed that materials learned later affect the recall of materials learned earlier, and that the degree of inhibition depends on the degree of similarity between the materials, moderate degrees of similarity having a greater effect than either dissimilarity or close similarity. Ranschburg's *Law of Fusion* states that similar elements tend to fuse in memory, and that different ones become even more differentiated. He related this to disorders in reading and writing and to underlying neural processes, stressing cohesion as the basic principle in nature. Ranschburg considered himself a forerunner of Gestalt psychology. His books of psychological importance are *Beiträge zur Psychologie des hysterischen Geisteszustandes* (1897, with L. Hajós), *Psychotherapy* (1900), *The Nature of Mental Functions* (1905), *The Mind of the Child* (1905), *Das Kranke Gedächtnis* (1911), *Psychology, Pathology, and Medical Pedagogy of Morally Abandoned Children* (1914), and *The Human Mind* (1923).

Biographic data: P. H. Schiller, Paul Ranschburg. *American Journal of Psychology*, 1947, 60, 444–446

WHITE, WILLIAM ALANSON

American psychiatrist
Rating: 14
Born: Brooklyn, New York, January 24, 1870
Died: Washington, D.C., March 7, 1937

Highest degree: M.D., Long Island College Hospital, 1891

Positions, honors: 1892, New York State Hospital at Binghamton; 1903, St. Elizabeth's Hospital, Washington, D.C.; professor of nervous and mental diseases, Georgetown University, George Washington University; president, American Psychiatric Association, 1924; the psychiatric research institutes, William Alanson White Foundation and William Alanson White Institute have been named in White's honor

White spent most of his professional life at St. Elizabeth's Hospital, where he was appointed to the position of superintendent because of the views he held concerning mental illness. During his tenure the hospital became one of the best known mental institutions in the world. White's foremost principle was that only humane and kind treatment is likely to produce improvement in the mentally ill. While emphasizing social pathology, White also conceived of the psychobiological organism as a whole and, on this basis, coined the term "mental hygiene." *Mental Hygiene of Childhood* (1919) presents the mental hygiene point of view within the psychoanalytic framework. White's other books were mainly in psychiatry and nervous diseases: *Outlines of Psychiatry* (1907), *Diseases of the Nervous System* (1915, with S. E. Jeliffe), *Essays on Psychopathology* (1925). In 1913, White founded *Psychoanalytic Review* (with S. E. Jeliffe), and, in general, was considered the leader of the Washington school of psychiatry, which included Karen Horney [434], Erich Fromm, Harry Stack Sullivan [474], and Frieda Fromm-Reichmann [461].

Biographic data: NCAB 38:565; W. A. White, *Autobiography of a Purpose,* 1938; S. E. Jeliffe, William Alanson White. *Mental Hygiene,* 1937, 21, 291–293; N. D. C. Lewis, William Alanson White. *Sociometry,* 1937, 1, 255–258

[317]

ADLER, ALFRED

Austrian physician

Rating: 27

Born: Vienna, February 7, 1870

Died: Aberdeen, Scotland, May 28, 1937

Highest degree: M.D., University of Vienna, 1895

Positions: 1897–1914, private practice; during World War I, physician in the Austrian army; after the war, organized child guidance clinics in Vienna; 1920, appointed head of first individual psychology clinic in Vienna; 1926–1929, lecture tours and visiting professorship at Columbia University; 1932, professor of medical psychology, later special lecturer and visiting professor, Long Island College of Medicine

Adler originated the school of Individual Psychology. He joined Sigmund Freud's [224] group in 1902 and was prominent among the psychoanalysts for some years. A controversy arose over Adler's emphasis on social factors in personality development and his underemphasis of the sexual factor, which led to Adler's parting ways with Freud in 1911.

Adler saw sex primarily as an attempt to obtain power over another person. Sexual abnormality is not the cause but the result of mental disturbance. Physical disease is the result of organ inferiority and of external demands on the organs; the basis of neurosis is in children's reactions to their feeling inferior to and dependent upon adults. Feelings of inferiority may lead to overcompensation or to submissiveness. The individual's characteristic way of expressing his individuality and of reaching his goals is his "style of life." Man's major goal is to strive for superiority. When inferiority is used as an excuse to give up attempts at compensation ("inferiority complex"), neurosis results. Adler emphasized ego functions and minimized the biological determinism implied in Freud's emphasis on the id. Man is motivated more by goals and future expectations; he thus creates his own personality. Adler emphasized the uniqueness of each individual and the creativity of the self. Adlerian psychotherapy is much briefer than Freud's psychoanalysis and concentrates on the patient's overt difficulties.

Adler wrote numerous papers and books, among the latter *The Science of Living* (1920), *Understanding Human Nature* (1927), *The Education of Children* (1930). Adler's work is carried on by the societies, practitioners, and journals of Individual Psychology.

Biographic data: EP 1:15; *IESS* 1:57–61; P. Bottome, *Alfred Adler, a Portrait from Life*, 1957; H. Orgler, *Alfred Adler: The Man and His Work*, 1965

LENIN, VLADIMIR ILYICH   ⌈318⌉

Russian communist leader and philosopher
Rating: (unrated)

Born: Simbirsk (now Ulyanov), April 22, 1870
Died: Gorkiĭ, Russian S.S.R., January 21, 1924
Education: Passed final examinations in law, University of St. Petersburg, 1891

Lenin developed the philosophical theory of dialectic materialism of Marx [136] and Engels, including the theory of reflection. The latter forms the basis of present-day Soviet psychology. It may be found in Lenin's *Materializm i empiriokrititsizm* (1909) and *Filofoskie tetradi* (1929–1930). According to this theory, matter is primary. Mind, consciousness, the psyche is secondary. Matter exists independently of consciousness, and the latter depends on matter. Consciousness is the highest product of matter organized in a special way. It represents the reflection, by the brain, of the objective, material world that exists outside outside the individual and independently of him. In *Materializm i empiriokrititsizm* Lenin criticizes Mach [174] and Avenarius [194] for viewing sensations as a neutral element, neither material nor mental, and for coming perilously close to Berkeley's [40] mentalism. According to Lenin, sensations are the fundamental source of knowledge about the world. They are representations of objective reality rather than signalling only that which inheres in the nerve fibers (Johannes Müller [121]) or being mere symbols of things (Helmholtz [143]). Reality inheres in cognition, and cognition and objective reference proceed from subjective sensation to action, and through action to objective reality.

Biographic data: *DSB* 8:183; *EP* 4:434; *IESS* 9:254

[319]

SMUTS. JAN CHRISTIAN

South African statesman, soldier, and philosopher
Rating: 13
Born: Bovenplaats, near Riebeeck West, Cape Colony, May 24, 1870
Died: Irene near Pretoria, September 11, 1950
Highest degree: Law degree, Cambridge University, 1894

As his first contribution to psychology, Smuts, as a student at Cambridge, wrote a psychological study of the life of Walt

Whitman (*Walt Whitman*, 1973). In 1926, he suggested the term "holism" to signify Gestalt psychology. The term, however, never caught on. Smuts related holism to evolution (*Holism and Evolution*, 1926) by postulating that the direction of evolution is toward better and more comprehensive wholes. Smuts's ideas in this respect resemble Bergson's [252] notion of *élan vital* and Morgan's "directing activity."

Biographic data: *DNB* 1941–1950; *EP* 7:464; W. K. Hancock, *Smuts*, two volumes 1962

RIGNANO, EUGENIO   [320]

Italian philosopher
Rating: 15
Born: Livorno, May 30, 1870
Died: Milan, February 9, 1930
Positions: University of Milan, professor of philosophy

Rignano's philosophy included psychology and biology. His studies range from those on metabolism and the behavior of lower organisms to psychic and social phenomena. The underlying theme of his many papers and books is that life is teleological. In his major work, *Psicologia del raggionamento* (1920, English translation, *The Psychology of Reasoning*, 1923), Rignano maintains that memory is the basis of all biological and mental phenomena. Reasoning is "a series of operations or experiences merely thought out simply," a concept similar to Mach's [174]. Life processes are finalistic as "nervous energy" in the form of memory is able to envision the future in terms of past experience and thus to adapt the organism to future eventualities. The developmental tendency is also found in moral life. The purpose of moral life is to satisfy the needs of all individuals and eventually to eliminate all conflict. Among Rignano's other books of psychological significance are *Sur la transmissibilité des charactères acquis* (1906; English translation, *Inheritance of Acquired Characters*, 1911), *La memoria biologica* (1922; English translation, *Biological Memory*, 1926), *Che cos' è la vita?* (1926; English translation, *The Nature of Life*, 1930), and *Problemi della psiche* (1928).

Biographic data: *EP* 7:199

American psychologist

Rating: 21

Born: Clinton, Iowa, June 18, 1870

Died: Palo Alto, California, May 29, 1955

Highest degree: Ph.D. in psychology, Cornell University, 1899, under E. B. Titchener [294]

Positions, honors: 1899, Cornell University; 1912, University of Illinois; 1928, Cornell University, Sage professor of psychology and head of Psychology Department; 1938–1940, consulting psychologist, Library of Congress; 1930–1931, chairman, Psychology Division, National Research Council; created Committee on Psychiatric Investigation, of which he was the chairman for several years; editorial work on *Psychological Index* (1916–1925), *Journal of Experimental Psychology* (1926–1929), *American Journal of Psychology* (1930–1950), *Journal of Comparative and Physiological Psychology* (1921–1935); president, American Psychological Association, 1925; honorary LL.D., University of Nebraska

Bentley's principal contribution to psychology was as a book reviewer: he had reviewed more than 250 books in his lifetime. In addition to this and his editorial work, Bentley was also a writer. He wrote 2 books (*The Field of Psychology* 1924; *The New Field of Psychology*, 1934), 11 editorials, and 157 articles and notes. Among his more notable scientific contributions are *studies of the memory image*, which led psychologists eventually to give up images as mental elements; *a study of wetness* (1900) in which Bentley synthesized wetness by combining cold with a uniform pressure, and which has hence served as a paradigm for similar experiments; a *study of learning* in Paramecium (with L. M. Day), which caused a controversy of twenty years' duration over the interpretation of its results; and additional studies in general, experimental, abnormal, and racial psychology, including a series of seventeen articles on illusions, in a Chicago newspaper.

Biographic data: *HPA* 3:53; *NCAB* 45:406; K. M. Dallenbach, Madison Bentley. *American Journal of Psychology,* 1956, 69, 169–186

German physiologist
Rating: 12
Born: Tübingen, Baden-Württemberg, June 19, 1870
Died: Rostock, Mecklenburg, January 14, 1911
Positions: 1894, University of Freiburg; 1902, University of Berlin; 1908, University of Rostock; physiological editor-in-chief of *Zeitschrift für Psychologie* for a time

Nagel was primarily interested in vision, but he worked also on the chemical senses and on touch. He published many papers in these areas in the *Zeitschrift für Psychologie*. Nagel was the editor of a *Handbuch der Physiologie* (1905–1910), of which the third volume is on the psychophysiology of sensation. Seven portions of this volume were written by Nagel himself. Other editorial work of Nagel's included his position on the board of editors of the third edition of Helmholtz's [143] *Handbook of Physiological Optics*. In connection with his work on color blindness Nagel invented an *anomaloscope* (1898) that is used even now to measure the Rayleigh equation for screening color blindness (red and green).

Biographic data: *Enciclopedia italiana*, vol. 24

American psychologist
Rating: 18
Born: North Truro, Massachusetts, August 24, 1870
Died: South Weymouth, Massachusetts, January 31, 1943
Highest degree: Ph.D. in psychology, Clark University, 1900, under E. C. Sanford [245]
Positions: 1901, Michigan State Normal College; 1902–1904, State Normal School, Los Angeles; various educational and school administrative positions between 1904 and 1923; 1923–1940, dean, College of Education, University of Maryland

In 1899, Small published a paper in which he described the study of the mental processes of the rat by means of a copy of the

Hampton Court maze in England. Small conceived of *the behavior of the rat in the maze* to follow the principles enumerated by Thorndike [353]. From then on, both the maze technique and the white rat were used more and more frequently until they became the standard technique and the perferred animal of the American student of animal learning. In Small's own opinion the most significant aspect of his work had been the possibility of translating thinking into motor and sensory terms.

Biographic data: *The Psychological Register,* 1932, vol. 3

[324]

MONTESSORI, MARIA

Italian educator
Rating: 21
Born: Chiaravalle, near Ancona, August 31, 1870
Died: Noordwijk, Netherlands, May 6, 1952
Highest degree: M.D., University of Rome, 1894
Positions: 1894, assistant physician at the Psychiatric Clinic, University of Rome; 1899, directress, State Orthophrenic School, Rome; 1901, Sculoa di Magistero Femminile, Rome; 1904–1908, University of Rome, chair of anthropology; 1906, La Casa dei Bambini

Montessori, first woman in Italy to receive a medical degree, discovered that certain methods of teaching would enable to the subnormal child to read and write like a normal child. She extended her method to normal slum children in the "children's houses" (Case dei Bambini). She described her work, begun with defective children in 1899, in the book, *Metodo della pedagogica scientifica applicata all'educazione infantile nelle case dei bambini* (1909; English translation, *The Montessori Method,* 1912).

The main features of the Montessori method are to attract the child's attention to a task using certain specified educational materials, ·allowing the child freedom of movement, and gearing the task to be learned to the developmental level of the child. The Montessori school is a "prepared environment" in which the teachers keep themselves in the background, providing only minimal guidance and discipline, and the children themselves are entrusted with keeping things in their places. They acquire concepts through sensory-motor exercises and activities with Montessori's educational materials.

From her observations Montessori derived certain generalizations concerning education and development: children go through certain "sensitive periods" during which they are particularly apt to learn certain things; they prefer to work with creative materials rather than play with toys; they are capable of extreme concentration if the situation is properly structured; they love orderliness, and under the conditions of a Montessori school no punishment is needed to maintain discipline. Montessori's approach to education was in the tradition of Rousseau [53], Pestalozzi [72], and Fröbel [104]. Although developmental in nature, it ran counter to Darwinism because of Montessori's emphasis of the importance of experience, behaviorism and its concept of learning as conditioning, fixed intelligence, and the psychoanalytic theory. Dewey's [253] progressive education eventually overshadowed the Montessori schools, but not before her works had been translated in many languages and schools had been set up in several countries. In the United States, a resurgence of interest in Montessori schools and the opening of many such schools occurred in the 1950s.

Biographic data: *IESS* 10:476; A. Maccheroni, *A True Romance*, 1947; E. M. Standing, *Maria Montessori*: *Her Life and Work*, 1958

WISSLER, CLARK [325]

American anthropologist
Rating: 14
Born: Wayne County, Indiana, September 18, 1870
Died: New York, New York, August 25, 1947
Highest degree: Ph.D. in psychology, Columbia University, 1901, under J. McK. Cattell [256]
Positions, honors: 1897–1899, Ohio State University, instructor in psychology; 1901–1909, Columbia University, psychological research until 1903, then instructor in anthropology; 1902–1942, American Museum of Natural History, ethnological research; 1924–1940, Yale University, psychological research to 1931, afterwards professor of anthropology; honorary LL.D., Indiana University, 1929

Wissler worked at first in the laboratory of his teacher, Cattell, and undertook to evaluate the results of Cattell's attempts to measure the mental ability of students at Columbia and Barnard by measuring their reaction time, movement time, and other simple sensory and mental processes. Wissler, using the measure of correlation developed by Spearman [274] just a few years earlier, found very low or near-zero correlations between academic standing and the tests, although students' grades in their different courses showed good correlation. Wissler's findings, published in a 1901 monograph, had the effect of undermining both Cattell's approach to mental testing and testing in general, although only temporarily since a different approach, that of Binet's [236], was soon to yield much better results.

Under the influence of Franz Boas [243], Wissler turned from psychology to anthropology. He became an authority on North American Indians and wrote more than two hundred scientific and popular articles in anthropology. Wissler's output in psychology was only about fifteen papers.

Biographic data: *IESS* 16:559; *NCAB* 33:20, E:168; G. P. Mardock, Clark Wissler. *American Anthropologist*, 1948, 50, 292–304

[326]   **YULE, GEORGE UDNY**

English statistician
Rating: 20
Born: Morham near Haddington, East Lothian, Scotland, February 18, 1871
Died: Cambridge, England, June 26, 1951
Highest degree: M.A., Cambridge University, 1913
Positions, honors: 1893–1899, University College, London; 1899–1912, City and Guilds of London Institute; 1902–1909, University College, London; 1912–1931, Cambridge University; president, Royal Statistical Society, 1924–1926; recipient of a variety of honors

Yule laid the foundation of the theory of partial correlation and linear regression for n variables, and described association in a 2 X 2 contingency table. He made numerous other contributions to statistics that were not directly related to psychological research. His *Introduction to the Theory of Statistics* (1911) was a well known text that by 1932 had seen ten editions.

Biographic data: *DNB* 1951–1960; *IESS* 16:589

American psychologist
Rating: 20
Born: Woburn, Massachusetts, February 20, 1871
Died: Tryon, North Carolina, April 8, 1942
Highest degree: Ph.D. in psychology, University of Halle, 1896, under Benno Erdmann [210]
Positions: 1898, Wesleyan University; 1924, Yale University; editorial work for *Psychological Bulletin* (1904–1910), *Psychological Review* (1910–1915), *Journal of Experimental Psychology* (1916–1920), *Psychological Monographs* (1927–1937), and others; president, American Psychological Association, 1916

Dodge was a productive and versatile general experimental psychologist. His main areas of research were motor performance (effect of alcohol), physiological psychology (vestibular reactions), military research during World War I (selection and training of Navy gunners), and many problems in vision and perception, particularly with respect to eye movements. He invented the *Erdmann-Dodge tachistoscope*, the *Dodge mirror tachistoscope* (1907), and *an apparatus for recording* horizontal and vertical *eye movements* (1901) using the photographic technique. He was first to measure and classify eye movements, and observed these in the study of reading and other visual tasks. Dodge wrote *Psychological Effects of Alcohol* (with F. G. Benedict, 1915), *Elementary Conditions of Human Variability* (1927), and *The Craving for Superiority* (1931).

Biographic data: HPA 1:99; NCAB E:8, 32:61; C. E. Seashore, Raymond Dodge. *Science,* 1942, 95, 472–473

German psychologist
Rating: 26
Born: Berlin, April 29, 1871
Died: Durham, North Carolina, March 27, 1938
Highest degree: Ph.D. in psychology, University of Berlin, 1893, under H. Ebbinghaus [207]

Positions, honors: 1897, University of Breslau; 1916, University of Hamburg, professor of psychology and director of Psychological Institute; 1933, Duke University; honorary degrees from Clark University (1909) and Wittenberg College (1928)

Stern was a versatile man. In 1898, he invented the Stern variator (*Tonvariator*), a device to produce tones of varying pitch. In a 1903 pamphlet he presented both the concept and the term of applied psychology as well as that of psychotechnics. He organized the Institut für angewandte Psychologie in Berlin in 1906 and a year later founded the journal, *Zeitschrift für angewandte Psychologie*.

In a three-volume work, *Person und Sache: System der philosophischen Weltanschauung* (1906), Stern presented a synthesis of laboratory psychology and "understanding psychology" advocated by Dilthey [164] and Spranger [411], by centering his attention on the total person ("critical personalism"). Every mental function is centered in a person, which is therefore the object of psychological study rather than the function. A person is a blend of the physical and the mental, of hereditary and environmental influences, and therefore can be adequately understood only by using both natural science methods and the cultural science approach. Stern's views of the person thus fit those of Brentano [176], James [184], and the contemporary humanistic psychologists. Stern's last statement on the psychology of personalism appeared in 1935 (*Allgemeine Psychologie auf personalistischen Grundlage*, English translation, *General Psychology from the Personalistic Standpoint*, 1938).

In the area of developmental psychology Stern published books (1907 and 1908) on observations made by him and his wife on their own three children. In 1914, he published *Psychologie der frühen Kindheit*, elaborating on a developmental theory proposed earlier in 1908, called the convergence theory. According to this theory, convergence or collaboration of inner and outer conditions of development in the emergence of any ability takes place, although these conditions never interact in a simple or direct causal fashion.

The one contribution that Stern is mostly known for is the *concept of the I.Q.* To estimate a child's intelligence on the basis of the Binet-Simon test independently of the absolute performance score and of his age, Stern proposed (in *Die psychologische Methoden der Intelligenzprüfung*, 1912) that the mental age score obtained on this test be divided by the child's chronological age, and to avoid fractions, the ratio multiplied by one hundred. This measure, which Stern called the mental quotient, was adapted by Terman [368] in his 1916 Stanford Revision of the Binet Scales.

Differential psychology was still another area in which Stern made a contribution. Starting his work before 1900, he published a volume, *Uber Psychologie der individuellen Differenzen*, in 1900. An expanded version of this book appeared in 1911 (*Die differenzielle Psychologie in ihren methodischen Grundlagen*). These were followed by *Psychologische Methoden der Intelligenzprüfung* (1912), *Intelligenz der Kinder und Jugendlichen* (1920), and *Psychologie und Schülerauslese* (1920). Stern wrote a total of 139 articles and books.

Biographic data: *EP* 8:15; *HPA* 1:335; *IESS* 15:262; G. W. Allport, William Stern. *American Journal of Psychology,* 1938, **51**, 770–773; H. D. Spoerl, William Stern, *Personalist,* 1938, 19, 309–311

MC DOUGALL, WILLIAM

[329]

English-American psychologist
Rating: 27
Born: Oldham, Lancashire, England, June 22, 1871
Died: Durham, North Carolina, November 28, 1938
Highest degree: M.D., St. Thomas Hospital, London, 1898
Positions: 1898–1904, Cambridge University fellow; 1900–1906, University College, London, reader; 1904–1920, Oxford University, reader in psychology; 1920–1927, Harvard University; 1927–1938, Duke University

Before beginning his work in psychology, McDougall had acquired a medical degree, with specialization in physiology and neurology, participated in the Cambridge University anthropological expedition to the Torres Straits, and studied with G. E. Müller [208] at Göttingen. McDougall's initial work was in general experimental psychology. He studied vision, attention, memory, fatigue, emotions, and the effects of drugs. He formulated a drainage theory of inhibition. He conducted psychological experiments at Oxford at a time when Oxford had no psychology chair or even recognized experimental psychology, and was thus instrumental in guiding British psychology in that direction. He wrote several psychology texts while at Oxford: *Physiological Psychology* (1905), *Introduction to Social Psychology* (1908), *Body and Mind* (1911), and *Psychology, the Study of Behaviour*

(1912). Of these, the most influential was his *Social Psychology*. It was reprinted twenty-four times, and continued to influence British psychology even after McDougall had moved to the United States. While the book was a pioneer effort in a new branch of psychology, the theory of instincts that it contained proved to be a controversial issue. McDougall described human behavior, including social interaction, in terms of a large number of instincts. He related each of these to some primary emotion, such as flight to fear, and suggested that experience overlays these with derived sentiments.

McDougall's purposive psychology or, as he called it later (1923), hormic psychology, postulates goal-seeking in all behavior. Instincts guide the organism towards goals. Cognition effects the guidance, which terminates when the goal is reached. Progression toward a goal is pleasant, being frustrated in such progress is unpleasant. While hormic psychology never became a school, it tied in with the psychology of those learning theorists who recognized purpose (such as Tolman [439]) and with dynamic psychology in general.

McDougall's work during World War I on shell-shocked patients resulted in an *Outline of Abnormal Psychology,* published in 1926. It contained a discussion of mental disorders in terms of instincts, repression, and conflict, a discussion of hypnosis, and a criticism of psychoanalysis. He criticized the latter more amply and trenchantly in *Psychoanalysis and Social Psychology* (1935). Soon after coming to the United States, McDougall made his systematic position known in his *Outline of Psychology* (1923). Many of his beliefs, however, made him less popular in the United States than in England because of the behavioristic aegis that this country was entering under at the time. These beliefs included his instinct theory, the beliefs in the superiority of the Nordic race, the existence of a soul, and in psychic research. In a famous experiment McDougall attempted to demonstrate the inheritance of acquired characters in white rats. His opposition to a mechanistic view of behavior brought McDougall into conflict with J. B. Watson [374], with whom he carried on an extended and famous polemic. The total published output of McDougall was 24 books and 167 articles.

Biographic data: *DNB* 1931–1940; *HPA* 1:191; *IESS* 9:502; D. K. Adams, William McDougall. *Psychological Review*, 1939, 46, 1–8; C. L. Burt, William McDougall, an appreciation. *British Journal of Educational Psychology*, 1939, 9, 1–7; J. C. Flugel, Professor William McDougall. *British Journal of Psychology*, 1939, 29, 320–328; F. A. Pattie, William McDougall. *American Journal of Psychology*, 1939, 52, 303–307; C. E. Spearman,

The life and work of William McDougall. *Character and Personality*, 1939, 7, 175–183; M. Smith, Obituary: William McDougall. *British Journal of Medical Psychology*, 1939, 18, 105–111; K. Zener, William McDougall. *Science*, 1939, 89, 191–192

DECROLY, OVIDE JEAN [330]

Belgian psychologist
Rating: 11
Born: Renaix, July 23, 1871
Died: Brussels, September 12, 1932
Highest degree: Dr. en médecine, University of Ghent
Positions, honors: 1920, University of Brussels; several medals, various honors

In a 1910 paper, published with J. Degand, Decroly reported on a study of the intelligence of Belgian children in which it was found that these children were a year and a half ahead of the Parisian children studied by Binet. It was soon realized that the difference was the result of the higher social class standing of the Belgian children, which, in turn, opened up the problem field of the relationship between social class and intelligence. Decroly continued working in the area of child psychology in which he published eight books between 1912 and 1930. These books reflect Decroly's research and thinking about the child that eventually found a concrete expression in what became known as the "Decroly method" in education, a set of educational principles based on psychological insights that deviated considerably from the traditional pedagogical prescription. Decroly published some one hundred thirty titles, most of them on child psychology, intelligence, educational psychology, and the exceptional child.

Biographic data: No readily available biographic references

WASHBURN, MARGARET FLOY [331]

American psychologist
Rating: 23
Born: New York, New York, July 25, 1871.

Died: Poughkeepsie, New York, October 29, 1939
Highest degree: Ph.D. in psychology, Cornell University, 1894, under E. B. Titchener [294]
Positions, honors: 1894, Wells College; 1900, Cornell University; 1902, University of Cincinnati; 1903, Vassar College, head of Psychology Department since 1908; editorial work for *American Journal of Psychology* (1903–1939), *Journal of Animal Behavior* (1911–1917), *Psychological Bulletin* (1909–1915), *Psychological Review* (1916–1930), *Journal of Comparative Psychology* (1921–1935); president, American Psychological Association, 1921; many honors, including membership in the National Academy of Science (second woman so honored) and an honorary D.Sc. from Wittenberg College

Washburn's main interest was in animal psychology. *The Animal Mind,* first published in 1908 (subsequent editions in 1917, 1926, and 1936), served as the standard comparative psychology text for the next twenty-five years and was translated in other languages. In her only other book, *Movement and Mental Imagery* (1916), Washburn broke with the Titchenerian tradition and presented her motor theory of consciousness. It was an attempt to reconcile introspection and behaviorism. She stated that consciousness comes from a certain balance between excitation and inhibition in a motor discharge. If excitation is at too low or at too high a level, consciousness is lessened. Visual imagery also depends on the simultaneous excitation and inhibition of a motor pathway. The association of ideas she thought occurred when the motor response to a stimulus was blocked and a weakened response or "tentative movement" took place instead.

Washburn published more than two hundred articles and reviews, among which is a series of sixty-eight Minor Studies, published from Vassar College between 1905 and 1938.

Biographic data: *HPA* 2:333; *IESS* 16:476; *NCAB* 30:248; K. M. Dallenbach, Margaret Floy Washburn. *Science,* 1939, **90,** 555–557; K. M. Dallenbach, Margaret Floy Washburn. *American Journal of Psychology,* 1940, 53, 1–5; R. S. Woodworth, Margaret Floy Washburn. *Biographical Memoirs of National Academy of Sciences,* 1948, 25, 275–295

[332]

CANNON, WALTER BRADFORD

American physiologist
Rating: 27
Born: Prairie du Chien, Wisconsin, October 19, 1871

Died: Franklin, New Hampshire, October 1, 1945
Highest degree: M.D., Harvard University, 1900
Positions: 1900–1942, Harvard University; many lectureships, consulting and research posts, trusteeships

Cannon first studied the physiology of thirst and hunger. With A. L. Washburn, he performed the classic experiment (1912) demonstrating the simultaneity of felt hunger pangs and stomach contractions. In both thirst and hunger Cannon stressed the importance of local stimulation. Local stimuli were the result of drive-related imbalance in the organism. Its subjective experience initiated action to restore the balance. Study of digestive activities led Cannon to the discovery of the effects of strong emotions on digestion. Further research led him to a broadened concept that included diverse adaptive changes in the physiology of the body under emotion, stress, and tissue need. It was presented in a well-known book, *Bodily Changes in Pain, Hunger, Fear, and Rage* (1915, revised edition 1929, 1946). The book presented an influential critique of James's theory of emotion, which had been the dominant one until then, and offered a substitute theory, now known as the *Cannon-Bard theory of emotion*. Cannon viewed emotion as an emergency reaction (emergency theory of emotion) which makes the body marshall available resources to cope with an emergency. Cannon's research on the hypothalamus led him to identify it as the control center in emotional behavior.

During World War I Cannon began the study of the effects of traumatic shock. He published his findings in *Traumatic Shock* (1923). Cannon also studied the effects of endocrine secretion on the functioning of the nervous system, particularly of the adrenal gland and its role in mobilizing the energy resources of the body under stress. He discovered and named the hormone *sympathin,* which stimulates heart activity. Other discoveries of the action of the autonomic nervous system followed, resulting in Cannon's formulating the *concept of homeostasis* (in *The Wisdom of the Body,* 1932, revised edition 1939), or the tendency of the body to maintain a steady internal environment. This concept has strongly influenced psychological thinking concerning motivation and learning.

Biographic data: W. B. Cannon, *The Way of an Investigator,* 1945; *IESS* 2:260–262; C. K. Drinker, Walter Bradford Cannon. *Science,* 1945, **102**, 470–472; L. G. Leibson, Walter Bradford Cannon. *American Review of Soviet Medicine,* 1946, 4,

155–162; H. E. Sigerist et al., Walter Bradford Cannon. *American Review of Soviet Medicine,* 1946, 3, 282–288

[333]

ACH, NARZISS KASPAR

German psychologist
Rating: 26
Born: Ermershausen, October 29, 1871
Died: Munich, July 25, 1946
Highest degree: Ph.D., University of Göttingen, 1902, under Georg Müller [208] ; also M.D.
Positions: 1902, University of Göttingen; 1904, University of Marburg; 1906 University of Berlin; 1907, University of Königsberg; 1922, University of Göttingen

A member of the Würzburg school of "imageless thought", Ach demonstrated experimentally that individuals have a predisposition to act or to react in accordance with the instructions for the task but without necessarily being aware of it. He named this predisposition "determining tendency" (*determinierende Tendenz* or *Bewustseinslage*). The Ach-Ducker law of special determination is named after him. Ach invented the term "systematic experimental introspection" to describe the research method used by psychologists of the imageless thought school to study awareness (*Bewusstheit*, a term also coined by Ach), or conscious contents that were neither images nor sensations. Ach is the author of *Uber die Willenstätigkeit und das Denken* (1905), *Uber den Willensakt und das Temperament* (1910), *Uber die Begriffsbildung* (1921), *Uber die Determinations-psychologie* (1933), *Analyse des Willens* (1935), *Lehrbuch der Psychologie* (1944).

Biographic data: *The Psychological Register,* 1932, vol. 3; *New Catholic Encyclopedia,* 1967, vol. 1

[334]

HENRI, VICTOR

French psychologist
Rating: 16
Born: 1872
Died: 1940

Henri was a collaborator and assistant of Alfred Binet [236]. With Binet and Beaunis, he was a cofounder of *L'Année psychologique* (in 1895). In the 1890s he coauthored with Binet several papers on individual differences, but did some work also in the area of psychophysics. He went to Göttingen, worked there with Georg Müller [208], and published *Uber die Raumwahrnehmungen des Tastsinnes* (1898), a classic work on the error of localization and the tactual two-point threshold.

Biographic data: No readily available biographic references

COGHILL, GEORGE ELLETT

[335]

American anatomist
Rating: 20
Born: Beaucoup, Illinois, March 17, 1872
Died: Gainesville, Florida, July 23, 1941
Highest degree: Ph.D. in zoology, Brown University, 1902
Positions, honors: 1902, Pacific University; 1906, Willamette University; 1907, Denison University; 1913, Kansas State University; 1925–1935, Wistar Institute of Anatomy and Biology, Philadelphia; president, American Association of Anatomists, 1933; editor, manager, *Journal of Comparative Neurology,* 1904–1941; three honorary degrees

Coghill was a developmental psychobiologist whose work on the behavioral development in embryos of the salamander Amblystoma became well known. Coghill observed the embryos from the time they began to respond to stimulation to the point of fully developed behavior. His conclusion was that reflexes, rather than being elementary phenomena, arise by differentiation from a preexisting behavior pattern. Coghill published his work in twelve parts as "Correlated Anatomical and Physiological Studies of the Growth of the Nervous System in Amphibia" between 1914 and 1936. A psychologically relevant book written by Coghill was *Anatomy and the Problem of Behavior* (1929). Coghill applied his conclusions also to the human fetus, which stirred a controversy concerning the universality of the principle of differentiation of reflexes.

Biographic data: DSB 3:331; C. J. Herrick, George Ellett Coghill. *Science, 1941,* 94, 202–204; C. J. Herrick, Biographical memoir of George Ellett Coghill. *Biographic Memoirs of the National Academy of Sciences,* 1943, 22, 251–273

BETHE, ALBRECHT

German physiologist
Rating: 16
Born: Stettin, April 25, 1872
Died: Frankfurt-am-Main, October 19, 1954
Positions: 1911, University of Kiel; 1915, University of Frankfurt

Bethe studied the histology and physiology of the nervous system and the sense organs, especially in the invertebrates (*Allgemeine Anatomie und Physiologie des Nervensystems,* 1903). In 1899, Bethe published (with Beer and Uexküll [277]) a paper ("Vorschläge zu einer objektivierenden Nomenclatur in der Physiologie des Nervensystems") proposing that mentalistic or psychological terms be discontinued in describing animal behavior and that objective terms like reflex, reception, and resonance be substituted. Earlier (1898), Bethe had written an article ("Dürfen wir den Ameisen und Bienen psychische Qualitäten zuschreiben?") denying ants and bees a psyche, their complex and seemingly intelligent behavior notwithstanding. In Bethe and others, Descartes's [48] view of animals as machines was finding support and furnishing impetus to the behavioristic view in psychology, soon to be launched by Watson [374].

Biographic data: *Enciclopedia italiana,* vol. 6

[337]

PILLSBURY, WALTER BOWERS

American psychologist
Rating: 21
Born: Burlington, Iowa, July 21, 1872
Died: Ann Arbor, Michigan, June 3, 1960
Highest degree: Ph.D. in psychology, Cornell University, 1896, under E. B. Titchener [294]
Positions, honors: 1897–1942, University of Michigan, head of Psychology Department since 1929; editorial work for *American Journal of Psychology* (1897–1960), *Psychological Review* (1910–1929), and *Journal of Social Psychology* (1930–1960); president, American Psychological Association, 1910; honorary LL.D., University of Nebraska, 1933

Pillsbury established a psychological laboratory at the University of Michigan, did some research there at first, then wrote his best known book, *L'Attention* (1906, translated into English in 1908). It was successful, which set Pillsbury on writing more books. He was an eclectic, and his textbooks (*The Essentials of Psychology,* 1911; *The Fundamentals of Psychology,* 1916) saw several editions. He wrote a well known *History of Psychology* (1929), seven additional books and sixty-nine articles.

Biographic data: *HPA* 2:265; *NCAB* 44:450; K. M. Dallenbach, Walter Bowers Pillsbury. *American Journal of Psychology,* 1961, 74, 165–173

KLAGES, LUDWIG

[338]

German-Swiss psychologist
Rating: 15
Born: Hannover, Germany, December 10, 1872
Died: Kilchberg, Zurich, Switzerland, July 29, 1956
Highest degree: Ph.D. in chemistry, University of Munich, 1900
Positions: University of Munich, 1901–1919; 1919, Seminar für Ausdruckskunde, Kilchberg, near Zurich

Klages contributed to the psychology of expressive movements, especially graphology. He founded the German Graphological Society in 1897, *Graphologische Monatshefte* (1897–1908), and in 1905 the Seminary for the Science of Expressions (Seminar für Ausdruckskunde), which became the main German center of characterology. Klages wrote *Die Probleme der Graphologie* in 1910 and *Einführung in die Psychologie der Handschrift* (1924, 2d edition, 1928), but it was *Handschrift und Charakter* (1916) that brought him fame. It saw twenty-four editions in forty years and, in the 1920s and 1930s, made Klages's name about as famous as that of Freud [224].

The term "characterology" (*Charakterkunde*) was coined by Julius Bahnsen (1867), but Klages became the foremost representative of characterology. Philosophically, Klages was a neo-Romanticist and anti-intellectualist, stressing instincts and life forces. He was influenced by such men as Carus, Goethe [77], Schopenhauer [108], Lipps [211], and Nietzsche [196]. Klages held that man differs from animals in his ability to represent sensations in images and by having acquired in his development a *Geist* or spirit. The *Geist* and nature (life) are engaged in a combat in man. A person's character is his relative balance between these forces. Klages assigned characterology the role of clarifying the relationship between spirit and nature. It should destroy the spirit and help man return to his primitive, undifferentiated, natural state.

Klages's main thesis was that "the body is a manifestation of the soul, and the soul is the essence of the living body." The psychic aspect of man can be apprehended only in the totality of the besouled body, i.e., expressive movements. Physiological psychology is useless in understanding personality. Expressive movements yield data that can be analyzed exactly, especially if they also yield a graphic record, such as a writing or a drawing. Although contributions to characterology were made also in other countries (Bain [138], Janet [249]), characterology, as exemplified by Klages, has remained a typically German development, and it is in Germany where it has played an important role in both theoretical and applied psychology.

Biographic data: *EP* 4:343; H.-E Schröder, Nachruf für Ludwig Klages. *Psychologische Rundschau,* 1957, 8, 75–76; R. Heiss, Ludwig Klages. *Zeitschrift für diagnostische Psychologie*, 1956, 4, 215–217

[339]

FERENCZI, SANDOR

Hungarian psychoanalyst
Rating: **19**
Born: Miskolc, 1873
Died: Budapest, May 22, 1933
Highest degree: M.D., University of Vienna, 1894
Positions: 1895, City hospital, Budapest; 1900, private practice, hospital appointments in Budapest; 1919, University of Budapest, professor of psychoanalysis

Ferenczi was one of the members of Freud's [224] inner circle. He was the founder and coeditor of the *Internationale Zeitschrift für Psychoanalyse,* the founder of the Hungarian Psychoanalytic Society (in 1913), and the holder of the first professorship of psychoanalysis. Ferenczi introduced two new methods of therapy. One, the active therapy method, was based on Freud's theory of privation. When patients resisted free association, Ferenczi ordered abstinence from eating, defecation, or sex, expecting the dammed-up libido to provide the energy needed for therapy and to clarify to the patient his defenses. Ferenczi abandoned this therapy by 1927 because it did not work, causing hostility in many patients, and switched to permissive therapy, which was based on the idea that a loving environment would provide the necessary therapeutic action by compensating for the lack of love and attention experienced by the patient in his childhood. Ferenczi's most important books are *Actual- und Psychoneurosen* (1908), *Introjektion und Transferenz* (1909, *Thalasso: Versuch einer Genital-theorie* (1924), and *Die Entwicklung der Psychoanalyse* (1924).

Biographic data: IESS 5:367; S. Radó, Sándor Ferenczi. *Psycho-analytic Quarterly*, 1933, **2**, 356–358; M. Balint, Sándor Ferenczi, obiit 1933. *International Journal of Psychoanalysis*, 1949, **30**, 215–219; P. Federn, Sándor Ferenczi. *International Journal of Psychoanalysis*, 1933, **14**, 467–485; S. Freud, Sándor Ferenczi. *International Journal of Psychoanalysis*, 1933, **14**, 463–466; B. R. Berkey & L. M. Roberts, Sándor Ferenczi: The man, his works, and evolving forms of active psycho-therapy. *Diseases of the Nervous System*, 1968, **29**(7), 457–461

JUDD, CHARLES HUBBARD [340]

American psychologist
Rating: 22
Born: Bareilly, India, February 23, 1873
Died: Santa Barbara, California, July 19, 1946
Highest degree: Ph.D. in psychology, University of Leipzig, 1896, under W. Wundt [161]
Positions: 1896, Wesleyan University; 1898, New York University; 1901, University of Cincinnati; 1902, Yale University; 1909–1938, University of Chicago; Judd taught psychology, philosophy, and pedagogy at all of these institutions, was chairman of the Department of Education at Chicago and chairman of its Department of Psychology from 1920 to 1925; president, American Psychological Association, 1909, National Society of College Teachers in Education, 1911, 1915

At Leipzig and at Wesleyan, Judd studied time and space perception and wrote several papers on these topics. He translated Wundt's *Grundriss der Psychologie* into English (1896). At Yale, he studied visual perception, motor processes, and learning. His interest in applying psychology, especially in the field of education, arose soon after his obtaining his doctorate. Judd's first book, written while at Yale, was *Genetic Psychology for Teachers* (1903). He next wrote a general psychology text (*Psychology: General Introduction,* 1907) and some laboratory manuals. It was at Chicago that Judd turned educational psychologist. He studied reading, problems of high school education, the number concept, formulated a social psychology for the educational setting, and published most of his books while at Chicago. Among them are *Psychology of High School Subjects* (1915), *Introduction to the Scientific Study of Education* (1918), *Silent Reading* (1923), *Psychological Analysis of the Fundamentals of Arithmetic* (1926), *Psychology of Social Institutions* (1926), *Psychology of Secondary Education* (1927), and *Educational Psychology* (1939). Judd insisted that, instead of applying findings from general psychology to education, educational psychology should derive its own principles from data of educational research, which should be as rigorous as any psychological research. At a time when rote learning and faculty psychology were still prevalent in education, Judd stressed the role of generalization in learning.

Biographic data: *HPA* 2:207; *IESS* 8:281; *NCAB* 42:678, A:252; G. T. Buswell, Charles Hubbard Judd. *American Journal of Psychology,* 1947, **60**, 135–137; F. N. Freeman, Charles Hubbard Judd. *Psychological Review,* 1947, 54, 59–65

[341]

MYERS, CHARLES SAMUEL

English psychologist
Rating: 21
Born: London, March 13, 1873
Died: Winsford, Somersetshire, October 12, 1946
Highest degree: M.D., Cambridge University, 1901, Sc.D., 1909
Positions, honors: 1904–1922, Cambridge University; 1903–1907, King's College, London; 1922, director, National Institute of Industrial Psychology, London; president, Seventh International Congress of Psychology, 1923; honorary Sc.D., University of Manchester, LL.D. from University of Calcutta, Sc.D. from University of Pennsylvania

Myers began his psychological career by participating, with Rivers [278] and McDougall [329], in the Cambridge University anthropological expedition to the Torres Straits in 1898. He studied the sensory discrimination and reaction time of the natives. Upon his return to Cambridge, Myers became a cofounder, with Ward [190] and Rivers, of the *British Journal of Psychology* in 1904. Later, he was able to obtain funds for a psychology laboratory, and opened one at Cambridge in 1913. As a director of the laboratory and lecturer in psychology at Cambridge, where many prominent British psychologists were trained, Myers was able to do much to change the emphasis in teaching psychology toward a more scientific approach. The experimental psychology text used in England in the 1910s and 1920s was *Textbook of Experimental Psychology* (1909) by Myers and Bartlett [444]. Myers also wrote *An Introduction to Experimental Psychology* soon after publishing the *Textbook* (1911).

As a result of his work during World War I on tests to select listeners for submarines, Myers became interested in applied psychology. He founded, with H. J. Welch, the National Institute of Industrial Psychology in 1921 and became the editor of *Occupational Psychology*, its organ. The several books that Myers wrote in the area of industrial psychology were also helpful in establishing a climate in Great Britain in which applied psychology was more readily accepted: *Mind and Work* (1920), *Industrial Psychology in Great Britain* (1926), *Ten Years of Industrial Psychology* (1923, with H. J. Welch), *Psychology as Applied to Engineering* (1942).

Biographic data: DNB 1941–1950; HPA 3:215; T. H. Pear, Charles Samuel Myers. *American Journal of Psychology*, 1947, **60**, 289–296; C. Burt, Charles Samuel Myers. *Occupational Psychology*, 1947,21, 1–6; F. C. Bartlett, Dr. Charles Samuel Myers, C.B.E., F.R.S. *Nature*, 1946, **158**, 657–658; M. S. Viteles, Charles Samuel Myers. *Psychological Review*, 1947, **54**, 177–181

CLAPAREDE, EDOUARD [342]

Swiss psychologist
Rating: 26
Born: Geneva, March 24, 1873
Died: Geneva, September 29, 1940
Highest degree: M.D., University of Geneva, 1897
Positions: 1897–1898, La Salpêtrière, Paris, neuropathologist; 1904, director, Psychological Laboratory, University of Geneva;

1915, University of Geneva, professor of psychology; secretary of the International Congress of Psychology for a number of years

Claparède's interests covered a wide variety of subjects. He did some early studies on sleep and on animal psychology, wrote sixty-two major articles, and, in 1901, founded the *Archives de psychologie* (with Théodore Flournoy [220]), which he edited till his death. Claparède's view of behavior was at first biological, then a functional and purposive one, stressing the adaptive response of the organism to the momentary situation ("law of momentary interest"). He shunned broad, theoretical speculations. Later, he became interested in child study. Claparède saw the study of the child as playing the same role as the clinical patient does for the medical researcher. He became a leader in establishing the scientific study of child psychology. His best known book is *Psychologie de l'enfant et pédagogie expérimentale* (1909), which has been translated into ten languages (English translation, *The Psychology of the Child*). In 1912, Claparède established the Jean Jacques Rousseau Institute, a teachers' training institute specializing in preschool and lower grade school children, as well as a child research center. Claparède's work has had a direct influence on Jean Piaget.

Biographic data: *HPA* 1:63; *IESS* 2:501; E. Lerner, Edouard Claparède. *American Journal of Psychology*, 1941, 54, 296–299; W. B. Pillsbury, Edouard Claparède. *Psychological Review*, 1941, 48, 271–278; H. T. Lovell, Edouard Claparède. *Australian Journal of Psychology and Philosophy*, 1942, 20, 81–85

[343]　　DREVER, JAMES, SR.

Scottish psychologist
Rating: 23
Born: Orkney Islands, April 8, 1873
Died: Edinburgh, August 11, 1950
Highest degree: D. Phil. in psychology, Edinburgh University, 1916
Positions: 1919–1944, Edinburgh University; War Office personnel selection position during World War II; president, British Psychological Society, 1935–1938; president, Twelfth International Congress of Psychology, 1948; editorial work for *British Journal of Psychology Monographs*

Drever's output of publications was modest. He worked in the areas of educational psychology (*Introduction to the Psychology of Education,* 1922), general psychology (*An Introduction to Experimental Psychology,* 1926; *Instinct in Man,* 1917; *Psychology of Everyday Life,* 1921, 11th edition, 1940), juvenile delinquency, and the psychology of the deaf. He also wrote *The Psychology of Industry* (1921) and a *Dictionary of Psychology* (1952, revised edition, 1964). Drever's main contribution was through teaching and the directing of the George Combe Psychological Laboratory at the University of Edinburgh. Between 1931 and 1944, Drever occupied the first chair in psychology at a Scottish university. The finest training in psychology in Great Britain in the 1920s and 1930s was to be had at Edinburgh, where Drever was placing a strong emphasis on experimentation in training psychologists.

Biographic data: HPA 2:17; M. Collins, James Drever. *Psychological Review,* 1951, 58, 1–4; J. Drever, Jr., James Drever. *British Journal of Educational Psychology,* 1951, 21, 1–2; B. Semeonoff, James Drever. *American Journal of Psychology,* 1951, 64, 283–285

CARR, HARVEY A.

[344]

American psychologist
Rating: **23**
Born: Indiana, April 30, 1873
Died: Culver, Indiana, June 21, 1954
Highest degree: Ph.D. in psychology, University of Chicago, 1905, under J. R. Angell [309]
Positions: 1906, Pratt Institute, Brooklyn; 1908–1938, University of Chicago, instructor to chairman of Psychology Department; president, American Psychological Association, 1926

Carr was an experimental psychologist and a leading exponent of the functional point of view in psychology, associated with the University of Chicago. In 1926, Carr succeeded James Rowland Angell, the first psychologist-functionalist, as chairman of the Department of Psychology at Chicago. Under his leadership the Chicago Psychology Department was the best in the United States. During Carr's time at Chicago, 150 Ph.D. degrees in psychology were granted, and 53 of these doctorates were directed by Carr.

Carr's views on functionalism are presented in his book, *Psychology, a Study of Mental Activity* (1925). By the time Carr wrote his book the period of controversy concerning functionalism was over, and the book served mainly to clarify further the meaning of function and of functionalism. The meanings of function as utility and as activity were said by Carr to be combined in psychology in that both implied what is meant in mathematics by $y = f(x)$, i.e., a functional or contingent relationship between psychological antecedents and their consequents. Functionalism was also amplified by Carr in his book in that to the antecedent-consequent relationship he added motivation as the guiding factor. Carr's viewpoint was representative of so many American psychologists even while Carr was at Chicago that he was able to maintain that functional psychology was American psychology. Carr did research in comparative psychology, systematic learning, and visual space perception. His work in the latter area is presented in his *Introduction to Space Perception* (1935).

Biographic data: *HPA* 3:69; H. L. Koch, Harvey A. Carr. *Psychological Review*, 1955, 62, 81–82; W. B. Pillsbury, Harvey A. Carr. *American Journal of Psychology*, 1955, 68, 149–151

[345]

BERGER, HANS

German psychiatrist
Rating: (unrated)
Born: Neuses near Coburg, Bavaria, May 21, 1873
Died: Bad Blankenburg, Thuringia, June 1, 1941
Highest degree: M.D., University of Jena
Positions: University of Jena, 1901–1941

Berger obtained a recording of the electrical activity of the brain in 1903, but it was not until 1924 that he attached electrodes to his young son's scalp, and using a vacuum tube amplifier and an optical galvanometer, was able to obtain a continuous record of the rhythmic electrical activity of the brain, *the electroencephalogram* (EEG). Berger published his work in an article in 1929. He named the most pronounced rhythm, the ten-cycles-per-second wave, *the alpha rhythm,* and related it to restful but not sleepy states of the subject. While Berger had always believed that mental states would reflect in the physical activity of the nervous system (*Über die körperlichen Ausserungen psychischer*

Zustände, 1904; *Trauma und Psychose,* 1915), his discovery came at a time when psychiatry was under the aegis of psychoanalysis, the organic viewpoint was in eclipse, and he was met by opposition and even ridicule. It was not until Adrian in England was able to duplicate Berger's results that EEG came into general use. In addition to medical uses, EEG has been finding ever wider application in psychological research: thinking, problem solving, states of consciousness, emotion, perception, sleep and dreaming, and other areas. The change in orientation that occurred in psychiatry and neurophysiology after 1929 was to no small extent due to Berger's discovery.

Biographic data: *DSB* 2:1–2; F. A. Gibbs, Professor Dr. Hans Berger. *Archives of Neurology and Psychiatry,* Sep. 1941, 514–516; Anon., Hans Berger. *New England Journal of Medicine,* 1941, 225, 205

MEYER, MAX FREDERICK [346]

German–American psychologist
Rating: 20
Born: Danzig, East Prussia, June 15, 1873
Died: Miami, Florida, March 14, 1967
Highest degree: Ph.D. in psychology, University of Berlin, 1896, under C. Stumpf [202]
Positions: 1901–1929, University of Missouri; 1929–1930, Central Institute for the Deaf, St. Louis, 1932–1940, University of Miami

On the subject of what psyhology is and how it should be studied Meyer expressed views that were very similar to those of the father of behaviorism, Watson [374], and he expressed them before Watson (*The Fundamental Laws of Human Behavior,* 1911). His best known work is *The Psychology of the Other One* (1921), whose point is that the task of psychology is the study of public data. Consciousness may be studied scientifically only if it is made public. Meyer's views never made quite the same impact as Watson's, however.

Meyer's contributions to empirical psychology were in the area of hearing and musical acoustics, where he published between the years 1899 and 1950. Meyer proposed a theory of hearing that was second-best known after Helmholtz's [143]. Like Helmoltz's theory, it made pitch a function of frequency of sound waves but excluded the factor of resonance. The theory also explained the perception of loudness of complex sound waves. The analysis of such waves Meyer placed in the inner ear rather than in the brain.

Biographic data: I. J. Hirsh, Max Frederick Meyer. *American Journal of Psychology* 1967, 80, 644–645

[347]

SIMON, THEODORE

French psychiatrist
Rating: 21
Born: Dijon, Côte d'Or, July 10, 1873
Died: Paris, September 4, 1961
Highest degree: M.D., University of Paris, 1900
Positions: 1899, intern at asylum of Perray-Vaucluse, Paris; 1901, intern, Saint-Anne Hospital, Paris; 1904, psychiatrist, Dury-les-Amiens and Saint-Anne hospitals; 1905, psychiatrist, Saint-You Hospital, Paris; 1920, medical director, Perray-Vaucluse colony; 1930–1936, medical director, Henri-Rousselle Hospital

A physician and a psychiatrist, Simon always had an interest in philosophy and psychology. Simon initiated a collaboration with Binet [236] in 1899 when Binet learned of the ready availability to Simon of child subjects, his patients. Simon joined Binet in producing the world's first intelligence test, *the Simon-Binet test*. He coauthored with Binet some twenty-eight papers and a book (*Les enfants anormaux,* 1907). Simon failed to develop the Simon-Binet intelligence test after Binet's death, but his interest in psychology continued. He devised his own intelligence scale for children below the age of two and a group intelligence scale that was developed at Perray-Vaucluse and called the P.V. In 1912, Simon became president of the Société Libre Pour L'Étude Psychologique de L'Enfant and editor of the Society's *Bulletin.* The name of the society was later changed to that of Société Alfred Binet. Through it, Simon sought to advance Binet's goal to understand man as well as to rectify the overuse and abuse of his intelligence test. Simon was also responsible for creating the first medico-psychological consultation for delinquent children brought before the courts.

Biographic data: T. H. Wolf, An individual who made a difference. *American Psychologist,* 1961, 16, 245–248; I.

Rapaport, In memoriam: Théodore Simon. *American Journal of Mental Deficiency,* 1962, 67 (3), 367–368

HOLT, EDWIN BISSELL [348]

American psychologist
Rating: 22
Born: Winchester, Massachusetts, August 21, 1873
Died: Tenants Harbor, Maine, January 25, 1946
Highest degree: Ph.D. in psychology, Harvard University, 1901, under William James
Positions: 1901–1918, Harvard University; 1926–1936, Princeton University, visiting professor of psychology

Holt advocated the study of behavior, but he is not counted formally among the behaviorists. The difference between him and Watson [374] was that Holt believed that one should study the "specific response relations" rather than muscular responses or reflexes. It was a more philosophically based and a more sophisticated view than Watson's (*The Concept of Consciousness,* 1914). The specific response relations were those between the organism's intents or purposes and the goals toward which action was directed. To Holt, responses were wholes and they had a purpose. In his most important book, *Animal Drive and the Learning Process: An Essay Toward Radical Empiricism* (1931), Holt shows that learning and memory can be considered in physical and psysiological terms. It presents, among others, *the reflex circle concept,* on which theories of language development were later built.

Holt's book on the Freudian wish (*The Freudian Wish and Its Place in Ethics,* 1915) is an important link in the development of dynamic psychology. Holt saw the Freudian wish as a concept that provided psychology with a dynamics since the wish as a specific response relation implied purpose and psychological causality. A wish is a course of action which the body is set to carry out. Holt, a determinist, saw the body as always executing behavioral acts which, impelled by the past, led to a future goal. Behavior thus always has a knowing, a meaning. Holt left a strong impress on Tolman [439] in the latter's formulation of purposive behaviorism.

Biographic data: EP 4:58; IESS 6:493; D. Katz, Edwin Bissell Holt. *Science,* 1946, 103, 612; L. Carmichael, Edwin Bissell

Holt. *American Journal of Psychology,* 1946, 59, 478–480; H. S. Langfeld, Edwin Bissell Holt. *Psychological Review,* 1946, 53, 251–258

[349]

TWITMYER, EDWIN BURKET

American psychologist
Rating: 14
Born: McElhalttan, Pennsylvania, September 14, 1873
Died: Drexel Hill, Pennsylvania, March 3, 1943
Highest degree: Ph.D. in psychology, University of Pennsylvania, 1902
Positions, honors: 1897–1943, University of Pennsylvania; honorary LL.D., Lafayette College, 1933

Twitmyer's doctoral dissertation was on the knee jerk. To signal the striking of the hammer on the patellar tendon he rang a bell, and thus discovered that eventually the ringing of the bell alone would cause the patellar reflex to occur. He reported his finding at the 1904 meeting of the American Psychological Association (Knee jerk without stimulation of the patellar tendon. *Psychological Bulletin,* 1905, 2, 43 ff.), but the significance of the first laboratory demonstration of the conditioned reflex was not then appreciated. Pavlov [206] published his findings with dogs the next year, persisted with his work and, having already won the Nobel prize, commanded more attention than Twitmyer. Discouraged by the indifferent reception, Twitmyer switched to other work, mainly in the area of speech. In 1914, the University of Pennsylvania special speech clinic was established, the first of its kind in America, and Twitmyer became its first director. In 1932, he wrote with Y. S. Nathanson a book, *Correction of Defective Speech.* In it he expressed the view that all disturbances of speech have a common etiology, namely a disturbance in the rhythm of breathing. The latter, being partly habitual, could be cured using the learning methods.

Biographic data: NCAB 33:193; S. W. Fernberger, Edwin Burket Twitmyer. *Psychological Review,* 1943, 50, 345–349; K. G. Ecob, Death of Dr. Edwin Burket Twitmyer. *Mental Hygiene,* 1943, 27, 331; R. A. Brotemarkle, Edwin Burket Twitmyer. *Journal of Consulting Psychology,* 1943, 7, 200–201; F. W. Irwin, Edwin Burket Twitmyer. *American Journal of Psychology* 1943, 56, 451–453

American psychologist
Rating: **20**
Born: Jersey City, New Jersey, May 27, 1874
Died: Los Angeles, California, October 14, 1933
Highest degree: Ph.D. in psychology, Columbia University, 1899, under J. McK. Cattell [256]
Positions, honors: 1899–1900, Harvard University, instructor in physiology; 1901, Dartmouth College, instructor in physiology and medical physics; 1904–1906, McLean Hospital for the Insane, Waverly, Mass., pathological physiologist and psychologist; 1907, George Washington University (St. Elizabeth's Hospital), professor of psychology; 1924–1933, editorial work for *Psychological Monographs* and *Psychological Bulletin* (1914–1924); University of California in Los Angeles, professor of psychology; honorary LL.D. and M.D.: president American Psychological Association, 1920

Franz pioneered in relating psychology to the physiology of the brain. He did this by using both the physiologist's method of extirpation of brain tissue and the psychologist's method of studying animal learning. The relationships studied by Franz were those between learned behaviors and their cortical localization. He found that a habit lost through extirpation could be relearned, lost again and so on several times. It suggested that neither the site nor the extent of brain damage in mental patients were directly related to the severity of behavioral impairment. Franz showed that complete frontal lobectomy in cats and monkeys led to loss of recent habits but not of old habits, that the lost habits could be relearned, and that the loss of one lobe only led to a decrease in the efficiency of the behavior involved, but not to its complete loss. Such findings, in addition to his demonstration that even the motor functions were not very precisely localized in the brain were quite surprising at the time. Franz jokingly began to refer to attempts to localize brain functions exactly as the "new phrenology." Karl Lashley [466], who worked with Franz at St. Elizabeth's Hospital, eventually took over from him and developed further this line of research, helping to swing the localization pendulum even further toward Flourens [113].

Biographic data: HPA 2:89; NCAB A:477; K. Dunlap, Shepherd Ivory Franz. *Journal of General Psychology*, 1934, **10**, 3; R. S. Woodworth, Shepherd Ivory Franz. *American Journal of Psychology*, 1934, **46**, 151–152

KRUGER, FELIX (E.)

German psychologist
Rating: **20**
Born: Posen, August 19, 1874
Died: Basle, Switzerland, February 25, 1948
Highest degree: Ph.D. in psychology, University of Munich, 1897, under H. Cornelius and T. Lipps [211]
Positions: University of Kiel, assistant; University of Leipzig, *Privatdozent;* 1906–1908, University of Buenos Aires; 1909, University of Leipzig; 1910, University of Halle; 1917, University of Leipzig, 1935 became rector of same, but retired for political reasons; in Switzerland since 1945

Krüger followed two great psychologists in their chairs: Ebbinghaus [207] at Halle and Wundt [161] at Leipzig (1917). At Leipzig, Krüger established the Leipzig Gestalt school of psychology (as contrasted with the Berlin school of Wertheimer [391], Köhler [447], and Koffka [438]), also known as *Ganzheitspsychologie* or holistic psychology (*Uber den Strukturbegriff in der Psychologie,* 1923). The school was influenced by the Graz or Austrian school of psychology (to which both Cornelius and Lipps belonged) and, while accepting the idea of wholes or *Gestalten* as basic, criticized the Berlin school for not including all psychological phenomena in its purview, such as emotions, feelings, and social and cultural phenomena. Krüger's goal was to study the totality of the person, which he later, in accord with Dilthey [164], named "structure." It included not only that which the phenomenologist studies but also all dispositional and determining tendencies which underlie mental events. In Germany, holistic psychology became the leading school of psychology in mid-20th century. Additional works of Krüger that present the ideas of holistic psychology are *Komplexqualitäten, Gestalten und Gefühle* (1926), *Das Wesen der Gefühle* (1928), *Ganzheit und Form* (1932), *Lehre von dem Ganzen* (1948), and *Zur Philosophie und Psychologie der Ganzheit* (1953).

Biographic data: *EP* 4:366

JOST, ADOLPH

German psychologist
Rating: **16**
Born: Graz, Austria, August 22, 1874

Died: Place and date unknown
Highest degree: Ph.D. in psychology, University of Göttingen, 1896, under G. Müller [208]

Jost worked with Georg Müller on human learning, using the method of right associates. The method was invented by Müller but published first by Jost. Jost's work on his doctoral dissertation (Die Assoziationsfestigkeit in ihrer Abhängigkeit von der Verteilung der Wiederholungen, 1897) led to the formulation of *Jost's law,* which is that of two associations of equal strength the older association will be strengthened more by repetition than the more recent one.

Biographic data: No biographies available

THORNDIKE, EDWARD LEE   [353]

American psychologist
Rating: 27
Born: Williamsburg, Massachusetts, August 31, 1874
Died: Montrose, New York, August 9, 1949
Highest degree: Ph.D. in psychology, Columbia University, 1898, under J. McK. Cattell [256]
Positions: 1898, Western Reserve University; 1899–1940, Columbia University; president, American Psychological Association, 1912

Thorndike was the first psychologist to study animal behavior experimentally in a laboratory. Thorndike began using chicks at Harvard, then moved to Columbia and did his dissertation study on cats. The study was published in 1898 and became part of the classical literature of psychology. Thorndike observed the escape attempts, or trial and error learning, of cats in puzzle boxes and arrived at the first general principles governing such behavior. *The law of effect* stated that those movements that led to satisfaction would be stamped in, and that those that led to an unsatisfactory state of affairs would be stamped out. Thus, from the random array of movements exhibited by the animal in the puzzle box only those leading to escape would be learned. Later on Thorndike discovered that noxious effects only suppressed behavior temporarily, but did not actually stamp it out.

The law of exercise stated that those associations that are practiced are stamped in and those that are not are extinguished. The law of effect was an empirically based restatement of what many philosophers and psychologists had previously said about the effects of pleasure and pain. The law of exercise restated how stimuli and responses become associated, hence hailed back directly to the associationistic doctrine. While Thorndike's two laws in their orginal form are not accepted today, most learning theories incorporate them in one modified form or another.

Thorndike's interest later turned on human learning. In 1901, he and Woodworth [312] published a classic paper that demolished the doctrine of formal disciplines by showing that transfer of learning takes place only if the same general principles or identical elements are involved. In 1903, Thorndike published his *Educational Psychology* (the second edition consisted of three volumes: *The Original Nature of Man*, 1913; *The Psychology of Learning*, 1913; and *Individual Differences and Their Causes*, 1914) in which the learning principles Thorndike had discovered in his work with animals were applied to the human educational experience. Education led Thorndike to mental measurement. He became a leader in that field, publishing his *Introduction to the Theory of Mental and Social Measurements*, in 1904, and later, with others, *The Measurement of Intelligence* (1927). The 1904 volume made statistical computations of test results available to the everyday user of such tests.

Additional efforts of Thorndike's included the construction of a scale to measure children's handwriting (1910), and a table of word frequency counts in the English language (*The Teacher's Word Book of 30,000 Words*, 1944, with I. Lorge [513]), of considerable utility to researchers who use dictionary words in their work. Thorndike was very prolific: he left a bibliography of over 450 articles and books. Additional important books that Thorndike wrote were *The Elements of Psychology* (1905), *Animal Intelligence* (1911), *The Fundamentals of Learning* (1932), and *The Psychology of Wants, Interests, and Attitudes* (1935).

Biographic data: HPA 3:263; IESS 16:8; NCAB 51:209; A. I. Gates, Edward Lee Thorndike. *Psychological Review*, 1949, **56**, 241–243; W. F. Russell, Edward Lee Thorndike. *Teachers College Record*, 1949, **51**, 26–28; G. Thomson, Obituary: Professor Edward Lee Thorndike. *Nature*, 1949, **164**, 474; G. Humphrey, Obituary notice: Edward Lee Thorndike. *British Journal of Psychology*, 1949, **40**, 55–56; F. L. Goodenough, Edward Lee Thorndike. *American Journal of Psychology*, 1950, **63**, 291–301; R. S. Woodworth, Edward Lee Thorndike. *National Academy of Sciences Biographical Memoirs*, 1952

BRILL, ABRAHAM ARDEN

American psychoanalyst
Rating: **18**
Born: Kańczuga, Galicia, October 12, 1874
Died: New York, New York, March 2, 1948
Highest degree: M.D., Columbia University, 1903
Positions: 1907–1912, studied at Paris, Zurich, and Vienna (under Freud); 1912, practice of psychoanalysis in New York, teaching at Columbia University and New York University

While the 1909 Clark University conference exposed Freud [224] and other European psychoanalysts to Americans physically, Brill was instrumental in presenting their ideas in printed form. The first translation of a book by Freud was done by Brill (*Selected Papers on Hysteria,* 1909), He translated nine more works by Freud and wrote several in which he expounded psychoanalysis: *Psychoanalysis—Its Theories and Practical Applications* (1921), *Fundamental Conceptions of Psychoanalysis* (1922), and *Freud's Contribution to Psychiatry* (1944). Brill was also responsible for founding the New York Psychoanalytic Society in 1911.

Biographic data: *NCAB* E:526; [Anon.] Abraham Arden Brill, M.D. *Psychoanalytic Review,* 1941, **28**, 1–11; A. A. Brill, A psychoanalyst scans his past. *Journal of Nervous and Mental Disease,* 1942, **95**, 537–549; S. Lorand, Abraham Arden Brill. *International Journal of Psychoanalysis,* 1948, **29**, 1–3; C. P. Oberndorf. Abraham Arden Brill. *Psychoanalytic Quarterly,* 1948, **17**, 149–154; F. Wittels, Brill—the pioneer. *Psychoanalytic Review,* 1948, **35**, 394–398

LINDWORSKY, JOHANNES

German psychologist
Rating: **15**
Born: Frankfurt-am-Main, January 21, 1875
Died: Essen, September 9, 1939
Highest degree: Ph.D. in psychology, University of Munich, 1915, under J. Fröbes [291]
Positions: 1920, University of Cologne; 1928, German University, Prague

Lindworsky studied thinking and emotion, and counted himself among the Würzburg psychologists of imageless thought. His main concern, however, was the will. In his first book, *Der Wille* (1919), Lindworsky presented a survey of the contemporary literature on the will as well as his own theory of the will, which was his most important contribution to psychology. According to this theory, motivation precedes willing. Motives are "everything which is represented to the mind as a value realizable through the voluntary act." All phenomena of volition are the voluntary direction of attention toward a complex of images. The will, not being a force but a switching mechanism, cannot be strengthened by repetition but by directing attention to motives. Will training occurs when an appreciation of values and motives is produced. In this context, Lindworsky interpreted the spiritual exercises of Ignatius Loyola, thus establishing a link between the school of imageless thought and Thomistic psychology. Lindworsky was also a good experimenter, wrote an *Experimentelle Psychologie* (1921, English translation, 1931) and numerous articles on a wide variety of subjects, many of them in popular magazines, *Theoretische Psychologie* (1932; English translation, 1931), *Psychologie der Aszese* (1935; English translation, 1936), and other books.

Biographic data: H. Misiak & V. Staudt, *Catholics in Psychology*, 1954, pp. 111–125

[356]

CARLSON, ANTON JULIUS

American physiologist
Rating: 12
Born: Bohuslan, Sweden, January 29, 1875
Died: Chicago, Illinois, September 2, 1956
Highest degree: Ph.D. in physiology, Stanford University, 1903
Positions, honors: 1903, Carnegie Institute of Technology; 1904–1940, University of Chicago; president, American Biological Society, American Physiological Society, other organizations; American Medical Association gold medal, many other honors; honorary degrees from eight universities and colleges

Of importance to psychology are Carlson's studies of hunger and hunger sensations. Between 1912 and 1914 he wrote about a dozen articles on the subject and later published *The Control of Hunger in Health and Disease* (1916). Carlson left behind about

Two hundred research reports and a well-known textbook of psysiology, *The Machinery of the Body* (1937, 2d ed. 1941), written with Victor Johnson.

Biographic data: NCAB 45:486

KENT, GRACE (HELEN)

[357]

American psychologist
Rating: (unrated)
Born: Michigan City, Indiana, June 6, 1875
Died: Silver Spring, Maryland, September 18, 1973
Highest degree: Ph.D. in psychology, George Washington University, 1911
Positions: 1906, Philadelphia Hospital for Insane; 1907, Kings Park State Hospital, New York; 1910, Government Hospital for Insane, Washington, D. C.; 1911–1912, State Hospital, Warren, Pennsylvania; 1920, State Training School for Feeble-Minded, Clinton, South Carolina; 1922–1926, Worcester State Hospital; 1928–1946, Danvers State Hospital; 1947–1948, University of Miami, visiting professor

Kent's name became a well-known one in connection with the publication of the Kent-Rosanoff Free Association Test in 1910. It was a psychiatric screening instrument that was one of the first to have objective scoring and objective norms. A patient's associative responses were compared with frequency tables prepared on a norm group of one thousand individuals. The test fell into disuse when it was realized that the associative response is also a function of the patient's socioeconomic status, age, education, and the like, not only of his psychopathology. Kent continued to work in the area of clinical psychometrics, producing additional instruments, the Kent-Shakow Formboards (1928), the Kent-Shakow Industrial Formboards (1928), the Kent Series of Emergency Scales for the quick and rough classification of psychiatric patients (*Series of Emergency Scales*, 1946), plus some twenty-five papers in this area. One of her last publications was *Mental Tests in Clinics for Children* (1950).

Biographic data: *The Psychological Register*, 1932, Vol. III; *American Men of Science*, 9th edition

JUNG, CARL GUSTAV

Swiss psychiatrist
Rating: 27
Born: Kesswil, Thurgau, July 26, 1875
Died: Küsnacht, Zurich, June 6, 1961
Highest degree: M.D., University of Basle, 1900
Positions, honors: 1900–1909, University of Zurich Psychiatric Clinic; 1905–1913, University of Zurich, lecturer in psychiatry; 1913–1933, in private practice; 1933–1942, Federal Polytechnical University, Zurich, professor of medical psychology; the C. G. Jung Institute Founded at Zurich in 1948; four honorary degrees and many other honors

Jung's first publication in 1902 on the psychology and pathology of occult phenomena set the tone for much of his later work. His earliest work, however, was experimental. Jung introduced the method of measuring the emotional content that words have for a subject by the subject's associative reaction time, a method still in use. When the subject showed no knowledge of the significance of an emotion-arousing word, Jung attributed this to the existence of a complex or unconscious psychic contents having functional autonomy. After reading Freud [224], Jung began to apply his ideas in treating his own patients (*The Psychology of Dementia Precox,* 1907). He met Freud in 1907; in 1911 he became the first president of the International Psychoanalytic Society and heir apparent to Freud. He also began to have doubts about some aspects of Freud's theory. While recognizing the importance of early sexual conflict situations, Jung did not place as much emphasis on sexual libido as did Freud. By 1914 Jung's views had grown sufficiently apart from those of Freud for him to sever his connections with Freud and the psychoanalytic movement. Jung began to call his own theory analytic psychology.

The book, *Psychological Types,* published in 1921, is the best known among the many that Jung has written. It introduced into common language the terms extrovert and introvert. The core of Jung's type theory of personality was that every psychological phenomenon implies the opposite of itself. Thus in addition to the opposition between extroversion and introversion, the psychological functions of thinking and feeling (the rational functions) are the opposites of sensation and intuition (the irrational functions). The dominance of one of these (the superior function) further determines the psychological type of an individual. The principle of opposites also implies that both manifest and latent tendencies need to be recognized and dealt with if man is to live in harmony with himself. Jung gave up his university position to devote his time to the study of the unconscious and its manifestations. He travelled in order to make cross-cultural studies, and studied the myths, religions, and symbols of many cultures and of different historical eras, including the lore of alchemy. Out of Jung's immense erudition emerged a complex view of man, which Jung presented in numerous volumes and monographs.

The Jungian individual consists of an ego (self-awareness), a persona (the expected social role played by him), the shadow (a concept not unlike the Freudian id), the animus (in a female) or the anima (in a male) (the unconscious attitude pertaining to the opposite sex), the self (the soul, in some respects similar to Freud's superego), and unconscious, consisting of a personal and a collective layer. The collective unconscious is a deposit of archetypes or fundamental modes of apprehension that are common to all humanity because of the universality of certain underlying experiences. The archetypes manifest themselves symbolically in myths, graphic representations, dreams, and the like. The process of attaining a healthy, creative personality, the process of individuation, involves the differentiation of as well as the compensatory balancing of the opposite facets of personality in relation to its central core, the self. Jungian analysis is based on this conception of man. Its purpose is to help the patient to achieve individuation, to become an integrated personality.

After the organization of the first Jungian training center in Zurich in 1948, additional training centers have been established in Europe and America. Jung's books have been translated into almost all European languages. There are seventeen volumes in the English edition of his collected works. They offer a view of man that, while psychoanalytically based, is an alternative to that of Freud's. Jung's influence on psychological thinking about the dynamics of human behavior and man as a symbol-using being has been far-reaching.

Biographic data: *DSB* 7:189; *EP* 4:294; *IESS* 8:326; C. G. Jung, *Memories, Dreams, Reflections,* 1961; W. Douglas, Carl Gustav Jung. *American Journal of Psychology,* 1961, **74**, 639–641; E. Harms,Carl Gustav Jung. *American Journal of Psychiatry,* 1962, 118, 728–732

DOWNEY, JUNE ETTA [359]

American psychologist
Rating: 14
Born: Laramie, Wyoming, July 13, 1875

Died: Trenton, New Jersey, October 11, 1932
Highest degree: Ph.D. in psychology, University of Chicago, 1907, under J. R. Angell [309]
Positions: 1905–1915, University of Wyoming, professor of English and philosophy; 1915–1932, University of Wyoming, professor of philosophy and psychology

Downey's book *The Will Temperament and Its Testing* (1924) and the will-temperament test it described attracted much attention at the time and stimulated research in personality, although the test itself was found to have considerable limitations. Downey was also interested in motor behavior, especially in the different aspects of writing, including graphology. She published many papers in this area and the book, *Graphology and Psychology of Handwriting* (1919). In a third area of her interests, aesthetics, she coauthored (with E. E. Slosson) *Plots and Personalities* (1922) and *Creative Imagination* (1929). Downey left behind a total of seventy-six publications.

Biographic data: R. S. Uhrbrock, June Etta Downey. *Journal of General Psychology*, 1933, 9, 351–364; J. E. Anderson, June Etta Downey. *American Journal of Psychology*, 1933, 45, 362–363

[360]

DUNLAP, KNIGHT

American psychologist
Rating: 22
Born: Diamond Spring, California, November 21, 1875
Died: Columbia, South Carolina, August 14, 1949
Highest degree: Ph.D. in psychology, Harvard University, 1903, under H. Münsterberg [272]
Positions: 1902, University of California at Berkeley; 1906, Johns Hopkins University; 1936–1947, University of California at Los Angeles; president, American Psychological Association, 1922

Dunlap was a versatile, general-experimental psychologist. In a paper on color vision (1915) he demonstrated the difference between actual and potential stimuli and that both kinds must be regarded as actually existing. In 1918, he and Madison Bentley [321] demonstrated that the nystagmic eye movements produced by head rotation could be modified or abolished. In 1921, Dunlap demonstrated the binocular transfer of momentary local blindness, which necessitated the revision of theories of nervous interaction. In these and other research studies Dunlap's interest was focused on the body-mind relationship. Assuming that one motor act or glandular discharge could serve as stimulus to another, he theorized that the same set of principles could explain the formation of both habits of thought and habits of action. Later his interest shifted to abnormal and social psychology and the psychology of religion (*Social Psychology,* 1925; *The Dramatic Personality of Jesus,* 1933). Dunlap wrote additional books on a wide variety of subjects: *A system of Psychology* (1912), *Psychobiology* (1914), *Habits: Their Making and Unmaking* (1932), *Religion: Its Functions in Human Life* (1946), and several others. He published a total of about two hundred titles. Dunlap was also the inventor of several pieces of apparatus: *Dunlap chronoscope, Dunlap chair for vestibular investigation, Dunlap steadiness plate,* and others. According to Dunlap himself, his contributions to psychology were: (1) attack on introspection, (2) insistence on response as the basis of mental processes, (3) attack on images and insistence that objects of perception are real objects rather than "psychic," (4) emphasis on periphery, rather than the brain, as the fundamental determiner of psychological qualities, (5) the elimination of the "instinct" concept, (6) the view of consciousness as an inference from response, and (7) changes in the view of heredity.

Biographic data: *HPA* 2:35; *NCAB* 39:21; K. G. Moore, Knight Dunlap. *Psychological Review,* 1949, 56, 309–310; R. M. Dorcus, Knight Dunlap. *American Journal of Psychology,* 1950, 63, 114–119

KUHLMANN, FREDERICK   [361]

American psychologist
Rating: 11
Born: Davenport, Iowa, March 20, 1876
Died: St. Paul, Minnesota, April 19, 1941
Highest degree: Ph.D. in psychology, Clark University, 1903, under E. C. Sanford [254]
Positions: 1903, Clark University; 1907, University of Illinois; 1910, director, Research Bureau, Minnesota School for the Feebleminded, Faribault; 1921, director, Division of Research, Minnesota State Department of Public Institutions

Intelligence and mental deficiency were Kuhlmann's chief interests (*A Handbook of Mental Tests*, 1922; *Outline of Mental Deficiency*, 1924; *Tests of Mental Development,* 1939). He extended the Stanford-Binet Intelligence Scale downward to the age of three months in 1912 (called *the Kuhlmann-Binet* and revised twice since), and constructed a group general intelligence test, *the Kuhlmann-Anderson Intelligence Tests* (1927). Kuhlmann also wrote eight significant articles on mental imagery and memory and numerous other articles and reports.

Biographic data: K.M. Dallenbach, Frederick Kuhlmann. *American Journal of Psychology,* 1941, **54**, 446–447; F. N. Maxfield, Frederick Kuhlmann, 1876–1941. Kuhlmann as psychologist. *American Journal of Mental Deficiency,* 1941, **46**, 17–18

[362]

BEERS, CLIFFORD WHITTINGHAM

American layman
Rating: **17**
Born: New Haven, Connecticut, March 30, 1876
Died: Providence, Rhode Island, July 9, 1943
Education: Ph.B., Yale University, 1897
Honors: 1932, Cross of Chevalier, French Legion of Honor; 1933, Gold Medal of the National Institute of Social Sciences; 1933, presented with a collection of tributes, published as *Twenty-five Years After: Sidelights on the Mental Hygiene Movement and Its Founder* (1934)

Beers was the founder of the mental hygiene movement. In a famous book, *A Mind That Found Itself* (1908), Beers described his mental breakdown and the poor and inhumane treatment he received in three Connecticut mental institutions over a period of three years. The book aroused interest and elicited help from the public and civic and scientific leaders, such as William James [184] and Adolf Meyer [292]. The latter suggested the term "mental hygiene" to describe the movement to educate the public in the area of mental disorders. The first Society for Mental Hygiene was organized by Beers in Connecticut in 1908 and the National Commission for Mental Hygiene in 1909. Beers became the leader of the mental health movement, which eventually achieved world-wide proportions when the First International Congress of Mental Hygiene was convened by Beers in 1930 and the International Committee for Mental Hygiene was founded by him. The mental hygiene movement has played an important part in the development of psychiatry, children's clinics, and other measures of prevention and diagnosis of mental disorders. The widespread interest and concern that Beers generated for it is attested by the twenty-six printings that Beers's autobiography had seen by the time of his death.

Biographic data: NCAB 34:40, E:430; [Anon.] Clifford Whittingham Beers. *American Journal of Public Health,* August, 1943; C. E. A. Winslow, Clifford Whittingham Beers. *Mental Hygiene,* 1944, 28, 179–185

YERKES, ROBERT MEARNS   [363]

American psychologist
Rating: 27
Born: Breadysville, Pennsylvania, May 26, 1876
Died: New Haven, Connecticut, February 3, 1956
Highest degree: Ph.D. in psychology, Harvard University, 1902
Positions: 1908, Harvard University; 1917, University of Minnesota; 1924–1944, Yale University; president, American Psychological Association, 1917

Yerkes and Thorndike [353] pioneered in the experimental study of animal behavior. Yerkes was primarily a comparative psychologist, although he called himself by preference psychobiologist. He wrote his first research paper in 1899, and it was followed by many others. He took charge of comparative psychology at Harvard in 1902. From then on, he was a leader in the field of comparative psychology, both in terms of the output of comparative studies on many species of animals, especially the primates, and his other activities related to the field. His name is associated with the operation of the first primate laboratory at Yale, the Yale Laboratories of Primate Biology, of which he was the director between 1929 and 1941, and later in Orange Park, Florida. The Orange Park laboratory was named the Yerkes Laboratories of Primate Biology (now the Yerkes Regional Primate Center of Emory University) when he retired in 1942.

Out of his work on animal behavior arose such statements as the *Yerkes-Dodson law,* which states that strong motivation interferes with learning a difficult discrimination problem but helps to learn a simple one. Yerkes developed such animal testing devices as the use of monochromatic light to study their color vision and the multiple-choice method to test concept formation. Later Yerkes also became interested in human abilities, developing a revision of the Stanford Binet Intelligence Scale in 1915, the *Point Scale*. During World War I Yerkes headed the group of psychologists whose task it was to measure the ability of army recruits in order to make decisions concerning their rejection or discharge, assignment to specific duties, or training. The group developed the Army Alpha and Army Beta tests which, by the end of the war, had been given to 1,726,000 men. Yerkes, however, is remembered mainly as a comparative psychologist who wrote such books as the *Great Apes* (1929, with Ada Yerkes) and *Chimpanzees: A Laboratory Colony* (1943).

Biographic data: *HPA* 2:381; *NCAB* A:109, 43:52; W. R. Miles, Robert Mearns Yerkes. *American Psychologist,* 1946, **1**, 175–178; R. M. Elliott, Robert Mearns Yerkes. *American Journal of Psychology,* 1956, **69**, 487–494; L. Carmichael, Robert Mearns Yerkes. *Psychological Review,* 1957, **64**, 1-7; E. G. Boring, Robert Mearns Yerkes. *Yearbook of American Philosophical Society,* 1956, 133–140; L. Carmichael, Robert Mearns Yerkes, psychobiologist. *Science,* 1957, **126**, 498

[364]   **WHIPPLE, GUY MONTROSE**

American psychologist
Rating: 20
Born: Danvers, Massachusetts, June 12, 1876
Died: Clifton, Massachusetts, August 1, 1941
Highest degree: Ph.D. in psychology, Cornell University, 1900, under E. B. Titchener [294]
Positions: 1898, Cornell University; 1914, University of Illinois; 1917, Carnegie Institute of Technology; 1919–1925, University of Michigan; 1915–1941, secretary-treasurer of National Society for the Study of Education and editor of its yearbooks; editorial work for *Journal of Applied Psychology* and *Journal of Educational Research*

Whipple started out as an experimentalist, but soon switched to educational psychology. By 1910 the testing movement had advanced so much that Whipple was able to publish a discussion of fifty-four tests and give directions for their administration (*Manual of Mental and Physical Tests,* 1910). In the same year

Whipple became a cofounder of the *Journal of Educational Psychology*. In 1915, at Whipple's instigation, the American Psychological Association expressed official disapproval of the use of psychological tests by unqualified individuals.

Being mechanically minded and before he turned to educational psychology, Whipple designed and constructed several pieces of laboratory equipment. The best known of these was the Whipple tachistoscope. It was described in the second edition (1914–1915) of his *Manual*. Whipple produced about fifty publications in psychology, many of them on educational psychology, and several books on educational problems.

Biographic data: *NCAB* 31:226; C. A. Ruckmick, Guy Montrose Whipple. *American Journal of Psychology* 1942, **55**, 132–134

GOSSET, WILLIAM SEALY [365]

English statistician
Rating: **13**
Born: Canterbury, Kent, June 13, 1876
Died: London, October 16, 1937
Education: Studied chemistry and mathematics at Oxford University
Positions: 1899–1935, Guinness, Son & Co., Dublin; 1935–1937, Guinness, Son & Co., London

Gosset produced his statistical work while working as a brewer and later as statistician for the famed Guinness brewing company, but was prohibited by the company's rules from publishing his research on the variability in the brewing process. The rules were relaxed to allow Gosset to publish under a pseudonym. Under the pseudonym of "Student," Gosset published a paper in 1908 ("The probable error of a mean") in which he pointed out that the distribution of the ratio of the mean to its standard error does not follow a normal curve if the sample is small. The statistic t (Student's t), now widely used in tests of differences between means of small samples, was contributed by Gosset.

Biographic data: *DNB* 1931–1940; *DSB* 5:476; *IESS* 6:211; R. A. Fisher, "Student." *Annals of Eugenics*, 1939, **9**, 1–9; L. McMullen, William Sealy Gosset, 1876–1937. I. "Student" as a man. *Biometrika*, 1939, **30**, 205–210

WIRTH, WILHELM

German psychologist
Rating: 14
Born: Wunsiedel, Bavaria, July 26, 1876
Died: 1952
Highest degree: Ph.D. in psychology, University of Munich, 1897, under T. Lipps [211]
Positions: 1898, University of Leipzig, editorial work for *Archiv für die gesamte Psychologie* (from 1905), *Vierteljahrsschrift für Psychologie und Medizin,* and *Psychological Abstracts* (since 1926)

Wirth did experimental work on geometric illusions, color contrast, perception, and psychophysics in search for a fundamental principle of phenomenology. He wrote *Vorstellungs- und Gefühlskontrast* (1900), *Fortschritte auf dem Gebiete der Psychophysik der Licht- und Farbenempfindungen* (1905), *Die experimentelle Analyse der Bewusstseinsphanomene* 1908)(which contains a theory of geometric illusions), and *Psychophysik* (1912).

Biographic data: HPA 3:283

BLONDEL, CHARLES

French physiologist
Rating: 11
Born: Lyon, October 10, 1876
Died: Paris, February 19, 1939
Highest degree: M.D., 1906, LL.D., 1913
Positions: University of Strasbourg; University of Paris

During his medical studies Blondel became interested in psychology and later in the contributions of anthropologists and sociologists, such as Lévy-Bruhl [230] and Durkheim [241]. In his *Introduction à la psychologie collective* (1928), Blondel opposes Durkheim's view that the personal and the collective consciousnesses in man are sharply separated and opposed to each other. Blondel asserted that the individual, being exposed to the influence of a group, becomes that group in his individual actions. Social phenomena determine perception, thinking, memory, and the will. In perceiving, an individual applies the yardsticks provided him by the society, for example. Additional psychological writings of Blondel include *La conscience morbide* (1914), *La psychoanalyse* (1924), *La mentalité primitive* (1926), *La psychologie de Marcel Proust* (1932), and *La suicide* (1933).

Biographic data: P. Guillaume & I. Meyerson, Charles Blondel. *Journal de psychologie normal et pathologique*, 1938, 35, 321–324; A Miotto, Charles Blondel. *Rivista di psycologia normale e patologica*, 1939, 25, 299–300

TERMAN, LEWIS MADISON [368]

American psychologist
Rating: 27
Born: Johnson county, Indiana, January 15, 1877
Died: Palo Alto, California, December 21, 1956
Highest degree: Ph.D. in psychology, Clark University, 1905, under E. C. Sanford [254]
Positions, honors: 1906, Los Angeles State Normal School; 1910–1943, Stanford University, head of Psychology Department, 1922–1942; president, American Psychological Association, 1923; four honorary degrees

Terman's major contribution to American psychology was his translation and adaptation to American circumstances of the Binet-Simon intelligence test in 1916 (*The Measurement of Intelligence*, 1916). One of Terman's changes was the introduction of Stern's [328] mental quotient to measure intelligence. Terman called it the *intelligence quotient*, or I.Q. Since Terman was at the time at Stanford University, the test became known as the *Stanford-Binet Intelligence Scale*. In 1937, Terman and Maude Merrill published the first revision of the Stanford-Binet which had been ten years in preparation(*Measuring Intelligence*, 1937). The last revision of the test was published after Terman's death (*Stanford-Binet Intelligence Scale: Manual for the Third Revision*, 1960). For a long time the Stanford-Binet was the most widely used and researched individual intelligence test in English. During World War I Terman, with a group of other psychologists, participated in the construction of the first group intelligence test, the Army Alpha, and the nonverbal Army Beta. The Stanford Achievement Tests (with T. L. Kelley [424] and G. M.

Ruch, 1923). and other psychometric instruments were the result of Terman's work.

Terman is also known for initiating a large-scale longitudinal study of the development of gifted children. Begun in 1921, the study encompassed an initial group of 1,500 California children with an I.Q. of 140 and above. The first report appeared in 1925. Terman continued the project until his death, and additional reports were prepared. Of the five volumes in the series, known as the Genetic Studies of Genius, the last one was published in 1959(*The Gifted Group at Mid-Life,* with M. H. Oden). Terman found, among other things, that the gifted were taller, healthier, physically better developed, superior in leadership and social adaptability, dispelling the often held notion to the contrary.

Biographic data: HPA 2:297; *IESS* 15:601; R. R. Sears, Lewis Madison Terman, pioneer in mental measurement. *Science,* 1957, 125, 978; E. R. Hilgard, Lewis Madison Terman. *American Journal of Psychology,* 1957, **70**, 472–479; W. B. Lewis, Professor Lewis Madison Terman. *British Journal of Statistical Psychology,* 1957, **10**, 65–68; W. M. Miles, Lewis Madison Terman. *Yearbook of American Philosophical Society,* 1957, 165–170; E. G. Boring, Lewis Madison Terman. *National Academy of Sciences Biographical Memoirs,* 1959, 33, 414–461

[369]

HORNBOSTEL, ERICH M. VON

German psychologist
Rating: **16**
Born: Vienna, Austria, February 25, 1877
Died: England, June 13, 1935
Highest degree: Ph.D. in psychology, University of Berlin, 1900, under C. Stumpf [202]

A Gestalt psychologist, Hornbostel worked with Stumpf in establishing the Berlin Phonogram Archive of records of primitive music. Eventually he took over the direction of the Archive from Stumpf. During World War I Hornbostel worked with Wertheimer on the detection of submarines by sound. In 1920, he published a paper on sound localization which introduced the time-theory of sound localization. In a 1925 paper Hornbostel established himself as a major spokesman for the unity of senses, asserting that certain attributes, such as intensity, are common to all senses.

Biographic data: *The Psychological Register,* 1932, Vol. III

HELLPACH, WILLY [370]

German psychologist
Rating: 12
Born: Öls, Silesia, February 26, 1877
Died: Heidelberg, July 6, 1955
Highest degree: Ph.D. in psychology, University of Leipzig, 1900, under W. Wundt [161]; M.D., University of Leipzig, 1903
Positions: 1906–1922, Technische Hochschule, Karlsruhe; 1926, University of Heidelberg, honorary professor

Hellpach was active in psychology, medicine, education, politics, and as a columnist, often at the same time. In addition, he was a prolific writer. He became internationally known in 1911 upon the publication of his book, *Geopsychische Erscheinungen,* in which he showed the effect of geography, climate, and other environmental conditions on behavior. His interest in this area continued (*Mensch und Volk der Grosstadt,* 1939), as well as in related areas, such as industrial psychology (*Das Problem der Industriearbeit,* 1925), in which area he was first in Germany to present academic lectures, and especially in ethnopsychology and social psychology. After Wundt's death, Hellpach was the only representative of ethnopsychology in Germany. His most important work, *Einführung in Völkerpsychologie* (1937), is in this area. He wrote several additional related volumes, such as *Elementares Lehrbuch der Sozialpsychologie* (1933), *Deutsche Physiognomik* (1942), *Der deutsche Charakter* (1954), *Kulturpsychologie* (1953), and others. Hellpach distinguished between "people as a natural fact" from "people as a mental Gestalt" and "people as a creation of the will." To understand the motivational, organizational, and developmental aspects of ethnic groups they must be considered on all three levels. Social groups are best studied using sociological and social-psychological methods. Social institutions may replace specific motives in individuals:

one acts according to the prescriptions of the society as they manifest themselves in its various institutions.

Biographic data: W. Witte, Willy Hellpach: zu seinem 80. Geburtstag am 26. Februar 1957. *Psychologische Beiträge,* 1957, 3, 3–20; W. Hellpach. *Wirken in Wirren,* 1948

[371]

FERREE, CLARENCE ERROL

American psychologist
Rating: **11**
Born: Sidney, Ohio, March 11, 1877
Died: Baltimore, Maryland, July 26, 1942
Highest degree: Ph.D. in psychology, Cornell University, 1907, under E. B. Titchener [294]
Positions: 1907, Bryn Mawr College; 1928–1942, Johns Hopkins University (Medical School), Director of Research Laboratory of Physiological Optics, lecturer in ophthalmology; honorary D.Sc. degree

With his wife, Gertrude Rand, Ferree did considerable work on vision and audition. He introduced the measurement of spectral energies in the study of vision, for which purpose he devised a special instrument. Ferree developed a precision perimeter and did considerable work on visual perimetry. His perimeter was adopted as standard by the American Ophthalmological Society and the International Congress of Ophthalmology. Appointed by the American Medical Association and the Illumination Engineering Society, Ferree studied lighting and eye fatigue. He devised new tests, publishing more than seventy-five papers on the subject of illumination and eye fatigue. Ferree showed that eye strain and fatigue lies in the eye muscles, not in the nerves. He did a large amount of additional work on vision in industrial settings, on reading, lighting and vision, and peripheral vision. There are 249 titles in his total scientific output.

Biographic data: *NCAB* 33:96; F. L. Dimmick, Clarence Errol Ferree. *American Journal of Psychology,* 1943, 56, 137–140; L. G. H. Hardy, Clarence Errol Ferree. *Archives of Ophthalmology,* 1943, 29, 668–669; G. K. Rand, Clarence Errol Ferree. *Journal of Optical Society of America,* 1943, 33, 423

ABRAHAM, KARL

German psychoanalyst
Rating: 20
Born: Bremen, May 3, 1877
Died: Berlin, December 25, 1925
Highest degree: M.D., University of Freiburg, 1901
Positions: 1901, Berlin Municipal Mental Hospital at Dalldorf;
   1905, Burghölzli Hospital (University of Zurich); 1908, private
   practice, Berlin

Abraham was one of Sigmund Freud's [224] senior collaborators.
In 1910, he organized the Berlin Psychoanalytic Society, the first
branch of the International Psychoanalytic Society, also founded
in 1910. Abraham elaborated Freud's views of the stages of
psychosexual development, asserting that adult personality can be
adequately described in terms of the results of fixation at one or
another stage of psychosexual development. Abraham described
the oral-passive, oral-aggressive, and the anal character. He studied
and described the basic obsessive personality traits in the anal
character; obstinacy, orderliness, and frugality. The explanation
of the adult's personality characteristics in terms of his childhood
experiences was Abraham's contribution to Freud's theory and
was accepted by Freud. In 1911, Abraham also offered the first
psychodynamic explanation of depression. Abraham's *Selected
Papers on Psychoanalysis* appeared in 1948.

Biographic data: *IESS* 1:1; *Encyclopaedia of Psychoanalysis*,
   1968

OGDEN, ROBERT MORRIS

American psychologist
Rating: 20
Born: Binghamton, New York, July 6, 1877
Died: Ithaca, New York, March 2, 1959
Highest degree: Ph.D. in psychology, University of Würzburg,
   1903, under O. Külpe [265]
Positions: 1903, University of Missouri; 1905, University of
   Tennessee; 1914, University of Kansas; 1916–1945, Cornell
   University, professor of education to 1939, professor of

psychology to 1945, dean of School of Arts and Sciences from 1923 to 1945; president, Southern Society for Philosophy and Psychology, 1912–1913; editorial work for *Psychological Bulletin,* 1909–1929, *American Journal of Psychology,* 1926–1958

Soon after the Gestalt theory became known in Germany, Ogden asked Kurt Koffka [438] to write a paper for *Psychological Bulletin* explaining it to American readers. Koffka's 1922 paper was instrumental in introducing Gestalt psychology in the United States. Ogden contributed to the dissemination of Gestalt ideas in America in other ways also, such as by translating Koffka's *The Growth of the Mind* in 1924 and by writing the first Gestalt-oriented book by an American, *Psychology and Education* (1926). Ogden also wrote *An Introduction to General Psychology* (1914), a book on *Hearing* (1924), and one on *The Psychology of Art* (1938). The contents of Ogden's approximately sixty scientific articles ranged from thinking and the Würzburg school to education, Gestalt psychology, and hearing.

Biographic data: NCAB 43:76

[374]

WATSON, JOHN BROADUS

American psychologist
Rating: 27
Born: Greenville, South Carolina, January 9, 1878
Died: New York, New York, September 25, 1958
Highest degree: Ph.D. in psychology, University of Chicago, 1903, under J. R. Angell [309]
Positions, honors: 1903, University of Chicago; 1908–1920, Johns Hopkins University; 1921–1946, with private firms; president, American Psychological Association, 1915; honorary LL.D., Furman University, 1919

A 1913 article by Watson, entitled "Psychology as a Behaviorist Views It," presented a view of psychology that totally departed from all views of the past and started a new school of psychology, behaviorism. In that article, Watson declared that psychology was an objective, experimental branch of natural science whose goal was to predict and control behavior. Introspection as a method was no part of it. Consciousness and the various mental states were to be made no reference to. The object of psychology, all psychology, was to study behavior. The study of soul and mental states was a difficult, irrelevant, and unreal task. The history of psychology up to that point proved it. Watson rejected both structuralism and functionalism.

Watson's article and subsequent writings had such an impact on American psychology that it emerged a new discipline. Many of Watson's radical statements were later modified, neobehavioristic schools arose, and behaviorism in its original form ceased to exist. Nevertheless, American psychology today conforms to Watson's conceptualization: it still defines itself as the study of behavior and, while admitting introspection in moderation and mind as a inference from behavior, largely eschews philosophy and speculation about subjective states. The influence of behaviorism in Europe and elsewhere was considerably weaker.

Watson did research on animals at Chicago, but his most important work was done at Johns Hopkins. Watson's 1914 book, *Behavior: An Introduction to Comparative Psychology,* advocated the study of animal behavior without resorting to mentalistic concepts. There was no reference in it to conditioning. Watson learned about conditioning in that year, and made it the topic of his presidential address to the American Psychological Association the next year. The concept of the conditioned reflex became a crucial one in behaviorism. In 1918, Watson began experimentation with children, a pioneering effort, and later wrote *Psychological Care of the Infant and Child* (1928). Watson's fame was such that he became an instant expert on child care and rearing, and his advice was followed by numerous parents.

In his 1919 book, *Psychology From the Standpoint of a Behaviorist,* Watson showed how the methods of animal study and the principles of behavior derived from them could be applied to man. Conditioning was given a particularly prominent role to play. Watson's last psychological publication was *Behaviorism* (1925, revised edition, 1930), a book intended for popular consumption.

Central to Watson's view of psychology was his S-R formulation of behavior. Behavior always involves a response of the organism to a stimulus, and the task of the psychologist is to predict from S to R. The responses are muscular contractions or glandular discharges, and the S-R units are simply reflexes. Reflexes are innate or conditioned, but there are no instincts in man. Not only are there no instincts, there are no other abilities that are transmitted genetically. Most emotions are conditioned reflexes. Given only three innate emotional responses—fear, rage, and love—all other emotions are conditioned elaborations of these. Watson's classic experiment of 1920 on the conditioning of fear in little Albert demonstrated the point. Sensations were treated by Watson as discriminatory behavior. The learning of habits is the formation of conditioned responses. Even speech is acquired through conditioning, and thinking is subvocal speech, Personality is but the combination of habit systems in an individual.

Biographic data: *HPA* 3:271; *EP* 8:279; *IESS*, 16:484; *NCAB* A:86, 48:548; B. F. Skinner, John Broadus Watson. *Science*, 1954, 120, 441–442; R. S. Woodworth, John Broadus Watson. *American Journal of Psychology*, 1959, 72, 301–310

[375]

BENUSSI, VITTORIO

Italian-Austrian psychologist
Rating: 20
Born: Trieste, Italy, January 17, 1878
Died: Padua, Italy 1927
Highest degree: Ph.D. in psychology, University of Graz, 1900, under A. Meinong[218]
Positions: 1902, University of Graz; 1914, University of Vienna; 1920, University of Padua

A member of the Austrian school of act psychology, Benussi was a productive and competent researcher who produced many studies on psychophysics, optical illusions, visually and tactually perceived movement, perception of time, and the perception of solidity. Although Austria's best experimentalist, Benussi was concerned with systematic issues only marginally. His theory of perception must be gathered from statements made in the various experimental articles. Benussi, following Meinong, stressed the role of the productive process (*Produktionsvorgang*) in perception, the higher psychic process that combines sensory elements into unitary wholes. With Ehrenfels [250] and Cornelius, Benussi developed the theory and thus the Austrian school of form quality. Benussi was the chief worker in this school through the first decade of the 20th century. In the second decade the school faded away as it was being replaced by the Gestalt school which took over and reworked some of its tenets.

Biographic data: *The Psychological Register*, 1932, Vol. III

Italian psychologist

Rating: 22

Born: Milan, January 18, 1878

Died: Milan, July 15, 1959

Highest degree: M.D., University of Pavia, 1902; Ph.D. in philosophy, University of Louvain, 1911; studied psychology under O. Külpe [265] at Bonn and Munich and under Kiesow [240] at Turin

Positions: 1914, University of Turin; 1922, Catholic University, Milan

Gemelli was a very productive psychologist (a bibliography of over four hundred items, dozens of books) who worked in several areas of psychology: perception, language (electro-acoustical analysis of speech), youth and developmental psychology, and areas of applied psychology. He was the founder (1921) and perpetual rector of the Università Cattolica del Sacro Cuore in Milan, and contributed to the development of psychology in Italy through research and teaching at that university. In 1920, he founded, with Kiesow, the *Archivio italiano di psicologia,* established a psychological laboratory at the Catholic University soon after its founding, and began to issue a series of publications from it, the *Contributi del Laboratorio di Psicologia della Università Cattolica del Sacro Cuore.* Later, in 1940, he also founded the *Archivio di psicologia, neurologia e psichiatria.*

Gemelli's most important contributions were in the area of applied psychology: criminal, military, industrial, and clinical. He acquired a name during World War I in connection with his work on pilot selection for the Italian armed forces. In 1952, he organized the first Italian symposium on clinical psychology, which gave a strong impetus to the development of clinical psychology in Italy, theretofore largely a province of the physician.

In his experimental work on the physiology of emotions in animals (using visceral deafferentation), Gemelli concluded that emotion is both a physiological and psychological phenomenon, inseparably so, and that it involves the whole organism. This conclusion developed into Gemelli's own way of thinking, the "personalistic orientation" or *soggettività,* according to which man is a biological entity in the first place. In addition, man is also an entity of personal, subjective experience, which is not merely a function of the biological structure but an independent, innate characteristic. Both the biological and the subjective aspects must be considered in order to understand man. This view led Gemelli to reject the behavioristic, the Gestalt, and the psychoanalytic schools of thought.

Biographic data: *HPA* 4:97; P. Bondioli, *Padre Gemelli*, 1930; H. Misiak & V. M. Staudt, *Catholics in Psychology*, 1954, pp. 126–152; L. Ancoa, Agostino Edoardo Gemelli. *American Journal of Psychology*, 1960, 73, 156–159

[377]

GUILLAUME, PAUL

French psychologist
Rating: 16
Born: Chaumont, Haute Marne, June 26, 1878
Died: Paris, January 4, 1962
Highest degree: Agregé en philosophie, Sorbonne, 1902; Dr. des lettres, Sorbonne, 1925
Positions: 1937–1947, University of Paris; president, Societé française de psychologie; editor, *Journal de psychologie normale et pathologique*

Guillaume was a representive of the French school of psychologie du comportement, or behavior psychology. Guillaume stressed the similarity between psychology and physics, and thought that the same methodology could be used in both disciplines (*Introduction à la psychologie*, 1942). In his *Manuel de psychologie* (1931), Guillaume broke with tradition in French textbook writing and presented psychology as a natural science, showing how psychology could solve real life problems.

Guillaume worked in four areas of psychology: animal psychology (primate research), philosophical psychology, psychological theory, and child psychology. *La psychologie de la forme* (1937) was a very popular introduction to Gestalt psychology. Along with Guillaume's translation of Köhler's [447] *Mentality of Apes,* it served to introduce Gestalt psychology in France. In 1936, Guillaume published a work on habit formation, *Formation des habitudes.* Guillaume's doctoral dissertation, published in 1926 as *L'imitation chez l'enfant,* presented a theory of imitation in children up to three years of age. This work resulted from Guillaume's study of his own two children, and contains many modern-sounding terms, like behavioral feedback, infantile stimulation, and control of behavior. In addition, the book was the beginning of Guillaume's influential work in psycholinguistics. He continued it in 1927 with two more books, *Les débuts de la phrase dans le langage de l'enfant,* and *Le développement des éléments formels dans le langage de l'enfant.* He was particularly interested in the emergence of first sentences in a child's language, and insisted that it was useless to apply adult grammatical categories to a developing child's speech.

Biographic data: I. Meyerson, Paul Guillaume. *Journal de psychologie normale et pathologique,* 1962, 59, 1–13; F. Bresson, In memoriam Paul Guillaume. *Psychologie française,* 1962, 7(3), 178–179

ROSANOFF, AARON JOSHUA

[378]

American psychiatrist
Rating: 15
Born: Pinsk, Russia, June 26, 1878
Died: Los Angeles, California, January 7, 1943
Highest degree: M.D., Cornell University, 1900
Positions: 1901–1922, State Hospital in King's Park, New York; 1917–1919, Army Medical Corps; 1923–1943, in private practice; 1925–1943, lecturer, University of Southern California; 1939–1942, California State Director of Institutions

In 1910, Grace Kent [357] and Rosanoff designed a psychiatric screening instrument that was based on word associations. It consisted of one hundred common words that had been found to elicit similar associations in a group of 1,000 subjects. The norms for the test were associative frequency tables for the various responses to each of the one hundred words. Schizophrenics were found, for instance, to give the less common responses. When it was discovered that word association frequency depends not only on pathology but a host of other factors as well, the test fell into disuse because of the impossibility to prepare adequate norms. *The Kent-Rosanoff list of associative frequency,* however, is still being used in learning experiments and other research involving verbal materials (*Free Association Test* 1927, with G. Kent).

Rosanoff's publications in the area of psychiatry included a wide range of topics: the relationship between heredity, constitution, and psychosis, degenerative brain diseases, war neuroses, organic psychoses, personality, and others. Rosanoff subscribed to the idea that psychoses basically have a genetic and constitutional basis. His theory of personality was based on this notion: mental disorders are hereditary patterns, and the origins of personality are seen in clinical types. Normal personality is an incomplete form of some clinical type, hence there are epileptoid, schizoid, etc. personalities, with no suggestion that the individual is epileptic or otherwise mentally disturbed. Among Rosanoff's other contributions may be counted the publication of a *Manual of Psychiatry and Mental Hygiene*, which saw many editions, the organization of a private mental institution, and planning of the construction of two mental hospitals, one in Los Angeles and one in San Francisco (the Langley Porter Clinic).

Biographic data: J. Kasanin, Aaron Joshua Rosanoff. *Journal of Nervous and Mental Diseases,* 1943, 97, 501–503

[379]

DEARBORN, WALTER FENNO

American psychologist
Rating: 12
Born: Marblehead, Massachusetts, July 19, 1878
Died: St. Petersburg, Florida, June 21, 1955
Highest degree: Ph.D. in psychology, Columbia University, 1905, under J. McK. Cattell [256]; M.D., University of Munich, 1913
Positions: 1905, University of Wisconsin; 1909, University of Chicago; 1912, Harvard University, since 1917 professor and director, Psychological Clinic of Harvard Graduate School of Education; 1947–1953, Lesley College, director of Psycho-Educational Clinic

Dearborn was an educational psychologist who did research on reading problems, the relationship between physical growth and intelligence, and on intelligence testing. He and his students produced many papers in these areas. In the area of testing, Dearborn produced *The Dearborn Group Tests of Intelligence* (1920). With J. W. M. Rothney he wrote *Predicting the Child's Development* (1941), which dealt with the correlation between mental and physical growth. Dearborn's studies showed that the correlation was a matter of individual differences and, on the average, so low as to be practically zero. With L. Carmichael [494], Dearborn wrote a well-known book on *Reading and Visual Fatigue* (1947). In *The Psychology of Teaching Reading* (1952), Dearborn stressed the role of motivation, emotion, and cognitive factors in learning to read.

Biographic data: H. S. Langfeld, Walter Fenno Dearborn. *American Journal of Psychology*, 1955, 68, 679–681

German-American neurologist
Rating: **26**
Born: Kattowitz, Upper Silesia, November 6, 1878
Died: New York, New York, September 19, 1965
Highest degree: M.D., University of Breslau, 1903
Positions: 1907–1915, University of Königsberg; 1916–1929, director, Institute for Research into the Aftereffects of Brain Injuries, University of Frankfurt; 1918–1929, University of Frankfurt, professor of neurology; 1929, director, Department of Neurology, Moabit Hospital, Berlin; 1933–1935, University of Amsterdam; 1936–1940, Columbia University, professor of psychiatry; research and teaching at New York State Psychiatric Institute and Hospital; chief, Neorophysiological Laboratory, Montefiore Hospital, New York; 1938–1940, William James lecturer at Harvard University; 1940–1945, Tufts Medical School, Boston, professor of neurology; 1946, visiting professor of psychology, City College of New York, New School for Social Research, Brandeis University

At both Frankfurt and Berlin Goldstein engaged in considerable clinical and organizational activity. He organized the University of Frankfurt Institute for Research Into the Aftereffects of Brain Injuries; he was a cofounder of the International Society for Psychotherapy and of the journal *Allgemeine ärztliche Zeitschrift für Psychotherapie*. He became affiliated with Gestalt psychology, and was, with Wertheimer [391], Köhler [447], Koffka [438], and Gruhle [397], one of the cofounders of the Gestalt-psychological journal *Psychologische Forschung* (1921). Influenced both by Gestalt thinking and the holistic tradition of German science, Goldstein began to use Gestalt concepts in his clinical neurology work. His experiences with cases of brain injury (*Die Behandlung, Fürsorge und Begutachtung hirnverletzter Soldaten*, 1919) led him to postulate that an organism must be considered as a whole whenever a particular aspect of its functioning is evaluated. The holistic-organismic theory was presented by Goldstein in his major work, *Der Aufbau des Organismus* (1934; English translation, *The Organism*, 1938). Goldstein asserted there was no localization of behavior in specific regions of the cortex; rather, behavior resides in the network of the central nervous system. The smooth functioning of each portion of the brain is guaranteed by the whole brain. Even when injured, the organism seeks to function adequately. There is only one drive in any organism, namely that of self-actualization. The organism realizes its particular nature when it reaches adequacy in the relationship between what it does and the environmental conditions (*Remarks on Localization*, 1946).

The Goldstein signs of brain injury include a rise in the threshold of excitation (slowing down of reactions), perseveration, disturbance of attention, blurring of figure and ground, and loss of the ability to abstract. Goldstein divided human acts into the abstract and the concrete. Impairment in abstract thinking (attention, planning, discrimination, hypothesizing) leaves concrete operations (those guided by the external stimulus properties) unaffected, and vice versa. The Goldstein-Gelb and Goldstein-Scheerer tests are test batteries that measure the ability to form concepts, and are used to diagnose brain lesions. Goldstein wrote some 250 papers, chapters in handbooks, and books. Several of his books have been translated into other languages.

Biographic data: *HPA* 5:147; *IESS* 6:197; J. Meiers, Kurt Goldstein. *Journal of Individual Psychology*, 1966, 22(1), 116–125

[381]

REVESZ, GEZA

Hungarian-Dutch psychologist
Rating: 23
Born: Siofek, Hungary, December 9, 1878
Died: Amsterdam, Netherlands, August 19, 1955
Highest degree: Ph.D. in psychology, University of Göttingen, 1905, under G. E. Müller [208]
Positions: 1908–1914, University of Budapest; 1919–1920, University of Groningen; 1921–1922, University of Utrecht; 1923–1955, University of Amsterdam; editor of *Nederlandsche Tijdschrift voor Psychologie*

With David Katz [428], who also received his doctorate from G. E. Müller only a year later, Révész performed some of the earliest experiments (1908) on form discrimination in birds. Later, at Amsterdam, where Révész established a psychological laboratory in 1939 and the Dutch Institute of Applied Psychologists, he cofounded with Katz the journal *Acta Psychologica* (1935). Révész's early work was on the tonality attribute of sound (*Grundlegung der Tonpsychologie*, 1912), to which he later added researches on genius and talent (*Psychology of a*

Musical Prodigy, 1925; *Talent und Genie*, 1951), the phenomenology of touch (*Die Formenwelt des Tastsinnes*, 1938), music (*Einführung in die Musikpsychologie,* 1946), psychology of the blind (*The Psychology and Art of the Blind*, 1950), vision, space perception, child, medical, educational, social psychology, and language and thought. Révész's name became well known, both because of his productivity (he wrote twenty books and more than one hundred articles) and because he wrote in several languages.

Biographic data: H. C. J. Duijker, In memoriam Géza Révész. *Acta Psychologica*, 1955, **11**, 357–359; H. Piéron, Géza Révész. *American Journal of Psychology*, 1956, 69, 139–141

JONES, (ALFRED) ERNEST

[382]

English psychoanalyst
Rating: 22
Born: Gowerton, Glamorganshire, Wales, January 1, 1879
Died: London, February 11, 1958
Highest degree: M.D., University of London, 1903
Positions, honors: 1903–1908, various hospital appointments; 1908–1913, University of Toronto; 1913, consulting physician; president, International Psychoanalytic Association, 1920–1924, 1932–1949, honorary president, 1949–1958; honorary D.Sc., Yale University, 1954

Jones came into contact with Freud [224] in 1908, became his disciple and member of the inner, "secret" committee that was to guide the destiny of the psychoanalytic movement (and which he himself had suggested). He became the leader of the English-speaking psychoanalysts and, at the death of Freud, the recognized leader of psychoanalysis worldwide. Among his contributions are the introduction of psychoanalysis in England, the defense of psychoanalysis against attacks during its early days of existence, and his successful efforts at keeping the psychoanalytic movement from splitting up. Jones founded the *International Journal of Psychoanalysis* in 1920 (and was its editor until 1939) and the *London Psychoanalytic Society* (later the British Branch of the International Psychoanalytic Association). His writings on psychoanalysis were collected in *Papers on Psychoanalysis,* and he published about fifty volumes of the *International Psychoanalytic Library*, a collection of standard works on psychoanalysis. Jones is best known, however, as the foremost biographer of Freud (*The Life and Works of Sigmund Freud*, 3 volumes., 1953–1957).

Biographic data: IESS 8:263, E. Jones, *Free Associations: Memoirs of a Psychoanalyst*, 1959; E. Glover, Ernest Jones. *British Journal of Psychology* 1958, 49, 177–181

[383]

KORNILOV, KONSTANTIN NIKOLAEVICH

Russian psychologist
Rating: **13**
Born: Tyumen, Siberia, March 9, 1879
Died: Moscow, July 10, 1957
Education: Graduated in philology from Moscow University in 1910
Positions: 1910–1921, Moscow University; 1921–1951, head, Psychology Department, V. I. Lenin Teachers College, Moscow; 1923–1931, head, Institute of Psychology, Moscow; vice-president, USSR Academy of Pedagogical Sciences, 1944–1950; editor, *Semya i Shkola*, 1946–1957, *Voprosy Psikhologii*, 1955–1957

One of Kornilov's first investigations concerned the strength of reactions. Noticing constant differences in the strength of handshakes, Kornilov contrived to measure both the reaction time and response strength with a "dynamoscope" of his own invention, and identified four types of reactions. He also worked in the area of child psychology and education, publishing a number of works, such as *Ocherk psikhologii rebenka dosh-kol'nogo vozrasta* (1917). When in the 1920s and early 1930s Bekhterev [226] campaigned against psychology and proposed the reduction of psychology to biology and sociology and the substitution of reflexology for psychology, Kornilov was the chief spokesman for psychology as an independent discipline. He also opposed, however, the Leipzig-trained Wundtian Chelpanov because of the latter's idealistic position. Kornilov proposed that a psychology based on dialectic materialism be established. He called it reactology, and presented it in *Uchenie o reaktsiyakh cheloveka (reaktologiya)* (1922), Psychology in the light of dialectic materialism (in Murchison's [453] *Psychologies of 1930)*, and *Uchebnik psikhologii, izlozhennoĭ s tochki zreniya dialekticheskogo materializma* (1926). The latter book went through five editions in as many years and was translated into several other languages. While reactology postulated, along with Karl Marx [136], that the nature of consciousness was determined by the conditions of social existence, it did not regard behavior only in terms of its mechanics but stressed the subjective aspects of it as well. The main features of reactology were the measurement of human reactions, emphasis on wholeness, and the economic determinants of behavior. Kornilov became the editor of the first purely psychological journal in Russian, *Psikhologiya* (founded in 1928). During the 1920s reactology, pedology, and psychotechnology flourished under Kornilov's leadership, but not for long. In the early 1930s, Soviet political leaders decided that reactology did not reflect the dynamic, active nature of Marxism-Leninism, and abolished it along with pedology and psychological testing. Kornilov lost his leadership but continued to be prominent in Soviet psychology. He shifted his interest back to educational and child psychology as well as the popularization of psychology, penning several volumes in these areas: *Psikhologiya* (with Teplov [488] and Shvarts, 1938), *Psikhologiya* (1946, a secondary school text), *Psikhologiya* (with Smirnov and Teplov, 1948), and others.

Biographic data: G. Razran, N. Kornilov, theoretical and experimental psychologist. *Science*, 1958, **128**, 74–75; N. F. Dobrynin, Konstantin Nikolaevich Kornilov. *Voprosy Psikhologii*, 1969, 15(2), 183–185

WALLON, HENRI PAUL HYACINTHE [384]

French psychologist
Rating: 12
Born: Paris, March 15, 1879
Died: Paris, December 1, 1962
Highest degree: Agregé en philosophie, Ecole normale supérieure, 1902; Dr. en médecine, University of Paris, 1908, Dr. des lettres, 1925
Positions: 1920–1927, University of Paris, Institute of Psychology; 1920–1949, director, psychological laboratory of l'Institut d'orientation professionelle; 1927–1937, Sorbonne; 1937–1950, Collège de France, director, Ecole pratique des hautes études

Wallon's early papers and books were on psychopathology. He then turned to child psychology, founding a center for medical and educational consultation for children in 1921 and a laboratory for child study in 1927. Wallon was an adherent of dialectic materialism and of Pavolv's [206] teachings. He opposed Durkheim's [241] school with its sharp distinction between the individual and the social. To Wallon, an individual becomes an individual only as a result of his interaction with his social environment. A person's consciousness cannot be separated from his behavior. The natural and the individual presuppose the social, like lungs presuppose a breathable atmosphere. Society is a necessity and an organic reality to the individual. Society, contrary to psychoanalysis and existentialism, does not repress that which is natural and does not make man lonely and desperate. Society is his natural habitat, and it grows more adequate to his human nature in the course of history.

In behavior, acts, mind, and behavior form a unity. To Wallon, psychology is the study of man as he interacts with objects and people. Thus the child's psychological development is determined by the particular physical and social environment of the age he is born into. Affective interaction between child and adult furthers the development of the clearly human qualities in the child. Emotional states are reflected in tonic, postural, and muscle states. These, in conjuction with external conditions of the moment, determine the nature of the clonic response or action. External behavioral relationships between parent and child eventually become internalized by the child and serve as guides to action.

Wallon authored the following books: *l'Enfant turbulent* (1925), *Psychologie pathologique* 1926), *Principes de psychologie appliquée* (1930), *Les origines du caractère chez l'enfant* (1934–1949), *l'Evolution psychologique de l'enfant* (1941), *Les origines de la pensée chez l'enfant* (1945), *La psychologie scolaire* (1953), and others.

Biographic data: R. Zazzo, Portrait d'Henri Wallon. *Journal de psychologie normale et pathologique*, 1963, 60, 386–400; L. I. Antsyferova, Anri Vallon i aktual'nye problemy psikhologii. *Voprosy psikhologii*, 1969, 15(2), 186–189

[385]

BUHLER, KARL

German-Austrian psychologist
Rating: 26
Born: Meckesheim near Heidelberg, Germany, May 27, 1879
Died: Los Angeles, California, October 24, 1963

Highest degree: M.D., University of Freiburg, 1903; Ph.D. in philosophy, University of Strasbourg, 1904

Positions, honors: 1906, University of Berlin; 1907, University of Würzburg; 1909, University of Bonn; 1913–1914, University of Munich; 1918, Technische Hochschule, Dresden; 1922–1938, University of Vienna, head, Psychology Department; 1939, Scholastica College, Duluth, Minnesota; 1940, St. Thomas College, St. Paul, Minnesota; 1945, Cedars of Lebanon Hospital and University of Southern California; president (honorary), sixteenth International Congress of Psychology, 1960

Member of the Würzburg school of imageless thought at one time, Bühler published important papers on the subject between 1907 and 1909. He started off criticism by using a method for studying thought processes that not everybody even within the Würzburg school entirely approved of. The method, the Ausfrage-methode, consisted of the experimenter posing complex mental problems to solve and the observer freely describing what was on his mind as he was solving the problem. Bühler proposed that a new mental element, thought, had to be accepted if all attributes of thinking were to be fully explained. Thought was believed by Bühler to be of three kinds: consciousness of rule, consciousness of relation, and intention, each corresponding to a different type of mental process.

In the 1920s, at the Psychological Institute in Vienna that they had founded, Bühler and his wife, Charlotte Bühler, were the center of child study in Austria. Bühler wrote *Die geistige Entwicklung des Kindes* (1918) and *Umriss der seelischen Entwicklung des Kindes* (1930), suggesting three stages of development, instinct, habit, and intellect, and emphasizing biological factors at the expense of social determinants of behavior. Instead of the IQ, the Bühlers suggested the concept of developmental age and the developmental quotient.

Bühler recognized that psychological research is not exhausted through the study of the inner subjective processes. He ventured into a semantic analysis of social relations, distinguishing information production (Kundgabe) from information reception (Kundnahme) in both man and animals. Human speech belongs to the group of semantic institutions that serve to guide humans in their relationships. Additional books authored by Bühler were *Die Gestaltwahrnehmung* (1913), *Kriese der Psychologie* (1926–1927), and *Das Gestaltprinzip im Leben der Menschen und Tiere* (1958).

Biographic data: IESS 2:199; H. Bolgar, Karl Buhler. *American Journal of Psychology*, 1964, 77, 674–678

WATT, HENRY JACKSON

Scottish psychologist
Rating: **19**
Born: Aberdeen, July 18, 1879
Died: Glasgow, 1925
Highest degree: Ph.D. in psychology
Positions: 1907, University of Liverpool; 1908, University of Glasgow

Watt was one of the prominent psychologists in the Würzburg school, engaged in the study of thinking along the lines of the leader of the "imageless thought" school, Oswald Külpe [265]. Watt, in explaining the thinking process, emphasized the importance of the task (Aufgabe) given the thinker. The conscious task or purpose of the thought problem brings about eventually an unconscious set (Einstellung) in the thinker, and the thinking process occurs without the thinker's being aware of what determines the course of his thoughts. Watt presented his main ideas in a 1905 paper (Experimentelle Beiträge zu einer Theorie des Denkens), but he wrote a fair number of papers on the subject in both German and English. Watt also authored *The Psychology of Sound* (1917), *L'économie et l'éducation de la mémoire* (1909), *The Common Sense of Dreams* (1929), and *The Foundations of Music* (1920).

Biographic data: *Who's Who*, 1925

LANGFELD, HERBERT SIDNEY

American psychologist
Rating: **20**
Born: Philadelphia, Pennsylvania, July 24, 1879
Died: Princeton, New Jersey, February 25, 1958
Highest degree: Ph.D. in psychology, University of Berlin, 1909, under C. Stumpf [202]
Positions, honors: 1910, Harvard University; 1924–1947, Princeton University, Psychology Department chairman, 1937–1947; editorial work for *Psychological Monographs*, 1931–1933, *Psychological Review*, 1934–1947; president, American Psychological Association, 1930; secretary-general, International Congress of Psychology, 1945–1951; secretary-general, International

Union of Scientific Psychology, 1951–1954; honorary doctorate, University of Montreal, 1954

Langfeld was the last American psychologist to study under the first generation of German psychologists. Unlike his teachers, Langfeld could not believe that consciousness could be separated for study in isolation. He subscribed to a motor theory of consciousness, which said that sensations, emotions, and thoughts are all bound to motor processes. In his best known book, *The Aesthetic Attitude* (1920), Langfeld appeals to a related idea to explain the emotional tone of works of art. Drawing heavily on Lipps [202] and his theory of sympathy, Langfeld asserted that while an emotional feeling originates in the perceiver it is immediately and unconsciously projected to the work or art, which then seems to possess that emotional quality. The origin of the perceiver's state of mind may be, Langfeld thought, incipient muscular movements.

Langfeld did experimental work on action, inhibition, vision, synesthesia, aesthetics, and emotional expression. He wrote *On the Psychophysiology of a Prolonged Fast* (1914), *Psychology for the Armed Services* (1945), and, with Floyd Allport, *An Elementary Laboratory Course in Psychology* (1916) that was widely used for some years. He was a coeditor of *Psychology for the Fighting Man* (1943), *Foundations of Psychology* (1948), and of the first four volumes of *History of Psychology in Autobiography*. With Boring [445] and Weld, Langfeld started the "BLW" series of psychological texts. He was much interested in the international aspects of psychology, and contributed to creating a greater interest in and acceptance of American psychological work in Europe.

Biographic data: C. C. Pratt, Herbert Sidney Langfeld. *Psychological Review*, 1958, 65 321–324; F. C. Bartlett, Herbert Sidney Langfeld. *American Journal of Psychology*, 1958, 71, 616–619

BRETT, GEORGE SIDNEY [388]

English-Canadian psychologist
Rating: 18
Born: Briton Ferry, Wales, August 5, 1879
Died: Toronto, Canada, October 27, 1944
Highest degree: M.A., Oxford University, 1902

Positions: 1908, University of Toronto, head of Psychology Department, 1926–1932, dean of Graduate School, 1932–1944

Brett's main contribution to psychology was his *History of Psychology*. Its three volumes (vol. 1, 1911, vols, 2 and 3, 1921) contained more than 1,100 pages and was the first history of psychology written in the English language. Before the appearance of Boring's [445] *History of Experimental Psychology* in 1929, Brett's was the principal history text used in English-speaking countries. Brett left behind more than 130 publications, most of them in areas other than psychology.

Biographic data: [Anon.] George Sidney Brett. *Bulletin of the Canadian Psychological Association*, 1944, 4, 71; H. Brown, George Sidney Brett, *Isis*, 1945–1946, 36, 110–114; J. A. Irving, George Sidney Brett. *Psychological Review*, 1947, 54, 52–58

[389]

VALENTINE, CHARLES WILFRID

English psychologist
Rating: 13
Born: Runcorn, Cheshire, August 16, 1879
Died: Birmingham, May 26, 1964
Highest degree: Ph.D., St. Andrews University, 1913
Positions: 1914, University of Belfast; 1919–1946, University of Birmingham

Valentine was the leader of Bristish educational psychology during his lifetime, but he worked in several additional areas as well. He founded the *British Journal of Educational Psychology* in 1931 and edited it for twenty-five years. His best known educational text is *Psychology and Its Bearing on Education* (1950). He published additional volumes on the psychology of education, such as *The Reliability of Examinations* (1932), *The Psychology of Early Education* (1942), *Intelligence Tests for Young Children* (1945), *Intelligence Tests for Children* (1950), *Psychology and Its Bearing on Education* (1950), and *Parents and Children*. Valentine also penned an *Introduction to Experimental Psychology in Relation to Education* (1915, second edition, *Introduction to Experimental Psychology* 1926), *Dreams and the Unconscious* (1921), *The Human Factor in the Army* (1943),and

Psychology and Mental Health, (1948). In 1913, Valentine wrote *The Experimental Psychology of Beauty,* presenting the results of his experimental work on the psychology of aesthetics. An enlarged version of the book appeared in 1919. It was at the time the only such book ever published, and it continued to be that until 1962 when Valentine published a final version of it. It remains the only text in a sparsely published field of psychology.

Biographic data: C. Burt & T. H. Pear, Obituary notice: Charles Wilfrid Valentine. *British Journal of Psychology,* 1964, 55, 385–390

WEISS, ALBERT PAUL [390]

American psychologist
Rating: 22
Born: Steingrund, Silesia, September 15, 1879
Died: Columbus, Ohio, April 3, 1931
Highest degree: Ph.D. in psychology, University of Missouri, 1916, under Max Meyer [346]
Positions: 1912–1931, Ohio State University; editorial work for *Journal of Genetic Psychology*

Weiss was one of the early behaviorists who advocated the abandonment of consciousness in psychology and the observation of behavior as its proper task. In *A Theoretical Basis of Human Behavior* (1925) Weiss asserted that all psychological phenomena could be reduced to physics, chemistry, social relations, or a combination of these. Consciousness, when analyzed behavioristically, vanishes into biology and social science. It is thus an objective phenomenon. It can be handled in biological and social terms, there being no need for mentalistic ones. Even so, there is no dichotomy between the biological and the social. Man, in addition to the "handling" responses, developed in the course of evolution a system of signaling responses or language. This response system accounts fully for all the human phenomena that have been traditionally attributed to nonphysical forces.

Weiss wrote only about twenty-five papers and two books, half of them theoretical and half experimental and applied, such as his *Psychological Principles of Automotive Driving* (1930).

Biographic data: R. M. Elliott, Albert Paul Weiss. *American Journal of Psychology,* 1931, 43, 707–709; S. Renshaw, Albert Paul Weiss. *Journal of General Psychology,* 1932, 6, 3–7

WERTHEIMER, MAX

German psychologist
Rating: 27
Born: Prague, Austria-Hungary, April 15, 1880
Died: New Rochelle, New York, October 12, 1943
Highest degree: Ph.D. in psychology, University of Würzburg, 1904, under O. Külpe [265]
Positions: 1912, University of Frankfurt; 1916, University of Berlin; 1929, University of Frankfurt; 1933, New School for Social Research

In 1910, Wertheimer made the discovery that if two identical visual stimuli are presented successively, then with appropriate exposure times for each and an appropriate interval between them they will appear as one object moving from one place to another. The significance of Wertheimer's discovery was not that it was new, because the phenomenon as such had been known for a long time, but because Wertheimer related his insights and his subsequent experiment, with Koffka [438] and Köhler [447] as subjects, in a novel way to perception and to the experience of physical phenomena in general. He wrote a paper in 1912 (Experimentelle Studien über das Sehen von Bewegung), which marked the beginning of a major school of psychology, the Gestalt school. Contrary to previous explanations of apparent movement, Wertheimer argued that it could not be explained entirely in terms of the properties of stimulation. The perceived movement was a new phenomenon, a whole, a Gestalt, not reducible to the elements that gave rise to it. It was the prior perception of the whole that determined how the parts would be perceived, not the other way around. Wertheimer performed additional experiments on apparent movement, drew upon the work of Schumann [273] and Rubin [443], and eventually applied the new way of looking at apparent movement to all perception. To publish works emanating from the new school, Wertheimer, Koffka, Kohler, Goldstein [380], and Gruhle [397] began publishing a new journal, *Psychologische Forschung*.

In 1923, Wertheimer published an important paper on the Gestalt principles of organization (proximity, similarity, closure, symmetry, regularity, good continuation), including the organization of the visual field into figure and ground, all subsumed under the general *law of Prägnanz,* or the tendency of experienced fields to become as articulated as possible. Underlying the law of Prägnanz, including the perception of apparent movement, Wertheimer thought were brain processes that in essence correspond to the perceived phenomena. This idea because the principle of isomorphism, later elaborated upon by Köhler.

With the years, Wertheimer became increasingly more interested in the analysis of thinking. Wertheimer's thoughts extending the idea of Gestalten to creative thinking were published posthumously in *Productive Thinking* (1945). In it, Wertheimer argues for the replacement of rote, associationistic kind of learning in schools, by methods that encourage flexible thinking and insightful solution of problems.

Biographic data: IESS 16:522; E. B. Newman, Max Wertheimer. *American Journal of Psychology*, 1944, 57, 428–435; W. Köhler, Max Wertheimer. *Psychological Review*, 1944, 51, 143–146

FREEMAN, FRANK NUGENT [392]

American psychologist
Rating: 11
Born: Rockwood, Ontario, April 17, 1880
Died: El Cerrito, California, October 17, 1961
Highest degree: Ph.D. in psychology, Yale University, 1908, under C. H. Judd [340]
Positions, honors: 1906, Yale University; 1909, University of Chicago, director, Orthogenic School; 1939–1948, University of California at Berkeley, professor of educational psychology, chairman, Department of Education, dean, School of Education; 1930, director, National Society for the Study of Education; member of various education-related organizations and institutions; honorary Sc.D., 1939

Freeman, an educational psychologist, wrote a number of books on education and on psychology (*Psychology of the Common Branches, How Children Learn, Mental Tests, The Effect of Environment on the Intelligence of Foster Children, The Handwriting Movement: a Study in the Motor Factors of Excellence in Penmanship*), of which the best known is one that he coauthored with H. H. Newman and K. J. Holzinger [478], *Twins—a Study of Heredity and Environment*. It presented data on the correlation between the IQs, personalities, and other traits of twins reared together and apart. The data have been incorporated in child and developmental psychology texts ever since.

Biographic data: The Psychological Register, 1932, Vol. III

American psychologist
Rating: 20
Born: De Witt, Nebraska, May 26, 1880
Died: Montrose, New York, September 17, 1956
Highest degree: Ph.D. in psychology, Columbia University, 1909, under J. McK. Cattell [256]
Positions, honors: 1909–1946, Barnard College; LL.D., University of Nebraska; president, American Psychological Association, 1927; Hollingworth Psychological Laboratories opened at Barnard College in 1954

Hollingworth contributed to psychology principally as a teacher of psychology and as a writer. He wrote twenty-five books and seventy-five papers on a wide variety of psychological topics, plus thirty-six book reviews. Some of his most significant volumes are *Vocational Psychology* (1916), *The Psychology of Functional Neuroses,* (1920), *Outlines for Experimental Psychology* (1913), *Applied Psychology* (with A. T. Poffenberger, 1917, rev. ed. 1923), *The Psychology of Thought* (1926), *Psychology, Its Facts and Principles* (1928), *Vocational Psychology and Character Analysis* (1928), *Abnormal Psychology* (1930), and *Educational Psychology* (1933).

Biographic data: NCAB 45:237; A. T. Poffenberger, Harry Levi Hollingworth. *American Journal of Psychology,* 1957, 70, 136–140

American psychologist
Rating: 25
Born: Alma, Wisconsin, June 21, 1880
Died: New Haven, Connecticut, May 29, 1961
Highest degree: Ph.D. in psychology, Clark University, 1906, under E. C. Sanford [254]. M.D., Yale University, 1915
Positions, honors: 1907, State Normal School, Platteville, Wisconsin; 1908, Los Angeles State Normal School; 1911, Yale

University; honorary D.Sc., Clark University, 1940, University of Wisconsin, 1953

After receiving his doctorate in psychology, Gesell became interested in the growth and development of children. He obtained a medical degree in order better to understand the physical basis of development. During his medical training he established the Clinic of Child Development at Yale University. He devoted the rest of his life to the study of the development of the child. In the course of his work he published some thirty books on the subject. The three-volume *Atlas of Infant Behavior* (1934) contains a vast amount of data and is representative of Gesell's work. The data are largely descriptive observations of children's behavior summarized in the form of developmental schedules. In his observations Gesell often used the film camera, which was one of the first instances of such use of the camera for scientific research. In the end, Gesell had filmed some 12,000 children.

From G. Stanley Hall [418], Gesell inherited an evolutionary outlook on development. He was a maturationist who assigned environment the role of the setting for growth but did not believe that environment played a major role in the child's development. Gesell felt that the tendency to grow was the strongest force in life and that it could not therefore be much affected by environmental influences. Gesell considered as his main task the description of the developmental stages that children passed through as they matured. Personality differences were explained by Gesell in terms of constitutional differences. In general, mental development in his view followed closely the development of the nervous system. This easy-to-understand approach to development appealed to parents, and Gesell soon became a popular authority on child development among parents, who eagerly used Gesell's developmental norms to check on the development of their own offspring.

Gesell received continued recognition for his work, notably in terms of some 195 research grants. Although behaviorism and psychoanalysis made their impact on developmental thought and child-rearing practices during the decades of Gesell's work, he was little influenced by them, persisting in his original viewpoint. In 1950, the Gesell Institute of Child Development was incorporated. It continues Gesell's developmental research work today. A well-known observational tool that has resulted from Gesell's and the Institute's work is the *Gesell Developmental Scales*. These are developmental inventories for infants and preschoolers measuring motor, language, cognitive, and social behavior. The Gesell

Institute's *Child Behavior* (by Ilg and Ames, 1951), a popular presentation of the Gesellian view of development, has sold over a million copies.

Biographic data: *DSB* 5:377; *HPA* 4:123; *NCAB* 49:119; L. B. Ames, Arnold Lucius Gesell: Behavior has shape. *Science*, 1961, 134, 266–267

[395]

AMES, ADALBERT, JR.

American ophthalmologist
Rating: 16
Born: Lowell, Massachusetts, August 19, 1880
Died: Hanover, New Hamsphire, July 3, 1955
Highest degree: LL.B. in law, Harvard University, 1906
Positions and honors: 1914–1917, research fellow, Clark University; 1919–1945, Dartmouth College; 1936–1949, director of research, Dartmouth Eye Institute; 1949–1955, Hanover Institute for Associated Research; LL.D., Dartmouth College, 1954; Optical Society of America Edgar D. Tillyer Medal, 1955

Dissatisfied with the practice of law, Ames turned to painting, which led him to the analysis of vision and to opthalmology. In 1936, he established the Dartmouth Eye Clinic, where he discovered and researched the phenomenon of aniseikonia and invented the *aniseikonic lenses* to correct it. A study of the effects of aniseikonic lenses in persons with normal vision as well as of other unique conditions of vision led Ames to the formulation of the view of *transactional functionalism* in perception. The philosophical basis for Ames's theory came from the philosophical theory of transactions of John Dewey [253]. The empirical support came from the demonstrations which Ames devised. They were set up to show how individuals transact with their environment, that is, experience the consequences of their own actions. They reveal the perceptual significance of action and the observer's assumptions about the perceptual world. To the transactionalist, the demonstrations show that objects derive their meaning at least partly from their participation in a total situation, and that the world we experience is the product of perception, not the cause of it.

The first demonstrations were set up in 1938. They include the distorted room, the trapezoidal window, aniseikonic lenses, size-distance phenomena in the "thereness-thatness" apparatus, and others. They were first set up at the Hanover Institute for Associated Research which Ames and Hadley Cantril organized in 1947, but were later placed in the Perception Demonstration Center at Princeton University.

Ames wrote thirty papers on vision but only seven on perception and *An Interpretative Manual for the Demonstrations in the Psychology Research Center, Princeton University* (1954). Otherwise his thinking appears in informal memoranda bound in six volumes, now at Dartmouth College and Princeton University.

Biographic data: *NCAB* 44:571; [Anon.] Adalbert Ames, Jr., Edgar D. Tillyer medalist for 1955. *Journal of the Optical Society of America,* 1955, 45, 333–337

BINGHAM, WALTER VAN DYKE [396]

American psychologist
Rating: 23
Born: Swan Lake, Iowa, October 20, 1880
Died: Washington, D.C., July 8, 1952
Highest degree: Ph.D. in psychology, University of Chicago, 1908, under J. R. Angell [309]
Positions: 1908, Teachers College, Columbia University; 1910, Dartmouth College, established psychological laboratory there; 1915, Carnegie Institute of Technology; organized and directed division of applied psychology and Bureau of Salesmanship Research there in 1916; 1924–1934, director, Personnel Research Federation, Inc.; 1924–1940, independent research and private practice in industrial psychology, summer teaching at Harvard and University of Minnesota, consultant to government agencies on personnel classification matters; 1940–1947, chief psychologist, Adjutant General's office; editorial work for *Personnel Journal* (1923–1937), *Journal of Consulting Psychology, Journal of Applied Psychology, Character and Personality,* and *Personnel Psychology;* president, American Association of Applied Psychologists, 1941

Bingham pioneered in the practice of industrial psychology, occupational guidance, personnel selection and classification, accident reduction, and psychological testing. Throughout his career he worked for the establishment of an industrial psychology based on experimental psychology, and thereby left an impress on the development of applied psychology in the United

States. Bingham exercised his influence through the study of many problems in applied psychology (he wrote more than two-hundred papers and books) and through participation in numerous governmental and civic bodies concerned with personnel problems, manpower, accident prevention, and applied psychology in general. Bingham was a cofounder of the Psychological Corporation in 1921 and one of its directors throughout his life. During World War I he was one of the seven psychologists who developed intelligence testing in the U.S. Army and he worked with W. D. Scott [308] on the classification of Army personnel. In World War II he also did personnel work for the armed forces. Two of his books of enduring value are *Aptitude and Aptitude Testing* (1937) and *How to Interview* (with B. V. Moore, 1931).

Biographic data: *HPA* 4:1; *IESS* 2:78; *NCAB* 39:524; H. E. Burtt, Walter Van Dyke Bingham. *Psychological Review,* 1952, 59, 403–404; L. W. Ferguson, Walter Van Dyke Bingham: Dean of industrial psychologists. *Heritage of Industrial Psychology,* 1963, No. 2, 12–23

[397]

GRUHLE, HANS WALTHER

German psychiatrist
Rating: 12
Born: Lübben, Saxony, November 7, 1880
Died: Bonn, October 3, 1958
Highest degree: M.D., University of Munich, 1905
Positions: 1912, University of Heidelberg; 1934–1946, director of sanatoriums; 1946–1952, Neurological Clinic, Bonn

Gruhle did research and wrote numerous articles and books on psychiatry, psychopathology (*Psychopathologie der Schizophrenie,* 1932), schizophrenia (*Psychologie der Schizophrenie,* 1929), psychology of criminality (*Geisteskrankheiten und Strafrecht,* 1927) and suicide (*Selbstmord,* 1940). He was a cofounder, with Wertheimer [391], Köhler [447], Koffka [438], and Goldstein [380], of *Psychologische Forschung* in 1921. In his *Verstehen und Einfühlen* (1953) he outlined a *verstehende* or *apprehending psychology* as a discipline concerned with inner experience, as well as a verstehende psychopathology.

Biographic data: *The Psychological Register,* 1932, Vol. III

MAYO, (GEORGE) ELTON

Australian-American psychologist
Rating: 11
Born: Adelaide, Australia, December 26, 1880
Died: England, September 7, 1949
Highest degree: M.A. in psychology, University of Adelaide, 1919
Positions, honors: 1911, Queensland University; 1923, University of Pennsylvania; 1926–1947, Harvard University, head, Department of Industrial Research, Graduate School of Business; honorary M.A., Harvard University, 1942

Mayo was responsible for the Hawthorne experiments of the 1930s (*The Human Problems of an Industrial Civlization*, 1933), famous in the annals of industrial psychology, industrial relations, and the social psychology of industry. One important aspect of this work was the discovery of informal groups in an industrial organization that had leaders not appointed by the management. Since these groups controlled production and occurred naturally everywhere, it became evident that the interests of these groups and those of the management should coincide. Later (1943), research in aircraft factories in California showed the cause of very high turnover to be the absence of primary groups among workers (*The Social Problems of an Industrial Civilization,* 1945). Mayo's theses that work is a group activity, that recognition and sense of belongingness are more important in determining morale than are physical conditions, that informal groups exercise strong control over the workers' behavior, that changes in the nature of the society at large continually disrupt the social organization of people at work, as well as others have been demonstrated by investigators elsewhere, repeatedly, and in different countries. Mayo's research was revolutionary at the time it was conducted, and later research in the social organization of work has been based on it.

Biographic data: *IESS* 10:82; P. E. Mayo, The work of Elton Mayo. *Occupational Psychology,* 1950, 24, 1–6

SACHS, HANNS

Austrian psychoanalyst
Rating: 13
Born: Vienna, January 10, 1881

Died: Boston, Massachusetts, January 10, 1947

Highest degree: Law degree from University of Vienna, 1904

Positions: 1918, private practice of psychoanalysis in Zurich, Switzerland; 1920, director, Psychoanalytic Institute, Berlin; 1932, training analyst in Boston, Massachusetts; faculty member of Harvard Medical School

After reading Freud's [224] works, Sachs joined his group in 1909 and became one of the ring-wearing members of Freud's inner group that was to guide the destiny of psychoanalysis. Sachs defended Freud constantly and, unlike such other members of the inner group as Jung [358], Adler [317], and Rank [421], never defected. At Berlin, Sachs became the first training analyst. He was a cofounder and editor of the psychoanalytic journal *Imago* (1912–1938). When it was suppressed, Sachs reestablished it in America as *The American Imago*. Sachs's early works were concerned with the interpretation of dreams, but he later shifted to the application of psychoanalysis to literature and art. Of Sachs's seventy-eight publications, the most significant monographs are *The Significance of Psychoanalysis to the Mental Sciences* (1916, with O. Rank), *Notes About the Psychology of the Film* (1925) (he helped direct an early film on Freud), *Psychotherapy and the Pursuit of Happiness* (1941), *The Creative Unconscious* (1942), and *Freud, Master and Friend* (1944).

Biographic data: F. Deutsch, Hanns Sachs. *The American Imago*, 1947, 3–11; R. M. Loewenstein, In memoriam Hanns Sachs. *Psychoanalytic Quarterly*, 1947, 16, 151–156; E. Jones, Hanns Sachs. *International Journal of Psychoanalysis*, 1946, 27, 168–169

[400]

SELZ, OTTO

German psychologist

Rating: 17

Born: Munich, February 14, 1881

Died: In a German concentration camp, 1944 (?)

Education: Studied at Munich and Berlin between 1899 and 1904, and at Bonn between 1909 and 1912

Positions: 1912, University of Bonn; 1923–1933, Handels-Hochschule, Mannheim; editorial work for *Archiv für die gesamte Psychologie* and *Psychotechnische Zeitschrift*

Member of the Würzburg school of psychology, Selz studied the organized thinking process *(Uber die Gesetze des geordneten Denkverlaufs,* 1913; *Zur Psychologie des produktiven Denkens und des Irrtums,* 1922; *Die Gesetze der produktiven und reproduktiven Geistestätigkeit,* 1924). In these books and some thirty papers and monographs on productive thinking, cognition, and Gestalt psychology, Selz stressed the notion that in thinking active processing takes place in the mind, and called for a psychology of thinking that would be concerned with processes rather than content. In opposition to the constellation theory of G. E. Müller [208], Selz theorized that responses are specific to the structured complex of the task. He emphasized that thinking is influenced by the thinker's set or "anticipatory schema," a concept similar to that of Aufgabe or task as used in the Würzburg school.

Biographic data: New Catholic Encyclopedia, Vol. 13

THOMSON, SIR GODFREY HILTON

[401]

English physical scientist and psychologist
Rating: 23
Born: Carlisle, Cumberland, March 27, 1881
Died: Edinburgh, Scotland, February 9, 1955
Highest degree: Ph.D. in physics and mathematics, University of Strasbourg, 1906; D.Sc. in psychology, Cambridge University, 1913
Positions, honors: 1906–1915, Armstrong College; 1920, King's College, Newcastle-upon-Tyne; 1925, Edinburgh University; president, British Psychological Society, 1945–1946; editorial work for *British Journal of Educational Psychology* and *British Journal of Psychology;* knighted, 1949

Thomson started his psychological work in psychophysics by analyzing the mathematical basis of threshold calculations. Later, he devised a test to select children who were to have free secondary education, the Northumberland Tests, now called the Moray House Tests, given every year in Britain to more than a million children. His last and most important contributions were in the area of *factor analysis.* Soon after Spearman [274] had presented his two-factor theory of intelligence, Thomson took issue with Spearman (1916, 1919) by pointing out that if there is one overlap among three or more variables (Spearman's G), there are additional, partial overlaps or group factors. Thomson was one of the men who developed the technique of factor analysis in the 1930s (*Factorial Analysis of Human Ability,* 1939). An important contribution to the field of psychological measurement was the book, *The Essentials of Mental Measurement,* written first (1911) by William Brown [406], but coauthored by Thomson in its second (1921) and third (1925) editions.

Biographic data: *HPA* 4:279; C. Burt, Sir Godfrey Thomson. *British Journal of Statistical Psychology,* 1955, 8, 1–2; J. Sutherland, Sir Godfrey Thomson. *British Journal of Educational Psychology,* 1955, 25, 65–66; J. Drever, Godfrey Hilton Thomson. *American Journal of Psychology,* 1955, 68, 494–496; L. L. Thurstone, Sir Godfrey Thomson. *Psychometrika,* 1955, 20, 171–172; W. Stephenson, Sir Godfrey Thomson. *British Journal of Psychology,* 1955, 46, 245–247

[402]

BINSWANGER, LUDWIG

Swiss psychiatrist
Rating: 19
Born: Kreuzlingen, Thurgau, April 13, 1881
Died: Kreuzlingen, February 5, 1966
Highest degree: M.D., University of Zurich, 1907
Positions: 1910–1956, psychiatrist and chief medical director, Sanitorium Bellevue, Kreuzlingen

Under the influence of Dilthey [164], Heidegger, and Husserl [248], Binswanger developed *Daseinsanalyse* or existential analysis, a combination of phenomenology, existentialism, and psychoanalysis. It was a reaction to the view that man is only an organism. Without denying the value of the natural science approach, Binswanger stressed the necessity to understand the present meaning-context of the patient since the past, the entire "world design," exists in the patient in the present, is the patient. Psychological knowledge is possible only if man communes with man lovingly. Besides several books on psychiatry, Binswanger wrote *Einführung in die Probleme der allgemeinen Psychologie* (1922) and *Wandlungen in der Auffassung und Deutung des Traumes* (1928).

Biographic data: *EP* 1:309.

SAUDEK, ROBERT

English psychologist
Rating: 11
Born: Kolin, Bohemia, April 21, 1881
Died: April 15, 1935
Education: Studied at Prague, Leipzig, and Sorbonne between 1899 and 1902
Positions, honors: Worked mostly as private consultant and lecturer; honorary Ph.D., 1928; founder and editor of *Character and Personality* (1932)

Saudek's main interest was graphology. He differed from Klages [338] in that he assumed that handwriting was not always an expression of a person's individuality but that it also reflected experience, education, culture, tradition, writing material, and other factors. In this area he wrote *Wissenschaftliche Graphologie* (1925) and *Experimentelle Graphologie* (1926, English translation, *Experiments with Handwriting,* 1929).

Biographic data: A. A. Roback, Dr. Robert Saudek. *Character and Personality,* 1935, 3, 263–269

PIERON, HENRI

French psychologist
Rating: 27
Born: Paris, July 18, 1881
Died: Paris, November 6, 1964
Highest degree: Doctorate in science, University of Paris, 1912
Positions, honors: 1907, Ecole pratique des hautes études; 1911, Sorbonne; 1923, Collège de France; editor, *L'Année psychologique,* 1912–1964, editorial work for many psychological journals; president, Eleventh International Congress of Psychology, 1937; numerous honors from world universities

After Binet's [236] death, Piéron took over the direction of the psychological laboratory at Sorbonne in 1910. In 1920, he established the Institut de Psychologie at the University of Paris, and remained its director until his retirement. During a large portion of his professional life Piéron was considered to be the leading French psychologist.

Piéron was physiologically oriented, but he did not reduce psychology to physiology. His view was that both the response of the total organism (psychology) and its partial responses (physiology) had to be considered. Before Watson [374] (1907, publication in 1908), Piéron stated that the subject matter of psychology is behavior. He was the originator of the French school of behaviorism, or *psychologie du comportement.*

Piéron was extremely versatile and productive. He produced a bibliography of some 500 items, many of which were books, some of them quite influential. They ranged in content from experimental psychology, sensation, and physiological psychology to individual differences and applied psychology. Piéron did research in general, animal, and especially physiological psychology. The psychophysiology of the senses was his main concern for some fifty years (*The Sensations, Their Functions, Processes, and Mechanisms, English translation* (1952). Piéron related psychology to physiology also by comparing and relating human and animal behavior. He believed that the governing principles were the same in man and animal (*De l'action à l'homme: Etudes de psychophysiologie comparée,* (1958). In the applied area, Piéron fostered psychotechnology all his life. He founded the Institut National d'Etudes du Travail et d'Orientation Professionnelle in 1928 and was also its director. He was the editor of a seven-volume series, *Traité de psychologie appliquée,* and the author of its first volume, *La psychologie différentielle* (1949).

Biographic data: HPA 4:257; A. Fessard, Henri Piéron, *L'Année psychologique,* 1951, 50, vii–xiii; Y. Galifret, In memoriam Henri Piéron. *Psychologie française,* 1965, 10(2), 113–118; D. Shakow, Henri Piéron. *American Journal of Psychology,* 1966, 79, 147–154

[405]

MICHOTTE (VAN DEN BERCK), (BARON) ALBERT EDWARD

Belgian psychologist
Rating: 26
Born: Brussels, October 13, 1881
Died: Louvain, June 2, 1965
Highest degree: Ph.D. in philosophy, science, and physiology, University of Louvain, 1900, under D. J. Mercier [212];

1905–1908, studied psychology at Leipzig with Wundt [161] and at Würzburg with Külpe [265]

Positions, honors: 1905–1956, University of Louvain; 1914–1918, University of Utrecht (University of Louvain was burned down); president, Fifteenth International Congress of Psychology, 1957; three honorary degrees; made baron 1954

During his lifetime, Michotte was the most prominent Belgian psychologist. He was interested in perception from the outset, and published his first monograph in that area in 1905 (*Les signes régioneux*). Before World War I, Michotte studied volition using the systematic experimental introspection method of the Würzburg school, but abandoned this approach when it proved to be inadequate. He then turned to the study of rhythm and movement and became interested in Gestalt psychology. Between 1918 and 1939, Michotte's laboratory produced research showing the development of motor and temporal Gestalten from a perceptual basis. In 1939, inspired by Gestalt psychology, Michotte embarked on a study of the perception of physical causality, which attracted international attention. In distinction from Jean Piaget who relied on children's introspections as he studied the development of the notion of physical causality, Michotte designed a mechanical device which portrayed two objects in varying degrees of collision, i.e., one apparently causing the other to move, and asked subjects to describe the type of interaction that they perceived to exist between the two objects. By varying the velocity of approach, duration of contact, and other variables, Michotte was able to relate perceived causality to physical stimulus dimensions. He concluded that the perception of causality was like any other perception, a direct experience, not an interpretation of experience, since even knowing that no actual causal relation exists does not preclude the perception of causality when the stimulus constellation is right (*La perception de la causalité*, 1946; English translation, *Perception of Causality*, 1963).

Michotte was very active in international psychology. He organized and participated in the activities of international congresses, unions, and societies. At Louvain, he organized the Institute of Psychology in 1944 and the Belgian Psychological Association in 1947.

Biographic data: HPA 4:213; J. R. Nuttin, Albert Edward Michotte van den Berck. *American Journal of Psychology*, 1961, 79, 331–341; In H. Misiak & V. S. Sexton, *Catholics in Psychology*, 1954, pp. 98–110

BROWN, WILLIAM

English psychologist
Rating: 11
Born: Slinfold, Sussex, December 5, 1881
Died: Oxford, May 17, 1952
Highest degree: D.Sc. in mathematics, University of London, 1910; D.M., Oxford University, 1918
Positions: 1914, University of London, reader in psychology; 1921–1947, Oxford University, Wilde readership in mental philosophy; 1925–1931, psychotherapist at King's College Hospital; 1936–1945, director of Institute of Experimental Psychology, Oxford University; president, British Psychological Society, 1951

In his most important work, *Essentials of Mental Measurement* (1911, revised editions, with Godfrey H. Thomson [401], in 1921 and 1925), Brown attempted to give a joint treatment to psychophysical methods and psychological statistics. He took issue with Spearman [274] on the question of interpretation of factor-analytical results related to intelligence measurement. Brown argued that the hierarchical order in matrices of intercorrelations could be produced by random overlapping of group factors, with no general factor in evidence. Later in his career, Brown devoted increasingly more time to abnormal psychology and psychiatry, emphasizing the importance of suggestion (*Suggestion and Mental Analysis*, 3rd edition, 1923; *Mind and Personality*, 1926; *Mind, Medicine, and Metaphysics*, 1936; *Psychological Methods of Healing*, 1938; *Psychology and Psychotherapy*, 5th edition, 1944; *Personality and Religion*, 1946). Even so, he is credited with establishing the first psychological laboratory (Institute of Experimental Psychology) at Oxford in 1936.

Biographic data: J. D. Sutherland, William Brown. *British Journal of Medical Psychology*, 1953, 26, 1

BROWN, WARNER

American psychologist
Rating: 11
Born: Greensboro, Georgia, February 9, 1882
Died: Berkeley, California, February 6, 1956

Highest degree: Ph.D. in psychology, Columbia University, under
R. S. Woodworth [312]
Positions: 1908–1952, University of California, professor, later
chairman of Psychology Department

Until his retirement in 1952 as professor emeritus, Brown was the
senior experimentalist at the University of California. In his day,
he was recognized as one of the leading experimental psychologists. Brown authored some thirty papers on perception, learning,
and memory. A number of them became classic references in
advanced psychology texts: papers on the probability of discrimination of small differences at threshold, reminiscence, the
whole-part meth∩d of learning, and maze learning in humans. He
also coauthored an *Introductory Psychology*.

Biographic data: NCAB 48:95; H. C. Gilhousen & J. W.
Macfarlane, Warner Brown. *American Journal of Psychology*,
1956, 69, 495–497

KLEIN, MELANIE   ⌈408⌋

German-English psychoanalyst
Rating: 17
Born: Budapest, Hungary, March 30, 1882
Died: London, England, September 22, 1960
Positions: 1921, child therapist, Berlin Psychoanalytical Institute;
1926, British Psychoanalytical Society, London

Although Klein never received an academic degree, she and Anna
Freud were the two most prominent child psychoanalysts in the
world. Klein's work with children led to the development of ideas
that did not always match those of Freud [224]. Klein placed the
development of the superego in infancy, for instance, believing
that the seeds of it are already to be found in the first and second
year of life. She thought that fear and aggressive tendencies were
also present at this age and held these to be more important in
understanding deviant development than psychosexual development. Not hewing to the classic Freudian lines created controversy around Klein, eventually leading to her forming her own
group of analysts within the British Psychoanalytical Society, the
"Kleinians." Of Klein's books the more significant ones are

Contributions to Psychoanalysis, 1921–1945 (1948), *New Directions in Psychoanalysis* (editor, 1955), *The Psychoanalysis of Children* (1960), and *Our Adult World and Other Essays* (1963).

Biographic data: IESS 8:415; R. E. Money-Kyrle, Melanie Klein. *Bulletin of the British Psychological Society*, 1961, 43, 29–30; S. Isaacson, Obituary: Melanie Klein. *Journal of Child Psychology and Psychiatry*, 1961, 2, 1–4; T. F. Main, Klein, Melanie. *British Journal of Medical Psychology*, 1961, 34, 163–166

[409]

BRIDGMAN, PERCY WILLIAMS

American physicist
Rating: 24
Born: Cambridge, Massachusetts, April 21, 1882
Died: Randolph, New Hampshire, August 20, 1961
Highest degree: Ph.D. in physics, Harvard University, 1908
Positions and honors: 1908–1954, Harvard University; 1946 Nobel prize in physics, numerous other awards, honors, and honorary degrees

In his 1927 book, *The Logic of Modern Physics*, Bridgman argued that any concept is equivalent to the set of operations by which it is obtained. A physical phenomenon is equivalent to the set of operations by which it is observed or measured. Concepts which cannot be tested by observation are meaningless. That which cannot be observed has no place in science. Thus the question of whether or not one person's red is the same as another's cannot be answered because sensory (subjective) qualities cannot be specified absolutely. Operationism, a form of logical positivism, was born at Harvard and popularized by Harvard psychologists, notably S. S. Stevens [517]. Psychologists, then under the aegis of behaviorism, were ready to accept operational definitions and reject nonobservable concepts, and thus operationism (which Bridgman did not name) was born. It did not become a school, and moderation having set in in its use after World War II, operational definitions are now being used as a technique and a means of clarifying one's thinking.

Biographic data: DSB 2:457–461; EP 1:368; NCAB 48:269

Italian psychologist
Rating: 15
Born: Milan, June 23, 1882
Died: Rome, January 9, 1960
Highest degree: M.D., University of Turin, 1911; studied psychology under F. Kiesow [240] at the same time
Positions: 1905, University of Turin, teaching psychology; 1931–1958, University of Rome, professor of psychology, head of the Institute of Experimental Psychology; president, Italian Society of Psychology, 1942–1958

Ponzo did research in the area of psychophysics of touch and taste, but turned to applied psychology after 1940, and pioneered in introducing applied psychology in Italy. He made contributions to aptitude testing and professional selection. His belief was that vocational guidance should be based on a consideration of personality characteristics and talent in addition to intelligence. Ponzo's bibliography numbers some 280 publications, most of them on the chemical senses, touch, temperature sensations, geometric illusions (*the Ponzo illusion* is named after him), and on breathing as a psychophysical behavior (observations on changes in breathing as a function of mental activity).

Biographic data: L. Canestrelli, Mario Ponzo. *American Journal of Psychology*, 1960, 73, 645–647

German psychologist, philosopher, and educator
Rating: 25
Born: Berlin-Grosslichtenfelde, June 27, 1882
Died: Tübingen, Baden-Württemberg, September 17, 1963
Highest degree: Ph.D. in philosophy, University of Berlin, 1909
Positions: 1911, University of Leipzig; 1920, University of Berlin; 1946, University of Tübingen

Spranger was one of Dilthey's [164] most faithful students. In 1913, he published a book that became his best known contribution to psychology (*Lebensformen,* English translation,

Types of Men, 1928). It was an attempt to present a plan for a psychology based on understanding (verstehende Psychologie), and thus followed Dilthey in its basic approach. A developmental psychology volume published a decade later (*Psychologie des Jugendalters,* 1924) bore the same seal of Verstehen. Spranger named his psychology the *psychology of structure* (Struktur-psychologie), to contrast it with Wundt's [161] elementism.

In addition to the physical and mental realms, Spranger postulated a third one, that of the spirit, and asserted that man can be understood only within the framework of the spiritual. The spiritual realm is reflected in group norms, contents of the collective unconscious, and other manifestations of culture. The psychological realm can be understood only in relation to the spiritual. Specifically, Spranger postulated six types of men, or personality as it is manifest within the six major areas of human activity, attitudes, and values: religion, science, social relations, aesthetics, economics, and politics. The predominance of one value may color the entire personality, and Spranger described the typical behaviors and attitudes of the six pure types.

While the postulation of a third mode of existence, the spiritual, is not accepted by most psychologists, that of the six realms of value has proved to be an attractive one. Soon after the publication of the English translation of Spranger's *Types of Men*, Allport [493] and Vernon constructed a value inventory (*Study of Values*, 1931) that has turned out to be a useful psychological instrument of considerable viability. More generally, Spranger, along with his teacher Dilthey, is counted among the forerunners of humanistic psychology.

Biographic data: EP 8:1; E. Croner, *Eduard Spranger,* 1933

[412]

MULLER-FREIENFELS, RICHARD

German psychologist
Rating: **15**
Born: Bad Ems, Hessen, August 7, 1882
Died: Weilburg, Hessen, December 12, 1949
Highest degree: Ph.D.; educated at Munich, Berlin, Geneva, Vienna, Tübingen, Paris, London, and Zurich
Positions: 1922, Kunst-Hochschule, Berlin; 1930, Pädagogische Akademie, Stettin; 1933, Wirtschaftshochschule, Berlin; 1946–1948, University of Berlin

Müller-Freienfels attempted to create an irrational-dynamic philosophical system (*Metaphysik des Irrationalen,* 1927) and to base his psychology, which he called *Lebenspsychologie,* or "life psychology", on it (*Lebenspsychologie,* 2 volumes, 1916; *Grundzüge einer Lebenspsychologie,* 2 volumes, 1924). Müller-Freienfels authored a considerable number of books, most of them in the area of social psychology and the psychology of personality. Some of them enjoyed considerable popularity and were reprinted several times: *Persönlichkeit und Lebensanschauung* (1919), *Psychologie der Religion,* 2 volumes (1920), *Psychologie der deutschen Menschen* (1922), *Psychologie der Kunst,* 2 volumes (1922), *Geheimnisse der Seele* (1927), *Hauptrichtungen der gegenwärtigen Psychologie* (1929, 3rd edition, 1933), *Allgemeine Sozial- und Kulturpsychologie* (1930), *Gedächtnis- und Geistesschulung* (1933, 6th edition, 1966), *Menschenkenntnis und Menschenbehandlung* (1940, 4th edition, 1951).

Biographic data: *The Psychological Register,* 1932, vol. III

JAENSCH, ERICH RUDOLF [413]

German psychologist
Rating: 25
Born: Breslau, Silesia, February 26, 1883
Died: Marburg, Hesse, January 12, 1940
Highest degree: Ph.D. in psychology, University of Göttingen, 1908, under G. E. Müller [208]
Positions: 1908–1910, University of Göttingen; 1913–1940, University of Marburg; president, German Psychological Society, 1936–1940

Although Jaensch was a student of Georg Müller, even his doctoral dissertation on visual perception had a strong phenomenological component (*Zur Analyse der Gesichtswahrnehmungen,* 1909). Its main topic was vision at short and long distances. Jaensch showed that visual acuity depends not only on the texture of the retina but also on additional, larger interacting systems. Jaensch discussed spatial vision in another monograph published two years later (*Uber die Wahrnehmung des Raumes,* 1911). It concerns the phenomenology of empty space and the perception of size in space. Later, Jaensch contributed still another volume on perception, *Uber den Aufbau der Wahrnehmungswelt* (1923). During his career Jaensch published a large number (269) of articles and several monographs on perception, especially visual perception.

Jaensch, however, is best known for his work on eidetic imagery. On this topic he published a book (*Die Eidetik*, 1925, English translation, *Eidetic Imagery*, 1930) and some thirty articles. Jaensch distinguished two human types, the B-type (later called the integrate type) and the T-type (later called the disintegrate type). The former was characterized by good eidetic ability that was under voluntary control and was caused by a hyperactive thyroid gland; the latter by afterimages not under voluntary control and caused by hypoactivity of the parathyroid. The descriptions of the character of each type were later adjusted by Jaensch to suit the National-Socialist ideology (*Zur Eidetik und Integrationstypologie*, 1941) and thus lost their value to science.

Biographic data: IESS 8:225; G. H. Fischer, *Erich Rudolf Jaensch zum Gedanken; sein Werk und Vermächtnis*, 1940 (ibid. in *Zeitschrift für Psychologie*, 1940, 148, 19–90)

[414]

BURT, SIR CYRIL LODOWIC

English psychologist
Rating: (unrated)
Born: Stratford-on-Avon, March 3, 1883
Died: London, October 10, 1971
Highest degree: D.Sc., Oxford University, 1906
Positions, honors: 1908, University of Liverpool; 1913–1915, Cambridge University; 1913–1930, psychologist, Education Department, London County Council; 1924–1931, University of London, professor of education; 1931–1950, University College, London, professor of psychology; during World War I employed by the National Institute of Industrial Psychology, Industrial Health Research Board, London School of Hygiene, and other bodies; honorary consulting psychologist to the Civil Service; 1953, editorial work, *Journal of Statistical Psychology*; two honorary LL.D. degrees; knighted 1946

Burt's primary contributions were to the areas of mental tests and statistical procedures over a period of about twenty years. Burt was one of the psychologists who in the 1930s developed the statistical technique of factor analysis. He held the position, common to factor analysts at the present time, that the various factor-analytical methods are basically reconcilable. His best known book, written in this area, is *The Factors of the Mind* (1941). Burt also revised and standardized the Binet intelligence test and other tests (*Distribution of Educational Abilities*, 1917; *Mental and Scholastic Tests*, 1921; *The Measurement of Mental Capacities*, 1927) and wrote in the areas of delinquency and mental retardation (*The Young Delinquent*, 1925; *The Backward Child*, 1937; *The Subnormal Mind*, 1935; *The Causes and Treatment of Backwardness*, 1952). In his last book, *The Psychological Study of Typography* (1959), Burt presented the results of his studies of the effects of typographic factors on the readability and aesthetic quality of type faces in use in children's books and scientific journals.

Biographic data: HPA 4:53

KAFKA, GUSTAV   [415]

German psychologist
Rating: 14
Born: Vienna, Austria, July 23, 1883
Died: Veitschochheim, near Würzburg, February 12, 1953
Highest degree: Ph.D. in psychology, University of Leipzig, 1906, under W. Wundt [161]
Positions: 1905–1916, University of Munich; during World War I set up psychotechnical services for the Austro-Hungarian army (with Géza Révész [381]); 1923–1935, Technische Hochschule, Dresden; 1947–1952, University of Würzburg; president, German Psychological Society, 1951–1953 (Kafka reestablished it after World War II)

Kafka's main interest lay in philosophy, but eventually he began to relate philosophy and psychology, for instance, by introducing concepts of developmental psychology in philosophy (*Geschichtsphilosophie der Philosophiegeschichte*, 1933). His psychological investigations were in the areas of developmental, comparative, and ethnopsychology. His text of comparative psychology (*Handbuch der vergleichenden Psychologie*, 3 volume, 1922) encompassed all three areas. *Was sind Rassen?* (1949) likewise touched all three areas. Kafka wrote many papers, a good number of which show him as an incisive critic of fundamental concepts in psychology. His aim for psychology was to go beyond mere accumulation of facts, to reckon with the concept of soul, and to add to psychology the dimension of Höhenpsychologie that would deal with human spirit and man as a whole, composed of body, soul, and spirit.

Biographic data: P. Lersch, Gustav Kafka zum Gedächtnis. *Jahrbuch für Psychologie und Psychotherapie*, 1953, **1**, 375–376; G. Révész, In memoriam Gustav Kafka. *Jahrbuch für Psychologie und Psychotherapie*, 1953, **1**, 373–375; W. J. Rivers, Gustav Kafka. *American Journal of Psychology*, 1953, **66**, 642–644

[416]

REYMERT, MARTIN LUTHER

Norwegian-American psychologist
Rating: 14
Born: Holmestrand, Norway, November 10, 1883
Died: Mooseheart, Illinois, June 2, 1953
Highest degree: Ph.D. in psychology, Clark University, 1917
Positions: 1918, University of Iowa; 1919, Iowa Child Welfare Research Station; 1920, State Agriculture College, Norway; 1925, Wittenberg College, head of Psychology Department; 1930, director of Research, Loyal Order of the Moose

During his last five years (1920–1925) in Norway, Reymert worked on the standardization of Norwegian IQ tests. At Mooseheart, Reymert established a psychological laboratory for child research, where he did educational counseling. In 1949, he established another laboratory to study age-related changes in behavior, this time in the aged, the Moosehaven Research Laboratory at Orange Park, Florida. Both institutions were financed by the Loyal Order of the Moose, and Reymert became its research director, supervising both laboratories. Reymert was a member of several advisory and similar boards having charge of children's institutions. He himself considered that his greatest contribution to psychology was the calling of two symposia on feeling and emotion, one at Wittenberg in 1928 and another in Mooseheart, Illinois in 1948 (*Feelings and Emotion*, 1928 and 1950, both edited by Reymert).

Biographic data: H. S. Langfeld, Martin Luther Reymert. *American Journal of Psychology*, 1953, **66**, 649–650

SAPIR, EDWARD

American anthropologist and linguist
Rating: 19
Born: Lauenburg, Pomerania, Germany, January 26, 1884
Died: New Haven, Connecticut, February 4, 1939
Highest degree: Ph.D. in anthropology, Columbia University, 1909
Positions: 1910, chief, Division of Anthropology, Canadian National Museum, Ottawa; 1925, University of Chicago; 1927, Yale University; president, Linguistic Society of America, American Anthropological Association

Sapir pioneered in advocating a closer relationship between anthropology, sociology, and psychoanalysis, and exercised considerable influence in this direction upon H. S. Sullivan [474]. Sapir is known, however, principally for his linguistic studies, especially of American Indian languages (1906), which he turned to under the influence of Franz Boas [243]. His ideas concerning the relationship between language and behavior appeared in a posthumous volume, *Selected Writings in Language, Culture, and Personality* (1949, edited by D. G. Mendelbaum). Sapir's most important work on linguistics is his *Language* (1921).

Biographic data: *IESS* 14:9; *NCAB* 33:507; H. S. Sullivan, Edward Sapir. *Psychiatry*, 1939, 2, 159

HALL, GRANVILLE STANLEY

American psychologist
Rating: 27
Born: Ashfield, Massachusetts, February 1, 1844
Died: Worcester, Massachusetts, April 24, 1924
Highest degree: Ph.D. in psychology, Harvard University, 1878, under William James [184]
Positions: 1882–1888, Johns Hopkins University; 1889–1920, Clark University, president and professor of psychology; president, American Psychological Association, 1892 and 1924

Although Hall received the first Ph.D. in psychology to be conferred in the United States and did considerable doctoral and postdoctoral work in physiology, his fame rests more on his organizational activities than his research. In 1883, at Johns

Hopkins University, Hall founded the second American psychological laboratory, then still another one at Clark University in 1889. Additional laboratories were founded elsewhere by those who had been Hall's students at Johns Hopkins. In 1887, Hall started publishing the *American Journal of Psychology*, first American psychological journal and first purely psychological journal in the English language. He also started the *Pedagogical Seminary* (now *Journal of Genetic Psychology*) in 1893, the *Journal of Applied Psychology* in 1915, and between 1904 and 1914 published the *Journal of Religious Psychology*. Most important of all was the founding of the American Psychological Association in 1892, an organization to which today more than one-half of the world's psychologists belong.

Hall was a pioneer of developmental psychology (he called it genetic psychology) in the United States. Influenced by Darwin's [127] evolutionary thoery, Hall came to think of the development of the child as reflecting the evolutionary history of mankind. He introduced the use of the questionnaire to study "the contents of children's minds." Hall published his findings in his own *Pedagogical Seminary*, the second psychological journal to appear in the United States. Inspired by Hall, enthusiasm for child study grew, and a child-study movement flourished for some years. Although it did not last, it established the notion of psychological development and the need for empirical work in child study. In a monumental two-volume work, *Adolescence,* published in 1904, Hall considered the later years of development. In it may be found Hall's cultural recapitulation theory, or the proposition that the child during its development repeats the evolution of civilization. Originally an idea of Rousseau's [53], it found no empirical support in spite of Hall's having it bolstered with evolutionary biology taken from Darwin and Haeckel [165]. Toward the end of his life, Hall considered old age and pioneered in gerontology by publishing a volume on *Senescence* (1922).

Hall was also one of the first American psychologists to become interested in psychoanalysis. In 1909, he brought Freud [224] and Jung [358] to Clark University for a conference, in spite of the suspiciousness with which psychoanalysis was viewed. By doing this and by teaching a course in psychoanalysis himself, Hall introduced psychoanalysis in the United States. In his later years interest in the psychology of religion led him to publish a volume of *Jesus, the Christ, in the Light of Psychology* (1917). Hall also pioneered in educational psychology, first through his public lectures on education in 1880, then by his child studies, by establishing a department of pedagogy at Clark University, and by providing an outlet for papers on educational psychology in his *Pedagogical Seminary*.

Biographic data: *DSB* 6:52; *IESS* 6:310–313; *NCAB* 39:469; G. S. Hall, *Life and Confessions of a Psychologist*, 1923; E. C. Sanford, Granville Stanley Hall. *American Journal of Psychology*, 1924, 35, 313–321; W. H. Burnham, The man, Granville Stanley Hall. *Psychological Review*, 1925, 32, 89–102; L. Pruette, *Granville Stanley Hall: A Biography of a Mind*, 1926

KLEMM, GUSTAV OTTO [419]

German psychologist
Rating: 20
Born: Leipzig, March 8, 1884
Died: Leipzig, January 5, 1939
Highest degree: Ph.D. in psychology, University of Leipzig, 1906, under W. Wundt [161]
Positions: 1906–1939, University of Leipzig

Klemm did laboratory research and wrote papers on a variety of psychological subjects. He also engaged in consulting and applied work out of Felix Krüger's [351] Institute at Leipzig and was a member of the Leipzig school of Ganzheitspsychologie headed by Krüger. Klemm did editorial work for several journals and was active within the German Psychological Society. Of the fifty-four titles in his bibliography by far the best known is his *Geschichte der Psychologie*, written in 1911. It was translated into English (1912) and several other languages and became highly popular. No other history of psychology was written in the German language for several decades.

Biographic data: *HPA* 3:153; G. W. Hartmann, Otto Klemm. *American Journal of Psychology*, 1939, 52, 308–309

MALINOWSKI, BRONISLAW KASPER [420]

Polish-British anthropologist
Rating: 22
Born: Cracow, Poland, April 7, 1884
Died: New Haven, Connecticut, May 16, 1942
Highest degree: Ph.D. in mathematics and physical sciences, University of Cracow, 1908; D.Sc. in anthropology, University of London, 1916

Positions, honors: 1914–1918, field work in anthropology in New Guinea and Melanesia; 1924–1942, University of London; 1939–1942, Yale University, visiting professor of anthropology; honorary D.Sc. Harvard University, 1936

Malinowski's work in anthropology centered on culture. He viewed culture as a system of collective habits that serves human needs. As man seeks satisfaction of his physiological drives, secondary drives arise that are also universal. The particular living conditions of a society give rise to motives derived from the secondary drives. All motives, however, rest basically on the physiological ones, and culture serves human needs. Malinowski found support for his views in psychology, especially in the ethnopsychology of Wundt [161], with whom he studied between 1908 and 1910, and in the work of Clark Hull [423], whose views also influenced him.

Malinowski acquired fame as a result of the thoroughness of his field work in the Trobriand Islands between 1914 and 1918. Of importance to psychology is his book, *Sex and Repression in Savage Society* (1927), which reports his observations on the sex mores of the Trobrianders. These observations failed to support the supposed universality and innate nature of some of the phenomena basic to Freud's psychology, notably the Oedipus conflict. Malinowski's observations paved the way for cross-cultural and eventually experimental testing of the tenets of the psychoanalytical theory.

Biographic data: *IESS* 9:541; P. Murdock, Bronislaw Malinowski. *American Anthropologist*, 1942, 45, 441–451

[421]

RANK, OTTO

Austrian psychoanalyst
Rating: 23
Born: Vienna, April 22, 1884
Died: New York, New York, October 31, 1939
Highest degree: Ph.D. in German philology, University of Vienna, 1912
Positions: Private practice; editorial work for *Imago* and *Internationale Zeitschrift für Psychoanalyse*, 1912–1924; founder and manager, Der Internationale Psychoanalytische Verlag, 1919–1924

Rank joined the psychoanalytic movement in the 1900s. He showed ability in applying Freudian concepts to the interpretation of mythology, art, dreams, and literary works, and was encouraged by Freud [224] to take a nonmedical degree. Rank became a member of the inner committee of six that guided the psychoanalytic movement.

Rank's early works were *Der Künstler und andere Beiträge zur Psychoanalyse des dichterischen Schaffens* (1907; English translation of an expanded version, *Art and Artist*, 1932), in which Freud's dream theory was used to explain artistic creation, *Der Mythus von der Geburt des Helden* (1909), and *Das Inzest-Motiv in Dichtung und Sage* (1912). After writing, with Hanns Sachs [399], *Die Bedeutung der Psychoanalyse für die Geisteswissenschaften* (1916), Rank published his most original contribution to psychoanalysis, *Das Trauma der Geburt* (1923; English translation, *The Trauma of Birth*, 1929), and began to interpret Freudian concepts in terms of birth trauma, the main points being that weaning causes anxiety because it represents separation from mother (as in birth), and that the male sexual urge represents the urge to return to the mother's womb. Rank's therapy consisted of helping the patient to reexperience the birth trauma. This reduced the duration of therapy to only weeks or months at most. While Freud tried to reconcile Rank's interpretations with his own theory as well as with the views of those that Rank opposed, Rank became disturbed by the conflict and left Vienna in 1924, settling in the United States three years before his death. Here he founded the Pennsylvania School of Social Work, in which his method of therapy was used. His last work was titled *Will Therapy* (English translation, 1936), which is one of the names of Rankian analysis.

Biographic data: *IESS* 13:314; J. Jones, Otto Rank: A forgotten heresy. *Commentary*, 1960(Sept), 30, 219–229

WELLS, FREDERICK LYMAN [422]

American psychologist
Rating: 11
Born: Boston, Massachusetts, April 22, 1884
Died: Belmont, Massachusetts, June 2, 1964
Highest degree: Ph.D. in psychology, Columbia University, 1906, under J. McK. Cattell [256]

Positions: 1907, assistant in pathological psychology, McLean Hospital, Waverly, Massachusetts; 1921–1938, chief, Psychological Laboratory, Boston Psychopathic Hospital; 1932–1950, assistant professor, Harvard Medical School; 1938–1950, psychologist, Department of Hygiene, Harvard University

Wells was a clinical psychologist under whose direction the first internship for psychologists in a mental hospital was established at the Boston Psychopathic Hospital in 1913. Wells's pioneering efforts in experimental psychopathology are documented in some of the approximately 150 psychological papers that Wells published. Wells's writing of *Mental Adjustments* (1917) marks the beginning of the "adjustment" literature that deals with the relationship between psychopathology and everyday life. In 1927, Wells provided one of the first summary accounts of the practice of clinical psychology (*Mental Tests in Clinical Practice*). In it, Wells criticized some of the common practices of the clinicians and was prophetic of the future development of clinical psychology. Wells was much interested in the use of psychological tests. Among his ventures in this field may be counted his revision of the Army Alpha test, first prepared during World War I (*Modified Alpha Examination*, 1941).

Biographic data: NCAB 51:155; L. F. Shaffer, Frederick Lyman Wells. *American Journal of Psychology*, 1964, 77, 679–682

HULL, CLARK LEONARD

American psychologist
Rating: 27
Born: Near Akron, New York, May 24, 1884
Died: New Haven, Connecticut, May 10, 1952
Highest degree: Ph.D. in psychology, University of Wisconsin, 1918, under V. A. C. Henmon
Positions: 1916, University of Wisconsin; 1927, Harvard University; 1929, Yale University; president, American Psychological Association, 1936

Hull's early interests in psychology were varied. He wrote a book on *The Evolution of Concepts* (1920), one on the *Influence of Tobacco Smoking on Mental and Motor Efficiency* (1924), one on *Aptitude Testing* (1928), and one on *Hypnosis and Suggestibility* (1933). The latter work in now a classic. In the 1930s, Hull became convinced that psychology could be an exact natural science and that behavior could be described in precise quantitative terms. He began research on conditioning, which he went about in a strictly systematic fashion, using the hypothetico-deductive method: logical statements clad in mathematical language were made, testable hypotheses deduced, tested empirically, and incorporated into the existing body of knowledge or revised and tested again. Hull at first limited this approach to rote learning (*Mathematico-deductive Theory of Rote Learning: A Study in Scientific Methodology*, 1940, coauthored with five others), but soon attempted to show that an objective, quantifiable general psychology was possible (*Principles of Behavior*, 1943). Hull modified his 1943 text eight years later (*Essentials of Behavior*, 1951) and extended it into *A Behavioral System* a year before his death.

Hull's system is highly quantified and elaborate. The early formulations of the theory stressed drive reduction as the main principle of learning. Later Hull began to emphasize drive stimulus reduction and secondary reinforcement. The reinforcement theme remained strong throughout his work. The theory proved to be very productive of research, although many of the more complicated postulates and corollaries were more programmatic than psychologically factual. Although his work was confined largely to learning, Hull's aim had always been to formulate a system of psychology in which all behaviors could be rigorously predicted. Hull provided much of the intellectual stimulus to a group of colleagues at Yale's Institute for Human Relations (Dollard, Miller, Mowrer, and Sears, among others). During his stay at Yale, Hull also put his stamp on his students, so that for a time one could speak of a Hullian school of psychology, at least in learning.

Biographic data: HPA 4:143; IESS 6:535; NCAB 41:69; K. W. Spence, Clark Leonard Hull. *American Journal of Psychology*, 1952, 65, 639–646; C. I. Hovland, Clark Leonard Hull. *Psychological Review*, 1952, 59, 347–350; F. A. Beach, Clark Leonard Hull. *Biographical Memoirs of the National Academy of Sciences*, 1959, 33, 125–141

KELLEY, TRUMAN LEE [424]

American psychologist
Rating: 21
Born: Whitehall, Michigan, May 25, 1884

Died: Santa Barbara, California, May 2, 1961
Highest degree: Ph.D. in psychology, Columbia University, 1914, under E. L. Thorndike [353]
Positions: 1914, University of Texas; 1917, Teachers College, Columbia University; 1920, Stanford University; 1931–1950, Harvard University

Kelley was a statistician and psychometrician who disagreed with Spearman's [274] approach to factor analysis by proposing the existence of group factors in addition to general and many specific factors, and thus a multiple-factor theory (*Crossroads in the Mind of Man: A Study of Differentiable Mental Abilities*, 1928). He also disagreed with Thurstone [448] on a number of points: he held that it was important to incorporate the value of a mental function in an analysis before executing it, so that important (useful) factors may be obtained rather than accurate but perhaps inconsequential ones; he analyzed the total variance of a correlation matrix rather than just the communalities; and favored orthogonal rotation rather than rotation to simple structure. Simultaneously with Hotelling, Kelley formulated the method of canonical correlation as well as his own form of the principal axes solution in factor analysis (*Essential Traits of Mental Life*, 1935). Kelley did much additional work on statistics, scaling and psychometrics, and individual differences in general. The books written by Kelley in these areas include *Educational Guidance* (1914), *Mental Aspects of Delinquency* (1917), *Statistical Method* (1923), *The Influence of Nurture Upon Native Differences* (1926), *Interpretation of Educational Measurements* (1927). *Tests and Measurements in the Social Sciences* (with A. C. Krey, 1934), *The Kelley Statistical Tables* (1938, 1948), *Fundamentals of Statistics* (1947), and *Stanford Achievement Test* (with others, 1953).

Biographic data: NCAB 49:443; IESS 8:358; [Anon.] Truman Lee Kelley. *British Journal of Statistical Psychology*, 1962, 15(1), 95–96

[425]

BLONSKII, PAVEL PETROVICH

Russian psychologist, educator, and philosopher
Rating: (unrated)
Born: May 26, 1884
Died: February 15, 1941

Education: Degree from the school of History and Philology,
University of Kiev, 1907
Positions: 1907–1913, psychology teacher in secondary schools,
Moscow; 1913, Moscow University; 1917, 1st and 2nd Moscow
Universities, Institute of Psychology

Blonskiĭ's *Ocherk nauchnoĭ psikhologii* (1921) was a first attempt
in the history of Soviet psychology to build a system of
materialistic psychology, based on dialectic materialism, the
evolutionary doctrine, and materialistic monism. In a collection
of essays, *Psikhologicheskie ocherki* (1927), Blonskiĭ wrote on
the evolution of consciousness, the nature of sleep, and on his
own research on the content of a base radical in the human saliva
as a function of the type of mental activity engaged in by the
subject. This paper led to additional research of the phenomenon
in the West. Blonskiĭ's most important psychological work was
Pamyat' i myshlenie (1935), a treatise on memory and thinking
that was complemented by a monograph on the development of
thinking in school children, *Razvitie myshleniya shkol'nika*
(1935). These works included Blonskiĭ's own research on thinking
in which he used the words "association technique." His *Ocherki
detskoĭ seksual'nosti* (1935) was a unique monograph in that,
with the exception of some published lectures and the *Book for
Parents* of the educator A. S. Makarenko, it was the only work in
Soviet education or psychology on sexual development and sex
education ever published. It continues to occupy that position.
Blonskiĭ wrote only twenty-seven articles, monographs, and
books in psychology, some of them in German, but his
educational writings contain much psychological material.

Biographic data: *Who Was Who in the USSR*, 1972

FLUGEL, JOHN CARL [426]

English psychologist
Rating: 16
Born: London, June 13, 1884
Died: London, August 17, 1955
Highest degree: D.Sc., University of London, 1908
Positions: 1909–1955, University College, London; president,
British Psychological Society, 1932–1935; secretary, Interna-
tional Psychoanalytical Association, 1919–1924

Flugel combined the academic psychologist with the psychoanalyst, believing that the two approaches, rather than being contradictory, had a common goal, a better understanding of human relations. He directed the work of the psychological laboratory of the University of London for over twenty years, but was as much interested in human and especially international relations. This attitude and his wide educational background enabled him to present psychoanalysis in a more objective and acceptable way than could many other adherents of Freud [224]. Flugel's first book, *The Psychoanalytic Study of the Family*, attracted much attention and introduced the concept of the Oedipus conflict to the general public. This was followed by a number of others: *Practice, Fatigue, and Oscillation* (1928), *The Psychology of Clothes* (1930), *An Introduction to Psychoanalysis* (1932), *Men and Their Motives* (1936), *Man, Morals, and Society* (1945), *Population, Psychology, and Peace* (1947), a total of about eighty publications. He is best known for a classic volume in the history of psychology. *A Hundred Years of Psychology: 1833-1933* (1933).

Biographic data: T. H. Pear, Dr. John Carl Flugel. *British Journal of Psychology*, 1956, 47, 1-4; R. W. Russell, John Carl Flugel. *American Journal of Psychology*, 1956, 69, 328-329; E. Jones, Obituary, J. C. Flugel. *International Journal of Psychoanalysis*, 1956, 37, 193-197

[427]

STRONG, EDWARD KELLOG, JR.

American psychologist
Rating: 20
Born: Syracuse, New York, August 18, 1884
Died: Menlo Park, California, December 4, 1963
Highest degree: Ph.D. in psychology, Columbia University, 1911, under J. McK. Cattell [256]
Positions: 1914, George Peabody College for Teachers; 1917, Army service; 1919, Carnegie Institute of Technology; 1923, Stanford University

Strong was prominent in vocational interest measurement. An industrial psychologist, Strong developed an *interest inventory*, the Strong Vocational Interest Blank (*Vocational Interests of Men and Women*, 1943; *Vocational Interests 18 Years After College*, 1955). It has been revised and extended several times, and is one of the most widely used interest inventories today. It compares the interest pattern of a person with the typical interest pattern for successful practitioners of many different occupations, and is used mainly in vocational counseling. The SVIB has been widely researched, and Strong himself wrote several research papers on it after the first appearance of the test. Strong's significance is measured by the thousands of young people who have been helped in their choice of a career through the use of the Strong Vocational Interest Blank.

Biographic data: *NCAB* 51:254; J. G. Darley, Edward Kellog Strong. *Journal of Applied Psychology*, 1964, 48(2), 73-74

KATZ, DAVID

German psychologist
Rating: 25
Born: Kassel, October 1, 1884
Died: Stockholm, Sweden, February 2, 1953
Highest degree: Ph.D. in psychology, University of Göttingen, 1906, under G. Müller [208]
Positions: 1906, University of Göttingen; 1919-1933, University of Rostock; 1937-1953, University of Stockholm; president, Thirteenth International Congress of Psychology, 1951

Katz was the first and prominent representative of experimental phenomenology in the 20th century. Although he was a student of Georg Müller's and worked for some time in the latter's laboratory after obtaining his doctorate, his researches were largely phenomenological. They yielded facts that were added to the store used by the Gestalt psychologists to argue their case. Katz himself sympathized with the Gestalt movement. He is best known for his study of the phenomenology of color. His important monograph on the modes of appearance of colors appeared in 1911 (Die Erscheinungsweisen der Farben und ihre Beeinflussung durch die individuelle Erfahrung, later published in book form as *Der Aufbau der Farbenwelt* (1930) and translated into English in 1935). Katz demonstrated that subjectively colors can be described as surface colors (those pertaining to objects), volume colors (such as those of colored liquids), and film colors (like the colors in a spectroscope), and that one mode of appearance may change into another, as when surface colors change to film colors when viewed through a small aperture and thereby lose the properties of the original mode, for instance, color constancy. Nativistic factors were stressed by Katz in his discussion of perceptual constancies, a phenomenon that runs as the main theme through his many and varied researches (he published more than one hundred titles, twenty of them books and monographs). In 1925, Katz's phenomenological study of touch (*Der Aufbau der Tastwelt*) appeared, similar in its conception to that of colors. Of Katz's books, some of the more significant ones are *Gespräche mit Kindern* (1927; English translation, *Conservations with Children*, 1936), *Hunger und Appetit* (English translation, *Hunger and Appetite*, 1932), and *Gestalt Psychology* (in Swedish, 1942).

Biographic data: *HPA* 4:189; *IESS* 8:352; T. H. Pear, David Katz. *British Journal of Psychology*, 1953, 44, 197–199; R. Arnheim, David Katz. *American Journal of Psychology*, 1953, **66**, 638–642; R. B. McLeod, David Katz. *Psychological Review*, 1954, **61**, 1–4

[429]

RORSCHACH, HERMANN

Swiss psychiatrist
Rating: 26
Born: Zurich, November 8, 1884
Died: Herisau, Appenzell-Ausser Rhoden, April 2, 1922
Highest degree: M. D., University of Zurich, 1912
Positions: 1913, post in a mental hospital in Russia; 1914, positions in four mental hospitals in Switzerland; vice-president, Swiss Psychoanalytic Society, 1919

Rorschach's life and work are completely overshadowed by the personality test he invented. Stimulus materials that are subject to different interpretation had been used previously to study imagination. Rorschach constructed symmetric ink blots to study personality structure, especially unconscious motivation. The need to measure unconscious phenomena arose from the work of Freud [224] and Jung [358]. The rationale behind the test is that, given an unstructured stimulus, the subject is more likely to reveal concealed, problematic, traumatic, or subconscious contents of his mind when describing what he sees in an inkblot than when asked direct questions about such matters. The test hinges on the interpretation of what is said, and lengthy training is required for a diagnostician to become proficient in the use of the test, even though Rorschach provided detailed scoring norms. Rorschach used the test beginning in 1911, but did not publish the ten ink blots that are presently being used, along with a manual, until 1921 (*Psychodiagnostics: A Diagnostic Test Based on Perception*, English translation, 1942). The test, as presently used, was developed by others. The *Rorschach ink blot test* was the first in a series of projective tests that were to appear afterwards. Even though there is serious doubt that the test is valid, it is being widely used, especially by those who consider personality to be an organic whole rather than a collection of traits. The published literature on the Rorschach test is enormous, and the inkblot has become so well known, even among laymen, that it is often used to represent all of psychology.

Biographic data: *IESS* 13:557; H. Ellenberger, The life and work of Hermann Rorschach (1884–1922). *Bulletin of the Menninger Clinic*, 1954, 18, 173-219

PINTNER, RUDOLF [430]

American psychologist
Rating: 18
Born: Lytham, Lancashire, England, November 16, 1884
Died: New York, New York, November 7, 1942
Highest degree: Ph.D. in psychology, University of Leipzig, 1913, under W. Wundt [161]
Positions: 1912, Toledo University; 1913, Ohio State University; 1921, Columbia University, Teachers College

While at Columbia, Pintner and his former student, Paterson, produced the Pintner-Paterson Scale of Performance Tests (*A Scale of Performance Tests*, 1917), an intelligence test intended for the deaf, the handicapped, and those whose native language was not English. It was the first major attempt to construct a series of performance tests with general norms. The scale consisted of fifteen subtests, some of which have been used repeatedly by others to construct similar scales. One-half of the Army Beta test items, for instance, came from it.

The construction of the performance test scale reflected one of Pintner's main concerns, the handicapped and especially the deaf child, and the improvement of his education. Pintner's scientific interests lay in the field of mental measurement, and his activity therein promoted the scientific study of individual differences in the United States. Pintner constructed several other tests, such as the Pintner-Durost Elementary Test (1941), Pintner Intermediate Test (1942), Pintner Advanced Test (1942), Pintner Non-Language Test (1945), and the Pintner-Cunningham Primary Test (1946). In 1923, he wrote *Intelligence Testing: Methods and Results*, and in 1941, *The Psychology of the Physically Handicapped* (with R. Eisenson and M. Stenton).

Biographic data: D. G. Paterson, Rudolf Pintner. *Journal of Consulting Psychology*, 1943, 7, 50–52; H. L. Hollingworth, Rudolf Pintner. *American Journal of Psychology*, 1943, 56, 303–305; S. Arsenian, *In memoriam: Rudolf Pintner*, 1953

[431]

HENNING, HANS

German psychologist
Rating: 20
Born: Strasbourg, February 15, 1885
Died: 1946
Highest degree: Ph.D., University of Strasbourg, 1910
Positions: 1914, University of Frankfurt; 1922, Technische Hochschule, Danzig

Henning is known for his research on smell. Up to 1915, the classification of smells used was that of Linnaeus [47], as modified by Zwaardemaker [233]. Although Henning kept most of the terms used by Linnaeus, he introduced (*Der Geruch*, 1916) a systematic conceptual change by placing all smells on the surfaces and edges of a prism (the Henning prism) whose six corners are the fragrant, putrid, ethereal, spicy, burned, and resinous smells. The essential features of the smell prism were subsequently verified experimentally by others. Henning also attempted to fit an organic chemistry to his prism. Although logically consistent, it, like all other attempts of this nature made after Henning, showed too many exceptions to claim that the smell stimulus had been finally identified. In a similar vein, Henning proposed a solution to the classification of the four basic tastes and how they relate to each other by placing them at the vertices of a tetrahedron and locating all intermediate tastes on its surfaces and edges. As in the case of smell, Henning also tried to fit a chemistry to his taste tetrahedron, with similar results.

Biographic data: *The Psychological Register*, 1932, vol. III

American psychologist
Rating: 16
Born: Speyer, Rhineland-Palatinate, Germany, April 28, 1885
Died: Boulder, Colorado, November 23, 1958
Highest degree: Ph.D. in psychology, University of Chicago, 1918
Positions: 1919–1922, industrial psychologist for Lakeside Press; 1923–1953, University of Colorado, assistant professor to chairman

At the University of Colorado, Muenzinger engaged in research on learning, working with rats in spite of his allergy to them. His contributions stem from carefully executed experimental studies rather than from theory building. Muenzinger's theoretical outlook was close to Tolman's [439]. The work on vicarious trial and error was done mainly by Muenzinger, while Tolman provided the theory. Muenzinger's researches were published in some forty papers. He also wrote an introductory text in psychology.

Biographic data: D. Krech, Karl Friedrich Muenzinger, *American Journal of Psychology*, 1959, 72, 477–479

Dutch physiologist
Rating: 13
Born: Brielle, June 6, 1885
Died: New Haven, Connecticut, June 9, 1940
Highest degree: M. D., University of Amsterdam, 1909
Positions: 1909, University of Amsterdam; 1911–1914, psychiatrist in a Meerenberg, Holland, asylum; 1919, professor of physiology at University of Utrecht and neurologist at St. Antonins Hospital, Utrecht; 1930, Yale University, Sterling professor of physiology; editorial work on *American Journal of Physiology* and *Journal of Neurophysiology* (also cofounder)

Dusser de Barenne became known for his work on the functional localization in the brains of cats, monkeys, and chimpanzees, for which he developed and used the technique of local strychninization. He contributed the chapter on the labyrinthine and postural mechanisms to the *Handbook of General Experimental Psychology* (1934).

Biographic data: *NCAB* 29:97; W. S. McCulloch, Joannes Gregorius Dusser de Barenne. *Yale Journal of Biology and Medicine,* 1940, 12, 742–746; J. F. Fulton & R. W. Gerard, Joannes Gregorius Dusser de Barenne. *Transactions of the American Neurological Association,* 1941, 67, 239–243

[434]

HORNEY, KAREN

German-American psychoanalyst
Rating: 23
Born: Hamburg, Germany, September 16, 1885
Died: New York, New York, December 4, 1952
Highest degree: M.D., University of Berlin, 1913
Positions: 1917, Institute for Psychoanalysis, Berlin; 1932, Chicago Institute for Psychoanalysis; 1934, New School for Social Research, New York; dean, American Institute of Psychoanalysis, 1941–1952

A neo-Freudian (she was a cofounder of the American Institute of Psychoanalysis), Horney accepted some tenets of the classical psychoanalytic theory, such as unconscious motivation and strict determinism, and rejected others, such as the primacy of biological and instinctive (sexual) factors in personality development and interpersonal relations. Horney's views resemble those of Adler [317] in that she stresses the role of the child's feelings of insecurity, his search for security and strivings for superiority, and the resulting conflict between attempted patterns of behavior, which may lead to neuroses. Her main theme is the development and expression of neurotic symptoms. Her view of the child-parent relationship allows for greater variability than in the classical psychoanalytic theory. The relationship does not always end in an Oedipus conflict but can be modified by a number of factors pertaining to the child's environment or his current fears, drives, and conflicts. The cultural context of a behavior can be crucial in that it can define the behavior as neurotic in one case and as adaptive in another. Horney was influential through her writing, especially in her books which are written in a style a nonspecialist can understand. Among them are

The Neurotic Personality of Our Time (1936), *New Ways in Psychoanalysis* (1939), *Self-Analysis* (1942), *Our Inner Conflicts* (1945), *and Neurosis and Human Growth* (1950).

Biographic data: *IESS* 6:513; N. Kelman. Karen Horney, M.D. *Psychoanalytic Review*, 1953, 40, 191–193; C. P. Oberndorf, Dr. Karen Horney. *International Journal of Psychoanalysis*, 1953, 34, 154–155

POPPELREUTER, WALTHER [435]

German psychologist
Rating: 16
Born: Saarbrücken, Saarland, 1886
Died: 1939
Highest degree: Ph.D. in psychology, University of Königsberg, 1909; M. D., University of Munich, 1915
Positions: 1919, University of Bonn; editorial work for *Zeitschrift für Psychologie, Psychotechnische Zeitschrift, Zeitschrift für Menschenkunde*

After writing *Die psychischen Schädigungen durch Kopfschuss*, (2 volumes, 1914–1918), the result of his experiences during World War I, Poppelreuter turned to industrial psychology, producing a number of publications in this area: *Allgemeine methodische Richtlinien der praktisch-psychologischen Begutachtung* (1923), *Zeitstudie und Betriebsüberwachung im Arbeitschaubild* (1929), *Leitsätze für den Zeitnehmer* (1929), and *Psychokritische Pädagogik* (1933). He later became an adherent of national socialism, producing such works as *Hitler als politischer Psychologe*. During his Bonn period, Poppelreuter founded and financed the Bonner Provinzialinstitut für klinische Psychologie, an institute of clinical psychology.

Biographic data: F. Baumgarten, Dr. phil. et méd. Walther Poppelreuter. *Travail humaine*, 1940, 8, 95–96

GUTHRIE, EDWIN RAY [436]

American psychologist
Rating: 26
Born: Lincoln, Nebraska, January 9, 1886

Died: Seattle, Washington, April 23, 1959

Highest degree: Ph.D. in philosophy, University of Pennsylvania, 1912

Positions, honors: 1914–1956, University of Washington, dean of Graduate School since 1943; LL.D., University of Nebraska, 1945; president, American Psychological Association, 1945; American Psychological Foundation Gold Medal, 1958

Guthrie worked in the fields of general psychology, social psychology, and the psychology of learning, but his most important contributions are in the latter field. Trained in philosophy, Guthrie combined the associationist doctrine with instrumental conditioning to formulate a new theory of learning (*The Psychology of Learning*, 1935, revised edition, 1952) that required only the contiguity of stimulus and response for learning to take place. "Stimuli acting at the time of a response tend on their reoccurrence to again evoke that response." The first significant theoretical paper introducing his ideas was "Conditioning as a principle of learning," published in 1930, which led to an attack by Pavlov [206] and a rebuttal by Guthrie, an exchange that placed Guthrie on the map.

Guthrie considered learning to be specific patterns of motor and glandular action called movements. When the learning situation remains ideal, only one trial is required for learning. Since, with each subsequent response, the stimulus situation is, however, slightly different, repetition may be necessary for learning to occur. Neither motivation nor reward are necessary conditions for learning, but are part of the stimulus pattern. Guthrie did not resort to any processes intervening between stimulus and response to explain learning. Reward forms a new stimulus set and prevents the formation of other associations. Extinction is the inhibition of an old response by subsequently learned one. *Cats in a Puzzle Box* (1946, with G. P. Horton) presents a specifically Guthrian notion, namely that of *stereotypy*. Once a particular movement pattern is learned, the tendency is to repeat it exactly.

Guthrie did not establish a formal, but rather an informal theoretical system. He deliberately avoided formalization, supporting his theoretical statements not by research findings but illustrations, actual or anecdotal, from everyday life. Guthrie also established for himself a reputation in abnormal psychology when he published *The Psychology of Human Conflict* (1938), in which he favored Janet's [249] views over those of the psychoanalysts.

Biographic data: IESS 6:296; F. D. Sheffield, Edwin Ray Guthrie. *American Journal of Psychology*, 1959, 72, 642–650

Russian psychologist
Rating: (unrated)
Born: Chukhlom, Kostroma province, January 21, 1886
Died: Leningrad, May 13, 1959
Highest degree: Doctor of medicine, University of Kazan, 1915
Positions, honors: 1911, University of Kazan; 1915–1917, military physician; 1921–1932, Leningrad Institute of Experimental Medicine, also Herzen State Teachers Training Institute; 1923–1928, Red Army physiological laboratories; 1925–1930, editor of *Trudy fiziologicheskikh laboratorii akademika Pavlova*; 1927, Leningrad University, in chair of physiology 1928–1940; 1932–1951, head of physiology departments of four medical and physiological research institutions; 1950, director, Pavlov Institute of Physiology, USSR Academy of Sciences; editor of numerous scientific publications, president of scientific societies; numerous orders, medals, and prizes

In 1926, Bykov and I. A. Alekseev-Berkman reported the first data on the formation of of conditioned urinary reflexes. In 1928, Bykov demonstrated that an interoceptive conditioned stimulus could cause a conditioned contraction of the striped muscles in dogs. He did a great deal of work on conditioning, especially interoceptive conditioning, afterwards. Bykov worked under Pavlov [206] between 1921 and 1932, publishing his main monographs in the 1940s: *The Cerebral Cortex and the Internal Organs* (2nd edition, 1944; English translation, 1957) and *The Corticovisceral Theory of the Pathogenesis of Peptic Ulcers* (1949, with I. T. Kurtsin; English translation, 1966). He published a total of some six hundred papers, directing fifty-five candidate (Ph.D.) and thirty-five doctoral theses.

In 1950, Bykov was instrumental in the "pavlovization" of Soviet science. Between June 28 and July 4, 1950, he served as the chairman of the Scientific Council on Pavlov's Physiological Theory of the USSR Academy of Sciences, and was one of the main speakers at the joint session of the USSR Academy of Sciences and the USSR Academy of Medical Sciences at which the development and application of Pavlov's doctrine was urged on physiologists and psychologists, and where the school of physiology represented by L. A. Orbeli and I. S. Beritashvili was denounced.

Biographic data: *Who Was Who in the USSR*, 1972; I. T. Kurtsin, K 70-letiyu so dnya rozhdeniya i 45-letiyu nauchnoĭ, pedagogicheskoĭ i obshchestvennoĭ deyatel'nosti Akademika K. M.

Bykova. *Zhurnal vyssheĭ nervnoĭ deyatel'nosti,* 1956, 6, 346–351; A. V. Solov'ev, Konstantin Mikhaĭlovich Bykov. *Zhurnal vyssheĭ nervnoĭ deyatel'nosti,* 1959, 9, 637–640

[438]

KOFFKA, KURT

German-American psychologist
Rating: 27
Born: Berlin, Germany, March 18, 1886
Died: Northampton, Massachusetts, November 22, 1941
Highest degree: Ph.D. in psychology, University of Berlin, 1909, under C. Stumpf [202]
Positions: 1911, University of Giessen; 1927, Smith College

Koffka was one of the founders of the Gestalt school of psychology. Before 1910, when he came in contact with Max Wertheimer [391], Koffka had studied imagery and thought with Stumpf. In 1910, Koffka and Wolfgang Köhler [447] served as subjects in a crucial experiment of Wertheimer's. A year later, Wertheimer explained the significance of the experiment to Köhler and Koffka. They immediately accepted Wertheimer's ideas, and became cofounders, with Wertheimer, of one of the major schools of psychology. These three, with Kurt Goldstein [380] and Hans Gruhle [397], founded the organ of the school, *Psychologische Forschung,* in 1921.

During his years at Giessen, Koffka wrote *Die Grundlagen der psychischen Entwicklung* (1921; English translation, *The Growth of the Mind,* 1927). In this book Koffka applied Gestalt notions to the problems of developmental psychology. While the Gestalt psychologists leaned in their theorizing more toward nativistic than empiricist explanations, Koffka stressed the interaction between innate capacities and environmental conditions, calling it the *convergence theory of development* (after William Stern [328], who had formulated the idea originally). Koffka extended the convergence principle to all psychological events, holding that there was a convergence of inner and outer factors in all such events. Reflexes, instincts, and learning were discussed by Koffka in Gestalt terms. Like Köhler, Koffka stressed the insightful nature of learning, to the point of denying that trial and error was a meaningful explanation of learning except in situations which allow no other alternative.

Of the three founders of Gestalt psychology, Koffka was the most prolific writer. He was also a propagandizer of the Gestalt theory. Before coming to the United States, Koffka wrote a long series of papers on Gestalt psychology, an article for the *Psychological Bulletin* in 1922 to introduce Gestalt psychology to Americans, and made several visits to the United States. He later wrote a comprehensive, ambitious, and difficult statement on Gestalt psychology, presenting it as a complete theory of behavior. The book, *Principles of Gestalt Psychology* (1935), is the only such presentation extant and a classic of psychological literature.

Biographic data: *EP* 4:353; *IESS* 8:435; W. Köhler, Kurt Koffka. *Psychological Review*, 1942, **49**, 97–101; M. R. Harrower-Erikson, Kurt Koffka, *American Journal of Psychology*, 1942, **55**, 278–281

TOLMAN, EDWARD CHACE   [439]

American psychologist
Rating: 27
Born: West Newton, Massachusetts, April 14, 1886
Died: Berkeley, California, November 19, 1959
Highest degree: Ph.D. in psychology, Harvard University, 1915, under E. B. Holt [348]
Positions, honors: 1915, Northwestern University; 1918–1954, University of California at Berkeley; president, American Psychological Association, 1937; American Psychological Association Distinguished Scientific Contribution Award, 1957

Tolman brought to psychology a systematic theory of learning that stressed cognitive factors. While basically behavioristic, the theory emphasizes significant units of behavior ("molar" behavior) rather than elementary reflexes ("molecular" behavior). Although Tolman was dissatisfied with the overly simple behavioristics of Watson [374], he developed his systematic views on the basis of his studies of maze learning in rats. Tolman, however, was also influenced by Gestalt psychology, and his theory of purposive behaviorism is a blend of neobehaviorism and Gestalt notions . *Purposive Behavior in Animals and Men* (1932) was Tolman's great work. It contains a glossary of 123 terms, many of them neologisms, that Tolman used to describe his theory.

The rat in a maze, instead of learning stimulis-response chains, learns sign Gestalten. These are cognitive representations of what leads to what. A pattern of such Gestalten is a cognitive map. It enables the animal to run a learned maze even when the stimulis-response connections no longer obtain, for instance, when other responses must be employed to obtain food, such as swimming in a flooded maze. Rats (and man) act for an end, i.e., with a purpose. Tolman, true to an objective and behavioristic psychology, never discussed purpose in teleological terms but rather as a descriptive term applicable to what the rats were doing in the maze. Disturbance in an animal when a different reward is given, search for food when none is found, and the results of latent learning experiments were used by Tolman as evidence that cognitive expectations constituted the essence of learning, not conditioned responses. Expectations allow for the substitution of responses when necessary, which is what is observed in animal learning rather than strictly stereotyped sequences of behavior. Latent learning experiments led Tolman to the conclusion that a distinction must be made between learning as acquisition and learning as performance. For learning as acquisition no reward is necessary. To establish whether learning has actually occured, perfomance of the learned task must be shown, for which reward is a prerequisite. Tolman called learning as acquisition an intervening variable, a concept that he introduced in American psychology and one that has been universally accepted. Intervening variables he called objective but unobservable variables that could be defined in terms of observable antecedent conditions and observable response.

Biographic data: *HPA* 4:323; *IESS* 16:95; *NCAB* F:327; R. S. Crutchfield, D. Krech, & R. C. Tyron, Edward Chace Tolman: A life of scientific and social purpose. *Science*, 1960, 131, 714–716; R. S. Crutchfield, Edward Chace Tolman. *American Journal of Psychology*, 1961, 74, 135–141; B. F. Ritchie, Edward Chace Tolman. *National Academy of Sciences Biographical Memoirs*, 1964

[440]

HOLLINGWORTH, LETA STETTER

American educator and psychologist
Rating: 12
Born: Near Chadron, Nebraska, May 25, 1886

Died: New York, New York, November 27, 1939
Highest degree: Ph.D. in education, Columbia Teachers College,
  1916
Positions: 1916–1939, Columbia Teachers College

Hollingworth's main interest was in individual, sex, and groups differences. Her research and investigations done between 1914 and 1920 are presented in *The Psychology of Subnormal Children* (1920) and *Special Talents and Defects* (1923). She realized that problem children suffer not only from lower intelligence but emotional problems as well, and that emotionsl problems play an even greater role in adolescence. Her research on the adolescent is summarized in *The Psychology of Adolescence* (1928), which was a standard text for a number of years. The discovery of gifted children among maladjusted ones led to her interest in gifted children. They became her focus of interest for the rest of her life. Hollingworth published seventy-five articles, of which about forty-five are concerned with giftedness. A major discovery and concern of hers was that giftedness does not preclude maladjustment (*Gifted Children,* 1926). Hollingworth became a champion of the cause of the gifted, as well as of clinical psychology, in which area she especially tried to raise the standards of test administration and of test administrators.

Biographic data: A. I. Gates, Leta Stetter Hollingworth. *Science,* 1940, 91, 9-11; A. T. Poffenberger, Leta Stetter Hollingworth. *American Journal of Psychology*, 1940, 53, 299-301; H. L. Hollingworth, *Leta Stetter Hollingworth, A Biography,* 1943; *Notable American Women 1607–1950,* 1971, vol. 2

GOODENOUGH, FLORENCE LAURA [441]

American psychologist
Rating: **20**
Born: Honesdale, Pennsylvania, August 6, 1886
Died: Saint Paul, Minnesota, April 4, 1959
Highest degree: Ph.D. in psychology, Stanford University, 1924,
  under L. Terman [368]
Positions: 1924, Minneapolis Child Guidance Clinic; 1925, Institute of Child Welfare, University of Minnesota

Goodenough was a prominent worker in the area of child psychology and child development. She is best known for her study of intelligence and children's drawings. In *Measurement of Intelligence by Drawings* (1926), Goodenough presented her *Draw-a-Man Test*, a non language intelligence test for children in which the subject is instructed to make a picture of a man and intelligence is evaluated in terms of the completeness of the drawing. In the 1940s it was the third most widely used psychometric instrument, and is still in use today. Goodenough wrote a number of papers on the subject of intelligence testing and related matters, as well as *Minnesota Preschool Scales* (1940, with K. M. Maurer and M. J. Van Wagenen), *The Mental Growth of Children from Two to Fourteen Years* (1942, with K. M. Maurer), and *Mental Testing* (1949).

Biographic data: The Psychological Register, 1932, vol. III

[442]

RUCKMICK, CHRISTIAN ALBAN

American psychologist
Rating: 17
Born: New York, New York, September 4, 1886
Died: Miami, Florida, 1961
Highest degree: Ph.D. in psychology, Cornell University, 1913
Positions: 1913, University of Illinois; 1921, Wellesley College; 1924, State University of Iowa; 1939, C. H. Stoelting Co., sales manager; 1942, U.S. Army Induction Station, Peoria, Illinois, chief civilian psychologist; 1943–1946, various training positions; 1946, superintendent of education, Ministry of Education, Ethiopia; 1952–1955, Univeristy of Miami

In psychological research, Ruckmick produced some one hundred publications on a wide variety of subjects. A considerable portion of his papers were on audition, GSR and emotion, and rhythm. Ruckmick invented the *affectometer* and other scientific instruments, but his main work was in connection with psychological publications and editorial activities. Books written by Ruckmick include *The Brevity Book on Psychology* (1920), *German-English Dictionary of Psychological Terms* (1928), *The Mental Life* (1928), *The Emotional Responses of Children to the Motion Picture Situation* (1933, with W. S. Dysinger), and *Psychology of Feeling and Emotion* (1936).

Biographic data: The Psychological Register, 1932, vol. III

Danish psychologist

Rating: 27

Born: Copenhagen, September 6, 1886

Died: Copenhagen, May 3, 1951

Highest degree: Ph.D. in psychology, University of Copenhagen, 1915.

Positions: 1916, University of Copenhagen, director of Psychological Laboratory since 1922; president, Tenth International Congress of Psychology, 1932

Rubin made a direct contribution to the raw material of which Gestalt psychology was made. His name is associated with the figure-ground phenomenon. Rubin started his research on this phenomenon in 1912. A first report on it was published in German in the proceedings of the Sixth Congress of Experimental Psychology, then in Danish (*Synslopevede figurer*, 1915), and finally, again in German, but in a monograph from (*Visuell wahrgenommene Figuren*, 1921). Rubin analyzed visual perception in terms of its two basic components, figure and ground. Figure is that which one pays attention to, which has a "thingness" about it, while the ground is that formless, less conspicuous extent upon which the figure is seen. Rubin's phenomenological analysis of figure-ground relationships and his demonstrations, the phenomenologist's *experimenta crucis*, of the role of attention in the perception of ambiguous, figure-ground reversal pictures ("vase-profile," "finger-claw") made his work eminently suitable material for Gestalt-theoretical analysis. In a paper presented in the early 1930s, however, Rubin denied the need for the concept of attention and attempted to explain figure-ground phenomena solely in terms of the structural properties of the visual field. Following his lead, Gestalt psychologists dropped the term in their writings until about 1960. The figure-ground concept is now part of general psychology, with usually no reference made to Rubin. It is applicable not only to the visual sense modality but all other modalities as well.

In addition to the figure-ground phenomenon, Rubin is also noted for the discovery, simultaneously with but independently of Goldscheider [244], of paradoxical warmth: he reported that stimuli just below skin temperature produced a weak sensation of warmth when applied to "warm" receptors. Rubin also studied visually perceived movement (1927) and other perceptual phenomena. Until his death, Rubin was Denmark's most distinguished psychologist.

Biographic data: D. Katz, Edgar Rubin. *Psychological Review,* 1951, 58, 387–388; W. C. H. Prentice, Edgar John Rubin. *American Journal of Psychology,* 1951, 64, 608–609

[444]

BARTLETT, SIR FREDERICK CHARLES

English psychologist
Rating: (unrated)
Born: Stow-on-the-Wold, Gloucestershire, October 20, 1886
Died: Cambridge, September 30, 1969
Highest degree: M.A. in moral sciences, University of Cambridge; mentors in psychology: W. H. R. Rivers [278] and C. S. Myers [341].
Positions, honors: 1922–1952, Cambridge University, reader in experimental psychology, director of psychology laboratory, first professor of experimental psychology; honorary doctorates from seven universities; editor, *British Journal of Psychology,* 1924–1948; knighted 1948

By heading one of the few British graduate programs in psychology for many years and by editing for twenty-four years the most significant British journal of psychology, Bartlett influenced the course of British psychology as an administrator and an educator. In his personal research, Bartlett is best known for his studies of memory and social psychology. His most significant and influential work is *Remembering* (1944), which examines the influence of social factors on memory in an experimental setting. Instead of the traditional nonsense syllables, Bartlett used meaningful materials to study the effects of past experience on the assimilation of materials. He showed how individuals, instead of merely reproducing the materials, reworked them in the light of their past experience. The notion of schema or a conceptual model originated with Bartlett. Although the schema is constantly changing, every new experience is absorbed by way of this preexisting model. While others found the schema idea a fruitful one, Bartlett seldom referred to it in his later writings. Bartlett's book marked a break with the German tradition in psychology and the advent of methods to study higher thought processes without the use of introspection. Other books written by Bartlett were *Psychology and Primative Culture* (1923), (with

C. S. Meyers) *Textbook of Experimental Psychology* (1925), *Psychology and the Soldier* (1927), *Political Propaganda* (1941), *The Problem of Noise* (1934), *The Mind at Work and Play* (1951), and *Thinking: An experimental and Social Study* (1958).

Biographic data: HPA 3:39; IESS 2:19; D. E. Broadbent, Sir Frederick Bartlett: An appreciation. *Bulletin of British Psychological Society,* 1970, 23(78), 1–3; O. L. Zangwill, Obituary notice: Sir Frederick Bartlett. *Quarterly Journal of Experimental Psychology,* 1970, **22**, 77–81; R. B. Buzzard, Sir Frederick Bartlett. *Occupational Psychology,* 1971, 45(1), 1–11; R. C. Oldfield, Frederick Charles Bartlett. *American Journal of Psychology,* 1972, 85, 133–140

BORING, EDWIN GARRIGUES [445]

American psychologist
Rating: (unrated)
Born: Philadelphia, Pennsylvania, October 23, 1886
Died: Cambridge, Massachusetts, July 1, 1968
Highest degree: Ph.D. in psychology, Cornell University, 1914, under E. B. Titchener [294]
Positions, honors: 1919, Clark University; 1922–1956, Harvard University; 1957–1968 Edgar Pierce Professor Emeritus; president, American Psychological Association, 1928; editor, *American Journal of Psychology,* 1920–1968; founder and editor, *Contemporary Psychology,* 1956–1961; president, Seventeenth International Congress of Psychology, 1963; American Psychological Foundation Gold Medal, 1959; two honorary Sc.D. degrees

Boring was a general-experimental psychologist who did research on a wide spectrum of phenomena. Some of the papers stemming from this work are classics, such as the paper on visceral sensitivity (1915), the moon illusion (1940), and visual size (1941). Boring wrote 176 papers, 202 editorials, and 45 book reviews. Only relatively few of the papers are papers on his own research. Most of them are theoretical, as is his book on *The Physical Dimensions of Consciousness* (1933), in which Boring discusses basic terms in psychology, such as consciousness and sensation, and shows how psychology could operate without reference to the body-mind dualism. The book marked his veering away from Titchenerian dualism toward a monism. Boring is best known for his work as a historian of psychology, however, He first published his *History of Experimental Psychology* in 1929. The theme of this book was the interaction between the spirit of the times and the individual scientist that spells out scientific development. The book soon became a classic. In 1950, the second edition of the text appeared, which is still the outstanding volume on the history of psychology. Boring's influence on generations of psychologists has been largely by way of his history book and his teaching of psychology at Harvard, especially of Psychology One, the introductory course. Boring's other historical text, *Sensation and Perception in the History of Experimental Psychology* (1942), while it brings together a prodigious amount of information, has had a much lesser impact. Because of his long association with general psychology and Harvard University, Boring became also well known outside of psychology, and was often referred to as "Mr. Psychology" in the popular press.

Biographic data: *HPA* 4:27; *IESS* 2:126; E. G. Boring, *Psychologist at Large*, 1961; S. S. Stevens, Edwin Garrigues Boring. *American Journal of Psychology*, 1968, 81, 589–606; J. Jaynes, Edwin Garrigues Boring. *Journal of History of the Behavioral Sciences*, 1969, 5(2), 99–112; A. Mace, Edwin Garrigues Boring: An appreciation. *Bulletin of the British Psychological Society*, 1969, 22(75), 99–100

[446] **UZNADZE, DIMITRII NIKOLAEVICH**

Georgian psychologist
Rating: (unrated)
Born: January 1, 1887
Died: Tblisi, Georgia, October 12, 1950
Highest degree: Ph.D., University of Leipzig, 1909
Positions: 1918, University of Tblisi; 1930, Pedagogical Institute, Tblisi

Uznadze, the most prominent Georgian psychologist, was a cofounder of the University of Tblisi in 1918. He established a Department of Psychology and an experimental psychology laboratory at that university. In 1941, he founded the Georgian Institute of Psychology under the auspices of the Georgian Academy of Sciences, one of the very few such institutes in the

USSR. After his death it was named the Uznadze Institute of Psychology to honor him for his scientific achievements.

Uznadze's main contribution to psychology was his theory of set. Originally applied to perception to explain deviation in perception away from the physical stimulus characteristics under the influence of the perceiver's set established by previous experience, expectations, instructions, and the like, the theory was expanded by Uznadze to account for most behaviors. The theory continues to be developed by Uznadze's students and coworkers. The Georgian school of psychology is based on Uznadze's theory. Uznadze also worked in the area of child psychology, especially the development of thinking.

Uznadze wrote several psychological texts in the Georgian language ([Fundamentals of Experimental Psychology], 1925; [General Psychology], 1940; [Child Psychology], 1947), including the first psychology text ever written in that language. He was also author of a number of papers and monographs in German. Russian translations of his work in connection with theory of set include *Eksperimental'nye osnovy psikhologii ustanovki* (1961) and *Psikhologischeskie issledovaniya* (1966).

Biographic data: *The Psychological Register*, 1932, vol. III

KOHLER, WOLFGANG

German-American psychologist
Rating: 27
Born: Revel, Estonia, January 21, 1887
Died: Enfield, New Hampshire, June 11, 1967
Highest degree: Ph.D. in psychology, University of Berlin, 1909, under C. Stumpf [202]
Positions, honors: 1910, University of Frankfurt; 1913, Anthropoid Station, Tenerife; 1920, University of Berlin; 1921, University of Göttingen; 1922, University of Berlin; 1935, Swarthmore College; president, American Psychological Association, 1959; American Psychological Association Distinguished Scientific Contribution Award, 1956

Köhler was one of the founders of the Gestalt school of psychology. Before 1910, when he came in contact with Max Werthcimer [391], Köhler had done important work with Stumpf on the perception of tones. In 1910, Köhler and Kurt

Koffka [438] served as subjects in a crucial experiment of Wertheimer's. A year later, Wertheimer explained the significance of the experiment to Koffka and Köhler. They immediately accepted Wertheimer's ideas, and became cofounders, with Wertheimer, of one of the major schools of psychology. The three of them, plus Kurt Goldstein [380] and Hans Gruhle [397] founded the organ of the school, *Psychologische Forschung,* in 1921. Köhler subsequently wrote several books presenting aspects of the Gestalt school of psychology: *Gestalt Psychology* (1929), *The Place of Value in a World of Facts* (1938), and *Dynamics in Psychology* (1940).

A major contribution of Köhler's was his work with chicks and chimpanzees in the Canary Islands during World War I. Köhler demonstrated the perception of and response to relationships (rather than absolute stimulus values) in chicks (later known as transposition) and insight learning (closure over psychological gaps) in chimpanzees. *Intelligenzprüfungen an Menschenaffen* (1917, English translation, *The Mentality of Apes,* 1924) was one outcome of his studies. They later led to much research and controversy over whether learning could be insightful or had to proceed by trial and error.

A second major contribution of Köhler's was the postulation of the principle of isomorphism. In a classic monograph, published in 1920 (*Die physischen Gestalten in Ruhe und im stationären Zustand*), Köhler first expanded Wertheimer's idea that in order to perceive actual and apparent movement as the same, brain processes in themselves must show properties of patterning or be *Gestalten* (configurations, structures). Köhler theorized that *Gestalten* exist not only mentally but physically as well. There is a correspondence in form between physical events in the brain, Köhler said, and the subjective events caused by them. The postulation of electrical fields in the brain, topologically equivalent to percepts, led to a well-publicized exchange of opinion and neurological experiments. While the existence of brain fields was never satisfactorily demonstrated, the field concept has been utilized and developed by individuals sympathetic to the Gestalt school (such as Kurt Lewin [468]) and others. A related line of enquiry that developed from the field theory concerned figural aftereffects, in which area a substantial literature has developed because of its theoretical importance to the question of how the brain works. The figural aftereffect phenomenon was first described and explained in terms of satiation of brain electrical fields in a paper written by Köhler and H. Wallach in 1944.

Biographic data: *EP* 4:354; *IESS* 8:438; S. E. Asch, Wolfgang Köhler. *American Journal of Psychology,* 1968, 81, 110–119

American psychologist
Rating: 27
Born: Chicago, Illinois, May 29, 1887
Died: Chapel Hill, North Carolina, September 29, 1955
Highest degree: Ph.D. in psychology, University of Chicago, 1917
Positions, honors: 1917, Carnegie Institute of Technology; 1924, University of Chicago; 1952, University of North Carolina; president, American Psychological Association, 1933; first president of the Psychometric Society; honorary doctorate, University of Göteborg, 1954

Thurstone was the most eminent psychometrician of his time. Thurstone's main contributions lie in the area of the application of statistics to psychological problems. In the United States, the development of the technique of factor analysis is connected mainly with his name (*Vectors of the Mind,* 1935; *Factorial Studies of Intelligence,* 1941; *Multiple Factor Analysis,* 1947). Thurstone factor-analyzed intelligence tests and tests of perception. In the area of intelligence, Thurstone's theory was that intelligence is made up of several primary mental abilities rather than a general and several specific factors. Spearman's [274] general factor he considered to be a second-order factor obtainable from a factor analysis of the first-order factors: verbal ability, number, spatial ability, perceptual ability, memory, reasoning, and word fluency. Thurstone's primary mental abilities (*Primary Mental Abilitiies,* 1938) have been used to construct intelligence tests which, unlike the general intelligence tests that yield a single score, yield a profile of the individual's performance on each of the ability tests.

The *law of comparative judgments in psychophysics* was a contribution that Thurstone himself considered to be his best. By introducing the concept of the discriminal dispersion, Thurstone produced a mathematical model that accounted for a set of comparative judgments made by a number of judges. Another contribution of Thurstone's was the construction of the earliest *attitude scale.* The scale was based on a modification of the psychophysical method of equal-appearing intervals. A series of statements on some subject are judged by a large number of judges. A person's score on the scale is the mean of scaled values of those items with which he agrees. The introduction of attitude scales did much to introduce quantification in social psychology

(*Measurement of attitudes,* 1929). Thurstone authored 23 books and monographs, 165 articles, 95 laboratory reports, and 47 tests.

Biographic data: HPA 4:295; *IESS* 16:22; D. A. Wood, *Louis Leon Thurstone,* 1962; D. C. Adkins, Louis Leon Thurstone: creative thinker, dedicated teacher, eminent psychologist. In N. Frederiksen & H. Gulliksen (Eds.), *Contributions to Mathematical Psychology,* 1964, pp. 1–39; D. Wolfle, Louis Leon Thurstone. *American Journal of Psychology,* 1956, 69, 131–134; J. P. Guilford, Louis Leon Thurstone. *Psychometrika,* 1955, 20, 263–265; P. Horst, Louis Leon Thurstone and the science of human behavior. *Science,* 1955, 122, 1259–1260; C. Burt, Professor Louis Leon Thurstone. *British Journal of Statistical Psychology,* 1956, 9, 1–4; H. Gulliksen, A tribute to Louis Leon Thurstone. *Psychometrika,* 1956, 21, 309–312; J. P. Guildford, Louis Leon Thurstone. *National Academy of Sciences Biographical Memoirs,* 1957, 30, 348–382

[449]

FERNBERGER, SAMUEL WEILLER

American psychologist
Rating: 18
Born: Philadelphia, Pennsylvania, June 4, 1887
Died: Philadelphia, May 2, 1956
Highest degree: Ph.D. in psychology, University of Pennsylvania, 1912, under F. M. Urban [313]
Positions: 1912, Clark University; 1920, University of Pennsylvania; editorial work for *Psychological Bulletin* (1918–1930), *Journal of Experimental Psychology* (1930–1946), and *American Journal of Psychology* (1925–1956)

Fernberger was a psychophysicist, but he contributed to many different fields in psychology. In psychophysics, several of his papers are classics. In 1914, he showed, for instance, that by changing the observer's attitude toward perceiving difference, the category of "equal" in the constant stimulus method may be eliminated. Most of his work in psychophysics was on lifted weights using the constant stimulus method. Fernburger wrote several oft-cited papers on facial expression in emotion, memory span, and the range of visual apprehension. He also did several statistical studies in the history of psychology and of the professional activities of psychologists. Fernberger wrote one book, an *Elementary General Psychology* (1936).

Biographic data: F. W. Irvin, Samuel Weiller Fernberger. *American Journal of Psychology*, 1956, 69, 676–680

BENEDICT, RUTH FULTON

[450]

American anthropologist
Rating: 16
Born: New York, New York, June 5, 1887
Died: New York, New York, September 17, 1948
Highest degree: Ph.D. in anthropology, Columbia University, 1923, under Franz Boas [243]
Positions, honors: 1922–1948, Columbia University; president, American Anthropological Association, 1947; honorary D.Sc

Benedict played a significant role in the development of an interdisciplinary approach to human behavior. The part of her work that is important to psychology is her theoretical writings on the relationship between personality and cultural forms, including the phenomena of deviancy and creativity. *Patterns of Culture* (1934), her best known work, has seen many editions and translations into other languages. Its theme, culture and personality, is treated in an analysis of three cultures, each dominated by a single motive. Here Benedict applies to groups, concepts reserved for the individual (group psychology): each culture selects a certain human characteristic and develops it to an extent impossible for a single individual.

Biographic data: *IESS* 2:48–52; *NCAB* 36:469; H. S. Sullivan, Ruth Fulton Benedict, Ph.D., D.Sc., 1887–1948. *Psychiatry*, 1948, 11, 402–403

DALLENBACH, KARL M.

[451]

American psychologist
Rating: (unrated)
Born: Champaign, Illinois, October 20, 1887
Died: Austin, Texas, December 24, 1971

Highest degree: Ph.D. in psychology, Cornell University, 1913, under E. B. Titchener [294]

Positions: 1913, University of Oregon; 1915, Ohio State University; 1916, Cornell University; 1948, University of Texas, professor, later chairman of Psychology Department

Of those students of Wundt's [161] who remained most faithful to him, Titchener was the most prominent. Dallenbach held the same relationship to Titchener. Dallenbach felt that psychology's first business was experimentation, although he did not necessarily use introspection as his main tool. Like Titchener, his main interest lay in sensation and perception. Dallenbach did not develop any major theories and he never wrote a book. He did contribute, however, almost 250 papers. Of these, almost 100 were contributions to scientific thought or new experimental data, most of them on sensation and perception, but also on attention, memory, and cognitive processes. His studies on facial vision and on retention during sleep belong to the classical psychological literature. A physical monument to Dallenbach the experimentalist is the psychological laboratory at the University of Texas, Mezes Hall, designed by Dallenbach and the building of which he supervised.

A contribution that is considered by some to have been an even greater one was Dallenbach's purchase, from G. Stanley Hall [418], and consequent rescue of the first American psychological journal, the *American Journal of Psychology,* in 1920. Dallenbach was the owner of this journal for the next forty-eight years and editor for forty-two. His involvement with the journal was such that he referred to its volumes as his "books."

Biographic data: *HPA* 5:59; E. G. Boring, Karl M. Dallenbach. *American Journal of Psychology,* 1958, 71, 1–40; R. B. Evans, Karl M. Dallenbach. *American Journal of Psychology,* 1972, 85, 463–476

[452]

GELB, ADHEMAR MAXIMILIAN MAURICE

German psychologist

Rating: 15

Born: Moscow, Russia, November 18, 1887

Died: Schömberg, Baden-Württemberg, Germany, August 7, 1936

Highest degree: Ph.D. in psychology, University of Berlin, 1910, under C. Stumpf [202]

Positions: 1909, University of Berlin; 1912, Academy of Social Sciences, Frankfurt am Main; 1915, Frankfurt Hospital for Brain Damaged; 1919, University of Frankfurt, director of Institute of Psychology since 1929; 1931–1933, University of Halle, teaching philosophy

Gelb was a Gestalt-oriented psychologist whose work with Kurt Goldstein [380] on soldiers with brain lesions resulted in numerous papers on the effect of brain damage on perception, speech, and color vision, as well as the book, coauthored with Goldstein, *Psychologische Analysen Hirnpathologischer Fälle* (1920). Gelb also did research on figure-ground. He is the discoverer of the *Gelb phenomenon* that a spot of colored light has a higher threshold when projected inside a figure than when projected upon the adjacent ground.

Biographic data: *The Psychological Register,* 1932, vol. III

MURCHISON, CARL   ⌈453⌉

American psychologist
Rating: 20
Born: Hickory, North Carolina, December 3, 1887
Died: Provincetown, Massachusetts, May 20, 1961
Highest degree: Ph.D. in psychology, Johns Hopkins University, 1923, under K. Dunlap [360]
Positions, honors: 1923, Clark University; 1936, manager, The Journal Press, Provincetown, Massachusetts; honorary degrees from Wake Forest College and the University of Athens

Murchison achieved distinction in psychology as the author, editor, and publisher of books, journals, and handbooks in psychology. First, upon Hall's [418] death, Murchison took over the editorship and management of *Pedagogical Seminary* in 1924. Under the name of The Clark University Press, Murchison founded, financed, edited, and managed *Genetic Psychology Monographs* (founded 1925), *Journal of General Psychology* (1927), *Journal of Social Psychology* (1929), and *Journal of Psychology*. Upon leaving Clark University Murchison established The Journal Press, which continued to publish the same journals. Later, *Social Psychology Monographs* and *Genetic Psychology*

Monographs were added and the name of *Pedagogical Seminary* was changed to *Journal of Genetic Psychology*.

Among Murchison's books are *American White Criminal Intelligence* (1924), *Criminal Intelligence* (1926), *The Case for and Against Psychical Belief* (1927), and *The Foundations of Experimental Psychology* (1929). In the 1930s, Murchison edited three handbooks: *The Foundations of Experimental Psychology* (1929), which was replaced by *A Handbook of General Experimental Psychology* in 1969, *A Handbook of Child Psychology* (1933), and *A Handbook of Social Psychology* (1935, 2nd edition 1967). Murchison was one of the five editors who prepared the first three volumes of *A History of Psychology in Autobiography* (vol. 1, 1930; vol. 2, 1930; vol. 3, 1936). Of lasting usefulness were also the two volumes of the *Psychological Register* (1928) and 1932), a Who's Who of the world of psychology.

Biographic data: J. P. Nafe, Carl Murchison. *American Journal of Psychology*, 1961, 74, 641–642

[454]

KROH, OSWALD

German psychologist
Rating: 12
Born: Beddelhausen, Westphalia, December 15, 1887
Died: Berlin, September 11, 1955
Highest degree: Ph.D. in psychology, University of Marburg, 1920, under R. E. Jaensch [413]
Positions: 1921, University of Göttingen; 1922, University of Braunschweig; 1923, University of Tübingen; 1938, University of Munich; 1942, University of Berlin; 1949, Free University of Berlin; president, German Psychological Society

During his Tübingen period, Kroh, under the influence of his mentor Jaensch, studied eidetic imagery and the associated Jaenschian typology (*Experimentale Beiträge zur Typenkunde*, vol. 1 1929, vol. 2 1932, vol. 3 1934). The work of Kroh and his colleagues in this area became known as the "Tübingen school." Kroh's most important work, however, was in developmental psychology. He theorized that in both phylogeny and ontogeny the primitive, instinctlike functions are gradually taken over by the cerebral cortex and made conscious and voluntary. This occurs in the course of sequential developmental stages. One such stage comprises the time between the point where the child begins to profit from school learning and the point of puberty. The theme of development during this period is the differentiation of mental life, which occurs through the overlaying of the older, emotional modes of experience and behavior by higher, rational mental functions. The developmental stages each differ in form and content, although the individual develops as a whole. Because of this educational programs must be adjusted to conform to the developmental specifics of individuals at a given developmental stage. Kroh's developmental views are contained in *Subjektive Anschauungsbilder bei Jugendlichen* (1922), *Phasen der Jugendentwicklung* (1926), *Psychologie des Grundschulkindes* (1928, his most widely used text that had seen twenty-two editions by 1944), and *Psychologie der Oberstufe* (1932, 10th edition 1944).

Biographic data: A. Wellek, Oswald Kroh. *Jahrbuch der Psychologie und Psychotherapie,* 1955, 3, 325–326; G. Kaminski & H. Märtin, Oswald Kroh und sein Lebenswerk. *Psychologische Beiträge,* 1956, 2, 226–238; P. Lersch, Nachruf auf Dr. Oswald Kroh. *Psychologische Rundschau,* 1956, 7, 55–57

MOEDE, WALTER [455]

German psychologist
Rating: 12
Born: Sorau, Prussia (now Zary, Poland), September 3, 1888
Died: Berlin, May 30, 1958
Highest degree: Ph.D. in psychology, University of Leipzig
Positions: 1921, Technische Hochschule, Berlin; 1951, Verwaltungsakademie, Berlin

Moede was a pioneer social psychologist who studied the effect of social variables in standard psychological experiments, such as threshold determination experiments. The study of the facilitating or inhibitory effects of other people on the performance of such tasks Moede dubbed "experimental mass psychology." Moede's work influenced Floyd Allport but not many others, since his work (*Experimentelle Massenpsychologie*), published in 1920, was never translated. Later Moede worked in industrial psychology, publishing a number of books in this area: *Lehrbuch der Psychotechnik* (1930), *Konsum-Psychologie* (1933), *Arbeitstechnik* (1935), *Eignungsprüfung und Arbeitseinsatz* (1943),

Betriebliche Arbeitswissenschaft (1954), *Psychologie des Berufs- und Wirtschaftslebens* (1958).

Biographic data: *The Psychological Register*, 1932, vol. III

[456] **KRETSCHMER, ERNST**

German psychiatrist
Rating: 26
Born: Wüstenrot, near Heilbronn, Baden-Württemberg, October 8, 1888
Died: Tübingen, Baden-Württemberg, February 8, 1964
Highest degree: M.D., University of Munich, 1914
Positions, honors: 1918, University of Tübingen; 1926, University of Marburg; 1946, University of Tübingen; honorary Ph.D., University of Bonn

Kretschmer made significant contributions to psychiatry, and wrote several volumes on abnormal psychology, such as *Hysterie, Reflex und Instinkt* (1923, English translation, 1960), in which he proposed that hysteria originates in conscious mechanisms that later become automated and unconscious; *Die sensitive Beziehungswahn* (1918); and *Medizinische Psychologie* (1922, English translation, *Textbook of Medical Psychology*, 1939). Kretschmer is important to psychology for his contributions to *the constitutional theory of personality*. The modern constitutional theory begins with Kretschmer. As a result of his psychiatric practice Kretschmer decided that physique had a bearing on behavior, especially behavior in two major types of mental disorders, manic-depressive psychosis and schizophrenia. Kretschmer devised an objective method for classifying individuals according to type of physique, and also related physique to normal behavior patterns. He established three basic body types: the asthenic, the athletic, and the pyknic. A fourth category, dysplastic, included markedly deviant physiques. After measuring the physiques of 260 psychotic patients, Kretschmer concluded that there was a "clear biological affinity" between manic-depressive psychosis and the pyknic physique on the one hand and the asthenic and athletic body build and schizophrenia. While Kretschmer assumed continuity between normal and abnormal behavior and therefore between physique and normal patterns of behavior, he never demonstrated such a relationship. Later, William Sheldon provided a much more sophisticated development of Kretschmer's idea. Kretschmer's constitutional type theory is presented in his *Körperbau und Charakter* (1921, English translation, *Physique and Character*, 1925).

Biographic data: *IESS* 8:450; [Anon.] Le professeur Ernst Kretschmer. *Revue de psychologie appliquée*, 1953, **3**, 43–48

HUNTER, WALTER SAMUEL [457]

American psychologist
Rating: **25**
Born: Decatur, Illinois, March 22, 1889
Died: Providence, Rhode Island, August 3, 1954
Highest degree: Ph.D. in psychology, University of Chicago, 1912, under J. R. Angell [309]
Positions: 1912, University of Texas; 1916, University of Kansas; 1925, Clark University; 1936, Brown University; during both World Wars was involved in Army testing and related work, for which he received the President's medal of merit; president, American Psychological Association, 1931; editorial work for *Comparative Psychology Monographs, Psychological Index*, and *Psychological Abstracts*

Hunter was a behaviorist who investigated representational processes in animals. For this purpose he invented the delayed reaction test for animals: food was placed in one of several boxes in plain sight of the animal but with access to allowed to the boxes only after a period of time. Phylogenetic differences in the toleration of delay become apparent in this test. Hunter did the delayed reaction test work for his doctoral dissertation; it was published in 1913, establishing him immediately as an investigator of note. In 1920, Hunter invented the temporal maze, which requires double or triple alternation of responses. This device shows phylogenetic differences in animals in their ability to "count" to two or three. In the same year, Hunter engaged in a polemic concerning behaviorism, penning several papers in the process. He suggested the use of the word "anthroponomy" as a synonym for behaviorism, to be used instead of psychology, in order to avoid the many mentalistic connotations of the latter term. Hunter wrote many papers on animal behavior and other psychological subjects.

Biographic data: *HPA* 4:163; *IESS* 7:8; *NCAB* 42:84; H. Schlosberg, Walter Samuel Hunter; pioneer objectivist in psychology. *Science*, 1954, **120**, 441–442; L. Carmichael, Walter Samuel Hunter. *American Journal of Psychology*, 1954, **67**, 733–734; J. McV. Hunt, Walter Samuel Hunter. *Psychological Review*, 1956, **63**, 213–217; C. H. Graham, Walter Samuel Hunter. *Biographical Memoirs of the National Academy of Sciences*, 1958, **31**, 127–155

[458]

TROLAND, LEONARD THOMPSON

American psychologist
Rating: **21**
Born: Norwich, Connecticut, April 26, 1889
Died: Mount Wilson, California, May 27, 1932
Highest degree: Ph.D. in psychology, Harvard University, 1915, under H. Münsterberg [272], E. B. Holt [348], and H. S. Langfeld [387]
Positions: 1916–1932, Harvard University; president, Optical Society of America, 1922

Troland was a very versatile scientist. He made contributions to several fields besides psychology. He wrote several important papers on life and life processes, published a book on physics, was a coinventor of the Technicolor movie process, and wrote papers on philosophy and metaphysics. His psychological papers were always begun and ended with a philosophical discussion. In psychology, Troland's most notable contributions were in the field of vision. His main interest here was to shape psychology after modern physics. Troland's vision research was formulated according to the "method of mathematical hypothesis," in which a process is first described by equations derived from a few simple mathematical premises. He published numerous papers in the field. In 1922, his book, *The Present Status of Visual Science* appeared. He participated in the translation of Helmholtz's [143] *Handbook of Psychological Optics* and contributed a chapter on vision to Murchison's [453] *Handbook of General Experimental Psychology*. His presidency of the Optical Society of America and the posthumous naming of the unit of retinal illumination, *the troland*, after him were the honorific results of his work on vision. Troland also attempted to extend the "method of mathematical hypothesis" to the field of emotion (*Fundamentals of Human Motivation*, 1928), although there it never went past a programmatic statement. His theory was hedonistic, postulating three kinds of receptors, one receiving pleasant stimuli, one painful stimuli, and one neutral stimuli. Receptors of painful stimuli were assumed to lead, by retroflex action of the thalamus, to a reduction in the conductance of cortical synapses. "Retroflex action" was a process postulated by Troland to stamp responses in and out, depending on the nature of stimulation. Pleasure or pain, Troland said, is experienced as the rate of cortical conductance at the synapses changes. A person's general affective makeup is thus determined by the accumulated total effect of retroflexive processes. Troland also wrote a popular book on psychology, *The Mystery of Mind* (1925), and a four-volume *Principles of Psychophysics* (1932, 1933).

Biographic data: J. Alexander, Leonard Thompson Troland. *Science*, 1932, 76, 255–257; J. G. Beebe-Center, Leonard Thompson Troland. *American Journal of Psychology*, 1932, 44, 817–820; A. A. Roback, Leonard Thompson Troland. *Science*, 1932, 76, 26–27

RUBINSHTEIN, SERGEI LEONIDOVICH

Russian psychologist

[459]

Rating: 12

Born: Odessa, June 6, 1889

Died: Moscow, January 11, 1960

Education: Graduated from Novorossiyskiĭ University, Odessa, in 1913

Positions: 1919, University of Odessa, head of Psychology Department since 1921; 1930, head, Herzen Pedagogical Institute, Leningrad; 1942–1950, Moscow State University, head of Psychology Department; editor of *Voprosy Psikhologii*

During the years of World War II, Rubinshteĭn organized the Psychology Department at the University of Moscow and also wrote a revised edition of his most significant work, *Osnovy obshcheĭ psikhologii*. It was published first in 1940, the second edition appearing in 1946. It was a text of general psychology based mostly on the work of Soviet psychologists, and it received a government prize. Rubinshteĭn's thinking, as expressed in this book, was also reflected in his defense of psychology during the so-called Pavlovian sessions that took place in Moscow in 1950. In defending psychology from attacks by those who chided it for not utilizing Pavlov's [206] teachings, Rubinshteĭn proposed a synthesis between dualism, as represented in psychology by the introspective approach to mind, and monism, as represented by behaviorism. He emphasized the unity of consciousness and behavior. Consciousness is not all internal, nor is behavior all external. They interpenetrate. Behavior reflects the inner world; objective reality is reflected in inner experience. Phylogenetically, development is first determined by the laws of biology. Later, however, development is also determined by the laws of history and the laws of social development. Man's activities transform his environment, and the environment, in turn, affects his development. It is a dialectic interaction. A further interactive system is seen in the relationship between the psyche and the nervous system and the psyche and the external world. The doctrine of reflection of Lenin [318] was applied by Rubinshteĭn to Pavlov's view of the reflexes by adding the notion of refraction: not only does organic matter reflect the external world but, by its own nature, it changes or refracts the action of the external world. Hegel [89] and Lenin also appear in Rubinshteĭn's concept of constitutive relationism: things and phenomena are determined by their relation to the surrounding reality. Hence mental processes have several different structures that relate mental activity to the brain and others that relate the brain to external reality. Relations are prior to the elements related, meaning is prior to words. Mental activities are therefore to be studied in relation to internal physiological and biochemical processes, which are material in nature, and in relation to external social processes, which are also material. Rubinshteĭn's was a two-faced materialistic monism. Rubinshteĭn continued to play the role of a major Soviet theoretical psychologist in writing three additional books during the last years of his career: *Bytie i soznanie* (1957), *O myshlenii i putyakh ego razvitiya* (1958), and *Printsipy i puti razvitiya psikhologii* (1959).

Biographic data: [Anon.] K 70-letiyu so dnya rozhdeniya Sergeya Leonidovicha Rubinshteĭna. *Voprosy Psikhologii,* 1959, 5(3), 143–146; [Anon.] Sergeĭ Leonidovich Rubinshteĭn. *Voprosy Psikhologii,* 1960, 6(1), 4–6, B. G. Anan'ev, Tvorcheskiĭ put' Sergeya Leonidovicha Rubinshteĭna. *Voprosy Psikhologii,* 1969, 15(5), 126–129; *Who Was Who in the USSR,* 1972.

[460]   **HUMPHREY, GEORGE**

English psychologist
Rating: 17
Born: Boughton, Kent, July 17, 1889

Died: Cambridge, April 24, 1966
Highest degree: Ph.D. in psychology, Harvard University, 1920
Positions: 1920, Wesleyan University; 1924, Queen's University, Kingston, Ontario; 1947–1956, Oxford University, director of Institute of Experimental Psychology since 1948; president, Canadian Psychological Association, 1942–1944

Humphrey did not leave very many experimental papers, but some are well known, for instance, that on inhibition. He did experimental work on conditioning, reinforcement, audiogenic seizures, and apparent motion, but his main effort was in the area of thinking. Humphrey at first tried to explain Freudian mechanisms and social psychological phenomena in terms of conditioning, then began to doubt the universality of application of conditioning principles, and gravitated toward the Gestalt viewpoint. In his best known book, *The Nature of Learning* (1933), Humphrey proposes that the organism is a system with a particular kind of organization; that an organism in the process of learning must be considered to be a four-dimensional entity, with time as the fourth dimension; that the same learning principles underlie the different types of learning; and that learning means achieving homeostatic equilibrium between an organismic system and its environment. Humphrey took up the problem of thinking in additional works, such as *Directed Thinking* (1948). One-half of the book, *Thinking: An Introduction to Experimental Psychology* (1951), written while Humphrey was the first occupant of a psychology chair at Oxford, is the first complete description in English of the work of the Würzburg school of imageless thought.

Biographic data: J. Blackburn, George Humphrey: Appreciation. *Canadian Journal of Psychology*, 1957, 11, 141–150; O. L. Zangwill, Obituary: George Humphrey. *Quarterly Journal of Experimental Psychology*, 1966, 18, 280; M. Argule & R. C. Oldfield, George Humphrey. *Bulletin of the British Psychological Society*, 1966, 19(65), 35–38

FROMM-REICHMANN, FRIEDA [461]

German-American psychoanalyst
Rating: 12
Born: Königsberg, East Prussia, October 23, 1889
Died: Rockville, Maryland, April 28, 1957

Highest degree: M.D., University of Königsberg, 1914

Positions: During World War I, cared for brain-injured soldiers on Kurt Goldstein's staff, University of Frankfurt; in early 1920s, at Weisser Hirsch sanitarium, near Dresden; later, psychoanalytic practice in Heidelberg, opened her own psychoanalytic sanitarium; 1930, Chestnut Lodge Sanitarium, Rockville, Maryland

Fromm-Reichmann was a neo-Freudian psychoanalyst whose theoretical stance was derived mostly from Harry Stack Sullivan [474] and the Washington School. Fromm-Reichmann emphasized the genetic approach to therapy, calculated to elicit, through interviews, dream analysis, and free association, the history and dynamics of the patient's maladjustment so as to bring about an insight and an intellectual and emotional grasp of the dynamics of the conflict by the patient. Fromm-Reichmann often preferred direct questioning to free association, so as to elicit more readily the "security operations" (ego defense mechanisms) used by the patient. Insight achieved by the patient through "working through" his problem was considered by Fromm-Reichmann to be the most significant factor in psychoanalysis, which she thought to be the only valid intensive psychotherapy. Her views are presented in *Principles of Intensive Psychotherapy* (1950).

Biographic data: [Anon.] Frieda Fromm-Reichmann in memoriam. *American Journal of Psychoanalysis*, 1957, **17**, 98; E. Weigert, In memoriam: Frieda Fromm-Reichmann. *Psychiatry*, 1958, **21**, 91–95

POLYAK, STEPHAN

Yugoslav-American anatomist

Rating: 12

Born: Northern Croatia, December 13, 1889

Died: Chicago, Illinois, March 9, 1955

Highest degree: M.D., University of Odessa, 1916; M.D., University of Zagreb, 1920

Positions: 1920–1928, University of Zagreb; 1921–1928, various research appointments at European universities and University of Chicago; 1928, University of California; 1930, University of Chicago

Polyak was a leading authority on the anatomy of the vertebrate visual system. He wrote three books on the subject. *The Main Afferent Fiber Systems of the Cerebral Cortex in Primates* (1932) considers normal and abnormal functions of the afferent somato-sensory, auditory, and visual systems in the brains of monkeys. *The Retina* (1941) describes the anatomy and histology of the human and primate retina. *The Vertebrate Visual System* (1957), a monumental work of 1600 pages, published posthumously, describes the origin, structure, and function of the visual system in vertebrates and man.

Biographic data: H. Klüver, Stephan Polyak, *American Journal of Psychology*, 1955, 68, 675–678

WERNER, HEINZ [463]

German-American psychologist
Rating: 24
Born: Vienna, Austria, February 11, 1890
Died: Worcester, Massachusetts, May 14, 1964
Highest degree: Ph.D. in psychology, University of Vienna, 1914
Positions: 1916, University of Munich; 1917, Psychological Institute, Hamburg; 1921, University of Hamburg; 1933, University of Michigan; 1936, Harvard University, visiting professor; 1937, Wayne County Training School; 1943, Brooklyn College; 1947–1960, Clark University, chairman of Psychology Department since 1949

Werner's early monographs were on aesthetics and music. During his Wayne County period he studied feeblemindedness, publishing some thirty articles. His work proved influential in the field of mental retardation. Werner, however, acquired prominence in the field of developmental psychology. His most notable work in this field was *Einführung in die Entwicklungspsychologie* (1926, English translation, *Comparative Psychology of Mental Development*, 1940), whose English version saw several editions and was translated into other languages.

Although our ideas about development include values placed on the developmental process, Werner believed that there are certain absolute, abstract truths that can be stated about it, which he called the *orthogenetic principle*: development proceeds from that which is global, undifferentiated, and unarticulated to that which is differentiated, articulated, and hierarchically integrated. Unlike many other developmental psychologists, Werner believed that development takes place along many different lines, but not necessarily on the same level. Werner added to the developmental picture such forms of functioning as aesthetics, expressiveness, and other "irrational" forms of knowing the world. The developed person has "mobility of operation" by having at his disposal more modes of knowing than the child. This includes the ability not only to function at a more differentiated level but also to move backward in one's developmental level and deal with to-be-cognized materials in an undifferentiated way. Werner believed that developmental psychology is a way of looking at all psychological phenomena, and sought to encompass all behavioral phenomena in a comprehensive system.

In 1949, Werner and Seymour Wapner formulated the sensory-tonic field theory of perception. The theory attempted to remedy a shortcoming of existing perceptual theories by incorporating the motor aspect of perception. It postulated the dynamic equivalence of sensory and tonic (motor) events and therefore an interaction and substitutability between them. The theory assumed the existence of only one kind of energy in the organism, sensory-tonic, which manifested itself in various ways. While the theory was only moderately productive of research, the demonstrations of the effects of motor events upon perception given by Werner and Wapner were impressive and led to such further developments as the rod-and-frame test, tilting room and tilting chair experiments, and the relationship between personality and styles of perception (field dependence and independence). Werner produced about seventy publications on perception while he was chairman of the Psychology Department at Clark University. During the four years between retirement and death, Werner published an additional twenty-five papers and a book (*Symbol Formation*, 1963, with B. Kaplan). After Werner's death, the Institute of Human Development at Clark University was renamed the Heinz Werner Institute of Developmental Psychology.

Biographic data: S. Wapner & B. Kaplan, Heinz Werner. *American Journal of Psychology*, 1964, 77, 513–517; H. A. Witkin, Heinz Werner. *Child Development*, 1965, 36, 307–328

[464]

FISHER, SIR RONALD AYLMER

English statistician
Rating: 20
Born: London, February 17, 1890

Died: Adelaide, Australia, July 29, 1962

Education: Studied mathematics and physics at Cambridge University, graduated in 1912

Positions, honors: 1918, Rothamsted Experimental Agriculture Station; 1933, University College, London, Galton professor of Eugenics; 1943, Cambridge University; 1957, University of Adelaide; knighted, 1952; numerous medals, honors

Although tests of the statistical significance of differences were performed before Fisher, Fisher's contributions were such that the era of contemporary analytical statistics begins with him. He was first to make a clear distinction between population parameters and sample statistics (his terms). He contributed heavily to the theory of experimentation. His two books most important to psychology (*The Design of Experiments*, 1935; *Statistical Methods for Research Workers*, 1925) contain largely his own findings. They are addressed primarily not to the statisticians but to research workers in different areas, and place powerful tools in their hands. Fisher developed the technique of analysis of variance. The F in the F statistic stands for Fisher. He also developed small sample and nonparametric techniques. Terms like "null hypothesis," "degrees of freedom," "randomized block design," and "treatment" were coined by Fisher. Fisher himself was instrumental in publicizing his work and in having it accepted, although in the course of these activities he developed vigorous controversies and polemic exchanges. While he wrote *Statistical Methods* in 1925, they did not begin to be applied by American psychologists until after his visit to the United States in 1931. Since then he has influenced psychologists' approach to experimentation more than any other person.

Biographic data: DSB 5:7; [Anon.] Sir Ronald Fisher. Obituary. *British Journal of Statistical Psychology*, 1962, 15(2), 197–198; G. A. Miller, Ronald Aylmer Fisher. *American Journal of Psychology*, 1963, 76, 157–158

WARDEN, CARL JOHN [465]

American psychologist
Rating: 19
Born: Hamilton, Missouri, March 18, 1890
Died: De Land, Florida, February 28, 1961
Highest degree: Ph.D. in psychology, University of Chicago, 1922

Positions: 1923, University of Wisconsin; 1924–1955, Columbia University; editorial work for *Journal of Genetic Psychology, Genetic Psychology Monographs,* and *Journal of Comparative Psychology*

Warden studied animal and human learning, and animal drives. He introduced the use of mazes that were simpler than the Hampton Court maze, such as the *U-maze* (*Comparative Psychology*, 3 volumes, 1935–1940, with T. N. Jenkins and L. H. Warner [501]), and standardized *the obstruction box*, hence much used in animal laboratories (*Animal Motivation: Experimental Studies on the Albino Rat*, 1931). Warden wrote several additional texts in comparative psychology: *A Short Outline of Comparative Psychology* (1927), *An Outline of Comparative Psychology* (1928), *Animal Drives* (1932), *The Evolution of Human Behavior* (1932), *Introduction to Comparative Psychology* (1934, with T. N. Jenkins and L. H. Warner), as well as an *Introduction to Psychology* (1928).

Biographic data: *New York Times*, March 1, 1961, 33:1

[466]

LASHLEY, KARL SPENCER

American psychologist
Rating: 27
Born: Davis, West Virginia, June 7, 1890
Died: Poitiers, France, August 7, 1958
Highest degree: Ph.D. in genetics, Johns Hopkins University, 1914
Positions, honors: 1915, St. Elizabeth's Hospital, Washington, D.C.; 1917, University of Minnesota; 1918, U.S. Interdepartmental Social Hygiene Board; 1920, University of Minnesota; 1926, Behavior Research Fund; 1929, University of Chicago; 1935–1955, Harvard University; 1942–1955, Yerkes Laboratory of Primate Biology; 1955–1958, emeritus professor; president, American Psychological Association, 1929; five honorary degrees; Warren medal in psychology, 1937; Elliot medal in zoology, 1943; Baly medal in physiology, 1953

Lashley's contribution to psychology was his studies of the cerebral localization of functions using learning and discrimination as the behavioral measures of the effects of ablation. He was responsible for pushing the localization-nonlocalization pendulum once more in the direction of nonlocalization. While Lashley was a student of Watson's [374] and a behaviorist, he seldom engaged in school-related polemics but dedicated his efforts to research in physiological psychology. Franz [350] had already indicated that functional localization in the brain was not as specific as had been thought, and Lashley did his postdoctoral work under Franz. They published together a paper on the effects of cerebral ablation on learning and memory in the rat. From here on, Lashley published a long series of papers dealing with the effects of extirpation of various sites in the rat's brain and of different amounts of brain tissue removed upon learning, memory, and discrimination. In doing so he introduced a new animal testing device that became known as the Lashley jumping stand. It has enjoyed wide use in the study of the rat's behavior. By 1929, Lashley was able to publish a book summarizing the results of his work (*Brain Mechanisms and Intelligence*). Two of the principles uncovered were that the rate and accuracy of learning is proportionate to the amount of brain tissue available (law of mass action), but that it is independent of the particular tissue that is available (principle of equipotentiality). These findings were revolutionary in view of the then current conception of the brain as a set of isolated neurons, reflex paths, and synaptic resistance, the nervous system being often compared to a telephone switchboard. Lashley did not completely deny localization, but stated that it was less precise and more complex than imagined before and that equipotentiality held sometimes (in the case of complex acts) but not always (especially for simple problems). Nevertheless, an antiphysiological trend set in because it seemed to many that there was little left for the physiological psychologist to study.

In addition to brain functioning and learning, Lashley studied other behavioral phenomena: color vision, instinctive behavior, and, as a remification of his ablation studies, pattern vision. In the latter area, his seminal idea that pattern vision may be explained in terms of interference or standing waves in the brain found a new life some forty years after its formulation. Lashley published more than one hundred major papers.

Biographic data: *DSB* 8:45; *IESS* 9:27; *NCAB* 44:198; D. O. Hebb, Karl Spencer Lashley. *American Journal of Psychology*, 1959, 72, 142–150; L. Carmichael, Karl Spencer Lashley, experimental psychologist. *Science*, 1959, **129**, 1410–1412

ROBACK, ABRAHAM AARON

American psychologist
Rating: **17**
Born: Poland, June 19, 1890
Died: Cambridge, Massachusetts, June 5, 1965
Highest degree: Ph.D. in psychology, Harvard University, 1917, under H. Münsterberg [272]
Positions: Brief academic appointments at University of Pittsburgh, Northeastern University, Harvard University, Massachusetts Institute of Technology, and Clark University; longer part-time appointments at Massachusetts Department of University Extension and Emerson College, Boston

Roback's contribution to psychology was primarily as a writer. He wrote some thirty books and about two thousand articles, although many of the articles were not on psychological subjects but Yiddish and Hebrew literature and folklore. *The Psychology of Character* (1927) was his book of most enduring value. Other significant books on psychology that Roback wrote were *Behaviorism and Psychology* (1923), *Behaviorism at Twenty-five* (1937), *History of American Psychology* (1952), and *History of Psychology and Psychiatry* (1961).

Biographic data: C. W. Allport, Aaron Abraham Roback. *American Journal of Psychology*, 1965, 78, 689–690

LEWIN, KURT

German-American psychologist
Rating: **26**
Born: Mogilno, Prussia, September 9, 1890
Died: Newtonville, Massachusetts, February 12, 1947
Highest degree: Ph.D. in psychology, University of Berlin, 1914, under W. Köhler [447]
Positions: 1922, University of Berlin; 1932, Cornell University; 1935, Child Welfare Research Station, University of Iowa; 1944, director, Research Center for Group Dynamics, Massachusetts Institute of Technology

Lewin began to study the effects of motivation on psychological processes before 1917. At Berlin, he became acquainted with the founders of the Gestalt school of psychology, and is sometimes counted as a member of that school. Lewin's contribution was to add and emphasize the factor of motivation within the Gestalt framework, especially the Gestalt concept of the field. In 1917, his first publication on the strength of association as a function of motivation appeared. Before he came to the United States, Lewin's students had already conducted a series of studies of the dynamics of behavior, which made him well known.

While Köhler applied the notion of fields and field forces to the physical and biological world to explain perception, Lewin applied these concepts to behavior in general. Each person lives in a psychological field, his life-space, which is the totality of his psychological reality as it exists at a given moment. To understand a person's life-space, it is unnecessary to include an account of that person's past history since the field, as presently constituted, is the totality of his present psychological reality and determines his actions completely. Actions are caused by the person's wishes. Actions are paralleled by locomotion within the psychological life-space. Since physical space and psychological space do not have a one-to-one relationship, Lewin postulated that psychological space is topological, i.e., it has no metric but only relationships of order. To preserve the advantages of a metric space, such as the possibility of quantitative prediction of behavior from quantified desires and wishes, which Lewin represented as vectors, he suggested that life-space was "hodological" or having differentiated paths.

The concept of field forces was explored experimentally by Lewin and his students in a variety of settings involving tension, such as the study by Bluma Zeigarnik of the influence of uncompleted acts upon their retention (the Zeigarnik effect); the effect of success and failure on the level of aspiration; reaction of children to frustration; the behavior of people in small groups; the effects of authoritarian, laissez-faire, and democratic leaderships, and others. The group dynamics field may be said to have been originated by Lewin. Group dynamics research and practical applications of the principles of group dynamics (T-groups, sensitivity training) originated with Lewin's work at the Massachusetts Institute of Technology. Conflict and conflict resolution was also analyzed by Lewin, and terms like "approach-avoidance conflict," "leaving the field," and others have become stock-in-trade terms in general psychology. Lewin thus contributed to the development of Gestalt psychology by including in it motivational factors, launched experimental dynamic psychology, and pioneered in experimental social psychology.

Lewin exercised his influence largely through his personality, charisma, and democratic leadership rather than his writings, which consisted mostly of articles and monographs and very few books. His first book was a collection of seven of his articles under the title, *A Dynamic Theory of Personality* (1935). *Principles of Topological Psychology* (1936) is the standard presentation of Lewin's theory. The representation and measurement of psychological forces is described in *Contributions to Psychological Theory* (1938). Lewin's *Resolving Social Conflicts* (1948) was published posthumously.

Biographic data: *EP* 4:454; *IESS* 9:266; D. Cartwright, Kurt Lewin. *International Journal of Opinion and Attitude Research*, 1947, **1**, 96–99; R. Likert, Kurt Lewin, a pioneer in human relations research. *Human Relations*, 1947, **1**, 131–139; R. Lippitt, Kurt Lewin. *Sociometry*, 1947, **10**, 87–97; E. C. Tolman, Kurt Lewin. *Psychological Review*, 1948, 55, 1–4; A. J. Marrow, *The Practical Theorist, the Life and Work of Kurt Lewin*, 1969

[469]

ZILBOORG, GREGORY

American psychoanalyst
Rating: **17**
Born Kiev, Ukraine, December 25, 1890
Died: New York, New York, September 17, 1959
Highest degree: M.D., Psychoneurological Institute, St. Petersburg, 1917; M.D., College of Physicians and Surgeons, Columbia University, 1926
Positions, honors: 1926–1931, Bloomingdale Hospital; 1929–1930, Psychoanalytic Institute, Berlin; 1931–1959, private practice in New York City; honorary D.Sc., National University, Ireland, 1954

Zilboorg published numerous articles on psychiatry and psychoanalysis in medical journals as well as some books of psychological interest: *Mind, Medicine, and Man* (1943), *Sigmund Freud* (1951), *The Psychology of the Criminal Act and Punishment* (1954), and *Freud and Religion* (1959). His best known work, however, was *A History of Medical Psychology*, which he published with G. W. Henry in 1941.

Biographic data: *NCAB* 43:310; L. Ancona, In memoria di Gregory Zilboorg. *Archivio di psicologia, neurologia e psichiatria*, 1959, **20**, 537–539

German-American psychoanalyst
Rating: 18
Born: Budapest, Hungary, January 22, 1891
Died: Palm Springs, California, March 8, 1964
Highest degree: M.D., University of Budapest, 1913
Positions: 1920, Berlin Psychoanalytic Institute; 1930, visiting professor of psychoanalysis, University of Chicago; 1932, Chicago Institute for Psychoanalysis: 1956–1964, director Psychiatric and Psychosomatic Research Institute, Mount Sinai Hospital, Los Angeles; 1957–1964, clinical professor of psychiatry, University of Southern California

Alexander was the most prominent representative of the neo-Freudian Chicago School of psychoanalysis, which sought to apply psychoanalysis in new situations more than it sought to add to psychoanalytic theory. Alexander and the Chicago School deemphasized the origin of neuroses in the psychosexual stages of childhood and stressed, in addition to early experience, heredity and actual difficulties of the patient created by situations that are beyond his control. Alexander defined neurosis as a relationship between personality and the social setting in which the personality finds itself. The aim of psychoanalysis is "to increase the patient's ability to find gratifications for his subjective needs in ways acceptable both to himself and to the world he lives in, and thus to free him to develop his capacities." Alexander's principle of surplus energy (derived from Ferenczi [339]) states that sexuality is a specific discharge of unused excitation in the organism. The therapeutic emphasis is on "corrective emotional experience" to release this surplus energy, which is a form of abreaction and a process central to the therapeutic process in the Chicago School. Planning and flexibility are two additional adaptions in the classical psychoanalytic procedure. The patient's free associations are not the main guideline in therapy. It is planned in accordance with the diagnosis and the personality of the patient and may change depending on the outcome of the therapeutic intervention, so that diverse methods may be used with different patients and with the same patient during his course of treatment. The work of the Chicago School centered around the Chicago Institute of Psychoanalysis, which Alexander founded. Alexander wrote some 120 articles and 18 books. Prominent among the latter are (with T. M. French) *Psychoanalytic Therapy* (1946), *Studies in Analytical Psychology* (1948), and *Fundamentals of Psychoanalysis* (1948).

Biographic data: *IESS* 1:262–264; *NCAB* H:385; T. M. French, Franz Alexander. *Behavioral Science*, 1964, 9(2), 98–100; W. M. Mendel, Franz Alexander, M.D. *Journal of Existential Psychiatry*, 1964, 4(16), 287–288; M. Grotjahn, Franz Alexander, M.D. *Journal of Nervous and Mental Disease*, 1965, 140(5), 319–322

[471]

ROHEIM, GEZA

Hungarian-American psychoanalyst
Rating: 11
Born: Budapest, Hungary, September 12, 1891
Died: New York, New York, June 7, 1953
Highest degree: Ph.D. in anthropology, University of Budapest, 1914
Positions: 1917–1919, professor of anthropology, Ethnology Department, Hungarian National Museum, Budapest; 1928–1931, field study of natives in Australia, New Guinea, Somaliland, and Arizona; 1932, Psychoanalytic Institute, Budapest; 1938, analyst at Worcester, Massachusetts State Hospital; 1940, private practice of psychoanalysis

Róheim was first to apply Freud's [224] ideas to anthropology. He later extended such application to folklore, mythology, prehistory, and social science in general. Otherwise Róheim was an orthodox Freudian who stressed the role of the sex drive in both psychoanalysis and in his treatment of culture. Róheim wrote some two hundred papers and books. Representative works are *The Origin and Function of Culture* (1943), *The Riddle of the Sphinx* (1934), and *The Gates of the Dream* (1952).

Biographic data: *IESS* 13:543; R. C. Bak, Géza Róheim. *American Psychoanalytic Association Journal*, 1953, 1, 758–759; M. Balint, Géza Róheim. *International Journal of Psychoanalysis*, 1954, 35, 434–436

[472]

PATERSON, DONALD GILDERSLEEVE

American psychologist
Rating: 15
Born: Columbus, Ohio, January 18, 1892

Died: St. Paul, Minnesota, October 4, 1961
Highest degree: M. A. in psychology, Ohio State University, 1916
under R. Pintner [430]
Positions: 1916, University of Kansas; 1917, U.S. Army, psychologist; 1918, Scott Company, consultants; 1921–1960, University of Minnesota; editorial work for *Journal of Applied
Psychology*, 1943–1954

Paterson was an applied psychologist who developed vocational
guidance techniques and became a leader in the field of student
counseling (*Men, Women, and Jobs*, 1936, with J. Darley;
Student Guidance Techniques, 1938, with G. Schneidler and E.
Williamson). Paterson worked extensively in the field of intelligence and ability measurement. He produced, with R. Pintner,
the Pintner-Paterson Scale of Performance Tests (1917), a
nonlanguage intelligence test. Additional tests constructed by
Paterson, with collaborators, were the Minnesota Mechanical
Ability Test (1930), Minnesota Mechanical Assembly Test
(1930), Minnesota Spatial Relations Test (1930), and the Revised
Minnesota Occupational Rating Scales (1953). Paterson did
additional work in applied psychology, such as the study of
legibility of type, which he published with M. Tinker (*How to
Make Type Readable*, 1940). A bibliography of Paterson's
publications contains more than three hundred items.

Biographic data: IESS 11:478

HECHT, SELIG [473]

American physiologist
Rating: 22
Born: Glogau, Silesia, February 8, 1892
Died: New York, New York, September 18, 1947
Highest degree: Ph.D. in physiology, Harvard University, 1917
Positions, honors: 1917–1925, Creighton University; 1926–1947,
Columbia University; recipient of the Frederick Ives medal,
Optical Society of America, 1941

Hecht was one of the principal contributors to modern vision
theory. His special contribution lay in the study and theoretical
formulation of photopigment processes in the retina. Hecht's
theory (1929) proposed that the Bunsen-Roscoe law of photochemical reaction is the sum of two chemical processes, each of

which is the other reversed: the decomposition of photopigments under light stimulation, and their reconstitution in the dark. Of particular importance was the development by Hecht of an apparatus and method to test for vitamin A deficiency, vitamin A being one of the elements of the photochemical reactions in the retina. Hecht extended his theory to include color vision. It included an explanation of increasing visual acuity with increasing light intensity in terms of the two populations of retinal elements, the rods and the cones, and their varied thresholds. Hecht and his coworkers contributed many papers to the field of retinal photochemistry, many of which are classics, such as the 1942 paper by Hecht, Schlaer, and Pirenne in which the visual threshold was related to the amount of light quanta stimulating the receptors. Books written by Hecht include *The Retinal Processes Concerned With Visual Acuity and Color Vision* (1931) and *La bas chimique et structurale de la vision* (1938). He also wrote "The nature of the photoreceptor processes" for the *Handbook of General Experimental Psychology* (1934).

Biographic data: *NCAB* 38:322; R. Kingslake, Doctor Selig Hecht, Ives Medalist for 1941. *Journal of the Optical Society of America*, 1942, **32**, 37–39; C. H. Graham, Selig Hecht. *American Journal of Psychology*, 1948, **61**, 126–128; B. O'Brian et al., Selig Hecht. *Science*, 1948, **107**, 105–106; M. H. Pirenne, Professor Selig Hecht. *Nature*, 1948, **161**, 673

[474]

SULLIVAN, HARRY STACK

American psychiatrist
Rating: 23
Born: Norwich, New York, February 21, 1892
Died: Paris, France, January 14, 1949
Highest degree: M.D., Chicago College of Medicine and Surgery, 1917
Positions: 1922, St. Elizabeth's Hospital, Washington, D. C.; 1923–1930, Shepard & Enoch Pratt Hospital, Towson, Maryland; University of Maryland; 1933–1943, president, William Alanson White Foundation; 1936, director, Washington School of Psychiatry; editor, *Psychiatry*, 1938–1949

Sullivan promoted a social-psychological theory that was based on his seven years' work with schizophrenics in Maryland. Sullivan began to formulate his theory in 1929, had it developed in the 1930s, but did not publish it in book form until 1947

(*Conceptions of Modern Psychiatry*). This was the only book he ever wrote. All others (*The Interpersonal Theory of Personality*, 1953; *The Psychiatric Interview*, 1954; *Clinical Studies in Psychiatry*, 1956; *The Fusion of Psychiatry and Social Sciences*, 1964) were published posthumously from his notes. The main influences on Sullivan's theory came from Freud [224], Adolph Meyer [292], George Mead [270], Edward Sapir [417], and Ruth Benedict [450], but it is otherwise an independent development within the group of sociopsychological theories of personality.

Sullivan's main tenet was that the concept of personality acquires meaning only in interpersonal relations. Personality is a hypothetical entity and can be observed only in interpersonal behavior. Personality processes include dynamisms, personifications, and cognitive processes. Dynamisms are the smallest units of recurrent behavior that can be used in studying behavior or habits. Most dynamisms develop to serve the basic needs, except the self-system which develops as a result of anxiety that arises in interpersonal relations. To reduce anxiety, the person takes protective or security measures, those that permit certain behaviors, or the good-me self, and those that forbid others, the bad-me self. These become the self-system. The self-system acquires autonomy and prevents objective evaluation of one's behavior. Personifications are self-images or images of others, formed in isolated instances of interaction, but influencing attitudes toward people in subsequent transactions. Shared personifications are stereotypes. Cognitive processes are prototaxic, parataxic, or syntaxic. Prototaxic experiences are an unconnected stream of consciousness which characterizes the infant's world; parataxic thinking sees causal connections between events that are only contiguous in time, and syntaxic thinking involves the exchange of symbols whose meaning has been agreed upon by a group of people.

Sullivan's personality dynamics explains the handling of tensions by a person and the use of the three modes of thinking. In personality development Sullivan stressed definite stages, characterized by developing interpersonal relations (he rejected Freud's notion of the libido and subordinated biological factors to social relations) and a hierarchical transition to higher forms of cognitive activity. Thus during early infancy the oral experience of food intake is colored by the infant's evaluation of the mother as good, bad, or rejecting, and the latent period in Freud's system becomes a very important one in Sullivan's because learning to behave appropriately in social situations or failure to do so is crucial to the person's future interpersonal relations.

Biographic data: *IESS* 15:396; A. F. Emch, Harry Stack Sullivan. *Psychiatry*, 1949, 12, 1

STONE, CALVIN PERRY

American psychologist
Rating: 16
Born: Portland, Indiana, February 28, 1892
Died: Palo Alto, California, December 28, 1954
Highest degree: Ph.D. in psychology, University of Minnesota, 1921, under K. S. Lashley [466]
Positions, honors: 1921, University of Minnesota; 1922, Stanford University; editorial work for *Journal of Comparative and Physiological Psychology* (1947–1950) and *Annual Review of Psychology* (1950–1954); president, American Psychological Association, 1942; honorary D. Sc., Indiana University, 1954

Stone's main interest was comparative and physiological psychology. He did his early work on instincts in animals, later on animal learning, maturation, and the effects of electro-convulsive shock. In this area his major topic of research was the physiology of reproductive behavior. Stone's second major interest was abnormal psychology. In 1923, he offered the first course on Freudian psychology as part of the regular curriculum of an American university. Stone's publications consist of a fair number of research papers.

Biographic data: *NCAB* 52:426; C. R. Carpenter, Calvin Perry Stone, investigator and teacher. *Science*, 1955, 121, 658–659; H. E. Rosvold, Calvin Perry Stone. *American Journal of Psychology*, 1955, 68, 326–329

WHEELER, RAYMOND HOLDER

American psychologist
Rating: 19
Born: Berlin, Massachusetts, March 9, 1892
Died: Wellesley, Massachusetts, August 24, 1961
Highest degree: Ph.D. in psychology, Clark University, 1915
Positions: 1915, University of Oregon; 1925, University of Kansas; 1947, Erskine College; 1948, Babson Institute of Business Administration

Wheeler defended Gestalt psychology against criticism, but he also modified it considerably, presenting it under the name of organismic psychology (*The Science of Psychology*, 1929, second edition, 1940; *The Laws of Human Nature*, 1932). Wheeler deviated from the original position of the Gestalt school so much that he belongs only on the periphery of that school.

Wheeler wrote several papers on synesthesia, on systematic psychology, and coauthored, with F. T. Perkins, a widely used educational psychology text, *Principles of Mental Development* (1932). Although the book contained some challenging ideas concerning development, it ceased to be influential, overshadowed by others.

Biographic data: *The Psychological Register*, 1932, vol. 3

CROZIER, WILLIAM JOHN   [477]

American physiologist
Rating: 18
Born: New York, New York, May 24, 1892
Died: Belmont, Massachusetts, November 2, 1955
Highest degree: Ph.D. in zoology, Harvard University, 1915
Positions: 1915, Bermuda Biological Station; 1918, University of Illinois; 1919, University of Chicago; 1920, Rutgers University; 1925–1955, Harvard University; editorial work, *Journal of General Physiology*, 1924–1955

Crozier influenced psychology through his theory and experimentation on animal behavior and the sensory processes. Crozier studied the different types of tropisms and the factors that influence tropistic behavior. He felt that his major contribution was the "parametric analysis" of behavior, by which he meant the identification and study of meaningful parameters in equations describing aspects of behavior so as to test hypotheses about the underlying mechanisms. In the area of sensory processsses Crozier wrote a chapter on chemoreception for the *Handbook of General Experimentation Psychology* (1934) and did a large number of experiments on critical flicker fusion. Crozier wrote a total of about three-hundred scientific papers.

Biographic data: H. Hoagland & R. T. Mitchell, William John Crozier, *American Journal of Psychology*, 1956, 69, 135–138

HOLZINGER, KARL JOHN

American psychologist
Rating: 13
Born: Washington, D.C., August 9, 1892
Died: Chicago, Illinois, January 15, 1954
Highest degree: Ph.D. in mathematics and education, University of Chicago, 1922
Positions: 1923–1954, University of Chicago; president, Psychometric Society, 1940; vice-president, American Statistical Association, 1933; editorial work for *Psychometrika* (1937–1948) and *Journal of Educational Psychology* (1949–1954)

Holzinger contributed to psychology in the area of factor analysis (with H. H. Harman, *Factor Analysis*, 1941). He was the main advocate of Spearman's [274] two-factor theory in the United States, but attempted to improve it by presenting his own bi-factor theory. In addition to the many papers and monographs that Holzinger wrote on statistical topics, he coauthored a well known developmental study in which factor analysis was used: *Twins: A Study of Heredity and Environment* (with H. H. Newman and F. N. Freeman [392], 1937).

Biographic data: H. H. Harman, Karl John Holzinger. *Psychometrika*, 1954, 19, 95–96

ENGLISH, HORACE BIDWELL

American psychologist
Rating: 14
Born: Eagle, Nebraska, October 1, 1892
Died: Columbus, Ohio, July 20, 1961
Highest degree: Ph.D. in psychology, Yale University, 1916
Positions: 1916, Wellesley College; 1927, Antioch College; 1930, Ohio State University; president, American Association for Applied Psychology 1937–1940

While English wrote in the area of child psychology (*Child Psychology*, 1952; *The Dynamics of Child Development*, 1961), he is best known for having written, with his wife, A. C. English,

A Comprehensive Dictionary of Psychological and Psychanalytic Terms (1958).

Biographic data: *The Psychological Register,* 1932, vol. 3

FEARING, FRANKLIN [480]

American psychologist
Rating: **12**
Born: Durango, Colorado, November 24, 1892
Died: Santa Monica, California, March 26, 1962
Highest degree: Ph.D. in psychology, Stanford University, 1926
Positions: 1926, Ohio Wesleyan University; 1928, Northwestern University; 1935–1960, University of California in Los Angeles; editorial work for *Journal of Psychology,* 1937–1962

Fearing worked at first in the area of physiological psychology. At Northwestern University he established a laboratory for the study of the inner ear in relation to the maintenance of balance and posture. He is best known for his volume on *Reflex Action* (1930). After moving to UCLA, Fearing began work in social psychology, specializing in mass communication.

Biographic data: *NCAB* 48:229

LINTON, RALPH [481]

American anthropologist
Rating: **19**
Born: Philadelphia, Pennsylvania, February 27, 1893
Died: New Haven, Connecticut, December 24, 1953
Highest degree: Ph.D. in anthropology, Harvard University, 1925
Positions: 1928, University of Wisconsin; 1937, Columbia University; 1946, Yale University

Linton brought to bear psychological theories and findings on his study of culture. His most important theoretical work, *The Study of Man* (1936), is a synthesis of sociological, anthropological, and psychological theories about culture. The effect of culture upon personality is considered by him in *The Cultural Background of Personality* (1945).

Biographic data: *IESS* 9:386; *NCAB* H:232

[482]

ROBINSON, EDWARD STEVENS

American psychologist
Rating: 16
Born: Lebanon, Ohio, April 18, 1893
Died: New Haven, Connecticut, February 27, 1937
Highest degree: Ph.D. in psychology, University of Chicago, 1920, under J. R. Angell [309]
Positions: 1920, Yale University; 1921, University of Chicago; 1927, Yale Univeristy; editorial work for *Psychological Bulletin* (1930–1934), *Journal of Social Psychology* (1935–1937), and *American Journal of Psychology* (1925–1935)

Robinson was a Chicago functionalist. His initial work was on learning, particularly retroactive interference (*Factors Determining the Degree of Retroactive Inhibition*, 1920). The Skaggs-Robinson hypothesis (so named by McGeoch [492] to give credit also to E. B. Skaggs who had conceived of a similar idea earlier, in 1925) states that positive transfer of learning is greatest when the successively presented material is identical, that dissimilarity of materials also facilitates transfer, but that intermediate degrees of similarity produce the greatest interference. Robinson wrote two books applying the functionalist analysis to some concrete and practical problems: *Practical Psychology* (1926) and *The Behavior of the Museum Visitor* (1928). He then presented an overview of *Association Theory Today* (1931). In this work Robinson showed how all the associative laws could be dimensionalized and quantified. These laws, as formulated by Robinson, as well as Carr [344], never caught on because they were too general, and were replaced by more specific ones, defined in terms of specific learning situations. Later, Robinson turned to social psychology believing that the functionalist approach could be applied in this field also. He lectured on law and psychology at Yale Law School, and published a book reflecting this phase in his thinking, *Law and the Lawyers* (1935). *Man as Psychology*

Sees Him (1932) and sixty-seven papers completed Robinson's bibliography when he died in an accident early in his life.

Biographic data: NCAB 28:304; R. P. Angier, Edward Stevens Robinson. *Psychological Review*, 1937, 44 , 267–273; H. A. Carr, Edward Stevens Robinson. *American Journal of Psychology*, 1937, 49, 488–489; J. R. Angell, Edward Stevens Robinson. *Psychological Bulletin*, 1937, 34, 801–805

SYMONDS, PERCIVAL MALLON [483]

American psychologist
Rating: 11
Born: Newtonville, Massachusetts, April 18, 1893
Died: New York, New York, August 6, 1960
Highest degree: Ph.D. in educational psychology, Columbia University, 1923
Positions: 1922, University of Hawaii, professor of education and psychology; 1924–1958, Columbia University, Teachers College, professor of education

Symonds published extensively in the area of educational and psychological measurement (*Measurement in Secondary Education*, 1927), personality assessment, psychology of adolescence (*Adolescent Fantasy*, 1949), and the psychology of the teacher. He stressed the importance of dynamic psychology (*The Dynamics of Human Adjustment*, 1946; *Dynamics of Psychotherapy*, 3 volumes, 1956–1958) and the importance of nonintellectual components in personality assessment in the educational system, such as free association and the Rorschach test. In his book, *The Ego and the Self* (1951), Symonds discusses personality in terms of the relationship between the self and the ego. Symonds defines the ego in the same way as Freud [224], and the self as the ways in which the individual reacts to himself in terms of his self-perception, self-cognition, self-valuation, and self-maintenance or enhancement. A person may not be aware of these aspects of the self and may hold contrary opinions of oneself, one conscious, the other unconscious, hence what the person says about himself may not be how he really feels about himself. If the ego is effective in mediating between external reality and internal demands the person will have a good opinion of himself; conversely, a high opinion of oneself in conducive to more effective ego-functioning. Symonds wrote twenty-one books, more than two hundred articles, and many inventories and questionnaires of attitudes, the psychology of the pupil, the teacher, and the like.

Biographic data: *NCAB* 46:7

[484]

KINSEY, ALFRED CHARLES

American biologist
Rating: 21
Born: Hoboken, New Jersey, June 23, 1894
Died: Bloomington, Indiana, August 25, 1956
Highest degree: Ph.D. in zoology, Harvard University, 1920
Positions: 1920–1947, Indiana University, teaching zoology; 1947–1956, director, Institute for Sex Research, Indiana, University

Kinsey's interest and research on human sexual behavior, which started in 1938, led to the establishment of the Institute for Sex Research at Indiana University. The results of 18,500 personal interviews concerning sexual behavior were published in *Sexual Behavior in the Human Male* in 1948 and in *Sexual Behavior in the Human Female* in 1953. These were the first large-scale empirical studies of sexual behavior. They presented quantified description of sexual behavior, showed an unexpected range of variation in such behavior, corrected misconceptions and upset many established opinions concerning human sexual behavior, and demonstrated that sexual behavior can be studied scientifically, objectively, and publicly.

Biographic data: *IESS* 8:389; W. B. Pomroy, *Dr. Kinsey and the Institute for Sex Research*, 1972

[485]

WIENER, NORBERT

American mathematician
Rating: 18
Born: Columbia, Missouri, November 26, 1894
Died: Stockholm, Sweden, March 18, 1964

Highest degree: Ph.D. in philosophy, Harvard University, 1913
Positions: 1919–1960, Massachusetts Institute of Technology

The idea for a new dicipline, cybernetics, grew out of Wiener's work in devising a system for the rapid direction of antiaircraft fire. The discipline was launched when Wiener published his book, *Cybernetics*, in 1948. He defined cybernetics as a discipline concerned with the comparative study of control mechanisms in the nervous system and high-speed computers.

Wiener's effect on psychology was twofold. One was in the form of a new type of model to pattern human behavior after—the human being as a computer. In *Cybernetics*, Wiener considers the automation of pattern perception, how to translate in computer terms the perception of invariants, as well as such broad topics as psychopathology and social psychology. The proliferation of computer models of form perception has been one direct effect of Wiener's book. The second effect was the introduction of the use of information theory in psychology. The information theory was presented simultaneously and independently in 1948 by Wiener and Claude Shannon. It gave, for the first time, the opportunity to quantify something that was of definite psychological interest but had theretofore been unquantifiable, namely information. Since information reduces uncertainty and learning may be considered a case of uncertainty reduction, information theory was relevant to learning. Since organization is about the same as redundancy, a cybernetic concept, and Gestalt psychologists talked about organization, their propositions could be tested quantitatively. Since any stimulus may be considered to contain information, the behavior of organisms could by treated as information processing behavior and quantified in addition, because all information could be converted to bits and added, regardless of the original form of the stimulation.

Cybernetic model building and the application of the information theory to psychological problems began immediately. They brought into psychology many terms that are now the coin of the realm: input, output, signal, signal-to-noise ratio, uncertainty, redundancy, bits and chunks of information, information processing, encoding, and the like. Of psychological interest are two other volumes of Wiener's *The Human Use of Human Beings* (1950) and *Cybernetics of the Nervous System* (1965).

Biographic data: *IESS* 16:545; N. Wiener, *Ex-prodigy: My Childhood and Youth,* 1953

HERSKOVITS, MELVILLE JEAN

American anthropologist
Rating: 13
Born: Bellefontaine, Ohio, September 10, 1895
Died: Evanston, Illinois, February 25, 1963
Highest degree: Ph.D. in anthropology, Columbia University, 1923
Positions, honors: 1924, Columbia University; 1927, Northwestern University; editorial work for *American Anthropologists,* 1949–1952; honorary D. Sc., Sarah Lawrence College, 1962, numerous honors and memberships in bodies related to anthropology, especially Negro anthropology

Herskovits contributed to psychology by his study of cultural influences on perception. His "carpentered" environment theory predicts that individuals living in such environments (as opposed to those living in the forest, round huts, caves or canyons) would tend to perceive the Müller- Lyer and other geometric illusions in perspective or as two dimensional representations of three dimensional objects and hence be more susceptible to such illusions. Dwellers in different types of "uncarpentered" environments would be more or less susceptible to the illusions depending on the specific environmental features and the nature of the illusion. The theory and a series of empirical studies with 1,878 subjects from diverse habitats are presented in *The Influence of Culture on Visual Perception* (1966) by M. H. Segall, D. T. Campbell, and Herskovits, which appeared after Herskovits's death. Herskovits contributed some twenty books on anthropology.

Biographic data: IESS 6:353

VYGOTSKII, LEON SEMENOVICH

Russian psychologist
Rating: 20
Born: Gomel', White Russia, 1896
Died: Moscow, June 11, 1934
Education: Studied at First State University of Moscow between 1913 and 1917, under K. N. Kornilov [383]
Positions: Second State University, Moscow; Institute of Psychology, Moscow; editorial work for *Voprosy defektologii, Pediatriya, and Voprosy psikhologii, pedologii, i psikhotekhniki*

Vygotskiĭ dealt with the development of consciousness in the course of evolution and in ontogeny. He considered the latter to be a qualitative change in the mind. Vygotskiĭ emphasized the role of education in psychological development, insisting that instruction must keep ahead of development. He conducted some of the first studies on concept formation in school children. He developed a test that bears his name, designed to test concept formation by having the subject group blocks according to different properties of the blocks. In his best known work, *Mysl' i rech'* (1934, English translation, *Thought and Language*, 1962), Vygotskiĭ considers the determining factor of a child's psychological development to be his social development, especially language development. In the course of the child's mental development his mental functions not only grow but, in a complex system of interrelations, develop new mental functional systems. The main change-producing factor is speech. The meaning of a word changes as a child grows up, which, in turn, brings about changes in his mental structure.

Vygotskiĭ also conducted psychopathological studies. He was one of the first psychologists to investigate conceptualization in schizophrenia. One of his main findings was that schizophrenics find it difficult, if not impossible, to use and understand metaphoric or figurative language. This finding forms the basis of a number of psychiatric diagnostic tests. Vygotskiĭ's work in pedology and defectology at the Institute for the Experimental Study of Mental Retardation in Moscow developed Soviet psychology in these areas and was used in applied situations of child care and training. Books written by Vygotskiĭ include *Pedagogicheskaya psikhologiya* (1926), *Pedologiya shkol'nogo vozrasta* (1928), *Etyudy po istorii povedeniya* (1930, with A. R. Luriya), *Pedologiya podrostka* (1931), and *Osnovy pedologii* (1934).

Biographic data: A. R. Luria, Leon Semenovich Vygotskiĭ. *Character and Personality*, 1935, 3, 238–240; A. R. Luria, Professor Leon Semenovich Vygotskiĭ. *Journal of Genetic Psychology*, 1935, 46, 224–226

TEPLOV, BORIS MIKHAILOVICH

[488]

Russian psycholgist
Rating: (unrated)
Born: Tula, October 21, 1896
Died: Moscow, September 28, 1965

Highest degree: Doctor of pedagogical sciences, 1947

Positions, honors: 1921–1933, various Red Army research estab-
lishments concerned with camouflage and visual perception;
1929, associate to head of research department, Institute of
Psychology, Moscow; lecturer at Moscow State University; chief
editor, *Voprosy Psikhologii*, 1958–1965; several awards, prizes,
other honors

After studying at Moscow University and graduating as an
engineer from a military school of camouflage in 1921, Teplov
did considerable work on camouflage, some of which was
published in journals of military technology. He extended his
work to problems of light and vision in architecture (*Tsveto-
videnie dlya arkhitektorov*, 1938), did an original study of the
psychology of the military leader during World War II (*Um i
volya polkovodtsa*), and wrote a widely used psychology text for
high schools that saw eight editions and was translated into
fourteen languages. Teplov then shifted to the study of individual
differences. In this area he wrote a book on the psychology of
musical abilities (*Psikhologiya muzikal'nykh sposobnosteĭ*, 1947),
and one on individual differences in general (*Problemy individual'nykhh razlichii*, 1961). Immediately after the 1950 "Pavlovian sessions" in which scientists were urged to incorporate
Pavlov's [206] teachings in their work, Teplov embarked on the
most sigificant portion of his career, the study of the properties
of the central nervous system. In contrast to other Russian
psychologists, Teplov stressed the study of types of the nervous
system, not of behavior types, his main thesis being that a
distinction must be made between types of the nervous system,
which are innately determined, and types of behavior, which are
alloys of innate temperament and experience, and that therefore
prediction of behavior from a knowledge of type of nervous
system alone is impossible, especially in man in whom language
plays a crucial modifying role. Teplov emphasized the study of
the strength parameter of the nervous system, and devised several
methods for assessing this and other parameters postulated by
Pavlov and elaborated by himself. Teplov's main publications in
this area are *O ponyatiyakh slabosti i inertnosti nervnoĭ systemy*
(1955), *Ob izuchenii tipologicheskikh svoĭstv nervnoĭ sistemy i
ikh psikhologicheskikh yavleniĭ* (1957), *Novye dannye po
izucheniyu svoĭstv nervnoĭ sistemy cheloveka* (1963), and the
four volumes of studies from his laboratory that he coauthored
and edited, *Tipologicheskie osobennosti vyssheĭ nervnoĭ
deyatel'nosti cheloveka* 1959–1965).

Biographic data: [Anon.] Boris Mikhailovich Teplov. *Voprosy Psikhologii*, 1965(6), **11**, 4–6

FENICHEL, OTTO [489]

Austrian psychoanalyst
Rating: 15
Born: Austria, 1897
Died: California, 1946
Highest degree:
Positions: 1924–1933, Berlin Psychoanalytic Institute; 1933–1938, private practice of psychoanalysis in Oslo and Prague; 1938–1946, private practice of psychoanalysis·in California

Fenichel was an orthodox Freudian psychoanalyst. He published seventy two papers and made more than two hundred oral presentations. His most notable book is *The Psychoanalytic Theory of the Neuroses* (1946).

Biographic data: E. Simmel, Otto Fenichel. *International Journal of Psychoanalysis,* 1946, 27, 67–71

LANDIS, CARNEY [490]

American psychologist
Rating: 16
Born: West Alexandria, Ohio, January 11, 1897
Died: New York, New York, March 5, 1962
Highest degree: Ph.D. in psychology, University of Minnesota, 1924, under K. S. Lashley [466]
Positions: 1926, Wesleyan University; 1930–1962, New York State Psychiatric Institute and Hospital, New York City, research psychologist; also professor of psychology at Columbia University.

Landis was a mainly a laboratory research psychologist, with a wide range of interests, of which the strongest was in psychopathology (*Modern Society and Mental Disease*, 1938; *Sex in*

Development, 1940; *Personality and Sexuality of the Physically Handicapped Women*, 1942; *Varieties of Psychopathological Experience* 1964). With W. A. Hunt, Landis penned a classic monograph on the startle response (*The Startle Pattern*, 1939) as well as a number of papers on the expression and physiology of emotion. He did additional work on personality inventories, psychosurgery, flicker fusion, and psychopharmacology.

Biographic data: W. A. Hunt, Carney Landis. *American Journal of Psychology*, 1962, 75, 506–509

[491]

BEEBE-CENTER, JOHN GILBERT

American psychologist
Rating: 19
Born: Boston, Massachusetts, March 19, 1897
Died: Cambridge, Massachusetts, December 6, 1958
Highest degree: Ph.D. in psychology, Harvard University, 1926
Positions: 1923–1958, Harvard University

Beebe-Center began his career in psychology by writing a brilliant thesis on affective equilibrium, one of the first investigations in the area that was later known by the name of adaptation level. He developed the topic in his 1932 book, *The Psychology of Pleasantness and Unpleasantness*, his major work. Beebe-Center spent the last years of his life in the study of taste, to which he was led by his study of the feeling value of odors. His researches on threshold determination and scaling of taste led to the development of a psychological scale of taste, with gust as the unit.

Biographic data: E. G. Boring, John Gilbert Beebe-Center. *American Journal of Psychology*, 1959, 72, 311–315

[492]

MCGEOCH, JOHN ALEXANDER

American psychologist
Rating: 20
Born: Argyle, New York, October 9, 1897

Died: Iowa City, Iowa, March 3, 1942
Highest degree: Ph.D. in psychology, University of Chicago, 1926
Positions: 1920, Washington University; 1928, University of Arkansas; 1930, University of Missouri, professor and head of psychology department; 1935, Wesleyan University; 1939, State University of Iowa, professor and head of psychology department; editorial work for *Psychological Bulletin* (1931–1942), *American Journal of Psychology, Journal of Psychology* (1935–1942)

McGeoch was a psychologist in the functionalist school who studied animal and human learning. He was first to formulate (1932) the basic ideas of forgetting in terms of interference, according to which an association becomes permanently stored after it is established and that forgetting is due to competition from associations that are already established or become established afterwards. Subsequent research on retroactive and proactive interference has lent support to the interference theory of forgetting. Another contribution of McGeoch's was his relating the different types of learning situations in terms of a hierarchy, from classical conditioning to problem solving, in which each higher type implies the existence of the lower ones. McGeoch's only book, *The Psychology of Human Learning,* appeared in the year of his death. Coauthored by A. L. Irion, the second edition of the book was published in 1952.

Biographic data: C. E. Seashore, John Alexander McGeoch. *Science,* 1942, 95, 293–294; [Anon.] Professor John Alexander McGeoch. *Psychological Bulletin,* 1942, 39, 199

ALLPORT, GORDON WILLARD   [493]

American psychologist
Rating: 27
Born: Montezuma, Indiana, November 11, 1897
Died: Cambridge, Massachusetts, October 9, 1967
Highest degree: Ph.D. in psychology, Harvard University, 1922, under Herbert S. Langfeld [387]

Positions, honors: 1924–1967, Harvard University editor, *Journal of Abnormal and Social Psychology*, 1937–1949; president, American Psychological Association, 1939; APA Distinguished Scientific Contribution Award, 1964

Allport was a personality psychologist who viewed the human personality as an evolving system of habits, attitudes, and traits (*Personality: A Psychological Interpretation*, 1937). Personality involves both physiological and mental processes. In man, motivational systems may become autonomous ("functional autonomy"), causing behavior that no longer depends on the original needs. The causes of behavior are thus in the present.

Allport favored the trait approach to personality (*Trait Names, A Psycho-lexical Study*, 1936). Traits, like habits, generalize to individuals and situations. There are traits that belong to the individual and traits that are common to some degree in most individuals. The unifying core of the personality is the proprium or self. The self's propriate striving is directed toward the realization of its potentialities and life goals. Allport's person is motivated more by social than biological factors (*Personality and Social Encounter*, 1960). He seeks new and higher goals, always trying to become something new and different, and is not satisfied with repeated reinstatements of homeostatic equilibrium (*Becoming: Basic Considerations for a Psychology of Personality*, 1955; *Pattern and Growth in Personality*, 1961). The adult personality is unique.

Allport contributed also to personality assessment methodology (*The Use of Personal Documents in Psychological Science*, 1942), originating such psychological instruments as the *A-S Reaction Study* (with Floyd Allport), and the *Study of Values* (1931, with P. E. Vernon; revised edition, 1951, with P. E. Vernon and G. Lindzey). The latter, based on Eduard Spranger's [411] classification of human types, has been widely used and researched.

Dedicated to a psychology that takes as its own the model of man as person, Allport was a cofounder of the Department of Social Relations at Harvard in 1946, and was counted among the "third force" or humanistic psychologists who reject both the behavioristic and psychoanalytic views of man. While Allport's output of publications was not very large (eleven books and about twenty papers), the influence he exercised through his writings and through his personality on his students and others was great.

Biographic data: HPA 5:1; T. F. Pettigrew, Gordon Willard Allport. *Journal of Personality and Social Psychology*, 1969, 12(1), 1–5

American psychologist
Rating: (unrated)
Born: Philadelphia, Pennsylvania, November 9, 1898
Died: Washington, D.C., September 16, 1973
Highest degree: Ph.D. in psychology, Harvard University, 1924, under W. F. Dearborn [379]
Positions, honors: 1925, Princeton University; 1927, Brown University; 1938–1952, Tufts College; 1953, secretary, Smithsonian Institution; 1964, chairman, Committee for Research and Exploration, National Geographic Society; president, American Psychological Association, 1940; president, American Philosophical Society, 1970–1973; twenty-three honorary degrees; two Presidential Citations

Carmichael's early interest centered on the psychobiology of development, in which area he published several important monographs and papers. In the 1920s and 1930s there appeared the oft-cited papers on the development of amblystoma and frog tadpoles in an anesthetic, the righting reflex in cats, behavioral development in guinea pigs as a function of fetal stimulation, and others. The main finding in these papers was that genetic determinants were more important in development than environmental ones. Carmichael also wrote chapters on prenatal behavior for several edited works, including a widely used *Manual of Child Psychology* (1946, 2nd edition, 1954), of which he was the editor. In 1935, he reported (with H. H. Jasper) the development of the electroencephalograh and the first recording of the EEG in America. Although Carmichael was mainly an administrator during his Tufts period, he did research on reading and eye movements, which resulted in the publication (with W. F. Dearborn) of the well-known volume on *Reading and Visual Fatigue* (1947). During World War II Carmichael recruited psychologists for the war effort. As director of the National Roster of Scientific and Specialized Personnel he eventually presided over a staff of over 400 people. He became involved in numerous committees, boards, etc., of the Armed Forces, the national government, and scientific organizations that were engaged in the management of scientific manpower resources, as well as in a very large number of civic organizations. His positions on various boards, as the chief executive of the Smithsonian Institution, and as government consultant, allowed Carmichael to present psychology to the public and to speak for it very effectively.

Biographic data: *HPA* 5:27; *NCAB* F:200

OBONAI, TORAO

Japanese psychologist
Rating: (unrated)
Born: Fukuoka, Iwate prefecture, April 25, 1899
Died: Tokyo, December 21, 1968
Highest degree: Bungakushi (in psychology), Tokyo Imperial University, 1924, under M. Matsumoto [284]; doctor of letters, Tokyo Bunrika University, 1952
Positions: 1926, Tokyo Koto-Gakko (National College); 1946, Tokyo Bunrika (Arts and Sciences) University; 1963, Nihon University; editorial work for *Psychologia* and *Journal of Genetic Psychology*

Obonai was an eclectic experimental psychologist who worked in all areas of psychology, leaving behind a bibliography of approximately 550 items. His strongest interest was in the area of perception. Between 1928 and 1968 Obonai authored some 120 papers on perception, most of them on visual perception, especially figural aftereffects, the geometric illusions, and other instances of illusory perception. In seventy-seven papers published between 1932 and 1968 Obonai offered a theory of "psychophysical induction" as well as experimental support for it. Its main features were Hering's [167] concept of anabolism and catabolism, Pavlov's [206] idea of excitation and inhibition, and Köhler's [447] field theory. The theory eventually exceeded its perceptual bounds as Obonai attempted to have it serve as an explanatory concept for most behaviors. Obonai's best known books are [*A Textbook of Psychology*] (1930), [*A Manual of Experimental Psychology*] (1950), [*Visual Perception*] (1955), and [*Memory and Thinking*] (1956).

Biographic data: T. Kaneko, The late professor Obonai and his psychological works. *Psychologia*, 1969, 12(3-4), 186–188; K. Sato, Professor Torao Obonai. *Psychologia*, 1969, 12(2), 63–64

BEKESY, GEORGE VON

Hungarian-American physicist
Rating: (unrated)
Born: Budapest, Hungary, June 3, 1899
Died: Honolulu, Hawaii, June 15, 1972
Highest degree: Ph.D. in physics, University of Budapest, 1923

Positions, honors: 1923–1946, acoustics researcher, Hungarian Telephone System laboratories; 1932–1946, on University of Budapest faculty; 1946, Karolinska Institute, Stockholm, Sweden; 1947, Harvard University, senior research fellow in psychophysics; 1966, University of Hawaii, professor of sensory sciences; honorary M.D. from University of Berne, 1959, Wilhelm University, Münster, Germany, 1955, University of Padua, 1962; honorary D.Sc., University of Pennsylvania, 1965; ten scientific medals; 1961 Nobel prize in medicine and physiology

Békésy spent his life studying the physics of sensory perception, especially that of hearing. He invented the tracking method of continuous recording of a subject's hearing as the subject controls the intensity of a tone around the threshold value. By this method a complete audiogram may be obtained in less than half an hour.

Békésy's major achievement was the observation of the actual operation of the basilar membrane of the cochlea as the ear was being stimulated by sounds of different frequencies. Using a microscope and a strobe light, Békésy saw that a sound sets up a traveling wave in the basilar membrane whose shape varies with the frequency, intensity, and complexity of the sound. High frequencies produce maximum displacement of the basilar membrane near the oval window, while low frequencies do so near the apex of the membrane. Békésy assumed that pitch is related to maximum displacement in the basilar membrane produced by the traveling wave. He constructed a model of the cochlea, and, assuming evolutionary similarity between the basilar membrane and the skin, stimulated the forearms of his subjects with this model, demonstrating very exact localization of the maximum stimulation produced by the piston-and-cylinder model in the subject's skin. Békésy's findings replaced the theory of hearing of Helmholtz [143], who thought that the cells of the basilar membrane resonated to sound frequencies according to their length.

Békésy wrote a chapter on the mechanical properties of the ear for Steven's [517] *Handbook of Experimental Psychology* (1951). In 1960, he presented his theory of neural quantum in the discrimination of loudness and pitch in his *Experiments in Hearing*. His second book, one on *Sensory Inhibition*, appeared in 1967. It reviews all of Békésy's work and describes the operation of the haptic senses, vision, audition, taste, and smell in terms of lateral inhibition, which Békésy believed to be a common feature of all sense organs. Between 1928 and 1967 Békésy published

121 papers, most of them on hearing and specifically the cochlear mechanics, but also some on taste and skin sensations.

Biographic data: *New York Times,* June 15, 1972, 44:4; E. B. Newman, George von Békésy: 1899–1972. *American Journal of Psychology,* 1973, 86, 855–857

[497]

FULTON, JOHN FARQUHAR

American physiologist
Rating: 14
Born: St. Paul, Minnesota, November 1, 1899
Died: New Haven, Connecticut, May 29, 1960
Highest degree: Ph.D. in physiology, Oxford University, 1925; M.D., Harvard University, 1927
Positions, honors: 1923–1925, Oxford University, demonstrator in physiology; 1929–1951, Yale University, professor of physiology, 1951–1960, head, Department of History of Medicine; nine honorary degrees, other honors

In 1926, Fulton published a book dealing with *Muscular Contraction and the Reflex Control of Movement.* Pursuing this topic further, Fulton discovered, in 1928, that the nervous structures called muscle spindles are triggered by stretching the muscle. In 1929, Fulton established the first primate laboratory for experimental physiology in America, and later founded, with Dusser de Barenne [433], the *Journal of Neurophysiology.* Fulton wrote additional books in physiology, including the revision of the 15th edition of *Howell's Textbook of Physiology* (1946). Of interest to psychology is his text on *Frontal Lobotomy and Affective Behavior* (1951).

Biographic data: NCAB 25:234

[498]

KRIS, ERNST

Austrian-American psychoanalyst
Rating: 11
Born: Vienna, Austria, April 26, 1900

Died: New York, New York, February 27, 1957
Highest degree: Ph.D. in art history, University of Vienna, 1922
Positions: Private practice; went to England in the 1930s; with BBC during World War II, left it to come to United States; coeditor of *Imago* from 1933

Kris was one of several ego-psychologists who extended the Freudian concept of ego to make it less dependent on the id. Kris held that both the id and the ego arise from a more primitive matrix, conferring greater functional autonomy to the ego than is possible in Freudian theory. In comparison with Freud [224], Kris attributed more functions to the ego that do not arise from conflict: movement, perception, reality testing, and thinking. Kris's ego regression theory develops Freud's idea of the nature of genius. The psychotic cannot control the eruptions from his unconscious and, since he does not elaborate on the contents of the unconscious, he does not communicate. A creative person who faces a problem may, on the other hand, regress to an earlier stage of development when the problem used to be less structured, restructure it, and formulate it in productive, communicable terms. By his emphasis on ego psychology Kris contributed toward a rapprochement between psychoanalysis and general psychology.

In England during World War II Kris studied German radio propaganda, and, on arriving in the United States, published his *German Radio Propagand: Report on Home Broadcasts During the War* (with Hans Speier, 1944). Kris applied psychoanalytic concepts to the study of art (*Psychoanalytic Explorations in Art*, 1952) and children. He initiated the Child Study Center at Yale University Medical School and the Gifted Adolescent Research Project at New York Psychoanalytic Institute to study the dynamic factors underlying children's behavior. In a discussion with Leopold Bellak, Kris suggested that children may be expected to identify more readily with animals than with humans. Bellak (and S. S. Bellak) constructed the Children's Apperception Test (1949) on the basis of Kris's idea.

Biographic data: *IESS* 8:452; R. M. Loewenstein, In memoriam Ernst Kris. *Journal of the American Psychoanalytic Association*, 1957, 5, 741–743; S. Ritvo, Ernst Kris. *Psychoanalytic Quarterly*, 1957, 26, 248–250; H. Hartmann, Ernst Kris. *Psychoanalytic Study of the Child*, 1957, 12, 9–15; W. Hoffer, Ernst Kris. *International Journal of Psychoanalysis*, 1957, 38, 359–362

American sociologist
Rating: 13
Born: Sac City, Iowa, June 6, 1900
Died: Cambridge, Massachusetts, August 24, 1960
Highest degree: Ph.D. in sociology, University of Chicago, 1930
Positions, honors: 1930, University of Chicago; 1931, University of Wisconsin; 1935, University of Chicago; 1946, Harvard University; president, American Sociological Society, 1952–1953; honorary LL.D., 1939, Sc.D., 1948

Stouffer pioneered in large-scale quantitative research in sociology. His principal contributions lay in the correlational and descriptive analysis of survey data, as exemplified by the four volume of *Studies in Social Psychology in World War II*. Stouffer was the senior author of the two volumes of *The American Soldier* (1949) and of volume 4 of the series, *Measurement and Prediction* (1950). He stuck close to the data, and ventured into theory only on a small-scale basis. One theoretical concept of considerable heuristic value that Stouffer stressed in *The American Soldier* was the concept of relative deprivation. Stouffer was influenced by such quantitatively oriented psychologists as Thurstone [448], as well as by Pearson [229] and Fisher [464], and, in turn, influenced psychologists by setting an example in field research and through his contacts with them in the Laboratory of Social Relations at Harvard University that he established.

Biographic data: IESS 15:277; D. S. Thomas, Samuel Andrew Stouffer. In American Philosophical Society, *Year Book: 1961*, 1962, pp. 192–196

German-American psychologist
Rating: 14
Born: New York, New York, June 10, 1900
Died: Lawrence, Kansas, October 19, 1961
Highest degree: Ph.D. in psychology, University of Hamburg, 1927
Positions: 1930–1933, University of Hamburg; 1936, University of Louisville; 1937, University of Columbia; 1940, Wells College, 1941, Brooklyn College; 1942, City College of New

York; 1947, New School for Social Research; 1948, University of Kansas

Influenced by Gestalt theory, Scheerer wrote *Die Lehre von der Gestalt* in 1931. He wrote a few papers, and his major contribution was the development, with Kurt Goldstein [380], who was also influenced by the Gestalt theory, of several tests of concept formation that were incorporated in 1941 in a series of five diagnostic tests: Goldstein-Scheerer Cube Test, Weigl-Goldstein-Scheerer Color Form Sorting Test, Goldstein-Scheerer Stick Test, Gelb-Goldstein Sorting Test, and Goldstein-Scheerer Object Sorting Test.

Biographic data: *New York Times,* October 20, 1961, 30:4

WARNER, LUCIEN HYNES [501]

American psychologist
Rating: 11
Born: Irvington, New York, September 9, 1900
Died: Las Vegas, Nevada, 1963
Highest degree: Ph.D. in psychology, Columbia University, 1927
Positions: 1926–1927, New York University; 1928–1930, National Research Council fellow in biological sciences; 1932–1934, research director, l'Oeil Qui Voie, Mont Pelerin, Switzerland; 1935–1937, Duke University; 1938–1941 Opinion Research Corporation, Princeton, New Jersey; 1942–1943, Office of War Information; 1944–1948, associate director of research, *Life* magazine; 1948–1958, Claremont Graduate School; 1959, business consultant.

Warner was a comparative psychologist. He coauthored several of his early papers with C. J. Warden [465], as well as two books, *Animal Motivation* (1931, with C. J. Warden and others) and *Comparative Psychology,* three volumes (with C. J. Warden and T. N. Jenkins). Warner wrote four more books and a fair number of papers on animal drives, learning, and discrimination. He contributed to the development of the method for training seeing-eye dogs.

Biographic data: *The Psychological Register,* 1932, vol. 3

NISSEN, HENRY WIEGHORST

American psychologist
Rating: **14**
Born: Chicago, Illinois, February 5, 1901
Died: Orange Park, Florida, April 27, 1958
Highest degree: Ph.D. in psychology, Columbia University, 1929
Positions: 1929–1956, Yale University research associate and professor of psychobiology; 1939–1958, Yerkes Laboratories of Primate Biology, associate director to director; 1956–1958, Emory University, professor of psychobiology.

Nissen, a comparative psychologist, was first to conduct experiments with chimpanzees in the late 1920s, continuing to work with this species throughout his career. Nissen studied perception, learning, as well as the more complex behaviors in chimpanzees. In a well known study (1951) Nissen and collaborators investigated the effect of tactual deprivation in a chimpanzee. Nissen wrote a chapter on phylogenetic comparison for S. S. Stevens's [517] *Handbook of Experimental Psychology* (1951) and a book, *The Great Apes* (1932). He wrote, himself or with others, some fifty papers, the majority of them on the behavior of chimpanzees.

Biographic data: *The Psychological Register,* 1932, vol. 3

RAZRAN, GREGORY

American psychologist
Rating: (unrated)
Born: Near Slutsk, Russia, June 4, 1901
Died: St. Petersburg Beach, Florida, August 31, 1973
Highest degree: Ph.D. in psychology, Columbia University, 1933, under R. S. Woodworth[312]
Positions: 1929–1940, Columbia University; 1938–1940, statistical consultant, Civil Aeronautics Administration; 1941–1944, consultant, Office of Strategic Services; 1940–1972, Queens College, CUNY, instructor to professor of psychology, chairman of department of psychology 1945–1966

Razran did extensive research and contributed more than fifty papers in the area of classical conditioning. A series of ten of these papers is concerned with the conditioned reflex as an index of meaning. Razran demonstrated in himself how the strength of the salivary reflex varies with the degree of proficiency in a language when words in different languages are used as the conditioned stimuli. Razran was also one of the very few individuals who, by way of review articles, kept American psychologists informed on developments in psychology in the Soviet Union. Two years before his death, Razran brought together his knowledge of conditioning, learning, and Russian psychology in the book, *Mind in Evolution* (1971), in which he attempted to integrate classical conditioning, instrumental conditioning, and sign learning within an evolutionary framework by relating the various types of learning to levels of evolutionary development.

Biographic data: *American Men of Science*

LOUTTIT, CHAUNCEY MCKINLEY [504]

American psychologist
Rating: **13**
Born: Buffalo, New York, October 9, 1901
Died: Detroit, Michigan, May 24, 1956
Highest degree: Ph.D. in psychology, Yale University, 1928, under R. Dodge [327]
Positions: 1928, University of Hawaii; 1930, University of Ohio; 1931, Indiana University; 1940, U.S. Navy, various psychological posts; 1945, Ohio State University; 1946, Sampson College; 1947, University of Illinois; 1954, Wayne State University; president, American Association for Applied Psychology, 1943; editorial work for *Psychological Abstracts,* 1947–1956, *Psychological Record,* 1937–1942, *Directory of Applied Psychology,* 1941, 1943

Louttit's 1936 book, *Clinical Psychology: A Handbook of Children's Behavior Problems,* was influential in the development of clinical psychology in the United States, and played a role in the growth of the field of child development. Louttit established a graduate training program at Ohio State University after World War II. It became a part of and impetus to the rapid growth of clinical psychology after World War II. Louttit also wrote several articles and notes on the use of literature in psychology, the classification of psychological literature, editorial matters, and was the 1952 chairman of the American Psychological Association committee in charge of preparing the APA Publication Manual.

Biographic data: J. W. Carter, C. M. Louttit, psychologist. *Science,* 1956, 24, 526–527; K. M. Dallenbach, Chauncey McKinley Louttit. *American Journal of Psychology,* 1956, 69, 682–685; F. C. Thorne, Chauncey McKinley Louttit. *Journal of Clinical Psychology,* 1957, 13, 99

[505] ANGYAL, ANDRAS

Hungarian-American psychiatrist
Rating: 13
Born: Hungary, June 21, 1902
Died: Boston, Massachusetts, December 31, 1960
Highest degree: Ph.D. in psychology, University of Vienna, 1926; M.D., University of Turin, 1932
Positions: 1932, State Hospital, Worcester, Massachusetts; 1945, private practice in psychiatry, Boston

Angyal was a representative of the holistic point of view in psychiatry and psychology. He recognized two basic motivational patterns in man: toward mastery (autonomy) and toward love (homonomy). Personality structure is a specific modification of these two trends. Causal examination of behavior is not very useful. Instead, personality should be considered as a system governed by the principles of autonomy and homonomy, and the connection between any two elements in this system is a function of the superordinate system to which they both belong. Thus the causal relationship of the past to the present can be reversed in system thinking: if the governing principles changes, relationships change and the present may determine the past as past events acquire different meaning. A personality is organized dualistically. Both health and neurosis function as a system. This "universal ambiguity" means that every person contains the seeds of both mental health and neurosis. Therapy consists of restoring dominance to the health system. Angyal's views are contained in his *Foundations for a Science of Personality* (1941) and *Neurosis and Treatment: A Holistic Theory* (1965).

Biographic data: IESS 1:302

American psychologist
Rating: (unrated)
Born: Bay City, Michigan, July 23, 1902
Died: New York, August 20, 1968
Highest degree: S.D., University of Michigan, 1928
Positions: 1927–1946, New York University; 1942–1968, American Museum of Natural History, associate curator and curator, Department of Animal Behavior; 1945–1958, adjunct professor, New York University; 1947–1968, adjunct professor, City University New York

Schneierla was the foremost representative of comparative psychology in America between 1930 and 1968. He was the chief opponent of Konrad Lorenz on theoretical questions. Schneierla stressed the impossibility of separating instinct from learning, urging the use of the terms maturation and experience, even though these too, he believed, could not be studied separately but were only conceptual conveniences. Schneierla's second basic idea was that of integrative levels of behavioral organization. These levels differentiate phylogenetic levels of animals in that qualitatively different behaviors may be observed under the same circumstances in two animal species. Schneierla's most significant contribution was his "biphasic A-W theory," which describes all existing behavior as well as the evolution and ontogeny of behavior in terms of approach and withdrawal with respect to points in the environment, weak stimulation from such points producing approach, strong stimulation withdrawal.

Schneierla's most important empirical observations were those on the behavior of the army ants, a subject that he began to work on early in his career (*Learning and Orientation in Ants,* 1928). With N. R. F. Maier, Schneierla wrote his most influential book, *Principles of Animal Psychology,* (1935). A classic text of comparative psychology, it is still being used, and most contemporary comparative psychologists have been brought up on it. In 1938, Schneierla and L. C. Crafts published *Recent Experiments in Psychology,* and L. R. Aronson and others edited and published posthumously (1972) *Selected Writings of T. C. Schneierla.*

Biographic data: *New York Times,* August 21, 1968, 42:1

DUNCKER, KARL

German psychologist
Rating: 18
Born: Leipzig, February 2, 1903
Died: Swarthmore, Pennsylvania, February 23, 1940
Highest degree: Ph.D. in psychology, University of Berlin, 1929
Positions: 1929–1937, University of Berlin; 1938-1940, Swarthmore College

Duncker was a Gestalt psychologist who contributed during his short life to the psychology of creativity and problem solving. Around 1930 he first proposed the concept of functional fixity as related to problem solving. In a 1935 monograph (Zur Psychologie des produktiven Denkens, English translation, On Problem-Solving, 1945) he gave a detailed description of the organization of problem solving: the establishment of the general range of the problem and its possible solutions, the stage of functional solutions, and the stage of specific solutions.

Biographic data: *The Psychological Register,* 1932, vol. 3

BRUNSWIK, EGON

Austrian-American psychologist
Rating: 26
Born: Budapest, Hungary, March 18, 1903
Died: Berkeley, California, July 7, 1955
Highest degree: Ph.D. in psychology, University of Vienna, 1927, under Karl Bühler [385]
Positions: 1927–1935, University of Vienna; 1935–1936, University of Ankara, visiting professor, established first psychological laboratory there (School of Education); 1936–1955, University of California at Berkeley

Brunswik's theoretical approach to psychology, probabilistic functionalism, is based on his belief that the method of psychology should rest on that of the physical sciences and that the matter of concern of psychology should be an analysis of how organisms adjust to the environment. To Brunswik, common methodology does not mean common laws, however. The aim of experimentation in psychology is the analysis of the organism's ability to estimate or "attain" the value of the distal stimulus, even though the proximal stimulus varies. Adjustment to the environment thus occurs under probabilistic, i.e., partly unpredictable conditions. In the utilization of environmental cues the perceiver therefore engages in a process resembling statistical reasoning, for instance, the weighting of probabilities. An organism attains increasingly more veridical perception by incorporating, through contiguity, new cues to an existing cue-family hierarchy. Much of this acquisition is unconscious. The degree to which a distal property and a proximal cue vary together determines the degree of the "ecological validity" of the cue with respect to that property.

Since the concern of psychology is the functional adaptation of organisms to the natural environment, the design of experiments should be not systematic, as in the physical sciences, but representative, i.e., their results should have validity in predicting, by statistical generalizations, behavior in the organism's natural habitat. Many of Brunswik's experiments were thus directed at the phenomenon of perceptual constancy and its achievement, which he conducted in natural settings. The Brunswik ratio, which predicts the matching of colors when stimulus and matching samples are under two different illuminations, was one outcome of his constancy research.

Brunswik and his probabilistic functionalism theory created no following, and his output of scientific papers was small, about twenty. His thinking, however, has exercised considerable attraction to psychologists, and Brunswik's ideas may be found, in one form or another, in writings of a considerable number of contemporary psychologists. Brunswik was the author of the following books: *Wahrnehmung und Gegenstandswelt,* (1934), *Experimentelle Psychologie in Demonstrationen* (1935), and *Perception and the Representative Design of Psychological Experiments* (1956).

Biographic data: *IESS* 2:156; E. C. Tolman, Egon Brunswik. *American Journal of Psychology,* 1956, 69, 315–324; in K. R. Hammond, *The Psychology of Egon Brunswik,* 1966

ZENER, KARL EDWARD

[509]

American psychologist
Rating: 15
Born: Indianapolis, Indiana, April 22, 1903
Died: Durham, North Carolina, September 27, 1964

Highest degree: Ph.D., in psychology, Harvard University, 1926
Positions: 1927, Princeton University; 1928, Duke University, chairman, Psychology Department since 1961; editorial work for *Journal of Psychology, Journal of Personality,* and *Character and Personality*

In the 1930s, Zener directed the work of a Pavlovian conditioning laboratory at Duke and, finding inadequacies in some of the Pavlovian formulations, introduced some changes. Most of Zener's scientific papers, which were not very numerous, were on problems in conditioning. He also studied motivation in relation to learning and perception, but the work for which he is best known was the phenomenological analysis of perceptual experience. This subject occupied Zener for the last fifteen years of his life. Zener analyzed the perceptual process that intervenes between the object and the central processes in the cortex into six phases, and considered this sequence of phases "as constituting an alternating and interlocking series of relatively isomorphic energy transformations and transmissions with interactions at the nodal regions of object surfaces, receptor mosaic, and successive synaptic relay regions." While in general approving of J. J. Gibson's approach to perception, Zener stressed the necessity to reexamine the experiential properties of the world instead of limiting oneself to an examination of the stimulus and the response alone. For this purpose Zener studied, both phenomenologically and using the eye movement recording technique, the experience and behavior of individuals as they looked at photographs and paintings in which the right and left sides or top and bottom were reversed. Zener's major theoretical statement may be found in a chapter that he wrote with Mercedes Gaffron on perceptual experience for *Psychology: A Study of a Science* (vol. 4, 1962).

Biographic data: *New York Times,* September 28, 1964, 29:5; E. E. Jones, Karl Edward Zener. *Journal of Personality*, 1964, 32, 511–513

[510]

SCHLOSBERG, HAROLD

American psychologist
Rating: 20
Born: Brooklyn, New York, January 3, 1904
Died: Providence, Rhode Island, August 5, 1964
Highest degree: Ph.D. in psychology, Princeton University, 1928

Positions: 1928–1964, Brown University, chairman of Psychology Department since 1954; 1953–1964, consultant to Surgeon General, U.S. Army

Schlosberg worked at first in the area of learning and conditioning, then made a major contribution in the area of emotion. In 1938, R. S. Woodworth [312] had developed a scale of emotions from judgments of posed photographs. Schlosberg used Woodworth's scale in 1941 and concluded that emotions vary along two bipolar dimensions: pleasantness-unpleasantness and attention-rejection. He then noticed that if these dimensions were placed at right angles to each other, photographs of posed emotions could be placed, according to their ratings, in an oval surface with the bipolar axes dividing it into four quadrants (1952). In 1954, Schlosberg added a third dimension to the surface of emotions, intensity, making it into a cone, with sleep at its apex.

Woodworth wrote the first edition of his *Experimental Psychology* (1938) alone. He invited Schlosberg to be a coauthor of the 1954 edition. "Woodworth and Schlosberg" became one of the great texts in American psychology, and for the next fifteen or twenty years most American psychologists were being exposed to it one way or another. Schlosberg wrote about seventy papers on a variety of psychological topics: conditioning, motivation, emotion, perception, play, laboratory experiments in an introductory psychology course, and others.

Biographic data: J. W. Kling, Harold Schlosberg: An appreciation. *Psychological Reports*, 1965, 17, 473–474; C. Pfaffman, Harold Schlosberg. *American Journal of Psychology,* 1965, 78, 148–152

VALENTINE, WILLARD LEE [511]

American psychologist
Rating: 13
Born: Chillicothe, Ohio, December 2, 1904
Died: Evanston, Illinois, April 5, 1947
Highest degree: Ph.D. in psychology, Ohio State University, 1929, under A. P. Weiss [390]
Positions: 1925–1928, Ohio Wesleyan University; 1929, Ohio State University; 1940, Northwestern University, professor and chairman of Department of Psychology

Valentine's main professional interest was the improvement of professional journals in psychology. He became business manager of the publications of the American Psychological Association in 1937. He changed the format of the APA journals to improve their appearance and legibility, and introduced the journal club plan for APA journals. Valentine was elected editor of *Science,* the organ of the American Association for the Advancement of Science, in 1945, where he instituted similar changes. Valentine held the position of Treasurer of the APA since 1936, and was instrumental in establishing the permanent headquarters of that organization in Washington, D.C.

Valentine was also interested in undergraduate instruction. He built up the introductory psychology course at Ohio State University, made several instructional films on psychology, and wrote a laboratory manual, a *Book of Readings in Experimental Psychology* (1931), and *Experimental Foundations of General Psychology* (1938).

Biographic data: F. C. Dockery, Willard Lee Valentine. *Psychological Review,* 1947, **54**, 233–236; W. R. Miles, Willard Lee Valentine, *Science,* 1947, **105**, 638–640; R. H. Seashore., Willard Lee Valentine. *American Journal of Psychology,* 1947, **60**, 446–447; D. L. Wolfle, *Scientific Monthly,* 1947, **65**, 91–93

[512]

KLUCKHOHN, CLYDE KAY MABEN

American anthropologist
Rating: 18
Born: Le Mars, Iowa, January 11, 1905
Died: Santa Fe, New Mexico, July 29, 1960
Highest degree: Ph.D. in anthropology, Harvard University, 1936
Positions, honors: 1935–1960, Harvard University; president, American Anthropological Association, 1947; honorary L.H.D., University of New Mexico, 1949; Viking Fund medal and award, 1950

Kluckhohn spent most of his life as an ethnographer of the Navajo Indians. He wrote two books and a number of monographs and articles on the Navajo. In the Harvard Department of Social Relations, which he helped to organize, Kluckhohn shared not only departmental affiliation but also ideas with the psychologists who were part of it: Allport [493], Mowrer, Murray, Sears, and others. His interests were in culture (*Culture,* 1952, written with A. L. Kroeber), the problem of values (Values and value-orientedness in the theory of action, in *Toward a General Theory of Action,* 1951), and the relationship between culture and personality. With H. A. Murray, Kluckhohn edited *Personality in Nature, Society, and Culture* (1948, 2nd edition 1953), a popular source book on personality formation in which personality was defined by the editors as "the continuity of functional forms and forces manifested through sequences of organized regnant processes and overt behaviors from birth to death."

Biographic data: *IESS* 8:419; *NCAB* H:238; G. P. Murdock, Clyde Kluckhohn. *Behavioral Science,* 1961, 6, 2–4; E. Z. Vogt, Clyde Kay Maben Kluckhohn. In American Philosophical Society, *Year Book: 1961,* 1962, pp. 133–137

LORGE, IRVING   [513]

American psychologist
Rating: 14
Born: New York, New York, April 19, 1905
Died: New York, New York, January 23, 1960
Highest degree: Ph.D. in psychology, Columbia University, 1930
Positions: 1927, Columbia University Teachers College; 1946, executive officer, Institute of Psychological Research

Lorge was an educational psychologist, known for his contributions to the measurement of intelligence (*The Lorge-Throndike Intelligence Tests,* 1954–1957; *The Columbia Mental Maturity Scale,* 1953, constructed with L. Blum and B. Burgmeister for use with cerebral palsy cases), but primarily for having established the frequency of occurrence of different words in general literature. These counts of semantic frequency (*The Teacher's Word Book of 30,000 Words,* 1944, written with E. L. Thorndike [353], and *Semantic Count of the 570 Commonest English Words,* 1949) have been used extensively by researchers in educational, learning, and other areas of research.

Biographic data: *The Psychological Register,* 1932, vol. 3

KELLY, GEORGE ALEXANDER

American psychologist
Rating: 17
Born: near Perth, Kansas, April 28, 1905
Died: Waltham, Massachusetts, March 6, 1967
Highest degree: Ph.D. in psychology, State University of Iowa, 1931
Positions: 1931–1944, Kansas State College; 1945, University of Maryland; 1946–1965, Ohio State University, 1946–1951 and 1963–1965, director of Clinical Psychology; 1965–1967, Brandeis University

Kelly developed a cognitive personality theory that he referred to as the psychology of personal constructs. He published a two-volume work under that title in 1955. It was a theory of cognition applied to the psychology of personality. Kelly attributed most human behaviors to thinking, expectations, and other cognitions rather than motives or needs. Each person's behavior is guided by the way he interprets a situation, by the way he constructs his own theory of reality. An individual is therefore able to control his own life to a considerable degree. Kelly denied that it was necessary to consider motivation in a personality theory. The most important and the only element of personality is the personal construct or idea about the world that is based on self-evaluation and the evaluation of factors that most influence an individual's life, especially relationships to significant others. Kelly's theory has led to the development of a number of therapeutic techniques, such as the fixed-role therapy. Kelly himself developed a personality test, the Rep Test, to assess the client's problems. Hundreds of papers have been published with personal constructs as their theme, while Kelly himself published only about twenty. *Clinical Psychology and Personality* was published posthumously, in 1969.

Biographic data: *IESS* 8:358; G. G. Thompson, George Alexander Kelly. *Journal of General Psychology*, 1968, 79, 19–24

GRAHAM, CLARENCE HENRY

American psychologist
Rating: (unrated)
Born: Worcester, Massachusetts, January 6, 1906

Died: New York, New York, July 25, 1971

Highest degree: Ph.D. in psychology, Clark University, 1930, under J. P. Nafe

Positions, honors: 1930, University of Pennsylvania; 1932, Clark University; 1936, Brown University; 1945, Columbia University; medals, awards, merit certificates from Society of Experimental Psychologists, American Psychological Association, Optical Society of America, National Academy of Sciences, American Academy of Arts and Sciences, President of the United States, honorary D.Sc., Brown University, 1958

While Graham worked on a variety of problems, the bulk of his work is in vision. He worked first on achromatic vision, then color vision, and, during his later years, on space and movement perception. His best known studies are those on color vision which he, in collaboration with Yun Hsia, contributed over a period of some twenty years while at Columbia University. Graham produced about ninety publications, of which the most important was *Vision and Visual Perception* (1965), written with Brown, Bartlett, Hsia, Mueller, and Riggs.

Biographic data: F. A. Geldard, Clarence Henry Graham. *American Journal of Psychology*, 1972, 85, 291–294

SEASHORE, HAROLD GUSTAV [516]

American psychologist

Rating: 11

Born: Swea City, Iowa, August 4, 1906

Died: White Plains, New York, June 13, 1965

Highest degree: Ph.D. in psychology, State University of Iowa, 1933

Positions: 1930, fellow, University of Iowa; 1935, Springfield College, Massachusetts, professor of psychology, chairman of Psychology Department; 1942, Psychological Corporation, research associate to vice-president

Seashore's contributions to psychology arose in connection with his work for the Psychological Corporation. By 1946 he was made director of the Test Division of the corporation. As a test specialist he participated in test construction, especially of aptitude tests, and wrote numerous articles on the various aspects of testing. He was co-author (with G. K. Bennett) of the Seashore-Bennett Stenographic Proficiency Test (1946) and of a battery of tests for educational and vocational guidance of high school students, the Differential Aptitude Tests (1952), among others.

Biographic data: NCAB 52:595

[517]

STEVENS, S. SMITH

American psychologist
Rating: (unrated)
Born: Ogden, Utah, November 4, 1906
Died: Cambridge, Massachusetts, January 18, 1973
Highest degree: Ph.D. in psychology, Harvard University, 1933, under E. G. Boring [445]
Positions, honors: 1936–1973, Harvard University; American Psychological Association Distinguished Scientific Contribution Award, 1960; Gold Medal, British Acoustic Society; Medal, Society of Experimental Psychologists

Stevens was the most prominent psychophysicist of the 20th century. His early work was in audition, which eventually led him to the formulation of the power law of psychophysics. In 1934, Stevens devised a method for equating tones on one attribute when they differed on a second, such as high and low tones with respect to volume, and was able to draw isophonic curves for pitch, loudness, volume, and density, the latter a new tonal attribute discovered by Stevens. It was a first demonstration that the criterion for differentiating sensory attributes was not independent variability but independent constancy.

Additional contributions in the area of audition followed during the decade of the 1930s. In scaling the continua of pitch and loudness using equal sense distances rather that just noticeable differences, Stevens created a unit of sense distance for pitch, the mel, and one for loudness, the sone (1938). In 1936, he had already demonstrated that using the halving method, a true ratio scale for loudness could be constructed. Stevens also studied auditory localization (1934), showing that it is equally good for tones of 1,000 and 10,000 Hz, but worse around 3,000 Hz because dichotic phase difference is effective for low tones and dichotic intensity difference works for high tones, but that these two processes do not overlap sufficiently at 3,000 Hz to make for good localization. In 1941, Stevens found evidence that the perception of pitch and loudness is quantal rather than continuous. Extending the reasoning of several other workers, such as Békésy [496], Stevens supported a theory of hearing that involved traveling waves in the entire basilar membrane, a form of resonance theory, but different from that of Helmholtz [143]. With H. Davis, Stevens wrote a book, bringing together his own work on audition and that of others (*Hearing,* 1938).

In his scaling work, Stevens abandoned the category scaling procedure used by Fechner [120] and others and developed some new ones, the direct scaling methods (magnitude estimation, ratio production, and others), and found that, when so scaled, most physical continua obeyed a psychophysical power law, $R = kS^n$, rather than the logarithmic law of Fechner's. Stevens argued that sensory continua are either qualitative (metathetic) or quantitative (prothetic), and that while the former (hue, pitch) may obey Fechner's law, most of them, being quantitative, obey the power law, equal stimulus ratios producing equal sense ratios. Much earlier, Plateau [122] had proposed a similar law, abandoning it in deference to Fechner. The power law was presented in the first chapter of the *Handbook of Experimental Psychology* (1951) that was edited by Stevens, and was subsequently bolstered by numerous research and theoretical papers. Stevens's work represented the most significant single attainment in psychophysics since Fechner.

A third area in which Stevens acquired distinction was that of philosophy of science. Not long after the appearance of Bridgman's [409] book, *The Logic of Modern Physics,* Harvard psychologists were talking about operationism. It was through the writings of Stevens that American psychologists learned about operationism and began to apply operational definitions of psychological concepts. Of the several papers that Stevens wrote on the subject, his 1939 paper, Psychology and the Science of Science, is the most comprehensive. Stevens wrote a total of more than 150 articles. He was also cofounder of the Psychonomic Society in 1959 and the founder of the journal, *Perception and Psychophysics* (1966).

Biographic data: American Men of Science

SPENCE, KENNETH WARTENBE [518]

American psychologist
Rating: 25
Born: Chicago, Illinois, May 6, 1907

Died: Austin, Texas, January 12, 1967

Highest degree: Ph.D. in psychology, Yale University, 1933, under R. M. Yerkes [363]

Positions, honors: 1933, NRC fellow, Yale Laboratories of Primate Biology, Orange Park, Florida; 1937, University of Virginia; 1938, University of Iowa; 1964, University of Texas; 1956 American Psychological Association Distinguished Scientific Contribution Award; other medals and awards

A neobehavioristic theoretician and experimentalist, Spence first worked on discrimination learning, emphasizing stimulus discrimination, then concentrated on conditioning. He extended Hull's [423] learning theory and modified some of its postulates. Spence's learning theory was a two-factor theory, involving both classical and instrumental conditioning. In classical conditioning, excitatory potential, $_SE_R$, is increased by two prior intervening variables, habit and drive. Habit is an associative variable and is a function of reinforced trials. The pairing of the conditioned stimulus and the unconditioned stimulus is sufficient to produce an increase in excitatory potential. For instrumental conditioning the contiguity of stimulus and response is all that is necessary to increase habit strength. Here the amount of reinforcement may increase $_SE_R$ without increasing habit strength. Spence's theory differs from Hull's in that for Hull there was only one kind of learning, and habit was a function of reinforcement only. For Spence delay of reward works mainly by affecting the amount of incentive rather than being independent of incentive, as in Hull.

Throughout his career, Spence was consistently and persistently engaged in the study of learning and conditioning phenomena, especially the dimensional analysis of conditioning. Spence, like Hull, attempted to formulate a general behavioral theory from the postulates of a learning theory (*Behavior Theory and Conditioning*, 1956). During his stay at Iowa, Spence exercised considerable influence on American psychology through the many (seventy-five) doctoral students who studied under him. The extensive experimental work on anxiety arose from the Iowa laboratory in testing Spence's concept of drive, especially in connection with the Manifest Anxiety Scale developed by Spence's student, Janet Taylor.

Biographic data: H. H. Kendler, Kenneth Wartenbe Spence. *Psychological Review*, 1967, 74, 335–341

French philosopher
Rating: **16**
Born: Rochefort, Charente Maritime, March 14, 1908
Died: Paris, May 3, 1961
Highest degree: Agrégé in philosophy, Ecole Normale Supérieure
   Paris, 1931
Positions: 1945, University of Lyons; 1948, Sorbonne; 1952,
   Collège de France

Merleau-Ponty was a philosopher and phenomenological psychologist, recognized for his originality and success in integrating philosophy and psychology. His psychologically most important works are *Structure du comportement* (1942, English translation, *The Structure of Behavior*, 1963) and *La phénoménologie de la perception* (1945, English translation, *Phenomenology of Perception*, 1962). In *The Structure of Behavior*, Merleau-Ponty proposes "to understand the relation between consciousness and nature." While nature is subject to causality, consciousness is not, even when considered as behavior. The appropriate method for studying behavior is systematic phenomenology of perception, not the methods presently used by psychologists. In *Phenomenology of Perception*, Merleau-Ponty derives a perceptual basis for his phenomenological philosophy. The essential characteristic of man is the dynamic interaction between consciousness and nature. This interaction or dialectic is reflected in the perceptual processes. Since perception "opens a window onto things," it is the starting point for the study of man. While in fundamental agreement with the emphasis on wholes of Gestalt psychology, Merleau-Ponty thought that the doctrine of isomorphism was by its very nature in error.

Biographic data: *EP* 5:279; T. Langan, Merleau-Ponty: in memoriam. *Philosophical and Phenomenological Research*, 1962-63, 23, 205-216; A. Robinet, *Merleau-Ponty, sa vie, son oeuvre avec un exposé de sa philosophie*, 1962

MASLOW, ABRAHAM HAROLD ⌈520⌉

American psychologist
Rating: (unrated)
Born: Brooklyn, New York, April 1, 1908

Died: Waltham, Massachusetts, June 8, 1970

Highest degree: Ph.D. in psychology, University of Wisconsin, 1934, under H. Harlow.

Positions: 1934, University of Wisconsin; 1935, Teachers College, Columbia University; 1937, Brooklyn College; 1951–1969, Brandeis University; president, American Psychological Association, 1968

Maslow was one of the moving forces behind what came to be called the "third force" in psychology or humanistic psychology (in addition to behaviorism and psychoanalysis). It was not until the middle of his life that Maslow began to produce writings that became the foundation stones of humanistic psychology. In his writings (*Abnormal Psychology*, 1941; *Motivation and Personality*, 1954; *Toward a Psychology of Being*, 1960; *Religion, Values, and Peak Experiences*, 1964) Maslow presents a holistic–dynamic theory of man that is based on a conception of man as healthy, normal, and having positive emotions and motives. There is a motivational hierarchy in which the higher motives are satisfied after the lower ones have been cared for. The lower motives are aroused by some deficiency (D-motives, such as hunger), the higher ones are to satisfy the higher needs of being (B-motives, such as self-actualization). Maslow makes self-actualization, a term coined by Jung [358], a central theme of his psychology. The striving to realize the highest potential of the inner self, part of which is universal and part individual, leads to an integration of the various aspects of personality into a healthy, creatively functioning whole. For psychology to be more complete, it needs to study individuals who have come near the ideal of complete self-actualization.

Biographic data: *American Men of Science*

[521]

MARQUIS, DONALD G.

American psychologist

Rating: (unrated)

Born: Two Harbors, Minnesota, June 22, 1908

Died: Cambridge, Massachusetts, February 17, 1973

Highest degree: Ph.D. in psychology, Yale University, 1932, under L. Terman [368]

Positions: 1933–1945, Yale University, chairman of Psychology Department since 1942; 1945–1957, University of Michigan, professor of psychology and chairman of Psychology Department; 1943–1945, director, National Research Council Office of Psychological Personnel; 1947–1950, chairman, Committee on Human Resources, Research and Development Board, U.S. Department of Defense; 1957–1959, staff member, Social Sciences Research Council; 1959–1973, Massachusetts Institute of Technology; president, American Psychological Association, 1947

Until about 1940, Marquis did research and published in the areas of conditioning and physiological psychology, especially the neurophysiology of vision. With E. R. Hilgard he wrote the widely used *Conditioning and Learning* (1940) text, and (with R. S. Woodworth [312]), a *Psychology* (5th edition, 1947). Work on personnel problems during World War II oriented him toward applied and organizational psychology, especially the management of science and technology, social psychology of organizations, and group decision making. Marquis published a number of papers in these areas, two books, *Successful Industrial Innovations* (1969, with S. Meyers) and *Factors in the Transfer of Technology* (1969, with W. H. Gruber), and was active on a number of committees and boards concerned with the problems of management of science and technology.

Biographic data: *American Men of Science*

FRENKEL–BRUNSWIK, ELSE   ⌈522⌉

Austrian-American psychologist
Rating: **19**
Born: Lemberg, Austria, August 18, 1908
Died: Berkeley, California, March 31, 1958
Highest degree: Ph.D. in psychology, University of Vienna, 1930, under K. Bühler [385]
Positions: 1931, University of Vienna; 1938, University of California, Berkeley

Else Frenkel married Egon Brunswik [508] upon her arrival in New York from Austria in 1938. They had been fellow students in Vienna and assistants to Karl Bühler. Her major contribution to the field of psychology was in connection with the development of scales of ethnocentrism and of authoritarianism (the F scale) and the study of prejudice, using new methods and testing new hypotheses concerning prejudice. The work was published in collaboration with others (T. W. Adorno, E. Frenkel-Brunswik, D. L. Levinson, and R. N. Sanford, *The Authoritarian Personality*, 1950). Frenkel-Brunswik's own specific contributions were the construction and analysis of the semistructured interviews with the subjects of the study. A concept developed by her in connection with the study of the authoritarian personality was intolerance of ambiguity. Her total scientific output was only about a dozen papers.

Biographic data: *IESS* 5:559; L. Lowental, Else Frenkel-Brunswik. *American Sociological Review*, 1958, 23, 585–586

[523] ## BOIKO, EVGENII IVANOVICH

Russian psychologist
Rating: (unrated)
Born: Elets, December 25, 1909
Died: Moscow, November 13, 1972
Highest degree: Ph.D., 1945; D.Sc., 1963
Positions: 1952, head, Laboratory of Higher Neurodynamics, Institute of General and Pedagogical Psychology, Moscow

Boĭko was an experimental psychologist and theorist in the area of conditioning and learning. He originated the theory of psychophysiological mechanisms of consciousness, and formulated the principle of temporary connections, based on the work of Sechenov [156] and Pavlov [206]. Boĭko studied the formation of such connections by measuring reaction time as a function of verbal stimuli. He concluded that verbal stimuli produce either facilitating or blocking impulses, which pass from the speech areas of the brain to the cortical projection areas, and in the process heighten or lower the excitability of the latter. Any goal-directed behavior of man is therefore not a one-way process of conditioning but a complex chain of interacting conditioned reflexes in which excitation spreads itself from the cortical projection areas into speech areas and back, continuously converging upon common points. This process creates new dynamic formations among previously formed connections based on sensory and verbal stimuli.

In addition to his [*Human Reaction Time*], Boĭko published as editor and co-author [*Materials on the Study of the Conditioned Reflex Basis of Man's Psychological Activity*], [*Questions on the*

Study of Higher Neurodynamics in Connection with Psychological Problems], and [Interdisciplinary Problems of Psychology and Physiology]. He was the author of more than fifty scientific papers.

Biographic data: [Anon.] Evgeniǐ Ivanovich Boǐko. Voprosy Psikhologii, 1973(1), 19, 190

RAPAPORT, DAVID [524]

Hungarian-American psychologist
Rating: 21
Born: Munkacs, Hungary, September 30, 1911
Died: Stockbridge, Massachusetts, December 14, 1960
Highest degree: Ph.D. in psychology, Royal Hungarian University, 1938
Positions: 1938, Mount Sinai Hospital, New York; Osawatomie State Hospital, Kansas; 1940, Menninger Clinic; 1948, Austen Riggs Center, Stockbridge, Massachusetts

Rapaport was a psychologist who made an attempt to make psychoanalysis into a global behavioral theory that harmonized with general psychology. His main concerns were thought processes, their development, organization, and pathology. Rapaport believed that psychoanalysis cast the most light on thought processes, but that it needed critical systematization. This he undertook to accomplish. There followed a series of books, reflecting his thinking and research: Emotions and Memory (1942), Diagnostic Psychological Testing (1945, with M. Gill and R. Schafer), Organization and Pathology of Thought (1951). The structure of psychonalytic theory: a systematizing attempt, in Psychology: A Study of a Science, vol. 3. In his psychology Rapaport attempted to incorporate and integrate ego psychology and social psychology and preserve, at the same time, Freud's [224] insights into the psychology if the id. Through his writings and lectures on psychoanalysis Rapaport exerted an influence in America that led clinicians away from IQ tests toward tests of thinking and personality and brought about a better appreciation of psychoanalysis and ego psychology. He collected papers were published posthumously, in 1967.

Biographic data: IESS 13:325; NCAB 50:91; M. M. Gill, In memoriam David Rapaport. In M. M. Gill (Ed.), The Collected Papers of David Rapaport, 1967, pp. 3–7

FITTS, PAUL MORRIS

American psychologist
Rating: 16
Born: Martin, Tennessee, May 5, 1912
Died: Ann Arbor, Michigan, May 2, 1965
Highest degree: Ph.D. in psychology, University of Rochester, 1938, under L. Carmichael [494]
Positions: 1938–1941, University of Tennessee; 1942–1944, assistant chief, Psychology Branch, Air Surgeon HQ, USAAF; 1945–1949, chief, Psychology Branch, Aeromedical Laboratory, USAF Air Matériel Command; 1949–1958, Ohio State University; 1958–1965, University of Michigan

Fitts's work was in human engineering, particularly in equipment design (editor, *Psychological Research on Equipment Design*, 1947). Fitts's experience with the Air Force oriented him particularly to problems encountered in the work of aircraft pilots. Both in the Air Force and later at the Ohio State University Laboratory of Aviation Psychology, Fitts contributed to the solution of problems related to cockpit design, radar operator training, and other related areas. His monograph (with J. A. Leonard) on visual pattern recognition (*Stimulus Correlates of Visual Pattern Recognition*, 1957) summarizes some basic work done by a group of investigators under the direction of Fitts in the area of visual form perception, but addressed to the solution of practical problems in visual information processing by aviation personnel. One result of this work was the contruction of a type of easily quantifiable and generalizable visual stimulus, the Ohio metric histoform. Another was one of the first instances of the use of information-theoretical measures in psychology, here applied to visual stimuli, especially in the form of redundancy measures. Fitts also wrote a chapter on "Engineering psychology and equipment design" for S. S. Stevens's [517] well-known *Handbook of Experimental Psychology* (1951), and a volume on *Human Performance* (1967).

Biographic data: *American Men of Science*

HOVLAND, CARL IVER

American psychologist
Rating: 23
Born: Chicago, Illinois, June 12, 1912

Died: New Haven, Connecticut, April 16, 1961

Highest degree: Ph.D. in psychology, Yale University, 1936

Positions, honors: 1936–1961, Yale University; 1942–1945, psychological research in Washington, D.C.; American Psychological Association Distinguished Scientific Contribution Award, 1957; Warren Medal, Society of Experimental Psychologists

Hovland's early research interests led to significant discoveries in the areas of retention, rote learning, and modes of resolution of motor conflicts. He was co-author of two psychological classics: with Clark Hull [423] and others, *Mathematico-Deductive Theory of Rote Learning* (1940), and with John Dollard and others, *Frustration and Aggression* (1939). Later Hovland's interests shifted to social psychology, especially communication, attitude, and later still, concept formation. His contributions in the field of social communication make him one of the outstanding social scientists of this century. Hovland's research on communication started during World War II when Hovland was on a government assignment to study military morale. In this four-year study Hovland, in addition to laboratory experiments, used groups of soldiers to test the effects of the different variables of communication using actual war-related issues. His *Experiments on Mass Communication* (1949) was the result of this work. After his return to Yale, Hovland and his former associates continued the systematic studies of factors affecting attitude change. *Communication and Persuasion* (1953), *Order of Presentation in Persuasion* (1957), *Personality and Persuadibility* (1959), *Attitude Organization and Change,* and *Social Judgment* (1961), which Hovland wrote with a number of other researchers in the Yale group, were the result of this period of Hovland's scientific activity. During the last decade of his life Hovland turned to thought processes, concept formation, and computer modeling of cognitive processes. Hovland's original and systematic studies advanced attitude research from mere demonstration of changes in attitude to the prediction of such attitude changes. His theorizing related this area of social psychology to the underlying fundamentals of the higher thought processes.

Biographic data: IESS 6:526; NCAB 52:263; [Anon.] Distinguished Scientific Contribution Award 1957. *American Psychologist,* 1958, **13**, 158–162; R. R. Sears, Carl Iver Hovland. *American Journal of Psychology,* 1961, **74**, 637–639; W. R. Miles, Carl Iver Hovland. In American Philosophical Society, *Year Book 1961,* 1962, pp. 121–125

INDEX

The entries in this index are terms mentioned in the preceding 526 biographies. These terms belong to the following categories:

1. Names of the various fields, subdivisions, and areas of investigation in psychology to which the biographees have contributed. These make it possible to list and otherwise treat all contributors to a given area of interest in psychology.

2. Names of psychological concepts, which allow the tracing of their development historically through the work of biographees.

3. Names of pieces of apparatus, discoveries, phenomena, special terms, eponyms, and laws and principles associated with particular individuals, which make it possible to ascertain their origin or priority of use.

4. Theories of body-mind relationship, which make it possible to group individuals in terms of their philosophical preferences.

5. Schools of psychology and psychological organizations.

6. Names of biographees where they are mentioned in biographies other than their own.

This index allows the reader to establish relationships among the biographees in tracing the development of an idea, as well as teacher-student genealogies in psychology. *The numbers appearing after each entry in this index are biography numbers, not page numbers.*

INDEX

Klages, L., 403
Knowing, 8
Knowledge, of the soul, 8, 35
    origin, 1, 7, 26, 28
    (*See also* Empiricism)
Koffka, K., 202, 351, 372, 380, 391, 397, 447
Köhler, W., 98, 202, 282, 351, 380, 391, 397, 438,
    468, 495
Kornilov, K. N., 487
Krüger, F., 419
Külpe, O., 4, 174, 186, 194, 258, 268, 274, 296,
    311, 373, 376, 386, 391, 405

L

Laboratories, psychological, 158, 159, 161, 184,
    186, 207, 208, 212, 226, 231, 234, 236,
    239, 240, 256, 258, 263, 265, 271, 272,
    275,284, 285, 286, 299, 304, 309, 337, 341,
    376, 418
Ladd, G. T., 280, 312
Lamarck, J. B., 48, 61, 88
La Mettrie, J. O., 42, 56, 80
Lange, C., 184
Langfeld, H. S., 458, 493
Language, 87, 377, 417, 487
Laplace, P. S., 80, 99, 116, 144
Lashley, K. S., 234, 350, 475, 490
Latent learning, 439
Lavater, J. C., 19
Law of comparative judgment, 448
Law of effect, 142, 353
Law of exercise, 353
Lazarus, M., 147
Leadership, 468
Learning, 8, 207, 208, 258, 352, 353, 423, 432,
    436, 438, 439, 447, 460, 465, 466, 482,
    492, 518, 526
Least squares method, 99
Lebenspsychologie, 468
Leibniz, G. W., 41
Leipzig Gestalt school, 351
Lenin, V. I., 89, 136, 174, 194, 459
Level of aspiration, 468
Lévy-Bruhl, L., 367
Lewin, K., 447
Liébeault, A. A., 152, 181, 228
Life space, 468
Life style, 302, 317
Light, 36
    adaptation, 153
Linnaeus, C., 233, 431
Lip key, 256
Lipps, T., 338, 351, 366, 387

Localization, auditory, 517
    of brain functions, 81, 149, 168, 173, 175, 198,
        200, 350, 380, 433, 466
    cutaneous, 334
Local signs, 135
Locke, J., 5, 20, 21, 26, 38, 40, 41, 45, 57, 60, 64
Locomotion, 23
Loeb, J., 303
Lorge, I., 353
Lotze, R. H., 103, 115, 155, 186, 190, 202
Lubbock, J., 282

M

McCosh, J., 129
McDougall, W., 192, 278, 293, 304, 341
McGeoch, J. A., 482
Mach, E., 185, 194, 229, 250, 318, 320
Magendie, F., 96, 131
"Magnetization," 46, 63
Maine de Biran, M. F., 112
Malthus, T. R., 146
Marbe, K., 265
Marx, K. H., 82, 89, 318, 383
Mass action, 466
Mastery method, 207
Materialism, 5, 24, 50, 54, 56, 80, 135, 156
    (*See also* Dialectical materialism)
Mathematical psychology, 37, 60, 67, 101
Matsumoto, M., 495
Maze method, 323, 439, 465
Mead, G. H., 474
Mechanistic psychology, 28, 50, 247
Medical psychology, 152, 170, 179
Meinong, A., 250, 314, 375
Mel, 517
Memory, 8, 16, 24, 28, 54, 109, 207, 208, 320, 444
    drum, 208
    traces, 8, 118
Mens rationalis, 41
Mental adjustment, 422
Mental chemistry, 125
Mental chronometry, 137
Mental disorders, 17, 71, 91, 179, 221, 223, 224,
    232, 249, 288, 292, 300
Mental hygiene, 292, 316, 362
Mental inheritance, 144
Mentalism, 26, 40
Mental measurement, 144, 406, 483
    (*See also* Intelligence tests; Mental tests)
Mental retardation, 98, 130, 262, 290, 299, 463
Mental tests, 19, 144, 256, 298, 307, 325, 357,
    401, 472, 516
Mercier, D. F., 405
Mesmer, F. A., 46